Granville Barker and
the Dream of Theatre

The golden fairies. Granville Barker's *A Midsummer Night's Dream*, Savoy Theatre 1914. Christine Silver as Titania, Dennis Neilson-Terry as Oberon.

Granville Barker and the Dream of Theatre

DENNIS KENNEDY

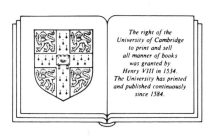

*The right of the
University of Cambridge
to print and sell
all manner of books
was granted by
Henry VIII in 1534.
The University has printed
and published continuously
since 1584.*

CAMBRIDGE UNIVERSITY PRESS

Cambridge
London   New York   New Rochelle
Melbourne   Sydney

Published by the Press Syndicate of the University of Cambridge
The Pitt Building, Trumpington Street, Cambridge CB2 1RP
32 East 57th Street, New York, NY 10022, USA
10 Stamford Road, Oakleigh, Melbourne 3166, Australia

First published 1985

Printed in Great Britain at
The University Press, Cambridge

Library of Congress catalogue card number: 84–28575

British Library Cataloguing in Publication Data
Kennedy, Dennis
Granville Barker and the dream of theatre.
1. Granville-Barker, Harley
I. Title
792′.0233′0924   PN2598.G655
ISBN 0 521 25480 9

WV

for Ann
who illuminates

Contents

Illustrations

Preface

Τ

HE THEATRE HISTORIAN attempts to create intelligible patterns out of the confusion and the midden of the past. The work would often be unstable and idiosyncratic without the aid of other thinkers; if I have avoided those faults, it is only by virtue of the many debts incurred in the construction. Chief among my creditors are the commentators on the Edwardian theatre: the major writers on Granville Barker discussed in the first chapter, and numerous critics, historians, biographers, and memoirists mentioned throughout the text. I have also benefited from the kindness of many people on a personal level, among them Attilio Favorini, William Frost, Frank Gardiner, G.B. Harrison, Dan H. Laurence, Patrick J. McCarthy, Jan McDonald, Margery Morgan, and Howard Stein. Eric Salmon has been particularly helpful in answering questions, and generously shared his work on Barker's life and letters at an early date.

Libraries and librarians far and near have unstintingly offered their services. I owe particular thanks to the staffs at the Bodleian Library, the British Library, the Theatre Museum of the Victoria and Albert Museum, the British Theatre Association (especially to Enid Foster), and to those at the universities of Michigan, Texas, and Yale (especially to Marjorie Wynne).

This work has been supported by research grants from Grand Valley State College in Michigan, where it was begun, and from the University of Pittsburgh, where it was completed. A year-long fellowship from the National Endowment for the Humanities allowed me freedom to accomplish the principal research, and was an invaluable benefit.

Quotations from the works of Granville Barker appear here through the courtesy of the Society of Authors as the literary representative of the Estate of Harley Granville Barker, Methuen London, Princeton University Press, and Batsford Ltd. Quotations from the works of Bernard Shaw appear through the courtesy of the Society of Authors on behalf of the Bernard Shaw Estate. For access to and permission to draw upon unpublished Granville Barker material, and for permission to reproduce original illustrations, I am grateful to the Curators of the Bodleian Library, Alexander Murray, the British Library, the Theatre Museum of the Victoria and Albert Museum, the British Theatre Association, the Harry Ransom Humanities Research Center of the University of Texas at Austin, the Department of Rare Books and

Special Collections of the University of Michigan Library, the Henry W. and Albert H. Berg Collection of the New York Public Library (Astor, Lennox and Tilden Foundations), Yale University Library, the Yale University Archives, and the Mander and Mitchenson Theatre Collection. I first worked out my ideas on Barker's plays in an article called "Granville Barker's Sexual Comedy" in *Modern Drama* 23 (1980), and I acknowledge permission from the editor and the University of Toronto to use portions of it.

The sources of photographs and drawings are cited in the list of illustrations. For those taken from Edwardian journals, I am grateful to: Bodleian Library for 1–4, 8, 11–18, 20, 22, 24a–b, and 26; *ILN* Picture Library for the frontispiece and 19; Theatre Museum, Victoria and Albert Museum for 5 and 36–8; British Theatre Association for 29; and the University of Pittsburgh for 39.

The staff at Cambridge University Press has been careful and cooperative, and I am happy to thank Andrew Brown, who encouraged me to write the book, and Sarah Stanton, who kept me at it. My colleagues Kathleen George and Robert Whitman read portions of the manuscript and made useful suggestions. Hazel Carr Leroy prepared the index. My greatest debt in this regard is to Anthony Parise, friend and former colleague, who was part of the work from the start. Whatever value the book may have, his help has made it better; his reading of various drafts saved me from numerous obscurities and follies, always with grace. Needless to say, the mistakes that remain are my own.

Finally, a word to my wife, who has not only put up with the work but has actively participated in it. She prepared the drawing for illustration 10, and made helpful comments over a long period: some debts are beyond the reach of words.

Documentation

Published sources are identified in the text, giving the author's name (when necessary, with a short title) and page number. Unpublished letters and manuscripts are identified by collection. In both cases the citations point to the list of References at the end, which stands also as a working – though hardly complete – bibliography of the subject. The numerous citations to the Edwardian press, however, are given in complete form in the text. The need for endnotes is thus drastically reduced, and those used are substantive rather than referential.

Many of Barker's letters quoted here will be included in Eric Salmon's eagerly awaited collection, entitled *Granville Barker and His Correspondents*. Though the editor has been most cooperative, press delays have made reference to that volume impossible; thus the majority of the letters I use are quoted from manuscript. (Through Salmon's generosity, however, I have been able to check my reading of Barker's difficult hand against the typescript of the collected letters.) C.B. Purdom prints a number of other letters in his biography of Barker, but often misrepresents the punctuation and the sense. In several places, therefore, I have quoted from manuscript sources rather than from Purdom's published versions.

In reconstructing performances I have drawn upon eye-witness accounts in press reviews, in letters, and in reminiscences. I have preferred to quote reviews from the original sources, even when (as in the case of Max in the reports in *The Times*, *The Stage*, and *The Era*. Beerbohm) the notices have since been collected. Promptbooks and other theatrical records have been heavily relied upon whenever available, and are detailed in the References. Statistical details of London performances have generally been derived from J.P. Wearing, supplemented by Desmond MacCarthy and P.P. Howe. When necessary cast lists and other factual items have been checked against programs (primarily in the Theatre Museum), and

Establishing texts for Barker's major plays is not an easy matter: there are three published versions of *The Voysey Inheritance* (1909, 1913, 1938), two of *Waste* (1909, 1926), and two of *The Madras House* (1911, 1925). Sometimes the revisions are improvements, sometimes not. Since the later versions are outside the period of Barker's active work, I have taken the simple course and used the original texts.

The director was a new official in the Edwardian theatre, apparent in the fact that a regular term for the position was lacking. Barker called himself a "producer," and that word eventually became standard – at least until after the Second World War, when the American term "director" achieved currency in England. But Shaw often used "stage manager," in the Victorian sense, as did many in the theatre; still others spoke of the "acting coach," or simply the "manager," or even the "stage director." I have attempted to lessen the confusion by using only *director* in the text. Except in quotations, I avoid the word "producer," and refer to the financial backer of a performance by the more comprehensive Edwardian term, *manager*.

Illustrations have been selected as an aid in documenting Granville Barker's productions: I have attempted to choose those that suggest acting and directing styles over those that are merely pleasing or biographical. Little selection is possible for the Court productions, but the choices become wider in Barker's later directing career, which explains the pictorial imbalance between the two halves of the book. A cautionary note: except for outdoor performances, the photographs reproduced were not taken in action or with authentic scene lighting. The technique of fast-speed indoor photography was not readily available until well after the First World War; thus there is often a stiff and artificial look to theatrical photographs of the time, and they cannot be trusted in the matter of lighting design.

The few abbreviations should be readily understood: *TLS* for *Times*

Literary Supplement and *ILN* for *Illustrated London News*, for example. One collection of correspondence, however, is referred to often enough to justify unusual abbreviation:

   SLB   Bernard Shaw's Letters to Granville Barker, ed. C.B. Purdom (London: Phoenix House, 1956).

                                                                        D.K.

University of Pittsburgh

1 Dreaming a theatre

On New Year's Day in the year of grace 1891, as if accompanying the decade with auspicious rites, the Novelist, aged forty-seven, traveled "a wet winter night in a windy Lancashire town" – Southport – for purposes theatrical. He was to pay homage at the altar of commerce, not of art: he wanted money quickly to secure time for his true calling. Fiction, in the Victorian view, was valuable, drama was not. Observing the conditions of the stage, he thought to turn a penny at a trade ancient and meretricious, to write down one of his exquisite tales so that it could be apprehended, in his famous phrase, "between dinner and the suburban trains." Like his own protagonists, he brought unexamined hopes to a world he deemed cynical and jaded, wishing to profit without capitulating to its massive dullness. He admitted that it was "the thirst for gold that is pushing me along this dishonourable path"; to his brother, a philosopher at Harvard and able to understand these things, he reported only "abject, lonely, fear."

So he made a debut as a playwright, with *The American* turned into a conventional late-Victorian comedy. William Archer was at the opening, having first respectfully asked permission to attend – William Archer who had been cajoling the best novelists to try the stage, to raise what he thought to be the appalling condition of contemporary English drama. The performance occurred; the Novelist bowed to the "gas-flaring indistinguishable dimness"; London beckoned. The play reached the Opera Comique Theatre in September, with Elizabeth Robins in the cast and a glittering transatlantic audience in attendance, including the American Minister and the Harvard philosopher. Reception was tepid. Thus began the abortive dramatic career of Henry James (Edel 287–8, 297–9). He made no money.

In March of that same year another foreign writer who had adopted London, Jacob Thomas Grein, founded a private society for the production of uncommercial plays. He called it the Independent Theatre, and chose for its model Antoine's Théâtre Libre, started in Paris only four years before. Grein's first production was the British première of *Ghosts*, which had of course been banned by the Lord Chamberlain. It was received with remarkable hostility, making its sponsor "the best-abused man in London" (Orme 88). Grein then looked for new English writing and found none of value. He produced an unexciting play by George Moore, an Irishman who had been promoting the notion of an alternative theatre in London, and he produced a few more foreign works. An unsuccessful novelist, another expatriate Irishman, finally came to his aid by literally dusting off an abandoned play begun long before with Archer's assistance. Grein presented it as *Widowers' Houses*, and started the long career of the most famous playwright of the twentieth century, Bernard Shaw – though it would be years before Shaw would have regular public productions in London and be accepted seriously.

In May of 1891 a young man of thirteen made his first public appearance in a play, at the Spa Rooms in Harrogate, as Dr Grimstone in something called *Vice Versa*. His mother was there to prompt him; she was by profession a reciter of popular poems in the drafty halls of provincial England, particularly noted for her imitation of birdsong. Her son, dressed in a sailor suit in earlier days, often was included in the act. He was Harley Granville Barker. He would spend the next twenty-four years working on the stage as an actor, director, manager, and playwright, then thirty years more working for the stage as a critic and theorist. He would establish Shaw as the first dramatist of his age. He would effectively invent the position of director in England and, building on Grein's model, create two of the most important theatre managements of the century. He would become a remarkable dramatist himself, and a highly influential interpreter of Shakespeare. Aided at first by Archer, he would show the way for the establishment of a national theatre, and struggle for it all his life. He would become the most versatile man of the English-speaking theatre in our time, and perhaps in history. He would dream of a theatre that even Henry James could turn to without shame.

Introducing Granville and Barker

Granville Barker has the most curious reputation of any major theatrical figure of the century. Acknowledged by 1914 as the premier theatre artist in England, he saw his fame decline after the war as he withdrew from active participation in the stage. He devoted the second half of his working life to the study, where he said he always wanted to be; but those who had fought the battle for a new theatre with him felt a rejection akin to betrayal. Lewis Casson, who learned his craft from the master at the Court Theatre, gave voice to that disappointment in the foreword to C.B. Purdom's biography: Barker was a hero who "gave up the struggle, threw off the dust of battle, and became a mere professor" (viii). For a generation of actors and playwrights, he was the lost leader.

If he had been killed in the war, he probably would be remembered with honor and regret for the impressive work he had already accomplished. But he survived, like E.M. Forster, another Edwardian personality whom the war made into a displaced person. All of Forster's novels but one were written by 1915, and after *A Passage to India* he became a reflective critic, an elder statesman of literature. Both Barker and Forster wrote with an emphasis on the hidden self, consistently promising, in the words of Auden's sonnet on Forster, that "the inner life shall pay." Barker had not begun as a writer, however, and in the eyes of his theatrical colleagues he not only left the fight he had started, he committed the unpardonable sin: he abandoned them for a wealthy American woman, ten years his senior, who loathed the theatre, turned him away from his friends and the source of his art, made him a dry pedagogue and a snob. In this view, his subsequent success as a critic could never make up for the action of a Coriolanus. Reputation is a flinty gravestone.

An ambivalent attitude has affected most subsequent attention to Barker, whatever aspect of his life is under discussion. The division in his work he emphasized himself by a change in the form of his name. The son of Albert James Barker and Mary Elizabeth Bozzi-Granville, christened Harley Granville in 1877, generally was known during his stage career as Granville Barker. After 1921, however, books were published with Harley added and a hyphen firmly in place. This might have been of no importance, but it became another sign to his abandoned friends of snobbishness and a rejection of the old life. "Mr Barker," as he had been in the press in the Edwardian years, ultimately signed some late essays "Harley Granville-Barker, LL.D." When he revised his Edwardian plays he added the new signature – though without the LL.D – and in some cases even omitted the cast lists of the first performances, as if denying their theatrical origins. (He claimed to his publisher that the revisions were new works – in a letter to Frank Sidgwick, in the Bodleian – and in a sense they are.) Since the majority of his writing after the war was scholarly and critical, "Granville-Barker" has become associated with his mere professor's life.

Strange, how much a hyphen can signify. It has become a flag for commentators, subtly used to indicate perspective. Without the hyphen the subject appears in his youthful, active state; with it added he becomes reserved and aloof, smelling of the lamp. J.L. Styan's *The Shakespeare Revolution* incorporates the split within two chapters: one is entitled "Barker at the Savoy"; the next, "Granville-Barker's early criticism." This is perfectly logical, but also suggests that two separate men were at large, one of whom did die in the war. Indeed, there are many students of literature, especially in America, who are amazed to discover that the author of the famous *Prefaces to Shakespeare* had a past as a great director as well. The extreme of this confusion occurred in a library I regularly use, when a much-handled copy was rebound. On the spine of the new binding are the names of the authors: "Granville and Barker."

Barker's reputation has been dogged as well by his chief spokesman, C.B. Purdom, who published the standard biography in 1955. Though he implies that he saw most of Barker's productions, Purdom was not well qualified to write this life. He was enabled to do so through the cooperation of Barker's first wife, Lillah McCarthy, who provided reminiscences and the most valuable documents, including the letters from Shaw which Purdom edited the following year.[1] Much of the evidence he uses, however, is undocumented; many of his quotations from manuscripts are incorrect; and though he provides essential information otherwise unavailable, the tone of the book is dull. Further, it is seriously marred by an uncritical acceptance of Lillah McCarthy's aggrieved view of Barker's second marriage, and echoes the received opinion of Casson and others that Barker destroyed his artistic self when he turned his back on the stage. A more dynamic treatment, or even a clearer one, might have rescued Barker's reputation at an early date. After giving all her aid, Lillah McCarthy was justly disappointed in the picture of Barker that emerged. She wrote Gilbert Murray that the book is "not a classic. Or even a pen portrait and there it is" (Bodleian). Fortunately a new critical biography by Eric Salmon, using newly discovered material, goes a long way to correct Purdom's errors and excesses. Greatly aiding the reevaluation is Salmon's edition of Barker's correspondence, due for publication soon.

Barker's work as a dramatist has not suffered the same critical fate. Margery Morgan's analysis of the plays in *A Drama of Political Man*, which appeared in 1961, is a mine of information and insight, and a number of essays have sought to secure a place for the plays, most notably a seminal article by Gerald Weales. Only recently, however, has the revival affected the theatre; in the last ten years the subsidized companies in England have shown that they can do justice to Barker's work, which had suffered a long neglect. It was a considerable surprise to hear a BBC announcer in 1979 introduce a production of *The Voysey Inheritance* as by "Harley Granville Barker, now generally recognized as one of the great dramatists of the century." Even allowing for television exaggeration, that is an opinion few in the past have held.

Though his achievement as a director of Shakespeare has been studied before, theatre historians have paid little attention to his directing as a whole. Even smaller attention has been given to how the multitudinous parts of his work fit together to make a single force for theatrical reform. Barker's active career from 1900 to 1915 was the conscious effort of an innovator seeking a new kind of theatre for the new century. His chief aim was to demonstrate, by theory and practice, the inevitability of an endowed repertory company in London: his consuming passion for a national theatre gave structure to his life, both before and after the Great War. Few men have entered the profession with as many talents as Granville Barker, and none in England or America has ever combined his resources to the same extent. His influence has been profound, more profound than is generally recognized, and continues to affect the life of the theatre in our time. To examine his contributions as a director, playwright, manager, and dreamer is to witness, in specific, the genesis of the twentieth-century English theatre, and to imagine with him another theatre that might have been.

Apprentice actor, apprentice playwright

He was set for a conventional stage career from birth, and had training and education for nothing else. After Dr Grimstone in 1891, his mother sent him for a few months to Sarah Thorne's drama school; there, on Margate sands, Barker connected. He found a literary collaborator in Berte Thomas, an actor nine years older; they began to write plays together in 1895, when Barker was seventeen. The first, *A Comedy of Fools*, was ripped up, but in the next four years they completed three more which have survived in typescript. None of them is very good, but they provide the best sight we have of Barker's early development as a reformer of the stage.

Despite his youth, Barker was dominant in the collaboration (Morgan, *Political Man* 41); in the end Thomas sat down and copied out scenes that his partner improvised. The earliest survivor, *The Family of the Oldroyds* (about 1895–6), is a hopeless tragedy about a young woman's need to break the bonds of sexual and social repression. Tessa Oldroyd strikes out to find her wild "destiny," an Italianate Hedda Gabler, but commits suicide when she discovers how her ignorance has deceived her about the man she loves. It need not detain us. *The Weather-Hen*, written in 1897, is more interesting and the only one of these unpublished plays to have been performed. Like its predecessor, it owes much to Ibsen. A woman named Eve Prior, trapped in a disastrous theatrical marriage, eventually learns to stand on her own and leave her husband. But she can arrive at the decision only after she has run off with a silly boy, and only after she has declared her love for, and been rejected by, an older man. Eve is a "weather-hen," a vacillating character, mocked by any wind. "Drifting boats can't be steered," says Jimmy Ferguson, her mentor. "You'll drift! Back to the very point from which you started today!" He urges her to stand alone, and at the end she accepts a low-paid acting job on tour as a step towards establishing herself.

The authors had no success in placing the work with a commercial management, so Barker sent a copy to William Archer for the New Century Theatre. He rejected it, but apparently gave an encouraging response, for Barker wrote him in April 1898 saying that he agreed about its "unsuitability to the public." He admitted its deficiencies, the principal one being that the two playwrights "failed to give definite expression to what was in our minds." He went on to "fear that with its refusal by the 'New Century' our last definite hope of production vanishes" (British Library). But still he implied that a more discerning audience might appreciate the work.

Their next play made many fewer concessions to ordinary theatrical taste and certainly is the most problematic of their joint efforts. *Our Visitor to "Work-a-Day"* – even the title is trying – was written in 1898 and 1899 with Barker in nearly complete charge. Thomas reported that as he took it down he understood almost nothing (Morgan, *Political Man* 41). It is an extreme example of subtle dialogue and obscure action, and since the authors were by now professional actors who knew the way of the world, they cannot possibly have thought that it would find a commercial production. Its subject, in a general sense, is that of all Barker's early work, sexual morality and its relationship to human happiness, but the technique sets it apart from the first two plays. *Our Visitor* experiments with devices put to fine use later in *The Marrying of Ann Leete*: glancing dialogue, indirect progression, incomplete statements, unexplained behavior. The technique has advanced from the nineteenth-century world of well-made melodrama, where everything fits the masterplan and explains everything else, to the twentieth-century world of uncertain knowledge, indeterminate action, unconscious desire.

The plot concerns the spiritual awakening of Griselda Greenhayes, brought about through her love for John Greatorex, a doctor in a bleak industrial town. She is newly married to Evelyn Gurth, a young poet and medical student, who once worked with John. The marriage founders and Griselda finds solace in John's stubborn dedication to the ordinary, the "work-a-day" world of dull routine. A sexual circle is completed when Evelyn has an unhappy affair with Vivien Lomax, John's former wife (or lover; the text is not clear). At the end, freer and wiser, Griselda reclaims her husband and rejects John. He will remain "the apostle of the commonplace"; Griselda has been but a visitor there.

The play is unsuccessful because its line of development is almost stubbornly opaque. Sexual passion is simmering everywhere, but how it affects the characters' hearts remains in doubt. Yet some scenes are very powerful, and at their best owe more to music than to conventional nineteenth-century drama. The contorted syntax of its dialogue is indebted to George Meredith, as Morgan points out (*Political Man* 49–50), and the ideas of the play may have been influenced by Maeterlinck's *The Treasure of the Humble*, as Salmon convincingly argues (53–8). Certainly Barker was impressed by both of those subtle investigators of the female character, and would stage their work later. As a young dramatist he was groping toward a new style: the subtle, thought-charged language of Meredith's fiction is combined in *Our Visitor* with the striking theatre images of Maeterlinck's static scenes.

Barker did not know that the manuscript survived. He lent it to Charlotte Shaw, and instructed her to destroy it after reading. She had it bound instead, and her husband eventually presented it to the British Museum. Shaw wrote Barker's publisher in 1946, after Barker's death, to announce that he possessed the forgotten play, "a very characteristic specimen of the early work which no manager would produce and which his critic-friends all declared they found unintelligible" (Sidgwick & Jackson Papers, Bodleian). It was a drama, whatever its faults, whose method looked for a theatre that did not yet exist.

If a new theatre was to be created, it would have to exist outside the Victorian notion of the stage. It was apparent to Barker very early in his career, as it had been to the leaders of the Free Stage movement in Europe and in England, that the conventional theatre strangled experimentation. What was needed was a completely new system, one that could be free of the high rents, the haphazard rehearsing, the long runs which deadened actors in their roles: the entire commercial structure, in fact, which made the stage subject to the marketplace. But how was such a change to be accomplished? Lacking a subsidized national theatre, Antoine's Théâtre Libre was the obvious model for an alternative, but it did not seem to work in London, perhaps because there had yet been no one with the talent and energy of Antoine to lead it. Grein's Independent Theatre Society struggled on until 1897, mostly in debt, and closed forever. Archer tried to continue the work with the New Century Theatre, a very small lamp indeed. These groups, and individual actors like Janet Achurch, her husband Charles Charrington, Elizabeth Robins, and Florence Farr, gave a tantalizing glimpse of a brighter dramatic scene. In 1895 Shaw had called them "the Impossibilists" (*Our Theatres* 1:20). Their task remained impossible so long as their work remained occasional. They were visitors to the work-a-day London stage.

Barker was unhappy about his work as an actor too. "Neither the plays he had to appear in nor the conditions of the theatre satisfied him," his biographer tells us; "he made next to nothing, was poor and shabby" (Purdom 7). Soon he would consider giving up acting entirely for playwriting and criticism. It is certain that at the end of the century there was little room in the theatre for a man of his type and promise. It would not have been surprising if he had left the theatre twenty years before he did.

Though it first seems a paradox, one of the most remarkable things about Barker's career as a reformer is that he began as a professional. Most of the dreamers and creators of a new theatre in the nineteenth and early twentieth centuries did not come from the stage. From Duke Georg of Saxe-Meiningen forward, they were men who saw the ancient value of the theatre more clearly for not having been forced to earn a living at the trade. Antoine, Otto Brahm, Stanislavsky, Jarry, Appia, Yeats – none of them emerged from a greenroom. It was especially true in England, where Moore, Grein, Archer, and Shaw were all journalists by profession. Of the major forces in the new theatre movement, only Craig, Meyerhold, Reinhardt, and Barker made their entrances as professional actors, and all abandoned the traditional stage as soon as they could.

In 1899 Barker was set on the road to his future work by exhibiting the talents thus far hidden from public display. Before his twenty-second birthday he would have a London production, act a major Shakespearian role for William Poel, and write on his own a new play of astounding quality. A few months after his birthday he would form a connection with a new group of Impossibilists that would provide his first opportunity for directing. It was an early age for accomplishments of this order. If none of the events had a marked significance at the moment, taken as a whole they show why Barker could in the next few years rise so swiftly to become the leader of the cause for a new theatre in England.

The Stage Society

The first happy occurrence was a special matinee of *The Weather-Hen* at Terry's Theatre on 29 June, organized by Madge McIntosh, who took the leading role. What function Barker had in the production is not recorded, but he did not act or direct. The play received a number of pleasant reviews and was successful enough to warrant a transfer to the Comedy Theatre, where it lasted for a two-week evening run. "Quite an exception among actors' plays," said Max Beerbohm (*Saturday Review* 15 July 1899:71). "Of course it does not appeal to the public, but the eccentric few find much that is good in it." A.B. Walkley thought the theme well worn, but handled freshly: "one or both of the authors have the sort of talent of which the theatre stands just now very much in need" (*Times* 1 July 1899:16). St John Hankin, writing in *The Academy* (15 July 1899:67), found it "extremely bold." But he cautioned that "it is possible to be too clever for the London stage and it is very easy to be too original. 'The Weather-Hen' is so fresh, so startling even in the novelty of its treatment, that I am afraid it may puzzle more people than it will charm."

Though the playwrights revised their work, it found no further productions. Barker was meanwhile struggling for a living as an actor, appearing in Mrs Patrick Campbell's revivals of those quintessential plays about the Woman with a Past, *The Second Mrs Tanqueray* and *The Notorious Mrs Ebbsmith*. In November, however, he was to exercise his talents in a more challenging way. William Poel selected him to play Richard II in a single matinee performance by the Elizabethan Stage Society, at the lecture theatre of the University of London in Burlington Gardens. It was Barker's first major role. "Mr William Poel had a surprise in store for the large audience," reported Walkley (*Times* 13 Nov. 1899:5):

the play had scarcely begun before it was clear that there was one player in the company whose talent would make the performance exceptionally interesting. A few months ago that oddly named piece *The Weather-Hen* showed Mr Granville Barker in the light of a promising dramatist. *Richard II* proved him to be also a well-graced and intelligent actor, with gifts especially fitting him for romantic drama. . . . Gay and princely in the first two acts, Mr Barker played the later scenes with a decided sense of character, and with pathos that seemed to touch every section of his rather difficult audience.

The audience was difficult not because of Poel's methods, as Purdom says (8), but because it was largely composed of schoolgirls studying the play for the Cambridge Local Examination, laughing and tittering at every excuse. Barker's achievement was powerful enough to overcome that distraction and some weak support from the amateur cast, who suffered from Poel's usual fault of slowness.

Barker learned much about directing from Poel, as he would acknowledge all his life, but his first opportunity to direct came from another source. The Stage Society, founded that same year, almost borrowed the name of Poel's group. But it was dedicated to a different object, the presentation of new and unproduced plays that were not commercially acceptable. Better organized and better subscribed than the Independent Theatre, it began with a clear social perspective. The founders, Janet Achurch, Charles Charrington, Walter Crane, Grant Richards, and Frederick Whelen (Wade 285), were Fabians who looked on the theatre as a powerful weapon for social change. Its opening production was Shaw's *You Never Can Tell*, just fifteen days after Poel's *Richard II*. Five more programs were presented in the initial season, and Barker was connected with four of them. He acted the roles of Eric Bratsberg in Ibsen's *The League of Youth* in February 1900 (Berte Thomas was Dr Fieldbo), Robert in Hauptmann's *The Coming of Peace* in June, and Marchbanks in Shaw's *Candida* in July. His first directing job was a triple bill of poetic plays in April.

Why was Granville Barker placed in charge of the Society's fourth production? The other presentations of the first season were directed by Achurch or Charrington, who had considerable experience with the advanced drama of Europe, whereas Barker had not yet fully proved himself in any way. Perhaps his intelligence and enthusiasm won over the governing committee. The plays he directed were Maeterlinck's *Interior* and *The Death of Tintagiles*, along with *The House of Usna* by Fiona MacLeod. Maeterlinck was an important writer for the European Free Stage movement in the nineties, principally because his misty symbolism provided an alternative to the dominant theatrical style, but had been rarely seen in London. *The House of Usna*, a treatment of the Concobar legend, was heavily influenced by the Belgian dramatist and by Yeats. It is a mournful threnody for Dierdre set against ruined backgrounds "vague in the moonlight" (F. MacLeod 409) and, like the Maeterlinck plays, gives wide scope to the director.

Fiona MacLeod was the pseudonym of William Sharp, then president of the Stage Society. In a note at the end of his collected works, his wife says that only a few people in the audience knew the truth of the play's authorship (454). Sharp went to great lengths to preserve the secret. He wrote a letter to the Society, dated 16 April 1900 (in the British Theatre Museum), purporting to be from Fiona MacLeod in Scotland, about arrangements for the production. It authorizes certain changes in the script, and requests reserved seats for Yeats, Ernest Rhys, and a box for George Meredith. Whether or not Barker was party to the secret, he must have found Sharp's presence trying.

Unfortunately nothing is known of the production. In its first season the Stage Society gave only one Sunday evening performance of a program and disallowed reviews in the press, so that no significant details have survived. Nonetheless it is apparent that Barker was marching to a different drum: the other plays of that opening year, though new to England, were examples of social realism. Barker's directing debut aligned him with Lugné-Poe and the Symbolists, rather than with Antoine or Brahm and their British followers.

His standing in the Society grew quickly. When *Candida* was being planned, Charrington, who was to direct and play Morrel, suggested him for the part of Eugene Marchbanks. For the rest of his life Shaw would claim the credit as the discoverer of Barker as an actor. In an obituary of his friend, Shaw remembered, "His performance of this part – a very difficult one to cast – was, humanly speaking, perfect" ("Granville Barker: Some Particulars" 8). But the plain fact is that Shaw did not at first want him for the role. He replied to Charrington on 6 June 1900, "I have often seen Granville Barker act, and as I cannot remember him in the least, and *can* remember [Henry V.] Esmond, I conclude that Esmond is the better man. . . . Unless I can get a Eugene of Esmond's standing, the play shall not be done" (*Letters* 2:170). He agreed to the casting only after he saw Barker in *The Coming of Peace*: "I withdrew my observations concerning G.B., whom I certainly never saw before" (2:172). After the performance, he crowed to Archer, "Yes: the poet – Granville Barker – was the success of the piece. It was an astonishing piece of luck to hit on him" (2:175). A collaboration had begun.

Within the next few years Barker would play Kearney in *Captain Brassbound's Conversion*, Napoleon in *The Man of Destiny*, Frank in *Mrs Warren's Profession*, and would assist the dramatist in directing *The Admirable Bashville*, all but one for the Stage Society. He became an early promoter of Shaw's plays as well; in September 1900 he was trying to arrange a series of matinees of *Candida* at the Comedy Theatre (letter to Charrington, Yale). To Shaw he soon seemed indispensable. "My only misgiving with regard to you," Shaw wrote in 1901, "is as to whether the Stage, in its present miserable condition, is good enough for you: you are sure to take to authorship or something of the kind" (*SLB* 8).

In 1903 he acted in Somerset Maugham's *A Man of Honour* and in Herman Heijermans' *The Good Hope* for the Stage Society. The second was staged by Max Behrend, another influence on Barker as a director. He also played Marlowe's Edward II for William Poel at Oxford. But aside from Shavian roles Barker's acting was less important than his directing. In 1901 he staged Israel Zangwill's *The Revolted Daughter*, in 1902 his own play *The Marrying of Ann Leete*, and in the next year S.M. Fox's *The Waters of Bitterness* (on the same bill with *Bashville*). His reputation shot forward. In 1904, in the few months before the start of the Vedrenne–Barker season at the Court, he directed Brieux's *The Philanthropists*, *The Two Gentlemen of Verona*, *Candida*, Euripides' *Hippolytus*, Yeats's *Where There Is Nothing*, and *The Pharisee's Wife* by George Paston. With the exception of *Two Gentlemen*, the productions played in matinees and very briefly, some for one performance only. They were sponsored by the Stage Society and its fellow Impossibilists, like the New Century Theatre and the matinees funded by J.T. Grein's newspaper, *The Sunday Special*. They made up the London constituency of theatre dreamers, attempting to do their new work, on whatever scale, outside the regular managements. Barker was already a chief representative. Later he would accurately name them "the Secessionist Movement" ("Theatre: Next Phase" 631).

Although the acutal productions are of limited historical interest, they demonstrated Barker's prowess with a variety of styles. His direction of a realistic comedy, *The Revolted Daughter*, even the discriminating Archer found "notably good" (*World* 27 Mar. 1901:25); and Grein praised Barker in a little speech after the curtain (*Stage* 28 Mar. 1901:14). The Yeats piece, a sprawling and uncontrolled work about an Irish St Francis, presented many challenges in casting and staging. Yet Barker managed to bring off this "odd, eccentric, and hardly ever dramatic play," according to *The Stage* (30 June 1904:13). *Hippolytus* (discussed in chapter 3) and *Two Gentlemen* gave him a different type of experience, foreshadowing a later involvement in redefining the classics.

A final point should be made about this period of Barker's apprenticeship. Many of the plays he chose to direct were about women, continuing his own interest as a playwright. *The Revolted Daughter*, *Ann Leete*, *The Waters of Bitterness*, *Candida*, and *Hippolytus* have female protagonists or significant female roles, and take some aspect of womanhood as their themes. *The Pharisee's Wife* is a quasi-feminist play – George Paston was the pseudonym of Emily Morse Symonds, author of a number of novels – about the relative sexual rights of a husband and wife. ("The audience at the Duke of York's Theatre on Tuesday afternoon was chiefly composed of ladies," reported *The Era* of 16 July 1904:13). This tendency of Barker's would become a permanent trait, and should be seen as another sign of his artistic singularity.

The Marrying of Ann Leete

The most important accomplishment of 1899 for Granville Barker was the completion of his first play without the help of Berte Thomas. The loss of his collaborator must have been liberating, for *The Marrying of Ann Leete* is not only a work of distinction, it also provided the structural model for Barker's subsequent comedy. Its stage history, however, is not indicative of its accomplishment. In the dramatist's lifetime it received only two private performances, and was not seen again professionally until David Jones revived it for the Royal Shakespeare Company in 1975, with Mia Farrow in the lead. Its absence from the stage for more than two generations was unfortunate for English drama: it is an extraordinary piece, adventurous, vital, light years ahead of Pinero, Jones, and Wilde, who provided the norms of literate drama in the nineties. And though its protagonist is a New Woman, the play shows no major influence from Shaw.

Set at the end of the eighteenth century (revolution in France, democracy on the rise, William Pitt in power), the play wishes to give distance to its subject. Ann is a New Woman a hundred years removed: "you want a new world . . you new woman," her brother says. The outer subject is public, as is so often the case with Barker's work. Carnaby Leete is a parliamentarian, failing in fortunes and in health, who sees a chance for political renascence in a family alliance with Lord John Carp. Carnaby had earlier disposed of his elder daughter Sarah to a member of the opposite party for similar reasons. Her marriage, now falling apart in bitter mutual contempt, is a negative example for Ann. Brother George, in a futile attempt to escape his father's transactions, married a simple country girl. But he made the mistake of bringing her into society, where she seems an embarrassment, a vulgar climber, a more caring precursor of Natasha in *The Three Sisters*.

The first act opens in literal obscurity: in the dark and with a scream. At Carnaby Leete's country house near Reading, the family and guests have been up all night. Lord John had just kissed Ann in the garden, part in desire, part in game, and part for a bet. As the day gets lighter, the game becomes serious. Carnaby skillfully manages a quarrel, supposedly over his daughter's honor, trapping Lord John into an unwanted duel. But the emphasis is not on the outward, public action, despite the political interest; rather it is on Ann's inner self. Her growth is hidden from the eyes of her family, like the sprouting of a seed, to take the play's central metaphor: it is her secret life that charges her character and determines her course. Though she does not recognize its implications until the climax, already in the opening we sense hidden power awakening within.

Carnaby is wounded in the arm by Lord John in the second act, and that dramatic catalyst has prompted the "victor" to capitulate and propose to Ann. Of course this was the politician's intention from the start, giving him, as he puts it, "an anchor in each camp . . There's a mixed metaphor." Ann, half in love and half in duty, agrees to the match: in deconstructive terms, she embraces the phallocentric world and her traditional place in it. "Look upon yourself – not too seriously – Ann, as the instrument of political destiny," explains George; "I suppose that a woman's profession is marriage," she admits (*Three Plays* 24–5). But as she begins to understand consciously how her father's world works and wants to use her, another less conscious awareness has been growing.

Acts 1 through 3 are set entirely in the garden; at subtle and crucial moments the gardener enters to carry out his work. He stands in direct contrast to the sophisticated, ultracivilized eighteenth-century life of the Leete family. Indeed his very name is about to blossom: John Abud: not John Carp. He had once courted Dolly, George's wife; her farmer-father thought the gardener beneath his daughter. Now Dolly is about to give birth, and thus George, despite himself, has a double connection to Abud, an interest in Dolly and a role in cultivating new life. "But it's great to be a gardener," Ann says, "to sow seeds and to watch flowers grow and to cut away dead things." At the end of act 2 the news arrives that Dolly has safely delivered twins. The garden abounds with fertility, and its caretaker is delighted. "I wonder that you can be pleased," Ann says in surprise. "It's life," Abud answers.

In the third act Ann's inner growth pokes through to her conscious mind. She sees finally what her worth is in her father's view of the world, mostly as a result of observing her sister's unhappiness. Her romantic, girlish notions of love for John Carp cannot alter the hard fact that she is property. The young protagonist faces a moral dilemma which is couched in sexual terms. Though Ann deeply loves her father, she refuses to sell her life for him: "I mean to disobey you . . to stay here . . never to be unhappy," she says. "I want to be an ordinary woman . . not clever . . not fortunate" (55). But she intuits that saying no is not enough, so she moves quickly from her refusal to an affirmation, grabbing what is at hand. Earlier in the act Carnaby had used the word "pellucid" to describe the rain, and wondered about its meaning. The parson explained, "Per . . lucere . . . letting light through." Now Carnaby's head is feverish from the wound and from wine. As the gardener passes by once more, Ann suddenly turns to him:

ANN: John Abud . . you mean to marry. When you marry . . will you marry me?
(*A blank silence, into which breaks* CARNABY's *sick voice*.)
CARNABY: Take me indoors. I heard you ask the gardener to marry you.
ANN: I asked him.
CARNABY: I heard you say that you asked him. Take me in . . but not out of the rain.
ANN: Look . . he's straight-limbed and clear-eyed . . and I'm a woman.
SARAH: Ann, are you mad?
ANN: If we two were alone here in this garden and everyone else in the world were dead . . what would you answer?
ABUD: (*Still amazed.*) Why . . yes.
CARNABY: Then that's settled . . pellucid.   (56)

In Barker's production, Abud, played by C.M. Hallard, "somewhat sadly accepted the situation" when he realized that Ann was in earnest (*Daily Chronicle* 28 Jan. 1902:6). Their pact is made with a determination equal to that of the first parents, for whom any doubts or questions about the meaning of love must have been irrelevant luxuries.

But Ann will not make her brother's mistake any more than her sister's. She intends to remain a gardener's wife, knowing the harsh toil her choice implies. She is the opposite of Chekhov's philosophizing characters like Astrov or Vershinin, who talk constantly of a better future while spending the precious present in stupid, wasteful lives. She will bring the future to the world now, herself a new Eve in the garden, if only as a frail gesture against the unlivable present. She will marry, but will not be married off.

Of course the world, like her sister Sarah, is convinced she is mad, and a wonderful wedding scene in the fourth act shows how class suspicions on all sides will prevent her gesture from having social value beyond her own life.

Barker's economy in writing did not extend this far. He requires an eighteenth-century manor house hall, and nine new characters for this scene alone, almost half the total cast. But the final moments of the play return to the elliptical style and reveal the true weight of Ann's impulsive action. The short last scene, one of Barker's finest and one of the best in modern English drama, takes place after the wedding party. The new couple have walked nine muddy miles to their new life. The bare plaster and red brick of Abud's cottage contrast to the opulence of Leete's polished hall in the previous scene. The spare, careful speech of the new partners similarly contrasts to the rich wit of the world Ann has abandoned:

ABUD: Out there's the scullery.
ANN: It's very cold.
ABUD: If we light the fire now that means more trouble in the morning.
    (*She sits on the settle*.)
ANN: Yes, I am very weary.
ABUD: Go to bed.
ANN: Not yet. (*After a moment*.) How much light one candle gives! Sit where I may see you.
    (*He sits on the bench. She studies him curiously*.)
ANN: Well . . this is an experiment.
ABUD: (*With reverence*.) God help us both.
ANN: Amen. Some people are so careful of their lives.   (76–7)

We are made strongly aware of the sexual implications of the bridal night, but Ann is poised on the edge of a spiritual precipice as well as a carnal one. In fact the incipient sexuality is used in the typical Barker way, as a sign of the secret inner life, and the outer subject of politics disappears entirely as the inner subject crystallizes. Ann Leete's marrying is her call to arms for a new world: "Papa . . I said . . we've all been in too great a hurry getting civilised. False dawn. I mean to go back" (79).

Her choice of Abud is not as precipitate as it appears. She wants to be connected to the soil, to the control of nature, turning her back on the etiolated life of her father for a life of peasant solidity. ("I'm a gardener," Abud says in act 2, "and there'll always be gardens.") Human happiness is found in risk-taking and personal commitment, and a sexual relationship like this one is its adequate sign. "Don't you aspire like George's wife," Ann cautions her husband. "I was afraid to live . . and now . . I am content" (79). The tense, disjointed dialogue is created by Barker's frequent employment of the ellipsis (in his characteristic usage, made up of only two dots), indicating quick pauses or changes of tone similar to those of Beckett and Pinter. The scene thus moves away from representational naturalism, and gives importance to theatrical symbols that suggest the inner world of the characters. The cold fireplace in the poor cottage, the dark steep stairs winding to bed, the single candle Abud holds to light Ann up them, all work to a final moment of great stage power, unusual in intensity and in scope.

Ann Leete has the balance of a sonata movement. It opens and ends in darkness – though the candle at the close is an important sign of hope for the future. It opens and ends with a man kissing Ann against her will, with the attendant sexual connotations. But John Carp's kiss, which leads to the outer action, is frivolous and playful. John Abud's kiss, which he takes out of duty and as his right, is serious and solemn, more a symbolic act than an act of love.

Like all of Barker's drama, the play is built around a great refusal with strong sexual ramifications, a personal version of what Dante called *il gran' rifiuto*. In refusing to be coin for her father, Ann refuses the accepted state of women as well as the life of aristocratic ease that seduced her sister. In itself hers is a naive, romantic refusal, but she transcends the sentimental by deliberately embracing a life of toil against all logic and advice. (John Carp's brother asks in the wedding scene, "But . . good heavens . . are we to choose to be toiling animals?") Ann's hard affirmation is not so much penance for her past as salvation for her future. Unlike Ibsen's Nora, she does not simply say no to what she learns is wrong, but goes on to say yes to what she will work to make right. The final scene presents the distillation of Ann's refusals and acceptances in sexual terms. Her bedding is also the beginning of a new century, a new world, hard, lonely, but green and untainted by the past.

The personal lives and sexual relations of Barker's characters are always more significant than the outer actions they provoke. His later work *The Secret Life*, published in 1923 but never produced, makes this concern overt; Eric Salmon's recent book, *Granville Barker: A Secret Life*, takes it for the theme of its subject's mind. All of Barker's plays, even the unpublished early ones, end with a scene in which a man and a woman discuss the sexual implications of their lives, though the tragedy *Waste* places this scene in the penultimate position. These sexual conclusions force the characters to consider how to continue in a world made complicated by the action of the play. The comedies also follow the structure used in *Ann Leete*: the protagonist is faced with a moral dilemma in which he or she is opposed by the father, refuses the negative example of close relatives, and ends by accepting a mate under difficult conditions. The pattern is of course similar to the classic one of New Comedy. Barker's major distinction lies in his insistence on the moral, inner significance of the protagonist's great refusal. Sexual relationship is not used as the symbol of a revitalized, perennial social order, but rather as a sign of the new world the hero strives to create.

We have seen how Barker's plays with Berte Thomas used female protagonists directed by external currents from a patriarchal world, like the weatherhen Eve Prior. Ann Leete at first is pulled by similar forces, but her awakening makes her a totally different character than her predecessors. Barker's second solo play, *Agnes Colander*, completed in January 1901, returns to the earlier model. It is unpublished; the author intended that it be destroyed. Agnes is a sieve-woman, floating from man to man while life drains through her, because she has lacked a conviction of her own value. Neither the character nor the play are near the level of accomplishment of *Ann Leete*, and

Barker would not use such a figure again. Yet Agnes struggles against conventional morality in a way new to English drama. She sincerely seeks a sexual identity in life, and is thus in direct contrast to Paula Tanqueray or Lady Susan, who seek social identity by denying their carnal pasts or carnal instincts. Agnes Colander approaches sexual life even more openly than Shaw's Sylvia Craven or Vivie Warren. "It comes to me," Agnes says at the end of the first act, "how one hammers eternally at the door of this sex question." The line amounts to a précis of Barker's theme as a playwright.

The Marrying of Ann Leete was presented by the Stage Society in 1902, the author directing, and its reception is indicative of the difficulty Barker's work could cause. Subtlety of language and insistence on inner action were not qualities generally admired in his time. "The motive of the play is obscure," said *The Stage* (30 Jan. 1902:21); "clever, daring – perhaps, impudent – inconclusive and unsound, but not uninteresting," allowed *The Sketch* (5 Feb. 1902:113). "But never, surely, did audience leave a theatre more completely mystified," thought *The Daily Telegraph* (28 Jan. 1902:5), disturbed by the social implications of the story as much as by the brisk dialogue. "Why in the name of reason and commonsense did Ann Leete throw over a young, presentable, impassioned, and entirely eligible nobleman for a husband socially so much her inferior as John Abud?" A.B. Walkley, as literate as any of the Edwardian critics, was so in the dark that he thought "an explanatory pamphlet" advisable: "It must be difficult to write a play in four acts . . . and throughout them all to keep your audience blankly ignorant of the meaning of it. . . . Granville Barker calls his piece a comedy. It might more suitably be termed a practical joke" (*Times* 28 Jan. 1902:7). Most critics praised Winifred Fraser's performance as Ann, but Walkley concluded that she "appeared to be suffering under the same disadvantage as the audience in not knowing what in the world the author was driving at."

Part of the fault may have been Barker's as director, working for an oversubtle style that did not sufficiently clarify the main action, though this is only a suspicion. The Edwardian stage was not ready for social problem comedies that departed significantly from realism. That is what troubled William Archer, realism's champion, who frequently complained about the work, and was still objecting two decades later that to him "the characters depicted, and the reasons for their sayings and doings, remained utterly enigmatic" (*Old Drama and New* 357). Shaw thought that judgment revealed Archer as "a hopeless philistine" (*SLB* 158), and in some ways Shaw was right.

Yet a few commentators suggest that the performance was equal to the excellence of the play. *The Daily News* thought it the most interesting work seen in London for several years, a rare example of "a play written with such evident knowledge of the theatre, and of what can be done in the theatre" (28 Jan. 1902:5). Arthur Symons, who could be expected to be sympathetic to a piece with affinities to Symbolism, thought it self-indulgent but fascinating.

"It is chaos," he said, "lit up by incessant flashes of lightning." Symons was especially impressed with the last scene:

A new thing on the stage, full of truth within its own limits; but it is an episode, not a conclusion, much less a solution. Mr Barker can write: he writes in short, sharp sentences, which go off like pistol shots, and he can keep up the firing, from every corner of the stage. (*Academy* 1 Feb. 1902:122–3)

Symons caught the flavor of the piece well. Since he saw the play only once, in a hastily rehearsed private performance, it is reasonable to conclude that *Ann Leete* was accessible enough in 1902 to those with ears to listen. It is much more accessible in our time, however. We are used to inconclusiveness, and probably expect it, so that we find the lack of a "solution" unobjectionable: another sign of Barker's advanced art.

2 Creating the New Drama

VICTORIA DRANK TEA, Edward drank champagne. It was a decade of champagne he led; the Edwardian rich served champagne, as J.B. Priestley remarks (61), on occasions when one would be perfectly content with a glass of barley-water. The theatre in general reflected the tastes of the new monarch well, uncorking case after case of intoxicating effervescence. The Free Stage movement, for all its importance, had little effect on the quality of dramatic life in London. Grein himself remained convinced that the public could not be made to accept serious new plays; the various Sunday and matinee producing societies failed to stimulate even a minor reawakening of English playwriting outside the accepted commercial realm. Shaw was the only writer strong enough and stubborn enough to row against the tide. By 1904 he had written and published eleven plays, at least half of them highly important works. He was well known to readers but almost unknown to audiences. In fact, until Barker took charge Shaw was the most important playwright in English and European history to have been snubbed by the regular theatres.[1] His fate, though clearly anomalous, stood as a warning to any serious writer thinking of the stage.

London needed some form of compromise between the societies and the commercial managements, a venue where new plays could be publicly performed without high costs and the need for long runs: not so much a Théâtre Libre as a Moscow Art Theatre. In the spring of 1903, at age twenty-six and with only a few productions to his personal credit, Granville Barker already possessed a transforming idea. He outlined a plan of remarkable perspicacity to William Archer in "a rather long letter":

> Do you think there is anything in this idea? To take the Court Theatre for six months or a year and to run there a stock season of the uncommercial Drama: Hauptmann – Sudermann – Ibsen – Maeterlinck – Schnitzler – Shaw – Brieux etc.
>> Not necessarily plays untried in England.
>> A fresh production every fortnight.
>> Not necessarily a stock company.
>> The highest price five or six shillings.
>> To be worked *mainly* as a subscription theatre.
>> One would require a guarantee of £5000 – if possible 50 people putting down £100 each. I would stake everything on plays and acting – not attempt "productions." (British Library)

The letter is a seminal document in the Edwardian reform of the stage. Most important is the motivating idea itself: an extended stock season at a small London theatre of drama that would not pay under ordinary circumstances. Barker's notion was to put the work of the producing societies on a regular basis, and change the bill often enough to avoid any suggestion that a play's run must be controlled by the box office. A subsidy was therefore necessary, and most of the audience would be subscribers, already pledged to whatever the theatre offered, like the members of the Stage Society. But the theatre would not be private; the general public could buy reasonably priced tickets (five or six shillings for the best seat would have been a bargain in 1903), and each play would last long enough for critical reaction to register. The chief drawback lay in the budget. Expenses would be heavily limited if they were to be kept at the proposed £250 a week, certainly requiring that the emphasis be on "plays and acting" rather than on "productions."

Barker saw that limitation as a virtue. It is characteristic that he planned even this simple project as a step towards something greater, and that his ultimate concern was to raise the level of dramatic writing in England. The letter continues, "It seems to me that we may wait a very long time for our National Theatre, and that when it comes we may have no modern National Drama to put in it. We must get vital drama from somewhere, and if we can't create it we must import it first." He was sure this vital drama would appeal to those who were "profoundly bored" by the current state of the theatre – the people, say, who read Shaw's plays with approval but stayed away from the regular playhouses. It would have the added value of invigorating the performers, for "our actors – and worse still our actresses – are becoming demoralised by a lack of intellectual work – the continual demand for nothing but smartness and prettiness." The last phrase is telling, nearly summing up the monarch's notion of the theatre as a place designed to keep him more or less awake between a heavy dinner and the midnight champagne supper.

Archer had been working for a quarter century to improve dramatic art in London, as a critic, as a translator, and as the founder of the New Century Theatre. But he was not a practical man of the stage. Barker was young, idealistic, and indefatigable; he was now an accomplished actor and a promising playwright. He was convinced that there was "a greater number of people interested in the pioneer drama" than ever before, but that the regular managers, "more timid and conservative than ever," would not act to change. The two men had a long talk, during which Archer apparently cooled some of his young friend's enthusiasm. A week later Barker thought that his scheme would come to nothing. But he retained the hope that "the National Theatre will hurry up and that it will fall into Liberal or even Radical hands and deliver us to some extent from the manager with the wooden head and the stage manager with the iron hand before another generation of actors (mine in this case) has gone to the devil artistically" (British Library).

But exactly a year later, in April 1904, and at exactly the theatre he wished, Barker was given the chance he had despaired of, and it was Archer who provided the connection. J.H. Leigh was a wealthy amateur who had taken a lease on the Court for the purpose of presenting a series of "Shakespeare Representations," mostly for the sake of his young wife, Thyrza Norman. The quality of the first two left Leigh dissatisfied, and Archer suggested that Granville Barker be hired to direct the next play (Purdom 19). *The Two Gentlemen of Verona* opened on 8 April, with Thyrza Norman as Julia, Berte Thomas as the Duke of Milan, Lewis Casson as Eglamour and the First Outlaw, and Barker himself as Speed.

The production was a long way from Barker's later Shakespeare revolution at the Savoy. He did not hesitate to trim the text and adjust scenes to simplify set changes, as was the custom. The script was arranged in four parts, with all the Verona scenes grouped in the first, the Milan scenes in parts two and three, and the forest scenes in the last. Schubert's incidental music was used throughout to provide mood (*Era* 16 Apr. 1904:12) as Irving or Tree might do. Nonetheless Archer thought the style was "very nearly the right mean between 'Elizabethan Stage' austerity and actor-manager prodigality" (*World* 12 Apr. 1904:633). A.B. Walkley was delighted (*TLS* 15 Apr. 1904:117–18), and the critics in general liked Barker's portrayal of Speed, which had "a vein of light and airy intellectuality almost Bernard-Shawesque in its modernity" (*Stage* 14 Apr. 1904:15).

The reference to Shaw was especially appropriate. Barker had agreed to direct *Two Gentlemen* on condition that Leigh lend the theatre and his business manager for a few matinees of *Candida* as well (D. MacCarthy 1), which, though written in 1895, had not yet been seen publicly in London. Shaw agreed when he was satisfied about the cast and finances; he had been anxious for Barker to repeat his Marchbanks ever since the Stage Society performance that had launched their association in 1900.

Candida opened on 26 April and played six afternoons in two weeks, with Kate Rorke again in the lead and Norman McKinnel as Morell. The production was a turning-point in the history of the English theatre. The matinees actually made a profit, which was not an easy trick, and demonstrated that Shaw could be appreciated by a small general public. One popular paper, acknowledging the "complete success" of the opening, noted in surprise that "peals of laughter succeeded each other, and there were moments towards the end when a feeling akin to pathos overpowered the audience" (*Daily Graphic* 27 Apr. 1904:372). To admit that Shaw was a playwright with power to move assembled spectators, not just a clever crank who had mistaken his vocation, was a significant departure from conventional opinion. But more significant was the possibility that a series of similar matinees of new plays might prove practical on a regular basis. Barker's idea for "a stock season of the uncommercial Drama" was about to to bear fruit. He struck an agreement with Leigh's business manager, John Eugene Vedrenne, and engaged the theatre for afternoons the following autumn.

The Vedrenne–Barker seasons

Looking back on the three years of Vedrenne–Barker at the Court it is easy to see the undertaking as momentous and to say, as Purdom does (26), that "no theatrical enterprise of this century has left a deeper mark upon the theatrical history of London." As a director and manager, Barker opened to his audiences a new world of drama, of acting, of production style, and of performance scheduling. In fact it was during these seasons that he created and defined the position of the modern director in England. But in 1904 none of this was apparent. The series of matinees announced for the Court Theatre appeared in the press to be like any other, commonly given since the 1870s by actors as opportunities for themselves, or by playwrights to introduce new work, or simply by managers interested in tapping an audience, principally female, who found the theatre a newly respectable source of entertainment. It was cheap to hire a theatre for a few off days, and there has always been an excess of actors looking for work.

The beginnings of the Court fell far short of Barker's dream for a new theatre. His key notion, that there existed a "a class of intellectual would-be playgoers who are profoundly bored by the theatre as it is," could only be tested if performances were given in the evenings. "Matinee productions," he had said to Archer, "don't touch these people (who are all workers) and Sunday evening is expensive and incapable of expansion" (British Library). Only by taking the movement away from the club could its strength be judged.

Perhaps Barker was fortunate that his ideal was not fulfilled immediately, for he was forced as a result to begin in a small way and with limited capital provided by friends and associates, much of it from Shaw himself. Had Barker followed his natural inclination and spent money unchecked by circumstances or Vedrenne, the project would have collapsed after a few months. Instead of regular evenings, performances were to be on Tuesday, Thursday, and Friday afternoons; each production was expected to run for two weeks regardless of its reception. According to Lewis Casson, who acted in the company from the first season, the total cost of a set of matinees was reckoned at £200.

With the Stage Society's procedure as model, actors at the Court were paid a guinea a performance and nothing for rehearsals. (It may seem impossible to us, in a profession that is strictly unionized, but it was not until after the First World War that rehearsal pay became common: see J. Macleod 130.) Casson remembers that "a very few of us actors were on low-salaried seasonal contracts, but most of the parts were played by first-rate important actors at one guinea a show – the theory being that they were earning their main salary at night in the more regular theatres" ("Court Theatre" 289). Barker counted on his actors working primarily for the love of good work and the chance to play roles otherwise unavailable; six guineas for an entire production's labor amounted to little more than a fee for expenses.

But the bargain rates did not extend to the audience. It proved impossible to place the ticket prices as low as he hoped, and the cost of a seat ranged from ten shillings and sixpence in the stalls to a half-crown in the pit, the same as in most London theatres. A small gallery was also available, at a shilling a head. An attempt was made to sell subscriptions (according to Borsa 113), but the plan did not succeed and was abandoned.

The director's choice for his first production was *Man and Superman*. It had been published the year before, and may well have been the most important work to be written for the English stage for a generation or more: Barker wanted to make it the drumbeat of the Court Theatre. But Shaw was not happy about the selection, fearing he could not get an adequate cast. Instead he wanted Ellen Terry to play the part written for her in *Captain Brassbound's Conversion*. "Unless you do it at least once," he wrote her, "posterity will never forgive you: you will go down to all the ages as the woman who made *il gran' rifiuto*; for there never was and never will be again such a part written for any mortal" (*Letters* 2:421). Terry responded that "it would have been pleasant to me to have played Cicely for a week for nothing, or at least next-to-nothing," but was already engaged to make money in the provinces (St John 296).

Shaw's mind then turned to material he was struggling with that summer, "a sort of political farce, of no use to anybody but cranks" (*Letters* 2:430), originally promised to Yeats for the Irish Literary Theatre. It was still unfinished when he wrote Barker in August, "I think the Superman would need a cast of more weight and splendour than Rule Britannia (provisional name for the Irish play)" (*SLB* 22). The Irish play, eventually called *John Bull's Other Island*, proved impossible for Dublin. But for the Court its advantages went beyond the theatrical, for it was concerned with one of the most pressing political questions of the time, Home Rule for Ireland. It could establish a social identity for the new theatre as well as an aesthetic one. But again Shaw saw a difficulty. His political sense made him realize that the date of the première was crucial: "It has only just occurred to me that it would be very bad business to produce Rule Britt. before parliament meets again. . . . You will sell a lot of stalls to the political people; and the Irish M.P.s will fill the pit" (*SLB* 25). The play was therefore held up until November.

Thus it came about that the first work presented by the Vedrenne–Barker management was not English and not new, but 2,332 years old and by Euripides: *Hippolytus*, which opened on 18 October 1904. Nor was the production new, as it was a remounting of the performance Barker directed for the New Century Theatre the previous May. Shaw's importance to the Court can hardly be overemphasized, but the accident of opening with a Greek play points to the other guiding spirit in Barker's professional and personal life, Gilbert Murray. It also indicates the significance that Euripides would have in Barker's career as a director and creator of a new stage. Murray, convalescing from ill-health and overwork between his professorships at

Glasgow and Oxford, began publishing rhymed verse translations of the
Greek dramatists in 1902. Barker was the first to stage them; four separate
plays by Euripides would be presented in the Vedrenne–Barker seasons, and
three new productions were to come in 1912 and 1915. Late in life Barker
called Murray "my professor of Greek – my only one" and admitted
that "Greek plays without your guidance are treacherous ground to me"
(Bodleian). With his professor's help, however, Barker was prepared to tackle
the challenge of antiquity.

Although *Hippolytus* passed with only polite encouragement from the
critics, the new Shaw piece marked the Court as the home of a new style of
theatre. *John Bull's Other Island* opened on the first of November, the first
Shaw play to be produced before publication since *Widowers' Houses*.
Despite its length – it played from 2:30 to 6:00, so that "the audience naturally
thinned towards the close" (*Daily Graphic* 2 Nov. 1904:454) – the effect was
instantaneous and enthusiastic. As Shaw predicted, the politicians rushed to
Sloane Square for seats; Beatrice Webb convinced the Prime Minister,
Arthur Balfour, to attend the fifth performance. That representative of high
Toryism was delighted, though with what it is difficult to say, for when the
play was revived in the spring he returned three times: once with the Leader
of the Opposition, Henry Campbell-Bannerman, once with H.H. Asquith,
both of whom would be, within a few years, Liberal Prime Ministers forced to
deal with the Irish question. On his third visit Balfour came alone, to enjoy
the wit, we may assume, without political rivalry.

Of course its topicality aided the play, but the production was what
advanced the management's reputation. Playgoers recognized that a balanced
ensemble performance could be more satisfying than one organized around a
single virtuoso. "Society," Desmond MacCarthy wrote, "on the eve of a
general election, came to laugh at Broadbent, and to listen to brilliant
discussions upon Irish and English character. They sat enthralled through a
play with no vestige of a plot, delighted by acting unlit by the light of 'a star,'
which was obviously and incomparably the better for that" (xiii). The
performance was far superior to any regularly available in London, yet Shaw
and Barker had cast the twelve difficult roles without using a single name well
known in the West End. *The Era* saw something new and admirable about the
acting of the minor roles: "they had an air of reality and first-hand observation
which made them genuinely interesting and artistic" (5 Nov. 1904:15).

Despite its popularity, Barker conscientiously removed *John Bull* from the
program after its six matinees to make room for the next scheduled production, Maeterlinck's *Aglavaine and Selysette*. This play about the conflict
between childish and sexual love seemed over-precious even to advanced
spectators. "A dramatised essay by Emerson," Walkley said (*Times* 16 Nov.
1904:7); "one gets sick of kisses." Archer thought its appeal too narrow for the
audience that the Court was seeking (*World* 22 Nov. 1904:862), and concluded
later that "it is the business of a progressive management to experiment, and it

is not to be expected that every experiment should succeed" (*V–B Season* 5). The autumn productions ended with a revival of *Candida*, which did well at the box office. Barker was confident of its appeal, for he added four extra performances, using, for the first time, Saturdays and evenings.

The Court was renovated during the next two weeks, the second attempt by Leigh since the summer to improve stage facilities and the comfort of the auditorium. The managers must have thought the expense warranted, for they expected to make money on their next offering, intended to attract the lucrative Christmas trade. *Prunella*, a delicate Pierrot play with music, written by Barker and Laurence Housman, took over the theatre afternoons and evenings from 23 December, mounted for a holiday run. Special investment had been necessary, including £200 from Gilbert Murray, as the piece was expensive to produce: twenty-two characters, music, singing, dancing, lavish period costumes and set. The investment was lost. Of its twenty-eight performances, only one paid for itself; Barker had to face the first of many financial disappointments in the battle to win public acceptance of unconventional dramatic art.

The failure was not without its lessons, and the director learned them quickly. "Our primary mistake," he wrote to Murray on the last day of 1904, "and a costly one – has been doing it as a Xmas play – it won't go down as that and our usual public is out of town or has over-eaten itself" (Bodleian). Advertised as a play "for Grown-up Children," it collapsed between two age groups. Aunties took their holiday charges expecting a panto, and instead found a bittersweet discourse on seduction, betrayal, and the power of sexual love. "Not quite the right thing for a Christmas occasion," pronounced J.T. Grein in *The Sunday Times* on Christmas Day (4); "it will not thrill the parents, and it will impel the little ones to ask awkward questions."

The second half of the season opened in February with a revival of *John Bull*. The plays were now presented for three weeks of matinees, giving nine performances instead of six. A triple bill of Yeats's *The Pot of Broth*, Schnitzler's *In the Hospital*, and Shaw's *How He Lied to Her Husband* followed; then Hauptmann's *The Thieves' Comedy (Der Biberpelz)* in March, and *The Trojan Women* in April. Though the receptions were uneven, the scope of the works proved that Barker was able to handle a wide range of material, none of which had previously been attempted on the London public stage, and to attract enough spectators to stay open. Archer, who thought the performance of Hauptmann's play equal to that of the original Berlin cast, was positive that the Court management was "full of promise for the future, both of English authorship and of English acting" (*V–B Season* 7, 10).

Ironically it was King Edward himself who insured the early success of the home of intellectual drama. At an evening command performance of *John Bull* on 11 March, the lines written by a teetotal vegetarian socialist, the opposite in all respects of the fleshly modern monarch, made the king laugh so hard that he broke his chair. Vedrenne's reaction was ambivalent, as he had spent precious pounds in renting furniture for the royal box (Stier 272–3). Shaw's reaction may have been ambivalent too; Henry James found it "humiliating" when a visit from the same august personage, then the Prince of Wales, resuscitated his first play in 1891 (Edel 298–9). But the lover of champagne had nonetheless done a royal service, for the Vedrenne–Barker season, if still viewed with suspicion, now had an unparalleled social cachet. In less than five months, Barker had become famous, Shaw accepted, and the New Drama given a home.

For the remainder of their first season the managers took over the Court completely for what amounted to the first Shaw festival. *John Bull's Other Island* was brought back for three weeks in the evenings from May Day, while *You Never Can Tell*, absent from London for five years, played matinees. *Candida* did an evening stint, followed again by *You Never Can Tell*, on its road to becoming the most persistently popular of Shaw's plays. Barker acted in each of them. He also acted in the season's leading piece, which was given matinees from 23 May: *Man and Superman*.

Shaw had hesitations about Barker in the role of John Tanner, but had withheld the play, even from the limited production of the Stage Society, primarily for the lack of an Ann Whitefield. Shaw knew that no "ultra-modern actress" could come near the demands of the role:

I wanted a young Mrs Siddons or a Ristori . . . I was in despair of finding what I wanted when one day there walked into my rooms in the Adelphi a gorgeously goodlooking young lady in a green dress and huge picture hat in which any ordinary woman would have looked ridiculous, and in which she looked splendid, with the figure and gait of a Diana. She said: "Ten years ago, when I was a little girl trying to play Lady Macbeth, you told me to go and spend ten years learning my business. I have learnt it: now give me a part." I handed her the book of "Man and Superman" without a moment's hesitation, and said simply, "Here you are." And with that young lady I achieved performances of my plays which will probably never be surpassed.

The young lady was Lillah McCarthy. The story, told in Shaw's preface to her memoirs, *Myself and My Friends* (5), has the ring of myth. Nonetheless it is essentially correct. He had reviewed her amateur performance as Lady Macbeth in 1895 (*Our Theatres* 1:139–40), and she took the advice and spent the intervening time in apprenticeship, some with Ben Greet, most in heroic parts around the world with Wilson Barrett. It was a remarkable fortune that brought her back to London, to Shaw and the Court, at the moment of sudden need for her "beautiful, plastic, statuesque" presence. Within the next few years she would also create the roles of Jennifer Dubedat, Doña Ana, and Margaret Knox, in addition to playing Nora, Gloria, and Raina. Shaw wrote Lina Szczepanowska in *Misalliance* for her (though she did not play it) and Lavinia in *Androcles and the Lion*. She became the mainstay of the Court company, and later Barker's partner in expanding the Court ideals in London.

Lillah McCarthy and Granville Barker were married in April 1906. One sign of the success of *Man and Superman* appeared in *The Sketch*, where the event was announced as "The Wedding of 'John Tanner' and 'Ann White-field' " (2 May 1906:74). That was a year after the play's first performances, but they received enough contentious notice to make a capstone to the initial Vedrenne–Barker season. It had been *annus mirabilis*: twelve plays (three of them one-acts), practically speaking all new to London, produced without subsidy, directed and acted with a sensitivity rarely seen anywhere.

Of course there were objections. William Archer was only voicing the most common when he found a "disquieting feature" in "the undue predominance of the works of Mr Bernard Shaw" (*V–B Season* 10). An Italian critic put it more directly: "Woe to the Court, if it should become a dramatic branch of the Fabian Society" (Borsa 118). But Shaw's predominance was not just, as Archer thought, "an outburst of latent or suppressed popularity." It was chiefly the result of the lack of any other good contemporary English plays. As Grein had gone to Shaw for the New Drama twelve years before, so Barker had to rely on him as well.

Prunella was the only other new English work in the first season – written quickly, in collaboration, and meant as an entertainment. Shaw suggested *The Weather-Hen* would be appropriate for the Court (*SLB* 25); that Barker disagreed, and refrained as well from producing *Ann Leete*, shows that he and Vedrenne were careful to keep the theatre from seeming a conservatory of Barker in bloom. Even so he was as visible as the old-fashioned actor–manager he disdained. He played major roles in all the Shaw plays, as well as the Henchman in *Hippolytus* and the protagonist in *Prunella*: seven important parts for a total of 191 performances. He assisted in the direction of Shaw's work, and directed the seven other pieces alone. He ran the artistic side of the theatre, controlling play selection, casting, and scheduling, and overseeing design, costumes, music, and the hundred details that make up the tone of a company. It was a prodigious amount of labor, and a marvel that Barker withstood it.

He was just as busy in the second season, which began in September 1905 with another recall of *John Bull*. Though he acted less, he directed more, and paid more attention to a policy for the theatre. "I am really a little frightened at the rush of work that is just coming on," he wrote Murray in January 1906, "and perhaps another straw might break this camel's back" (Bodleian). Shaw delivered *Major Barbara*, the first masterwork prompted by the Court, and Ellen Terry at last played in *Captain Brassbound's Conversion*. There was a production of *The Wild Duck*, the first in English in London since 1897: "I'm wild-quacked to death," Barker wrote Murray (Bodleian), and then resigned the role of Hjalmar after three performances to play Tanner again in the evenings. *Electra* had its première, and *Prunella* was encouraged in a revival. Most important, however, there were new plays not written by Shaw.

The only one of lasting significance was Barker's own *The Voysey Inheritance*, which opened to high acclaim in November, the same month as *Major Barbara*. By then there could be no doubt that the Court was a theatre of social concerns. In September a highly promising work, *The Return of the Prodigal*, had cut deeply into the fabric of Edwardian convention. It was written by St John Hankin, a journalist, who also wrote *The Cassilis Engagement*. (Hankin committed suicide in 1909; Barker dedicated *Three Plays* to his memory as a "fellow-worker.") His play is excellent social satire, Oscar Wilde ten years later and without the sentiment, and deserves renewed attention. It provides flashing glimpses of the terrors of poverty and hunger alive in the land, all the more powerful because seen through the eyes of a rich man's son.

The other new works of the second season were less successful. Two poetic romances by the popular novelist Maurice Hewlett were artificial and stale. R.V. Harcourt's *A Question of Age* (on a bill with a short play by Frederick Fenn) was a solid failure, the only offering removed before its initial performances were completed. The audience was bewildered by its confusing plot and was not aided by the actors, who omitted a crucial section of dialogue on the first afternoon (D. MacCarthy 26). But a pattern had been created nonetheless: concentration on new English plays, and on new interpretations of the classics, with dominant attention to ensemble playing rather than to stars. A new play was now given only two matinees a week for three weeks, which eased the burden on the company, and the successes were moved into the evening bill. The policy allowed continued risk and experimentation in the afternoons, yet provided the best work a showing at night where it was accessible to all. This further complicated casting, as many of the better actors were engaged elsewhere for evening curtains. Barker could not use Arthur Whitby as the Peasant in *Electra*, for example, "without sacrificing him when the play is done in the evening" (Bodleian), for he was already in a comedy at the Garrick. Thus the Court was a long way from true repertory. But it was working.

In the third season the enterprise flowered. Though there was no Euripides, Shaw provided his fourth première, *The Doctor's Dilemma*, as well as *Don Juan in Hell* and the first public showing of *The Philanderer*. Barker cut back his acting to only three roles, even giving up Keegan to William Poel and Tanner to Robert Loraine. Instead he devoted his time to directing plays by new writers: Galsworthy's *The Silver Box*, Hankin's *The Charity That Began at Home*, Cyril Harcourt's *The Reformer*, John Masefield's *The Camden Wonder*, and a feminist work by Elizabeth Robins, *Votes for Women!* Though most were first plays, it was a roll call that few theatres in Europe could match for range, power, or social concern. "The management of Messrs Vedrenne and Barker, indeed, is the best thing that has happened to the stage in our time. It has let ideas into the theatre." That praise, on the front page of *The Referee* (14 Apr. 1907), was a brisk summary of a three-year saga. Thirty-two plays for 988 performances[2]–the Thousand Performances, J.C. Trewin says they were called (*Edwardian Theatre* 4) – made the Court a white arc light in the Mauve Decade.

Vedrenne–Barker at the Savoy

The problems, however, were enormous. Aside from the debilitating load of work, there were serious limitations that became more apparent as the experiment succeeded. The Court Theatre had been an ideal choice at the start; it was out of the West End, yet accessible by underground railway, was intimate, comfortable, and architecturally delightful. Its seating capacity (about 642) was right for the matinee audience, but became restrictive when the emphasis switched to evenings. In fact, the entire basis of the project had changed in the second season. Actors who would gladly accept matinee work for expenses had to be paid more for regular evening runs, if they were available at all. Further, the Court had cramped storage and rehearsal space, making the change from a 2.30 to an 8.15 performance very difficult, and full repertory scheduling impossible. Early in the third season Barker was already planning to move to larger premises which would have scope for a big play: "I would very much like to make 'Peer Gynt' the first Vedrenne–Barker matinee at the new theatre," he wrote to Archer, "and it's really only a question of when, for we obviously can't go on here much longer" (British Library). Both managers wanted a bigger operation, but for different reasons. Vedrenne wanted to make the "uncommercial Drama" pay as well as its rival, Barker wanted to build his success into a subsidized national repertory theatre.

In 1904 Barker had helped Archer to write a proposal of revolutionary vision, called *Scheme and Estimates for a National Theatre*. It had been rumored, as Lewis Casson reports, that Andrew Carnegie would build such an institution "if a complete scheme were laid before him" ("Court Theatre" 291). In this expectation, the authors assiduously printed and distributed the book privately, but the money did not appear. Now, in August 1907, with the Court behind him, Barker added a new preface and published the work, forlornly hoping that his personal example would shake coins from the tightly drawn purse of Edwardian philanthropy. The book, a justification for an endowed theatre as well as a detailed plan for its construction and operation, provided a theoretic foundation for expanding Barker's practical work on a national scale.

For their different reasons, then, Vedrenne and Barker moved their now famous names to the Savoy Theatre in September. It proved a disastrous change. Like many successful enterprises, the Court had acquired a mystique, vaguely defined but palpable, and the *genius loci* did not travel. The Savoy, only some 350 seats larger than the Court, nonetheless made intimate playing difficult, and the pioneer audience felt uncomfortable in the heart of theatre land. The bigger house meant higher rent, higher costs, higher risks for each production; and the management, as it knew well, had to be more and more concerned with business.

Unfortunately business was poor. *You Never Can Tell* was trotted out to start the evening bill; Shaw derided Barker for aping the regular theatres by playing the National Anthem at the opening (*SLB* 104). Galsworthy's *Joy* was given eight matinees, a family drama without the social bite or character insight of *The Silver Box*. Though Walkley liked both play and production (*TLS* 26 Sept. 1907:294), *The Nation* found it "baffling" (28 Sept. 1907:1085), and the majority opinion was summed up by *The Illustrated London News* of the same date: "disappointing" (438). *The Devil's Disciple* opened in October with Barker as General Burgoyne, amazingly its first production in London proper, despite its publication and transatlantic success a decade earlier. It ran six weeks, then transferred to the brand new Queen's Theatre, where Barker switched to Dick Dudgeon. He had been hopelessly miscast as Burgoyne, whom he played as if he were "the chaplain of his own regiment," as Max Beerbohm had it (*Saturday Review* 26 Oct. 1907:510). When *Arms and the Man* followed in December it looked as though the management was exploiting Shaw in open-ended runs, contradicting the first principle of the Court.

In fact the management was about to break up in acrimony and debt. Vedrenne and Barker now disagreed about many things, especially about the goal of establishing a repertory company. Barker must often have been moody and difficult, as Purdom claims (69), but his partner brought their relations to a crisis when he refused to cast Lillah McCarthy in the best roles because she was Barker's wife. ("This habit of getting married is the ruin of theatrical art," Shaw wrote to Ellen Terry about her third marriage in October; "Vedrenne and Barker are almost shipwrecked by it already": St John 319). Vedrenne absolutely rejected Masefield's powerful new work, *The Tragedy of Nan*, because Lillah was to have the lead, and refused to allow her to play Medea. She wrote pitiable letters to Murray, begging him to insist on her. "Harley cannot cast me for parts, as I am his wife, and Mr Vedrenne prefers not to unless it is the author's first wish"; and later, "*Don't* give up the fight with Mr Vedrenne till you *really must* – perhaps he is only trying to see how much *you* really want me to play . . . I really am broken hearted" (Bodleian). Whatever Murray may have done, she was not given the job, and did not act at the Savoy until *Arms and the Man*. Compounding Barker's distress was the censorship of his own play *Waste*. Along with *Joy* and *Nan*, it had been expected to carry the weight of the new season. Suddenly theatrical riches had been stolen away, and the Savoy seemed like an empty jewel case.

Literal riches were disappearing as well. Though the three Court seasons actually made a small profit, their continuation was possible only by the most rigorous economies. "As a rule of course we limit our expense to what I assure Vedrenne is absolutely necessary," wrote Barker, "and we especially pare away at any sort of decoration or accessory" (British Library). The resulting emphasis on text and acting suited the smaller enterprise well, though there were complaints about poor scenery; Robert Loraine, for example, loathed the Court for the "shabbiness" of the *Man and Superman* sets (*SLB* 87). The move to the Savoy simply compounded the money problems of an under-capitalized venture. As the chief provider, Shaw suffered with grace, for he was benefiting in reputation with each of the plays produced by the firm. Still it is saddening to read over Vedrenne's receipts for Shavian emergency loans (at Texas): £2,000 in September, £1,000 in October, £500 in December, £500 in March, £200 and then £300 in June, and so on: eventually a total of £5,250, most of which was lost. In August Shaw wrote, "The purse of Fortunatus is empty" (*Letters* 2:807).

A web of reasons, then, led to the dismantling of the most important theatrical experiment of the era. London was not ready to support the New Drama on a large scale, but London would never be ready until it was adequately forced: mistakes and contradictions from within were as much to blame as antipathy without. The flourishing artistic enterprise was resistant to transplantation.

Barker was made bitterly aware of the change in attitude in an incident that can stand as a symbol of the failure of the Savoy. At the opening of *Arms and the Man* at the end of the year, making his entrance as Sergius Saranoff, he was greeted by a jarring demonstration from the gallery, "a loud chorus of shouts of 'No Fees!'. . . presumably as a protest against a charge being made for programmes" (*Pall Mall Gazette* 31 Dec. 1907:4). At the socialist Court the programs, beautifully printed on heavy paper, had always been free, and a large notice had usually been inserted in red that announced "No Fees." But the Savoy was run like a commercial theatre, and the old audience – that precarious amalgam of Shavians, Fabians, feminists, lovers of the Court idea, theatrical pioneers – was repudiating its leader for invading the West End.

Acting and directing

The rapid acceptance of the Vedrenne–Barker seasons could never have been possible without the excellence of acting consistently found in them. If new plays were the matter, new acting was the manner of the venture. Drawing on the experience of the Secessionist Movement, and on the methods of Frank Benson and Ben Greet, Barker was able to establish a style for his actors that was malleable enough to suit the highly varied plays he offered. But whether the work required passionate elocution like *The Trojan Women* or understated realism like *The Silver Box*, acting at the Court was known from the start for its natural quality.

It is important to understand that the "naturalness" associated with the Court company does not mean Naturalism in its nineteenth-century, deterministic sense. Barker's style was not like the early work of Antoine, though the two directors shared certain beliefs; acting appropriate for Zola at the Théâtre Libre would not do for *Prunella* and would be impossible for Shaw. Barker's aim, in Desmond MacCarthy's catch-phrase, was "truth as opposed to effect." The actors of the New Drama recognized that "to make others feel you must feel yourself, and to feel yourself you must be *natural*" (3). It was not possible to be natural, MacCarthy argued, under the normal conditions of the Edwardian stage, when a play was usually chosen because "a prominent actor" saw in it an opportunity to exploit his talent. Casting was commonly handled the same way: the actor–manager gathered his subordinates around him as he gathered his texts, carefully reflecting the light on himself, where it belonged by practice and by right.

Most commentators saw the difference at the Court immediately, and found pleasure in the balanced nature of the performances. The care over small roles, the attention to detail, the distinct speech, the overwhelming service to the play: these were new production values in London. The company proved at last that native talent was equal to any in Europe. "Give us the plays," cried Grein, "we have the actors" (*Sunday Times* 28 May 1905:4). The credit for the value of the acting belongs to Barker, and, to a lesser extent, to Shaw, who were together forging the new office of the director in England. MacCarthy notes that Court actors, when they appeared elsewhere, "seemed to sink again to normal insignificance" (2), indicating that it was the management that made the difference. But it would be vastly incorrect to suggest that Barker used actors as raw material for his own directorial constructions, like Craig's *Übermarionetten*. An actor himself, Barker always insisted that the actor was the center of theatre. From his fugitive interviews in the press to his most considered scholarly writing late in life, he stuck to the notion that good acting is the soul of drama, and that good acting came from within the actor, not from his director.

Nonetheless Barker could take just credit for the most important accomplishment of any director: creating an atmosphere where good acting could flourish. In his own summary of the achievement of the Court, at a festive occasion given to honor the two managers, Barker emphasized the ensemble work of the actors. "I would rather think of them as a company than as individuals . . . it is the playing together of a good company which makes good performances," he said (*Complimentary Dinner* 12). The players agreed. Edith Wynne-Matthison, representing them at the same dinner that marked the end of the Court seasons, noted that the actors did not think of Vedrenne and Barker as "employers of labour" but as members of the same company, "quite common working-men like ourselves" (20).

That the actors were happy in their employ is obvious. They stayed on, despite low pay and overwork, and generally seemed prepared to accept any role assigned them. Lillah McCarthy wrote that she turned down a highly paid offer from Charles Frohman so that she might continue "wearing the 'twelve pound look' of the Court Theatre" (83). Many of the company were used to the new methods. As Jan McDonald has shown ("Promised Land" 78–80), a number of important Court actors had been raised in the 1890s and early 1900s with Frank Benson, who was strenuously opposed both to the star system and the long run. They included A.E. George, Lewis Calvert, Madge McIntosh, Harcourt Williams, and Dorothy Minto. Others had worked often for Ben Greet, William Poel, J.T. Grein, The New Century, and the Stage Society, where they gathered in the air of theatre revolution as well as the skill of learning new parts quickly and for few performances. In one sense Barker was able to expropriate the acting lessons of the Secessionist Movement and transmit the spirit of committed players to a larger audience. Lillah McCarthy describes it best:

> When we went elsewhere, the part was everything; but at the Court, the whole was greater than the part! Any of us would cheerfully take a small role, for we knew that even so we should not have to be subservient, negative and obsequious to the stars – for . . . there were no stars. We were all members of a theatrical House of Lords: all equal and all lords. (90)

Lords, but hardworking nobles indeed. The rehearsal period was necessarily short – between two and three weeks, if the calendar of productions is a guide – but finding times when the entire cast could be present was especially difficult. Frequently an actor would be preparing a new role while performing two older ones. With six evening performances and three or four matinees per week, scheduling actors was a nightmare responsibility, and many rehearsals were at odd and often very late hours. Theodore Stier, musical director for the company, records (259) that he was forced to move away from Sloane Square to get some sleep – when he was nearby he would often be awakened in the middle of the night to settle a musical question raised by a rehearsal still in progress. Edmund Gwenn provides an example of the full life of a Court actor. In the autumn of 1905 he acted six parts, five of them new, or new to him, in two and a half months: Hodson in *John Bull*, the butler in *Prodigal*, a small role in *The Wild Duck*, Colpus in *Voysey*, Bilton in *Major Barbara*, and Enery Straker. And he played them well. Desmond MacCarthy (5–6) picked Gwenn out for special praise for his few minutes on stage as the butler, as effective in its small way as his famous portrayal of Straker.

Two noteworthy characteristics further distinguished the quality of the acting. The first, the diction of the speakers, was a matter of technique. A large number of Vedrenne–Barker plays depended on eloquence for their chief support. The long rhythmic lines of Murray's Euripides, the musical passages in *Prunella*, the rhetorical brilliance of Shaw, the public speeches of *Votes for Women!* – all required technical excellence of diction and great vocal control. Lewis Casson says that Barker and Shaw could not have accomplished what they did without a stock of actors who had been rigorously trained in stage elocution. They were

> speakers who had grown up in a tradition that there is an art of stage speech as definite and distinct from the speech of the street and drawing room as the art of opera or ballet is from everyday life . . . It included a much wider range of pitch, much more use of melody in conveying significance and meaning, and definite unwritten rules on phrasing (rhetorical punctuation one might call it) . . . There were good and bad actors of this tradition, but they were all audible, and the good ones could, under it, give the illusion of "natural" speaking, though with far more significance. ("Court Theatre" 291)

Because their speech was precise, Casson concludes, the actors who formed the backbone of the Court were "perfect instruments in the hands of an inspired director." They could quickly adapt to the requirements of a new style without sacrificing naturalness to clarity. Wynne-Matthison could move from Andromache and Electra to Mrs Baines in *Major Barbara*; Dorothy Minto could cover Prunella, Hedvig, Jenny Hill, and Silvia Craven; Edmund Gwenn could stretch from realistic roles to others in *Prunella* and *Pan and the Young Shepherd* and encompass Felix Drinkwater as well. And they are but a few examples of the range of the Court actors.

The second characteristic was intellectual. Put simply, these actors were bright people, interested in improving their profession and the world in which they acted and lived. Jan McDonald has shown, in an important article called "New Actors for the New Drama," how extensive their concerns were. Some were Fabians, some Suffragists, some (following Barker's lead) became involved in the reform of the Actors' Association. They combined a socially aware conscience with a vital interest in the theatre. Their intelligence infused their acting at the Court, giving it the quickness and naturalness that set it apart.

There were occasional complaints that the pace of the productions was too slow. That could well have been the result of Barker's attention to detail, without sufficient rehearsal time to compensate. There were also complaints that the actors, in their emphasis on naturalness in realistic plays, spoke too softly to be heard. The gallery shouted even at Mrs Patrick Campbell to "speak up" in *Hedda Gabler* (*Stage* 7 Mar. 1907:17; and *Era* 9 Mar. 1907:15). One is tempted to think that, as with Barker's Shakespeare a few years later, the fault lay more with the audience's expectation of volume than with the voices of the players. But Shaw also warned the director about the problem in *Voysey*: "And dont suppress your people too much. Remember the infernal acoustics of the theatre" (*SLB* 58). Those lapses aside, the acting was habitually superior, even when the plays were not. *The Academy*, for example, in dismissing Hewlett's poetic work, was surprised to find that it acted well. "Is there anything," the reviewer asked, "that Mr Barker *couldn't* stage?" (3 Mar. 1906:207).

Max Beerbohm had no doubt about the answer. For him, Barker's actors succeeded because they were "very carefully stage-managed" (*Saturday Review* 11 Nov. 1905:620), and his assessment was frequently echoed. Admiring Mrs Pat's Hedda, Desmond MacCarthy said, "it speaks wonders for the Court Theatre management that she did not act the others off the stage" (43). Soon, said *The Referee*, "to have acted at the Court will be, as it were, to have taken an academical degree in acting" (12 Apr. 1907:2).

Much of the surprise over the balanced productions was the result of a novel approach to what theatrical production meant. In the second half of the nineteenth century, when the actor–manager rose to power in England, control of performance shifted away from text to the interpreter. There were exceptions, of course; the dictatorial methods of W.S. Gilbert and H.A. Jones, who prohibited the slightest deviation from stage directions, intimidated actors into a kind of submission to the playwright's will. As late as 1930, long after the directors' battle had been won, Pinero, another dramatist–dictator, thought that the "producer" was a "modern excrescence of the theatre" (*Two Plays* viii). In general, however, the dramatist and the "stage manager" were employees and neither had the preemptive authority of the Victorian star actor, who regularly conditioned a production to suit not the script, but his own virtuosity. Usually the authority was pleasantly exercised, with the employer commissioning work to fit his need, or hiring adaptors to arrange Parisian plays for London sensibilities. But if the case ever came to court, with a live actor suing a dead playwright for possession of property – as it did, in Shaw's view, whenever Irving took action against Shakespeare – there was no doubt that the aggressive and living plaintiff would prevail.

London acting in 1904 was at the end of two stylistic traditions, both reaching back deeply into the previous century. Irving's dark, kingly romanticism was atavistic, listening to the echoes of Edmund Kean. It could hope for no true line of succession, despite the prince pretender, Beerbohm Tree. The more modern mode, originated by Tom Robertson and nourished by the Bancrofts, was still practiced in both high comedy and society drama at the Haymarket, the Criterion, and the St James's. It stressed underplaying and subtle control, what Robertson called "reserved force" (see Rowell 55–6), and touched at least one side of Barker's own methodology. But it was Irving who was the architect of the late-Victorian stage. Though his manner was old-fashioned at the start of his career, and his mannerisms so egregious as to inspire cartoonists to absurdity, Irving remained at the turn of the century the unmistakable genius of the London theatre. In the teeth of realism, he could play magnificently to the Victorian fondness for strong passion and astounding shows.

Neither of these styles, which Barker called "the Irving idea and the Bancroft idea," would suit Shaw or the New Drama of the new century. Both had flourished from 1860 to about 1880, and were exhausted. "The Irving idea was conditioned by the personality of Irving, and its force has not survived his loss." As to the Bancroft idea, Barker thought

it has given us a method of production perfect in the letter, less perfect in the spirit. . . . So that we have now in England a school of actors as highly trained in the good manners of the stage as any comedy of manners can require, well trained also in the expression of certain emotions. But . . . carefully train your actor to do certain things mechanically well, then as carefully write your plays to make no further demands on him that this training will respond to, not only will he learn nothing fresh, but in time even what he has learnt will grow stale to ineffectiveness.

That was written in 1909, with the Court still fresh in mind ("Repertory Theatres" 492, 496–7). Instead of the vicious circle of the Bancroft tradition, or a hopeless imitation of Irving, Barker developed a new model. Carefully planned in advance and based on confidence in the text, it had essential respect for the use of detail to develop character, gave importance to small roles, found its power in understatement and its definition in ensemble acting. "Mr Barker founded a tradition, and justified it by success," concluded *The Spectator* (28 Mar. 1908:499–500). "Mr Barker tried the bold experiment of treating his audience as if they were composed of rational human beings who knew the difference between rant and eloquence, who were more interested in people than puppets, and who had their wits about them."

At the time of the Court his notions about directing, still in their developmental stage, were in some ways similar to those of Stanislavsky, who had begun his serious work about five years earlier. There was no possibility of actual influence; the two pioneer directors were unaware of each other, and did not meet until Barker paid a short visit to Moscow in February 1914. Nonetheless both were striving at about the same time for an inner truth of performance that was actor-centered and based on psychological depth rather than histrionic effectiveness. Both found extra-textual speculation useful for actors, and both preferred to work without stars and the star mentality. But there were important differences. Barker, much to his regret, never had the luxury of long rehearsal common at the Moscow Art Theatre, nor the subsidy that kept Stanislavsky free of constant stress over the box office and free from bankruptcy. Neither did Barker ever have a fully continuous acting company or artistic staff. More important, as a director he thought of himself as an interpreter of the text rather than an independent creative force; the actor is the center of the play, but the director's first responsibility is to the dramatist. Chekhov frequently complained that Stanislavsky misunderstood his intentions; it is unlikely that Barker could have been accused of the same fault.

He may have seen Antoine's company briefly in London in June 1904, but had not been to Paris to study Antoine's methods systematically. Barker was more clearly influenced by the methods of Max Behrend, the director of the German Theatre in London, who stressed ensemble acting and careful rehearsing. He also drew from William Poel, who strove in his idiosyncratic way for a clear interpretive line in a production, though often falling far short in the result. Finally, however, Barker created the modern notion of the director's office by experiment. In the fast current of activity at the Court, he sought and discovered suitable means of guiding good actors to better performances by helping them to see the whole play and their parts in it more clearly. As Salmon points out (110), his ideas are commonplaces now; so thoroughly have we learned the lessons that Barker taught, we are apt to forget that in 1904 they were still revolutionary in Europe and practically unknown in England and America.

Indeed, the case for directors had not yet been made convincing to the profession. Their virtues had been demonstrated only fitfully in London, chiefly in the controversial work of Gordon Craig in the two years prior to the

Court seasons. Before Barker, no English company had operated under the continuous artistic control of a modern director. Throughout the Edwardian period *The Stage* put the words "producer" and "produced by" in quotation marks, treating them with distance and a certain disdain. Lennox Robinson (27) says that Barker "earnestly begged" him, as late as 1910, to put the director's name on the programs at the Abbey when he took charge. It was not until after Max Reinhardt's visit to London in 1911 and 1912, and after Barker's work in the years just before the war, that the director began to be accepted as a regular part of the English theatrical scene.

In the mass of praise about Barker as a director at the Court, two of his qualities stand out. He began with a complete knowledge of every play, even a new play, "the whole thing at his fingers' ends at the first rehearsal" said Harcourt Williams (*Old Vic Saga* 164); and he had an extraordinary ability to communicate with actors. This second matter may have been the crucial one, for good directors are marked not by the authority that they can exercise, as is so often supposed, but rather by their rapport with actors. Barker's rapport gave his actors the confidence to use "their own imaginative ideas" (Casson again, speaking as one of them, *DNB* 320), so that the director was in turn able to incorporate their contributions by "blending and moulding them within the framework of the play as he saw it." When he encountered a recalcitrant player he would use unconventional means to achieve what was needed. "I have known him change readings and positions from day to day," Williams wrote (163), "without explaining why he did it, on purpose to break down the inhibitions of some actor, and at last, out of the subconscious if you will, would emerge the right way of doing it."

In Barker's usage, the director was a guide rather than a dictator or an underling. In the rush of mounting the Thousand Performances he was sometimes forced to make command decisions; but after the Court period he regretted that necessity and tried to avoid it. He was not on hand to teach acting, however; as Sacha Guitry's Deburau says (in Barker's translation, 209),

> A professor
> Of acting can only teach you his faults.

But he could take his larger knowledge of the play to show the actor how to make independent contributions part of a luminous whole. "A producer's business," he wrote ("Repertory" 501), "is to help an actor in the study of his part, especially to help him find the relation of his part to the whole play." This was difficult to achieve when the director was also acting; Barker later concluded it was impossible. At the Court he acted primarily in Shaw's plays under Shaw's direction, and took roles in his own productions only when unavoidable. He told Murray in 1905 that he did not want to play Orestes because "my acting is getting worse every day and the production is so important and my mind will be upon that and not upon a part" (Bodleian). Harcourt Williams got the role, by the way, his first at the Court.

One of the most helpful suggestions about this period comes from Theodore Stier (259), who saw Barker's work as analogous to his own as musical director. Barker extended care to every word of the text and to every moment of performance as a conductor must to every note of music. "I want a tremendous *crescendo* here," Barker would say. "A sudden stop. A *firmata*. Now – down to pianissimo!" To another actor he lamented, "You deliver your lines as if you were the trombone, whereas you really are the oboe in this *ensemble*." But a conductor only leads his players, if he knows what is good for him; he is not a one-man band. Barker coached, but the actors made the music. He heard the harmonies on paper and shaped the performance through diligent rehearsals and marking good time. Casson concludes, "He was a perfectionist but no dictator, criticizing to the last inch and the last rehearsal, always with good humour, every tiniest movement or vocal inflection, until the whole play became a symphony in which every phrase, rhythm, melody and movement reached as near perfection as he could make it" (*DNB* 320). Some actors found this perfectionism trying and intimidating. Further, sometimes Barker worried too much about the notes, which prevented his full attention to the shape of the symphony – but not often. And, as G.B. Harrison wrote me, "without a perfectionist you don't get perfection."

The ultimate job of a director is to vivify the play, to take it off the printed page, "where it lies inanimate, incomplete," as Barker said in the introduction to *Deburau* (5). A director cannot hope to accomplish the task alone, though Gordon Craig sometimes thought so. It is in the crucible of rehearsals that he is tested, not in the coolness of his designs or pre-production plans: a director may be more properly thought of as a gardener than a god. Barker proved his talent and superiority in actual relationships with actors, even early in his career, and he maintained the same focus all his life. Though written much later, the best summary of his vision of the director's job is in the introduction to *Prefaces to Shakespeare* (1:5). He clearly means there to include all drama, from high literature to ephemeral entertainment:

> The text of a play is a score waiting performance, and the performance and its preparation are, almost from the beginning, a work of collaboration. A producer may direct the preparation, certainly. But if he only knows how to give orders, he has mistaken his vocation; he had better be a drill-sergeant.

Audience

The spectators at the Court were as unusual as the productions. Barker set out to entice "intellectual would-be playgoers who are profoundly bored by the theatre as it is," and he seems to have gathered them. When he moved to the Savoy he was followed by a boom in special matinees that imitated the Court seasons: at least four regular managers were planning them, including Charles Maude, Lena Ashwell, and Otho Stuart (*Tribune* 26 Nov. 1907:8).

Tree's Afternoon Theatre soon arrived, using the same Tuesday and Friday schedule that Vedrenne and Barker had begun. "The plain fact is," said *The Referee* during the first Court season, "Mr Vedrenne has succeeded in drawing to the theatre a class of playgoer for whom too scant consideration is shown by the theatrical managers; playgoers, I mean, with a purely artistic taste for the theatre" (16 Apr. 1905:2). The growing sales of Shaw's published plays might have suggested that an audience was ready to see them, but few commentators had actually expected them to come.

Shaw insisted the Court spectators were not an audience but a congregation (Henderson, *Playboy* 444). His boast is supported by F.C. Burnard, who counted twelve women to one man in the house for a matinee of *Major Barbara*, with "not a theatre-going, but rather a lecture-going, sermon-loving appearance." Though as the editor of *Punch* (13 Dec. 1905:422) Burnard may have exaggerated the statistical ratio, other evidence agrees that unconventional women were dominant. When that same play moved to the evening bill, *The Bystander* remarked that "the Court Theatre is now become a cult. The matinee-goers are an audience apart. . . . Outspokenness brings no blush to their cheek. They are mostly women" (10 Jan. 1906:72). At the Savoy evening performances women continued to be dominant, if illustration 1 is to be trusted, especially in the circle and the gallery.

Obviously many men attended the Court as well. Balfour was at the first afternoon of *Barbara*, in a box with Sir Oliver Lodge and the Webbs, heading "a brilliant and intellectual audience" (*Stage* 30 Nov. 1905:17). And the women did not pay to see matinee idols (unless Barker was one), or to be idly entertained; they paid to see the play. The educated daughters of the Victorian middle class, products of large families like the Huxtables in *The Madras House*, found the Court a haven for new ideas. Nothing shows their seriousness more than their acquiescence to the Vedrenne–Barker request that they take off their hats. Shaw had railed against the inconsiderate absurdities of matinee headgear in 1896 (*Our Theatres* 2:77–8); the Stage Society asked women to sit bareheaded. Yet critics were amazed at *Hippolytus* to see women in a public theatre "cheerfully conforming to the new Edict" (*Referee* 23 Oct. 1904:2). This audience had come to see rather than be seen. They had found a theatre that was as stimulating as reading, and they were using their leisure for profit and learning.

The evening performances were naturally available to a wider spectrum of people and the plays had to be carefully selected to succeed there. Shaw filled the nights, along with a few realistic dramas; many other works that did well in matinees could not draw at all. The three Euripides plays, for example, were essentially afternoon phenomena. In its original six matinees in January 1906, *Electra* took in an average of nearly £100 per performance, a respectable box office for minority fare. Yet when the play ran for two weeks in the evenings in March, the game was not worth the candle: the six evening performances of its first week averaged only £26 each. "The business so far is

Shavians at the Savoy

(1) In the Stalls (Half a Guinea)

(2) In the Circle (Seven and Sixpence)

(3) In the Pit (Half a Crown)

(5) One of our future Monuments?

(4) In the Gallery (A Bob)

1   Shavians at the Savoy. The audience at *You Never Can Tell*, 1907. Note the predominance of serious women (sketch by Charles Sykes)

suicidal," Barker wrote the translator. "It is all the fortune of war, war with the public" (Bodleian). *Hippolytus*, happy as the initial Vedrenne–Barker matinee, did even worse than *Electra* when it was tried at night in April.[3] Even the contemporary realistic comedy of *The Return of the Prodigal* could not make the jump from afternoons and was replaced halfway through its scheduled evening run in 1907. The audience with a "purely artistic taste" was limited. The afternoon and evening presentations acquired two distinct followings, related but far from identical.

As usual Shaw had something to say on the subject. Disturbed by the failure of *Prodigal*, he protested to Vedrenne that Barker was making a number of errors about play selection and a more fundamental error in judging the nature of his audience:

I am greatly disturbed by this Prodigal business, because it shows that neither of you understand what has made the Court possible. I have given you a series of first-rate music hall entertainments, thinly disguised as plays, but really offering the public a unique string of turns by comics and serio-comics of every popular type. Calvert as Broadbent and William, Gwenn as Straker, Lewis as B.B., Yorke as Bill, with the sisters Clandon and the Irish character turns and the newspaper man have done for the Court what George Robey and Harry Lauder have done for the halls. Make no error V.D. that that is the jam that had carried the propaganda pill down. Even in Voysey it was the Booth turn, the Clarence turn, the wicked solicitor and the comic old woman that consoled the house for the super drama.

(*SLB* 77)

If that analysis is true, the Court was a long way from Barker's dream of a group of enlightened playgoers who would cheerfully support a repertory theatre. The analysis is heavily biased, however, for Shaw was trying to convince Vedrenne to produce *The Philanderer*, as the listing of his own successes implies. The failure of the Savoy might seem to lend support to Shaw's assertion: the larger audience was not prepared to asist at the birth of an art theatre in London. But, as we have seen, the Savoy failed for complex reasons. The Court showed that a magnificent start could be made.

3 The Court productions

GRANVILLE BARKER'S NAME has been conventionally associated with realist Edwardian plays. A general impression has developed that as a director and a dramatist he was most successful in the muted style dominant at the time, and was not suited artistically or temperamentally to the larger gestures in acting and directing of pre- and post-realist drama. Yet his work at the Court belies this common notion. He regularly presented four distinct types of plays, each requiring a different production style; the realist play, while important, was only one of the pillars of his theatre. The other three led him away from realism to the innovative open staging that marked his later directing career: the translations of Euripides; the poetic, non-representational work of Maeterlinck, Hewlett, Masefield, and *Prunella*; and the "ideational comedies" of Bernard Shaw.

Shaw's plays, though often judged by his contemporaries in terms of realism, require instead an athletic, robust production that we can now compare to the demands of Brecht. Shaw was perfectly aware of the nature of his challenge, and Barker had much to do with the formation of an appropriate style for the plays. *Major Barbara*, which in its time was Shaw's most adventurous foray into a rhetorical form of drama, was written for the Court company, and written after Barker had proved it capable of rising to the playwright's needs. But Shaw's part in the story is so vast that his work will be discussed separately, in the next chapter, along with Barker's own Court play, *The Voysey Inheritance*. Here I will take examples of the other three types, as studies of Barker's first major achievement as a director.

Euripides

The revival of Greek drama in English in this century originated from a fortuitous friendship. Barker had met Gilbert Murray in 1899 when he played in the scholar–poet's *Carlyon Sahib*, and they remained close until Barker's death. Superficially opposites, they admired and envied each other's gifts. Murray, with immense learning and a quick pen, sought practical experience of the stage to bring life to his Euripides; Barker, without formal education and congenitally short of time, longed for the professor's reflective life. Their affection was fraternal, deep, and productive. They were well matched to collaborate on the enterprise of naturalizing an ancient playwright to Edwardian London.

Barker's productions were, practically speaking, the first professional presentations of Attic drama in English. Greek plays were not completely unknown on the English stage, though nearly forgotten. At the time of Barker's *Hippolytus*, the students of Bradfield College played *Alcestis* in their outdoor arena (which Barker would use in 1912), and Sophocles' *Electra* was presented at the Court by Greek actors (reviewed in *The Referee* 29 May 1904:2–3). But both of these events were amateur, in Greek, and symptomatic of the antiquarianism that had previously conditioned whatever attention had been given to the drama of Athens. As translator, Murray was reaching for a different goal. He hoped to leap the centuries, to provide a voice for antiquity that would make it speak clearly in the present. His overwrought, Swinburnian cadences now seem stiff and unnecessarily archaic:

> Nay, mountainward but now thy hands
>   Yearned out, with craving for the chase;
> And now toward the unseaswept sands
>   Thou roamest, where the coursers pace!   (*Hippolytus* 23)

But in their own era they were admired both for their beauty and speakability. Judging from the critical response, they succeeded in the theatre better than most newer versions do today. They captured for the Edwardian ear some of the lost music of Euripides.

Murray had published his first translation in 1902, and William Archer brought about its production. His New Century Theatre backed *Hippolytus* for four matinees at the Lyric Theatre in May 1904, with Granville Barker as director. Archer, champion of psychological modern drama, saw in Euripides a kindred spirit. Reports of the productions comment on the modernity of the plays; the emphasis on women and on abnormal passion made the ancient playwright seem doubly contemporary. In fact, Murray says in his preface to *Electra* (5) that Euripides was a forerunner to the psychology of Ibsen, and Grein's review of *Hippolytus* calls Euripides "the poet Ibsen of his day" (*Sunday Times* 29 May 1904:6). The theatrical renditions took their cue from that modern element. Desmond MacCarthy, commenting on the absence of the "archaeologically sentimental" in the productions, found that they were presented "as though they had been written for the modern stage" (11–12). Barker himself put it succinctly: "I want to make the plays come as naturally to the theatre as possible" (Bodleian).

But Greek plays can never be natural to a modern audience in the way that Ibsen is natural. In fact, Euripides provided Barker with his chief early opportunity to experiment outside the realistic style, with lighting, scenery, costumes, movement, music, as well as acting. In general he was successful in meeting the challenge. Only the Chorus, a difficulty even for Euripides and a bugbear ever since, defeated Barker's resources and powers of invention.

The director's uncertainty about how to stage the Chorus continued for all four of the plays he presented. For the first, *Hippolytus* at the Lyric, he used eight women. The leader and ninth member was Florence Farr, whose "cantilation" so pleased Yeats, and who had composed the music for the odes. She struck occasional chords on her psalteries (see illustration 2), leading the group in a monotone "series of Gregorian chants" (*Daily Telegraph* 27 May 1904:7) that were nonetheless heavily criticized for being too modern. Shaw chided her for rambling "up and down staircases of minor thirds in a deplorable manner. . . . the effect is modern, cheap and mechanical" (*Letters* 2:519). Barker was never happy with Farr, whom he thought self-consciously arty, and for the first matinees of the plays at the Court in October he replaced her with Tita Brand. But he was forced to use Farr's music and her psalteries, having nothing else; to get them he had to include her in the Chorus, now increased to twelve. The addition of four actresses was unfortunate, as the Court stage was much smaller than the Lyric and gave the production a cramped feeling.[1]

The new arrangement was patently unsatisfactory, so Florence Farr was

2 *Hippolytus*, Lyric 1904. Hippolytus (Ben Webster) appeals to Theseus (Alfred Brydone) across the body of Phaedra. Florence Farr with psalteries at left, Barker as Henchman at far right (drawing by A. Boyd)

back in charge of *The Trojan Women*, leading a Chorus of six: Walkley heard only "the twanging of instruments . . . as unmusical as a Japanese orchestra" (*TLS* 14 Apr. 1905:121). This time Barker tired of "her jejune harmonics" for good, and desired to replace "her muddling with a little real training of the chorus" (Bodleian). For the remaining productions at the Court, Gertrude Scott was engaged to lead a Chorus of eight. *Electra*'s music was composed by Theodore Stier, under the direct supervision of Barker and Murray (Stier 261). Still complaints arrived that "the melodic chanting and some of the concerted singing sounded much too modern" (*Daily News* 17 Jan. 1906:4), with suggestions that the Chorus should either speak their lines simply or be provided with a full operatic score. Desmond MacCarthy's original review condemned the Chorus as "a non-conductor of emotion" (*Speaker* 27 Jan. 1906:412), blocking rather than connecting the spectators to the action.

The most serious drawback to these half-musical Choruses was the difficulty in distinguishing the words. Murray naturally was disturbed by the problem and finally chose clarity over the Florence Farr system of a "good unintelligible song" (Purdom 51). The director went to work early on a "new idea" for the last Greek play, *Medea*, produced at the Savoy in 1907. Almost a year before he could write to Murray, "we are on the right track at last . . . It is very simple and dignified, you can hear the rhythm, and you get something of a choric effect" (Bodleian). Instead of music or chanting, the Chorus now rhythmically spoke their lines in unison, sometimes as an ensemble, other times in sections. Though the words were definitely clearer, the effect was still controversial. Despite the care taken with voices and dynamics, Archer wondered if the new Chorus was really an improvement (*Tribune* 23 Oct. 1907:5). Grein held that it caused "irrefutable hilarity" (*Sunday Times* 27 Oct. 1907:4): "imagine nine maidens all demure, woebegone . . . imagine nine board-school girls laboriously and staccato reciting a piece of poetry." Obviously the Chorus, after its fourth leader, Penelope Wheeler, and its third system of delivery, was intractable. Barker was not to solve the problem fully until he presented the plays in outdoor arenas in America in 1915.

In light of the size of the difficulty, the general success of the four Greek dramas is all the more remarkable. Though the praise was never unanimous, again and again we can read about the power of acting, about the impressive but simple scenic effects, and about the unexpected dramatic surprises of the plays themselves. Audiences sat enthralled, especially at *Hippolytus*, which was more familiar because of Racine's version. Indeed, audiences on occasion found the emotion overpowering; Barker, acting the role of the Henchman describing the death of Hippolytus, sent "a lady in the pit into hysterics" (*Pall Mall Gazette* 19 Oct. 1904:11), requiring her "to be conducted sobbing from the house" (*Daily Graphic* same date:266).

Other actors achieved equal if less violent results. Edith Wynne-Matthison made a particularly impressive Electra, "now stately and statuesque, now mere womanly, and again a passionate semi-hysterical revoltée" (*TLS* 19 Jan.

3   Edith Wynne-Matthison as Electra, Court 1906

1906:21), winning "her triumph by sheer force of diction" (*Standard* 17 Jan. 1906:4). Illustration 3 suggests her noble simplicity and muted grace, encased in the rough black cloth of a peasant's wife. Her Andromache was also highly praised. Edyth Olive appeared in all the plays, as Phaedra, as the mad Cassandra, as a "cringing and remorseful Clytemnestra" (*Daily Graphic* 17 Jan. 1906:233). Though powerful in these roles, her Medea fell short. (See illustration 4.) She was "bizzare with her dark complexion and her reddish robes" (*ILN* 26 Oct. 1907:588), but could not "rise to the tigerish rage" needed for the second half (*Daily Graphic* 23 Oct. 1907:313). Barker relied heavily on these two actresses for their elocutionary training and striking appearances, characteristics essential if the verse and intense passions were to be mastered.

The men held up their side. Ben Webster as Hippolytus, Harcourt Williams and the romantic Henry Ainley, who both played Orestes, Lewis Casson as Castor and the Messenger in *Medea*, were tackling roles that gave them fine opportunities. But the Greek plays chosen are principally women's plays, and offered actresses tragic range and dramatic variety far surpassing most other work in the Vedrenne–Barker repertoire. The Choruses are all female, which gave the stage in each case a consistent women's perspective. *Hippolytus*, somewhat more interested in male characters, calls for a second Chorus of Huntsmen; Barker used seven men in these roles for the Lyric production, almost balancing the male–female proportions. (Some of the men can be seen in the sketch in illustration 2.) But for the revivals at the Court, the Huntsmen were omitted, so that women predominated in that play as well. Barker's early predilection for women's plays has already been noted; these four works of Euripides are a continuation of an established pattern of mind.

Of them *The Trojan Women* is the most concerned with revealing women under tension. Its structure is simply a series of set pieces on sorrow, delivered by a quartet of sufferers left alive to bear the result of male destruction. The play develops no plot, contains practically no suspense, and is constantly in risk of static lamentation. Murray began his introduction, published just before the first performances, with that acknowledgment: "Judged by common standards, the *Troades* is far from a perfect play; it is scarcely even a good play" (5). Many reviewers agreed; Max Beerbohm's "an afternoon of wailings" (*Saturday Review* 22 Apr. 1905:521) catches the general tone. It was certainly not the most loved of the Greek plays. Yet its production was representative of Barker's methods, and can demonstrate how he faced the problems of essentially "undramatic" material.

He began, as usual, worrying about actors: correspondence with the translator is filled with concerns about casting, and about Florence Farr's "tin-pot choruses" (Bodleian). The question of Gertrude Kingston for Helen put Barker "into a cold sweat," though she was finally accepted for "her cleverness" and ability to "get the meaning of the speech." He ultimately concluded that Greek plays were especially hard on actresses; only a special type was suited for the major roles, which mainly required physique, "with technical skill to back it" (Bodleian). In rehearsals Barker worked to get the players to understand their speeches thoroughly on their own, so as to avoid depending on mere declamation. Euripides encourages melodramatic voice projection – "woe, woe" is the refrain of *The Trojan Women* – and Barker had particular trouble restraining Marie Brema. She was a dangerous choice for Hecuba, for she was principally a Wagnerian mezzo-soprano, and the character must be on stage throughout, the framework and continuity of the tragedy. Brema was determined to open with an outpouring of grief that left no room for development (Thomas 297). To judge by the records, the director was never able to diminish her expressions of grim terror; she never worked for him again.

As to production, Barker's first reaction to the script set the tone of his

4   Edyth Olive as Medea, Savoy 1907

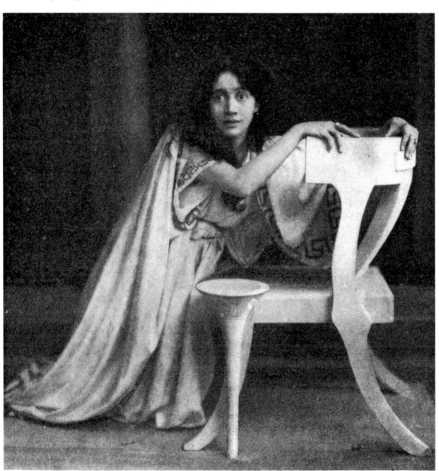

approach: "my disposition is to believe in it dramatically. Certainly it has no action but the situation is tremendous" (*Bodleian*). In a drama of situation, the director's choices determine most of the effect. Barker chose to light the play symbolically to accent its mood of despair. The scene was in "almost total darkness" at the beginning for the conspiracy of Poseidon and Pallas Athena, and again at the end for the burning of Troy (*Stage* 13 Apr. 1905:10). In the body of the play, color was used to distinguish the separate lamentations. Barker was not happy about the opening effect: "I can get nothing but a red dawn and the dawn isn't red," he told Murray (*Bodleian*). Still the variety of light on the set gave gradations of tone to a piece much in need of them.

The set was a "great gateway" in front of the ruined city, itself represented by a painted backcloth, with "the white towers of Troy standing out against the blue sky and the blue waters in the distance" (*Stage*). It seems that Barker did not use the huts called for in Murray's text; thus the stage was dominated by the fixed architectural feature of the gate, in front of a two-dimensional perspective controlled by plastic lighting. Though no photographs or drawings of the production have been discovered, this conclusion is consistent with the sets for the other Greek plays. Illustration 2, for example, shows a painted background of trees behind the massive portico and palace of Trozen, with the palace on a raised platform. In front of this the varying shades of costumes easily could be used to add pictorial weight to the climactic scene. The disposition of the actors also shows Barker's early control of a sizable group (though of course the artist may have improved the stage picture). Further support comes from *Electra*, where the set consisted of a "straw-thatched hut in the midst of a grove of cypress trees, whose trunks and lower branches stand out simply but grandly against a distant view of valley, river, and mountain" (*Tribune* 17 Jan. 1906:5). With footlights discarded, the scenic effect of that play reminded one critic of Gordon Craig (*Sketch* 24 Jan. 1906:46).

Costumes were treated in a similar manner, using simple materials and designs that allowed actors to make a large statement or remain unobtrusive when required. Designs were often conventional, like the Greek key pattern on the borders of the garments in illustrations 2 and 4. The main figures of *The Trojan Women* were provided with distinctive flowing robes that characterized them individually. Gertrude Kingston as Helen, for example, marked her difference from the Trojans by wearing "her pink garments with a modern air, as if it were a new-fashioned opera cloak" (*Daily News* 12 Apr. 1905:4). Her poses suggested she had "studied the records of Greek art" (*Pall Mall Gazette* same date:5). The Chorus was clothed in deep reds and browns to reduce its prominence when on stage but not in the direct action.

The distinguishing costumes and lighting allowed each character to make dramatic sense of her extended scene. The actresses were also helped by Murray's verse, which is more suited to this play of arias than to the brisk stichomythia of *Hippolytus*. Edyth Olive, for example, handled Cassandra's disjointed song with frightening intensity:

> Awake, O my feet, awake:
>> Our father's hope is won!
>>> Dance as the dancing skies
>>> Over him, where he lies
>> Happy beneath the sun! . . .
> Lo, the Ring that I make . . .   (*Trojan Women* 28)

She waved her lighted torch of Hymen like a weapon here, with "indication of madness, of spiritual imagination, of dire purpose" (*Standard* 12 Apr. 1905:5). Edith Wynne-Matthison effected her grief as Andromache so well that when the child was ripped from her arms to be tossed from the walls, "the theatre became as still as a church in prayer" (*Sunday Times* 16 Apr. 1905:4).

The production was "somewhat costly," as Barker wrote to Murray's wife, and he was not satisfied with it. The play may have been too great a challenge for actors and audiences unused to Euripides:

Well we've done our present best with the Troades but that best isn't good enough for me – the truth is we're not big enough people for it – How it gives us away that our idea of representing grief is to weep and howl and that anyway we can grieve over a baby but we can't grieve over a city.   (Bodleian)

But if the conventions of a difficult ancient play were not completely managed, *The Trojan Women* nonetheless showed Barker's courage and control as a director. What he learned from the production was applied to further Greek plays, including his 1915 remounting of this one, when he had a fine Hecuba in Lillah MacCarthy and the background of the First World War to echo the pacifist theme.

Meanwhile, in three years the Vedrenne–Barker seasons had reclaimed a great playwright for the stage, and by extension rescued an entire literature from theatrical oblivion. Frank Benson, who had been touring the *Oresteia* in English when the Court opened, had not dared to risk the capital. After Barker broke the ground, however, Benson brought the trilogy to the suburban Cornet Theatre in 1905 (reviewed in *Academy* 11 Mar. 1905:242–3). Poel directed Murray's version of *The Bacchae* in 1908 with Lillah as Dionysus, and Barker's work prepared England for the famous Reinhardt production of *Oedipus* at Covent Garden in 1912, which also used Murray, and Lillah McCarthy.

Yet not all commentators were won over to the cause. Max Beerbohm objected to the handling of Euripides from the start, on the premise that a modern audience could never hope to recapture the spirit of ancient Athens as long as it remained in a modern theatre – an idea similar to Poel's regarding Shakespeare. Only in an outdoor theatre, and with the play spoken in its original language, Beerbohm thought, could we detach ourselves sufficiently to accept the demands of antiquity. In a review of *Hippolytus*, he noted that "some of the ladies in the chorus evidently wore corsets beneath their draperies; and that seemed to me a symbol of the whole matter" (*Saturday Review* 4 June 1904:716).

Presenting the plays in ornate Victorian theatres was a grave drawback. In making an important point, however, Beerbohm missed a larger one. Barker's use of modern stagecraft to solve some of the problems of Euripides might look like a poor substitute for the freer conventions of the Theatre of Dionysus. (Especially when the director used a transparency for the vision of Castor and Polyderces, projected in a tree above Electra's hut.)[2] But his aim was to make the plays speak after years of silence, and to do that he had to cut through great, turgid indifference. A.B. Walkley sensed the essence when he wrote that the aim of the Savoy *Medea* was "to make us . . . forget the religious character of a Greek theatrical performance and the growth of a play from choral dialogue, and judge it solely as a play, a dramatic work which will or will not appeal to us by its power" (*Times* 23 Oct. 1907:8). And judged as a play, Walkley continued, *Medea* "is enormously, even horribly, impressive."

The preponderance of the evidence supports that view. Barker would be the last to judge success by the box office, and the Greek plays never could equal the popularity of Shaw or some of the realist pieces at the Court. Yet they achieved a sizable matinee audience, and a persistent one. The sign of Euripides' acceptance appeared in *The Bystander*, a popular pictorial weekly. In its theatre guide for 11 April 1906, when *Hippolytus* was in the evening bill, the magazine recommended it along with frothy Edwardian comedies and musical entertainments. "You will like it," the notice read (72), "without any necessity of posing as an earnest student of the drama."

Non-representational drama

Poetic plays constituted the smallest of the four groups in the Vedrenne–Barker management, and were the least successful. Barker had brief experience with the genre in his work for the Stage Society; if we add the Savoy Shakespeare productions to the category, it becomes clear that he had important contributions to make in the staging of non-representational plays. But at the Court the material barely rose above the banal. Maeterlinck's *Aglavaine and Selysette* was a poor choice to represent the Symbolist movement on the stage. In offering it as his third production, Barker showed the eclectic tastes of his theatre, but audiences can be forgiven for resisting five acts of stasis, even when the acts are brief. The only work by Yeats, *The Pot of Broth*, was submerged on a bill with Shaw and Schnitzler. Maurice Hewlett's two plays opened no doors, and were a sign of the novelist's inflated reputation.

John Masefield's first play, *The Campden Wonder*, was a different matter. Masefield found the Court by accident, and was encouraged to try his hand because of the fine work he saw there. Based on an incident from Cotswold history, 1669, he wrote a grim and uncompromising tale of dogged revenge. A stupid and drunken failure perversely confesses that he, his younger brother, and their mother have murdered a missing villager. The man adheres to the lie to the end, merely for the satisfaction of seeing his brother dragged "lower than dirt" (96). In the last of three short scenes, they are taken off one by one to be hanged, just before the supposed victim's wife arrives with the news that her husband has returned. As a study of pertinacious hatred it has few rivals. The language is charged with strong, authentic Gloucestershire dialect, an attempt at an English *Riders to the Sea*; in Barker's words to Archer, "the beginnings and more than the beginnings of good English drama of the soil" (British Library).

As the elder brother, Norman McKinnel gave a powerful performance, hugging himself in the death cell "with a kind of insane, sardonic rapture at his triumph" (D. MacCarthy 33). But the story proved too dark even for Court tastes, and Barker compounded the difficulty with injudicious programming. He mounted it with Cyril Harcourt's *The Reformer*, the most ill-matched partner imaginable, a lightweight play not for the Court at all. "One of those aberrations of which only clever people like G.B. are capable," wrote Shaw (Babington Smith 94). The pairing destroyed the chances for *The Campden Wonder*, and damaged the chances for a vigorous poetic drama.

Only one of these plays was both worthy of the enterprise and succeeded enough to demonstrate the director's ability in the genre. *Prunella, or Love in a Dutch Garden*, written by Laurence Housman in collaboration with Barker, ultimately became more popular than any other play with Barker's name on the title page. It was performed each year at the Court, was revived in 1910 for the Duke of York's Repertory Theatre, and was regularly produced for some years thereafter by professionals and amateurs.

Barker's exact share in the composition is difficult to determine; certainly the play is unique in his output,[3] and the internal evidence suggests that the songs and much of the dialogue came from the poet–partner. Yet Housman told Margery Morgan (*Political Man* 82) that he and Barker worked together on six or seven plays, though only *Prunella* acknowledged the fact. (One of them was *The Chinese Lantern*, produced under Barker's management in 1908 and probably directed by him.) In Housman's account in *The Unexpected Years* (131–2 & 241), Barker asked for "a grown-up fairy-tale play" for the Court, and he agreed on condition that they do it together. "Barker was a wonderful coach; he knew exactly when to bully me, and when to leave me alone." From this "happy collaboration," *Prunella* was born.

The theme of the play was congenial to Barker; as Morgan points out, it bears important similarities to *The Marrying of Ann Leete*. Both center on the sexual awakening of a young woman, confined by convention and family, who escapes through the sudden appearance of a sexual figure outside her social world. Both are set in gardens, both use gardening for metaphoric value, both conclude that selfless love can overcome its cynical opponents through sacrifice and pain. In addition, both are costume plays that glow with the romantic shimmer of remote settings. But where *Ann Leete* is based on the harsh realities of English politics and upper-class morality, *Prunella* is a timeless fantasy that goes for the heartstrings rather than the head.

The project gave Barker unusual control of its total artistic effect: as part-author, director, chief actor, fundraiser, and manager. Further, he participated in the planning of the music, which was written by Joseph Moorat. As Barker coached Housman in the writing, so he coached Moorat in "the task of fitting his music to dramatic moments. . . . Barker knew exactly how much music was wanted to accompany words and action at certain points of the play, and how much music could be allowed for atmosphere, without action, at other points" (Housman, *Unexpected Years* 230–1). The music charmed most commentators, even when they gave the play rough judgment.

In fact the whole piece had a musical treatment that, while consistent with the director's usual methods, made it unlike any other at the Court. The tale itself, with the simplicity of a ballet, was appropriate material for choreographic handling. Prunella, ripe but restrained, is kept at dull lessons and duller tasks by her aunts Prim, Prude, and Privacy (and their maids Queer and Quaint), who fear the outside will break through the gate and seduce their charge. Prunella's mother ran off to ruin with a French architect, and is their exemplum; a statue of Cupid which he built is a barren curiosity in this trim and self-contained garden world. The single set at the Court showed severe high hedges and the façade of a Dutch house with red bricks and cypresses beyond: a realistic, proper locale for the dream-like fantasy of the action. Suddenly a troupe of noisy mummers arrived, dressed in bright *commedia* motley, led by an anarchic Pierrot. The aunts at the Court flew into the house before "a shower of confetti" from over the hedge (*Daily Graphic* 24 Dec. 1904:1205), leaving the white-faced Silenus time for a single, passionate kiss.

In the second act, Pierrot returned in moonlight, the realistic garden now transformed into a magic world of make-believe and love, with "dark and solemn flame-like cypresses dark against the deep blue of an Italian night" (*Pall Mall Gazette* 24 Dec. 1904:5). He carried Prunella, wrapped in a cloak, down a ladder from her high window to the fountain. The Statue of Love drew his bow across his stone fiddle and blessed her:

> And in thy heart thou hear'st the chime
> Of Love whose feet shall outrun time. (51)

As the Statue, Lewis Casson "showed to the audience a quiet and private sense of dignity, and . . . of mystery" (*Pall Mall Gazette*), prompting Prunella to capitulate to love's power. "Ah, where am I since yesterday?" she cried, in the voice of Thyrza Norman. The act ended with a *coup de théâtre*: the Columbines took off her cloak to reveal her dressed as one of them, ready for the harlequinade of life:

PIERROT: What you have dreamed to-night, do not forget.
        Farewell, Prunella!
PRUNELLA: I am – Pierrette! (53)

At this point she was "garlanded with roses white and red" and "carried away amid shouts of a laughing crowd" (*Daily Graphic*).

In a later version of the play (Sidgwick & Jackson, 1930), the authors provided an extra act here, showing the troupe on the road two years later and the inevitable fading of Pierrot's love. The original text at the Court, however, asked the audience to imagine the interim and may have achieved more power by compression. The last act, three years later, is also in the garden, but without its summer clothes: "the dry leaves scuttle drearily down the weedy garden paths," in Desmond MacCarthy's words (32), the fountain covered with moss, all but one of the aunts dead. A new tenant arrives to take possession. It is Pierrot, dressed in black, losing his looks and liveliness, a Don Juan who has heard the Commendatore's knock. His followers are with him, "all querulous, dishevelled, lame, but still trying to affect mirth" (*Saturday Review* 11 May 1907:584) – all but Prunella. He callously abandoned her the year before, and now has come to grieve for his loss, to try to recapture the joy he vaguely remembers he once found in the garden.

At the moment of his greatest need, when he is vulnerable for the first time in his player's life, Prunella appears, a ragged and dirty beggar girl. Transfigured in the moonlight, is she a ghost? Pierrot risks death to embrace her, and the Statue of Love "flooded with light," again "plays upon his viol, while all the garden grows loud with song" (stage direction, 89).

Despite the verse-songs and the music, there was little actual singing in the production, which gave it a peculiar bitterness, as if the actors were deliberately withholding the full joy of song. Instead, the orchestra supplied "throughout a running commentary of music" (*World* 27 Dec. 1904:1111), which "may be said to elucidate, and not impede" the plot (*Stage* 29 Dec. 1904:19). Theodore Stier, who conducted, said that the music had been composed "to fit the rhythm of the verse, so that I had to keep my eyes fixed irrevocably on the mouths of the speakers in order to ensure exact synchronization" (255). Some critics held that the play would have been better as an opera or musical, just as others wanted less realism in the acting and set: they wanted pure fantasy, bloodless symbols. But the unusual blend of dreaming and waking was partly achieved by the combination of speech and music. It made the play a distant cousin of *The Winter's Tale*, encompassing betrayal and regeneration through the mysteries of music and love.

The autumnal feeling, a taste of burnt almonds, led papers like *The Daily Express* to call *Prunella* "imitation Bernard Shaw cynicism" (24 Dec. 1904:5). It was the flavor that Granville Barker gave to his portrayal of Pierrot, disturbing to so many spectators of the first Christmas performances. Of the three actors to take the role at the Court, Housman thought Barker's the best, though "the least popular; it had too much 'bite' in it – audiences preferred a Pierrot whom they could like – and forgive – more easily" (*Unexpected Years* 243). Grein objected to Barker's lack of "the warm tone which renders a love-scene vital" (*Sunday Times* 25 Dec. 1904:4); E.A.

Baughan wanted acting "with a little less realism" (*Daily News* 24 Dec. 1904:9). But Barker gave the precise quality needed for the play, arresting a slide into sentimentality. (Exactly two years later in St Petersburg, Meyerhold would play Pierrot in Blok's *The Fairground Booth* with a similar lack of sentimentality, and under a musical conception. See Braun, *Meyerhold* 70–2). The happy ending of *Prunella*, like the end of *The Threepenny Opera*, was thereby suffused with the cynicism of the character, holding the mixture in suspension. "Funambulesque," Walkley called it (*Times* 24 Dec. 1904:10): a tightrope act of emotions, the one, elegant example from the Court company of unabashed theatrical virtuosity.

Realist plays

Barker's letter of intent to William Archer in 1903 proposed a season of Hauptmann, Sudermann, Ibsen, Maeterlinck, Schnitzler, Brieux, and Shaw. In the event, the Court produced few European plays in the realistic tradition: one comedy by Hauptmann, a sketch by Schnitzler, and two of Ibsen's tragedies. Chekhov and Strindberg may seem striking by their absence, but they were almost unknown in England and would be slow to arrive. Other foreign writers were kept off the stage by the competition from Shaw and Euripides, and there was no need for the theatre to support Ibsen more than it did. He would never be popular, but his work had become part of the fabric of English life by the turn of the century.

Ibsen's two productions were nonetheless important reminders of where the modern movement had begun. The performance of *Hedda Gabler*, with Mrs Patrick Campbell and Lawrence Irving (Lövborg) fitting into the Court ensemble, showed the theatre could use stars without star treatment. The play got seven matinees, and – despite Mrs Pat's objections – that was an end to it. *The Wild Duck*, with an exceptional Hedvig in Dorothy Minto (who played Prunella in the revivals), was a workmanlike presentation of a play infrequently seen by London audiences. Some of Barker's staging, "in flat defiance of Ibsen's directions," angered Archer, the translator (*World* 24 Oct. 1905:680), but on the whole it was received without comment.

The sparse European repertoire, together with the Court's receptiveness to engaged drama, served to draw native talent to the English stage. The last season saw the debuts as playwrights of two artists who had already acquired a degree of success in other endeavors: John Galsworthy and Elizabeth Robins. Their contributions to the Court merit extended comment.

Galsworthy had received a measure of acclaim as a novelist just a few months before with the first Forsyte book, *The Man of Property*, in which he had struck out against English privilege and caste. Back in the autumn of 1905, Edward Garnett had suggested that his friend try a play for the Vedrenne–Barker management. Galsworthy was evidently intrigued by the idea, for he wrote a script quickly in early 1906 and sent it off in March. It arrived on Saturday, Marrot relates (189–91), was read by Barker and by Shaw on Sunday, and accepted on Monday. The haste was justified. Galsworthy would write better plays but never a more compact one: *The Silver Box* is a shrewdly detailed skein of Edwardian life that broadened the Court's range of subjects. As Walkley said of its spring revival, it "is one of the welcome plays which restore one's confidence in the power of the drama to deal squarely and fairly with life and remain a work of art" (*Times* 9 Apr. 1907:5).

The play had much to recommend it to Barker's theatre. It treats its characters unsentimentally and provides excellent opportunities for ensemble playing, especially in the much-praised police court scene. Though Galsworthy is overly schematic about its thesis – one law for the rich and another for the poor – he is careful to balance his anger with comedy and irony. John Barthwick, for example, is no conniving hypocrite, but a Liberal MP with convictions, who is sincerely disturbed by his son's behavior. Jack is a worthless example of Edwardian high life. He has stolen a purse from his evening's sexual game, out of spite; stumbling in a champagne haze at his door, he needs help from the charwoman's husband, Jones, to find the keyhole. Tired and hungry from a day looking for work, Jones accepts Jack's invitation for whiskey, gets quickly drunk, and steals the purse in turn, as well as a silver cigarette box. He too does it out of spite, but with vastly different results.

Barthwick eventually learns most of the truth, and thinks Jack should take his punishment. "You and your sort are . . . a nuisance to the community," he shouts at his son about the woman's purse. "Why, a poor man who behaved as you've done . . . d'you think he'd have any mercy shown to him?" (Galsworthy 14). Propriety makes demands, however: faced with a scandal, Barthwick concludes that discretion might be his better part. But it is too late to stop prosecution for the parallel theft. Suspicion has fallen on Mrs Jones, and a tussle occurs between her husband and a detective when the silver box is discovered in their room. So Jones is sentenced to a month's hard labor; Mrs Jones, now jobless and penniless, is left to support their child; while Jack, saved by his father's money and a clever solicitor, suffers a minor family embarrassment.

The problem of reconstructing the Court performances is often acute. No promptbooks have survived for these plays; there are very few pictures or set designs, and even fewer that reveal anything significant about production. Because realism was the dominant mode of the time, reviewers rarely gave details of the staging or the setting for a new realist play. Even with the acting they tended to remark on verisimilitude or nothing; indicative is Desmond MacCarthy's judgment on *The Silver Box*: "very seldom has a performance so careful had at the same time so much the air of a play that acted itself" (24). Most reviewers devoted their space to plot summary and commentary on the literary and dramatic value of the play. While this is only just, it is difficult for the theatre historian. On the other hand, Galsworthy provides detailed stage directions in the printed text, and enough evidence exists to suggest that Barker followed them. Taken with a few revealing press comments, we can get glimpses of the production.

Barker set the mood at the opening with lighting. The first scene was in "semi-darkness" (*Stage* 27 Sep. 1906:16), projecting sharp shadows on young Jack, in evening dress and carrying the stolen blue "reticule"; and on Jones, with "hollow cheeks, black circles round his eyes, and rusty clothes," as the stage direction describes (3). Jack, "perfectly played by Mr A.E. Matthews . . . enters in a state of sordid exhilaration" (D. MacCarthy 24). The actor, who regularly played aristocratic rakes at the Criterion and St James's (Matthews 105–6), presented an exaggerated contrast to Norman McKinnel's unemployed workingman, whose keynote was "smoldering revolt," as Galsworthy told the director (Marrot 192). The brief scene, two pages in print, established the two worlds of the play with quick strokes in the Court production. The rest could follow with ironic inevitability.

Though most of the characters are accessible types, Barker kept control of the performance by restraining the acting. Only Irene Rooke as Mrs Jones was out of place, "too self-conscious and theatrically conventional," said Baughan, who went on to explain that he would not have noticed but for the remarkable ensemble performance of the rest of the cast (*Daily News* 26 Sep. 1906:4; she was replaced for the revival in April). Sydney Fairbrother played the Unknown Lady who comes for her purse the morning after, revealing to Barthwick the degree of his son's prodigality. The part could easily have been exaggerated, but the actress kept her head. The result was that she became a powerful outside witness to the tension between father and son, with "a touch of genius about her silent acting in the scene" (*Academy* 29 Sep. 1906:312).

The third act received the most attention, usually for Barker's directing of the courtroom crowd. "The almost continual coming and going in the police court is a stroke of genius" (*World* 2 Oct. 1906:655), accenting the harsh truth that Jones's case was merely one of many similar cases. "You will hardly see better acting in London" (*Nation* 13 Apr. 1907:261), and many reviewers noted the fidelity of the minor actors to their life models. McKinnel's portrayal of Jones was gripping for the same reason, "a really masterly sketch of the brutalised man whose vices are merely the outcome of his unfortunate conditions," said *The Daily Graphic* (27 Sep. 1906:1221). "He gave us the real living man, never exaggerated, as is so often the case with low-class types on the stage, but full of weight and power."

At the end Jones is termed "a nuisance to the community," the very words of Barthwick to his son in the first act. His final shout – "Call this justice?" – is cut short by the prisoner's door. "We will now adjourn for lunch!" declares the magistrate: and wretches hang that jurymen may dine. With such a subject, consistent with the early traditions of European Naturalism, it is not surprising to find a critic equating the Court to "the Parisian Théâtre Antoine" (*Athenaeum* 29 Sep. 1906:376). Its title, its attention to small detail, its social statement, all imply that the play and its production shared the Naturalist motivations of the Free Stage movement.

But sifting the evidence leads me to think that Barker's style was a significant departure. Antoine was of course capable of much subtlety and passed beyond Zola's determinism, with its patronizing suggestion that depravity was the usual condition of the lower classes. Even so Antoine's directing, acting, and repertoire were based in Naturalism; Barker's work never was. Though *The Silver Box* can be exaggerated, it is at heart not like Zola, Hauptmann, or even Gorky. Barker invested it with delicacy and restraint, with what Purdom calls "a poetic tragedy–comedy quality, utterly different from the treatment it has since received" (59). Though the phrase sounds a bit like Polonius, the idea is clear. The play is a tragicomedy of the two Englands, written with intelligence and sensitivity, balanced by Galsworthy's legal mind. Barker saw its dangers as well as its virtues, and avoided the heavy hand that could make it a mere tract. He was the ideal director for Galsworthy, and helped the new dramatist to even finer work in *Strife* and *Justice*.

The matinees of *The Silver Box* were successful enough to justify a three-week evening run in April 1907. While it played nights, another social piece played days, one with even more topical and political reference. Elizabeth Robins, the American actress who carried Ibsen's banner in London in the nineties, had since become a novelist of some merit. Like Lillah McCarthy, Edith Wynne-Matthison, and others at the Court, she was also a feminist. *Votes for Women!* was her first play, and one of the first plays in England devoted to the Suffragist cause.

It is not surprising that a literary actress should eventually write a play. Nonetheless I suspect that it was again the open door of the Court that sparked Robins into creating the piece as a "dramatic tract," as she called it in the subtitle. (A novelistic version, *The Convert*, was published later the same year, and reprinted in 1980 with a valuable introduction by Jane Marcus.) Letters from Granville Barker (at Texas) demonstrate that the play arrived unfinished and in need of polish. In February 1907 he was uncertain about it, though his sympathies were engaged. "I would very much like to read the whole play again to see how it strikes me as a play," he told the author, "for I am so strongly prejudiced in favor of its subject." By 6 March it had been accepted, still without a title; Barker himself suggested *Votes for Women!*, from the banner spread in the meeting scene. A good title in itself, he thought, and "from a business point of view I should think it's good too." The director suggested cuts in acts 1 and 3, and for act 2 "a great deal of patter for the crowd will want writing in. Will you do this, or would you rather leave it to me." Robins apparently gave him permission to cut and rearrange; the day before rehearsals began he said he had "chopped about considerably" with act 1, "though as considerately as I was able," and during rehearsals made further suggestions for changes that were followed.

It was not Barker's practice to exercise dictatorial control over a script in the manner of Henry Irving: the Court was a playwright's theatre. Of course most new plays need some objective attention; Barker suggested at least seven pages of cuts for *The Silver Box* (Marrot 192). But the Robins case was different because the dramatist did not begin with adequate charge of her material. Even after rewriting, *Votes for Women!* remained imperfect. Despite its topicality and one marvelous scene, it was a type of play overly familiar in the nineteenth century, a late version of the Woman with a Past drama that ran from *Camille* to *The Second Mrs Tanqueray* and beyond. The story centers on Vida Levering, an ardent campaigner for the women's cause. She was played appropriately by Edith Wynne-Matthison, "the woman I most wanted" for the part, as Robins wrote her supporter Henry James (*Theatre and Friendship* 265). Vida had once conducted a liaison – as Pinero would put it – with Geoffrey Stonor, and subsquently suffered his betrayal and an abortion. (Stonor was played by Aubrey Smith, at home with the type in the Society Drama preferred by John Hare and George Alexander.) Ten years later Vida meets the man accidentally at a country house; he is now an important Tory parliamentarian engaged to a young heiress, Beatrice Dunbarton. This situation is the framework for an argument about women's rights that is both aggressive and compelling. But the act is soured by melodramatic devices: coincidences, a dropped handkerchief with an embroidered initial, eyes meeting by chance, significant silences. The resolution is equally unsatisfying, involving a conversion of Stonor to the feminist movement and an (opportunistic) pledge to support universal suffrage in the House.

The women's cause was heating up quickly in 1907. The press that spring often carried sensational stories of actual Suffragist meetings, demonstrations, and disturbances. Many reviewers, already anxious about a gathering tide they did not understand, ridiculed the weaker spots of the play, using it as an example of what they saw as the deficient fabric of the movement itself. Despite their objections and its own shortcomings, however, *Votes for Women!* is an interesting work even today. As Samuel Hynes points out, it goes beyond the call of its title to deal with the general exploitation of women through "the sexual viciousness of men" (202). It opened an area of Edwardian life that the theatre almost passed by, the insistence from some women that they would no longer be dull slaves to male domination. "Votes for Women and Chastity for Men" was one of Mrs Pankhurst's more telling slogans. Elizabeth Robins, herself on the governing committee of the Women's Social and Political Union, had heard that shout and charged her drama with a vision of bitter understanding.

When Stonor acknowledges that he owes a debt to women because of his treatment of Vida, we may reasonably conclude that a social problem has been solved by a dramatic fantasy – as if Helmer suddenly understood Nora and vowed to change his ways in the future. But for some members of the original audience the happy resolution at least served a legitimate function of fiction, for it suggested that an improvement in women's status was possible and that it could be accomplished by changing the minds of a few powerful men. If this seems improbable now, knowing the Liberal Party's dithering with female suffrage, in 1907 it remained one of the chief hopes of the movement.

WSPU activists cheered the play on, as Barker guessed they would, following the action "with rapt attention" (*Times* 10 Apr. 1907:5). They were especially noticeable in the pit and gallery, clapping "with bare hands" and stamping their feet "in what you may call a manly style," protested *The Referee* (14 Apr. 1907:1). With the Court "crowded in every corner," policemen were "hovering about uneasily in the offing" (*Daily Mail* 10 Apr. 1907:5). But the only suffrage riot was on the stage.

Even when commentators damned the play's ideas thoroughly, they readily admitted its great attraction, the public meeting in Trafalgar Square in act 2. It was the heart of the production, and proved that Elizabeth Robins, whatever her failings as a dramatist, had a wonderful ear for crowd oratory. Entirely devoted to four speeches and the interposed reactions from onstage auditors, the scene was a triumph for Barker as a director. Max Beerbohm, who picked holes in the work with his usual anti-feminist bias, announced nonetheless that "I shall attend every performance for the sake of the play's second act" (*Saturday Review* 13 Apr. 1907:465).

The scene is luckily preserved in a posed action shot, illustration 5, one of the very few taken of Court productions on stage. (The play created enough stir that the picture was printed the same week in two magazines.) The audience faced the base of Nelson's Column, shown up to the first frieze, flanked by the eponymous banners; Trafalgar Square is on a painted backcloth upstage. At least forty-eight actors are visible in the photograph, filling the narrow space. The crowd of listeners forms a thin line along the footlights, interspaced with police constables, facing the row of committee members and speakers on the plinth. Vida Levering delivers the climactic speech. She had been preceded by a character called only Working Woman (played by Agnes Thomas, in a black dress immediately to the left); by a young convert to the cause, Miss Ernestine Blunt (Dorothy Minto, to the right); and by a Labour Party leader, Mr Walker (Edmund Gwenn, hatless).

No doubt the dynamics of performance lessened the academic symmetry of the photograph. Stonor, in the left foreground in white motoring duster and cap, forms a pleasing group with Lady Wynnstay and Miss Dunbarton. Their position allowed their whispers to further the story while the oratory continued. But the most important feature of the scene is the placement of the crowd. Aligned in a halfway space between the speakers on the platform and the audience in the house, the crowd functioned like a Greek chorus, ritually standing for the spectators as they reacted to the principals in front of a *skena*.

Each of the speakers had provoked rowdy responses, giving the scene a sense of spontaneous reality. Here is Ernestine Blunt on sex roles:

MISS E.B.: Do you know that out of every hundred women in this country eighty-two are wage-earning women? It used to be thought unfeminine for women to be students and to aspire to the arts – that bring fame and fortune. But nobody has ever said it was unfeminine for women to do the heavy drudgery that's badly paid. That kind of work has to be done by *some*body – and the men didn't hanker after it. Oh, no.
(*Laughter and interruption.*)
A MAN ON THE OUTER FRINGE: She can *talk* – the little one can.
ANOTHER: Oh, they can all "talk."
A BEERY, DIRTY FELLOW OF FIFTY: I wouldn't like to be 'er 'usban'. Think o' comin' 'ome to *that*!
HIS PAL: I'd soon learn 'er!

(58–9)

When Walker's Cockney speech prompted the taunt of "What do you know about it? You can't even talk grammar," he responded, "I'm not 'ere to talk grammar but to talk Reform" (66). In fact the crowd took control of the act, bringing into focus not only the argument for female suffrage but also the variety of responses to it. From Lady Wynnstay and Geoffrey Stonor to a "Vagrant" and a "Threatening Voice," the sequence showed the spectrum of Edwardian society face to face with its most intractable political issue.

5   Trafalgar Square in *Votes for Women!* Court 1907

The liveliness of the crowd was the result of Barker's insistence on a company style. These milling auditors were not supers jobbed in for the occasion, as Irving or Tree would have done; though their names did not appear on the program, Hamilton Fyfe noticed that many were experienced actors and actresses (*World* 16 Apr. 1907:666). At least some, like Trevor Lowe, were regular Court troupers, the best possible sign of a company dedicated to submerging individual personalities for the sake of the ensemble. Reviewers tripped over each other to praise the effect of the scene: "a marvel of verisimilitude akin to that which might be achieved by a joint use of megaphone and cinematograph," said *The Observer* (14 Apr. 1907:4); "not the Saxe-Meiningen crowds, not the coster mob in *The Lights of London* at the old Princess's were so perfectly and absolutely illusive," said *The Era* (13 Apr. 1907:13). "Mr Tree's *Julius Caesar* crowd is quite eclipsed, and M. Antoine at his best could not have done better," reported *The Sunday Times* of 14 April (4). "Bravo! Mr Granville Barker!"

On the platform, Edmund Gwenn had the best role as Mr Walker. (In the published text his name was changed to Pilcher, perhaps to avoid the association with Shaw's bully, Bill Walker.) Gwenn worked himself up "to a frenzy of rhetoric" (*Daily News* 10 Apr. 1907:12), relying on his well-exercised technique for portraying working-class characters. He walked to and fro along the steps of the column with a "rolling gait . . . hands thrust down in his pockets, and his chin thrust forward, and his face cocked to one side and shining all over with the good-humour that comes from absolute belief in oneself" (*Saturday Review* 13 Apr. 1907:456). Wynne-Matthison's speech was less exciting, but she gave a tenseness to Vida Levering that deepened the character. Caught between the public assurance of a committed revolutionary and the private uncertainty of her own unhappy past, the actress made profit out of the moment when Stonor appeared in the crowd with his fiancée: past, present, and future in one shooting glance.

For three weeks in April, on Tuesdays and Fridays, a Londoner could see *Votes for Women!* and *The Silver Box* on the same day, two very different examples of English social realism, and both unlike anything the capital had offered before. Then *Prunella* came back in the afternoon, while the Robins play had an evening run. The Court venture closed with five weeks of its most important piece, *Man and Superman*, with Robert Loraine as Tanner; paired with it in matinees, the première of the detached act, *Don Juan in Hell*. It was an unforgettable finale of three years that changed the contours of London theatre and English drama. Desmond MacCarthy's book on the Vedrenne–Barker seasons, published just a few months later, was a testimony to their value and importance. MacCarthy wittily summed up the three years in an epigraph from an earlier London playwright:

TOUCHSTONE: Wast ever at the Court, shepherd?
CORIN: No, truly.
TOUCHSTONE: Then thou art damned.

4 Shaw's natural son

"INEVITABLY, no doubt, a legend ran round London that Granville-Barker was G.B.S.'s son, though no mother was ever mentioned. When I first heard it, I suggested to my informant that the strongest refual of it was G.B.S.'s failure to boast about it . . . " So St John Ervine (344) sketched a notion that has persistently colored the picture of Shaw and Barker. From their heads of red hair and their relative ages (Shaw was born in the same year as Barker's official father) to their falling out over Barker's choice of a second wife, the most famous pair in Edwardian theatre has been touched by a form of paternity case. Shaw, who did indeed love the younger man like a son, could treat the charge with comic indifference. "Others hint that he is my natural son," he wrote of Barker in 1910, "but most of them reject this hypothesis on the ground that I am physically incapable of parentage" (*Letters* 2:912). Commentators from Archibald Henderson on have felt compelled to discuss their relationship. "Among Shaw's younger friends," Henderson wrote, "the others were treated like nephews by the genial and friendly Shaw; but Barker received from him all the tender interest and straight-from-the-shoulder handling of a son" (*Man of the Century* 795). Speculation has continued to the present. Even Eric Salmon, usually so cool-headed, begins his book with a fantasia on the possiblity of parentage, complete with photographic evidence.

Whatever the biological facts, it is certain that the two shared a theatrical genesis of utmost propinquity. From the start of the century until the First World War, their careers were thoroughly intertwined. Shaw found in Barker first the juvenile actor he wanted, then the manager and co-director he needed; for sixteen years Barker was his chief stage resource. Shaw gave his plays, parts, advice, and money as freely as a father to a son. Barker returned the investments many times over, all but the money. Without Shaw, Barker would have had insufficient material to base his reforms on; without Barker, Shaw might well have remained unproduced in London until after the war.

Shaw's own attempts to reform the theatre are well known. His three years as drama critic of *The Saturday Review* were "a siege laid to the theatre of the xixth Century by an author who had to cut his way into it at the point of a pen" (*Our Theatres* 1:vii). In the Mayfair problem play, "Sardoodledom," and in decorated Shakespeare, Shaw saw only dead branches in the sacred wood òf drama. He objected to the theatres of the nineties because they were not taken seriously:

Only the ablest critics believe that the theatre is really important: in my time none of them would claim for it, as I claimed for it, that it is as important as the Church was in the Middle Ages and much more important than the Church was in London in the years under review.

(viii)

But he never wished to make the theatre over from nothing. Barker, like Antoine and Stanislavsky and Meyerhold, wanted a new type of actor for the New Drama. Shaw always hoped that older performers, with the older styles he so admired, would abandon their folly at last and present contemporary plays of merit.

Shaw ceaselessly castigated his two favorite actresses, Ellen Terry and Ada Rehan, for dissipating their talents in the reactionary service of Henry Irving and Augustin Daly. Yet when he came to write plays, though they were different from any plays yet written, Shaw often wrote them for famous actors of the old school. *Captain Brassbound's Conversion* (and perhaps *Candida* as well) were designed for Ellen Terry in the flower of her grand manner; *The Devil's Disciple* was for the hero of Adelphi melodrama, William Terriss, who fell asleep when Shaw read it (Milward 117–18); William the Waiter was for Cyril Maude; *Caesar and Cleopatra* for Forbes Robertson and Mrs Patrick Campbell. As early as 1895 Shaw had aspirations to the Lyceum itself, but Irving passed up *The Man of Destiny* for the Sardoodledom of *Madame Sans-Gêne*. Until Granville Barker established Shaw's reputation, none of these actors responded to the gage thrown down before them. Then Ellen Terry undertook Lady Cecily, converting not Irving but J.H. Barnes at the Court; "by that time," the dramatist wrote, "Irving had passed out of her life, and indeed out of his own" (St John xxvii). Shaw was fulfilled, though Terry was too old and forgot her lines. Forbes Robertson did his play in New York the same year, and in London the next, with Gertrude Elliott as Cleopatra. Shaw's commercial acceptance was complete when Mrs Pat and Beerbohm Tree gave *Pygmalion* at His Majesty's in 1914, the year that ended an era. By then most of the old guard whom he had provoked in the nineties had disappeared from the boards, and Shaw himself was fifty-seven.

Acting and directing Shaw

One of the great examination questions of theatre history surely is this: why were the plays of the most important British dramatist since Sheridan consistently refused by London managers? The answer, clearly, is not simple. And it may be that the most obvious answers, including those advanced by Shaw's contemporaries, are not the most important ones. The problem of an audience, for example, was often mentioned as the major stumbling-block to producing Shaw's work. It is true that audiences on occasion did find the plays long and difficult, but they did not find them impossible and rarely un-entertaining. Critics might rail that this was not a play – the cry of critics against most new ideas in the theatre – but the laughter in the house belied them. It is unlikely that the Unpleasant Plays could have achieved a following in the decade of their composition (no chance for *Mrs Warren*, banned until 1925), but the rest of Shaw's work might have succeeded much earlier had an important manager offered it under the right conditions. With Shaw himself directing, *Arms and the Man* ran for two months at the Avenue Theatre in 1894; its reception suggests that the Pleasant Plays were accessible to audiences already attuned to the satire of Gilbert and the inverted wit of Wilde. Richard Mansfield's small achievement with that same play in New York, his much larger success with *The Devil's Disciple* in 1897, and Agnes Sorma's success as Candida in Germany, provide further evidence that the difficulty was not essentially one of resistant spectators.

The real problem lay with the theatrical system itself. Had there been a manager willing to risk Shaw, no company of actors was capable of presenting his work. Shaw's plays demand a style of performance that did not exist in London before the Court enterprise, a style both older and newer than that practiced in the commercial theatres. On the one hand, Shaw needed actors thoroughly schooled in traditions of nineteenth-century melodrama and romantic comedy. Martin Meisel has shown how Shaw depended on the forms and styles of the Victorian stage; with the fiery Barry Sullivan as his model actor, the playwright naturally sought homes for his work in the theatres of Terriss and Irving.

On the other hand, Shaw needed actors of quick intelligence who were capable of understanding how his plays exploded their nineteenth-century models; actors, more importantly, capable of projecting a socially critical attitude inside comic characters. It is almost as common now as then to think of Shaw's plays as dramatized essays, but they are much more than that. For them to appear more, however, requires a tight ensemble and a directing mind able to force broad performance into a controlled style: ideational comedy, it might be called. "What you have always wanted for a leading man," Barker wrote him in 1922, "is a Barry Sullivan with your brains. But do the two things ever go together?" (Texas).

Shaw recognized this as the major problem posed by his work almost from the beginning. After the production of *Widowers' Houses* in 1892, he began his second play, *The Philanderer*, with the Independent Theatre Society again in mind. "But even before I finished it," he admitted in the preface to *Plays Unpleasant*, "it was apparent that its demands on the most expert and delicate sort of high comedy acting went beyond the resources then at the disposal of Mr Grein. I had written a part which nobody but Charles Wyndham could act, in a play which was impossible at his theatre" (*Plays* 1:19). The lighthearted *You Never Can Tell* was written in a deliberate attempt to break into the commercial theatre, capitalizing on "the popular preference for fun, fashionable dresses, a little music, and even an exhibition of eating and drinking by people with an expensive air, attended by an if-possible comic waiter" (*Plays* 1:376). Cyril Maude put it into rehearsal in

1897, but the actors were immediately at sea. Though the play seems the simplest of Shaw's early work, the Haymarket cast had no experience about how to proceed and no will to learn. Had Shaw been directing the task might have been manageable; as it was, his presence as author further disturbed the equilibrium. J.H. Barnes, who had no trouble with the play a decade later at the Court, threw over his part after the first reading of the first act, and Fanny Coleman followed, protesting "no laughs and no exits" (Maude 213). Shaw, who recounted the tale with humorous grace in the persona of Maude, cut his losses and withdrew the play.

The end of the century gave Shaw no quarter, because he wrote from outside the theatrical system, and from outside the conventions of society in an age when Society was of utmost importance to the theatre. In 1898 he noted that the "intense energy necessary for the establishment of the New Theatre . . . could be set free only by the genius of the actor and manager finding in the masterpieces of the New Drama its characteristic and necessary mode of expression, and revealing their fascination to the public" (*Plays* 1:16). The Vedrenne–Barker seasons provided what was otherwise not available: a committed facility. At the Court, Shaw was able to experiment with a corps of actors who had become at ease with his plays. Lewis Casson, Edmund Gwenn, Agnes Thomas, Louis Calvert (despite himself: he detested and almost ruined *Major Barbara*), Lillah McCarthy, and Granville Barker gave the dramatist what seemed impossible, a single venue capable of both *The Philanderer* and *Man and Superman*.

Shaw found the encouragement to enlarge his dramatic world; the mature voice of his work after 1905 came in part from his direct experience with Barker's acting companies. Once *Man and Superman* had prospered, Shaw's style was liberated. *Major Barbara*, his first play written for a specific company with production assured, quickly stretched his technique while it expanded the boundaries of English comic acting. *The Doctor's Dilemma* pushed the boundaries even farther, though perhaps with less satisfactory results, and the plays that came later exploited the discoveries at the Court.

A list of the Shavian plays presented under Barker's various managements shows how intimate were the fates of the two men.

WORLD PREMIERES:

John Bull's Other Island	1904
Man and Superman	1905
Major Barbara	1905
The Doctor's Dilemma	1906
Don Juan in Hell	1907
Getting Married	1908
Misalliance	1910
Fanny's First Play	1911
Androcles and the Lion	1913

FIRST PUBLIC PERFORMANCES IN LONDON:

Candida	1904

How He Lied to Her Husband	1905
Captain Brassbound's Conversion	1906
The Philanderer	1907
The Man of Destiny	1907
The Devil's Disciple	1907
Caesar and Cleopatra	1907

In addition, *You Never Can Tell* was presented at each of the four seasons at the Court and Savoy (it had been publicly performed for six matinees in 1900), and *Arms and the Man* was also revived at the Savoy.

The great majority were produced under the Vedrenne–Barker management. At the Court 11 of the 32 plays, and 701 of the 988 performances, were Shaw's; "The Shaw Repertory Theatre" was a quip about the Court with much truth. During the 1907 season at the Savoy, four Shaw plays were seen between September and December, and *Getting Married* came on at the Haymarket in May 1908. Thereafter the association was less frequent. The great logjam, dating back to 1893, had been cleared, Shaw's output slowed, and he found productions elsewhere. (The 1907 *Caesar and Cleopatra*, for example, was actually Forbes Robertson's production, presented under the Vedrenne–Barker name.) But the connection remained. Barker was acting on tour in 1908 with his original productions of four Shaw plays. *John Bull* reappeared at the Kingsway in 1912, and Barker revived *The Doctor's Dilemma* in 1913–14, and in New York the next year, along with *Androcles*. From 1900 to 1915, in fact, not a season had gone by for Barker without some connection with at least one of Shaw's plays.

The connection began because of Barker's acting. Shaw often denigrated Barker's predilection for "worms" in life and art:

When will you understand that what has ruined you as a manager is your love for people who are "a little weak, perhaps, but just the right tone." The right tone is never a little weak perhaps; it is always devastatingly strong. Keep your worms for your own plays; and leave me the drunken, stagey, brassbowelled barnstormers my plays are written for.

(*SLB* 115)

But despite his manly avowal, Shaw actually created a series of roles that needed the delicate tone of weakness and strength congenial to Barker's personality on and off stage. From the early Stage Society productions, Barker provided for Shaw what no other English actor could have accomplished. Eugene Marchbanks, Frank Gardner, Valentine, Keegan, John Tanner, all dreamers and lovers, all outsiders, might have been designed for Barker's peculiar gifts: his lyrical voice "with its haunting, half-mocking intonations, and its power of suggesting unutterable things" (*Spectator* 28 Mar. 1908:500); his penetrating eyes; his quiet manner that implied secret passion just under control. In fact the "critical intelligence" which "marred his performance of more ordinary characters" (wrote Lewis Casson in *DNB* 320), was especially "valuable in detached parts" in Shaw's plays. His Tanner, made up with red beard to look like a young Bernard Shaw

6   Lillah McCarthy and Barker as Ann and Tanner, *Man and Superman*, Court 1905

(illustration 6), was one of his most praised successes. Barker capitulated to Ann at the end, wormlike, with a wonderful sense of tragic defeat; according to Winifred Loraine (89), this was something Shaw could never get her proud husband to do.

Of course those roles had not been designed for Barker; but Adolphus Cusins and Lewis Dubedat were. Though based on other men (Cusins on Gilbert Murray and Dubedat at least partly on Alfred Gilbert), both contain a good deal of Barker himself. Shaw admitted that he had made Cusins a worm, "the reverse in every point of the theatrical strong man" (*Letters* 2:566); "nobody else except Barker could touch it or make the public accept it" (549). Some of his attractive weakness is apparent in illustration 7: the drum, the Salvation Army uniform, the Gilbert Murray glasses acting as shields against the gunpowder ruggedness of Undershaft. And Purdom holds (60) that, with the exception of the turquoise blue eyes, the stage direction introducing Dubedat fitted Barker at age thirty exactly.

"He is always useful when a touch of poetry and refinement is needed," said Shaw (quoted in Pearson, *Actor–Managers* 73), making light of what John Gielgud called Barker's "extraordinary power and repose" (*Stage Directions* 54). Dover Wilson thought Barker's "the finest voice I ever heard on or off the stage" (327), though most observers thought it limited in range and too high-pitched, leading him into underplaying. Yet one after another contemporary critics attested to Barker's power, "without whose aid," in the jibe of *The Daily Telegraph* (24 May 1905:7), "Mr Shaw's plays would be even less explicable than they are." Shaw always appreciated how important Barker's acting was to his dramatic career, and frequently pressed him to accept roles he did not want, even when Barker had begun to withdraw from performing. Very late in life, Shaw wrote to Alan Downer that "my plays were the decisive and at first sole V.B. stock-in-trade. I produced them all with Barker as my leading juvenile actor; and my throw-back to the art of Barry Sullivan and Italian Opera, and my method of rehearsal, must have influenced him considerably" (Meisel 107–8).

But acting was clearly not Barker's only contribution to Shaw's Edwardian advance, and not the most important. In addition to providing the theatrical company and performing in the major plays, Barker shared in their direction. This is a contentious point, and requires explanation in the face of Shaw's claim to Downer above. At the dinner in honor of the Vedrenne–Barker seasons in July 1907, Barker acknowledged that "Bernard Shaw produces his plays himself" (*Complimentary Dinner* 13). Yet it is apparent that at the Court and elsewhere Barker aided in the preparation of most of Shaw's plays, sometimes carrying out the playwright's instructions, on occasion assuming the complete responsibility of the director.

Given their close personal relationship, it is natural that they would offer each other advice and confer deeply about productions that concerned them both. But Barker's value went further than friendship. Shaw, for all his native

7   Banging the drum for Shaw. Lewis Calvert as Undershaft and Barker as Cusins, *Major
      Barbara*, Court 1905

acting skill and self-training in the ways of the stage, was not a professional man of the theatre. Even when he possessed very clear ideas about staging his work, he needed Barker to manage practical and technical details. This seems to have been the case from the beginning. For the Stage Society production of *The Admirable Bashville* in 1903, for example, Shaw apparently left the preparations to Barker, who was directing S.M. Fox's *The Waters of Bitterness* for the same program. Correspondence (*SLB* 12–15) reveals Shaw passing on theatrical ideas, implying that Barker was responsible for their execution, but also suggesting that together they might "coach the company up to the mark." Purdom is convinced that Barker directed the play on his own, yet the Stage Society program for this triple bill (Theatre Museum), which lists Ian Robertson as the director of his own play, *The Golden Rose*, and Barker as the director of *The Waters of Bitterness*, is silent about the director of *Bashville*. It was Shaw's usual practice to omit his name when he directed. The promptbook (British Library, Add. MS 50613) has few instructions, but they are in Shaw's hand.

Shaw directed a few productions, like *Getting Married*, *Misalliance*, and *Fanny's First Play*, without assistance. Barker was responsible for *Androcles and the Lion* and for the revivals of *The Doctor's Dilemma*. Generally, however, the early "Shavian" style of performance was developed by the two men working together. Shaw's busy schedule kept him from some rehearsals, whereas Barker was always at the Court, able to take charge; Shaw trusted him to keep to the outline he had established. This was true even for his pet project, Ellen Terry's appearance in *Brassbound* (see *SLB* 56–9).

Sometimes the results did not please the master. Barker rehearsed *You Never Can Tell* while the playwright was abroad in 1906, and Shaw hated the first two acts when he saw it, as well as Henry Ainley as Valentine (*SLB* 65). Barker revived the piece at the Savoy in 1907, again to Shaw's dismay. "I should have come up for the last few rehearsals," he wrote after the opening; "the combination works better than the single cylinder. You are so afraid of their acting badly that you make them afraid too" (*SLB* 105). That combination engine was well suited for the task: Barker emphasized subtle characterization and significant detail, Shaw went for broad strokes and flamboyant gestures.

Occasionally Shaw depended on his coadjutor to prepare a production carefully so that he could deliberately turn it on its head; for the sake of the actors, the two assumed opposing roles. This was apparent for *The Devil's Disciple* in 1907, when Shaw wrote, "I suppose I must take John Bull in hand and leave you to bend all your energies on the D's D. I do not intend to interfere really with that, except to produce an effect of upsetting everything at the end, if it seems firm enough to stand that treatment" (*SLB* 107–8). Though Shaw often complained that Barker's methods were not suited to his operatic style – he liked to compare his own plays to Verdi and Barker's to

Debussy – it seems clear enough that together they managed to achieve what neither could have done so well separately.

Shaw's method as a director began and ended with worries over acting. Lewis Casson, who observed it firsthand, held that Shaw never took "any serious practical interest in anything beyond the casting and the acting. All the rest, including scenery, costumes, lighting and groupings, was of very minor importance" ("G.B.S." 16). That this is an exaggeration even a cursory reading of Shaw's letters will confirm, for he was full of descriptions of scenery, sketches of costumes and sets, lists of props, and of other practical suggestions. Yet it was casting and acting that concerned him beyond any other matters. Shaw's rehearsal notebooks, fortunately preserved in the British Library, support the essential truth of Casson's view. Six pocket notebooks, looking like prayer books, are given to the Vedrenne–Barker productions of his plays. They contain extremely detailed notes for actors: line readings, movements, gestures, and Shaw's most common direction, instructions for one actor to "play to" another.[1] The *Major Barbara* notebook even offers advice for Barker's production of *The Wild Duck*, in rehearsal at the same time. (True to form, Shaw complains about underplaying: "Gregers not taken aback enough at the Do they go shooting.")

The slowness of London to accept Shaw can be ascribed, then, partly to the lack of a company willing to suit his needs. But, despite Barker's absolute importance, Shaw held for the rest of his life that his surrogate son was the wrong director for his plays. "His taste for low tones, which made his productions of Galsworthy's plays and of his own exquisite, did not suit mine: that was how . . . I had to upset his arrangement of Androcles" (Meisel 108). That story, gleefully related by Hesketh Pearson ("The Origin" 804, and *Bernard Shaw* 289–90), is frequently cited as evidence that Barker could not manage raw emotion and open theatricality. After working for weeks for restraint and pacing, he saw Shaw appear at the final rehearsal in full evening dress, straight from a romantic visit to Mrs Pat, and exaggerate the piece until a controlled comedy had become a Shavian extravaganza. Granted that Barker's inclination for delicate effects did not mesh with the intentions of *Androcles*, it is possible that the two were once again assuming their agreed-upon roles. Barker's tight rein on the actors may have been just the preparation needed for Shaw to let them slip the traces. "A bit of training does them no harm," he wrote Barker in 1907; "it will enable me to let them rip all the more recklessly next time" (*SLB* 106).

An astute critic noticed the precise distinction between the directing styles of the two men, when both as usual were using the same company for disparate ends. Comparing Barker's production of *Justice* to *Misalliance*, which Shaw had directed alone, *The Spectator* found that Shaw had devised "a new convention of acting, rather formal, and tending a little to caricature – the very opposite of the acting in *Justice*, but admirably suited to *Misalliance*"

(26 Feb. 1910:339). Nonetheless it would have been very strange if Barker, whose hallmark was complete understanding of a playwright's aim, had missed Shaw's. Barker knew the shape and tone of the writing quite thoroughly, even if the exaggerated gesture of his friend's style was not personally congenial. Shaw himself, in an out-of-the-way place (*London Music* 28), recorded that appreciation. "Harley Granville Barker was not far off when, at a rehearsal of one of my plays, he cried out 'Ladies and gentlemen: will you please remember that this is Italian opera.' "

Don Juan in Hell: performance

The most obviously operatic of Shaw's plays, *Man and Superman*, was shorn of its openly musical act when first produced. The dramatist was convinced that the dream scene in the Sierra Nevada made the work too long even for congregational endurance, unless "performed under the conditions which prevail at Bayreuth and Oberammergau" (*Plays* 2:798), and thereby took the heart of the philosophy out of his comedy. It was not until 1915 that Esmé Percy risked the play in its "infernal entirety." A decade earlier it was accompanied at the Court by only one piece of appropriate entr'acte music, the overture from *Don Giovanni*. The remaining orchestral offerings were standard theatrical fare, selections from the *Nutcracker*, a movement from a Schubert symphony. Thus the great comic overtones of an Edwardian Don Juan, chauffeured by a Cockney Leporello, disputing with a stone-statue Roebuck Ramsden, and a Doña Ana searching the void for Superman, were lost.

They were recovered for a month in 1907 when *Don Juan in Hell* played matinees while the parent acts played evenings. Though awkwardly billed with *The Man of Destiny* (with Dion Boucicault and Irene Vanbrugh), the night on Mendoza's mountain filled some June afternoons with a most unusual London entertainment. A quick look at the production can reveal Shaw at work as a director at the Court, collaborating again with Barker to find a theatrical expression for his most verbal piece.

Their whole approach to *Don Juan* was musical. The text calls for orchestral accompaniment from Mozart, of course, both to set the ghostly scene and to create character leitmotifs. Gounod's Mephistophelean chords introduced the Devil; Mozart's statue music announced the tread of the Commander. He was not the Ramsden from the evenings, but Michael Sherbrooke instead, declaiming "his sentiments in an admirably military manner" (D. MacCarthy 116). Shaw also used Handel in the production (Loraine 90), and attended Juan's rhapsody on love and beauty with the "immortal minuet" from *Don Giovanni* (*Pall Mall Gazette* 5 June 1907:4). But actual music was only the entrance point; the production relied on using speech as operatic song. Robert Loraine, who was playing Tanner in the evenings, took Tenorio also. As his wife reports, "Shaw annotated *Don Juan* like a symphony for Robert. The margin in the book twinkled with crotchets, crescendoes, and minims; with G clefs, F clefs, and pianissimos" (Loraine 90). In order to understand his instructions, the actor was forced to learn to read music.

Shaw regularly cast his plays according to vocal attributes; he wanted the contrast between tenor and bass, soprano and mezzo to reinforce characterization, as it does in Mozart and Verdi. His quartet of speakers in *Don Juan* must rely almost entirely on vocal prowess, straining mind, throat, and memory beyond normal duty. Like singers, they must play their voices as musical instruments – "a family of viols," in Meisel's phrase (50). For the sake of the music Shaw violated the operatic tradition of the *père noble*, always a bass or baritone, and made the Commendatore a counter-tenor. He worked hard in rehearsals to get the balance and variety right, and apparently succeeded, for many reviewers praised the delivery and vocal resourcefulness of the cast. Norman McKinnel and Lillah McCarthy, as the Devil and Doña Ana, had the benefit of full Court Theatre practice to draw on, but Loraine matched their talents and was frequently singled out for his eloquence.

Visual elements were also guided by an operatic hand. The stage was draped in black velvet, and was framed by electric lights "which created the illusion of still further darkening it" (*Pall Mall Gazette*). Black velvet covered the actors' stools as well. The opening scene took place in pitch blackness (*Stage* 6 June 1907:16), though later a dazzling white light picked out the characters from the void. Charles Ricketts had created a setting that suggested infinite space: "richly dark, Hell stretches impenetrably on and on," said Max Beerbohm, "so that we really believe ourselves there" (*Saturday Review* 8 June 1907:713). Lillah McCarthy "looked like a dream of Velasquez" (*Pall Mall Gazette*) in her costume, its brilliant colors standing out against the black velvet like a night blossom. As she describes it (108–9), the dress was "rose silk covered with black lace and silver trimming. In my hair a flame feather." Ricketts' costumes were simple but richly elegant. Purdom reports (63) that their cost nearly broke Vedrenne's heart.

The simplicity achieved by these effects served the play well. The rolling arias held the audience, who were not distracted by a fussy setting. The eye was satisfied and the mind engaged. Desmond MacCarthy realized that "a few well-chosen details go further to create a scene than all the usual resources of a lavish London management" (8). Centering attention on acting, the Court had created a new production style, vastly different from the Victorian costume spectacle still prevalent at His Majesty's. The speeches of *Don Juan* became musical compositions, and the characters, conventionalized as operatic voices, became symbols with cosmic implications. Returning to a simpler, presentational style of performance, the production found an expression for the complex ideas of the text that was more appropriate than the realist mode. As Shaw wrote to Ricketts:

It seems to me that we . . . hit on a most valuable and fascinating stage convention. William Morris used always to say that plays should be performed by four people in conventional costumes, the villain in a red cloak, the father in a bob wig, etc., etc., etc., and I have always loved Harlequin, Columbine, Sganarelle. . . If only we could get a few plays with invisible backgrounds and lovely costumes like that in a suitable theatre, with fairy lights all round the proscenium, there would be no end to the delight of the thing.

(*Letters* 2:698)

I cannot pretend that 8 matinees of *Don Juan* were as important to the Court venture as the 176 performances of the rest of *Man and Superman*. It was not its philosophic underpinnings that made the play popular, but rather the romantic charm of the New Woman chasing the Edwardian Revolutionary. *The Illustrated London News* was being representative when it declared that *Man and Superman*, "for all its high-sounding Nietzschean title and its Schopenhauerian philosophy, is just a very pleasant light comedy in which a charming woman is seen capturing an amusing young misogynist" (3 Nov. 1906:619). Loraine's performance emphasized romance, and helped the play to a further 192 performances at the Criterion in 1911 and 1912. (His tone had been set on the American tour in 1905–6, when the company traveled in two white railway carriages emblazoned with the title, and Loraine rode a white charger into every new town.) *Don Juan*, on the other hand, was caviare to the general, appealing more to the Euripides coterie than to the *John Bull* crowd. It was nonetheless a fitting farewell to London's art theatre. As a theatrical experiment it demonstrated the vitality of Shaw's directing, and canonized the simple staging that Barker made the hallmark of the Court. It also proved that an audience could sit still for two hours of complex talk without the benefit of spectacle, love interest, or plot.

The Voysey Inheritance

After the first Court season the relationship of Shaw to Barker was much discussed at large in London. At a time when even intellectual theatrical figures were considered newsworthy, the press found a new subject in Shaw's literary and personal importance to Barker's cause. In the popular view, Barker was often cast as chief disciple, the promoter of the devilish ethics of his master. Given Shaw's genius for self-publicity and the rapid strides Barker made in presenting his plays, it is not surprising that they were snidely appointed by journalists as captain and lieutenant of the advance guard of drama. Barker's Court play with a social subject was therefore almost certain to be viewed as the result of a diet of vegetables and Fabianism.

Even the serious critics agreed about *The Voysey Inheritance*: Barker was "a disciple of Ibsen, of Schnitzler, of Bernard Shaw," said Grein (*Sunday Times* 12 Nov. 1905:4). "Yes, decidedly the Court is our 'Shavian' theatre," agreed Walkley (*TLS* 10 Nov. 1905:384); "Mr Shaw's own plays are shown there nightly, and in the afternoons they give you new plays by younger men" with the "faint aroma" of Shaw. Baughan held that the character Alice Maitland "has stepped from the pages of Mr Shaw" (*Daily News* 8 Nov. 1905:8). Max Beerbohm thought the play masterly, yet found Alice an imitative creature: "all the young ladies in Mr Shaw's plays are exactly like her" (*Saturday Review* 11 Nov. 1905:620). As Dixon Scott wrote later (159), the general opinion was that "G.B. was simply G.B.S. *minus* S."

It is difficult now to take the confusion seriously. The style of *Voysey* is utterly different from Shaw's, its ideas and social focus original, its combination of inner and outer actions unique. The play does have ideas, of course, and that fact may have convicted it in some popular reviewers' minds, along with its length and verbosity, which were frequent subjects of complaint. ("Incidentally it was also brought home to me," Grein added, "that life is short and *ars longa* – terribly *longa*.") But even Alice is unlike Shavian characters. She takes some control of the protagonist at the end, and prompts him to propose marriage, but as a New Woman she is a far cry from battlers like Ann Whitefield or Barbara Undershaft. In fact *The Voysey Inheritance* could be seen as a declaration of independence, proof that Barker was, as *The Daily Chronicle* put it, "something more than a mere Elisha to Mr Bernard Shaw" (8 Nov. 1905:7). And that one paper's praise, at least, was unqualified: "a work of original and unmistakable genius – a full-grown, masterly, and very possibly epoch-making play."

To be fair, contemporary opinion did not overly object to the supposed Shavian connection, once it had been noted. It might even have aided the work's popularity. Certainly the reception and stage history of *Voysey* prove that it is the most accessible of Barker's plays, both during the Edwardian period and after. Before the First World War, *Ann Leete* and *Waste* each received only 2 performances, *The Madras House* 10, but *Voysey* had a total of 115. It has been revived much more often than the others. One or another of its three published versions has been in print regularly since 1909, and it is frequently included in anthologies.

The reasons for its popularity are not hard to find. More than any of Barker's plays, *Voysey* uses a surface of conventional realism as its operating mode. Its outward subject is immediate and contemporary, its characters recognizable representatives of the Edwardian middle class, and its action is suspenseful. It has little of the truncated, elliptical dialogue that marks *Ann Leete*; in fact it strives to avoid obscurity, sometimes losing tightness as a result. Though the last act offers no resolution, generally the play holds immediate interest even on a superficial level. Adding to its accessibility are its comic scenes and characters, especially the deaf old Mrs Voysey, and the portrait of the military in Major Booth Voysey ("what England wants is Chest!"). William Archer professed an incapacity to understand any of Barker's early plays, but *The Voysey Inheritance* sent him into raptures. "A new force enters the dramatic field," announced his original review (*World* 14

Nov. 1905:823); "one of the sanest, largest, most human and vital plays of our time."

Voysey is Barker's first play to use a male protagonist. From Tessa Oldroyd and the weather-hen Eve Prior to Ann Leete and Agnes Colander, Barker had concentrated attention on the "sieve-woman"; in *Voysey* he entered the male world of law and finance, with a booming Army officer for good measure. The dramatic question also derives from values firmly in the hands of men. Edward Voysey is not a theatrical strong man, however; he is, in fact, a "worm," not nearly so powerful as Ann Leete. The play operates as it does because of his moral qualms and vacillating decisions. "I cannot get rid of the superstition that a good man on the stage must always be a strong one," Barker complained to Archer, referring to trouble with Thalberg Corbett in the part of Edward, "and that a sensitively weak character cannot be interesting" (British Library). It is upon that weak character that the inheritance of the title descends. His changes and his growth make up the real action of the play.

Edward's father, old Mr Voysey, is his opposite in strength, a self-willed powerhouse, a "buccaneer," who has spent his life secretly defrauding his clients' trust funds for the excitement of the gamble and for personal profit. When the curtain rises we watch Edward's queasy reactions as he realizes how

8 *The Voysey Inheritance*, act 4. Arthur Wortner as Edward, William Farren as George Booth. The original picture editor inserted Mr Voysey (Edmund Maurice) at the bottom, brooding over the scene. The Kingsway revival, 1912

his family has blithely and ignorantly existed on rotten foundations while enjoying the fruit of the old man's criminal genius. Thus at the start the play announces middle-class hypocrisy as its theme, and proceeds to expose the depth of corruption through a protagonist almost incapable of dealing with the dilemma his father passes to him. Edward's impulse is to reject his inheritance entirely – even though it has come, at least in part, from his grandfather – and when old Voysey dies after the second act, Edward looks forward to an imminent "smash" and prison.

In act three he reveals the nature of the inheritance to the family immediately after the funeral. For its clash between Edward's high ethics and the more ordinary practicalities of the other survivors, Max Beerbohm called this "the finest scene of grim, ironic comedy in modern English drama" (*Saturday Review* 11 Nov. 1905:621). Edward wants the family to renounce the money old Voysey has left so that the son can restore as much as possible of the funds bilked from the poorer clients. He wants, in effect, to purify his tainted soul by offering himself as a sacrifice for past wrongs: "it'll be a relief to clear out this nest of lies, even though one suffers one's self. I've been ashamed to walk into that office, Alice . . I'll hold my head high in prison, though" (*Three Plays* 155). Prison is actually the easy way out of a crushing position, and Edward prefers instant scandal to a life of secret hope that he might survive without discovery.

It is at this point that the similarity of *Voysey* to the earlier plays becomes significant; the style may be different, but the theme remains the same. Edward, like Ann Leete, is motivated by *il gran' rifiuto*: his instincts all tell him to refuse absolutely his unwanted "inheritance." But Edward finds total abdication more complicated than Ann. Public admission of two generations of wrongdoing would satisfy his urge for transcendent heroism but bring financial destruction to family, firm, and to innocent clients as well. Alice Maitland (like John Abud, another punning name) functions as a deflator, making Edward see that true heroism lies not in saying no, but in finding a way to say yes. She has previously rejected his offers of marriage, knowing him to be a worm and "a well-principled prig" (207). But now she intimates that he has a task before him that can alter his character and her attitude. Her "gentle hint," as a stage direction terms it (158), is that if Edward will work to restore the squandered money, she will work to restore him.

The climax in act four comes when he is forced to tell George Booth, the firm's most important client and old Voysey's closest friend, that the man he loved as a brother had stolen half his property (illustration 8). Mr Booth finds the revelation incredible and accuses Edward of the theft, to which he replies, "I've not the ability or the personality for such work, Mr Booth . . nothing but principles, which forbid me even to lie to you" (178). Edward encourages the old man to prosecute and rid him of his intolerable burden:

MR BOOTH: Perhaps you'll be put in prison?

EDWARD: I *am* in prison . . a less pleasant one than Wormwood Scrubs.   (180)

But in the fifth act George Booth proves that he is just as worldly and practical as the elder Voysey brothers. He will agree not to prosecute if Edward will, out of the profits of the firm, restore his lost capital in installments at a faster rate than the restorations made to other clients.

This double hypocrisy is too much for Edward. He laughs at the proposal and decides to end the grand charade, a desire for martyrdom returning with new force. The model of *Ann Leete*, however, now comes fully into play. Alice reminds him that he has "still given up proposing" (206), and makes him see that hard work is a more courageous though less dramatic course. She encourages him to accept his father's mantle and better him, to rectify the past, not by denying it, but by brilliant fiscal management that will save all the clients' future. His inheritance, therefore, gives him the chance to overcome himself, and her the chance to guide him to success. The pattern of *Ann Leete* has been repeated: Edward stands opposed by his father, trapped in an impossible moral dilemma, but rises above it, and above the compromising example of his older brothers, by virtue of an amatory commitment.

In the final scene the man and woman are again left alone to chart out the personal implications of their new world. Edward worries that if his clients learn of George Booth's proposal, "they might syndicate themselves and keep me at it for life" (209); Alice replies, "What more could you wish for?" Like Ann, she offers herself to him and to the secret Sisyphean task ahead. One trouble here is that Alice, unlike Ann, often seems a flat character, though her function in this scene is crucial. In a revival at the Kingsway in 1912 Barker worked to make her more alive. She was played by Jean Sterling Mackinlay, the wife of Harcourt Williams, himself cast as Hugh Voysey. Williams records that "Barker dragooned her not a little, but finally got the result that he wanted" (*Old Vic Saga* 164). The result was that Alice appeared "more human than that rather too sensible young woman has ever been before" (*Observer* 8 Sept. 1912:10); "a more normal, jollier girl than we imagine her from the text" (*Stage* 12 Sept. 1912:19). The play could thus end in a sexual agreement, sanctified by moral purpose, in which the partners were approximately equal in strength.

Viewing the ending, William Archer thought that the dramatic problem was meant to be solved in sexual terms. After the opening performance in 1905, Archer wrote the playwright with the suggestion that the lengthy finale would be improved by stopping at the moment when Alice and Edward come to an agreement to work together for the future: "If you don't think me your equal as woman to man," Alice says, "we'll never speak of this again. But if you do . . look at me and make your choice. To refuse me my work and happiness in life and to cripple your own nature . . or to take my hand" (207). Ending the play there, with Edward grasping her hand, would have saved some five minutes in performance and left no doubt that the ultimate subject was marriage and personal happiness. Bur Barker was adamant. He replied to his friend:

I am so very glad you think well of the play, but I won't, won't, won't bring the curtain down on the handclasp at the end. The scene seems long because I cannot knock the point of it into Thalberg yet and therefore he does it wrong, but the last bit is a necessary finish to the play which has been about Edward's Inheritance and not about his love for the girl. If you could read the thing I am sure you would see this in a moment. Of course they play the last scene six times too slow.

(British Library)

Despite Barker's trouble with the production, the last scene remains slow in reading as well. For while it is true that the play is principally about the inheritance, the conclusion is presented in sexual terms. Ultimately the play is about the effect of the inheritance on Edward's future life, and his future life is to find its form in a dedication to Alice. Thus he leaves his old family, like a protagonist from Greek New Comedy, but creates a new sexual order for the purpose of correcting the old order's mistakes. Or at least he plans to. In fact, Edward accomplishes almost nothing during the play, though he talks a great deal. He is, as Ashley Dukes noticed long ago, an example of the new stage type created by Barker, "the hero-raisonneur, a person who does little, but talks heroically" (138–9). In that talking the play is at its weakest. The power and compression of *Ann Leete*'s last scene, where the future is apparent in a concise and present action, is here dissipated in discursive argument.

Voysey is always a discursive play. Its settings are locations of talk: two acts in a solicitor's office, three around a dining-table. Barker apparently wanted to use the physical locations to pin his actors, a favorite directing technique of his whenever the language of a scene dominated. "The VOYSEY dining-room at Chislehurst," reads the stage direction for act 2, "is dining table and very little else" (102). The production at the Court gave small room for the actors to move. Complaining about Loraine's changes to the set of *Man and Superman* in 1907, Shaw wrote that "the motor car is now – I was going to say in the middle of the stage, but as a matter of fact it is all over the stage, like your dining table in Voysey" (*SLB* 85).

A photograph of the 1912 revival (illustration 9) shows the spread of the table, with Edmund Maurice as Mr Voysey at the head, his daughter Ethel on his knee. The table occupied most of the width of the stage, and forced the actors into formal positions. Like chessmen they might move from one square to another, but could not have free range across the board. The characters were therefore treated as discussants, and the audience was to focus on their dialogue. Another photograph of this production (in Scott 156, of poor quality for reproduction) records the act 3 setting. Edward now sat at his father's place at the head of the table and led a family seminar about the old man's thievery. As a director Barker liked to begin rehearsals with the actors reading around a table; in *Voysey* he wrote a play where most of the action never leaves it.

Barker's theatrical intuition is also apparent in a symbolic use of sceno-graphy, parallel to *The Cherry Orchard*, written at the same time. Stanislavsky advised Chekhov to set his last act in the nursery of act 1, thus achieving a significant, iconographic irony in the change of the appearance of the room. What was at the beginning a warm and expectant environment becomes at the end a locale of farewell and regret for what is lost: walls and windows bare, furniture removed, suitcases piled high. In *Voysey* the dining-room of act 2 may reflect middle-class hypocrisy but is cheerful and full of vitality, a center for family and friendship, with Mr Voysey presiding in genial despotism. Illustration 9 reveals how faithfully the 1912 production followed the set directions in the text, down to the port, the filberts, the portrait of grandfather Voysey, the red-papered walls, and the clock on the "black marble sarcophagus of a fireplace."

In the next act, however, "the dining room looks very different in the white light of a July noon." The type of food and drink, the absence of decoration, the position of the tablecloth, "denote one of the recognized English festivities" (133), a funeral. Thus the lunch after the burial, a scene of truth-telling and unmasking, is to be played in a set which constantly reminds us of old Voysey's powerful absence. And in the fifth act the same room, now in its Christmas finery, emphasizes the irony of the occasion. Outwardly festive and joyful, the walls seethe with secrets breaking from their middle-class solidity. All the aspects of bourgeois life, the play suggests, eventually appear at table.

9   The Voysey dining table "all over the stage," Kingsway 1912

The setting reinforces the inheritance theme: Edward strikes his bargain with Alice under his father's watchful portrait (which has replaced his grandfather's) and over his father's mahogany furniture.

The contrast between acts 1 and 4 works in a similar way. Mr Voysey's office in Lincoln's Inn "radiates enterprise" (83): polish on everything, a sparkling fire, a fresh bunch of roses. When the room becomes Edward's, it has "lost that brilliancy which the old man seemed to give it" (160). The fire is dull, the windows are dull, there are no flowers. One thing remains constant, however; the room is still an enclosure, trapping its occupants into talk. George Booth learns of the fraud like a prisoner strapped to his chair, waiting for his tormentor to admit it is all a joke. In the 1912 performance, William Farren played him "perilously near the border of senility" (*Stage*). He was almost frozen in shock, suddenly a much older man (illustration 8), preferring the unknown, cheerful lie of the past to the horrible grey reality of the moment. But the setting is a place of talk, and Mr Booth is forced to talk until the truth is taken in. Like *Don Juan in Hell*, both in text and in production *Voysey* works as an orchestrated debate where the speakers are required to remain until the problem has been talked out.

As I suggested earlier, the length of the talk presents the major difficulty for the play, especially in the static last scene. A number of commentators have felt this a serious debility: a work that begins with the savage insight of *Volpone* ultimately wastes itself in inconclusive verbosity. As Arnold Bennett said, "Certainly the man who could write the first three acts of *The Voysey Inheritance* must be something of a genius, but the man who could write the fourth and fifth acts must be a fool" (*Letters* 2:324). Barker himself was aware of the problem, which led him to revise the text for the 1912 performance. But he had written himself into a corner, and the last scene remained. He indicated his dissatisfaction with Edward and Alice the next year:"I too am sick of the eternal feminine drawing him upward on and on" (Purdom 151). Though he thought in 1928 "it is certain that I'll never re-write Voysey" (letter to Frank Sidgwick, Bodleian), he did revise it again for a 1934 production at Sadler's Wells, with Harcourt Williams now playing Edward and sharing the directing. The author tinkered with much of the script, but the structure was unchanged and the last scene was burdened with the usual difficulty.

Despite the unsolved problems, the play survives. In a good production it holds its own thoroughly, both as a picture of Edwardian life and as a study of human life. Even the ending can work if Edward and Alice are well cast. The première at the Court suffered from Thalberg Corbett's uncertain portrayal, yet Grein said the acting proved the Court to be "the promised land of the London stage" (*Sunday Times* 12 Nov. 1905:4). A revival in 1906, with Barker as Edward, firmly established the play's reputation; the production at the Kingsway, with Arthur Wortner in the lead, eclipsed the original, according to Desmond MacCarthy (*Eye-Witness* 12 Sept. 1912:403). Its power at the time seemed to justify the large claim of *The Observer* (8 Sept. 1912:9) that *Voysey* "is the finest comedy of modern times ('The Playboy of the Western World' and 'Man and Superman' not excepted)." Whatever our judgment now, the play contributed immensely to Barker's Edwardian reputation. It gave him a literary success equal to his directorial successes at the Court, increasing his authority as a reformer of the stage, more Shaw's equal than his son.

5 The man of affairs

A FEW DAYS after the close of the Court seasons, a dinner was held at the Criterion Restraurant for J.E. Vedrenne and Granville Barker, in celebration of their accomplishment and in anticipation of their transfer to the Savoy. It was summer, and hopes were running high; Barker still had plans to christen his new theatre with *Peer Gynt*. He, Shaw, Gilbert Murray, and others of like convictions, ate from a vegetarian menu and abstained from the wine. Lord Lytton gave the toast to the guests of honor. At the end of his talk, when he offered the hope that the Court and Savoy would lead to the creation of a national repertory theatre, there were loud cheers from the diners (*Times* 8 July 1907:11). The managers responded, Vedrenne briefly, Barker incisively. Herbert Beerbohm Tree, of all people, soon to be a knight, gave a long and witty toast to the authors of the Court. Shaw's reply, in which he attacked the press for its retrograde reviews of new plays, was longer and wittier. Many more celebratory speeches were to follow.

It was twenty minutes past eleven. It was Sunday night. It was England. The police arrived, stone guests at the feast, to inform the restaurant management that this festivity violated the establishment's license and must end immediately. Authority was pounding at the door, making its harsh presence felt in the world of art. It was a sign of things to come.

Politics and social affairs engaged Barker deeply, both in his writing and in his civic activities. If his plays ultimately focus on personal matters, their outer subjects are usually public and often derive from careful observation of government in action. From *Ann Leete* to *His Majesty* he was fascinated with politicians, especially with their ready concession of ideals. Margery Morgan devotes her book on Barker's plays to this theme, calling it *A Drama of Political Man*. On the practical level, he was actively involved with a number of dissenting groups in the first decades of the century, among them the Fabians, the Suffragists, the reform wing of the Actors' Association, and the anti-censorship forces. He was greatly (though quietly) opposed to the war, and all his life grappled in the public forum to obtain funding for a national theatre.

After his second marriage, to an American millionairess, his commitment to social reform seemed suspect, crowded out of his consciousness by a country squire's estate in Devon, an elegant flat in Paris, and a life in the thirties in the luxury hotels of Europe. He seemed to cast aside social beliefs as easily as he cast aside his vegetarianism, his total abstinence, and Bernard Shaw. But in the Edwardian years there is little doubt that Barker was sincere in his dedication to social justice. He labored hard in the Fabian Society, for example. He was a member of the Executive from 1907 to 1912, and took, according to Edward R. Pease (186–7), the long-time secretary, "a large share in the detailed work of the Committees, besides giving many lectures and assisting at social functions." In fact, Archibald Henderson thought that Barker's conversion to socialism in 1901 was the transforming event of his life. His attitude to his work underwent a revolutionary change, for "he became profoundly imbued with the necessity of organizing the theatre, of making it a great instrumentality in the social life of our time" (*European Dramatists* 388). In Henderson's view, the Court seasons and Barker's subsequent work for a national theatre were "a direct outcome of Socialist conviction."

The connection of social reform to theatre was the important one for Barker, whose life from the start was the life of the stage, distinguishing him from the bedrock Fabians. One Sunday afternoon in 1905 he and Shaw called on the Webbs to discuss "their really arduous efforts to create an intellectual drama." Beatrice Webb became fascinated with the young "intellectual actor," as so many of her contemporaries were; she wrote that he "dislikes the absorption in mere acting and longs to mix with persons actually in affairs or intellectually producing" (311). In 1909, convinced of Barker's genius, she and Sidney pestered him to make a play out of their Minority Report of the Commission on the Poor Law. Understandably, he refused, saying that was more Galsworthy's line. (Galsworthy declined, and John Masefield as well: see Hynes 127–8 and MacKenzie 367.)

What must have convinced Beatrice Webb that Barker was the man to compose the ideal Fabian play was not his committee work, but his brilliant analysis of the machinery of government in his tragedy *Waste*. He had been kept from writing for most of the three years of the Court seasons; *Voysey* was drafted in 1903, and merely revised for production. His honeymoon with Lillah McCarthy in 1906 was the first opportunity "to tackle seriously" his new play (Bodleian), which he was still writing the following year. "Absenting myself to write Waste," he admitted to St John Ervine, "and the general strain of that affair, were one of the chief causes of the break up of that management" (Texas). The play was expected to be the principal new work of the Savoy season, and had been announced for eight matinees starting 19 November 1907. No doubt the managers hoped it would move into the evening slot. But the Commendatore knocked at the door, in the person of one G.A. Redford, Examiner of Plays. He refused to grant the work a license, and, according to the law of the land, there was no appeal. *Waste* could not be publicly performed.

The censor's official objections centered on "the extremely outspoken reference to sexual relations." He further demanded that the playwright "eliminate entirely all reference to a criminal operation" (Purdom 73–4), though he had not objected to the reference to abortion in *Votes for Women!* earlier that year. There remained more than a suspicion that the true reason for the ban on *Waste* was political: the play could embarrass party leaders on both sides by its exposure of the cynical inner world of parliamentary power. Dramatic censorship had been established in England, after all, because Henry Fielding had dared to attack governmental corruption on the stage. As Shaw pointed out in 1898, "the serious drama is perhaps the most formidable social weapon that a modern reformer can wield. . . . Mr Redford is not appointed to make the theatre moral, but solely to prevent its having any effect on public opinion" (*Our Theatres* 3:366–7). That certainly was the result with *Waste*. "Our greatest modern tragedy," in the eyes of William Archer (*Old Drama and New* 360), it was kept off the regular stage well beyond its own time. Not licensed until 1920, it was not publicly performed until 1936.

Waste: the play

The mixture of sex and politics that roused the censor is at the heart of Barker's play. Ostensibly a tragedy about the destruction of a valuable public figure, the key to the work is again found in the protagonist's secret life. Henry Trebell has drafted a bill for the disestablishment of the Church of England, which would dedicate its funds to the service of a great new educational system. He has a holy devotion to social reform; he wishes to recapture the ancient and sacred teaching function of the church and apply it to secular use, to build an earthly palace for the kingdom of the spirit. He sees a vision of a priesthood of teachers, well trained, properly paid, to provide salvation from ignorance. Trebell is an eminently dedicated statesman who has sharpened his mind and his instincts to realize the dream that consumes his life. "Hard-bitten, brainy, forty-five, and very sure of himself" (*Three Plays* 231), he has made virtues of his aloofness and aloneness. Even party loyalties matter little to him. Elected as an independent, he aligned with the Liberals; now he offers himself to the Conservatives, who are expected to return to power shortly, in exchange for a seat in the cabinet and a promise to carry his disestablishment scheme through Parliament.

But Trebell's personal life, which he has controlled so thoroughly that it is almost invisible, tumbles him from power into death. At a weekend party in the first act, called to smooth over his alliance with the Tories, he finds himself idle for a few moments and responds to the flirtations of the charming Amy O'Connell, "if by charming you understand a woman who converts every quality she possesses into a means of attraction, and has no use for any others" (213). Their moment of passion, which electrifies the end of the act, is easily forgotten by Trebell. Amy, however, finds herself intrigued by the cold attentions of the politician; she also finds herself pregnant. As she lives apart from her Irish scholar-husband (his speciality, ironically, is thirteenth-century statutes), she comes to Trebell for help in getting rid of the child neither of them wants.

Trebell's horrified reaction surprises her, and she suddenly sees him as the enemy, as an example of the stubborn male oligarchy that controls the country. But she has arrived at a difficult time, for Trebell is about to have a crucial discussion with the cabinet representative of High Church interests who must be satisfied if his measure is to pass. Barker prepares a tense scene: Trebell implores Amy to wait in an adjoining room while he battles wits with Lord Charles Cantelupe. Thus the intellectual drama of Trebell's political life is played against a challenge to his self-assurance that arises from his sexual life. He wins over Cantelupe, but in the process loses two lives.

Amy does not wait, and goes off to a back-alley abortion that kills her. The threat of scandal promises to ruin Trebell in the party's eyes, but his dalliance and its consequences still seem to him a minor obstacle on the road to disestablishment. "You know we're an adulterous and sterile generation," he says to his antagonistic colleagues. "Why should you cry out at a proof now and then of what's always in the hearts of most of us?" (293). The third act, set in the house of the Tory leader, Lord Horsham, is an informal cabinet council, the scene that most effectively lays bare the cynical machinery of Edwardian politics. The first part of the act centers on the attempt to keep the matter private, and climaxes with an unintentional meeting between Trebell and Justin O'Connell, Amy's husband. O'Connell eventually promises to remain quiet about the paternity of the child at the inquest. With that settled, the oligarchy turns to the question of Trebell himself. Finding a series of objections to taking on an uncompromising man and his uncompromising bill, the shadow cabinet concludes that the unsavory affair provides a convenient excuse to drop both. The scene ends at night with Horsham posting a note to Trebell about the decision.

The final act bears more resemblances to Euripides than to realistic tragedy. It places the violence offstage, and though it does not avoid the reporting of gruesome details, it does not show them. Further, the bulk of stage time is given to the reasons for Trebell's suicide, as if his death were part of an ancient myth that required interpretation. While waiting for Horsham's note, Trebell occupies himself with reflections on the significance of Amy's abortion and its after-effects, first with his closest friend, Gilbert Wedgecroft, a kind of choric figure, and then with his sister Frances. He waits alone through the night with a copy of *Huckleberry Finn*. When the message arrives in the morning, he already feels dead to the world as he knew it. "I've reasoned my way through life," he says to Frances; but his dark night of the soul has revealed how reason has deceived him. Now, armed with a new "comic courage" gained from Mark Twain, he says that "something has happened . . in spite of me," echoing Amy's phrase about the conception of the baby. "My heart's clean again. I'm ready for fresh adventures" (337). He welcomes suicide not as an escape from scandal or political disappointment, but as the logical outcome of a failure in his secret life. He has looked in himself for comfort, and found only a "spirit which should have been born, but is dead" (335). As Agnes Colander realizes in Barker's unpublished early play, "Suicide's easy when there's so little left to kill."

Trebell's inability to love amounts to a tragic version of the great refusal. He discovers that he could never care for Amy nor for himself nor for anyone – only for the idea of the dead child. He is lost in himself, in what should have been, and has no mate to extract him. His sister tries to provide what he needs, in an almost incestuous offer of commitment: "Let's go away somewhere," she begs, "I'll make demands" (334). But her power is not strong enough to overcome the opposite pull he feels, and he chooses to be united with the mother and child in a ghastly parody of the Holy Family. Unlike Barker's comic protagonists, he can make no affirmation because he has not been taken out of himself by love. Edward Voysey can say yes to life after being saved by Alice from emotional celibacy; Trebell, lacking sexual salvation, can say yes only to death.

Waste in performance

The play was already in rehearsal, with Norman McKinnel in the lead, when license was denied. The Stage Society immediately arranged two private performances at the Imperial Theatre on 24 and 26 November. Just prior to opening, however, McKinnel was forced to withdraw. The program courteously announced that "great pressure of work" prevented him, though in fact he was prevented by Lena Ashwell, who had him under contract at the Kingsway (Purdom 74), where he was appearing in a long run of a now forgotten drama. The pervasive power of the censor is evident here: Miss Ashwell was happy to see her actor in a regular Vedrenne–Barker matinee, but apparently did not wish to risk association with a prohibited play. In the sudden emergency Granville Barker himself took the role of Trebell.

Instead of becoming the management's centerpiece at the Savoy, *Waste* was relegated to the theatrical scrap heap. Though it probably got a longer rehearsal than most Stage Society productions, the dramatist was not the right actor for Trebell, especially when he was also directing. Nonetheless the performance was often praised, making the play and its censorship rapidly into a *cause célèbre*. *The Athenaeum*, often hostile to Barker's work at the Court, called it "the most important event of our recent theatrical history" (30 Nov. 1907:699). "English drama has broken ground at last," held *The New Age* (same date:99). "But Waste, Waste!" said Robert Ross (*Academy* same date:196); "it is for nothing we have a great writer for the stage in England. His work has to be rendered twice in a moral catacomb."

Despite my emphasis on the importance of the play's symbolic overtones and its concern for the inner worlds of its characters, *Waste* is a realist drama

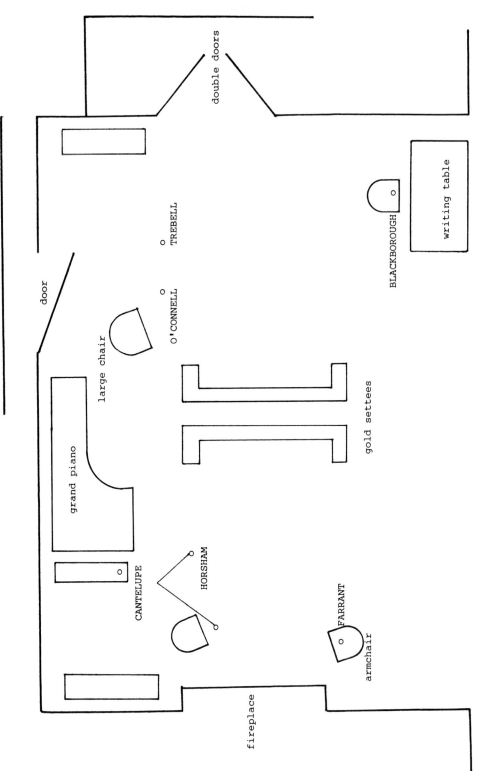

10 Groundplan for *Waste*, act 3. The entrance of Trebell, with the "tennis net" in the center. The playing

in style. It requires three separate interior settings, each of which is environmentally significant and firmly tied to physical details. Barker's production naturally gave the work an appropriate treatment. The prompt-book contains a long list of borrowed furniture and props: vases, bowls, clocks, lamps and shades, carpets, rugs, settees, a Chippendale armchair, and so on. Trebell's study was overflowing with furnishings, from bookcases and a live fireplace to a very large writing-table in the middle of the set, reminiscent of the dining-table in *Voysey*. The groundplan reveals that there was little room for actors to move in acts 2 and 4, though a myriad of places to sit. The table was piled high with authentic materials of a politician's life, parliamentary Blue Books, a dispatch book, a plotting pad. The property plot is almost pedantically precise about inkstand, pens, drafts of bills, a set of reference books, twelve parcels, and "100 Letters Various."

The upstage left wall contained a practical window with curtains and blind. Outside a balustrade could be seen, with street backing beyond. Up right a set of double doors opened to a small lobby which separated the main set from the secretary's room, clearly visible through a second door, and itself containing a bookcase, table, and chairs. It was here that Amy was sent to wait in act 2. Horsham's drawing-room in act 3 was equally laden with furniture, including an Aubusson carpet, a grand piano, and gold armchairs (see illustration 10). In the center of stage, two large gold settees were placed back-to-back. With interior backing behind practical doors, the general result was without question a standard naturalistic set.

Yet it was typical of Barker's use of the traditions of realism that the set became a method of controlling the actors' performances. The promptbook records that movements were worked out in detail and that the furniture was deliberately placed in difficult positions that required precise actor placement. In 1936, when Michael MacOwan enticed Barker to direct the first weeks of rehearsals for the revised version of the play, a similar set was arranged for act 3, the two settees again back-to-back. Barker explained that they would "form a tennis net, something to keep the two factions in the scene separate, and for them to fight across." The tennis net also stopped the actors from making grand, sweeping movements across the stage. "It's good for them to have something difficult to manage; keeps them awake," the director said (MacOwan 7). He put a large chair near the main door, like the one up center in the 1907 groundplan in illustration 10, to prevent actors from "making an exit."

The overfurnished sets, therefore, were not an uncritical use of the naturalistic mode but part of a general campaign against sloppy acting. MacOwan reports that Barker constantly demanded alertness, struggling against "all that was slothful, automatic, easy, anything that went by itself without the full mind of the actor behind every syllable and every action." He kept actors unsettled on purpose, to challenge their limits and to maintain freshness.

Intelligent and varied performances would be especially needed in a production of *Waste*, both to follow the subtlety of the text and to avoid overblown moments. As writer, Barker had been careful to point the surface action and dialogue to deeper concerns, to what we might call the overplot of Trebell's spiritual crisis. Like Chekhov in his last plays, Barker works toward traditional moments of high drama, to "big scenes," and then pulls back from them. The audience is thus denied the comfort of an expected or conventional emotional release, and is forced to look to the meaning of the action. The best example involves the suicide itself. At the opening of act 4 Trebell says to Wedgecroft, "If my life as I've made it is to be cut short . . the rest of me shall walk out and slam the door . . with the noise of a pistol shot" (320). In the penultimate scene, after Frances leaves him alone, his eyes fall on the pile of unanswered letters that arrived in the post with Horsham's note. He carries them carefully to the inner room and arranges them on his secretary's desk. "On his way out he stops for a moment," the stage direction reads, "then with a sudden movement bangs the door" (338). When the lights again come up Frances and Wedgecroft are discussing his death: the slam of the door is the pistol shot, and the suicide, instead of being melodramatic, becomes a philosophic piece of stage business.

The original production emphasized Trebell's isolation by marking him off from the start from the normal life around him. Barker portrayed him with a "pale student face, firm mouth, an abrupt virile cynical speech, careless dress" (*Times* 27 Nov. 1907:8). His natural red hair was hidden by a black wig. Though he looked "too boyish" (*Daily Graphic* same date:797), the playwright–actor–director made the protagonist a stiletto of ice amid the older, meatier members of the ruling caste, like Berte Thomas's Wedgecroft or Henry Vibart's Horsham. "Trebell has no *sunshine* in him," Barker wrote to

11   The seduction, *Waste*: Barker and Aimée de Burgh. The censor, G.A. Redford, rushes on to stop the play, in a sketch by H.M. Bateman

Nicholas Hannen, who played the role in 1936. "That is his tragedy; that is why he kills himself. Can you come on the stage and *not* impart an extra cheerfulness to the proceedings?" (Salmon 155). Even the passionate seduction of Amy was tempered by distance. Illustration 11 is a cartoon version of the end of act 1, but the picture is supported by the promptbook and the text. Trebell easily overpowered the willing Amy; their kisses actually caused her to faint, and he carried her "swooning into the garden" (*Observer* 1 Dec. 1907:4), a cold conquerer in possession of the spoils.

A number of critics objected to the open treatment of sex in this scene, among them William Archer, who held that the last half minute was "unnecessary and inartistic" and "distinctly chilled the audience" (*Tribune* 27 Nov. 1907:6). Such a comment from Ibsen's champion makes it easier to understand how the censor could ban the play for the reasons he cited. *Pace* Archer, Aimée de Burgh's performance as Mrs O'Connell served to clarify the sexual center of the play. She was a "brainless, dangerous, flirting little woman" in the first act (*Daily Graphic*), thinking of little but her ability to attract the man of the moment. She was utterly bored with the other women's political discussion, and languidly resorted to smelling-salts in their company. "She walks across the room with the voluptuous undulation of a nautch-girl," said Walkley. On her visit to Trebell's study, however, she was "in a piteous state, haggard, broken, in a frenzy of fear" (*Times*). Her change prepared for the later change in the protagonist, and balanced her personal catastrophe against the larger weight of Trebell's.

In the final act the production attempted to cut to the poetic core. "A feeling of brooding tragedy hangs over it," said Austin Harrison of *The Observer*. The suicide appeared as a foregone conclusion, and thus the three scenes became like the separate movements of a piece of chamber music, incorporating changes of key and tempo but retaining the unity of a single, symbolic theme. Alone at the end of the first scene, Trebell sat with his book, looked at it, put it down, and then stared into space. The promptbook gives a full count of ten before the curtain: a long freeze of silent isolation, with the dark night visible through the window behind him. The moment anticipated the ending of one of Samuel Beckett's plays half a century later. Barker used a similar position in the next scene when he read Horsham's dismissal (illustration 12). He sat completely still among scattered papers, the remnants of his old life, holding the note, staring out. His sister's angry outburst, given full vent by Henrietta Watson, served to give more focus to this anesthetic stillness. It was as if death had already paid his call.

The censorship campaign

The censorship of any work is galling to its author, but in the case of *Waste* Barker felt especially rejected. He had identified strongly with his protagonist; Trebell's consuming dream for a reformed society based on advanced education bears obvious resemblances to Barker's passion for a new theatre. The banning of the play, unfortunately, made the cases all too similar, and the playwright's ensuing despair was great. At the end of November he wrote Murray, "'Waste' has wasted me, and I am finding it difficult not to leave undone the things I ought to be doing" (Bodleian). Like Trebell, he had been dismissed by the authority of the realm, and his best work lay silent.

The reaction to the performance in the conservative press, where the censor's action was generally approved, made matters worse. Even J.T. Grein patronizingly held that plays like *Waste* should not be presented in an ordinary theatre accessible to the "unthinking and still imperfectly educated

12   Trebell gets the note. Henrietta Watson and Barker in act 4, scene 2 (sketch by Bateman)

crowd of woman, man, and child" (*Sunday Times* 1 Dec. 1907:4). E.A.
Baughan in the Liberal *Daily News* (27 Nov. 1907:8) headed his review "The
Censor Justified." "If such matters are to be treated on stage," he said, "they
need not be underlined and emphasized." But Walkley's judgment was the
most difficult to swallow. His long notice treated the work with sensitivity and
respect:

The play is a work of extraordinary power, dealing with some of the most fundamental
facts of human life with an unflinching truthfulness and at the same time blending these
facts with certainly the most vivid and probably the most authentic presentation we have
yet had on the English stage of great social and political questions that come home to all
Englishmen's business and bosoms. No one who has seen *Waste*, and who is familiar with
the ordinary limitations of drama, will, we believe, dispute Mr Barker's right to take a
foremost place among English dramatists.

After that shining compliment, the conclusion came like a blow to the
stomach:

For our part, we have no hesitation in approving the Censor's decision. The subject-matter
of *Waste*, together with the sincere realism with which it is treated, makes it, in our
judgment, wholly unfit for performance under ordinary conditions before a miscellaneous
public of various ages, moods, and standards of intelligence. While we gratefully recognize
the artistic value of the play, we would remind Mr Barker, as well as his brother authors
who are clamouring just now for a "free" stage, that questions of art are one thing and
questions of public policy and expediency are another thing.

(*Times* 27 Nov. 1907:8)

It was an extraordinary statement for a sophisticated man of letters in the new
century. Not only was government censorship justified when a work infringed
on the methods or manners of the governors; indeed, if the work was as
powerful as *Waste*, the censor had a positive duty to prevent it. As H.W.
Massingham wrote in *The Nation* (30 Nov. 1907:301), if the play were as
valuable as Walkley held, "its performance would seem to be a matter not for
State prohibition, but for State patronage and endowment."

But the outcry over *Waste* was louder than any defense of its ban. Earlier in
the year a play by Edward Garnett called *The Breaking Point* had been refused
license because the plot concerned an unmarried girl's pregnancy and suicide.
A stilted and moralistic work, which Barker had refused for the Court
(Purdom 91), it nonetheless raised Redford's gentlemanly hackles. Garnett
had created a small stir by revealing the censor's petty-minded morality in a
preface to the play, which of course could be published without hindrance.
When *Waste* was also prohibited, Redford's power seemed overweening and
action seemed imperative.

The first event in Barker's campaign was a call to arms. Seventy-one
prominent dramatic authors appealed to the Prime Minister, who agreed to
receive a delegation in a month's time to discuss changes in the operation of
the censor's office. Their demand for the abolition of theatrical censorship
was published in *The Times* (29 Oct. 1907:15). The group included

playwrights of every stamp: Barker, Barrie, Galsworthy, Gilbert, Housman, Jones, Masefield, Maugham, Murray, Pinero, Shaw, and Synge. It also included luminaries whose principal work was in other literary fields: Conrad, Hardy, Hueffer, James, Meredith, Swinburne, Symonds, Wells, and Yeats.

The chief objection expressed was a scarcely veiled attack on Redford himself. The signatories asked "to be freed from the menace hanging over every dramatist of having his work destroyed at a pen's stroke by the arbitrary action of a single official neither responsible to Parliament nor amenable to law." Like many English institutions, the office of the censor had grown by default. The 1843 Theatres Act, like Walpole's eighteenth-century version, had placed absolute power to license plays in the hands of the Lord Chamberlain. But the Lord Chamberlain was (and is) a member of the Royal Household, holding office by hereditary right and at the Monarch's pleasure, over whom Parliament had no control whatsoever. In practice the Chamberlain delegated his licensing powers to an appointed servant, who had in himself no legal standing or authority, and thus the Examiner of Plays was another step removed from parliamentary oversight. The Commons could neither reprimand his actions nor cut off his funds. The dramatists' charge was true: the censorship was legal, but the censor acted outside of the reach of the law.

The Liberal government, whenever faced with a difficult question, prevaricated. The delegation was not received until the following February, and not by the Prime Minister but by the Home Secretary, Herbert Gladstone ("an ass," said Barker: Purdom 78). He was not encouraging. Then in 1909 two Shaw plays were banned, *The Shewing-Up of Blanco Posnet* (for blasphemy) and the trifle *Press Cuttings* (politically embarrassing). In both cases the prohibition was patently ridiculous, and Shaw made capital in *The Times* out of Redford's growing hubris and folly. (Shaw's letters are reprinted in *Plays* vol. 3.) Further, Robert Harcourt, whose play *A Question of Age* had been produced at the Court, was now a Member of Parliament continuously asking questions about the censorship. The pressure mounted until Asquith finally appointed a Joint Select Committee to investigate the matter. Hearings began in July from a large body of witnesses, including the major dramatists, critics, and managers. Redford easily demonstrated his ignorance of the Act under which he exercised his power; indeed, it appeared that he had not read it. The Lord Chamberlain himself chose not to testify.

The Committee published a report of some half-million words in November. "Few books of the year 1909 can have been cheaper and more entertaining," wrote Shaw (*Plays* 3:675), and the volume remains enlightening today. The full story need not be recounted here; it has been treated by a number of writers, especially well by Samuel Hynes.[1] We can note, however, that Granville Barker's testimony was some of the most telling. His status as an actor, manager, and major dramatist who had been hurt by the censor gave him a unique platform, which he used to place himself as the leader of the assault. He spoke eloquently of the double jeopardy a playwright must endure, first in long uncertainty as to whether his play will be accepted by a manager, then in a second uncertainty as to whether it will please the Lord Chamberlain's man. He pointed out that the result of capricious censorship was bound to be self-censorship; that as a manager himself he had at least half a dozen times in the last four or five years warned a writer off a valuable subject out of fear of the Examiner's power to destroy the work. Thus the total effect of the present system was to lower the quality of dramatic art. In his own case, he recalled how Redford had refused to specify the offending passages in *Waste*, relying, as he usually did, on the principle that it was not his job to edit, but the writer's job to create a "licensable" play.

The evidence of the authors seems now to provide an overwhelming case, but there were powerful forces on the opposite side. The critics divided, some expecting a flood of "objectionable" plays from unscrupulous managers as soon as the gates were lowered. Walkley testified about his concern for theatrical propriety, earning him Barker's private sobriquet of "popinjay" (Purdom 95). In an age that remained Victorian in its official morality, the fear of the critic of the conservative national newspaper was damning. Yet it was the managers who most swayed the Committee. They approved of the existing system because it meant that a play, once licensed, was free from attack by the police or local authorities. Though that was not strictly true, in practice it was true enough. Abolishing the censor would mean that drama, on the same footing as any other form of public expression, would be subject to indiscriminate libel actions from private interests and closures from the police. A license was, in their view, a helpful protection of valuable investment.

Barker agitated everywhere he could against censorship. Much of his energy in 1908 and 1909 was dedicated to the cause; he often seemed a desperate man working out of desperation. No real improvement in the theatrical system was possible, he felt, if capricious authority was to determine what could be staged. "I share your feeling of sorrow for poor Barker," Pinero wrote to Shaw, "and agree with you that he ought to be working at his play, and recovering his health in the country. I begin to think that the preservation of the drama is engaging so much of the dramatists' time that soon there will be no drama left to preserve" (*Letters of Pinero* 219–20). The result of Barker's efforts, however, was more waste. The Committee recommended that the system remain in place but, accepting the compromise of Gilbert Murray, that applying for a license be made optional. Since almost all of the managers wanted the security of imprimatur, the recommendation was equivalent to marching in place to the accompaniment of fanfares and drums. "The art of contriving methods of reform which will leave matters exactly as they are": that was Shaw's summing up (*Plays* 3:677).

In any event, the Liberals did not care to move on the question. André Maurois concluded (299) that their inaction stemmed from an unwillingness to ask further concessions from the King when the government was already forcing his hand to curb the power of the Lords with the Parliament Bill. The Prime Minister, despite his friendship with the Barkers and with other artists, did not think censorship all bad. In fact the prosecutor in the famous Vizetelly obscenity trial in 1888, over the English publication of Zola's *The Soil*, had been none other than H.H. Asquith himself. Besides, the official sanction of the Lord Chamberlain meant better business for the theatres, a circumstance that did not escape the notice of other businessmen. In 1912, while authors were clamoring for liberation, publishers were petitioning for stricter censorship of books (Hynes 260, 306). As Barker wrote to Edward Marsh, if new legislation were needed "we might as well ask the Government for it directly as ask for the moon" (Berg).

The next significant battle in the campaign occurred in November 1911 when Redford resigned his post – not in disgrace, but to become the first British film censor. He was replaced by Charles Brookfield, whose appointment raised howls of protest and derision. Brookfield was the author of just the sort of popular plays most condemned by serious dramatic artists: adaptations of French bedroom farces, which cynically exploited sex by innuendo, pretending all the while to be harmless bits of fun. *Dear Old Charlie*, for example, which was revived by Charles Hawtrey at the Prince of Wales's in order to capitalize on its playwright's new position, had been mentioned in the Committee hearings as especially offensive. Though the text is lost, we know that the protagonist was a character who regularly seduced his friends' wives. But that was all right: as *The Observer* noted (25 Feb. 1912:7), clearly thinking of *Waste*, "you may show a flagrant and cheery adulterer so long as you do not suggest that any harm can come to him." Brookfield was openly hostile to the drama of ideas, and had gone so far as to insult Barker directly by referring in his farce to a play called "Sewage" by a "Mr Bleater." Massingham pointed out in justifiable anger (*Nation* 9 Mar. 1912:944) that the work of sincere moralists like Shaw, Brieux, and Tolstoy "may be and is turned off the English stage by the author of the worst piece now being played in London."

Barker immediately set to work against Brookfield by a series of telegrams and letters to supporters. The day after the appointment was announced, Laurence Housman's *Pains and Penalties* had a private performance, directed by Edith Craig. The play had been refused by Redford because he insisted that it defamed Queen Caroline. (If was a ridiculous charge, but Redford had banned Housman's *Bethlehem* in 1902 because of its biblical subject.) With the playwright's approval, Barker turned one of the intervals "into an indignation meeting" to denounce Brookfield's appointment (Housman, *Unexpected Years* 209). Agitation in the Commons began again. On 30 November Mr A. Lynch rose with a question on censorship for the Home Secretary: "Is the right hon. Gentleman aware that the existing tendency in this Department is to repress the development of the higher forms of art by a system of pachydermatous ignorance and inspissated Pharisaism" – but unfortunately he was cut off by the Speaker for "making a speech" during question time (Hansard 1911, 32:582). The Lord Chamberlain grandly ignored the protests, and the appointment stood.

A few months later Brookfield acted in keeping with the Redford tradition. *The Secret Woman*, a novel by Eden Phillpotts about Devonshire adultery and revenge, was the inverse of *Dear Old Charlie*. The book had been published in 1905, and Phillpotts dramatized it at Barker's suggestion. The new censor refused the play a license unless certain "improper" lines were cut, which were specified. Barker, who planned to direct, felt "obliged to make a firm stand against any interference," and accordingly arranged for a committee of prominent writers to present six matinees of the play, inviting the public to attend without charge. Barrie promised to guarantee the cost of production. "We keep just to the windy side of law in doing so," Barker wrote Murray, asking for his cooperation (Purdom 134). Another group letter went to *The Times* (14 Feb. 1912:10) protesting the ban. On the same page a note from Barker revealed that Phillpotts could have changed the offending lines without damaging the piece, "but it has seemed to every one concerned that a far more important question is involved," that of artistic freedom. As a novelist, Phillpotts had proceeded unmolested; as soon as he turned his attention to the stage he found the road barred. The production was to be at the Kingsway, which was under Barker's management. But Lena Ashwell, who owned the theatre, again stepped forward. She applied for a High Court injunction against the free performances, forcing Barker in the end to give only two private matinees, in the manner of the Stage Society (Mander and Mitchenson, *Lost Theatres* 234–7).

The result smacked of hasty preparation and an inadequate cast, especially in Janet Achurch's portrayal of the lead role, and the critics were not over-kind. The play itself did not make the best case for the cause it was forced to serve, and Phillpotts readily admitted, in a letter to the director, that his work was "very faulty" (Texas). For Barker, however, the protest was the significant action. He reprinted the *Times* letter in the program, and spoke before the curtain about the importance of the undertaking. The two matinees attracted a "remarkable audience" (*Standard* 23 Feb. 1912:10), which included writers, high-ranking members of society, and two clerks from the office of the Lord Chamberlain (*Daily Telegraph* same date:9). One of Barker's masterstrokes was to get the press to print a list of important people who attended the opening of the forbidden play. His intention was to make Brookfield look as ridiculous as possible, and he succeeded. The Liberal *Daily Chronicle* announced on 23 February on the first page that the event was "an expression, by the most distinguished audience of the season, of contempt for the Censorship such as makes it inconceivable that the author of the immoral play now permitted at the Prince of Wales's can dare to tamper any longer with the sincere work of healthy-minded playwrights."

While still in rehearsal Barker attacked on a new flank: he tried to get a summons against a music hall for presenting, without a license, what were technically stage plays. The music halls depended on sketches and short plays to fill their variety bills; they did not submit the works for license, and the Lord Chamberlain's office ignored this clear infringement of the law. If the halls were required to obtain permission, the censor would be unable to cope with the thousands of turns and playlets; if he did manage to read them, many surely would not pass moral inspection. Barker wished to summon a music hall manager before a magistrate and force the Lord Chamberlain into an impossible position by obtaining a conviction. He asked Shaw, Galsworthy, and Murray to support the legal costs, and planned to take the summons out in his own name (letter to Murray, 13 Feb. 1912, Bodleian). Like many of his battles against the censorship, however, the idea did not get support and died.

Individually or as a group, artists did not carry sufficient weight to change a system as powerful and as ingrained in English life as this one. Winston Churchill, Home Secretary during part of the censorship campaign, is reputed to have said that demonstrations in Trafalgar Square might possibly attract the government's attention to the cause, but letters to *The Times* would do nothing (Maurois 299). Brookfield thus continued to tamper with sincere work, and the censorship stumbled on until 1968. Barker's failure to rid the theatre of its heavy curse was one of the deep disappointments of his life, nearly equal to his disappointment over a national repertory company and clearly related to it. The dream of a free stage in England was as distant as the national theatre itself.

6 The limits of naturalism

I N March of 1908 Granville Barker sailed across the Atlantic with
William Archer. Barker had been invited to become the director of a
"Millionaires' Theatre" in New York, a new enterprise sponsored by
wealthy admirers of drama, devoted to performing in repertory. He
longed for such a post, and an end to his life of financial and artistic
uncertainty, even if it meant leaving England. The hope was that Archer
would become his literary advisor, and be appointed professor at Harvard or
Columbia (letter to Archer, British Library). The travelers needed only one
look, however, to see that the building was hopeless. It had been constructed on opera house scale, making it impractical for ensemble playing
and for works with limited appeal. "The theatre will be entirely too large
for comedy or the intimate form of drama," Barker told the *Dramatic
Mirror* (11 Apr. 1908:2) in New York, "and larger than necessary even for
classic tragedy." They returned to England on the next tide.

The disappointment was particularly acute, coming as it did hard upon the
failure of the Savoy and the débâcle over *Waste*. Three years at the Court
seemed to have led nowhere: a national repertory theatre in London was as
distant as ever, and Barker was unemployed and penniless again. Back at
small work, he directed matinees of Masefield's *Nan* for the Pioneers in May.
At Shaw's insistence, Vedrenne had at last overcome his stubbornness about
Lillah McCarthy and agreed to sponsor additional performances. The title
role had been designed for her, and she made a strong impact as a country girl:
"the best piece of work which she has yet done," said *The Academy* (6 June
1908:863). Barker helped Housman with another play, *The Chinese Lantern*,
with music again by Joseph Moorat, and presented it for a few matinees in
June. Meanwhile Shaw directed *Getting Married*, which played in the
evenings during the same period. The three productions were at the
Haymarket and carried the Vedrenne–Barker name, now in association with
Frederick Harrison. But they were a last stand against the inevitable. The
management, without a home, was effectively ended. Much against his will,
Barker was forced on tour in the autumn with *Man and Superman* and *Arms
and the Man* in an attempt to pay off some of his debts.

His state of mind soon had a physical concomitant. While playing in
Manchester he drank infected milk and contracted typhoid fever, which laid
him on his back for eight weeks in Dublin, where he almost died. He needed a
long recuperation, and was not ready for work until well into the new year.

(Barker refers to the incident in *Red Cross* 12, and it is related by Purdom 87.) Back in America in 1915 he would say, "I think that bad drama is just as bad as typhoid fever" (*NY Times* 31 Jan. 1915, 5:19), insisting on a relation between the health of society and the kind of plays seen every day by the mass of people. Near death in Dublin, his inability to effect a permanent change in social health through the theatre might have sent his personal health into further decline. He was brought through the crisis, to round off the analogy, only when Lady Gregory provided him with the Abbey Theatre's own physician.

The Duke of York's repertory

Barker's insecure position can be deduced from the fact that in the nineteen months from June 1908 to February 1910 he directed only one play. For a man already recognized internationally, this was an anomaly, to say the least. The play was Galsworthy's *Strife*, presented by Charles Frohman for matinees at his London theatre, the Duke of York's, in March of 1909. Frohman was a strange man to be involved with the New Drama. The archetypal American impresario, a great power in the Theatrical Syndicate, he had spent his life making money out of the commercial stage. His connection with Barrie's plays, however, provided an opening to the artistic side of the business, as he might put it. Barrie convinced him that a repertory theatre was now feasible in London, and that Barker's record at the Court demonstrated his ability to lead it. Thus, about the time of *Strife*, Frohman announced that the Duke of York's would soon become a full-scale repertory theatre, with emphasis on the best new plays.

The announcement must have seemed too good to be true. Indeed another repertory plan, sponsored by Lord Howard de Walden, which Barker was also invited to direct, was proclaimed at the same time and came to nothing (Purdom 97–9). But arrangements went ahead for Frohman's, and Barker devoted much of the autumn to preparation, while trying to finish his own new play. Other dramatists were busy too; in addition to the works actually produced, Frohman intended to present Masefield's *Pompey the Great*, Galsworthy's *The Eldest Son*, Murray's translation of *Iphigenia in Tauris*, and *The Outcry* by Henry James. Significant revivals were part of the plan, including three plays each by Barrie and by Pinero, *Voysey*, *The Silver Box*, *Nan*, *Major Barbara*, *Man and Superman*, and *The Doctor's Dilemma* (handbill announcement, Feb. 1910, Theatre Museum). It was an optimistic and ambitious program, designed to attract attention by the volume of productions as well as by the quality of the plays. "A repertory theatre may be likened in method to a juggler," wrote P.P. Howe in a book that records the enterprise (157); "certainly it may, within reason, be judged in the same way, by the number of things it can keep going." At the outset Frohman intended to keep as many things going as possible.

Barker may have been the illuminating force, but he was not in complete charge. The works from the Court dramatists were clearly his responsibility, but Frohman's hand is evident in the equal emphasis on older, more established writers. Barker's authority was further diluted by the presence of Dion Boucicault, who regularly staged plays for Frohman, and who was engaged to share the directing duties. Though no one's position was fully specified, Barker was not given the power of a manager. As he wrote to Murray, "I am not, of course, in any absolute authority" (Bodleian).

Yet the opening of "The Repertory Theatre," with its title in large red letters on the program's face, seemed like the apotheosis of the Court. The three chief Court dramatists, Shaw, Galsworthy, and Barker, were joined by Barrie to create an exceptional start to the first modern repertory in London. *Justice* was chosen to lead off on 21 February, directed by Barker, followed by *Misalliance* two days later, directed by Shaw. In the second week a triple bill was added: *Old Friends* and *The Twelve Pound Look* by Barrie, directed by Boucicault, and an unfinished comedy by Meredith, *The Sentimentalists*, directed by Barker. This two-scene fragment had been discovered among the novelist's papers after his death, and arranged by Barrie for performance (Barker, "Tennyson" 187). The third week saw the première of Barker's own *The Madras House*. Four separate bills were then running in rotation:

March 7	Monday	Triple Bill
8	Tuesday	*Misalliance*
9	Wednesday	*The Madras House*
10	Thursday (mat.)	*Misalliance*
10	Thursday (eve.)	*Justice*
11	Friday	*Justice*
12	Saturday (mat.)	*The Madras House*
12	Saturday (eve.)	Triple Bill

The program was exactly the kind that Barker had wanted but had hitherto been unable to offer: contemporary plays in true repertory, representative of the best new English dramatists.

But by the end of the week it was already clear that the venture would fail financially. *Justice* was a success in spite of its gloomy subject, but critics and audience alike thought the other three confusing and tedious. *Misalliance*, said *The Standard*, "is quite the most incoherent and irrelevant thing that even Mr Shaw has written" (24 Feb. 1910:8). "Tittle-tattle about everything, and nothing in particular, for three and a half hours, with no profit, no illumination, no palliation by purpose or aim," said Grein (*Sunday Times* 27 Feb. 1910:4). In a review of the triple bill, *The Stage* urged Frohman "to put into his programs as speedily as possible more of the joy and sanity of life. Here on Tuesday was another bill in which the morbid and the sour-visaged predominated" (3 Mar. 1910:20). The notices of *The Madras House* were not much better, as we shall see. Faced with heavy losses, Frohman reacted according to instinct and removed the offending plays. *Misalliance* got only eleven performances, *Madras* ten, and the triple bill a mere six. The great majority of the remaining slots were given over to the safety of *Trelawny of the "Wells"*, which ultimately made up one-third of the total performances given in the project. Though other revivals were added – including *Prunella* – adventurous new plays were no longer trusted and the repertory idea was perverted. "Poor Miss Alliance has been jilted by Charles Frohman," said Shaw (*Letters* 2:922–3). King Edward's death in May gave Frohman a convenient excuse to terminate the proceedings. The last night was 17 June, the repertory having presented 10 plays in 17 weeks for 128 performances: a long way from the Thousand Performances at the Court.

The Duke of York's was an experiment that should have succeeded. Performances were excellent, and the mix of plays more varied than the critics allowed. The company was exceptional. Though Shaw could not acquire Lillah McCarthy and Robert Loraine for *Misalliance* as he wanted (*SLB* 159–62), the actors eventually engaged provided a tight ensemble of players, willing to accept repertory casting and profit from its opportunities. Some of the best people from the Court were joined by actors of equivalent talent: Lewis Casson, Dennis Eadie, Edmund Gwenn, Florence Haydon, and Edyth Olive were side by side with Lena Ashwell, Charles Maude, Sydney Valentine, and Irene Vanbrugh.

Why, then, did it fail so quickly? Some of the reasons were the results of insufficient planning and inadequate commitment on Frohman's part. The chain of command was confused, no one person being in steady or clear control. The Duke of York's was not a suitable house for repertory; like many London theatres, it had no storage facilities for scenery, a significant debility when six separate plays were performed in a single week, with another in rehearsal. The barrage of publicity and the grandiose intentions Frohman attached to the venture actually worked against it, for it was soon evident that the project had overextended itself and could not fulfill its promise.

But the chief reasons for failure were programmatic, and at least partially Barker's fault. *Misalliance* and *The Madras House* are brilliant companions, now recognized as masterworks of the Edwardian era. In 1910, however, the general audience was not ready for lengthy discussion plays: "A Debate in One Sitting" is Shaw's subtitle. Three of the four opening bills seemed overly intellectual, talky, and emotionally dry – the old charges against the New Drama again. *The Daily Graphic* wondered after the première of *Madras* if the Duke of York's "is to be wholly given up to works which are discussions and not plays" (10 Mar. 1910:958). *The Sentimentalists* was a trying selection – a fragment can be interesting but not much more – and *Old Friends* is a weak play by any standards. Another of the pieces directed by Barker, *Helena's Path* by Anthony Hope and Cosmo Gordon Lennox, lasted for two performances only, a disastrously written frivolity that did not belong in the company. Perhaps Barker's impatience to run a repertory theatre got the better of him. A more cautious opening schedule, one that balanced a challenging new piece against a familiar one, might have saved the project from its sudden death.

The ultimate and intractable problem was repertory scheduling itself. Never having it before in living memory, London needed time to accustom itself to the notion of a constantly changing bill, and time, of course, is what a commercial management cannot afford. Frohman gave up quickly because, for all his high intentions, he was not a philanthropist. Archer chided him for refusing to nurse *Misalliance* and *Madras* to success ("Theatrical Situation" 744), but might as well have reprimanded night for not being day. The box office receipts for *Misalliance* (at Texas) show an almost continual decline in the takings, from £203 12s 0d for the opening to £64 17s 6d for 17 February. A repertory theatre has a theoretical obligation to nurse good new work along; insulating unpopular but important plays from the harshest aspects of the box office is one of the major reasons of its existence. But when the businessman saw what that obligation would cost, he became rapidly unconvinced of the virtues of repertory.

While Barker had proved that the system of repertory could be made to work in England, he also proved that it could not work at a profit. Shaw wrote him that "Charles has not played the game for a single moment. . . . the R.T. [Repertory Theatre] is not an R.T. in our sense; and all we have succeeded in doing is to prove the impossibility of a high class theatre under a commercial management" (*SLB* 165). Either a major subsidy, or strictly curtailed production expenses as at the Court – those were the alternatives for an "R.T." Frohman was not about to provide the first, and neither he nor Barker wanted to revive the second. A commercially based national theatre was an impossibility.

Strife and *Justice*

The plays produced in the Duke of York's experiment, except for *Prunella*, were all grounded in a naturalistic style. Even *Misalliance* and *The Madras House*, neither of which represents a slice of liife, are rooted in the here and now of space and time. But they differ from nineteenth-century plays by using naturalism as a springboard to an expanded realm. Something similar might be said about Galsworthy. He is much more photographic than Shaw or Barker, and often has the confident appearance of European naturalism, yet finally even his work is more concerned with ideas than with social problems. As Archer noted of *Strife*, "the whole play produces a symbolic effect . . . Superficially it is a picture . . . but fundamentally it is the utterance, the embodiment, of a thought" (*Nation* 13 Mar. 1909:892). In directing Galsworthy and *The Madras House*, Barker was perfecting the naturalistic mode as he pushed it towards a new symbolism. In the next few years he would recognize the limitations of a representational style and seek to open his stages to a freer and more theatrical form.

After the failure of *Joy* at the Savoy, *Strife* reestablished and solidified Galsworthy's reputation as a playwright. "At last we have a dramatist who counts," said Baughan (*Daily News* 10 Mar. 1909:7), probably meaning one who counts in the list of European realists. The impassioned treatment of the conflict of labor with capital made it accessible as a contemporary problem play, but it was its irony that attracted Barker and provided the key for his production. Ultimately the work is more about unshakable will than class struggle; the two leaders see themselves as isolated heroes maintaining what is right, classic antagonists engaged in a personal tragic action. Norman McKinnel played old John Anthony, the monumental chairman of the board of the tin works, "with immense, quiet, slow, magnetic force" (*Daily Chronicle* 10 Mar. 1909:7). He was "indomitable, though weak of voice and tottering in gait" (*Stage* 11 Mar. 1909:18), a dying man incapable of relinquishing his Darwinian view of labor and of life. As the strike leader Roberts, willing to sacrifice everything for the cause, including his wife's life, J. Fisher White gave a "remarkable piece of nervous portraiture, quite admirable in its fiery impetuosity" (*Standard* 10 Mar. 1909:8). In the end the two rivals understand that they have both lost, swept aside in a compromise that undermines their authority: "They've done us both down, Mr Anthony," admits Roberts (Galsworthy 155). At this moment McKinnel rose with difficulty, faced Fisher White, then bowed in a gesture of respect "to his opponent before staggering out, a beaten man" (*Era* 13 Mar. 1909:17).

The production achieved its power from Barker's attention to the ensemble, and commentators were often reminded of the careful playing at the Court. The cast of twenty-three speaking roles was supplemented by a large number of extras for the strike meeting in act 2, yet throughout "every actor . . . knew exactly at every moment the right thing to do . . . The smallest parts were rendered with as complete a mastery as the most important" (*Spectator* 27 Mar. 1909:499). About thirty-seven men were on stage for the strike debate, according to the promptbook, spread in a crowd facing the speakers upstage, as in the Trafalgar Square scene in *Votes for Women!* A painted curtain representing a barge on a canal was the backdrop; two bargemen stood on an elevated towpath, divided from the main acting area by a barbed wire fence four feet high. The platform was located at a corner formed by the junction of the fence with the wall of the works, behind which (upstage left) was a large chimney rising above the strikers. The "starving, shouting men, swayed hither and thither by the orators" (*Standard*), were thus visually dominated by a sign of the force of industry, silent and threatening.

The groundplan for the previous scene in Roberts's cottage shows a simple set of table and two chairs, a fireplace, and a door. The bare stage conveyed the poverty of the workers, and allowed the scene to be placed inside the set of the larger one to follow, speeding up the change. Performed at the extreme edge of the stage, it gave quiet intimacy to the strikers' tragedy and a contrast

13   Lillah McCarthy as Madge Thomas in *Strife*, Duke of York's 1909

to their public side in the loud meeting. Lillah McCarthy played the working-class girl Madge Thomas (illustration 13), who tries to comfort the dying Annie Roberts and to stop the confrontation between men and management that Annie's husband insists upon. The scene was especially poignant because of Jan Thomas, her young brother of ten, who enters near the end. In the middle of the anger and sorrow in the cottage, the small child, "all heedless of the trouble, plays, absurdly, on a pipe," as Walkley reported (*Times* 10 Mar. 1909:10); "a stroke of art, this touch of the incongruous-trivial in the storm-laden air." Barker's directing found the delicacy and balance of the script in moments like this, making the performance as powerful in the small, human scenes as in its big crises.

Strife sees the outcome of social struggle as fated, or nearly so – implacable at least, beyond the control of those who suffer from it. *Justice*, on the other hand, attacks specific inequities of English law and penal custom with a reformer's fire. Before it was produced, Galsworthy had begun to wage a campaign in the press on the horrors of solitary confinement (Marrot 249–51). *Justice* is his most committed play, and one of the few examples in the history of theatre where a production actually forced a change in public policy. It is little wonder that Beatrice Webb was impressed with the piece. Attending the Duke of York's repertory, she thought *Misalliance* and *Madras* socially backward, "obsessed with the rabbit-warren aspect of human society." But *Justice* was the Fabian play she had wished for, "great in its realistic form, great in its reserve and restraint, great in its quality of pity" (447, 449). Its première on the same day as the State Opening of Parliament in 1910, whether by accident or design, emphasized its political nature. Shocked by the prison scenes and the fate of the prisoner, a number of critics hoped that the play would affect the authorities; Grein's review made a direct appeal to Parliament to reform the penal system and the use of solitary confinement (*Sunday Times* 27 Feb. 1910:4).

The new Liberal Home Secretary was Winston Churchill, probably the only holder of the office to have been in prison: he spent a month in a Boer jail in South Africa. He saw the play four times, and arranged an introduction to the playwright (Cross 162). *The Bystander* reported that Churchill was soon "flooded with tear-stained letters imploring him to abolish solitary confinement" (9 Mar. 1910:478), prompted by *Justice*. He made a number of visits to prisons as a consequence, to confirm his opinions, reducing sentences when he found cases of injustice. In July he announced in the House that the government would institute a program of prison reform, greatly limiting the statutory periods of solitary confinement. If the Duke of York's repertory died with King Edward, *Justice* at least created a living memorial to its social worth.

Given the immediacy of the subject, the realism of presentation came foremost in the audience's mind. Max Beerbohm noticed that the illusion of the courtroom in act 2 was so perfect that when the jury retired to consider its verdict, the spectators in the auditorium took up the "buzz of conversation" from the stage, becoming "honorary 'supers'" in the production (*Saturday Review* 5 Mar. 1910:297). "Certainly the most accurate reproduction of a criminal trial yet seen on our stage," held *The Times* (22 Feb. 1910:10). Indeed *The Pall Mall Gazette* (same date:5) complained that realism went too far when the counsels for prosecution and defense addressed the jury with their backs to the audience. The play has a scenic exactness that is almost cinematic. The first and last acts are in a fully realized lawyer's office (Barker used a large writing-table in the center of the stage, reminiscent of *Waste*); the second act is the courtroom; and three separate prison scenes constitute the third act. When a film was made of the play in 1917, directed by Maurice Elvey, with Gerald du Maurier as Falder, little alteration of the script was necessary.

The most telling scenes in the production, however, were achieved by visual techniques that were supra-naturalistic. Barker's method was to take the solidity of the realistic moment and invest it with poetic or symbolist overtones that passed beyond the immediate. His production placed *Justice* in the company of *The Wild Duck* or *Hedda Gabler*, where the representational scene frequently carries a transcendent charge, though the realist style is not violated. In Barker's handling, details that might be mundane became luminous.

The best example of the method occurred in the trial scene, where Falder is convicted of forgery and sentenced to three years' penal servitude. As evening closed in, the light from the set's windows gradually failed. The effect provoked "heaviness in the air, the hush, the indistinctness as the hour for lighting-up the court gradually approaches" (*Referee* 27 Feb. 1910:2). A clerk moved through the courtroom, slowly lighting green-shaded reading-lamps; the room was "penetrated by the even, precise impartiality of his Lordship's voice" (*Spectator* 26 Feb. 1910:339), played with quiet assurance by Dion Boucicault. While the trial moved to its climax, the figures in the crowded court, as well as the voice of the judge, became "more than a little indistinct" (*Referee*). The actions leading up to Falder's sentencing, in other words, were organized to convey successive emotions of expectation, stillness, and finally sorrow. Each separate production value was executed under a careful plan: lighting, speech, movement, crowd noise, even "the audible dropping of a book" (Howe 189–90), were precisely engineered. This was more mood choreography than naturalistic directing. The realistic effect came, not from "fidelity to fact," as St John Ervine said (343), but from imaginative reconstruction of an emotional state. Details of fact became hinges to the realm of spirit.

The prison scenes succeeded for similar reasons. The first one, in the Governor's temporary office on Christmas Eve, was an ordinary box set except for an overwhelming detail: a portion of one wall was transparent, looking on to the exercise yard. As the characters in the room went about their business, the audience saw through a "wire-blind" (Max Beerbohm's words) "a blurred glimpse of certain automata, quickly revolving – the convicts at exercise." The third scene of the act was a magnificent opportunity for Dennis Eadie as Falder: a silent view of the prisoner alone in his cell, consisting entirely of mime action. Galsworthy's stage direction (260–1) gives clear instructions to the actor and is moving even on paper. Having learned in abstract of the prison system, we now observe the specific man, caught in the law's cold trap, becoming a caged beast. Dennis Eadie's acting was very powerful, and his performance differed enough from the stage direction to warrant attention. Here is Ashley Dukes's contemporary account:

> And in the hour before dawn we see William Falder, an indistinct figure in the grey light, leaning against his kennel wall, feeling along it with vague, twitching movements of a blind man, pacing up and down with a soft pad, pad, faster and faster; then drawing irresistibly nearer to the door, hesitating, moving away and back again, and at last beating his clenched hands upon it, gaining the confidence of madness, battering fiercely until the madness spreads, until the creatures in the other kennels are roused, and an answering volley of thuds rolls down the corridor and fills the prison.   (*New Age* 3 Mar. 1910:426)

The scene was, as *The Daily Graphic* insisted (22 Feb. 1910:719), "a thing to haunt you."

Eadie's portrayal of the hapless Falder, who commits suicide rather than risk further imprisonment, was universally praised for its "sheer nervous horror" (*Daily Chronicle* same date:5). His bearing and the look in his eyes made him like "the caged beasts at the Zoo" (*Bystander*), a quality reflected in a miraculous portrait of the prisoner, illustration 14. It was made by Alvin Langdon Coburn, perhaps the greatest of Edwardian photographers, and remains a signpost to the nature of Eadie's high-strung performance. Yet the chief feature of the production was "its moderation, its quiet" (*Pall Mall Gazette*). As with *The Silver Box*, the director created tension in a tightly wound but controlled style. Even *The Stage*, still suspicious of "producers," had to admit that the "ensemble throughout is practically flawless, the master hand of Mr Granville Barker counting for much in this" (24 Feb. 1910:18).

Interestingly, Barker did not like the ending of the play. In place of Falder's death, which he found too melodramatic, the director wanted to close on his rearrest – to suggest the future rather than to dramatize it. Galsworthy revised the scene according to Barker's wishes and submitted the alterations to Gilbert Murray, who much preferred the elevated tragedy of the original (Marrot 252–3). Barker gave in with good grace, but his desire to turn down the volume of the play demonstrates again his emphasis on the delicacy and overtones of the dramatist's work.

The Madras House

". . . this fantasia of talk about the family affairs of a firm of London drapers . . ." (*Athenaeum* 12 Mar. 1910:319): a fair summary of the con-

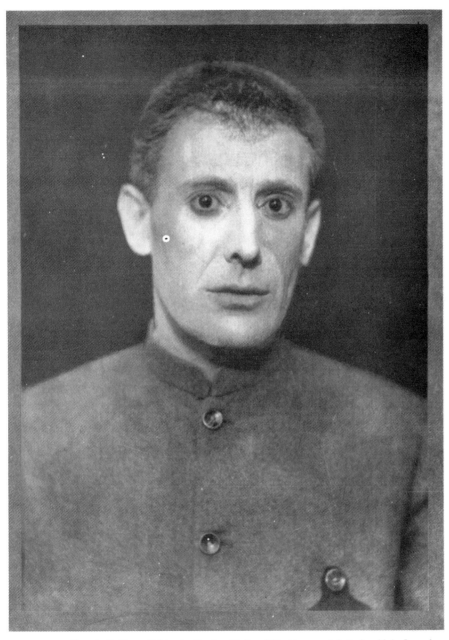

14 Dennis Eadie as Falder in *Justice*, Duke of York's 1910 (photo by Alvin Langdon Coburn)

temporary response to Granville Barker's most accomplished play. Many notices thought it clever, and in the Edwardian period the term was almost always derogatory. *The Standard* (10 Mar. 1910:8) was weary of cleverness: "here is yet another of the diabolically clever examples of the decadent drama with which we are in danger of being surfeited." Cleverness and talk, that meant Bernard Shaw. *Misalliance* was dismissed as talky Shaw, *Madras* was a copy. Those who liked it were deeply impressed but few, merely "a certain class of fussy people, a class so small that it is not worth a theatrical manager's serious consideration," asserted *The Referee* (13 Mar. 1910:2), and Frohman had to concur. Those who were not impressed, like J.T. Grein, detested it (*Sunday Times* same date:4); it was a bloodless, sexless, abstract dissertation to him, three and a half hours of "durance vile."

But the relationship of *Misalliance* to *The Madras House* was the reverse of what some reviewers assumed. Hearing Barker read the first draft of his play, Shaw went away to write his own treatment of the theme (Purdom 103), adopting some of Barker's characters, the eastern backdrop, and the drapery trade. (Morgan discusses the two plays shrewdly in *Playground* 187–99). Barker repaid Shaw's compliment by pointed references to the companion piece in the dialogue, directing the Duke of York's audience to think of the two works together.[1] Much of the thematic interweaving seemed lost on the original audience, unfortunately; the reviews rarely mentioned connections between the two plays beyond noting that they were both filled with talk, and distasteful talk at that.

The Madras House could nonetheless be called Barker's least Shavian play, in that it extends Barker's characteristic concerns farther than any other. It deals even more openly with sexual matters than *Ann Leete* or *Waste* and does so with a new bitter insight. The play as a whole is occupied with the position of women, and particularly their economic condition, in a highly charged sexual environment. For the first time in Barker's mature work the protagonist is already married. Philip Madras's relationship to his wife Jessica, although not dramatized until the last act, provides the central action, just as marriage is the central theme. The outer movement is slight and static: in the opening scene Philip announces his intention of leaving the family drapery business, and in the last scene he confirms his decision. He is the quintessential example of the "hero-raisonneur," a sharper version of Edward Voysey, a "worm" *par excellence*. In place of a forceful action, in other words, Barker made more room than usual to deal with inner concerns.

The concerns are wide in scope and, though they touch at tender points, do not come together in a substantial resolution. Instead of being teleological or plot-driven, the play is a series of layers, a composite. Each act shows a different type of sexual problem connected with business, marriage, or family, and all involve women's economic dependence upon men. This was a new technique for the time, as Archer's review noted, consisting of "several incidents in process . . . not a slice [of life], but a section, like that which we see when a railway cutting lays bare three or four different strata of rock" (*Nation* 12 Mar. 1910:910).

In the first act, the top stratum, we observe the six unmarried daughters of Henry Huxtable, a successful draper and Philip's uncle, at home in Denmark Hill after Sunday church. They are cut off by their extended maidenhoods from conventional fulfillment, and they must waste their vitality because class restrictions discourage any expression of worth outside marriage. They are kept more tightly leashed than the shop assistants in the drapery trade; metaphorically they are sexless assistants in their father's domestic establishment. The second act is chiefly concerned with Miss Yates, a live-in assistant of the family firm, who has become pregnant despite the prim housekeeper who watches over her charges like a eunuch. Her stubborn refusal to reveal the identity of the father gives Miss Yates a delightful freedom that no other character shares. Act 3 shows the pashas of the drapery trade, enthroned in the "Moorish rotunda" of the Madras House itself, reducing women to sexual automatons for economic exploitation in *haute couture*. Finally, Philip attempts to bring the themes of the play home in the standard Barker way, by discussing in the last scene the challenges of sexual relationships with his wife.

A superficial unity of the four layers is achieved by the protagonist's presence, moving through the play like a picaresque hero, sometimes in the forefront, sometimes quietly reserved. Dennis Eadie made a marvelous repertory leap from Falder to play "a rather 'precious' and priggish Philip" (*Stage* 17 Mar. 1910:18), attempting to deal with business and personal problems with what Barker's stage direction calls "light-hearted logic" (*Madras* 52). He was at his best in the second act, facing the problem of Miss Yates in the ugly waiting-room of the Roberts and Huxtable establishment (illustration 15). The light streaming in from the stage right window caught Mary Jerrold in her prominent position at the table with him, emphasizing the character's natural charm and self-possession. She gave Miss Yates a "wonderful naturalness, spirited in its quietude, restrained in its exaltation," according to *The Standard*, which liked the acting while condemning the play. The housekeeper, Miss Chancellor (Geraldine Oliffe, looking like Queen Victoria), had seen her kissing Brigstock, another employee; when Miss Yates's condition becomes known, this guardian of public morality accuses him of being the father.

Brigstock was played by Lewis Casson as a typical draper's assistant, with "quite remarkable fidelity to life" (*Bystander* 23 Mar. 1910:594). He must desperately defend his private and his professional positions before his wife (Mary Barton, at the left of the picture) and his employer. Unknown to the firm he has been married four years – the conditions applying to living-in made it awkward for him to reveal the union. (H.G. Wells showed those conditions well in his 1905 novel, *Kipps*.) Philip thus becomes a formal judge of sexual behavior, ruling from behind the table on conflicting claims. The problem of assessing the correctness of his employees' sexual lives serves to point out the difficulty in his own.

Though Philip is the central character, looming broadly over the play is *il gran' rifiuto* from another quarter: his father abandoned England and refuses to take any further part in western civilization. After a successful life in business, Constantine Madras suddenly became a Mohammedan and retired to Hit, "a village on the borders of Southern Arabia," where he treats his women in happy Koranic fashion. He has returned to London only to negotiate the sale of the drapery firm that bears his name. Constantine admits that he was driven away from England at least partly by the very purpose of the Madras House, the provocative dressing of the female sex, for he has in his time been an incorrigible philanderer, especially with shopgirls. He had abandoned his wife long before, as he abandoned conventional morality; but in the end he found temptation debilitating as well as distracting.

In the last act we incidentally learn that on a previous visit it was Constantine who seduced Miss Yates; it is left to her to put him in his place, as Philip calls it, by refusing him the child and refusing his money. This European state of sexual affairs, where a woman can first offer a man temptation and later deny him control of the result, is intolerable to him. "You keep an industrial seraglio," he says to his brother-in-law Henry. "What

15   *The Madras House*, act 2. Lewis Casson as Brigstock, Mary Jerrold as Miss Yates, Dennis Eadie as Philip. Duke of York's 1910 (sketch by Bateman)

Much Ado About a Kiss

else is your Roberts and Huxtable but a harem of industry. . . . You buy these girls in the open market . . . you keep them under lock and key." Aware of how western society exploits women under the guise of freedom, and exploits men as well in a mutual pretense, Constantine has chosen a simpler course:

> But you coin your profits out of them by putting on exhibition for ten hours a day . . . their good looks, their good manners, their womanhood. . . . And when you've worn them out you turn them out . . . forget their very names . . . For such treatment of potential motherhood, my Prophet condemns a man to Hell. (105–6)

His is an unashamedly sexist viewpoint, of course. But like Henry Trebell's, his life reveals not so much a desire for unconventional love as an inability to love. The unsatisfactory nature of his sexual relationships (at least his western ones; he is happy in Hit) points to his more general failure as a father and husband. Constantine Madras, imperial in name and in bed, is a comic absurdity in London. Yet his great refusal is one of the most significant nay-sayings in all of Barker's plays and cuts deeply into the sexual hypocrisy of Edwardian England, with its elevation of the idle lady to white goddess of the marketplace, dressed by men in the costume of a French whore.

In production, the third act most successfully demonstrated the complicated treatment of the sexual theme. Sydney Valentine played Constantine with "a calm dignity and assured affability" (*Era* 12 Mar. 1910:17), wearing a long beard, velveteen jacket and aesthetic tie, affecting a long cigarette-holder. He was made up to look like William Morris, according to *The Daily Telegraph*'s critic (10 Mar. 1910:13). "Lolling in armchair, poising a Turkish cigarette and puffing out polygamy" (*New Age* 24 Mar. 1910:497), he raised a superior and bemused eye at the fashion parade. The only women to appear in the act are three mannequins who model new French creations, "beautifully dressed and superbly shaped young ladies" (*Bystander*), whose costumes accented their sexuality. Charles Maude gave Mr Windlesham, the house designer, an androgynous air, yet even he treated the mannequins as objects, or "as if they were domestic animals rather than human beings." Describing the origin of the fish-basket hat worn by one, he snatched "it from her head as he might take his own hat from the rack" (*Bystander*). The men in the scene constituted a "committee upon the problem of sex," in Ashley Dukes's phrase (*New Age*); the three models were only the most obvious examples in the play of the marketing of sex as a commodity.

Philip is a member of the committee, but decides to resign. When the American purchaser of the Madras House offers him a directorship, he says no to it; his great refusal is similar to his father's and at the same time a conscious denial of him. The son has also grown to see the family business as a parasite attacking what is weakest in women while encouraging them into further exploitation. But Philip, who lacks his father's sexual passion, is trapped by intellect; Jessica thinks her husband may be "only an intellectual edition" of Constantine (133). He seeks salvation by abandoning the firm for the London County Council – "to save my soul alive" is his expressed reason

(134). He cannot, however, find his father's inner peace by abandoning one culture for another. For Philip the real challenge is still sexual and on uncompromising western terms. The Edwardian lady – his wife – remains for him both virgin mother and scarlet woman, an unsettling reminder of the Victorian adulation and fear of the female sex. "As the son of a quarrelsome marriage," he says, "I have grown up inclined to dislike men and despise women" (126). His emotional reticence, which again recalls Henry Trebell, is the greatest indication of his limitations. Like Barker's other male protagonists, he is coldly intellectual: desperately trying to deny his need for sexual love, caught between abnegation and desire.

The pattern of the play repeats that established in the earlier works. Though Philip's dilemma is never great, the moral questions certainly are; and his father stands in stark opposition to his moral sense, as Carnaby Leete or old Voysey do to their offspring. Philip denies the fleshly examples of his dull uncle Henry Huxtable and his hot cousin Major Thomas. He says no to sexual exploitation and yes to the obscure work of a small civic drudge. He wants to cut back on the expense of living, both literally and metaphorically; to teach his daughter "sensible" things; to become democratically common "even if it's an uncomfortable business" (136). Like Ann Leete he thinks we have been in too great a hurry getting civilized. He means to go back.

And like all Barker's comic protagonists, he goes back with a mate. Philip carries home his two days' intellectual travels, rounding off the sexual theme by bringing its major concerns to the hearth. He would be happier without sex in the world – "I do so hate that farm-yard world of sex," he says (142) – and with women completely liberated from dependence on men, though his program gets barely beyond an insistence on work. But he is on sensitive ground when he gives Jessica his ultimate confidence: "I treat you as a man would treat another man . . . neither better nor worse. Is the compliment quite wasted?" Jessica has no real answer. Despite the long discussion, Barker implies there is none, for he leaves the two characters with an unconcluded argument, staring into their fire. The final stage direction reads, "for really there is no end to the subject."

Whatever the truth of that assertion, an audience might justly ask for a more specific example. Indeed the first-night crowd, which greeted the third act curtain with loud cheers, felt greatly let down by the ending. The last act was twenty minutes too long for Archer (*Nation* 12 Mar. 1910:910); Max Beerbohm advised his readers not to stay for it at all, lest they spoil a delightful evening (*Saturday Review* 19 Mar. 1910:363). Barker was aware of the difficulty from the start. When the first draft was finished he wrote Murray that he was depressed over the play (Purdom 94). He made a number of new drafts (they have survived in the Theatre Museum – see Ritchie), and in December 1909 he was still unhappy with the last act. He tried to rectify the problem in the 1925 revision, which sharpens the criticism of Constantine in the concluding scene and clarifies Philip's desire for an asexual relationship with his wife. It also gives Jessica two important new lines about women: "But you can't be wise for us," and "I suppose we've still to set ourselves free."

Applaud those notions as we may, it is unlikely that the Jessica we are given would willingly set herself free of anything that would reduce her physical comfort. In both versions the play ends not with Nora's slammed door or Ann Leete's valiant opened one, but somewhere in between, with a hopeful accommodation. Since life goes on, there is time for argument another day. "Male and female created He them," shrugs Philip, "and left us to do the rest" (143–4).

Doing the rest: it could stand as comment on *The Madras House*, and on each of Barker's comedies, concerned as they are with completing the act of sexual creation, finding out what it means for the sexes to be different. *Vive la différence*, a Johnny Tarleton might say, treating *homo sexus* with broader and more operatic strokes, as indeed Shaw did in *Misalliance*. "The moment a woman becomes pecuniarily independent," Johnny says, "she gets hold of the wrong end of the stick in moral questions" (*Plays* 4:251). Nowhere is the difference between the two dramatists more evident than in their companion works for the Duke of York's, and we are reminded that Shaw liked to compare his plays to Verdi and his friend's to Debussy. If Barker never sounds the clear brass notes of Shaw, he makes us far more conscious of the intricacies of sexual harmony and the importance of overtones to moral acts.

Madras is the most musical of Barker's plays. Its four parts cohere like the movements of a symphony of profound thought. Even the last act is satisfying when considered on a musical level, a quiet ending instead of a tympanic resolution. The juxtaposition of moments within the acts, especially in the third, conveys an awareness of the musical power of contrast, dynamics, and rests. The dialogue often presents a similar quality, sometimes abandoning the connotative value of speech for the effect of pure sound, as in this general chorus from the close of act i:

PHILIP: Good-bye, Clara.
CLARA: Good-bye, Philip.
MR HUXTABLE: You really won't stay to dinner?
PHILIP: Good-bye, Laura.
THOMAS: Thanks, no. We meet to-morrow.
   (*The general-post quickens, the chorus grows confused*).
LAURA: Good-bye.
THOMAS: Good-bye.
JANE: Good-bye.
THOMAS: Good-bye.
PHILIP: Good-bye, Emma – oh, pardon.
   (*There has been the confusion of crossed hands. Apologies, withdrawals, a treading on toes, more apologies.*)
EMMA: Good-bye, Major Thomas.
PHILIP: Now good-bye, Emma.
THOMAS: Good-bye, Mrs Madras.
PHILIP: Good-bye.
THOMAS: Good-bye.   (36)

Clearly the writing here moves beyond naturalism, however it is defined. It makes a world out of sonorities and dance.

Barker's directing struggled within the confines of commercial managements to be true to the choreographic qualities of the play. Marie Ney, who played Emma in the 1925 production at the Ambassador's Theatre, said he spent an entire week rehearsing the entrances and exits of the Huxtable family in act 1 (Morgan, "Edwardian Feminism" 84). John Gielgud saw the performance and was "bowled over by . . . the movement and shape of the production, especially in the elaborate first act, though everything seemed quite spontaneous" (*Actor and His Time* 183). In 1910 the director's emphasis seems to have been similar. Lennox Robinson attended rehearsals at the Frohman season, and reported that Barker used a stagecloth marked with one-foot squares like a giant checkerboard, on which actors were to move in designed measures. The tactic smacks of the worst excesses of director's theatre, though the musical method of the play might well require the precision of a dance ensemble. "But woe betide you if you ended up on the wrong square," Robinson wrote. "Every move was part of a pattern, so was every gesture, every speech" (26). The delicacy and subtlety of *Madras* require a highly disciplined company; the play can show its art only in a performance informed by rhythm and control. Barker's two productions, like most of his directing work, were personal attempts to create from scratch a company that was equal to the demands of the text. It is significant that the only other major production of the play has been by the National Theatre in 1977, using the full resources of its subsidy and artistic support – exactly the kind of sustained repertory company that Barker wrote for but never had.

The McCarthy–Barker management

Lillah McCarthy was not associated with Frohman's project and, seeing the unhappy results of his dabbling in the world of art, decided to take the means of production in her own hands. At the end of January 1911 she presented the first of "Miss Lillah McCarthy's Matinees" at the Court, under her husband's direction. The play was *The Witch*, an adaptation by John Masefield of Wiers Jenssen's *Anna Pedersdotter*, a moody psychological melodrama with a powerful role for her. (Barker had directed it at the Glasgow Rep. the previous autumn, with a different cast, while he was acting Tanner there.) The performance, which reminded Walkley of Holbein and Dürer in its visual effect (*Times* 1 Feb. 1911:12), was an experiment in shadowy lighting; the final act showed a "dimly-lighted Cathedral, with long candles above the bier" (*Stage* 2 Feb. 1911:18). *The Witch* was performed for ten Tuesday and Friday afternoons. It was followed by *Nan* for four matinees, paired with the première of Barker's one-act farce called *Rococo*. Using the Court for matinees stirred memories, though the plays were not up to the old standard. Barker continued to be dissatisfied with his life, and began to think of leaving England for a country like Germany, where he might have a chance with serious theatre (Purdom 121).

Lillah effected a sudden coup to keep him home. Using her considerable persuasive charms, she secured £1,000 from Lord Howard de Walden. Supplemented by £500 from her friend Lily Antrobus and an equal amount from Shaw, she determined to become a manager herself. Without her husband's knowledge she signed a lease for the Little Theatre in Adelphi and invited him to be its director. The theatre, recently built by Gertrude Kingston, was in business trouble; Lillah knew it was available because the Barkers were living in a flat above it (Purdom 122). The house had no galleries or tiers and sat but 250, though it had generous amenities. There were no scene cloths and no orchestra pit, and the stage was illuminated by "Horizant" lighting after the method of Reinhardt (Mander and Mitchenson, *Lost Theatres* 243–5). It was an ideal chamber theatre for serious playgoers.

The Lillah McCarthy–Granville Barker management was inaugurated on 11 March 1911 with Schnitzler's *Anatol*, "paraphrased" by Barker with the help of his friend, Dr C.E. Wheeler. "Not ten words of German do I know!" admitted the paraphraser, in a letter to Martin Harvey (Theatre Museum). *Anatol* is a sequence of dialogues on sexual affairs, tied together by the cynical title character, a role exquisitely suited for Barker himself. With Nigel Playfair as Max, Barker's performance was an easy success, though it was to be his last on the London stage. In February three of the playlets had been given on variety bills at the Palace Theatre, a different one each week; six of the seven that Barker eventually published made up a delightful evening at the Little. Near the end of March *The Master Builder* was mounted for about a month, with Norman McKinnel and Lillah McCarthy. Both productions were designed by Norman Wilkinson, whose visual sense supplemented Barker's direction and encouraged him to a freer use of stage space. Wilkinson put Post-Impressionist paintings on Anatol's walls, and a fragmentary fireplace at the footlights (*Times* 13 Mar. 1911:10). The fall of Solness had "a sky of purple hue above the tree tops" (*Stage* 30 Mar. 1911:17) as a suggestive backdrop.

In addition to his £500, Shaw had given his latest work to the venture. *Fanny's First Play, An Easy Play for a Little Theatre*, opened on 19 April with Playfair, Harcourt Williams, and Lillah McCarthy in the cast. It was an immediate success. Kingston had established a policy of withholding the dramatist's name until after reviews appeared, to give unknown writers, especially women, a better chance. Shaw not only presented *Fanny* anonymously, he would not admit to owning it throughout the run. The authorship was never much of a secret, however, and Shaw's pretense was little more than a game with the press. In fact the daily advertisements in *The Times*, which announced the play as "By ******* ****," quoted a critic on the next line: "It was Bernard Shaw – at his best." Barker was not connected with the production and was slightly disturbed by its instant popularity, for the management had intended to renew the Court principle of short runs. But the play had such vitality that he capitulated, and *Fanny* amassed 623 performances, making it, Shaw said, "the Charley's Aunt of the new drama" (Purdom 129). Lord Howard's reaction was incredulous. "Is it possible," he asked Lillah McCarthy (138), "that I am to be connected with a theatrical enterprise and not lose all my money?"

One of the results of the success was that the landlady raised the rent. Finding this unacceptable, the Barkers, with Lord Howard's help, took a 25-year lease on the Kingsway Theatre from Lena Ashwell. It was a small house too, though more than twice the size of the Little, and had been newly redecorated: a pleasant home for the management, which clearly intended to stay in business. At last Barker began to escape the depression that had haunted him since 1907. He directed matinee revivals of *Nan* and of *The Sentimentalists* while still at the Little. He then went outside his theatre to direct a comic opera at the Queen's in September: *Bonita*, "a Portuguese Romance" about the Peninsular War, was designed by Wilkinson. With *Fanny* securely transferred to the Kingsway in December of 1911, Barker could again look for challenging work without the constant threat of bankruptcy.

The project that most intrigued him was *Iphigenia in Tauris*, which had been waiting for performance since Frohman announced it for the repertory. After numerous false starts, the time at last seemed right. But Murray and Barker agreed that their old system of Greek production was unsatisfactory, especially with regard to the Chorus. The barbarism of *Iphigenia* needed a new approach.

In 1910 Barker had traveled to Berlin to see Max Reinhardt at work, studying the rehearsals of *Oedipus* among other productions. In January of 1912 Reinhardt brought his vast staging to Covent Garden, using an adaptation of Murray's translation, with Martin Harvey in the lead. Barker did not assist in the directing, as Murray hoped he would, but did attend some rehearsals and strenuously coached Lillah McCarthy in her role as Jocasta.[2] *Oedipus* was Reinhardt's third spectacular performance inside of four months in London, and attacked a number of conventional English attitudes to theatrical production.

It also opened doors that Barker entered. When the critics saw *Iphigenia* two months later at the Kingsway, they had little doubt about the influence: "it is Reinhardt's spirit that hovers over the whole picture," concluded Grein (*Sunday Times* 24 Mar. 1912:5). Indeed, many of the physical conditions of the stage were similar to those used for *Oedipus*. A forestage was built out over the orchestra pit and the front three rows of the stalls. The Temple of Artemis, against the upstage wall, was elevated by five steps from the main stage floor like a Greek *skena*. Two massive doors were in the center of the shrine. No curtain was used, and some entrances and exits were made through

16 Lillah McCarthy as Iphigenia, raising the figure of Artemis, Kingsway 1912

the house on a "sloping gangway" (*Observer* same date:7) from the stalls to the stage.

Covent Garden was about four times larger than the Kingsway, however, so that Barker's set was much less monumental and much more intimate than the one used by Reinhardt. Further, Norman Wilkinson designed a color scheme that was distinctive as well as appropriate to *Iphigenia*. The set was scarlet around the blood-stained altar in the center of the main playing area (*Times* 20 Mar. 1912:11); the steps and the walls of the Temple were deep red, decorated with yellow double-headed axes. The only substantial relief from the red glow came from the large gilt doors, painted with "a naive, formal pattern in black and white" (*Daily Telegraph* same date:14). The Chorus of eleven captive women, dressed in brown hoods and "bluish-purple" robes, made a daring effect against the blood-red setting (*Nation* 23 Mar. 1912:1020).

Even the light was dull red, and all of it came from above. Instead of Reinhardt's four distracting limelights that "chased Mr Martin Harvey about the floor of Covent Garden" (*Pall Mall Gazette* 20 Mar. 1912:5), Barker used large stationary lamps. Some were concealed in the roof of the Temple portico; others were mounted on the square side columns, and two funnel spots were hung in view from the top of the proscenium arch (*New Age* 11 Apr. 1912:565). The lighting controlled the mood: it was kept dim while Orestes was under the threat of death, and brightened when the crisis was past (*Daily News* 20 Mar. 1912:5).

17 *Iphigenia* at Bradfield College, a Greek theatre in an old chalk pit, 1912. Design by Norman Wilkinson

"I want the Taurians almost comic," Barker wrote the translator (Bodleian), and he devised an acting style to emphasize the savagery of a play about human sacrifice. A small crowd of Taurian extras would dash through the house to the stage, "savage warriors, florid with greasepaint, hot with a sprint from the box-office and sultry with body odours," said Huntly Carter (*New Age*). As the Herdsman, Jules Shaw was "a little too barbaric, too crouching and aboriginal" (*Nation*). "Bare-legged, bare-armed and shaggy" (*Observer*), he and the soldiers of King Thoas "gibber like so many angry apes" (*Daily News*). The land of the Taurians was a violent place.

Lillah McCarthy presented a calm contrast. Her Iphigenia was stately and monumental, "as if a statue had come to life," said Grein. Her costume supported her dignity, despite her cruel function in Tauris: a short white tunic with blood-red wavy lines, and a white robe and skirt decorated with large teardrops of blood, a golden fillet on her head (*Stage* 21 Mar. 1912:20). Over her robe she wore a heavily embroidered ceremonial vestment. In illustration 16 she raises the statue of Artemis above the altar, grasping it with hands wrapped in black silk, dressed in the full regalia of her priestly office. Her tragic destiny stood in vivid distinction to the barbarity of her surroundings.

For the first time in his work with Euripides, Barker seemed to have solved the problem of the Chorus. Discarding the methods used at the Court and the Savoy, and Reinhardt's method of a massive Chorus speaking in unison, the director had music composed by S.P. Waddington to guide the odes. It gave structure to the Choral parts without killing their vitality. The music was "malleable stuff," Barker wrote Murray (Bodleian), "conceived in the loosest form possible." The Chorus alternately spoke in recitative and chanted in unison; occasionally one or two members would take a strophe alone. The dances, arranged by Margaret Morris, were simple patterns of movements, often far downstage. Massingham found them "symbolic, and rather Indian" (*Nation*). A significant point was noticed by *The Daily Telegraph*: because of their dark purple costumes, when the Chorus moved into the shadows they faded into the background. Thus Barker could bring them into prominence when required, but could also avoid the awkwardness of eleven unoccupied ladies hindering the sightlines when the action resumed.

Iphigenia was no more popular than Euripides at the Court. It got only nine matinees at the Kingsway, yet had a large effect on London and on Barker's reputation. If the production appeared derivative to some commentators, it showed that the new staging ideas from Germany could be applied at home. *The Standard* (20 Mar. 1912:9) concluded that it conveyed "a note of reticence and restraint which is English." Its success prompted Tree to invite Barker to remount it for a matinee at His Majesty's as part of the annual Shakespeare Festival, where a larger audience saw it on a larger stage.

Then for three afternoons in June *Iphigenia* moved to the Greek theatre built in an abandoned chalk pit at Bradfield College. Special trains with reduced fares were provided from Paddington to Theale (program note, at Texas) and the performances "were under blue skies to a full chalk pit," as Lillah remembered (307). Illustration 17 suggests how the staging readily adapted to ancient conventions. At the Kingsway the Chorus danced on the extended forestage; at Bradfield they were of course in the *orkestra*. The original set with its five steps leading up to the Temple seems to have been rebuilt as a *skena* in the Greek style. Granville Barker played Orestes for these performances, his last public appearance as an actor. (He and Bridges-Adams as Pylades are partially hidden at the left of the photograph, being led away under guard. Lillah McCarthy is in the center of the procession.) Directing Euripides outdoors at last was a delight and inspiration for Barker. The open theatre, the open style of the play, were liberating. Much of his subsequent active work was an attempt to find equivalent and appropriate stages for the various styles of plays under his direction. As he wrote Murray (Purdom 144), "you know after Bradfield I swore – Never in a stuffy theatre again."

7 Shakespeare alive

A WHITE GLEAM. White floors, white pilasters. Dead gold back curtains. Bright white light, hygienic, austere, democratic light, from "search-lamps" mounted at the dress circle in view of the audience. Footlights gone. A platform extension over the first rows of the stalls. Non-realistic backgrounds on painted silk drops. Eclectic costumes, recalling Beardsley, Bakst, Art Nouveau, Byzantium, the Chelsea Arts Club Ball, in emerald, magenta, lemon, and scarlet. Two proscenium doors. Stylized movement. Swift speaking. No delays between scenes. Full text, one interval. It is 21 September 1912, the Savoy Theatre, Granville Barker's *The Winter's Tale*, and Shakespearian production will never be the same.

"Post-Impressionist Shakespeare": so A.B. Walkley would have it (*Times* 23 Sept. 1912:7). Like many critics he was affected by the scenic aspects as much as by the strictly dramatic. (The paraphrases in the first paragraph are from reviews identified below.) The innovations were numerous but it was the look of the thing that was most unsettling. Barker professed not to understand the critical reaction, especially when it was hostile, but surely he could have anticipated a conservative response from audiences whose visual tastes were acquired from Irving and Tree – the splendid irrelevant pageantry, the illusionist backdrops, the fully upholstered settings. So much was new that the critics struggled for points of reference, finding progenitors behind every European bush and English hedgerow. Barker testily denied his indebtedness to anyone except, indirectly, Poel and Craig. In a letter to *The Daily Mail* (26 Sept. 1912:4), which had printed an abrasive review, he appealed to playgoers to abandon "artificially stimulated prejudices. There is no Shakespearean tradition," he wrote."We have the text to guide us, half a dozen stage directions, and that is all. I abide by the text and the demands of the text and beyond that I claim freedom." It was a creed, a new gospel, and there is no more succinct expression of it.

Some of the hostility to the production was actually hostility to the play. The last full performance of *The Winter's Tale* in London had been in 1887, when the American actress Mary Anderson doubled Hermione and Perdita for the first time in history. Tree gave a violently shortened version in 1906–7 (with Ellen Terry as Hermione), cutting about half the lines. It had never been a popular play, despite the opportunities for spectacle, and its uncertainties of time and place especially bothered the nineteenth century. The 123 geography of Bohemia so disturbed Charles Kean's sense of archeology that in 1856 he fixed the time at 300 BC and changed the locale to Bithynia, where he could have a seacoast with impunity. To choose *The Winter's Tale* to carry the banner of a new Shakespeare was a bold act, reckless in its disregard for conventional approval. It is a "bad work," opined *The Referee* (22 Sept. 1912:3), "one of the plays least worthy of reverence." The difficult metaphysical verse, the romance plot, the sixteen-year gap in the time scheme, the allegorical figure of Time, a bear in the cast: the play was ill-suited for stages given over to decorated realism.

But if a new theatre for Shakespeare was to be created, it needed "new" Shakespeare plays. *The Winter's Tale* offered a chance to show the power of taking an unbroken text swiftly, to show the value of open staging, and to concentrate on Shakespeare's own method of characterization. Perhaps for the first time since the closing of the theatres, Shakespeare was presented on a commercial London stage in a manner designed to exhibit his craftsmanship as a dramatist. Barker did this by the simple expedient of concentrating on the text; that is, he used elements of production, from acting to lighting, to support a consistent interpretation rather than as isolated items separated from the whole. To these he added an important reform: he redesigned the physical stage to permit a graceful acceptance of Shakespeare's own conventions. John Palmer went so far as to say that this *Winter's Tale* was "probably the first performance in England of a play by Shakespeare that the author would himself have recognized for his own since Burbage – or, at any rate, Davenant – retired from active management" (*Saturday Review* 28 Sept. 1912:391). Those commentators who got beyond the shock of the visual tended to agree. Even when the production made them uncomfortable, the best knew that something exciting, indeed revolutionary, was happening before their astonished eyes.

Staging *The Winter's Tale*

Barker was indebted to Poel (as he was to Craig and Reinhardt), though he had no intention of alienating the audience with antiquarianism. A museum reconstruction of an Elizabethan theatre would not do, nor would Poel's eccentric, academic approach to production. But Barker did intend to create, within the serious limitations of a late nineteenth-century building designed for Gilbert and Sullivan, an acting space with some of the most important freedoms that Shakespeare's stage provided. For all three of his Shakespearian productions, two in 1912 and one in 1914, he used the same stage architecture, a refinement of the Kingsway method for *Iphigenia in Tauris*. A narrow false proscenium was built upstage, which created a raised acting area similar to the Elizabethan "inner stage," but larger and more flexible. (For Leontes' palace this housed the white pilasters and the throne;

in Bohemia the shepherd's cottage sat there.) Four steps lower and down-stage, a center space, on the main stage floor, extended to the permanent proscenium arch. Most important, however, was a third area, built two steps lower again by constructing a curved apron out over the orchestra pit and into the stalls, wider than the arch, and twelve feet deep in the center. Proscenium entrances were provided through two former boxes, left and right. The footlights gone, this elementary thrust stage allowed at least some of the intimacy between actor and audience so important in Barker's view of Shakespearian performance. Many scenes, soliloquies, and set speeches were played there, frontally, outside the picture-frame and only a few feet from the first row of spectators.

Bemused by the outlandish decor, a number of critics failed to notice the significance of the stage alterations. But John Palmer, already a dedicated follower, saw Barker's intent. Sitting in the front, "in direct, almost personal, contact with the players," he recorded, "I had no illusion, and could wait receptively for Shakespeare himself to build it." As J.L. Styan has shown in *The Shakespeare Revolution*, Barker's work aimed at reestablishing the non-illusionist relationship between actor and audience that characterized Shakespeare's theatre. The modified stage alone could not do it, of course, but could aid actor and audience alike, give them an imaginative shove in the right direction. "The value of Mr. Barker's revival – apart from the acting – rests almost wholly upon his production [*sic*] of the stage into the auditorium," Palmer went on, "for thereby hangs all that distinguishes Elizabethan plays and playing from Restoration comedy." Abolishing the footlights, breaking down the picture-frame, were actions that took the audience back to an older sense of the theatre and its purpose. The foots and the arch, the crutches of the drama of illusion, had trapped Shakespearian actors for more than two centuries in a box that, whatever its size, was always constricting. In an interview in *The Observer* (29 Sept. 1912:9), Shaw noted that Barker's additional apron, actually quite small in dimension, had "apparently trebled the spaciousness of the stage. . . . To the imagination it looks as if he had invented a new heaven and a new earth."

In *Winter's Tale* only two full-stage sets were used: Leontes' palace (altered slightly for the Court of Justice scene) and a thatched cottage for the sheepshearing festival. All the other scenes were played in front of painted drop curtains, which provided varying depths of stage, and which were suggestive of time and place but were not scenically realistic. According to the Account Book, there were nine of them in different colors: for the prison, for winter scenes, for summer, and so on. A "ship cloth," 48 by 24 feet in size, was used for the Cleomenes and Dion scene in act 3, with a large cutout removed. The drops allowed the play to proceed without interruption and at a speed unthought of in the carpenter-dominated theatres of Irving and Tree. Scenes could thus be transferred with the directness of the Elizabethan stage, the new location established primarily by the actors themselves. As Walkley noted,

"the act-drop occasionally descends upon the actors when they are speaking
. . . so that they begin a speech in mid-stage and finish it before the curtain."

Norman Marshall says (151) that the effect of the drops was "very different
from the glum austerity which we nowadays associate with a curtain setting.
They were of light, expensive materials, frequently silk, painted with formal
designs." Norman Wilkinson was responsible for them as part of the "decoration." Barker refused the word *scenery*: "as to scenery, as scenery is mostly
understood – canvas, realistically painted – I would have none of it" (*More
Prefaces* 24–5). Albert Rothenstein, who changed his name to Rutherston
during the war, was the costumier; in a lecture in 1915 he described the drops:

> These curtains were meant to be suggestive only of the time, place, and mood of the action
> that took place in front of them. There was no attempt at scenic illusion, only such colour
> and form being employed as were sufficient and appropriate both to the material being
> used, and the suggestion which had to be implied.   ("Decoration" 19)

The material was not only of good quality but voluminous. Designs were
hand-painted with dyes, and the curtains hung in large folds.

The drops were used for the shorter scenes like that on the Bohemian
seacoast, which was represented by a white curtain with designs of windswept
trees. Occasionally they were lowered and raised immediately to indicate a
passage of time. Scene changes were effected swiftly: "the last words of one
scene were not spoken before the curtain fell and the people were all busy in
front of them carrying on the play" (*Standard* 23 Sept. 1912:4). W. Bridges-
Adams gives a good glimpse of the production style the drops created. Their
use was revolutionary in itself, but the manner of their use increased the
shock: "Even the fantastic draperies," he remembered (*Lost Leader* 10),
"came down with a defiant flop, as if Barker himself had hurled them at us
from the flies, saying, 'There! What d'you think of that?'" Time the Chorus,
in fantastic gold wig, blue cashmere gown with green and gold trim, emerged
only halfway from the decoration, speaking his piece while grasping the white
act-curtain.[1]

The statue scene, surprisingly, was also played in front of a drop and has
been recorded in a revealing picture (illustration 18). A black and silver
geometrically patterned curtain was well downstage, partially draped on
Hermione's pedestal and canopy. The effect, so far as one can judge, was
marvellously ceremonial and secret. The formal mood of the scene, implying
gestures of mystery and gravity ("it is required / You do awake your faith")
was enhanced by the designs on the cloth, yet softened by the delicate folds
and the human figures carefully posed in front of it. This scene, the last of the
play, with all its opportunities for illusion – special lighting, music, a statue
that comes to life – is even today regularly mounted in a full set with Hermione
well upstage. Indeed it seems made for the tricks of the theatre, and
Shakespeare himself may have taken advantage of some of them, especially in
the performances at the court of James I where sophisticated stage machinery
was available. It is therefore especially significant that Barker was confident

enough in his non-illusionist methods to place it in front of a drop, downstage of the proscenium, a few feet from the spectators' eyes. The Account Book records that the arc lights and the dress-circle lights were on full.

Drop curtains often look flat and uncompromising when mixed with three dimensional settings, but in the hands of Wilkinson and Barker this did not happen, for the two full-stage sets were themselves non-realistic. Leontes' palace, "a simple harmony of white pilasters and dead gold curtain" (*Times*), used movable benches and seats arranged in symmetrical patterns. The set, while striking, remained backdrop for the action. The white marble floor, running to the edge of the stage, served to highlight movement and the physical relationship of characters. *The Daily Graphic* (23 Sept. 1912:6) found much expression in "a series of impressive tableaux" against the atmospheric set, particularly in the scene when Leontes sends Hermione to prison. The art critic of the same paper, sent to review the production as a

18 *The Winter's Tale*, statue scene. Lillah McCarthy as Hermione, Esmé Beringer as Paulina, Henry Ainley as Leontes. Savoy 1912

visual object, held that since the play deals with questions of purity it was appropriate that it be set in white. Leontes, the disturbing element, jarred visibly in a royal blue and silver robe (2 Oct. 1912:4).

In fact the very eclecticism of the costumes served a valuable purpose. Critics were driven to wild comparisons – *The Daily Mail* found they ranged from "Layard's Nineveh to the Nice carnival" with some courtiers dressed "like Highlanders dipped in ink" (23 Sept. 1912:5) – but the value of Rothenstein's dressing was to remove the play from any definable time and place and put it where it belongs, in the world of fancy, fantasy, and romance. The costumes were prompted by the paintings of Giulio Romano, "that rare Italian master," as Paulina calls him, whose statue of Hermione was of course never carved. His "Renaissance-classic, that is, classic dress as Shakespeare saw it" (Barker, *More Prefaces* 24), gave Rothenstein a point of reference and a freedom. That no one ever wore "Renaissance-classic" clothes, except on the stage, is immaterial; no one, except on the stage, ever lived in a snowy Sicily when there was an Emperor of Russia and called on both the Delphic Oracle and Giulio Romano. Kean's archeological sense betrayed the play; Rothenstein's exaggerations were an imaginative type of fidelity. Perhaps Hermione's arresting entrance with candles under a gold *umbrellino* best demonstrates (illustration 19): this was not a real world but a world of art.

19 Post-Impressionist Shakespeare: Hermione's entrance. Design by Norman Wilkinson

That cannot quite be said for the visual effect of act 4, the great autumn festival. Explaining his intentions for the original audience, Barker wrote that "Bohemia is pure Warwickshire, and there are signs that Autolycus was something of a portrait" (*More Prefaces* 21). Accordingly the backdrop was close to realistic: a three-dimensional thatched cottage surrounded by wattled fencing ("a model bungalow from the Ideal Home Exhibition with Voysey windows," quipped Walkley). The costumes were identifiably Elizabethan with outlandish peasant hats. The half-naked satyrs wore garlands of flowers and hybrid masks. Actors disported over the full stage, romping in vigorous rustic dances – too vigorous for most of the commentators – accompanied by pipe and tabor. There was, of course, no orchestra (and no space for one), itself a significant departure for London Shakespearian production.

Even in this long scene some of the visual, non-illusionist convention was maintained. Camillo in disguise provides the best example; he merely held a black mask with distorted features in front of his face (illustration 20). The device "answers its purpose admirably," wrote P.G. Konody (*Observer* 29 Sept. 1912:9); "the impossible will be immediately and unquestioningly accepted." Many others, however, were less sure about the total effect of the Bohemia scenes, often thinking that the acting faltered or that the Warwickshire setting was a mistake. Desmond MacCarthy, otherwise enthusiastic, argued that Bohemia belongs not to rural England but to the continent of fancy. He summed up his objections to the specified locale in a memorable phrase: "happy the country which has no geography!" (*Eye-Witness* 3 Oct. 1912:501). Perhaps it would have been better had Barker maintained the full thrust of geometrical "decoration" throughout.

Barker's visual reforms extended to the lighting as well. With the footlights gone, front illumination was provided by an unusual set of spots or projection lamps – "search-lamps" Walkley called them – hung from the dress circle in full view. High-wattage bulbs were focused through funnels onto the stage. The technique was not as innovative as the commentators assumed: Barker used a similar method at the Kingsway; Reinhardt and others had preceded him; and even Poel tried a form of horizontal illumination in 1910 (see Mazer, *Shakespeare Refashioned*). Nonetheless the lighting was new to most of Barker's audience, raised on the soft flattering glow of the foots. The white background, said Barker, was purposefully designed to give "as much reflected light as possible" (*Evening News* 24 Sept. 1912:4).

George Moore told Arnold Bennett (*Journals* 2:52) that the light made the stage look like a public lavatory. The habitués of the Lyceum and His Majesty's did not care for the "egalitarian brilliance" of the Savoy either, according to Bridges-Adams; this new light did not flatter, and made supers seem as visually important as stars. Barker's style replaced the boot-and-saddle romance that hung about the Victorian theatre with the tidy fastidiousness of a drawing-room. But "the hygienic whiteness of the setting and the absence of vegetation in the pastoral scenes were not, as some wickedly said, a sop to the Fabian planners," continued Bridges-Adams ("GB and the Savoy" 30); "they were part of an endeavour to recapture the daylight, and the austerity, of the Globe." Barker's search for a new theatre for Shakespeare again made him see solutions in a modern adaptation of Shakespeare's own methods. Later he would argue that new theatres should be built with provisions for performances in daylight (*Exemplary Theatre* 206), but for the moment he made do with an electrical suggestion of the light at the Globe. (Not for every case, however. In a night scene in the second act, a brazier lit the stage; all other lights were out, the Account Book records, except a blue circle light and a blue stage left light, both very dim.)

Barker never did want a new Globe; he knew that Poel's way, for all its importance, was ultimately self-defeating. "We shall not save our souls by being Elizabethan. . . . To be Elizabethan one must be strictly, logically or quite ineffectively so. And, even then, it is asking too much of an audience to come to the theatre so historically-sensed as that." Thus he reassured his audience, in a letter to the *Play Pictorial* in 1912 (21.126:iv). But the actor had a freedom in Elizabethan performance subsequently lost when he was enclosed within walls and within the proscenium. The power of the solioquy

20   The Shepherd's cottage. Camillo (Stanley Drewitt) in disguise, Cathleen Nesbit as Perdita, H.O. Nicholson as the Shepherd, Dennis Neilson-Terry as Florizel

in Shakespeare came from the actor's intimacy with the audience, just as the speed of action derived from the bare platform stage. Barker knew that his task was to restore them somehow, and thus the visual qualities of his *Winter's Tale* were designed to regain lost freedom. They were shocking as items in themselves, but the overall effect was disturbing because it provided a swiftness and intimacy that violated the accepted conventions of the Victorian and Edwardian theatre. "To invent a new hieroglyphic language of scenery," Barker wrote, "that, in a phrase, is the problem." Everything that an actor does is conditioned by the visual frame of the space that contains the acting. The new hieroglyphic language sought to place the text in primary position, but could achieve that only by presenting a radical physical context: one that returned, conscious of the twentieth century, to the dramatic simplicity of the sixteenth.

Acting *The Winter's Tale*

A designer must interpret a play according to his own light, but if he finds himself "competing with the actors, the sole interpreters Shakespeare has licensed, then it is he that is the intruder, and he must retire." So Barker wrote in 1930 (*Prefaces* 1:407). It is possible that his own designers in 1912 violated this principle; some of the reviewers thought so. But most agreed that the acting contained in the "decoration" was fresh and remarkable. Barker's chief strength as a director, apparent since his work at the Court, was an ability to elicit exceptional performances from his players. The confidence they gained merged the company into an ensemble that served the play rather than individual moments or individual actors. He rehearsed everyone at the Savoy extremely hard, often until three or four in the morning (Nesbitt 60). He "drove poor Henry Ainley almost demented," according to Purdom (141), but got from him the performance of a lifetime. John Palmer again: "Mr Ainley's Leontes is the finest piece of Shakespearian acting I have yet seen. It was absolutely in the spirit of the platform stage."

Ainley, a former member of Frank Benson's troupe, flourished under Barker's care as he never had before or would after. A half-century later Bridges-Adams remembered that "Ainley's voice and physique with Barker's mind in charge of them, begot a Leontes that came as near greatness as makes no matter" ("GB and the Savoy" 30). Indeed there are suggestions that Barker made Ainley into a surrogate for himself – a "Trilby to Barker's Svengali," was Felix Aylmer's view (32). Cary Mazer, in an interesting discussion of the question ("Actors or Gramophones"), says that the actor became the director's *doppelgänger*. However it was achieved, Ainley gave the role a Freudian sense of mental derangement: he was a "neurasthenic" (*Sunday Times* 22 Sept. 1912:7) or a "modern neurotic, speaking in gasps" (*Standard* 23 Sept. 1912:4). In the night scene the great brazier picked him out from the red shadows, a "snarling, skulking wolf of a jealous king" (*Observer* 22 Sept. 1912:9). His passionate portrayal of unreasoning jealousy set the standard for the production, and his delivery set the pace.

The pace was swift to the extreme and, after the decor, caused the most comment. The text, played entire except for five small cuts of obscure dialogue,[2] was broken by only one interval, in the logical place after act 3. Barker took the verse allegro, much faster than his audience was prepared to accept. *The Tatler* (9 Oct. 1912:41) chided:

> Mr Barker's way of producing Shakespeare in a hurry as it were gives the impression not so much of witnessing "The Winter's Tale" as a winter's whirlwind. Everybody speaks at such a rate that often they are inaudible. They stand reciting Shakespeare's lovely verses as if Mr Barker stood behind them with a whip and they were within five minutes of closing time.

A number of critics claimed that the verse was reduced to a meaningless "gabble." *The Referee* (21 Sept. 1912:3) suggested Barker might just as well have cut in the traditional way since a third of the dialogue was unintelligible; J.T. Grein (*Sunday Times*) concluded that the audience "*saw* something of the Bard, but they *heard* him not."

A few commentators got the point about the verse speaking. Desmond MacCarthy emphasized that the rhythm of the whole passage is more important than the comforting "titum titum" of the individual lines; dramatic verse is meant to express character in action, not sound "like the voice beautiful from the lectern." If there were moments when understanding was difficult they were due as much to ears as to mouths. A decade later Barker wrote that "our ears are out of practice for such speech, even when tongues are trained to it. . . . Shakespeare's language has, in fact, to be learned before it can be rightly listened to, and playgoers must put themselves to that much trouble" (*More Prefaces* 57). A new theatre implied a new audience, or a made-again old one.

But learning takes time, and *Winter's Tale* descended like a winter's whirlwind. Further, the verse in the play is often difficult: highly condensed, often referential, suggestive of secret motives and hidden desires. In fact in a letter to *The Nation* some seven years later (27 Sept. 1919:767), Barker admitted that while he cut a few passages on grounds of intelligibility, he consciously retained some of Leontes' more obscure lines, like the speech "Affection! Thy intention stabs the centre" (1.2.138–146):

> Though they are certainly wild and whirling words, they are . . . the more indicative of Leontes' quiet pathological state of mind. An intentional obscurity surely, and a quite legitimate dramatic effect. We must remember that Shakespeare worked with words and not with "business," as a modern playwright might.

Once first-night jitters were over, the speaking settled down to an efficient clip, justified by the total thrust of the production as well as by "legitimate dramatic effect." Harcourt Williams, himself accused of gabbling in his productions at the Old Vic in the early 1930s, suggested that the negative reaction to *Winter's Tale* was due not so much to the speech as to the general pace (*Four Years* 36). Critics, used to frequent pauses and long intervals for scene shifting, found the continuous playing left them breathless. Most reviewers of the time were conservative in their dramatic tastes, and should not be completely trusted about challenging innovation. Other artists and men of artistic sensibility were not as suspicious. Edward Elgar, for instance, wrote Barker that "a lot of preposterous nonsense has been written" about the production; he found the entire evening a "great joy" (British Library Add. MSS 47897). Lawrence Binyon was delighted by the speed: "the relief to have no footlights, no beastly tootlings between the acts, no drawling of voices and dragging of feet!" (quoted in L. McCarthy 159).

But the speech was fast, and Barker worked his company to get it right. Cathleen Nesbitt, who played Perdita, remembered (63–5) that he wanted "tremendous speed and clarity, a difficult combination." While he allowed the actors great freedom of interpretation and in movement, "the only thing he ever bullied one about was *speech* . . . " Barker chose her for the role because of her innocent manner; he saw Perdita not as a princess but as a simple country girl raised by a shepherd, the queen of curds and cream. When Nesbitt was carried away with the beauty of the verse, he would tug her back to character. "Remember – be not poetical. Be *honest*, always. Don't ever listen to yourself sing." Ainley objected that with such rapidity the audience would never follow the sense of difficult passages. "They don't have to understand with their ears," the director replied, "just with their guts."

Lillah McCarthy resisted the fast tempo, according to Grein, and was generally praised for her dignified portrayal of Hermione. It would of course be out of character to take the role at headlong speed. Dignity had always been associated with her acting, especially in classical roles; she was called statuesque long before she played the statue scene in *Winter's Tale*. It is possible that she kept emotion too distant, but this must have contrasted well with Ainley's raw passion. And after the first act Hermione has little reason for tenderness.

Barker's attention to small roles shows his general care. He convinced Nigel Playfair to take the Third Gentleman, on stage for about five minutes in act 5, paying his full salary (Nesbitt 62). It is a crucial part in a difficult scene, for Shakespeare gives him the moment the play has worked for: he narrates the reunion of Leontes with Perdita and Polixines. The scene, regularly cut in the nineteenth century, was made both hilarious and dramatically satisfying by Playfair's experienced acting.

Extras received the same kind of attention, insuring that they formed a part of the overall stylistic treatment. While set speeches were delivered at the very edge of the apron extension and addressed directly to the audience, "several scenes were presented in pure profile, clear cut against that wonderful white curtain," the actors passing across the stage "with scarcely a turn to the audience at all" (*Daily Graphic* 2 Oct. 1912:4). Walkley noted that "squads of supers have symmetrical automaton-like movements which show the influence of *Sumurūn*." The effect was both non-illusionist and balletic. Barker's urge was to take the audience to the realm of fancy; the acting joined with the decoration to build a bridge to the imaginative world of the play. Photographs, though poor evidence for acting, attest that gestures, postures, and movement were at least sometimes stylized, especially at moments of crisis or high passion. When Hermione collapsed at the end of the trial scene, for example (illustration 21), the distraught state of the courtiers was exhibited in their contorted stances. Their bent bodies and extended arms, and Ainley's crouched posture, emphasized the disaster in an expressionist style.

The visual overtones led Walkley to the appellation "Post-Impressionist," a term that has stuck to the production ever since. Desmond MacCarthy thought it was mistaken, since the costumes lacked the "synthesis, simplicity, generalisation" of the artists associated with the movement (*Eye-Witness* 3 Oct. 1912:500). MacCarthy knew what he was saying for he had been secretary to the first Post-Impressionist exhibition held in England, at the Grafton Galleries in November 1910 (it was titled "Manet and the Post-Impressionists" and included many works by Gauguin and Cézanne). Along with Roger Fry he can be credited with inventing that "somewhat negative label."[3] A second Post-Impressionist show would open on 5 October 1912, a fortnight after Barker's *Winter's Tale*; clearly the electricity of a new art was in the London air. Walkley's use of the term was critically imprecise – though the term itself is hardly exact – but his review makes clear what he meant: "Yes, there is no other word for it save the word that in popular usage denotes a special kind of artistic assault on conventionalism; it is Post-Impressionist Shakespeare."

It was visually exciting, it was unconventional certainly, it was new; most of all it was vital. W.A. Darlington recaptures the spirit well. For him as a young man even Forbes Robertson's impressive Hamlet, the epitome of acting for a generation, seemed like "a service in a great cathedral, conducted by a pious and eloquent bishop" (69). But his visits to the Savoy in 1912 changed everything: "It was as if I had been looking at a wax figure in a glass case, when Barker came and whisked away the glass to show me that what I had mistaken for a cleverly moulded dummy was in fact a living and breathing man" (65).

Vitality was what Barker most sought after. If his methods struck some spectators as exaggerated and disrespectful, he was prepared to risk the accusation in order to breathe life into the play. He fixed last-minute typed cards to his actors' mirrors, just before opening. Arthur Whitby's (Autolycus) read: "BE SWIFT. BE ALERT. BE DEXTEROUS. PITCH THE SONGS HIGH. BE SWIFT. BE ALERT" (Trewin, *Shakespeare* 53). Cathleen Nesbitt's: "Be swift, be swift, be not poetical" (Nesbitt 65). In an interview in *The Evening News* (24 Sept.

1912:4) Barker was straightforward enough: "The first thing I aimed at was to get the thing alive at any cost. You can't get that without swiftness." His cost did not include betraying the playwright; he understood something more important than some directors who have trudged after him. Shakespeare is alive in the theatre if he is given half a chance on his own terms. Barker's vitality, in fact, stemmed primarily from his conviction that Shakespeare knew his job as a dramatist and man of the theatre, that Shakespeare's judgments are to be trusted and his words respected.

That is a belief he never abandoned, even much later when he was an elderly scholar detached from the turmoil of the stage. In the introduction to *Prefaces to Shakespeare* (1:4) he maintained what he had started with in 1912: "Besides, what is all the criticism and scholarship finally for, if not to keep Shakespeare alive? And he must always be most alive – even if roughly and rudely alive – in the theatre." Most spectators, sometimes despite

21   The trial scene, *The Winter's Tale*, with expressionist gestures. Costumes by Albert Rothenstein

themselves, felt excited by the vitality and strength of *Winter's Tale*. Norman
Marshall (158) sums up their reactions: "Talking to those who saw Granville-
Barker's Shakespearian productions one invariably finds that the quality that
is most vividly remembered is the air of freshness and spontaneity." Perhaps
Desmond MacCarthy best hit on Barker's contribution when he headed his
review

STARTLING DISCOVERY AT THE SAVOY:
SHAKESPEARE ALIVE!

The *Winter's Tale* got more attention than Barker could have hoped for.
Even though much of it was uncomplimentary, the controversy itself should
have insured a reasonably long life. The performances were well attended,
according to Purdom (140), but clearly they were not attended enough: the
production suffered a heavy loss and was taken off the evening bill after only
six weeks. It is difficult to understand why Barker acted so hastily. He
replaced it in less than two weeks with *Twelfth Night*, using many of the same
actors, and continued *Winter's Tale* at matinees until the end of November. It
is logical that the two could have shared a repertory bill equally that might, in
time, have gained *Winter's Tale* greater public acceptance. Barker was
responding a bit like Frohman; there appears to be no satisfactory explanation
of why he did not try to nurse the play along. Perhaps he was simply piqued:
he wrote to Harcourt Williams on 24 September that those who were "carping
and cavilling . . . don't really like Shakespeare, or poetry, or acting" (Purdom
140). Shaw said something similar in an interview (*Observer* 29 Sept.
1912:9): "What they didn't like was Shakespear. It will take them ten years to
acquire a taste for Shakespear's later plays and learn his language." Or
perhaps Barker simply saw no reason to risk more money and to jeopardize
future productions when the play had already made its mark. But despite the
short run it must be acknowledged as one of the four or five most important
Shakespearian productions of this century. As the first of them, it has a
undeniable place in the theatre history of our time.

Twelfth Night

There were no doubts about the popularity of *Twelfth Night*, which opened in
mid-November to enthusiastic applause: "the cheers were long and loud at
the close" (*Standard* 16 Nov. 1912:10). It played 139 performances in the
next four months. The editor of *Play Pictorial* (21.126:50), a magazine
usually concerned with commercial success, proclaimed it "a performance of
sheer delight, wonder and surprise! . . . The traditions of a life-time
torpedoed into infinity!" Most of the "carping and cavilling" critics of
Winter's Tale had already shouted their assent, some self-righteously assuming that Barker had corrected his errant ways under their instruction. "A
blessing was pronounced, and *Twelfth Night* has drawn society ever since,"

said Leonard Inkster (22). "On one occasion lately three persons [were] sitting together the sum-total of whose previous visits amounted to something near a hundred." Barker's methods were milder but no different in kind; simple familiarity with them and their results seemed to ease conventional playgoers. Familiarity with the play, however, was the chief reason for the acceptance of "Barkerized Shakespeare." Even when the production flew in the face of tradition, the comedy itself, lighthearted and comfortably worn, never presented the challenging shock of *Winter's Tale*.

In the Savoy lobby the audience could buy sixpenny acting editions of each of the three plays as they were presented, with short "Producer's Prefaces" in which Barker outlined the principles that governed his work. (They are reprinted, with other uncollected Barker essays, in *More Prefaces to Shakespeare*, used here for ease of reference.) These proto-prefaces are close to the theatrical moment, for they refer to the critical reaction and to discoveries being made in rehearsal, yet they are clearly the products of long study and thought. In the *Twelfth Night* edition, Barker contrasts the general mood of his first two productions:

The Winter's Tale, as I see its writing, is complex, vivid, abundant in the variety of its mood and pace and colour, now disordered, now at rest, the product of a mind rapid, changing, and over-full. I believe its interpretation should express all that. *Twelfth Night* is quite other . . . its serious mood is passionate, its verse is lyrical, the speaking of it needs swiftness and fine tone; not rush, but rhythm, constant and compelling.

(More Prefaces 32)

The play was accordingly given a mounting that emphasized its romantic, youthful essence, contrasting to the febrile fire and ice of *Winter's Tale*. The stage architecture was the same, three levels coming down in widening steps to the apron extension. Drop curtains were used again to establish place, and the dresses were equally flamboyant, though this time Norman Wilkinson designed both setting and costumes and achieved a more unified effect. Lighting, pace, text, all followed the form we have seen. But the feel was very different. Barker sensed that *Twelfth Night* was "the last play of Shakespeare's golden age" and gave it tender treatment.

"Spring-cleaning Shakespeare" – the phrase from *The Referee* (17 Nov. 1912:3) captures the director's urge. Barker wanted to strike off the nineteenth-century traditions that had settled on the play like layers of London soot, especially in the form of exaggerated comic business for Malvolio, Toby, and Andrew. But he bent his greatest efforts towards showing off Viola in what he considered to be her proper clothes. As one of the chief "breeches parts," actresses since the Restoration had used the role to gain sexual or comic advantage by exploiting the woman under the doublet. Here was a clear case, Barker thought, where remembering the Elizabethan practice was essential:

Viola was played, and was meant to be played, by a boy . . . To that original audience, the strain of make-believe in the matter ended just where for us it most begins, at Viola's entrance as a page. Shakespeare's audience saw Cesario without effort as Orsino sees him; more importantly they saw him as Olivia sees him.   (*More Prefaces* 28–9)

Thus for an actress to center her portrayal on "childish by-play as to legs and petticoats or the absence of them" is not only "dramatic bad manners," it is also to knock "for the sake of a little laughter, the whole of the play's romantic plot on the head."

This is a crucial point. Barker sought to return to Shakespeare's own convention because Viola's dramatic value in the play at large is superior to her incidental comic value, however delightful that might be. In his emphatic opinion, Shakespeare was the master craftsman of plays, not of striking turns for a star. To realize his notion of the main role Barker relied on Lillah McCarthy, and she succeeded admirably. In her memoirs (161) she reveals that she wanted to "let Viola betray the woman in her." Eventually, however, she agreed to the director's interpretation; she captured the spirit of Viola as a boy and freshened the play with simplicity and innocence.

With pageboy hair and green brocade doublet, it must have been difficult to recognize the same woman who was playing an elegant Hermione in the afternoons of November 1912. Most photographs of the production attest to her physical plainness in the role, though illustration 22 shows her boyish immaturity best. The contrast between Orsino and Viola was not merely one of height. His ornate costume with a Persian flair emphasized the strength of passion in his stance and eyes, while Lillah stood quiet, rapt, slightly awkward in her new position and sex. The moment portrayed (act 1, scene 4: "I have unclasped / To thee the book even of my secret soul"), the first occasion they are on stage together, requires the actress to straddle her two roles delicately. As Cesario she must manfully accept the Duke's charge to woo Olivia for him, and yet must remind the audience that she is Viola and is herself in love with her new master: "Who'ever I woo, myself would be his wife." For an actress to play this without relating that her own sex is the same as Viola's is certainly to choose the harder way.

Barker never paled before a task because it was hard. On the other hand, as a practical man of the theatre he certainly did not seek unnecessary difficulties. Clearly he thought the case of the Elizabethan boy actor significant and integrally tied to a modern approach to Shakespeare in the theatre. Thinking of Shakespeare's women characters as women, he wrote much later, adds to their literary and psychological dimension, but does not help the actress. Shakespeare does not represent women so much as present characters as women-played-by-boys. (Barker did not employ this Brechtian phrase, but he would have understood its aptness.) Therefore the real charms of femininity are superfluous for the actress: "The 'serpent of the old Nile,' realistic in the flesh, will but obscure Shakespeare's Cleopatra. To tell a woman to begin her study of how to play a woman's part by imagining herself a boy may seem absurd; but this is the right approach nevertheless" ("Shakespeare's Dramatic Art" 55–6).

22 Lillah McCarthy and Arthur Wortner as Viola and Orsino in *Twelfth Night*, Savoy 1912

In the twentieth century, the Shakespearian boy actor points the same moral as the sceneless stage. We need not reproduce either, but we must recognize how they both differ from our modern practices, and why. Actresses should first "achieve the selfless skill and beauty" the parts require, then they may add "charm and the rest." (Charm seems to be Barker's delicate word for sex.) "Shakespeare's Rosalind is – very naturally! – not self-conscious in her doublet and hose," Barker continues, "his Viola casts no sheep's eye at Orsino, and Beatrice conquers Benedict by her wit, nothing more primitive." A vital actor, it might be objected, male or female, can never entirely lose that something "more primitive," but Lillah McCarthy managed to subdue it at least. John Palmer (*Saturday Review* 23 Nov. 1912:638) held that she restored "Shakespeare's magically written part for the principal boy-player of the company of Burbage." In so doing she broke a tradition of 250 years and restored something of the freshness of the play.

It was freshness that controlled Barker's approach to the comic characters as well. Throughout the nineteenth century the comic business associated with the two knights had assumed larger and larger proportions until Toby the drunken lout and Andrew the vacuous gull dominated much of the play with interpolated riot. Barker returned to both characters a bit of their gentlemanly status and gave them a significance that took account of their positions in the scheme of the play. Toby is not just "a bestial sot"; drink and fellowship are his relief from boredom in a household in mourning. Andrew is slow and vain but not "a cretinous idiot," he wrote in the acting edition. Like them, Feste is not young: "There runs through all he says and does that vein of irony by which we may so often mark one of life's self-acknowledged failures" (*More Prefaces* 29–30).

The main line followed for the three characters is exemplified in the drinking scene, or "kitchen" scene, which had in the past become the focal point of much accumulated comic business. (Fortunately the promptbooks for *Twelfth Night* and *Midsummer Night's Dream* have survived – that for *Winter's Tale* is lost – and they are a wellspring of information.) Barker set the scene in a tapestried inset (15 ft wide by 6 ft deep, according to the Account Book). The small space kept the characters confined and their movements limited, and gave a fine suggestion of late-night revelry in the otherwise dark house of Olivia. Toby and Andrew entered in darkness with their shoes off, one to light candles, the other to stub his toe on a chair. The quiet beginning set up a gradual crescendo of humor, which followed the scene as written rather than as recorded in the standard prompt copy of the day. For the first song, "O mistress mine," Feste accompanied himself on the virginal quietly. But the singing soon increased to "caterwauling," prompting Maria's entrance, then Malvolio's (illustration 23).

As the text directs, Toby was singing "O the twelfth day of December" just before the steward appeared, but the tune was actually "The Twelve Days of Christmas." Throughout Malvolio's speech Toby sang lines ironically timed to Malvolio's words: after "My masters, are you mad," for example, he gave out, "Ten asses racing." Toby and Feste sang the snatches that follow, and on "Sir Toby, there you lie," Feste tipped his partner out of his chair onto the floor (promptbook 26, 30). This was all fresh business, all attached to character, none of it stopping the progress of the action. John Masefield wrote to Barker that he liked "the way you made the drinking scene a concert, another bit of seeing with W.S.'s mind" (Purdom 143). The end of the scene returned to the quiet of its opening. The lights dimmed and the curtain fell for the first interval (there were two, of ten minutes each) on Toby and Andrew attempting to blow out the candles above their heads (*Oxford Times* 30 Nov. 1912:14).

Malvolio himself had been the subject of much Victorian tampering, of course, because the role offered such temptations to the great actor–managers. Irving's sentimentalized, near-tragic figure, close to his Shylock, is well known. In 1901 Tree played him followed about by a quartet of sub-Malvolios, dressed as their master, mimicking his gait and gestures. Though

23   The drinking scene, in a small tapestry inset. Entrance of Malvolio (Henry Ainley)

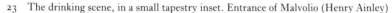

Barker does not discuss Malvolio in his preface, his approach is easy to ascertain; he simply looked at the text to discover the outlines of the figure and kept his actor within them. By all accounts Henry Ainley was superb: supercilious yet dignified, self-controlled yet vulgar and venomous in flashes. In tossing aside the burden of fustian tradition, Ainley became for Palmer the "first Malvolio of this generation that does not seem to have walked on to the stage from some municipal museum of theatrical bric-à-brac." In the drinking scene, for example, he did not wear the time-honored nightshirt but plain black garments (illustration 23). In prison he avoided exaggeration and thus kept the audience from sympathizing too closely with him as the victim of a joke that seems cruel to modern eyes. He generally kept a portion of control – "a quietly, if inordinately, conceited man, and no magnificent monster" (*Times* 16 Nov. 1912:10) – more Polonius than Leontes, more Holofernes than Lear.

But he did not become a pallid figure. The character is interesting psychologically because he believes utterly in himself and his absolute rectitude. Ainley's Malvolio, cross-gartered and in brave attire, gave full force to his self-importance after the smiling interview with Olivia: "O, ho! do you come near me now? No worse man than Sir Toby to look to me!" The promptbook (60) reveals something of his plumped-up frenzy: he crossed right, then left, and then upcenter, where he executed a double cross – a spin – and finished leftcenter by a seat. His costume was a Puritan's illicit dream: grey velvet brocade tunic, trimmed with pearls; yellow stockings, of course; black velvet hat with a large white feather; and a black velvet cape trimmed with reflective silver rays (Account Book). Two photos from separate sources, when placed together, recreate the moment of his twirling (illustration 24). Ainley turned like a fashion model to display what Bridges-Adams called "the dazzling radiation of Malvolio's cloak, which drew a gasp from the women in the house when he turned upstage" (*Lost Leader* 11).

The best example of Barker's treatment occured in the final scene. As Fabian explained about the forged love letter, Ainley tore it up, again and again, into tiny pieces, to the general laughter of the company. Then, according to Masefield, Barker had Feste "blaze out at Malvolio and Malvolio flame up in reply." Malvolio's reply, of course, is his famous exit line, "I'll be revenged on the whole pack of you." On this he flung the pieces of paper – the material remnants of his shame – in Feste's face (promptbook 95). The moment captured many sides of the complex character and his place in the play: the self-righteous Puritan, the angry peacock, the hypocrite unmasked, the fool driven from the feast. Under it all was a swift, unsettling glimpse of a human being cut down by a self-blindness we all share, another scapegoat condemned to the desert so that life might rush on to the mystery of union, the magic of love.

Some of the magic came from Feste and his music. Barker made an inspired choice for the part in Hayden Coffin, a musical comedy star who had never acted in Shakespeare before. The music included the eighteenth-century songs by Thomas Arne, orchestrated for the occasion by W.H. Squire. "Come away, Death," for instance, was accompanied by a quintet of onstage musicians, dressed in black cloaks and cowls, playing old stringed instruments. Coffin notes (174) that they were required to play from memory and without benefit of a conductor, which was most unusual for theatre musicians at the time; Coffin himself had to learn both the virginal and the Morris pipe for the role. The effect of the unusual casting was to return to Feste some of his Elizabethan status as a professional entertainer, another fidelity to the text that illuminated it.

Winter's Tale had driven a deep wedge into the resistance to Barker's methods, so with *Twelfth Night* there were fewer complaints about the speed of speech or the pace of the production. In fact it is astounding how quickly critics and public were converted after the first blast of conventional dismay; no doubt that is a sign that the time was ripe for a new approach to Shakespeare. Again Barker used a nearly complete text. The only cuts, about twenty lines in all, were of obsolete jokes he thought hindrances to the movement of the play. It should be mentioned, however, that most of these cuts were also bawdy or scatological, like Toby's jests to Andrew in the first

24   a–b   Malvolio in brave attire . . . and dazzling cape

act: "and I hope to see a huswife take thee between her legs and spin it off," or "I would not so much as make water in a sink-a-pace." Barker of course knew that Shakespeare's audience was not squeamish about sex, but he believed that if contemporary viewers were made uncomfortable by an obscene joke, and lost the thread of the play for the next five minutes out of embarrassment, Shakespeare's purpose was not served (*Prefaces* 1:21).

And again Norman Wilkinson's design allowed graceful and swift scene changes, which *Twelfth Night* needs much more than *Winter's Tale*: "The scene changes constantly from anywhere suitable to anywhere else that is equally so," Barker wrote in the acting edition; "Scenery is an inconvenience" (*More Prefaces* 27). Six separate drops were used, in addition to the act curtain, and most were non-realistically painted. Their rapid flying in throughout the performance recaptured the spirit of Shakespeare's unlocalized stage. Two examples must suffice. The play opened in front of a cubist-patterned yellow and black drop that represented Orsino's palace ("Duke's cloth" the promptbook calls it). At the end of the scene Orsino walked off left, finishing his line on the exit, and immediately the "sea cloth" came down in front as the next set of characters entered and Viola spoke "What country,

25   Orsino's court: Come away, death. Hayden Coffin as Feste

friends, is this?" As this short scene concluded, the drop rose to reveal the full-stage set with Toby and Maria already in place and in the midst of conversation. A more interesting case occurred at the start of the second part of the production with the "Come away, Death" scene, again in front of the Duke's cloth (illustration 25). The act curtain descended for the first few lines of the next scene; Fabian and the knights discussed their revenge on Malvolio on the forestage. At Andrew's line "it is pity of our lives" (2.5.10), the curtain rose to reveal the full set: Maria was already in place and the three men walked upstage to her as Toby said "Here comes the little villain" (promptbook 39). The characters carried place with them in true Shakespearian style, but the drops helped an audience unaccustomed to the open stage to understand what the place was.

Only one full-stage set was built, showing Olivia's formal garden, and it was even more non-illusionist than the sets for the previous play. Illustration 26 shows most of its spread, from a line upstage of the permanent proscenium. It was painted in violent, unexpected colors; *The Sketch* (27 Nov. 1912:239) referred to its "pink pagoda, its dead-white sky and steps, its gold seats, and its clipped yews of most unnatural green." The floor was white marble, and the checkerboard tiles below the baldechino were pink and black. The futuristic space needles, representing the box trees of the text, were dominant by their size and lurid color. Critics saw them as items from a child's Noah's Ark and

26   The futurist *Twelfth Night*: Olivia's garden. Design by Norman Wilkinson

liked to compare the set to confectionery. But it was a highly useful set, versatile by virtue of its rigid conventions.

It also showed off the costumes to advantage. Wilkinson used a color scheme to contrast the mourning of Olivia's house, principally in black, to the mooning passion of the Duke's court, principally in carmine. For the scene in illustration 22, Orsino wore a cerise velvet tunic with silver braid, cerise velvet knickerbockers, black stockings, and a heavy cloak of a lighter shade (Account Book). Wilkinson said that he sought after "romance and smartness" in the costumes (*Evening News* 12 Nov. 1912:7) by combining a basic Elizabethan style with the exoticism of a Persian seraglio, apparent in Orsino's cape and turban. The style is clearer in Antonio's costume and Andrew's baggy pantaloons in illustration 27, the duel scene in front of a painted drop. Viola and Toby were in modification of Elizabethan dress, while Fabian looked like a policeman with garters. The presence of blackamoors in Olivia's retinue increased the Oriental feeling. For the final scene a pair of golden gates was inserted at midstage level, the box trees and baldechino having been struck; the gates and their wall had an East–West hybrid look that matched that of the clothes. The Duke's soldiers here were like Swiss Guards, with high Spanish helmets and shiny breastplates.

27   The mock duel. Wilkinson's eclectic costumes before a patterned drop

Barker's chief rule as a director of Shakespeare might be expressed in Hippocrates' charge to physicians: above all, do no harm. Throughout the production, the promptbook indicates, there was no stage business or movement unless dictated by the text or by clarity. There were long passages during which the characters were still, the verse carrying the weight of the play. Barker also kept the ending simple, rejecting, as we would expect, an operatic finale. The principals went out through the golden gates, lined on either side by the company. After the general exit the black servants shut the gates and Feste began the closing song. A slow curtain fell as he neared the end, and he finished the last stanza with his head through the center of the drapery (promptbook 96).

"The whole production dwells in my mind still as a single unique quality, indissoluble and unanalysable as the pungent sweetness of an aroma." So wrote Wilson Knight (22) half a century later. St John Ervine, whose compliments to Barker came hard, could say simply that it was the most beautiful production he had ever seen on any stage anywhere (344). But the most telling testimony to the lyrical power of the performance comes from G.B. Harrison, who, as a freshman at Cambridge, saw it in January 1913 and wrote me as I was preparing this book: a living connection with Barker, an unbroken memory of seventy years. "So beautiful," Harrison wrote, "that at the end one wanted to go by oneself and weep!"

8 A wide-awake dream

Shakespearian influences

TO THE PROMOTERS of a new theatre in the new century, English production of Shakespeare had been an embarrassment for over a generation. They attacked the old ways whenever they could, and with great intellectual force. Ultimately the assault became so successful that much of the value of the great actor–managers has been dismissed in twentieth-century theatre histories. Only recently have scholars attempted to correct the balance; we are particularly indebted to Alan Hughes for work on Irving, to Ralph Berry on Tree, and to Cary Mazer's general reassessment of Shakespeare in the Edwardian era. But to Shaw and to Barker, no such balance was desirable or deserved.

Shaw let fly his arrows as soon as he was installed at *The Saturday Review*. All aspects of contemporary Shakespeare appalled him. If Burbage were to appear at the Lyceum, he wrote in 1895, "he would recoil beaten the moment he realized that he was to be looked at as part of an optical illusion through a huge hole in the wall, instead of being practically in the middle of the theatre" (*Our Theatres* 1:199). Shaw admired Forbes Robertson, but not his *Romeo and Juliet*: "one has to listen to the music of Shakespeare . . . as one might listen to a symphony of Beethoven's with all the parts played on the bones, the big drum, and the Jew's harp" (1:214). On Daly's *Two Gentlemen*: "Mr Daly has proceeded on the usual principles, altering, transposing, omitting, improving, correcting, and transferring speeches from one character to another" (1:179). When he saw Beerbohm Tree's *Henry IV* in 1896, he thought Tree lacked only one thing for Falstaff, "to get born over again as unlike himself as possible" (2:137). And he summed up his objections to the master in a review of *Cymbeline*: "A prodigious deal of nonsense has been written about Sir Henry Irving's conception of this, that, and the other Shakespearean character. The truth is that he has never in his life conceived or interpreted the characters of any author except himself" (2:208).

In Shaw's view the Victorian actor treated Shakespeare as raw material to be manufactured. The production was not a collaboration between dramatist and performer, but a conquest of one by the other: Irving "positively acted Shakespeare off the stage." It was only just beginning to occur to some younger actor–managers that they could present the plays as written, he said in 1898, "instead of using them as a cuckoo uses a sparrow's nest" (*Plays* 1:26).

Though Barker arrived too late to see Irving in his prime, he followed Shaw's lead in condemning the disciples. In 1910 Barker wrote that the conventional idea amounted to this: "If Shakespeare had had our modern scenic resources he would have been only too thankful to arrange his plays to fit them. Unfortunately the poor chap is dead, so we must do it for him." Since the audience prefers scenery to poetry anyway, the "production-mongers" make scenery into the protagonist of the play ("Repertory Theatres" 493–4). Once a heavy expense has been made for carpentry and crowds of extras, a long run is essential, which then deadens the actors. Under these conditions, anything that does not draw sixty or seventy thousand people is a failure.

Despite the work of Frank Benson at Stratford, gorgeous Shakespeare became the Edwardian style. It was an age of conspicuous consumption; Thorstein Veblen could have used Tree's *Twelfth Night* (1901), with real fountains and the famous grass carpet, as an example of the irresponsible show of wealth. And yet as early as 1881 an alternative had appeared. In that year William Poel gave the first of his performances, *Hamlet*, at St George's Hall; using a bare platform and Elizabethan costumes, Poel thus began a lifetime of cranky persistence in the cause of an authentic Shakespeare in the theatre. Poel's urge was always to return to the conditions of original performance, whether involving the physical stage, the costumes, the text, the lighting, or the speaking of the verse. His ideas were sometimes based on misunderstandings or faulty scholarship, sometimes merely eccentric, and sometimes the result of a blind and fanatic hatred for the commercial theatre, but there is no doubt that he followed them with the absolute sincerity of a great reformer. His influence on Barker was simple and profound. Despite the charm of the Poel story, it is only that influence that concerns us here.

Their first direct contact occurred in 1899 when Poel chose Barker to play Richard II, his first major role in London, and one of the luminous points of his life. Thirty years on he sent Poel a copy of *Prefaces to Shakespeare* with this note:

You won't agree with much of it. Never mind. A dull world it would be in which we all found ourselves in agreement. But such light as has shone for me on W.S. dates from an earlier day on which you came to York Buildings to see me and shook all my previous convictions by showing me how you wanted the first lines of *Richard II* spoken.

(Speaight 149)

Four years after Richard, he played Edward II for Poel at Oxford. There-after, their ways parted as Barker struck out on his own directing career, though certain early lessons had a permanent effect.

What Barker got from Poel is clear enough: emphasis on actor's speech, the open stage with extended platform, lighting that evoked the open air, absence of scenery, respect for the text, avoidance of stars. These are large debts, and Barker never failed to acknowledge them. In his acting edition of *Midsummer Night's Dream*, for example, Barker remembered that "in the teeth of ridicule

[Poel] insisted that for an actor to make himself like unto a human megaphone was to miss, for one thing, the whole merit of Elizabethan verse . . . Poel preached a gospel" (*More Prefaces* 36). To Max Reinhardt, he wrote that Poel taught "more about the staging of Shakespeare and the spirit of playing it, I think, than anyone else in Europe" (Theatre Museum). Though Barker might have come upon some of his reforms even without an antecedent, Poel's importance cannot be ignored.

Too often, however, commentators tend to gloss over the differences that marked the two men. The most important one was a radical divergence regarding the audience. Poel went his own way and let the public be damned; like a bristling professor he suspected that popular approval necessarily implied betrayal of principles. There was always the air of the academy about him and at least the appearance of dry scholarship about his productions. Barker, on the other hand, understood that Shakespeare was a vital popular dramatist, and intended to take his discoveries as far into the popular realm as he could. He wanted a theatre for the present, one where the national poet might live, not a museum replica. Poel's antiquarianism was stiffened by a mortal respect for the outward conditions (or what he took to be the outward conditions) of the Globe. Barker knew that vitality was to be found inside the plays themselves.

Nothing reveals Poel's limitations more than his method of casting and rehearsing. He strove for the meaning and emotion behind Shakespeare's language, but often had to settle for second-rate actors. As a result he felt he had to teach his players by rote every intonation, every phrasing; and he locked them in the rehearsal room late at night until they satisfied his notion of the music of the verse. He cast each part according to a preconception regarding the voice of the character, like a conductor orchestrating a chorus. For his *Twelfth Night* in 1897 he attempted to make Viola a mezzo, Olivia a contralto, Orsino a tenor, Sebastian an alto, Malvolio a baritone, Toby a bass, and poor Andrew a falsetto. He seemed to care little for the actual playing so long as the vocal music was right. In 1910 he produced *Two Gentlemen* at His Majesty's, having been invited into the armory of the enemy by Tree for the annual Shakespeare Festival. Dissatisfied with the voices of all the men he auditioned for Valentine, in the end he gave the role to a woman because she had the right music. Nugent Monck was assistant stage manager for the production, and at his first meeting with Poel found the lady before him in tears. The director's voice rose in anger: "I am disappointed," he said, "very disappointed indeed. Of all of Shakespeare's heroes Valentine is one of the most romantic, one of the most virile. I have chosen you out of all London for this part, but so far you have shown me no virility whatsoever" (Speaight 111, 121).

Barker, whose authority in the profession meant he could always get excellent actors, also strove for a musical blend of voices but achieved it by prompting and correction instead of slavish imitation. The music came from the player instead of the conductor. He achieved the swiftness of speech that eluded Poel; and he kept the play alive in the only way that matters, by the liveliness of the acting.

"We shall not save our souls by being Elizabethan": as we have seen, Barker did not want to follow Poel's lead regarding the physical conditions of the Globe either. After the opening of his *Twelfth Night*, Barker said he was "trying to establish a simple method of staging, to create a simple shell into which you can put your ideas. I don't go as far as Mr Poel; I think his method is somewhat archaeological; there is somewhat too much of the Elizabethan letter, as contrasted with the Elizabethan spirit" (*Evening News* 3 Dec. 1912:4). Later he would disassociate himself even more from the barren aspects of his mentor. "Mr Poel shook complacency. He could not expect to do much more; for he was a logical reformer." So wrote the author of *Prefaces to Shakespeare* (1:3), who was far from strictly logical at the Savoy. Barker took what he could and used it when he could, concerned with the total theatrical effect rather than with a philosophic manifesto. While it is important to understand Shakespeare as an Elizabethan dramatist, he thought, it is more important to recognize that Shakespeare has become much more than that to us. As we cannot turn ourselves into Elizabethans, so we cannot "thrust him back within the confines his genius has escaped." To ignore the changes in the theatre since 1600 is as blind as to ignore the nature of the soliloquy.

The "logical reformer" did not always work logically. In the matter of the text, for instance, Poel's practice was inconsistent at best. For his 1897 production of *Twelfth Night* in the Hall of the Middle Temple, the supposed site of the original production in 1601, Poel cut a large chunk of Sebastian's soliloquy in the fourth act. Embarrassed by the baiting of Malvolio, he removed the entire prison scene, as Daly and Tree did. (Lillah McCarthy played Olivia; Ben Greet immediately engaged her for a tour, during which she met Barker, who played Paris to her Juliet. The world of Shakespeare was small at the turn of the century.) In fact Poel habitually and cavalierly cut the text. Consider, for example, his 1899 *Richard II*: from the last great soliloquy in prison, the center of the fallen king's tragic knowledge and growth, Poel unaccountably cut forty-seven lines. This was mayhem egregious, considering what the sensitive and intelligent young Harley could have done with the speech. (This evidence is all from Speaight 103–4, 111, 151.) What the future director gained from Poel was great, but it is hardly baffling that he often disagreed with Poel's methods.

Barker was also influenced from an entirely separate direction, yet the same qualifications must be made. Gordon Craig was of course a reformer with a much larger brief than Poel's and his reforms have been effected more completely. Yet both, vastly different in temperament and intention, were alike in detachment from the day-to-day working of the London stage. From Craig, Barker learned that the alternative to realistic scenery was "decoration" to establish and control mood. But Craig's monolithic settings, deliberately reducing the actors to *Übermarionetten*, were not right for Shakespeare's swift scene changes and rapid character development, as Hugh Hunt notes (45). Barker insisted that the actor was the beginning of theatre, and he knew that Shakespeare shared this view. As he selected what was useful from Poel, so he took a potent idea from Craig and discarded the rest as unworkable. Craig "will have no less than the dramatic kingdom of heaven on earth," Barker wrote. "I, on the other hand, am but a plodding theatrical shopkeeper" (letter to *Daily Mail* 26 Sept. 1912:4). The result was a blending of two distinct theories into a new coherence. Barker's controlling attitude was that the spirit of the open stage was necessary for Shakespeare. His practical awareness was that the unit set and symbolic drops would fit into a Victorian theatre, and sufficiently transform it for a new kind of performance.

He denied the debt, but Barker was probably more affected by Max Reinhardt than by Craig. In 1909 Martin Harvey brought Reinhardt's *The Taming of the Shrew* to London; it was a non-illusionist production, with a forestage over the footlights and simple, symbolic backdrops (Styan, *Reinhardt* 54). The next year Barker visited Berlin, where he met Reinhardt and was impressed by his directing, as well as his managing of state-supported theatres. In 1911 Reinhardt directed two works in London: the highly stylized *Sumurūn* was at the Savoy in October, a wordless play (based loosely on *The Arabian Nights*) that Walkley compared to Barker's *Winter's Tale*; and "a wordless mystery spectacle," *The Mystery*, was at Olympia in December. We have seen in chapter 6 how Barker coached his wife when she took Jocasta in Reinhardt's *Oedipus* at Covent Garden in early 1912, and how the staging affected Barker's *Iphigenia*.

These productions, however, with their vast crowds, enormous stages, and misty settings, were antithetical to Barker's ultimate intentions. It is more to the point to note that Reinhardt had used geometrical sets and suggestive drops for Shakespeare in Berlin some time before the Savoy season. His *Winter's Tale*, for example, designed by Emil Orlick in 1906, and *King Lear*, designed by Carl Czeschka in 1908, used patterned drop curtains and monochrome columar sets that anticipated Norman Wilkinson's decoration. (Photos of both are in Fuerst and Hume, vol. 2.) And Reinhardt himself had been influenced by Craig, as well as by other sources. A few years earlier Georg Fuchs had published *The Stage of the Future* in Berlin, which asked for a wide playing space rather than a deep one, divided into three areas: an extended forestage for most of the action; a middle stage, which could be used with a painted drop; and a rear stage. Each area, Fuchs said, should be marked off by shallow steps (see Braun, *Director* 114–15).

In many ways, then, Barker was the recipient of wireless messages from Europe: the New Stagecraft, as it came to be known, was in the Continental air. England's old insularity in art was being battered by forces exciting and strange, from the Post-Impressionist exhibitions to Leon Bakst and the

Russian Ballet. "On or about December 1910," in Virginia Woolf's famous phrase, "human character changed" (quoted in Hynes 325). In the theatre a more accurate date is the end of 1912. By then Diaghilev had brought his company to London twice (*The Rite of Spring* was still to come), Reinhardt was a household word, and Barker's first two Shakespeare productions had been widely discussed. As Mazer points out (*Shakespeare Refashioned* 85–8), the European forces were brought together in Huntly Carter's *The New Spirit in Drama and Art*, an extensive brief for artistic internationalism, published that year. Carter did not care for Barker's work, but Barker was nonetheless part of a large new movement. His Shakespeare gained power from Modernism as well as from Elizabethanism.

Prefaces to Shakespeare

With the help of these philosophic and practical predecessors, Barker devised his own theory of Shakespearian production. It was not a rigid theory, and at the time of the Savoy season it was experimental: he shaped it as he went along, adapting, modifying, seeking a satisfactory result in the laboratory of artistic success and public response. When he came to refine it into a coherent whole, when the hurly-burly was done, it remained a stage-centered theory. Barker was the man most responsible for the shift away from the literary–historical approach in Shakespearian criticism to the theatrical approach that has begun to flower in recent years. As such, he was one of the most important influences on modern Shakespearian study; certainly he was the only major figure of the century to have successfully spanned the active and the contemplative sides of the subject. The intellectual work he took up after his retirement from the stage, which became the principal work of the remainder of his life, was rooted in and illuminated by his practical experience. In his best critical writing he most resembles his own methods as a director: suggestive rather than philosophic, seeking always what will work in the theatre rather than in the mind. "And the prefaces themselves," he wrote at the start of their composition in 1923, "may best be thought of as the sort of addresses a producer might make to a company upon their first meeting to study the play" (*More Prefaces* 43). He set out to offer the scholarship and reflection preliminary to production, though not the specific plans for one. He knew that work could only be done in the theatre itself, in the crucible of collaboration with designers and actors.

Barker's *Prefaces to Shakespeare* span nearly the entire time of his retirement from the theatre. The history of their making is both interesting in itself and a model of Barker's working methods as a writer. They were originally conceived by Victor Gollancz, who embarked on a series of expensive and beautifully illustrated books for collectors under the imprint of Ernest Benn. Included in the project were the plays of Shakespeare, to be printed in old spelling in the First Folio text to celebrate the tercentenary of its publication. Barker was engaged to write a preface for each play from the theatrical perspective. Called the Players' Shakespeare, seven volumes were printed in limited editions within five years: *Macbeth*, bound with a general introduction, *The Merchant of Venice*, and *Cymbeline*, all in 1923; *A Midsummer Night's Dream* and *Love's Labour's Lost* the following year; *Julius Caesar* in 1925; *King Lear* in 1927. From a publishing standpoint the venture failed and was abandoned. The large volumes are impressive but contradictory in purpose: ostensibly presented from the view of the stage, they were far too expensive for ordinary readers and too precious for stage use. Even the drawings, by artists like Albert Rutherston and Norman Wilkinson, are book illustrations rather than set and costume designs.

But in 1927 Barker signed an agreement with the firm of Sidgwick and Jackson, who had been his early publisher, that all his books would henceforth be printed by them. Out of this union the *Prefaces to Shakespeare* were born, produced in five volumes in a score of years. Two things about their writing are particularly characteristic of Barker's methods: he relied whenever possible on work he had already done, and he revised that earlier work slowly, constantly, painfully. The first series appeared in 1927 and contained revisions of the prefaces to *Love's Labour's Lost*, *Julius Caesar*, and *King Lear* from the Players' Shakespeare, and a much revised version of the general introduction. For the second series, published in 1930, Barker considerably reworked his *Merchant* and *Cymbeline* prefaces and wrote new ones for *Romeo and Juliet* and *Antony and Cleopatra* based on lectures given at Aberystwyth. *Hamlet* took a long time, became a book in itself, and stood alone in 1937. Barker intended it to be the last; while struggling with it he wrote to Frank Sidgwick, "There ain't going to be no Fourth Series. No, *sir*! When I am very old I might write a squishy book on Shakespearean Comedy" (Bodleian). The squishy book was never written, but a fourth series did appear, and a fifth. *Othello* (1945) was based on lectures given at Harvard during the war, and *Coriolanus* (published posthumously in 1947) on the Alexander Lectures at Toronto. The earlier essays were revised again for the two-volume edition of the complete *Prefaces* brought out by Princeton University Press in 1946–7.

Throughout his life Barker provided something unique among Shakespearian commentators of the time: he believed in the power of the stage. His unswerving principle was that Shakespeare is understood best and appreciated fully only in the theatre. To that service he brought the high value of his experience and thought, charging his Shakespearian criticism with an awareness of the demands and strengths of the theatre. Two examples of this critical approach must serve, and the first concerns an essential matter, the integrity of the text. We have already seen what Barker's practice was here: he believed that the case for Shakespeare as a dramatist could not be proved by fashioning a text of convenience in the common style of actors since the

Restoration. The responsibility is firmly on the director's shoulders to make sense of the play without large-scale recourse to the knife. Some of us, he wrote, "are not such very skillful surgeons; nor is any surgeon to be recommended who operates for his own convenience." Of course there must be exceptions; one is the "pornographic difficulty" he encountered with *Twelfth Night*. But even that does not mean that a director should be free to clean up everything – he especially should not touch licentious passages that are dramatically important, like those in *Measure for Measure* or *Othello*. Topical allusions present another difficulty and can often be lost, though each case must be treated separately. "In general, however, better play the plays as we find them. The blue pencil is a dangerous weapon; and its use grows on a man, for it solves too many little difficulties far too easily" (*Prefaces* 1:21–2). In the Shakespearian theatre, playing complete or nearly complete texts is a severe challenge, and few directors have been willing to follow Barker's courageous lead. For him it was a challenge that simply must be accepted. Trust Shakespeare before the director.

The second example concerns the importance of the actor in a non-illusionist setting. Shakespeare's "capital dramatic discovery" was that physical action in itself is an ineffective thing on stage. The moment of murder or love over, excitement quickly passes. What matters dramatically are the thoughts and reasons behind physical action. Shakespeare managed to convey deep psychology on a stage of "flagrant publicity" – in daylight, on an open platform, with spectators aware of each other – by focusing on the power of the actor. "Let all other aid to illusion be absent and the illusion lodged in the actor himself will only grip us the more strongly" ("Shakespeare's Dramatic Art" 68). The "true gain of the bare stage" is that the drama becomes attached "solely to its actors and their acting." Just as in *Antony and Cleopatra* the characters "carry place and time with them as they move," so throughout Shakespeare the focus is never on outer things but on the inner, secret soul:

Man and machine . . . are false allies in the theatre, secretly at odds; and when man gets the worst of it, drama is impoverished; and the struggle, we may add, is perennial. No great drama depends on pageantry. All great drama tends to concentrate upon character . . . on the hidden man.   (*Prefaces* 1:7)

Actors alone on a platform: that is the irreducible mode of Shakespearian drama. As a critic, Barker began to restore the "bare stage" to the study as he had earlier restored it to the theatre.

Those two examples from Barker's criticism are in key with his work as a director. At a time when both the text and the company were regularly submerged under the weight of machinery and the star, Barker returned the play to the playwright. The closing of the introduction to the *Prefaces* (1:22–3) best summarizes his position:

Lastly, for a golden rule, whether staging or costuming or cutting is in question, and a comprehensive creed, a producer might well pin this on his wall: Gain Shakespeare's effects by Shakespeare's means when you can; for, plainly, this will be the better way. But gain Shakespeare's effects; and it is your business to discern them.

The notion that the director is a servant of the playwright, responsible to the play before the production, was and remains revolutionary. It is a luminous point of twentieth-century dramatic policy, though it has not always been followed. At the Court Barker created a theatre for contemporary writers; at the Savoy one for a Renaissance writer. The criticism that followed was intended to consolidate and extend his stage work.

King Lear

The *Prefaces* had a wide and immediate effect. Directors as varied as Harcourt Williams, Bridges-Adams, John Gielgud, and Tyrone Guthrie speak of their debt to them, and often used them as plans for productions. One such performance occurred in 1940, when Lewis Casson mounted *King Lear* at the Old Vic, with Gielgud in the lead. Casson, of course, knew Barker since the heady days at the Court, and Gielgud had struck a professional friendship with him. In fact Gielgud had often asked Barker to return to active work. His reply was always the same: written words would have a greater and longer effect than the ephemeral few weeks of a production ("G.B.'s Shakespeare"). But for some reason Barker agreed to help with *Lear*.

He planned the production with Casson and the designer based on his Preface, then returned to Paris while Casson and Tyrone Guthrie worked with the cast under his postal advice. Barker came back to London for ten days to supervise final rehearsals, and his hand helped make the performance one of the most successful revivals of the play in the twentieth century.

Gielgud read the part for him at their first session. "You got two lines right," Barker said. "Now we will begin to work." Further: "Lear is an oak. You are an ash. We must see how this will serve you." The comment is typical of Barker's directorial method. He took the actor as given and shaped the role around him. Despite his thorough preparation and knowledge of each character, he always left room for the player's own notions and for the spark of collaboration. His first concern was still Poel's, "the speaking of the verse and the balance of the voices." The actors had "immediate respect for his authority," Gielgud reports, though they were dismayed by his high standards and devotion to hard work:

For the moment they appeared to begin to satisfy him in one direction, Barker was urging them on to experiment in another. Tempo, atmosphere, diction, balance, character – no detail could escape his fastidious ear, his unerring dramatic instinct and his superb sense of classic shapeliness of line.   (*Stage Directions* 51, 53)

He remained impersonal with the actors, never shouted, was never angry, never tired. His whole bearing quietly demanded perfection. He had lost nothing of his genius for the stage despite the years of disuse.

Barker's notes were "brilliantly suggestive." As transcribed by Gielgud they provide a rare sight of the collaboration of a great actor with a great director. Lear was to enter in the first scene with a "huge staff which he uses to walk with," strike it "impatiently on the floor," and rap out his command to Gloucester, "pleased. Happy." Later, when mad at Dover, he was to recall this sovereignty: "Happy King of Nature. No troubles. Tremendously dignified. Branch in hand, like staff in opening scene, walk with it." The line "let copulation thrive" should be "almost jolly. Swing staff above head" (121, 128). Another source, an unpublished account of the production by Hallam Fordham, records further details for the scene. At first Gielgud had tried "realistically doddering movements" but Barker corrected him. "The entrance to be a caricature" of the opening, but the "prevailing note must be kingly dignity; always, when in doubt, return to that." When Lear is sent to prison with Cordelia, Gielgud was instructed to be "delighted. Really happy. Dance the whole speech like a polka. Music up and down. Variety. Exit hand in hand with her, triumphant" (*Stage Directions* 129).

In the Preface Barker emphasizes the majesty and strength of Lear in the final scene, deliberately recalling the opening of the play. He is "the same commanding figure; he bears the body of Cordelia as lightly as ever he carried robe, crown and scepter before" (*Prefaces* 1:299). Almost the same characters are present; "even Regan and Goneril are here to pay him a ghastly homage" (1:277–8). The king's dignity and surprising strength were apotheosized at the end of the production, for Gielgud entered bearing Cordelia in one arm. Her weight was supported by a sling over his shoulder, hidden by the costume, that allowed his other arm free for gestures. Fordham reports that Barker was excited and pleased by his invention, and with justification. That type of incandescent detail, that opens possibilities for the actor and yet is true to the character, shows him at his best.

The cast was impressive. It included Harcourt Williams as Albany, Nicholas Hannen as Gloucester, Jack Hawkins as Edmund, Jessica Tandy as Cordelia, and Casson as Kent. Cathleen Nesbitt, Barker's Perdita in 1912, was Goneril. The costumes were Elizabethan, designed by Roger Furse; the text virtually complete, with one interval; the reaction highly favorable. Barker did not wish to claim the production, however, and refused to allow his name on the program as director. He saw himself as a consultant: he had become a thinker and offered thoughtful advice. In fact he did not even see a performance, for he returned to Paris after the dress rehearsal. It is tempting to read this as a sign of his utter detachment from the affairs of the theatre, but the truth is more complicated than that. His second wife, alone in their apartment, had been writing him daily with justified worries about the war (Salmon 287–8). Less than a month later France was occupied, and the Barkers escaped barely in time.

Gielgud went so far as to rejoice in Barker's retirement from the stage, because the result was a much wider and more permanent dissemination of his value as a Shakespearian interpreter. And of course that is how he is best remembered today: for most Shakespearian students the *Prefaces* come to mind more readily than the Savoy performances. That is an irony that Barker himself sought, but unfortunate nonetheless; the three Savoy productions were significantly more important to the theatre of our century than any commentary that he wrote. Whatever effect criticism and theory might have, battles in the theatre are ultimately won or lost in the theatre.

A Midsummer Night's Dream

We return to the battle, which, like all battles, cost money. The Savoy casts did not receive large salaries, but the productions were expensive; despite the decent reception of *Twelfth Night*, Shakespeare was not going to pay his own way very long. In fact the venture had been possible at all only because of subsidy. Lillah McCarthy had used her wondrous ability to extract funds from the rich whenever she could. She met Lord Lucas at a party in 1911; he readily admitted that he had been in love with her since seeing her as Mercia in *The Sign of the Cross* at Oxford years before (L. McCarthy 196). One morning soon after, preferring Barker's pearls to his own swine, he sold his pig farm and arrived with a check for £5,000. Shakespeare from sausages, a wag might remark: in many ways, the absurd paradigm of what finance for serious theatre would become in the twentieth century. Barker, called smiling and dripping from his bath, wrapped in a towel as if girding his loins for the fray, characteristically said the amount would have to be doubled (Purdom 139). It was 1912, a spring filled with promise.

Winter's Tale and *Macbeth* were rehearsed through the summer: the intention seems to have been for the McCarthy–Barker management to get to the great tragedies quickly. Plans were made for *Antony and Cleopatra* as well, and in Henry Ainley and Lillah the director certainly had a fine pair for the leading roles. "I pored over Shakespeare," Lillah said of her youth, "and longed to be Juliet and Imogen, and above all, Lady Macbeth" (quoted in *The Theatre* May 1915:252). The Account Book shows that scenery for *Macbeth* was constructed; Felix Aylmer (32–3), who played in the Savoy season, says that he later found it used as the Ogre's castle in *Puss in Boots* at the Birmingham Repertory. But when *Winter's Tale* proved sticky at the box office, *Twelfth Night* was offered instead.

Barker was preoccupied by a series of new plays and a short repertory experiment throughout 1913. Included was Arnold Bennett's dramatization of his popular novel *Buried Alive*, produced as *The Great Adventure* in March at the Kingsway with Ainley in the lead. Perhaps Barker intended to bring on *Macbeth* soon after, but Bennett's play was a roaring success – it ran for almost twenty months – and Ainley was engaged as Ilam Carve the entire time. In the event Barker decided to go ahead with another comedy. He was worried about money in November 1913, when he wrote Ottoline Morrell asking for five or six thousand pounds for *Midsummer Night's Dream* (Texas). But the Kingsway success eased the tension. Financially the management was more secure than ever; it seems deliciously appropriate that *The Great Adventure* could pay for Shakespeare, and Barker was properly grateful. "I am against long runs on principle," he wrote to Bennett, "but *thank you* for this for it has enabled me to devote a lot of time to fussing about elsewhere with your rival W.S." (Yale).

And "fussing about" is exactly what many reviewers thought he was doing with *A Midsummer Night's Dream*. If the reaction to *Twelfth Night* tempered Barker's usual opinion of critics, he must have felt at home again the morning after 6 February 1914. The battlefield was confused, some critics disliking what others praised, many happy with one thing and vitriolic about another. Barker converted J.T. Grein, who had been hostile to the two previous plays ("the eccentricities have mellowed into a new and definite manifestation of Art" – *Sunday Times* 8 Feb. 1914:6), but lost John Palmer, his staunchest supporter ("Shakespeare being slaughtered to make an intellectual and post-impressionist holiday" – *Saturday Review* 14 Feb. 1914:202). Desmond MacCarthy struck the best balance. Dissatisfied after his first visit, he "had the sense to go again," and recommended his readers do the same. The first time he was distracted by the setting, but then discovered that the merits of the performance were more notable when "surprise at the scenic effects" had subsided (*New Statesman* 21 Feb. 1914: 629). He saw that the virtue of the production was Barker's success in capturing the dramatic qualities of a work usually thought of as a romantic poem or a pretext for canvas and paint. But Walkley wrote what would become the classic sentence for the occasion (*Times* 7 Feb. 1914:8). "The mind goes back to the golden fairies, and one's memories of this production must always be golden memories."

The fairies received much critical attention, and quite properly. They are the secret to establishing a style for the play, and their treatment exemplifies the general tone of any production. "The fairies are the producer's test," Barker wrote in the sixpenny preface, admitting that "a hope of passing that test" had partially prompted him to undertake the project. "Foolhardy one feels in facing it. But if a method of staging can compass the difficulties of *A Midsummer Night's Dream*, surely its cause is won." Using the same method of staging as before, he took the fairies to an extreme of non-illusionist portrayal. What seemed important to him was that they be instantly appre-hended as beings separate from the mortals. "They must not be too startling. But one wishes people weren't so easily startled. I won't have them dowdy. They mustn't warp your imagination – stepping too boldly between Shakespeare's spirit and yours. It is a difficult problem" (*More Prefaces* 35, 38). His solution – with the aid of Norman Wilkinson again – was bound to displease many, and some of that displeasure distracted from the other values of the production. It is the risk a director runs in electing any new and distinctive style. One wishes people weren't so easily startled.

Three days before the opening he invited Arnold Bennett to "come early before all the gold has rubbed off the fairies, for it is going to be rather pretty" (Yale). Most commentators did not think *pretty* was the word; *fantastic* might catch the mood better. For Desmond MacCarthy they were "ormolu fairies, looking as though they had been detached from some fantastic, bristling old clock." For Walkley they were "Cambodian idols," and others repeated the thought: Oberon "a painted graven image" (*Punch* 18 Feb. 1914:136), Titania "a quaint little golden idol from an Indian temple" (*Referee* 8 Feb. 1914:3). But gold they certainly were, from head to foot, gold and bronzed-gold. And there was indeed some danger of the gold rubbing off, for their faces and necks were also gold. A voyeuristic reporter watched Titania's preparations for the New York version and discovered the makeup was gold leaf, applied from small sheets with the fingers, at a cost of thirty-five cents per sprite (NY *World* 21 Feb. 1915). Lillah McCarthy says the cost was a shilling in England; for economy's sake the fairies had to stay gilded between matinees and evening performances (175). The fairy king and queen wore fantastic gold crowns and long, translucent, shimmering trains, hers an iridescent mauve, his copper-gold tinsel. The color photographs of Oberon and Titania, reproduced here as the frontispiece, provide the best pictorial evidence we have of the visual effect. Wigs, and some beards, were of curled gold buckram looking like wood shavings or unsprung clock springs; gloves were copper; shoes, a book, a quill and scroll, a four-foot scimitar, a seven-foot scepter, were all gold.

This golden woodland was violated by one brilliant flash of color: Puck was costumed in flaming scarlet. He wore heavy rouge, exaggerated black eyebrows, and a stiffened orange wig, spotted with red berries; red ballet slippers and anklets of red berries; on his left breast, a large blue flame. "Oberon and Titania are romantic creations: sprung from Huron of Bordeaux, etc., say the commentators; come from the farthest steppe of India, says Shakespeare. But Puck," Barker insisted, "is pure English folklore" (*More Prefaces* 38). The acting of Donald Calthrop matched his physical appearance. Avoiding a lyrical portrayal, he accented the hobgoblin, the prankish side of Robin Goodfellow, which is to say that Barker followed Puck's position in the action rather than in the poetry. According to Desmond MacCarthy, he read "I'll put a girdle round about the earth in forty minutes" as "fantastic bombast" (that word again), and strutted off "extravagantly kicking out his feet in a comic swagger." Though MacCarthy thought he unnecessarily denied the other side of Puck's nature ("there is nothing of Nature in him, nothing of Ariel"), the effect was calculated to emphasize his masculinity: an important matter, for Calthrop was the first grown man on record to play the role in England.

This was systematic visual shock, but with a point. Like the white world of

Winter's Tale or the Futurist trees of *Twelfth Night*, Barker's fairies were meant to unblinker the spectators' eyes; the audience was to see the substantial immortals that Shakespeare created, instead of the precipitate of moonlight preferred in the nineteenth century. Few items of the pre-war imagination were as trammeled by Victorian sensibility as fairies. One result was that readers believed *Midsummer Night's Dream* to be the supreme example of Shakespeare's mistaken vocation; to them the work was a lyric poem, to be realized only in the mind, where the fairies had free roam over time and space. When the play was put on the stage, it tended to become a sad spectacle of the body's failure to equal the mind's dreaming. No play of Shakespeare's came with more expected trappings: Mendelssohn's music, realistic outdoor scenery (for Tree, live rabbits), hyperbolic stage illusions, children for the elfin folk, Puck and Oberon played by women, and the full-bodied plot of the rustics reduced to a series of music hall intermezzi. Ralph Berry (44) suggests that Tree's version, first produced in 1900, belonged to the same genre as Walt Disney. Barker attacked all of this, and with more force than he used in either of his previous Shakespearian plays. He indeed meant to prove his method by direct assault on the accepted way. The fairies were the golden key.

And how they came on! Not in moonlit woodland mist but in three-quarter white light, in front of the proscenium and a conventionalized forest drop, making full use of the forestage. From opposite sides in five distinct entrances

28   Entrance of the fairies: *A Midsummer Night's Dream*. The forestage extension is clearly visible. Savoy 1914

the two camps moved, in a lightly choreographed and comic ceremony leading to the swift arrival of their king and queen, accompanied by trumpets (promptbook 18–19). Illustration 28 shows the twelve-foot extension with Puck and others on it, a total of thirty-one fairies across the stage. If the picture looks a little stiff, or mocks some of the recorded descriptions, it should be remembered that it was of necessity posed, not shot in action. But clearly there was no illusion there, no attempt to "*realise* these small folk who war with rere-mice for their leathern wings." Whatever they were, they were not little Victorian girls. Barker used only four children, for "Cobweb and Co.," recognizing that there is no modern equivalent of Elizabethan choir schools and thus no tradition of trained children's singing voices (*More Prefaces* 35–6). The rest were adult actors, individualized as much as possible. The promptbook gives names to many: the scimitar-wearer is the Major, the book-bearer the Professor, and there were the Twins, an Old Man Fairy (with rope beard to the floor), and a Doctor. Movements were often synchronized and abstract, but strong. It was a vigorous, passionate elfland. The fantastic appearance was the distancing device.

The fairies successfully defined as separate beings, the way was clear to point out their parallels to the mortal world. So long as Oberon was an actress, attended by another actress, it was difficult to see relationships between the kingdom of Athens and the kingdom of sprites. Yet the text is at pains to establish them, marital harmony being the desired end of all the plots of the play – including what might be called the super-plot, if the work was indeed written to celebrate a great noble wedding. Julia Neilson-Terry, who impersonated Oberon in Tree's productions, could hardly have been engaged to turn in a virile performance. But her son Dennis, as irony would have it, took the role for Barker and was by most accounts a match for the Thesean virtues of Baliol Holloway. (I am obliged, however, to report that *Punch* [18 Feb. 1914:138] found son Dennis "a curiously effeminate figure for those who recalled the manly bearing of his mother in the same part." Tastes differ.) Oberon's followers, almost all men, emphasized the sexual contrast further.

Barker insured that the parallels between the two kings would be evident: the ceremony of the opening scene in Theseus' palace, also held on the forestage in front of a drop (illustration 29), was echoed in the meeting of Titania and Oberon. Titania's mostly female band, though they shared her anger, acknowledged him as their ruler. At the end of the scene they scurried after the queen, but first each one bowed ceremoniously to the king (promptbook 21). Later Barker wrote that in this play of transformations only "Oberon remains master of himself . . . he is kinglier than Theseus" (*More Prefaces* 114, 117). His authority is unchallenged within and without. Barker restored him to his rightful position, and he is now commonly played by a leading actor.

What was swept aside gave room for a new approach to the entire play. Mendelssohn's incidental music of course had to go. In its place Cecil Sharp arranged old English folk songs, claiming (in his introduction to the printed score) that they have more universality than Elizabethan music or music composed in the Elizabethan idiom. Sharp also choreographed the dancing; fairies and rustics alike stepped to traditional English tunes. The clowns, usually made farceurs, were played as simple countrymen, in accord with the text. Shakespeare discovered, Barker held, that "set down lovingly, your clown is better fun by far than mocked at" (*More Prefaces* 34). Like Toby Belch and Andrew in his *Twelfth Night*, the rustics abandoned outworn comic business for their place in the architecture of the drama. Barker had himself made the simplest of discoveries: left alone, Shakespearian comedy plays better than when mugged, hammed, or forced. "By being kept in proportion and played quite naturally," *The Observer* noted (8 Feb. 1914:9), the rustics "rouse roars of laughter while they are before us, and leave us longing for more of them."

The settings followed the equally simple pattern established in 1912; obviously, Barker would have no truck with rabbits. The first scene took place in front of a gray curtain with grapevine patterns (illustration 29). Quince's house was suggested by dropping a rose-pink curtain in front of this, with painted doors and windows and a sketch of a town's skyline. Though less than 400 lines of the play had passed, Barker took a five-minute break here, then ran the entire night in the wood uninterrupted, from act 2 through the arrival

29 The court of Theseus. Opening scene, with Evelyn Hope as Hippolyta and Baliol Holloway as Theseus

of the hunting party in act 4. The third scene of the play, the fairy meeting, was in front of the forest drop of illustration 28.

Titania's bower (illustration 30) was the first full-stage set. It consisted of a green mound in the center, high over which was hung a large wreath of colored fairy lights like glow worms. A cylinder of gauze dropped inside it to the floor, to encase her while asleep. The backdrop was a semi-circle of semi-abstract woodland curtains, strips of cloth for trees, which kept the action relatively forward: the center of the mound was no more than ten feet upstage of the proscenium, to judge from the photographs. Frosted light illuminated these scenes from the dress circle, according to the promptbook, dimmer than that used for the fairy meeting, and some colored light was added from a source overhead in the flies. But the light never sought illusion; in the view of *Punch* it was a "pitiless light that poured point-blank upon the stage from the 12.6 muzzles protruding from the bulwarks of the dress circle. There was no distance, no suggestion of the spirit-world, no sense of mystery (except in regard to Mr Barker's intentions)."

Mr Barker's intentions are easier for us to discover: in such a setting stage

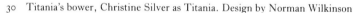

30   Titania's bower, Christine Silver as Titania. Design by Norman Wilkinson

tricks would be ridiculous and redundant. To be invisible the fairies had only to step back and observe the mortals' folly: "I am invisible," says Oberon. Despite their fantastic appearance, or perhaps because of it, the audience easily accepted the convention so important to the plot. "They group themselves motionless about the stage," Desmond MacCarthy wrote, "and the lovers move past and between them as casually as though they were stocks or stones. It is without effort we believe these quaintly gorgeous metallic creatures are invisible to human eyes." The promptbook reveals, as it does for *Twelfth Night*, that there was little movement during long verse passages in the forest. Barker held that Shakespeare's chief delight was in "the screeds of word-music" of the immortals rather than in character (*More Prefaces* 37). Indeed in this play, as in *King Lear* and in *Antony and Cleopatra*, "Shakespeare's stagecraft is at issue with the mechanism of the modern theatre" (94).

The four lovers, who are close to anonymous in the text, were individualized as something like a stockbroker and poet matched to a minx and a fool (Bridges-Adams, *Lost Leader* 11). The importance attached to them can be

31   Puck (Donald Calthrop) leads out Bottom (Nigel Playfair), translated

assumed from the fact that Lillah McCarthy played Helena. She would have made an obvious Titania, but Barker wanted lightness there. Lillah wore a wig of long flaxen tresses; some critics caviled that the nordic look did not suit her dark Irish features, but she appears ravishing in the color photographs.[1] So does Laura Cowie, a thoroughly modern Hermia, "like a résumé in one person of the prettiest and most up-to-date ladies on recent posters" (*Athenaeum* 14 Feb. 1914:240). Her Greek dresses would have been acceptable for street wear.

The final scene of the play, which brings all the characters together in an epithalamium, deserves some attention. The night in the forest completed, Barker allowed a fifteen minute interval and provided a new set. This second full decoration used the entire depth of the Savoy stage and was dominated by seven heavy white pillars with black bands, elevated on a high platform at the rear (illustration 32). Behind them, silver stars on a night sky cyclorama. Seven steep white steps led down to the proscenium, occupying most of the middle stage. "These modern theatres with their electric lights, switchboards and revolving stages are all well enough but what is really needed is a great white box." So Barker spoke the following year in New York. "That's what

32   Theseus blesses the lovers, act 5

our theatre really is. We set our scenes in a shell" (*Harper's Weekly* 30 Jan. 1915:115). At the Savoy the white box held black and silver costumes for the last scene that echoed the set: even the motif on the base of the pillars was repeated at the hem of attendants' tunics.

A simple but significant set change was effected during the scene. When Theseus announced that he would hear the rustics' play, four large couches were brought on by stewards and placed along the arc of the forestage extension, immediately in front of the spectators. From them the nuptial sextet watched "Pyramus and Thisbe," which was played at the top of the steps (illustration 33). The front lighting was concentrated on the clowns; Theseus and his court, half in shadow, blended almost imperceptibly into the paying audience behind. This novel arrangement gave the comic sketch its due – it received high and frequent praise – but also kept it fully inside its dramatic function in the larger play. Its hilarity in performance has often obscured its basic and ironic purpose, the fact that the story of star-crossed lovers is an inversion of the sexual celebration, a magnificently inappropriate wedding present. Barker's staging emphasized that Peter Quince's very tragical mirth is presented to the Court first, then to us. For the Bergomask ("it never came out of Bergamo, but is right Warwickshire . . . with vigorous kickings in that part of the anatomy meant for kicks" – *Times*), the couches were removed and positions reversed. The dance took place

33   Pyramus and Thisbe on the top platform, the court audience on couches on the forestage. Quince (left) echoes the stance of Philostrate (right)

downstage center and the lovers were on the platform and steps watching it.

The scene had begun ceremoniously with large lighted torches; at the end formal ceremony returned. Hippolyta, Hermia, and Helena made their exit upcenter, accompanied by Amazons and bridesmaids with torches, followed by Lysander and Demetrius. The remaining attendants, all bearing torches, ranked themselves into a guard of honor as Theseus walked up the steps alone (promptbook 83). Then the fairies. Barker believed that a song was missing at the end and, with apology, used the nuptial verses from the opening of *The Two Noble Kinsmen*, with music and dancing by Cecil Sharp:

> All dear Nature's children sweet,
> Lie 'fore bride and bridegroom's feet,
> Blessing their sense.

The dance is recorded in illustration 34, high up on the top platform. Walkley can do the honors for their final moments: "In the end the golden fairies play

34   Final dance of the fairies

hide-and-seek round the columns of Theseus's palace. Gradually their numbers dwindle. At last only one, a girl, is left – the last patch of gold to fade from sight, and to leave on the mind the strange, new impression of the play as golden." The lights faded, the curtain fell. Puck spoke the epilogue in front of it and disappeared through the center in a flare of trumpets.

It was not somnolent, it was not romantic, it certainly was not insouciant. It was a clear-headed vision; in the words of *The Nation* (14 Feb. 1914:826), an "original and very wide-awake 'Dream.'" It was calculated to awaken the audience, to disturb old notions. What the traditionally-minded critics objected to best reveals what was new. *The Standard* (7 Feb. 1914:8) merits quoting at length for a condemnation of the apron stage, which

is becoming something of an infliction. For one thing, the audience is aware constantly of the shuffle of the actors' feet on the boards. And they come up much too close to the mere spectator. One is tempted to say "Ha, ha! I can see the joining of your wig!" or even to lean over and shake hands with somebody. After all, it is best to keep the time-honoured gulf between spectator and actor. . . . The average theatre goer craves illusion.

Peter Brook would be interested in that: at the end of his famous *Dream* (1969), much the grandchild of Barker's, the actors did invade the audience to shake hands. *The Standard*'s man was not the first reviewer to feel uncomfortable with the sheer physical presence of the actors at the Savoy, and his reaction helps us to see how Barker was assaulting the conventions of the time. Illusion was, it seems, a powerful and addictive drug: "the average theatre goer craves illusion."

A writer of much greater insight, G.C.D. Odell, had a similar reaction to the New York version, one year later. Odell grew purple about the forest curtains; he was incapable of apprehending the non-illusionist premise of the production, noting three times that the scene curtains "waved, to the loss of all illusion." Like his colleague William Winter (281), Odell thought Barker an upstart, an artistic anarchist, whom history would pass by. In 1920, at the end of his history of Shakespearian staging, he expressed the hope that "this silly and vulgar way of presenting Shakespeare died with all other vain, frivolous, un-simple things burnt up in the great war-conflagration" (2:468). How Barker's work could be seen as frivolous or unsimple is difficult for us to grasp, and our difficulty demonstrates that Barker's way became the way of the twentieth century. But if the great conflagration did not burn up the new method, it nonetheless brought an end to Barker's active work with Shakespeare. When the *Dream* closed in May 1914 the guns of August were already primed, and soon he would cease directing entirely.

9 Opening the stage

W HILE the new Shakespeare flourished, the McCarthy–Barker management continued to present modern plays at the Kingsway. Barker had not been so busy since the time of the Thousand Performances. As *Winter's Tale* was in preparation in 1912, he directed a highly praised revival of *The Voysey Inheritance*; *Fanny* was switched to matinees to make room. Just a week after *Twelfth Night* opened, *Voysey* was replaced by Galsworthy's *The Eldest Son*. This new work seemed pale after *Strife* and *Justice*, however; to Desmond MacCarthy it was "the least successful of all Mr Barker's productions" (*New Witness* 19 Dec. 1912:211). Shaw then restaged *John Bull*, which played until the following March, when Bennett's *The Great Adventure* settled in for the longest run of any work Barker ever directed. Henry Ainley and the music hall star Wish Wynne helped to make it deeply popular; its 674 performances would probably have been even greater had the war not ended them. Barker, used to notoriety, proved immune to popular success; as we have seen, he used the profits to underwrite the *Dream* at the Savoy.

With the Kingsway again given over to a long run and the Savoy dedicated to Shakespeare, Barker was ready to take on another theatre. He was at the height of his reputation as a director; the time had never been more auspicious for the fulfillment of the Court ideals on a permanent basis. Though the great eruption of English playwriting seemed over, Shaw at least was prepared: he had written a new ideational comedy for the management, with a major role intended for the manageress. Lord Howard de Walden reaffirmed his financial interest, and made possible a four-month lease on the St James's. Barker was about to take two momentous steps: the establishment of his own repertory company, and the expansion of his directing into new areas of presentational work.

St James's Theatre

George Alexander's theatre, the most socially prestigious in London, was not the obvious venue for a Shavian extravaganza with feminist implications. (Indeed Barker went to some trouble to counter the upper-class traditions of the St James's. A sign was affixed near the box office, stating that "we should like our patrons to feel that in no part of the house is evening dress indispensable" – reported in *The Standard* of 3 Dec. 1913:8). The home of Wilde and Pinero echoed with a more robust humor on the night of the first of September, when *Androcles and the Lion* took the stage. "Of course it is the lion's evening," wrote Walkley (*Times* 2 Sept. 1913:6). "Was ever beast so fortunate? . . . we mean in being the one character in the whole range of Shavian drama who never talks." The lion, played by Edward Sillward, romped delightfully, and O.P. Heggie gave the title role a "touch of saintly drollery" (*Standard* same date:7). The butchery of the Colosseum proceeded as in "the modern music hall, with a very casual call boy, who announces the number of each turn" (*Era* 3 Sept. 1913:14). In acting Lavinia, even the dignified Lillah McCarthy suggested a parody of her heroic role in *The Sign of the Cross*, the one that had devasted Lord Lucas so long ago. Walkley thought it was "all good fun."

Many spectators disagreed. "Vulgarity," "blasphemy," and "childish" were the words heard by the reviewer for the *Manchester Guardian* (2 Sept. 1913:6) as he left the theatre. He was sure the play would scandalize "the most characteristic part" of the audience; "we English cannot conceive being serious about a thing without being solemn about it." The antagonism of the ordinary playgoer must have been increased by what *The Standard* called "the militant suffragist flavour" of the piece. That taste is lost now, though noticeably present on opening night, when feminists took the persecution of the Christians as a direct reference to their own cause. Christians, says the Roman Captain, have only their "own perverse folly to blame" if they suffer. Since a Christian need only perform a simple ceremony to the gods in order to be freed, "every Christian who has perished in the arena has really committed suicide" (*Plays* 4:594–5). When Ben Webster delivered these lines, the play was interrupted by "suffragette cheers from the gallery" (*Manchester Guardian*). Shaw's play found few child-like spirits in St James's Square. "An enormously clever insult thrown in the face of the British public": *The Standard* again, probably unaware that it echoed Ruskin's infamous phrase about Whistler.

The St James's was a large house, seating about 1200; the production had been expensive and began losing money almost immediately. Hesketh Pearson, who played Metellus, insists that it failed because of the piece harnessed to it in a double bill ("The Origin" 804), and there is some truth to the charge. *Androcles* is long enough to fill an evening now, but Barker thought it too short for the time. He gave it a companion in *The Harlequinade*, written by Dion Clayton Calthrop in collaboration with the director himself. The subject was promising, a theatrical history of Harlequin, but it became a stiff and arid work, a bit patronizing and pedantic. Walkley was dismissive: "the theatre audience is in no mood for these subtleties." It bears more resemblance to Calthrop's history of *English Costume* (1906) than to *Prunella* or any of Barker's own plays.

Though Barker put his name to the work, a letter to Calthrop (Texas) makes clear that the composition was not his. Concerned about the billing, Barker said "certainly I cannot appear as writer. On the other hand I have contributed rather more than a producer does." Because Barker had an unusually large role in creating the piece through his direction, Calthrop agreed that he should receive part of the royalties. But there was a worry over the appearance of professional malfeasance. "As manager of course I have to disclose to the people interested exactly what I take," the letter explains, "and if I take a share of the royalties while my name only appears as a producer, as it does in Shaw's play, frankly it will look like blackmail." The solution – not a very satisfactory one – was to credit Barker in the program and in the published text as part author.

The Harlequinade cost almost as much as its partner to produce, according to the Account Book. If it caused or contributed to the failure of the bill, the intention was nonetheless worthy. By pairing Shaw's play with one that was patently fanciful, Barker expected to show the audience that the style of *Androcles* was a departure from the usual realism of the St James's or any fashionable theatre of the age. Those unable to appreciate a lighthearted treatment of serious matters were trapped in the very mode Barker was hoping to supersede.

Barker's directing of *Androcles* was turned on its head by Shaw at the last moment, as we saw in chapter 4. Pearson was convinced that Barker was inappropriate to the exuberance of the play, and Shaw agreed, at least officially. But if Barker sought more delicacy and subtlety in the acting than the playwright would allow at the dress rehearsal, the basic architecture and general mood were already in key with the open staging of the Savoy Shakespeare. Albert Rothenstein designed *Androcles* with suggestive scenery and costumes which were "the grotesque of the historical" (*Sunday Times* 7 Sept. 1913:6). A Reinhardt-style revolve was used for the major set change, from the interior of the Colosseum cages to the arena and Emperor's box. Thus the script could be played without interruption, and most of the stage was left free for unrestricted actors' movements.

The opening scene, "a gaudy Rothenstein forest" (*Observer* 7 Sept. 1913:5), was a painted drop hung far downstage. Illustration 35 shows its high contrasts: a forest of dreams, a preliminary version of Norman Wilkinson's set for Titania's bower. Actually it was a series of hangings, with sections in the main drop cut away to reveal strips of distressed cloth behind, giving the setting depth. There was a Chinese feel to the painted designs, "rather like the design on an Oriental china plate," said the *Manchester Guardian*. In 1913 it was the most presentational setting yet used for any of Shaw's plays.

"You are caught in the usual cleft stick. If you take off Androcles," the dramatist wrote on 4 October, "you will confess failure where there really has been a record success; and the chances of improving matters by a revival of The Witch or anything else are obviously quite desperate" (*SLB* 192). Shaw's claim that his play was a triumph may have simply meant that it was in the wrong theatre for the New Drama. The gate averaged £850 a week (Purdom 146); at the Little or the Kingsway the house would have been packed. In any case, Barker was forced to replace it, and with *The Witch*, at the end of October.

More significantly, however, he used his final month at the St James's to create the first full repertory experiment under his own management. Starting at the beginning of December, he directed seven plays in five bills; when the tenancy of the theatre expired at the close of the year, he moved the repertory to the Savoy, where it continued for another month. Only the rehearsals for *Dream* ended the experiment. John Palmer found the "Repertory Justified" (*Saturday Review* 20 Dec. 1913:773–4), noting that the St James's had been kept open four months "without yielding an inch to the speculative manager's view of what the public is supposed to want."

The Witch and *The Doctor's Dilemma* were the mainstays of the program. The other bills got only eight or nine performances each, but were varied enough to insure the vitality Barker believed essential. A rather bland and

35   *Androcles and the Lion*: forest curtain. Design by Albert Rothenstein. St James's 1913

under-rehearsed *Wild Duck* opened the repertory, and two unusual double bills completed it: *Nan* was paired with Molière's *Le Mariage Forcé*; a solid revival of *The Silver Box* was made an unlikely afterpiece to *The Death of Tintagiles*. Realistic plays put together with works of opposite styles – the director was again stretching his audience's received opinions.

The best of England's non-representational stage artists were called upon to assist the stretch. *Mariage* had a "toy-like setting" (*Stage* 4 Dec. 1913:22) by Rothenstein: "yellow buildings, with dead-black windows, green roofs, and green penthouses" (*Pall Mall Gazette* 3 Dec. 1913:5). *Tintagiles*, which Barker had directed for the Stage Society in 1900, now had its first public performance in London, with music by Vaughan Williams and an exceptional performance by Lillah McCarthy. Charles Ricketts designed a semi-circular drapery on a traverse rod, perhaps influenced by the forest drop for *Androcles*, that opened to the massive, mortal door: "high cobweb-silvery curtains" to Desmond MacCarthy (*New Statesman* 27 Dec. 1913:372).

MacCarthy noticed how the repertory system improved the performers. The company was essentially that used for the Savoy Shakespeare, and some actors discovered new depths in their range. Arthur Whitby, for example, who played Autolycus, Toby Belch, and Quince, was Uncle Edgar in *The Harlequinade*, Master Johannes in *The Witch*, Pancrase in *Mariage*, Barthwick in *The Silver Box*, and Sir Ralph B.B. Lillah McCarthy remained center stage, taking Lavinia, Anna Pedersdotter, Nan, Ygraine, and Jennifer Dubedat. The McCarthy–Barker management was proving good for actors. It employed some of the company more or less steadily for four years.

The Dynasts

The war of course transformed the theatre. The darkened streets and the early closing ordinance made a new London overnight; attendance suffered drastically, and soon many theatres would close or alter their offerings beyond recognition. In the first months, however, while a pretense lived that the hostilities would end quickly, it was still possible to gather actors and audiences for sophisticated entertainment, especially for worthy causes. One such event occurred on 5 November 1914, when Elizabeth Asquith organized the Arts Club Fund Matinee at Covent Garden, to aid "distressed members of the artistic professions" whose livelihoods were affected by the war. The event included a recitation by Lady Tree of Kipling's "For all we have and are," *Le Carnival* performed by the Russian Ballet, Bach's comic opera *Phoebus and Pan*, and a symphonic poem by Saint-Saëns. The orchestra was conducted by young Thomas Beecham. The last item on the long program was Masefield's verse drama *Philip the King*, with music composed by Gustav Holst, and directed by Granville Barker.

In the style of *The Persians*, Masefield presents Philip and his subjects

waiting for and receiving news of the Armada. Ricketts created an idealized
Escorial, a vast symbolic set for the vast opera house. "I remember with
pleasure," he wrote to Lillah, "the huge semicircle of curtains, the monumental doors studded with coffin nails, the huge crucified Christ I painted in the
manner of El Greco" (quoted in Purdom 161). Philip's study was raised on a
platform about ten feet above the floor, so that he was seen "through a gigantic
window, as it were" (*Daily News* 6 Nov. 1914:7), while the people were below
him on a conventionalized street. The background was in reds and grays; the
Spaniards in black, silver, and gold; and the Indians appeared only in dim
ghostly light.

The cast, taken from the McCarthy–Barker company, included Henry
Ainley as Philip and Lillah as the Infanta. Barker went to enormous trouble
for the single performance, perhaps because he felt so strongly about the
destructiveness of the war. The result was magnificent, though some of the
effect was spoiled by spectators leaving because of the late hour.

A more significant war play was presented at the Kingsway a few weeks
later, after the close of *The Great Adventure*. Thomas Hardy's *The Dynasts*,
published between 1903 and 1908, was intended for a theatre of the mind.
Hardy's preface shows the suspicion of the theatre common to the Victorian
man of letters, though he does suggest that a presentation behind misty gauze
curtains might serve his mighty theme. As J.C. Trewin says, *The Dynasts*
was "the ultimate closet play" (*Edwardian Theatre* 126). But Barker saw an
opportunity to stage portions of it, making a connection between the present
and past examples of European aggression. Hardy willingly agreed, and
composed a new prologue and epilogue, printed on the program and widely
published in the press. The purpose of the production, the poet intoned, was

> To raise up visions of historic wars,
> Which taxed the endurance of our ancestors,
> That such reminders of the feats they did
> May stouten hearts now strained by issues hid.

Barker's own attitude to the war might suggest a distaste for the chauvinism of
the poem, but apparently he was not averse to some patriotic drum-beating.
The Dynasts is ultimately a warning against congenital belligerence; perhaps
the director felt that Hardy's lines, amid the early mania for battle in 1914,
could clarify the "issues hid" on the European scene.

Hardy altered some of the cinematic stage directions and dumb shows, but
the main work of abridgment and arrangement was done by Barker. The
script, which survives in the promptbook at Harvard, shows that his solution
to the vast scale of the poem was simple. Though he retained the original three
parts, Barker's principle was to cut out anything not connected with England's role in the Napoleonic Wars. Thus there was no room for the Prussian
King, the Czar, the Austrian Emperor, Josephine, Marie-Louise, or even the
Prince Regent. The cosmic implications of Hardy's verse were severely

curtailed, in favor of a picture of the English people struggling against the
militarism of Bonaparte.

The challenges of time and space were handled with a similar directness.
Barker used the stage as an open platform for a series of episodic scenes,
presented in front of a fixed architecture. The stage was built out beyond the
proscenium at the right and left sides; in the center, five steps lower than the
main floor, Henry Ainley sat at a desk with an open book (illustration 36).
Dressed in a black regency jacket "with a long grey scarf flowing to the knees"
(*Stage* 3 Dec. 1914:22), Ainley read the long stage directions, his sonorous
voice calling up the scene. He carried the major burden of the three-hour play.
Esmé Beringer and Carrie Haase sat on either side in gray-green niches, like
Sibyls in marble draperies, portraying the Chorus. These "two forbidding
ladies" (*Standard* 26 Nov. 1914:6) were Barker's solution to the Spirits of
Hardy's text. They recited sections of the verse commentaries in unison, or
individually as Strophe and Antistrophe.

Norman Wilkinson designed the production to allow swift movement of the
narrative. Having worked with Barker on three Shakespeare decorations, and
having profited from the recent work of Ricketts and Rothenstein, Wilkinson
developed a method quite in accord with Barker's directing. Though the cast
of fifty-two was already large for the Kingsway, most of the actors took two or
three roles, and no attempt was made to create spectacular crowd effects
or scenic illusion. Costumes were representational but the episodes were
handled presentationally, the actors often delivering speeches on the forestage, directly to the house. The players "frankly assume that the audience

36   *The Dynasts* company on stage. Henry Ainley as the Reader at the desk, downcenter.
Kingsway 1914

is the English Channel, a Royal review, or a procession of Mr Pitt to the Guildhall," reported the *Manchester Guardian* (same date:8). The neutral backdrop gave prominence to the actor on a human scale, in Elizabethan style.

The full stage was used for larger scenes, like the death of Sir John Moore or the climactic battles, without major scenic additions. The locale was thus created by the Reader's narrative and by the actors' presence. Occasionally simple props or small set pieces helped to specify place and suggest environment. For the inn scene in part 1, a fireplace was moved on to the center steps; Villeneuve's ship at Trafalgar was "a painted wooden railing" (*Bystander* 16 Dec. 1914:394); campfires, illuminated by interior lights, were spotted on stage for night scenes in part 2 (promptbook). The Duchess of Richmond's ball at Brussels (illustration 37) used the raised inner opening as well, but the blocking put most action far downstage, keeping the Chorus integrated in the scene for the speeches of the Spirit of the Years and the Spirit of the Pities. The noise of war in these full scenes was as imaginary as the crowds – "Waterloo is without the boom of cannon," said *The Stage*. Lighting was generally non-illusionistic, though at the end of the final battle the lights were darkened so that no character was visible.

One result of the staging was to give heroic actions a rare intimacy. The upstage opening was used for smaller scenes, domesticating great events. Sometimes a formal drop on the back wall indicated locale: a deserters' den in the Peninsular Campaign had a painted door and window; Napoleon's palace

37   The ball in *The Dynasts*, using the full stage

at Fontainebleau (illustration 38) was provided with an elegant panel. For the death of Nelson, a cabin in the *Victory* was indicated by dropping a ship's lantern above the inner stage.

The production sought to convey the sweep of events, their cumulative power rather than their monumental substance. The overall effect was more medieval than Elizabethan, despite the physical layout of the stage and Hardy's synthetic Shakespearian verse. It seemed a rapid journey through a historical age, pointed to the present, an approximation of the expressionist style. The incidents were shown "not kinematographically, not with any kind of mechanical realism," concluded *The Times* (26 Nov. 1914:5), "but by groups of typical figures saying essential things and no more." *The Dynasts* was an experiment that codified many of Barker's discoveries of the previous three years, and showed the way to a new type of staging and a new form of drama. As Ainley narrated events and characters' emotions while actors portrayed them on a bare stage, the production boldly looked forward to the theatre of Bertolt Brecht.

New York repertory and Euripides outdoors

The Dynasts played until the end of January 1915, its seventy-one performances a reasonable success in light of the emergency. Though no one suspected at the time, it would prove to be Barker's last major production in

38   Napoleon (Sydney Valentine) at Fontainebleau, *The Dynasts*, using the "inner stage"

London. When it closed, however, the director had already begun a new repertory program in America. Barker had been invited by the New York Stage Society to head a season, with a guarantee fund provided by prominent citizens; since there was nothing for him in England, he was interested in establishing a permanent theatre under his control elsewhere. The British government apparently looked on his visit as propaganda for the war effort, and Asquith encouraged him to accept (Purdom 170).

He opened *Androcles and the Lion* on 27 January at Wallack's Theatre in New York, with Rothenstein's set, imported from England. Lillah McCarthy and O.P. Heggie repeated their parts, but they were the only members of the company to make the crossing; the other actors, some English and some American, were discovered on the spot. Barker thought the cast superior to London; Phil Dwyer made "a most admirable lion," he wrote to Shaw (British Library), better even than Sillward.

The companion play was also new. Having learned a lesson with *The Harlequinade*, Barker preceded Shaw's piece with a more appropriate work in *The Man Who Married a Dumb Wife*, Anatole France's version of a medieval story. The main roles were taken by McCarthy and Heggie, and the designer was a young American named Robert Edmond Jones. The New York Stage Society had previously intended to present the play, and Jones had already made sketches; Barker appreciated his talent immediately and decided to direct (*Harper's Weekly* 27 Feb. 1915:209). The setting, Jones's first professional assignment, became such a landmark in theatre history that only a brief discussion is necessary here. The designs and photographs have been reprinted in many places (including Salmon 245).

Barker built a forestage out over the orchestra pit and front rows of seats, as at the Kingsway and the Savoy. Two lower stage boxes were turned into proscenium entrances (Eaton 189). Jones's design took particular advantage of the extension, for it turned the set around: the street, which France intended to be upstage of Master Bortal's room, was directly in front of the audience, who looked at the exterior of the house. When the blind fiddler sat on the edge of the extension, said William Winter (283), "his bare feet were, practically, in the lap of spectator sitting before him." The street characters thus passed between the audience and Bortal's study, which was elevated slightly and seen through a window opening in the façade. The room was a ten-foot cube, crowding the actors into physical proximity. The colors of the set were dull, set off by bright items of contrast, like a red library ladder. The costumes, however, many of them constructed by Jones himself, were vibrant orange, yellow, and red: "bits of colored glass in a kaleidoscope," according to *Vogue* (Mar. 1915:105). Lighting for all the productions came from the flies and from a battery of powerful lamps mounted on the first balcony. The footlights were gone, of course, and the side border lights were not used; this was unusual, apparently, since many critics commented on it.

The extended forestage had not been used at the St James's for *Androcles*; it was built into Wallack's for the benefit of repertory. *A Midsummer Night's Dream* began to share the program in mid-February, the golden production essentially unchanged, though only Lillah was from the original cast. The New York reviews were *déjà vu* to Barker; the general reaction was the same mixture of hostility and amazement that had greeted Shakespeare at the Savoy. But whether belligerent or laudatory, the American press was filled with stories about the production and the Barkers. As E.F. Coward reported in *The Theatre* (Apr. 1915:197), one man stopped reading the daily papers entirely because "they contain nothing but war news and Barker." All the attention, however, did not bring crowds to the theatre. Though on the program for two and a half months, *Dream* was given only twenty-two performances, and half of them were matinees. In the final month of the season it was seen on Saturday afternoons only. *Androcles* and *Dumb Wife* fared better with the public, playing seventy-seven times, over two-thirds of the total number of performances given in the venture; the bill went on tour later.

Walter Pritchard Eaton (234) believed that the scheduling confused the New York audience. "Totally unused to repertory since Mansfield died," they assumed that a play was a failure unless it ran continuously. Barker wanted to forge ahead anyway, but was forced to slow down. He wrote Shaw just after *Dream* opened that he had worked the actors too hard and had to allow a rest before mounting the third play, otherwise "the company would either strike or die" (British Library). Doubts were creeping in: "I don't trust the public here," he went on, "I think they are most alarmingly fickle."

He intended to add *The Witch* and *The Madras House* to the season; both plays were announced on the first programs, and he wrote Shaw in January that he would probably have to play Philip Madras himself (British Library). He must also have hoped to do *Philip the King* and *Le Mariage Forcé*, for the costumes and sets had been shipped from England.[1] But the voice from the box office was clear, and expenses were mounting. The last bill was offered on 26 March: *The Doctor's Dilemma* in the St James's production. Nicholas Hannen was brought over for Dubedat, Heggie took B.B., and Lillah McCarthy kept Jennifer, which she had played since 1906. Audiences did not find it amusing. They laughed a little at *Androcles*, Lillah reports, but at *Doctor's Dilemma* "they got up and walked out of the theatre" (186). Wallack's had been scheduled for demolition before Barker moved in, and the season ended on the first of May.

When the wrecking ball struck, he was already busy directing Greek plays outdoors at five eastern universities, on a scale unprecedented in the modern theatre. Barker had no specific plans for Euripides when he left England, though he wrote Gilbert Murray on 6 November 1914 that he had his eye on *The Trojan Women* for America (Bodleian). During a visit to New Haven, he was hit with the idea of using the Yale Bowl as a gigantic Greek theatre (Smith 409). He wired Murray at the end of February with a proposal; on the same day letters went to established academics inviting cooperation. Eventually an overseas version of the McCarthy–Barker management was created to sponsor the plays, with a $10,000 guarantee fund provided by New York supporters. A committee of professors and university administrators was established to coordinate the arrangements, under the chairmanship of George Pierce Baker of Harvard.

Barker wrote Murray in March that he hoped to do *Iphigenia in Tauris*, *Trojan Women*, *Alcestis*, and *Hippolytus* (Bodleian). In the end only the two Trojan War plays were produced, and their relevance to the European war was not missed. (Maurice Browne of the Chicago Little Theatre was touring Murray's translation of *Trojan Women* in the midwest at the same time, under the auspices of the Women's Peace Party, billed as "the World's Greatest Peace Play," according to the tour circular). The choices were partially determined by the available company. Edith Wynne-Matthison sailed over to perform Andromache again, but the other roles were cast domestically. Lillah played Hecuba, looking "like the Queen of the Belgians," as Barker said to Murray (Bodleian), and repeated her Iphigenia; Lionel Braham, who acted in all four plays at Wallack's, took Thoas and Poseidon. Barker considered sending for Penelope Wheeler to lead the chorus, as she had at the Savoy in 1907 and the Kingsway in 1912. But the expense was prohibitive, and he was content with a local replacement in Alma Kruger. The Atlantic had become

39 *Iphigenia* in the Yale Bowl, 1915. The stage house is placed about one-third of the way along the field

dangerous water, of course, and a crossing could not be contemplated lightly; when the *Lusitania* was sunk on 7 May, one of those lost was Charles Frohman.

Norman Wilkinson's problem was as immense as the undertaking: to design a set that was large enough for a football stadium yet capable of being transported in ordinary baggage cars. In addition, the set had to work both in the Yale Bowl, which could hold 71,000 people, and in a new stadium in New York one-tenth that size. His solution was a portable stage house of wood and painted canvas, 100 feet wide by 40 feet high, that could be placed anywhere along the length of the field. This enormous *skena*, raised five steps from the ground, contained a narrow platform for the actors and three sets of doors. Arranged at the appropriate point in the stadium to cut off unwanted portions of the stands, it created arena seating similar to that at Epidauros (illustration 39). Between the *skena* and the audience was a circular dancing place 100 feet in diameter, with a raised altar in the center. It was made of canvas groundcloth, decorated with formal figures of circles and squares.

Iphigenia opened at the Yale Bowl on 15 May with more than 10,000 people in attendance. The performance began at 4.30, "shortly after the dual track meet with Harvard" (*Yale Daily News* 15 May 1915:1), and was timed to end about two hours later at sunset. In the next four weeks that play and *The Trojan Women* were each shown five times more at universities: at Harvard, the College of the City of New York (two performances of each), Pennsylvania, and Princeton. There was an additional performance of *Iphigenia* at the Piping Rock Country Club on Long Island before a much smaller audience. The best evidence suggests that well over 60,000 people saw the plays (Elberson 162). One estimate (*Vogue* July 1915:52–3) held the number to be as large as 100,000.

The conditions of performance approximated those of ancient Greece. But the urge was not antiquarian, any more than it had been with the Savoy Shakespeare. Rather, the vast outdoor setting was meant to enliven the plays for the present, returning to them some of the essential majesty that a proscenium theatre always diminishes. "The mere transference from outdoors in will prove deadening," Barker wrote ("On Translating Greek Tragedy" 240). Similarly, Wilkinson needed broad effects and striking colors to register in the surroundings and did not care if he was historically correct. A number of the costume designs were based on the records of antiquity, but his free treatment of shape and color was not constricted by archeological exactitude.

The *Iphigenia* costumes were modeled on his designs for the Kingsway, but electrifyingly emboldened. The twenty-one women of the Chorus were in "sweeping drapery of black and orange" (Smith 412), which trailed across the *orkestra* as they danced. Thoas, with high double crown and red beard, was a nightmare monarch of mythic savagery. His soldiers, in patterned tights and tunics, wore headdresses and skirts of flaming red: "union suits of black and white adorned with whisk brooms of the hue of tomato bisque", said the *New York Times* (16 May 1915, 2:10). Illustration 40 shows the Taurians aligned on the *skena*, as Lillah McCarthy carries out the sacred image of Artemis. Lionel Braham's large gesture, and his ten-foot scepter adorned with birds, give some suggestion of the broad nature of the performance. The costumes for *Trojan Women* were more subdued, predominately in black, purple, and gray. Hecuba wore a kind of papal tiara, and rich colors on a heavy cloak.[2]

Barker's previous work with Euripides had been mostly at small theatres. The scale of the American productions required a modified approach, and the key was in a version of ritualized performance. The *Iphigenia* promptbook shows that while movements were vigorous, the director paid close attention to formal, ceremonial patterns. Near the end, for example, when Thoas sends his troops after the Greeks, there was a great deal of activity: seven soldiers leapt off the platform with their spears in the air, split into two sections, and shouted loudly on their way off. At that moment Athena appeared – in the form of a large statue at the top of the stage house, *dea ex machina* in gold and crimson – and spoke with an actress's voice projected through a megaphone. All the rapid movement suddenly ceased, and the Taurians stood in organized

40   The Taurians and Iphigenia before the temple doors, Yale. Design by Norman Wilkinson.

groupings for her long speech (promptbook 86). A number of cuts were made in the dialogue and the odes to emphasize the essential action; Athena's monologue was reduced by sixteen lines.

Inside the controlled movements, the acting was large in scale. The Messenger's speech about the escape of the Greeks, sixty-eight lines long, was delivered without major stage movement; yet Philip Merivale held the moment with an intense portrayal. A photograph (in Smith 415) shows him on one knee before a threatening King Thoas, arms widely outstretched, in a posture reminiscent of one of Henry Ainley's in *The Winter's Tale*. In other episodes, the performance sought passion as a means of projecting to the vast crowds. In the recognition scene, Orestes (Ian Maclaren) was instructed to "let it rip" (promptbook 45). The basic style of both plays remained thoroughly non-representational. The burning of Troy in *Trojan Women*, for example, was accomplished by symbolic action: the Greeks lit three huge braziers on the stage, and black smoke rose upwards (*Harper's Weekly* 19 June 1915:594).

A separate promptbook for the Chorus of *Iphigenia* is extremely detailed about movement for the dances. Patterns were always symmetrical, and the geometrical design of the groundcloth allowed precise placement of the dancers. The women would hold a figure for the start of an ode, then move during the chant to new positions, where they remained in place for another short time. They carried wooden staves with green leafy hangings, which were raised and lowered in choreographed gestures: "choric weavings" said one observer (*Outlook* 26 May 1915:169). David Stanley Smith composed the music for both plays, as accompaniment to the Chorus. (It has survived in the Yale Music Library, and is reproduced in Elberson 300–24.) Like that used at the Kingsway it is flexible and kind to actors, consisting mainly of a monophonic line with occasional drums and cymbals. It was played by a small group of strings and woodwinds, placed out of view.

Lillah McCarthy reports (309) that the acoustics at Yale were "so perfect that there was no need to shout or strain the voice." There were frequent hearing problems notwithstanding, as well as complaints about sightlines (at Pennsylvania, where the stands of the arena in the Botanical Gardens were too low), the weather (it was cold and wet at Harvard), and the behavior of the younger members of the audience. It was probably a mistake for the coordinating committee to invite as many schools as they did. The performances in New York were subsidized by the city as part of inaugural festivities for the Adolph Lewisohn Stadium on Amsterdam Avenue, and graduating students of all the city high schools were required to attend. For each production 2,000 seats were reserved for them, at a special price of fifteen cents (Smith 415). Everywhere the plays were performed the students became restless and embarrassed, and often disturbed the more mature spectators.

Lionel Braham's booming voice and outlandish appearance were obvious targets for youthful derision and undergraduate humor. He was six and a half feet tall and had a method, Barker said, "like an overgrown good-natured bull" (British Library). On his first entrance at New Haven there was such a flutter in the stands that he forgot his lines; as he could not hear the prompter through the massive double doors, he just roared, repeatedly, causing further hilarity (*NY Times* 30 May 1915, 7:8). Adults also found reasons to laugh. The same writer reports that when the sun dropped below the rim of the Yale Bowl, hundreds of men rose to put on their overcoats, accompanied by multiple titters and jests about the seventh-inning stretch.

The problems encountered, however, were simply the problems attendant on outdoor performance. By creating a modern equivalent of the Attic festival, Barker united his spectators around a theatrical event that was more comprehensive than art, entertainment, or sport. It was a joyful combination of all of them, with the seriousness of tragedy joined to the communal anarchy of a football game. The occasion was not religious, of course, nor was it a true civic festival, despite civic sponsorship. Further, the plays remained distant in years and in their conventions, and the verse is always challenging to listeners. But with a growing and horrifying war as the backdrop, and a pacifist mood at large in America, Euripides may have spoken more directly than at any time since the defeat of Athens. To gather 10,000 people at a single performance of a play in the twentieth century is itself an accomplishment of significance; to have them also feel the power of an ancient poet is almost unheard of. And they did feel it: Montrose J. Moses said there was "an overpowering sense of the dignity of Greek tragedy" in the stadium (*Independent* 7 June 1915:396). The distractions of the outdoors became part of the tone of the event, as they are at a historical pageant, a parade, or an athletic competition.

The costs were high, much higher than Barker anticipated, and the large attendance did not cover expenses, for he had gravely underestimated the amount of skilled labor needed to run the performances. After calling on the guarantee fund, Barker suffered a loss of almost $7,500, according to a letter he sent to Paul Cravath, the chief organizer (quoted in Elberson 175). This was a personal disaster which caused considerable distress in his life for the next two or three years, and contributed to his decision to leave the stage. Neither England nor America was in the mood for a permanent art theatre of the kind Barker could direct. The time was out of joint, and he would soon be required to join the war effort more thoroughly, as a soldier.

The eclectic director

When Granville Barker returned home in June of 1915, he sailed as the chief man of the theatre of the English-speaking world. Since entering into management with his wife in 1911, he had shown a steady and remarkable advance as a director; his work had never been restricted to one style, but in this period its range expanded enormously. He was now equally at home with realist plays, with the symbolism of Maeterlinck and Masefield, with Shakespeare and Shaw, with farce, and with the expressionist pageant-show of *The Dynasts*. In addition he had succeeded in mounting two war plays by Euripides on a scale that even Reinhardt and Meyerhold would not match. Whatever Barker's financial liabilities, his position as a theatre artist was unassailable.

His general urge in these years was to free his stages from the conventions of Edwardian naturalism. Most of the works he directed after the move to the Kingsway were written in a non-realist mode; almost every one in America was presentational. (The exception was *The Doctor's Dilemma*, and even its production bore resemblances to *The Winter's Tale*, especially in Rothenstein's costumes for Jennifer.) But the emphasis on open staging was not accompanied by a change in directorial principles or in working methods. He remained firmly grounded in fidelity to the dramatist. Barker never carried a brief for an exclusionary production style; like Reinhardt he believed that each play made its own demands. The director's job was to discover an expression appropriate to the moment, and appropriate to the text under his charge.

"One great truth about my husband is that there is not a Granville Barker school, or manner of treatment," Lillah McCarthy said in an interview in New York; "every new play is a new problem" (*Theatre* May 1915:253). Barker himself repeated the notion often: Shakespeare needs a different treatment than do realist modern plays, where even the dreaded footlights "may be essential" (quoted in NY *Morning Telegraph* 21 Feb. 1915:2); Ibsen uses physical details in a sharp way to define character, whereas Shakespeare and Aeschylus do not (*On Dramatic Method* 19, 171). The director may be the controlling intelligence, but must be subject to a sympathetic understanding of the playwright.

And the director, in Barker's view, must recognize the limits to his authority and know when his stylistic control should be loosened. Once he determined the mode of a play, Barker picked the artist "best qualified to decorate it" and left the details to him. So too with actors: "I suggest the general lines I want them to follow and leave the filling in to them. I am the architect and they build upon my plans. This is what I conceive to be directing as opposed to driving" (*NY Times* 21 Feb. 1915, 7:5). He often demonstrated how he wanted a scene played, but did not ask for slavish imitation, which would have contradicted his zeal for vitality and spontaneity. Harcourt Williams said that "he never gave you intonations and accents but the reason why and where the emphasis should be made" (*Old Vic Saga* 184). Florence Gerrish, one of Titania's attendants in New York, reported that he communicated in dynamic and unconventional ways, acting out scenes in the guise of animals, and conveying emotion like an orchestral conductor by waving his arms, snapping his fingers, and swaying his body: "the original human dynamo," she said. He demonstrated line phrasings for Peaseblossom by kneeling beside the small actress while she spoke, "whistling and chirping like a bird until the child catches his meaning and the words are said in little thrills and warbles" (*Evening Sun* 16 Feb. 1915). A director's "simple rule," Barker wrote ("Rehearsing a Play" 4), should be that, while "he may veto, say definitely what is not to be done, he may never dictate what is to be."

In fact sometimes the director's job might be to refrain from doing too much. The "over-conceptualizing" common in later twentieth-century theatre was not one of Barker's faults. He wrote to Arnold Bennett that his "principal virtue" in directing *The Great Adventure* "has been the negative one of not putting the play into corsets, and painting its face until it has lost its humanity and became [*sic*] like any other old theatrical harridan" (Yale). He achieved results by being a source of suggestive ideas rather than by being a puppetmaster. For realist plays he commonly fleshed out the life history of small characters for the benefit of the actors. As Pearson points out (*Actor–Managers* 75), the result was an expanded vitality passed on by the performer to the audience. Barker gave comparable attention to small roles in Shakespeare: naming the lesser fairies was one of the methods, but chiefly he insisted that the smallest role in a crowded scene be played with confidence and conviction. During rehearsals for *Dream* in New York, he sat in the balcony with assistants; he checked the principals, they the supers. Critiques at the end of each act ran to as many as a hundred pages of notes, but Barker carefully passed them all on with attention, actually spending more effort on the supers than on the leads (*NY Times* 21 Feb. 1915, 7:5).

Wilson Knight (227) saw Barker as an Apollonian artist: a powerful bearer of light and intellect, but one who ignored the Dionysian side of existence. Thinking of Barker's aborted *Macbeth*, Bridges-Adams feared that the Weird Sisters would have been those "of a man who didn't hold with Witches" (quoted in Speaight 201). In so far as Barker was Apollonian he was a figure of the era, sharing the illuminator's urge with Shaw, Galsworthy, Murray, Archer – all friends – the Fabians, and lesser lights. As a director he strove for clear lines of portrayal, for an uncluttered style. "I get to believe more and more in the open air – in feeling if not in reality," he wrote Maurice Browne in 1915, "and [shapeful?] clean cut, finely disciplined things. I think that all art must ultimately stand that test" (Michigan). He was a proto-modernist; already a mature artist when the war came, he was not transformed by it the way Pound was, or Stravinsky or Meyerhold. In this sense his subsequent writer's life was an acknowledgment of the pedagogue that had always been within, shedding light. "Ah, sir," he wrote to G.B. Harrison in 1935, "had I been a professor what a dry-as-dust I should have been!" (Michigan).

So it is with surprise that we come again and again upon evidence that reveals Barker as a deeply mysterious force, unrivaled in England or America as a guiding spirit, guru, saint, and mystic of the theatre. His ability to inspire actors was unmatched; part of the explanation for his curious reputation may be found in the inexplicable loss fellow workers felt when he left them. John Gielgud's discussion of the 1940 *King Lear*, for example, is inspired by unspoken regret. The mere ten days Barker gave to the production "were the fullest in experience that I have ever had in all my years upon the stage," Gielgud wrote (*Stage Directions* 52). The superlative was attached to him so regularly as to become redundant: by those who worked with him, like Harcourt Williams (*Old Vic Saga* 184), A.E. Matthews (197), and Charles Ricketts (Purdom 161); and by almost anyone who wrote about his directing, from Desmond MacCarthy and P.P. Howe, to the daily reviewers who admitted his genius even when objecting to it. The same Bridges-Adams who thought Barker's work "hygienic" and "fastidious" could also speak of the "holy hush" of some of his scenes (*Lost Leader* 6). If he was Apollo, all this might suggest, his light on occasion was reflected by Diana.

"All arts are mysteries," he wrote in 1931 (*On Dramatic Method* 7); "the way into their services is by initiation, and the adept hugs his secret." They are not the words of a Fabian realist. Barker hugged his secret self, as Eric Salmon has shown so well, and made it the foundation of his work as a dramatist. As a director he also used the secret life to capture the elusive mystery of great plays, recognizing that art comes from hidden sources. "A play, in fact, is a magic spell; and even the magician cannot always foresee the full effect of it" (*Prefaces* 1:6). A magic spell, spoken in a charmed circle by initiates: his *Iphigenia* and his *Trojan Women* come to mind, presented in broad daylight while suggesting the darkness of the war. "British Are Losing 1000 Men a Day," reported the *New York Times* (1 June 1915:6), while Hecuba lamented the fall of an ancient city in modern New York.

The Greek plays, the Savoy Shakespeare, and his other late work showed that mystery could live in the theatre without mystification. Barker banished the shadows and illusionism of the nineteenth-century stage; in so doing he lost some of the churchly connotations and popular appeal of an Irving or a Tree. His gains, however, were coins of fierce value. More than anyone in England or America, Barker taught the new century about the power of the open stage, the virtues of swift speaking and restored texts, the force of simple decor and non-representational color and shape. For realist plays, his example demonstrated how careful attention to luminous detail could invest the performance with symbolic and mysterious overtones – the quality we now call "Chekhovian." To this list must be added his most consistent principle, that the responsibility of the director is always first to the playwright.

Perhaps most of all, Barker's contribution as a director was to rediscover the power of the unvarnished actor: not the star but the craftsman–actor, himself dedicated to the service of the communal experience that is the play. Barker found that by dismissing tricks of lighting and scenography he could make the actor more honest and yet more deeply mysterious. The ultimate paradox of the theatre is not that we mistake the mask for the person, but that we know the mask to be a mask. The barefaced actor in daylight challenges a deeper part of our theatrical response than the mesmerist on a darkened indoor stage. "The art of the theatre is not a reasonable art," said the Apollonian ("Heritage" 73). "A play's dialogue is an incantation, and the actors must bewitch us with it."

10 Ploughing the sands: the dream of a national theatre

HARLEY GRANVILLE BARKER was everywhere that drama mattered in England in the first sixteen years of the century, but nowhere was his power of thought and action more evident than in his fight for a national theatre. Though Barker was the champion of the cause for many years, his efforts are not well remembered, perhaps because the cause did not prevail in his time – a wounding disappointment all his adult life. Yet his part in the history of the establishment of a British national theatre is a drama of its own, a tale of protracted struggle against those perennial enemies of art: prejudice, vested interests, both theatrical and financial, and the intellectual torpor of the mass audience. While the final victory was clearly the accomplishment of many, Barker's work was indispensable: through his vision the lines of the eventual institution were drawn. To trace his concern with a national theatre is to see the evolution of a social and artistic idea, as well as to summarize his life's work.

The national theatre movement reaches back to the mid-nineteenth century (it has been studied by Elsom and Tomalin, and by Emmet), but the serious modern campaign began in the year of Barker's birth. While still living in Edinburgh in 1877, the young William Archer collaborated on an anonymous sixpenny pamphlet called *The Fashionable Tragedian*, attacking the mannerisms and wasted talents of Henry Irving just before the great man was to appear in that city. Irving's genius, Archer wrote, had been destroyed by long runs and "indiscriminate adulation." If actors must continue to seek the long run for survival, they will be ruined like Irving: "the only remedy lies in a national theatre, with good endowment, good traditions, good government" (5). Though Archer's opinion of Irving mellowed – he wrote a complimentary monograph in 1883 – he continued to attack the destructiveness of the commercial system.

George Moore entered the fray a few years later with concerns about the state of English drama that shared Archer's theme. Moore was perhaps the first writer in England to appreciate the Théâtre Libre; in a paper called *The Hawk*, edited by his brother Augustus, he promoted the value of a London imitation as early as 1888. (The essential articles were reprinted in *Impressions and Opinions* in 1891.) Moore hoped that a private patron would come forward to endow an art theatre as a matter of social conscience: "the man who gives pleasure is as charitable as he who relieves suffering. . . . it would be equally meritorious to endow a theatre as a hospital" (213).

Schemes and estimates

The endowment did not come, of course, but it was through the Secessionist Movement that the idea of a national theatre took first root in London. When Barker appeared in 1900, the same qualities that brought him to quick prominence in the Stage Society also recommended him for work on the campaign. A committee was formed that year to consider steps towards a national theatre; Barker became a member, along with Archer, Gilbert Murray, and A.C. Bradley. They met several times to no effect. Barker recalled the gatherings more than twenty years later in *The Exemplary Theatre* (v–vi): "I trust I sat silent. I was impatient – the scheme seemed likely to be long in coming to birth. I am sure I looked forward to a national theatre in being within the next year or so." His impatience was seized on by Archer. "We must get something on paper," Archer insisted; "what you and I have to do is draw up a practical scheme, and these other fellows may amend it if they know how." With the rumor abroad that Andrew Carnegie might endow a theatre under the right conditions, there was some urgency to the task. Barker, almost unknown outside the Stage Society, was already Archer's most likely collaborator in the endeavor.

The practical plan they wrote, forthrightly titled *Scheme and Estimates for a National Theatre*, was privately printed in 1904 and referred to as the "Blue Book." It was a careful and prudent proposal, highly organized and financially detailed – it should have appealed to Carnegie – covering all aspects of the subject from endowment to pension fund. Even ticket prices and refreshments were included in its scope. The authors assumed a company of actors consisting of forty-two men and twenty-four women, and one house with 1,500 seats. They were deliberately cautious in the sample repertory, omitting the provocative names of Ibsen and Shaw, emphasizing Shakespeare and drama within the late-Victorian tradition. The season would open with the Henry IV cycle, and though it would include Restoration comedy, Yeats's *The Countess Cathleen* was the most adventurous new play suggested. "It is not an 'Advanced' Theatre that we are designing. . . . experiment would not be its primary function" (36–7).

Aside from the idea itself, the only radical notions in the Blue Book are the proposal for a training school and dramatic college as part of the national theatre, and the insistence on a new and specially designed building to house all of the functions related to it. The collaborators wrote that "our estimates presuppose a theatre-building wholly different from any now existing in London. We believe that such an enterprise would be almost impossibly handicapped in any building not specially designed for this particular purpose" (2). They suggested that the London County Council or Parliament offer one of the sites at their disposal on favorable terms, and they anticipated a private donor for the entire capital expenditure, estimated to be about

£330,000. It would be "a waste of time" to ask Parliament for the money.

As noted in a "Postscript-Prologue," several critics thought the estimates too low. But the theatre the authors desired was "not a combination under one roof of His Majesty's, the St James's, and the Haymarket." It was not, therefore, to be a competitor to the commercial theatres, even the best of them, using their methods and running to their expenses. Rather it was to be a totally new enterprise, a full repertory institution "which shall show what artistic results are possible under a wholly different system." Further, it would be a theatre that could be imitated "in any of the great cities of the provinces or the Empire . . . Therefore *we regard economy not merely as a necessity likely to be forced upon the Theatre for lack of a lavish endowment, but as the indispensable means to an artistic end*" (xxii–xxiii). It was a socialist ideal: not a monument glorifying the nation but a democratic theatre for the people of the nation, showing the best plays at accessible prices.

Remarkable a document as the Blue Book is, it is even more remarkable that it received the support of famous figures in the commercial realm. An endorsement printed in the book, certifying that "such an institution is urgently needed, and that it could in all probability be successfully established on the general lines here indicated," was signed by Henry Irving, Squire Bancroft, J.M. Barrie, Helen d'Oyly Carte, John Hare, H.A. Jones, and A.W. Pinero. The notion of a national theatre in England had been bandied about haphazardly for some time, but the Blue Book was the first detailed proposal of what it should actually look like. It has remained the best, according to Elsom and Tomalin (36), and has influenced planners ever since.

The details of finance and the private distribution suggest that Archer and Barker expected the plan to be realized immediately. But though Archer worked on his fellow Scot, Carnegie did not provide the money and Barker suffered the first of many disappointments over the dream of a national theatre. In the hope that a wider dissemination might prompt another donor, the authors published the book in 1907, now with its title reversed: *A National Theatre: Scheme and Estimates*. The text remained the same, but Barker added a new preface in the form of a letter to Archer; it indicates clearly how his personal authority had grown. Most significantly he notes that they now can name the new dramatists to be played at the national theatre without fear of being labelled radicals: "I should unhesitatingly . . . advocate the inclusion in our repertory list of every author whom we so carefully excluded four years ago – Ibsen, Hauptmann, d'Annunzio, Shaw and the rest. I hope I could even find other names to add" (xi).

What emboldened him to risk those inflammatory names was, of course, the Court Theatre. As the Thousand Performances progressed, commentators recognized that they were witnessing an artistic renovation accomplished almost entirely outside the mainstream of the commercial stage. In a review of *The Silver Box*, Hamilton Fyfe, one of the members of that committee in 1900, admitted that his earlier agitation for a national theatre was "absurd," since there were no new English plays to justify it. "What would be the use of a Bank of England if we had no money to keep in it?" (*World* 2 Oct. 1906:655). But with Shaw, Barker, and now Galsworthy on the scene, Fyfe said, all that has changed utterly. No single venture had a more lasting effect on the search for a national theatre than the Court seasons. Barker's particular genius was to provide both theory and practice. The Blue Book was supported in such strength by his own acting, directing, writing, and managing that in three years he had himself become the most persuasive argument for a subsidized repertory theatre.

Yet while the new drama fought for breath, audiences at Drury Lane "gladly queued six hours" to see *Ben Hur*, said Charles Landstone (quoted in Trewin, *Edwardian Theatre* 90), or *The Bondman* with Etna erupting and real cows milked on stage, or *The Sins of Society* with the sinking of a troopship. Barker knew that, whatever the value of his work, it would never pay. A true repertory system would mean a large, permanent company of actors, directors, designers, musicians – all impossible without a major endowment. In July 1907, at the dinner celebrating the achievements of Vedrenne and Barker, the Earl of Lytton offered a toast to the imminence of a national repertory theatre. In his reply, Barker was less sanguine:

I feel very strongly, as I think everyone must, the necessity for a change in the English theatrical system. To my mind no drama and no school of acting can long survive the strangling effects of that boa-constrictor, the long run. What is needed, of course, is a repertory theatre, but the difficulty of establishing one in London would be very great, greater than Lord Lytton thinks. As a good Socialist I am glad to be able to sum up the chief of those difficulties in the one word rent.   (*Complimentary Dinner* 12)

He went on to say that it might be necessary to look to Manchester or Birmingham for the first repertory, in order to avoid those high costs – until, that is, a patron was convinced of the value of creating a national theatre in the capital.

The unfortunate season at the Savoy took some of the gloss off Barker's name as the leader of the campaign, though pointing out again the necessity of subsidy. The censorship of *Waste* added a personal disaster: it must have seemed that the government, hitherto simply indifferent, was suddenly hostile to Barker's cause. None of the proposals of the time seriously argued that the nation underwrite the national theatre, along the lines of the Comédie Française or the German state theatres. The English stage had been commercial in nature since the suppression of the Corpus Christi cycles in the late sixteenth century, when drama ceased being a civic experience and became metropolitan entertainment. The Edwardian Liberal government was firmly committed to free trade, and would have considered a grant to establish or maintain a theatre a most inappropriate waste of public funds. St John Hankin put the matter in focus in 1907 when he wrote that "the British Parliament is about as likely to subsidise dramatic art as it is to subsidise the prize ring. Less likely, in fact" (814).

Thus attention was repeatedly drawn to the need for private contributors, and Barker or his wife often led the fund drive. Lillah McCarthy, princess of promoters, secured a single donation of £70,000 from Carl Meyer in 1908. Lord Howard de Walden, sponsor of a number of theatrical enterprises, including Herbert Trench's seasons at the Haymarket, was an obvious target. Archer wrote Trench at the end of 1907, soliciting support from Lord Howard for a national theatre; he insisted that "Granville Barker is quite clearly *the* indispensable man to such an undertaking," now that he has proved "his genius as a producer, and his tremendous power of work" (quoted in Whitworth 61–3). Barker's visit to New York in 1908 was a similar search. "Why not do four years there," Shaw wrote, "and then come back and found the national theatre and opera house of this country? . . . Eventually, simultaneous operations on both sides of the Atlantic might be possible" (*SLB* 83). But Meyer's generosity was never matched; Lord Howard, helpful later, was not willing to commit a large amount to a permanent institution; and the American idea proved another bubble on the stream.

Before he sailed for New York, Barker was interviewed by the *Pall Mall Gazette* (14 Mar. 1908:7), on the last day of the Savoy performances. The venture failed, he said, because Vedrenne and Barker could not compete with commercial managements on the same basis; the only solution for an art theatre was to be endowed at least with rent, rates, and taxes. He noted with sarcasm that "some people are going to raise as much as £200,000 on a statue of Shakespeare. This is more than half the sum that would endow and run for ten years a national répertoire theatre in London."

The "some people" were the members of the Shakespeare Memorial Committee, organized a few years earlier when Richard Badger offered a large contribution toward a Bardic memorial in London. In March of 1908 the Committee had announced a competition for a "sculptural or architectural" monument; instead of receiving the designs hoped for, the Committee received scorn and derision. As Cary Mazer points out ("Treasons" 3), the ensuing debate on the form of the memorial succeeded in undermining the statue party. The Shakespeare Memorial Committee agreed to merge with the agitators for a national theatre, and the Shakespeare Memorial National Theatre committee was created, with the support of the major figures of the Edwardian stage.

The new group published an illustrated handbook of its purposes in 1909, based on the *Scheme and Estimates*. The SMNT suggested the construction of a building "wholly different in character and aspect from any existing theatre," dedicated to the production of Shakespeare and other plays. An appeal for a half million pounds was launched with little success (Whitworth 82–90; Elsom and Tomalin 41–52).

The SMNT committee was a difficult amalgam of opposing forces, and the acceptance of the Barker model did not come without struggle. Since its members included Shaw, Archer, Barker, Pinero, and Beerbohm Tree, it is hardly surprising that meetings were often divisive. Shaw wrote Barker about one such conflict in which the Blue Book was attacked because of the power it placed in the hands of a single authority: "neither Esher nor any other man experienced in public affairs will hear of the scheme in the Archer–Barker book, as it is quite openly planned to make the Director supreme" (*SLB* 144). The Blue Book does give the director "absolute control of everything in and about the Theatre" (12), except in the selection of plays where he has one vote in a reading committee of three. But the root problem in the committee was not whether one man should be supreme but who that man might be, and on this question the forces of the old guard lined up against the new.

Using the records of the SMNT, Mazer demonstrates that Tree attempted to maneuver the committee into supporting the annual Shakespeare Festival at His Majesty's as a *de facto* national theatre, with himself as the director. Tree had much to lose if a new theatre dedicated to Shakespeare appeared in the capital. Had his purpose succeeded, the result would have been an official sanction of realist Shakespeare as the appropriate mode for England, a coup of the most reactionary kind. Though Tree was forced by the committee to end his intrigues, he and the other actor–managers remained opposed to Barker's modern methods and his endowed theatre. A major subsidized company in London would have been an open threat to the commercial stage – in business terms, an unfair practice. When the work of the SMNT was shelved by the war, a great chance had already passed. Just at the moment when a national theatre might have materialized, rivalry and disagreements over what it should look like added decades to its delay.

The value of repertory

While the committee squabbled, Barker set out to prove the social and artistic benefits of a national theatre by personal example. In November 1909, as the Frohman season approached, he published an article called "Repertory Theatres" in Desmond MacCarthy's *New Quarterly*. It is a succinct expression of the deadly effects of commercial acting, and we have had cause to refer to it before. His text is that "a civilised man needs a home; a sensitive nature needs change" (491). The application to the theatre was clear. "A play must have a home, an actor must have variety. Only the repertory system – the opposite of the long run – can provide either. A repertory system is the next step, is a necessary step in the progress of English drama" (499). Freshness and vitality remained the essence of good acting, yet the regular stages operated on a monetary principle that expressly denied the chance of variety; indeed, in the long run system, if an actor changed roles frequently he was a professional failure. "If acting cannot seem spontaneous, it is nothing," he concluded. "It can only seem so by the actor coming fresh to his work, his whole personality like a sensitive plate, which he exposes untouched to the light of his conception of the part" (501).

The Duke of York's experiment was a working example of the freshness and value of repertory acting, even if it did not draw the necessary houses. Barker took his lessons with good grace and remained convinced that only an endowment could secure a national theatre. In a lecture given in June 1910, just before Frohman terminated the performances, Barker announced with optimism that "the theatre is at last being brought to a sense of its needs" ("Theatre: Next Phase" 635). He expected that some enlightened "rich man's money" would soon enable drama to flourish in England as it deserved. We must, he said, open a Shakespeare National Theatre "at the very latest the day after to-morrow." Much as Tree would disagree, Barker held that "we cannot get Shakespeare as we want it by private enterprise. . . . We never have; and what signs are there that we ever shall?" He suggested, for the first time, that admission to the national theatre should be free, as at the National Gallery and the British Museum: it would always be "full of people who really wanted to see the plays" (636). The Duke of York's had shown that "a Repertory Theatre cannot be made to pay in the commercial sense of the word," but despite the losses and setbacks "the practicality of modern repertory has been proved, and the public now knows by demonstration what a Repertory Theatre is" (639). The financial failure of the Frohman scheme, in other words, made the case even plainer: repertory was essential and so was beneficial funding. The health of the nation depended on it.

Barker visited Germany later in 1910, surprised and delighted at how seriously theatre was taken there. Returning from a rehearsal of Reinhardt's *Oedipus*, he wrote Murray: "theatre here so alive and interesting – it makes me ashamed" (Purdom 115). He reported on his travels to Berlin in a series of articles for *The Times*, pointing out how German subsidies provoke excellence. Reinhardt, he wrote, "though brilliantly creative, is still sane. He has one great safeguard. He spends brains on his work instead of money" (19 Nov. 1910:6). In the *Fortnightly Review* he cited the Deutsches Theater and the Düsseldorfer Schauspielhaus as models of a national theatre and a regional theatre supported by public funds. Why was this not possible in the land of Shakespeare? Even if the government would not finance the institution, he wished that it would give benediction to the national theatre scheme: "until the theatre in England receives some public recognition there will be little credit in disinterestedly investing money in it" ("Two German Theatres" 61).

Seen in light of the search for a permanent public theatre, the McCarthy–Barker management between 1911 and 1914 becomes much more than a passing venture. Barker's work with modern plays at the Little and the Kingsway, with Shakespeare at the Savoy, and with repertory at the St James's and the Savoy, fulfilled many of the artistic requirements of a national theatre. Three houses, excellent programming, a stable company (of actors, designers, and musicians), first-rate productions: the director was providing a personal version of a national repertory theatre. His subsidy was not large, he was subject to rents and leases, he had no assurance of stability, but the management continued in operation nonetheless. The long runs of *Fanny* and *Great Adventure* violated repertory principles, though under the circumstances they were practical necessities; and the public response was occasionally disappointing. But London had witnessed nothing like this variety and vitality in the history of the modern stage.

"Well, ladies and gentlemen, is this repertory to continue?" So Barker asked before the curtain of the St James's on the night when the last production had been added to the repertory program. He was answered by cheers and cries of "yes." He took pride in what had been done, he said, but only by contributions could the work go forward. "I am prepared to stake whatever reputation I may have acquired in the service of the theatre that repertory, real repertory, is the only path out of the evils which beset the theatre." He appealed to a thousand Londoners to pledge £25 each for three years to guarantee a company:

In Heaven's good time (but hardly within the next three years) we are, I hope, to have a National Theatre in being. [More cheers.] But that is only an institution, however fine, and to-night I am pleading for a whole system. Besides, we must prepare for our National Theatre. If we do not, then when it comes, and we on our part are not used to its methods and you on yours are not accustomed to its aims, it will be in danger of settling down as a mere museum of theatrical antiquities. [Laughter.] No, if we are to save our dramatic souls we must begin to save them now.[1]

The old impatience and messianic fervor are in the speech, but tempered by awareness that public support was not yet sufficient for a national theatre. "Hardly within the next three years": it would be very much longer.

Meanwhile Barker planned for his private subscription scheme. Papers were drawn up giving him sole artistic control; the money was to be placed in the hands of trustees (Barrie, Murray, and Lord Howard de Walden). The response was good, but was rendered moot by the war. Writing in *The Stage Year Book* for 1915, E.A. Baughan called the St James's experiment "an astonishing success" (7) that would have prompted a new repertory scheme if the fighting had not intervened. Barker's own opinion was that the national theatre was "on the verge of accomplishment" in 1914 (letter to Ervine, Texas). But the dream of theatre rapidly faded as the nation turned to the more pressing business of killing. He cried out to Murray in September (Bodleian): "My principal admirers are alien enemies."

The year 1916 was the tercentenary of Shakespeare's death, yet a national theatre was further away than at any time in Barker's life. The London stage was given over to musical frivolity (*Chu-Chin-Chow* opened in August and ran for five years) and there would have been no place for him even had he not been forced to serve in the war, first in the Red Cross and then in Army Intelligence. The Shakespearian commemoration, he recalled later, brought with it "the bitterness of my realization – sharpened by the occasion – of the theatre's utter and ignominious failure during the war to lift its head into any region of fine feeling and eloquence" (*Exemplary Theatre* viii). He suffered a number of personal difficulties too, the most immediate being the financial losses of the American tour.

All of these forces came together in the most important decision of his life, made during the war and partly because of it. On his 1915 trip to New York he had been attracted to an older American woman, Helen Huntington, a minor poet, novelist, and wife of Archer Huntington of the railroad family. The progress of their relationship is not relevant here, except to note that, since Helen was also attracted to Barker, it did progress. After much pain and delay, Lillah McCarthy was convinced to sue for divorce, and Barker married Helen in London in 1918. Archer Huntington unexpectedly settled a large income on his former wife; Barker's world changed permanently. Helen provided him with the security he sought, and any price he paid he apparently paid willingly. She disliked the theatre, distrusted actors, and detested Shaw. Barker, already disgusted with the state of the world and of the stage, at Helen's urging made his own *gran' rifiuto*: he abandoned the theatre. His magnificent career as an actor, director, manager, and active playwright was over. Henceforth he would be a man of leisure and a man of letters.

That at least is the standard version, the Barker myth, given voice by Casson and Purdom. The truth is more complicated. For one thing, Salmon has shown that Helen Huntington did not bewitch Barker with her money; he fell deeply in love with her, perhaps for the first time in his life, and remained a devoted husband. For another, Barker had been saying for a number of years that he wanted to stop directing and cultivate his writing: he found the two tasks irreconcilable. Before the war began he told Dixon Scott that he had given up writing for directing when he was thirty, and was determined to give up directing for writing when he was forty. Once the new repertory scheme was underway, "you would see me back at my desk like a shot" (154).

He wrote Shaw an even clearer expression of his intentions in 1915. Disappointed by the financial results of the Wallack's season, he was no longer interested in working on a commercial basis:

> I have been thinking things over well, and have come now to a decision – either repertory or nothing. By nothing I mean that I will go through with the ANDROCLES and DOCTOR'S DILEMMA committments, and after that no more management; no more producing. Somebody else must do the job. It will be an enormous relief: for American conditions, though better in some ways, make me chafe under the yoke even more than English ones do.
>
> (British Library)

With the addition of the outdoor Greek plays, Barker's resolve was more or less kept. On his return to London he was in an unassailable position as the greatest director in the English theatre, yet was without a structure that permitted him to work. Germany thought Reinhardt important enough to continue his subsidy through the war; indeed the period from 1914 to 1919 was one of his most fruitful. But Barker was not so lucky. He gave up the lease on the Kingsway and permanently retired from management.

While his departure was an inestimable loss to the theatre, it was not Helen who forced him to go. All his life had been directed to bettering the art. But the theatre is an art that needs large support, and Barker was not interested in producing popular successes to finance the higher work. Neither was he temperamentally capable of writing popular plays, as Shaw was. The only hope, as he saw it, was in a theatrical system specifically devoted to excellence. This theatre, as he had argued for half his life, must be at least partially free of the terrors of finance. "As to the producing of plays," he explained to St John Ervine,

I made up my mind sometime before 1910 that it was futile to plough the sand i.e., in this connection, to make a production and then disperse it, the play to semi-oblivion, the actors to demoralisation. On the personal count I made up my mind even earlier to give up acting when I was 30 and producing when I was 40.   (Texas)

When the war wiped away the foundations he had so carefully laid, he saw no reason to continue the active fight for a cause that, even if successful in the end, would waste him personally. He was forty in 1917. He washed off his makeup and took up his pen.

Reconstructing the theatre

"So in place of ploughing the sands," he continued to Ervine, "I cast my bread upon the waters." Most of what he wrote from his retirement until his death remained concerned with the dream of theatre, *hors de combat*; he was a wounded general, advising the fray. The military metaphor was one he used immediately, in an article for *The Times* called "Reconstruction in the Theatre" (20 Feb. 1919:11), in which he reported on the growing interest in England in amateur community theatres on the American model. He saw a role for them in "reconstructing" the stage along non-commercial lines. That same year he became the first chairman of the council of the British Drama League, established by Geoffrey Whitworth as a central aid station for amateur and small professional groups. In the initial issue of the League's magazine, *Drama*, Barker restated a familiar position: excessive repetition, whether in rehearsal or performance, is deadly for an actor. "No man can act Hamlet eight times a week, he can at best repeat it" ("Rehearsing a Play" 4); repertory theatre is the only salvation for the actor and his public.

A few years later, in a preface to Laurence Housman's *Little Plays of St Francis*, Barker went further in condemning the theatrical establishment: "there is an art of the theatre and there is a theatrical industry," and their interests rarely coincide (vii). Housman's work had been widely performed by amateur groups, demonstrating that there are "bodies of people so hungry for a little, simple, wholesome, unhocussed dramatic art, that, denied it by the professional providers, they are ready to see to the supply themselves" (xi). Of course Barker's own clean break with the profession was the strongest possible condemnation. That the complete man of the theatre should have retired to a study in Devon was a standing challenge to those who remained on the stage.

In 1922 Barker published his first theoretical book, *The Exemplary Theatre*. If the Blue Book was over-specific, this one went to the opposite extreme: instead of schemes and estimates, it dealt with the philosophic and social aspects of dramatic art. The opening chapter is a long debate between two opposing characters on public subsidy for the theatre. "The Man of the Theatre," a kind of crypto-Barker, argues the virtues of a national theatre with "The Minister of Education," who insists that he has better things to do with the state's money. Barker's urge was to provide an "educational basis" for a paradigmatic theatre which would justify its existence, or rather make its existence essential, in any society concerned with its own emotional and psychic health. The theatre should be a great teaching force for the nation, as well as a depository of its dramatic culture and a seminary for its future practitioners.

But it would have a teaching responsibility to its actors too. How can we explain "the undoubted impoverishment of English acting," Barker asked, "in the presence of as undoubted an enrichment of English drama?" The answer is simple: "the present lot of English-speaking actors do not know their business" because they have not been properly trained. Acting "has fallen to dullness; a quite unforgivable sin. . . . the art of acting was the beginning of drama. Before ever the literary man and his manuscript appeared acting was there" (82–3). The long run kills the vitality of playing, but more than repertory is needed to revive it. The actor must be trained like any artist, and trained vigorously; so Barker again insisted on a school as an integral component of the national theatre. But this dramatic training college would teach more than acting and stagecraft. Its chief responsibility would be to provide a liberal background for young actors, who otherwise might be denied the chance to learn anything of the larger world in a systematic way. Though actors must learn their craft, they must also study life off the stage if they are to portray living people on it.

The proposals for the architecture of the theatre were a departure from the past as well. Where the Blue Book assumed a single, conventional auditorium, *The Exemplary Theatre* insisted on two unconventional ones. Two houses allow more performances, of course, and permit the retention of a larger company, but Barker was mainly interested in greater dramatic flexibility. The two theatres would provide not only "the picture stage, but a platform with footlights abolished and suitable entrances for Elizabethan plays." For Greek drama, the second house must be able to convert "part of the stalls into an arena for a Greek chorus" (204). He also asked for a removable proscenium that could be lifted into the flies, and for provisions for performing in daylight (206) – a wonderfully radical notion. Set decoration, especially for Shakespeare, must be kept simple and never distract attention from the text or from the actors (201). To encourage a sense of community in the audience, the seats should be arranged in a horseshoe shape so that spectators never quite lose consciousness of each other: "the relations of the spectators among themselves are part of their united good relations to the play," and people should feel free to turn around to strangers and speak without restraint (202). As the playhouses must be flexible, so the choice of plays must be inclusive. A library stocks all authors, an exemplary theatre presents all drama, including the whole of Shakespeare (258). "The business of any true theatre is . . . to build up a library of living drama" (262).

The Exemplary Theatre is a significant book that seriously influenced thinking on the national theatre question, even if, as usual, it had no immediate practical effect. However, Barker's highmindedness and insistence on an educational basis disturbed many readers. His old collaborator Archer, a great defender of popular drama, thought the character of the Man of the Theatre "too resolutely high-browed," though admitting he had read only the first chapter (British Library). In fact there is something dry about the book that interferes with its persuasiveness. Purdom says that Barker considered it his most important work (199), though I can find no justification for the assertion; most evidence suggests that he did not much care for it. He wrote Shaw that "the form is damnable," mainly because he began it in 1914 "as a short pot-boiler," then after the war "discovered that the theatre I had nicely outlined would be no sort of use" (Texas). In 1937 he told Frank Sidgwick that "it is a pretty poor book – though there is sense in it" (Bodleian). It could be that Barker's departure from the theatre, still new when he completed the work, lent a detached tone.

Detachment may have affected him as a dramatist as well. The two plays of his retirement are often thought to smell of the lamp, an ironic condition for a man who learned his dramaturgy on the stage from the bottom up. Barker's plays had always been labelled intellectual, but *The Secret Life* (1923) is much more subtle than any of his earlier published work. The title is the clue to the chief difficulty: it is obsessed with the inner life of its characters and the action is therefore covertly dramatized. Barker apparently did not expect it to be performed. Archer wrote him that "in this play you seem to be drifting away from, not towards, the theatre that is understanded [*sic*] by the people – even the fairly intelligent people" (British Library). *His Majesty*, started in 1923 but not completed and published until 1928, is more conventionally playable, but its scale and length present major theatrical challenges. Neither of the two late plays has yet been professionally produced.

The standard interpretation is that Barker had lost touch with his theatrical instincts or was frankly writing closet drama: the opinion of both John Russell Taylor (114–15) and Allardyce Nicoll (393). A more likely assessment is that he was frankly writing for the national theatre to be. He knew the difficulties in the way of performing *The Secret Life*; his reply to Archer insisted that the problem was not with the play, but rather that "there is no English company of actors so trained to interpret thought and the less crude emotions, nor, as a consequence, any selected audience interested in watching and listening to such things" (British Library). The difficulties would be overcome, in other words, by the kind of theatrical system the two men had spent their lives fighting for. "The Heritage of the Actor," an article that posits a new kind of subtle acting based on mood instead of overt action, was originally intended as a preface to the play. (It became too long to be included: Salmon 271.) Read *The Secret Life* as "an orchestral symphony," he advised Ervine (Texas); plays like it can serve "to set actors new problems and to widen the theatre's appeal. It needs widening."

The subtle theme, the introverted protagonist, the use of recurring images and indirect dialogue would require a long, intimate rehearsal time and a slow, sympathetic process of development – the kind of treatment Stanislavsky could give to Chekhov, or that Barker would have given as a director had he been free of the usual pressures of production. When he visited Moscow in 1914, Barker was overwhelmed by Stanislavsky's ability to rehearse a work until it was ready, heedless of production schedules. "I have postponed a play a bare week and my business manager has nearly wept at the cost and the complication," he remembered ("At the MAT" 659–60). He praised those long, careful rehearsals in his graduation address to the American Academy of Dramatic Arts in 1915 (reported in NY *Telegraph* 20 Mar. 1915). As he recognized in *The Exemplary Theatre*, it was Stanislavsky's unhurried rehearsals that created the characteristic emphasis on subtle, psychological portrayal.

His Majesty was licensed on 26 March 1927 for performance at the Theatre Royal, Brighton (Nicoll 682), but was not produced, and it is possible that Barker prevented it for the same type of reasons. In 1933 Harcourt Williams proposed a production at the Old Vic; though Barker was willing, he felt it unlikely that the play could be adequately cast. "It would be pleasant to find myself working with you," he wrote, "but I have held it back, and shall, from every other rut of chance" (Purdom 240). These two plays, then, whatever their successes or failures, can be considered as unusual further arguments from Barker's pen for the necessity of a national theatre.

The living dream

The last major development in the plot occurred in 1930 when Sidgwick and Jackson published a short book entitled *A National Theatre*. Archer, who died in 1924, had talked about revising the Blue Book, but in the end Barker was left to do the job alone. The new version is the most readable and most cogent of his many attempts at the subject, and its effect on public opinion, according to Geoffrey Whitworth, was "prompt and permanent" (181). It brought the *Scheme and Estimates* up to date in matters of finance, though it retained the basic philosophy and proposals. The two houses of *The Exemplary Theatre* were discussed in more detail, with sample plans included, drawn by W.L. Somerville, who had won a competition sponsored earlier by the British Drama League. They show two proscenium theatres with seating in modified Greek arenas (the "Bayreuth plan"), holding 1,800 and 1,000 spectators. Barker even included a third small theatre or studio, seating a few hundred, "for student performances and for very experimental plays" (52, where the idea is credited to H.M. Harwood).

In the past he had insisted on a dramatic training college as part of the national theatre, but now he was able to abandon that proposal since "several schools of reputation" had been established in London. He suggested an agreement through which some of them would provide advanced students for small roles and as understudies; the theatre in turn would provide opportunities for graduates to join the company (112). Thirty years of thought and experience had dictated changes in the size of the company as well, now much larger than before: seventy-one men and thirty women, though many of them would be apprentices. The large company was necessary for a large repertory; idealistic as ever, Barker suggested a profligate forty-five to fifty plays a year, figures no modern English troupe has been able to match. But repertory was not only the distinguishing mark of this theatre, it was to be its moral character. "With a repertory theatre, constantly changing its bill," he wrote, "it is the theatre itself that we get into the habit of visiting" (50).

Perhaps the most significant difference in this version is the proposed method of funding. The estimate for the site, construction, and initial operating costs had leapt from the £330,000 of 1904 to £1,000,000 in 1930. Raising that by private subscription "would be a pretty formidable task," and it could not be expected that the government would put "such an item nakedly" in the budget either. The way out was to take a portion of the BBC radio license fees and vest them for a national theatre, and ultimately for a national opera as well, instead of putting all the money in the general fund. In the few years the BBC had been operating, those profits averaged about £400,000 annually, certainly a large enough sum for the task (30–4). A generation of disappointment over rich men's largesse, then, made Barker see the fiscal future in public money. The time for state subsidy in England had not arrived, yet he was optimistic enough to end his preface with the ultimate hope: "it really looks as if the National Theatre were on its way" (xvi). They are sad words, evoking an entire life of waiting. It was on its way, yes, but slowly, slowly: another forty-six years, almost another life.

A National Theatre is a book that seems amazingly prescient. The British National Theatre as finally built contains three houses roughly equivalent to Barker's (the Olivier Theatre holds only 1,160, about two-thirds the number he recommended, but the Lyttleton seats 890, and the Cottesloe, with a variable audience arrangement, between 100 and 400). His preference for a site on the South Bank is not far from where the new building now stands. And his sample repertory, emphasizing Shakespeare (eight or ten productions a year), classic English plays, and new works (a dozen or more a year), anticipates the selections made by the National Theatre Company since 1976. But Barker was less prescient than simply right: a lifetime of work and thought brought him to conclusions not only profound but almost inescapable. It is no occasion for wonder that others deep in the work of the stage should have built and run a real institution according to the designs of his dream.

Though he spent most of the rest of his life quietly, writing about Shakespeare and translating Spanish plays with his wife, he never abandoned the dream. The translations were of relatively lightweight comedies, by Gregorio Martinez Sierra and by the prolific brothers, Serafin and Joaquin Alvarez Quintero; yet even here Barker worked with some direction. The popularity of these writers in Spain was a sign that a healthy dramatic culture could exist when the theatre was in the hands of gifted playwrights, who truly understood the people, rather than commercial managers who guessed at what the public wanted for the sake of profit (Martinez Sierra vii–viii). Barker came to see the struggle against commerce in the theatre in larger terms, as part of a general condition in a changing world. In a speech to the Society of Authors in 1931, for example, he extended his case to literature as a whole. Publishers can no longer afford to print books that sell a hundred copies in one year and fifty in the next, a dangerous condition for new writers interested in quality and experiment. He suggested a private "endowment fund for the

41   Harley and Helen Granville Barker in front of the Alvarez Quintero fountain, Seville, 1927. A postcard sent to his publisher, Frank Sidgwick. Barker jokingly identifies two passers-by as "?Serafin" and "?Joaquin." The message on the reverse notes that the empty shelves in the fountain are for the works of the dramatists: "with a dishonest public, how good for the publishers!"

subsidy of important work which cannot expect to make an immediate or popular appeal" ("Help" 56–7).

On a few occasions he was tempted back into the theatre: for revivals of his own plays, for *King Lear* in 1940. Of these instances, the most revealing occurred in 1934 when Harcourt Williams, after trying for *His Majesty*, got him to agree to a production of *The Voysey Inheritance* at Sadler's Wells. Barker revised the text and assisted at rehearsals. Though the performance was decently received, it did not palliate his dissatisfaction, as a subsequent letter to Williams reveals: "Well, there it is! another ploughing of the sands – and I fear not worth the trouble and fatigue it was to us all. Things have not changed in 40 years. For our sort of play and our sort of attitude to the theatre – yours and mine – *real* repertory and a permanent company are the only solution" (Purdom 242–3).

Much of what he wrote and did for the remainder of his life is singed by disappointment, though it would be wrong to imply, as Purdom does, that he considered his later career a failure. He left the theatre because its conditions were antagonistic to his genius, and he became less and less willing to compromise his ideals. When the SMNT gathered enough momentum in 1937 to think its appeal would succeed, Barker was invited to become the first director of that version of the national theatre. He refused, however, principally because he insisted that two houses were essential and the committee, for reasons of economy and practicality of site, proposed only one (Whitworth 203–4).

In 1943 the Barkers were convalescing in Arizona – neither had been well, and they spent most of the war years in America – when Lord Esher asked for a letter favoring the amalgamation of the SMNT committee with the governors of the Old Vic. Barker replied that the idea was unwise. What was needed now, as always, was a new theatre, untrammeled by what he called the "third-rate" traditions of the Old Vic or Stratford, and "above all you must have your two auditoriums and be perfectly prepared to argue for three." Old Vic productions might be preparatory to a national theatre but not part of it, and his insistence on quality was unbending: "I personally would not give a straw for a National Theatre which did not set out to be *better* (just that) than the theatre round the corner" (Purdom 269–70). When he returned to England in May 1945 he was asked to be chairman of this very amalgamation: for forty years he had remained the prime candidate for the same job. But he was seriously ill and, philosophic disagreements aside, had to refuse.

So the drama ends. The year of Barker's death, the year after the war, the political and social climate suddenly changed and the London County Council presented a new site on the South Bank. The National Theatre Bill passed through Parliament in 1949, and in 1951 Queen Elizabeth (now the Queen Mother) laid a foundation stone next to the Festival Hall. Not until 1963 was a company performing under the magic name – ironically for Barker, at the Old Vic – and Great Britain would wait until 1976 for the much-delayed building that Archer and Barker had known to be essential seventy-four years before. By then the capital had two major subsidized companies, and one of them was maintaining two houses in Stratford as well as two in London.

Barker went to a French grave, his tombstone blank save for his name and dates, self-exiled from his land and its theatre: in his lifetime the dream had been dust in the wind. Yet he had been the most important single force in the movement, and without his work, on the stage and on the page, and behind the scenes as well, the country would have waited even longer. He was a visionary who came too early for public subsidy. In his half-century the theatre was still seen as an industry – and most industries in Britain were not nationalized until 1946.

The theatre, as Barker said himself ("Theatre: Next Phase" 635), is "a democratic and a rather vulgar art." It has always suffered from a two-edged purpose, to uplift and to entertain. Because it entertains it can make money; when it makes a lot of money, its other purpose is easily neglected. But it survives in an age of electronic competition for reasons that Barker also understood: not because it entertains better, but because "it satisfies some emotional hunger" that is not satisfied by other forms, like "the new mechanical drama of the Movie and the Talkie" (preface to Housman's *Little Plays* viii). "Uplift" is a poor word for the perennial virtue of dramatic art, which might be defined as a connecting of human minds previously separate. To join the unjoined, to enfranchise the disaffected in spirit, surely these are ends that most societies would consider admirable. The best theatre has a social benefit that easily outweighs its cost, yet it has taken a very long time for English-speaking countries to acknowledge this by public funding, and the struggle is far from over. Granville Barker's ultimate contribution may be that he persistently held to his creed. His dream of theatre was a dream to change what drove him out of the theatre. Through a broken career, in a broken world, his life was a testament to the importance of the stage: not so much a great refusal as a great and joyful affirmation of the social value of art.

Wren's memorial in St Paul's reads *si monumentum requiris, circumspice*. The real National Theatre on the South Bank owes Barker a great debt, and such a plaque would not be out of place in the lobby, dedicated to its dream-architect. But playwrights and directors, especially dreamers, do not require concrete monuments. The National's production of *The Madras House* in 1977, the centenary of Barker's birth, was a more appropriate memorial. So also were productions of *Waste* in 1985, and of *Ann Leete* a decade earlier, by the Royal Shakespeare Company, Britain's second national theatre. Other such payments would be an adequate epitaph.

Appendix: Granville Barker's productions

A few productions not directed by GB are included here [enclosed in square brackets], when they were presented under his management or on multiple bills with his work. Unless specified, the Shaw plays were jointly directed by GB and the dramatist: see chapter 4 for details. Matinees and evening performances are distinguished when the information is significant, and very short runs (usually for private societies) are indicated with the total number of performances. When GB acted in his own productions, his roles are noted (in parenthesis) after the title. The theatre season begins each September and continues through the following summer; thus in the 1904–5 season, 1 Nov. was in 1904 and 2 May in 1905. Two lists contained in Purdom, giving GB's acting roles and his productions, are incomplete and occasionally inaccurate. Full details of venues, casts, and lengths of runs are contained in Wearing for most of these productions.

Season & Date	Author	Play	Theatre and management
1899–1900			
29 Apr.	Fiona MacLeod	The House of Usna	Globe (Stage Society 1 perf.)
	Maeterlinck	Interior and	
		The Death of Tintagiles	
1900–1			
22 Mar.	Zangwill	The Revolted Daughter	Comedy (J.T. Grein 1 mat.)
29 Mar.	Shaw	The Man of Destiny (Napoleon)	Comedy (1 mat.)
1901–2			
26 Jan.	GB	The Marrying of Ann Leete	Royalty (Stage Society 2 perfs.)
1902–3			
7 June	S.M. Fox	The Waters of Bitterness	Imperial (Stage Society 2 perfs.)
	[Ian Robertson]	The Golden Rose, dir. Robertson]	
	Shaw	The Admirable Bashville	
1903–4			
31 Jan.	Brieux	The Philanthropists	King's Hall (Stage Society 2 perfs.)
8 Apr.	Shakespeare	The Two Gentlemen of Verona (Speed)	Court (J.H. Leigh)
26 Apr.	Shaw	Candida (Marchbanks)	Court (J.H. Leigh 6 mats.)
26 May	Euripides–Murray	Hippolytus (Henchman)	Lyric (New Century 4 mats.)
26 June	Yeats	Where There Is Nothing	Court (Stage Society 3 perfs.)
12 July	"George Paston"	The Pharisee's Wife	Duke of York's (1 mat.)
1904–5			
18 Oct.	Euripides–Murray	Hippolytus (Henchman)	Court (Vedrenne–Barker mats.)
1 Nov.	Shaw	John Bull's Other Island (Keegan)	mats.
		[revived 7 Feb. for mats. and again 1 May for eves.]	
15 Nov.	Maeterlinck	Aglavaine and Selysette	mats.

Date	Author	Play	
29 Nov.	Shaw	Candida (Marchbanks)	mats.
	[revived 22 May for eves.]		
23 Dec.	Housman & GB	Prunella (Pierrot)	eves.
28 Feb.	Yeats	The Pot of Broth	mats.
	Schnitzler	In the Hospital	
	Shaw	How He Lied to Her Husband (Lover)	
21 Mar.	Hauptmann	The Thieves' Comedy	mats.
11 Apr.	Euripides–Murray	The Trojan Women	mats.
2 May	Shaw	You Never Can Tell (Valentine)	mats.
	[revived 12 June for eves.]		
23 May	Shaw	Man and Superman (Tanner)	mats.
	[privately performed on 21–2 May for Stage Society]		
1905–6			
11 Sept.	Shaw	John Bull's Other Island (Keegan)	eves.
26 Sept.	St John Hankin	The Return of the Prodigal	mats.
12 Oct.	Ibsen	The Wild Duck (Hjalmar)	mats.
23 Oct.	Shaw	Man and Superman (Tanner)	eves.
7 Nov.	GB	The Voysey Inheritance	mats.
	[revived 12 Feb. for eves. with GB as Edward]		
28 Nov.	Shaw	Major Barbara (Cusins)	mats.
	[revived 1 Jan. for eves. and 13 Feb. for mats. without GB in cast]		
16 Jan.	Euripides–Murray	Electra	mats.
	[revived 12 Mar. for eves.]		
6 Feb.	Robt. Harcourt	A Question of Age	2 mats.
	Frederick Fenn	The Convict on the Hearth	
27 Feb.	Maurice Hewlett	Pan and the Young Shepherd and	mats.
		The Youngest of the Angels	
20 Mar.	Shaw	Captain Brassbound's Conversion	mats.
	[revived 16 Apr. for eves.]		
26 Mar.	Euripides–Murray	Hippolytus (Henchman)	eves.
24 Apr.	Housman & GB	Prunella	mats.
9 July	Shaw	You Never Can Tell	eves.

Season & Date	Author	Play	Theatre and management
1906–7			
17 Sept.	Shaw	John Bull's Other Island	eves.
25 Sept.	Galsworthy	The Silver Box	mats.
	[revived 8 Apr. for eves.]		
23 Oct.	St John Hankin	The Charity That Began at Home	mats.
29 Oct.	Shaw	Man and Superman (Tanner)	eves.
	[revived 27 May for eves. without GB in cast]		
20 Nov.	Shaw	The Doctor's Dilemma (Dubedat)	mats.
	[revived 31 Dec. for eves.]		
8 Jan.	Cyril Harcourt Masefield	The Reformer The Campden Wonder }	mats.
5 Feb.	Shaw	The Philanderer	mats.
11 Feb.	Shaw	You Never Can Tell (Valentine)	eves.
5 Mar.	Ibsen	Hedda Gabler	mats.
9 Apr.	Elizabeth Robins	Votes for Women!	mats.
	[revived 11 May for eves.]		
29 Apr.	St John Hankin	The Return of the Prodigal	eves.
7 May	Housman & GB	Prunella	mats.
4 June	Shaw	Don Juan in Hell and The Man of Destiny }	mats.
1907–8			
16 Sept.	Shaw	You Never Can Tell	Savoy (Vedrenne–Barker eves.)
24 Sept.	Galsworthy	Joy	mats.
14 Oct.	Shaw	The Devil's Disciple (Burgoyne)	eves.
	[transferred to Queen's, with GB as Dudgeon]		
22 Oct.	Euripides–Murray	Medea	mats.
24 Nov.	GB	Waste (Trebell)	Imperial (Stage Society 2 perfs.)

Date	Author	Play	Venue
25 Nov.	[Shaw	*Caesar and Cleopatra*, dir. Forbes Robertson]	Savoy (Vedrenne–Barker eves.)
30 Dec.	Shaw	*Arms and the Man* (Sergius)	eves.
12 May	Frederick Fenn	*The Convict on the Hearth*	
	[Shaw	*Getting Married*, dir. Shaw]	Haymarket (Vedrenne–Barker & F. Harrison)
24 May	Masefield	*The Tragedy of Nan*	
	"George Paston"	*Feed the Brute*	
	[transferred to Haymarket by Vedrenne–Barker & Harrison]		Royalty (Pioneers 5 perfs.)
16 June	Housman	*The Chinese Lantern*	Haymarket (V–B & Harrison mats.)
1908–9			
9 Mar.	Galsworthy	*Strife*	Duke of York's (Charles Frohman)
	[transferred to Haymarket and to Adelphi]		
1909–10			
21 Feb.	Galsworthy	*Justice*	Duke of York's Repertory (Frohman)
23 Feb.	[Shaw	*Misalliance*, dir. Shaw	
1 Mar.	Meredith	*The Sentimentalists*	
	[Barrie	*Old Friends* and *The Twelve Pound Look*, dir. Boucicault]	
9 Mar.	GB	*The Madras House*	
13 Apr.	Housman & GB	*Prunella*	
	[Barrie	*The Twelve Pound Look*]	
3 May	Hope & Lennox	*Helena's Path*	
	[Barrie	*The Twelve Pound Look*]	
1910–11			
10 Oct.	Jensen–Masefield	*The Witch*	Royalty, Glasgow (Glasgow Rep.)
31 Jan.	Jensen–Masefield	*The Witch*	Court (Lillah McCarthy's Mats.)
6 Feb.	Schnitzler–GB	Three dialogues from *Anatol* (Anatol)	Palace (one each week for 3 weeks)
21 Feb.	Masefield	*The Tragedy of Nan*	Court (Lillah McCarthy 4 mats.)
	GB	*Rococo*	

Season & Date	Author	Play	Theatre and management
11 Mar.	Schnitzler–GB	Anatol (Anatol)	Little (McCarthy–Barker)
28 Mar.	Ibsen	The Master Builder	eves.
19 Apr.	[Shaw	Fanny's First Play, dir. Shaw]	
	[to 29 Dec. 1911, then transferred to Kingsway: eves. to 10 Sept. 1912, mats. to 20 Dec. 1912]		
16 May	Masefield	The Tragedy of Nan	Little (McCarthy–Barker mats.)
1911–12			
23 Sept.	Peacock & Fraser-Simson	Bonita	Queen's
3 Oct.	Barrie	The Twelve Pound Look	
	GB	Rococo	Little (McCarthy–Barker mats.)
	Meredith	The Sentimentalists	
22 Feb.	Phillpotts	The Secret Woman	Kingsway (McCarthy–Barker 2 mats.) mats.
19 Mar.	Euripides–Murray	Iphigenia in Tauris	
	[on 4 June: 1 mat. at His Majesty's. on 11 June: 3 mats. at Bradfield College with GB as Orestes]		
1912–13			
7 Sept.	GB	The Voysey Inheritance	Kingsway (McCarthy–Barker eves.)
21 Sept.	Shakespeare	The Winter's Tale	Savoy (McCarthy–Barker)
15 Nov.	Shakespeare	Twelfth Night	Kingsway (McCarthy–Barker)
23 Nov.	Galsworthy	The Eldest Son	
26 Dec.	[Shaw	John Bull's Other Island, dir. Shaw]	
25 Mar.	Bennett [until 7 Nov. 1914]	The Great Adventure	
1913–14			
1 Sept.	Shaw	Androcles and the Lion	St James's (McCarthy–Barker)
	Calthrop–GB	The Harlequinade	

Date	Author	Title	Theatre
29 Oct.	Jensen–Masefield	The Witch	St James's Repertory (McCarthy–Barker)
1 Dec.	Ibsen	The Wild Duck	
2 Dec.	Molière	Le Mariage Forcé ⎫	
2 Dec.	Masefield	The Tragedy of Nan ⎬	
6 Dec.	Shaw	The Doctor's Dilemma ⎭	
17 Dec.	Galsworthy	The Silver Box ⎫	
17 Dec.	Maeterlinck	The Death of Tintagiles ⎬	
		[the above 5 bills were continued in rep at the Savoy in Jan.]	
6 Feb.	Shakespeare	A Midsummer Night's Dream	Savoy (McCarthy–Barker)
1914–15			
5 Nov.	Masefield	Philip the King	Covent Garden (Arts Fund 1 mat.)
25 Nov.	Hardy–GB	The Dynasts	Kingsway (McCarthy–Barker)
27 Jan.	Shaw	Androcles and the Lion	Wallack's, New York (repertory)
27 Jan.	France	The Man Who Married a Dumb Wife ⎫	
16 Feb.	Shakespeare	A Midsummer Night's Dream ⎬	
25 Feb.	Shaw	The Doctor's Dilemma ⎭	
15 May	Euripides–Murray	Iphigenia in Tauris	Yale Bowl (McCarthy–Barker)
		[then at Harvard Stadium on 18 May, Piping Rock Country Club on Long Island about 25 May, the College of the City of New York on 31 May & 5 June, the Univ. of Pennsylvania on 8 June, and Princeton Univ. on 11 June]	
19 May	Euripides–Murray	The Trojan Women	Harvard Stadium (McCarthy–Barker)
		[then at CCNY on 29 May & 2 June, Pennsylvania on 9 June, and Princeton on 12 June]	
1920–1			
16 Sept.	Martinez Sierra–GB	The Romantic Young Lady	Royalty
8 Jan.	Maeterlinck	The Betrothal	Gaiety
1921–2			
2 Nov.	Guitry–GB	Deburau	Ambassador's
1925–6			
30 Nov.	GB	The Madras House, rev. vers.	Ambassador's

Season & Date	Author	Play	Theatre and management
1927–8 26 Oct.	Martinez Sierra–GB	*The Kingdom of God*	Strand
1933–4 3 May	GB	*The Voysey Inheritance*, rev. vers. [dir. with Harcourt Williams]	Sadler's Wells
1936–7 1 Dec.	GB	*Waste*, rev. vers. [dir. with Michael MacOwan]	Westminster
1939–40 15 Apr.	Shakespeare	*King Lear* [dir. with Lewis Casson]	Old Vic

Notes

1: Dreaming a theatre

1. Purdom was lent or given most of Barker's prewar papers by Lillah McCarthy, which Barker had apparently abandoned at the time of their divorce. When she died, Purdom kept them, and a great amount of valuable material was ultimately sold at Sotheby's by the biographer's estate in 1965. Some of the material that Purdom used has disappeared, though new documents have come to light. Of chief interest to my work are the promptbooks; he wrote G.B. Harrison in 1956 that he had those of *Twelfth Night* and *A Midsummer Night's Dream* (which Harrison acquired for the University of Michigan and which have been available for some time), *The Madras House*, the American production of *The Trojan Women*, and *Strife*. My searches have brought up all of these but *Madras*, and a few more, detailed in the list of References which follows. Perhaps Purdom was not entirely at fault for the condition of the biography; he told Harrison in the same letter (Michigan) that because of the small interest in Barker in England, his publisher forced him to cut 40,000 words from the text.

2: Creating the New Drama

1. Of Shaw's plays only *Arms and the Man* had a regular run in London, at the Avenue Theatre in 1894, directed by the playwright. The rest were seen briefly in matinees and private performances, as detailed in chapter 1. I have omitted mention of suburban, provincial, and foreign productions, which were growing in number and importance. Mander and Mitchenson's *Theatrical Companion* lists reasonably accurate information on the stage history.

2. This is Desmond MacCarthy's imaginative calculation, derived by counting each one-act play as a separate performance, even though it was given on a double or triple bill. Thus *Don Juan in Hell* and *The Man of Destiny*, for example, which were presented together for eight matinees in June 1907, are considered by MacCarthy to total sixteen performances. To be precise, only 946 performances were actually given by Vedrenne–Barker at the Court, not 988. But MacCarthy's number has stuck. (The first six matinees of *Candida*, sponsored by J.H. Leigh, are not included in the figures.)

3. Box office statements from Vedrenne, dated 3 February, 19 and 26 March, 2 and 8 April 1906, in the Gilbert Murray Papers, Bodleian. The figures for the original matinees of *Hippolytus* in 1904 have not survived, but in 1906 the evening performances averaged about £25 each.

3: The Court productions

1. Noticed by three reviewers: *Daily Telegraph* 19 Oct. 1904:11; *Sunday Times* 23 Oct. 1904:5; and *Observer* of same date:6. But the number of men on the stage had been reduced by seven, as discussed later in this chapter; GB was therefore making some attempt to accommodate to the smaller stage.

2. At least this is what he proposed in a letter to Murray of 14 Dec. 1905 (Bodleian). I

have found no proof that it was actually accomplished. Murray's stage direction simply says that the vision of Castor and Polyderces "appears in the air" (*Electra* 80).

3. *Prunella* does bear similarities to *The Harlequinade*, a collaboration with Dion Clayton Calthrop, produced in 1913. But as we will see in chapter 9, GB did not really participate in the composition of that play; his name was on the title page for reasons other than writing.

4: Shaw's natural son

1. Bernard Dukore has given an account of Shaw's general technique as a director in what is an excellent compendium of his relationship to the practical theatre. Admirably researched, *Bernard Shaw, Director* demonstrates the modernity of Shaw's methods as well as his large understanding of theatrical art. A reader might legitimately wish, however, that Dukore had reconstructed a specific production or two and dealt with them individually. By gathering evidence from many sources, the book tends to suggest that Shaw's directing entered the world full-grown and never changed. In fact, at the Court Shaw gradually developed a director's skill that grew as he grew as a playwright, and Barker's role in that development was a large one.

5: The man of affairs

1. Hynes has a valuable chapter on general censorship and morality in the period, as well as a chapter on the Lord Chamberlain. Other treatments include an Edwardian book by John Palmer, and one by Frank Fowell and Frank Palmer. A 1967 survey by Richard Findlater was published as the controversy flared up again, before the licensing of plays was finally abolished.

6: The limits of naturalism

1. The interconnections of *Misalliance* and *Madras* went further. Barker, overwhelmed with directing duties, had yet to complete his third act as the date of production approached. Shaw did it for him, with a meeting between Constantine and Miss Yates – renamed Miss Knagg – in which she rejects his offers of assistance on stage. Barker was "infuriated," according to Shaw, and "finished the act in his own way at once." The MS of Shaw's mock ending is at Texas, and was first published by Dukore in "*The Madras House* Prefinished." It has since been reprinted in Shaw's *Plays* 7:609–12.

2. Lillah McCarthy recorded Barker's notes after the dress rehearsal of *Oedipus* on 11 January 1912 in her copy of the play, which has survived, and is now also at Texas. The suggestions are very specific, often asking the actress to pull back from overstated emotion. Purdom prints a selection from the notes (130–1); as usual he makes a number of errors in transcription, but the gist is correct.

7: Shakespeare alive

1. The costume details for Time, and for other characters in the Shakespeare productions, are taken from the records in the Account Book, now in the British Theatre Association library. Some of the original designs for *Winter's Tale* are beautifully reproduced in color in Ruthertson's *Sixteen Designs for the Theatre*, which includes the sketch for Time. Bartholomeusz (163) prints a photograph of Herbert Heweston in the role, hanging on to the drop curtain, as well as other valuable production shots that space prevents me from using.

2, Bartholomeusz (139) worries over the confusion regarding the omissions in *Winter's*

Tale: Purdom (139) says six lines were cut; Styan (*Shakespeare Revolution* 87) says three cuts were made, adding up to eleven lines; *The Sunday Times* (15 Sept. 1912) reported fifteen lines would be missing. This is an unnecessary confusion, for the Heinemann acting edition that Barker prepared clearly indicates the excisions. Five spots were affected, totaling about fifteen lines, three from the verse of 1.2 and two from the prose of 4.4. The only cut of the slightest significance occurred at 1.2.201–6 (Arden edition), where one of Leontes' vulgar sexual images was omitted.

3. See Alan Bowness's introduction to *Post-Impressionism* 9. Desmond MacCarthy discusses the naming of the exhibition in "Roger Fry," *Memories* (London: MacGibbon & Kee, 1953), 181.

8: A wide-awake dream

1. The color pictures are from *ILN* 11 Apr. 1914, supp. 602–3, and are captioned "Untouched Instantaneous Photographs Specially taken for 'The Illustrated London News' by the Polychromide Process at the Dover Street Studios." They include the two of Oberon and Titania used here as the frontispiece, and were taken in front of studio backdrops, not the set. The shades generally match the descriptions in reviews and in the Account Book. The large two-page spread shows the Lion, Puck, and some of the lesser fairies as well.

9: Opening the stage

1. A letter to Maurice Browne of 24 Oct. 1915 (at Michigan), written when Barker was back in America for lecturing, lists the material he had in the country at his disposal: the entire *Dream* production; the costumes and hangings for *Philip the King*; the set of *Le Mariage Forcé*; the costumes and props for the two Greek plays (the huge set went to Yale); and the entire *Doctor's Dilemma*, the set of which had been newly built for Wallack's. *Androcles* and *Dumb Wife* were still on tour at the time.

2. The details of the costumes are primarily derived from Smith (411–14), whose article was written before the close of the Greek tour, and who seems the most trustworthy of the contemporary reviewers. A number of Wilkinson's designs are reproduced in it, along with helpful photos. Many pictures of *Trojan Women* are in *Theatre* July 1915:12–13.

10: Ploughing the sands: the dream of a national theatre

1. "Transcription of a speech made by Granville Barker at the St James's Theatre on Wednesday, December 17th," single page handbill, 1913. A copy is in BL, pressmark 1865.c.3; another is at Texas. I have parenthetically inserted the audience's responses based on reports in *The Standard* (18 Dec. 1913:10) and *The Times* (same date:10). Portions of the speech are quoted by Purdom (148), who adds that Barker talked too long and "without the necessary enthusiasm," but the newspaper accounts belie that judgment. Salmon (134–9) discusses the business details of the appeal.

References

Unless otherwise specified, the place of publication is London.

Manuscript sources and collections

a. Unpublished plays by Granville Barker

The Family of the Oldroyds (c. 1895–6), with Berte Thomas. British Library, London [BL].
The Weather-Hen (1897), with Berte Thomas. Lord Chamberlain's Plays, BL.
Our Visitor to "Work-a-Day" (1898–9), with Berte Thomas. BL.
Agnes Colander (1900–1). BL.
A Miracle (c. 1900). Lord Chamberlain's Plays, BL.

b. Promptbooks and theatrical records

Waste, Imperial Theatre, 1907. BL (c.116.g.11).
Strife, Duke of York's Theatre, 1909. Lincoln Center Library of Performing Arts, New York Public Library.
Twelfth Night, Savoy Theatre, 1912. Univ. of Michigan, Ann Arbor.
A Midsummer Night's Dream, Savoy Theatre, 1914. Michigan.
Account Book for Savoy and St James's seasons, 1912–14. British Theatre Association, London.
The Dynasts, Kingsway Theatre, 1914. Harvard Theatre Collection.
A Midsummer Night's Dream, Wallack's Theatre, New York, 1915. Harvard.
The Trojan Women, USA 1915. Humanities Research Center, Univ. of Texas at Austin.
Iphigenia in Tauris, with a separate promptbook for the Chorus, USA 1915. Texas.
King Lear, Old Vic, 1940: Hallam Fordham, "Player in Action: John Gielgud as King Lear," manuscript account with notes by Gielgud. Folger Shakespeare Library, Washington, DC.

c. Correspondence. The major collections referred to:

Berg Collection, New York Public Library: to various recipients.
Bodleian Library, Oxford: to Gilbert Murray (Gilbert Murray Papers); to and from Frank Sidgwick (Sidgwick & Jackson Papers).
British Library: to and from William Archer (Add. Mss 45290); to Bernard Shaw (Add. Mss 50534); to and from John Masefield (Add. Mss 47897).
Harvard Univ.: to George P. Baker.
Univ. of Michigan: to Maurice Browne and G.B. Harrison.
Univ. of Texas: to Shaw, Helen Huntington, and many others.
Yale Univ.: to Arnold Bennett, John Drinkwater, Murray and others.

d. Theatre collections

Theatre Museum, Victoria & Albert Museum, London: records of London theatres, scrapbooks, manuscripts, photographs, and some letters.
Lincoln Center: records of American productions.

Published works by Granville Barker

Anatol. See Schnitzler.
"At the Moscow Art Theatre," *Seven Arts* 2 (1917):659–61.
The Exemplary Theatre. Chatto & Windus, 1922.
Granville Barker and His Correspondents, ed. Eric Salmon. Detroit: Wayne State Univ. Press, expected 1985.
The Harlequinade. See Calthrop.
"Help for 'Unpopular' Literature," *The Author* 41.2 (1931):56–7.
"The Heritage of the Actor," *Quarterly Review* 140 (1923):53–73.
His Majesty. Sidgwick & Jackson, 1928.
The Madras House. Sidgwick & Jackson, 1911. Rev. vers. 1925.
More Prefaces to Shakespeare, ed. Edward M. Moore. Princeton: Princeton Univ. Press, 1974.
A National Theatre. Sidgwick & Jackson, 1930.
A National Theatre: Scheme and Estimates. See William Archer.
"Notes on Rehearsing a Play," *Drama* 1 (1919):2–5.
On Dramatic Method. Sidgwick & Jackson, 1931.
"On Translating Greek Tragedy," in *Essays in Honour of Gilbert Murray*, ed. J.A.K. Thomson and A.J. Toynbee. Allen & Unwin, 1936.
Preface to *A Midsummer Night's Dream: An Acting Edition*. Heinemann, 1914.
Preface to *Twelfth Night: An Acting Edition*. Heinemann, 1912.
Preface to *The Winter's Tale: An Acting Edition*. Heinemann, 1912.
Prefaces to *The Players Shakespeare*. 7 vols. Ernest Benn, 1923–7.
Prefaces to Shakespeare. 2 vols. Princeton: Princeton Univ. Press, 1946–7.
Prunella. See Housman.
The Red Cross in France. Hodder & Stoughton, 1916.
"Repertory Theatres," *The New Quarterly* 2 (1909):491–504.
The Secret Life. Sidgwick & Jackson, 1923.
"Shakespeare's Dramatic Art," in *A Companion to Shakespeare Studies*, ed. Barker and G.B. Harrison. Cambridge: Cambridge Univ. Press, 1934.
"Tennyson, Swinburne, Meredith – and the Theatre," in *The Eighteen-Seventies*, ed. Barker. Cambridge: Cambridge University Press, 1929.
"The Theatre: The Next Phase," *The English Review* 5 (1910):631–48.
Three Plays: The Marrying of Ann Leete, The Voysey Inheritance, The Madras House. Sidgwick & Jackson, 1909.
"Two German Theatres," *Fortnightly Review* 89 (1911):60–70.

Other published works

Archer, Charles. *William Archer*. New Haven: Yale Univ. Press, 1931.
[Archer, William.] *The Fashionable Tragedian: A Criticism*. Edinburgh: Thomas Gray, 1877.
Archer, William. *The Old Drama and the New*. Heinemann, 1923.
   "The Theatrical Situation," *Fortnightly Review* 88 (1910):736–50.

The Vedrenne–Barker Season, 1904–1905. Pamphlet printed for the Royal Court Theatre. London, 1905.

Archer, William, and Granville Barker. *A National Theatre: Scheme and Estimates.* Duckworth, 1907. Rpt. Port Washington, NY: Kennikat Press, 1970.

Armstrong, William A. "George Bernard Shaw: The Playwright as Producer," *Modern Drama* 8 (1966):347–61.

Aylmer, Felix. "The One That Got Away," *Drama* NS 86 (1967):31–3.

Babington Smith, Constance. *John Masefield: A Life.* Oxford: Oxford Univ. Press, 1978.

Bartholomeusz, Dennis. *The Winter's Tale in Performance in England and America, 1611–1976.* Cambridge: Cambridge Univ. Press, 1982.

Bennett, Arnold. *The Journals of Arnold Bennett,* ed. Newman Flower. 2 vols. Cassell, 1932.

   Letters of Arnold Bennett, ed. James Hepburn. 2 vols. Oxford: Oxford Univ. Press, 1968.

Berry, Ralph. "The Aesthetics of Beerbohm Tree's Shakespeare Festivals," *Nineteenth Century Theatre Research* 9 (1981):23–51.

Borsa, Mario. *The English Stage of Today,* trans. Selwyn Brinton. John Lane The Bodley Head, 1908.

Bowness, Alan (ed.). *Post-Impressionism.* Weidenfeld & Nicolson, 1979.

Braun, Edward. *The Director and the Stage.* Methuen, 1982.

   The Theatre of Meyerhold. New York: Drama Book Specialists, 1979.

Bridges-Adams, W. "Granville Barker and the Savoy," *Drama* NS 52 (1959):28–31.

   The Lost Leader. Sidgwick & Jackson, 1954.

Byrne, Muriel St Clare. "Fifty Years of Shakespearian Production: 1898–1948," *Shakespeare Survey* 2 (1949):1–20.

Casson, Lewis. "G.B.S. at Rehearsal," in Mander and Mitchenson, *Theatrical Companion* [which see].

   "Granville Barker, Shaw and the Court Theatre," in Mander and Mitchenson, *Theatrical Companion* [which see].

   "Harley Granville-Barker," *The Dictionary of National Biography, 1941–1950.* Oxford: Oxford Univ. Press, 1959.

Coffin, Hayden. *Hayden Coffin's Book.* Alston Rivers, 1930.

The Complimentary Dinner to Mr J.E. Vedrenne and Mr H. Granville Barker: A transcript of the proceedings. Copy in BL (010825.ff.50). Rpt. as appendix to Weintraub's edn of D. MacCarthy's *The Court Theatre.*

Cross, Colin. *The Liberals in Power.* Barrie & Rockliff, 1963.

Darlington, W.A. *Six Thousand and One Nights.* Harrap, 1960.

Dukes, Ashley. *Modern Dramatists.* Frank Palmer, 1911.

Dukore, Bernard F. *Bernard Shaw: Director.* Seattle: Univ. of Washington Press, 1971.

   "*The Madras House* Prefinished," *Educational Theatre Journal* 24 (1972):135–8.

Eaton, Walter Prichard. *Plays and Players.* Cincinnati: Steward & Kidd, 1916.

Edel, Leon. *Henry James: The Middle Years.* Philadelphia: J.B. Lippincott, 1962.

Elberson, Stanley Denton. "The Nature of Harley Granville Barker's Productions in America in 1915." Dissertation, Univ. of Oregon, 1968.

Elsom, John, and Nicholas Tomalin. *The History of the National Theatre.* Cape, 1978.

Emmet, Alfred. "The Long Prehistory of the National Theatre," *Theatre Quarterly* 6.21 (1976):55–62.

Ervine, St John. *Bernard Shaw.* Constable, 1956.

Euripides. See Murray.

Findlater, Richard. *Banned! A Review of Theatrical Censorship in Britain.* MacGibbon & Kee, 1967.

Fordham, Hallam. See *King Lear* under Manuscript sources b.

Fowell, Frank, and Frank Palmer. *Censorship in England*. Frank Palmer, 1913.

Fuerst, Walter René, and Samuel J. Hume. *Twentieth-Century Stage Decoration*. 2 vols. New York: Knopf, 1929. Rpt. New York: Blom, 1969.

Galsworthy, John. *The Plays of John Galsworthy*. Duckworth, 1929.

Gielgud, John. *Gielgud: An Actor and His Time*. New York: Potter, 1980.

"Granville Barker's Shakespeare," *Theatre Arts* 31 (1947):49.

Stage Directions. Heinemann, 1963.

Glasstone, Victor. *Victorian and Edwardian Theatres*. Thames & Hudson, 1975.

Guitry, Sacha. *Deburau*, trans. Granville Barker. Heinemann, 1921.

Hankin, St John. "How to Run an Art Theatre in London," *Fortnightly Review* 88 (1907):814–18.

Henderson, Archibald. *Bernard Shaw: Playboy and Prophet*. New York: Appleton, 1932.

European Dramatists. Cincinnati: Steward & Kidd, 1913.

George Bernard Shaw: Man of the Century. New York: Appleton-Century-Crofts, 1956.

Housman, Lawrence. *Little Plays of St Francis*. Intro. by Granville Barker. Sidgwick & Jackson, 1922.

The Unexpected Years. Indianapolis: Bobbs-Merrill, 1936.

Housman, Lawrence, and Granville Barker. *Prunella: or Love in a Dutch Garden*. A.H. Bullen, 1906.

Howe, P.P. *The Repertory Theatre: A Record and a Criticism*. Martin Secker, 1910.

Hunt, Hugh. "Granville Barker's Shakespearean Productions," *Theatre Research* 10 (1969):44–9.

Hynes, Samuel. *The Edwardian Turn of Mind*. Princeton: Princeton Univ. Press, 1968.

Inkster, Leonard. "Shakespeare and Mr Granville Barker," *Poetry and Drama* 1 (1913):22–6.

Jackson, Anthony. "Harley Granville Barker as a Director at the Royal Court Theatre, 1904–1907," *Theatre Research* 12 (1972):126–38.

Kelly, Helen. "The Granville-Barker Shakespeare Productions. A Study Based on the Promptbooks." Dissertation, Univ. of Michigan, 1965.

Knight, G. Wilson. *Shakespearian Production*. Faber, 1964.

Loraine, Winifred. *Robert Loraine*. Collins, 1938.

MacCarthy, Desmond. *The Court Theatre 1904–1907*. A.H. Bullen, 1907. Rpt. Coral Gables, Florida: Univ. of Miami Press, 1966, ed. Stanley Weintraub. [References are to original edn.]

McCarthy, Lillah (Lady Keeble). *Myself and My Friends*. Thornton & Butterworth, 1933.

McDonald, Jan. "The Promised Land of the London Stage," *The Role of the Actor in the Theatrical Reform of the Late 19th and Early 20th Century*, ed. Milan Luke. Praha [Prague]: Univerzita Karlova Praha, 1976.

"New Actors for the New Drama," *Drama and the Actor*, ed. James Redmond (Themes in Drama 6). Cambridge: Cambridge Univ. Press, 1984.

MacKenzie, Norman and Jeanne. *The Fabians*. New York: Simon & Schuster, 1977.

MacLeod, Fiona (pseud. for William Sharp). *Poems and Dramas*. Heinemann, 1910.

Macleod, Joseph. *The Actor's Right to Act*. Lawrence & Wishart, 1981.

MacOwan, Michael. "Working with a Genius," *Plays and Players* July 1955:7.

Mander, Raymond, and Joe Mitchenson. *The Lost Theatres of London*. New York: Taplinger, 1968.

A Theatrical Companion to Shaw. Rockliff, 1954.

Marrot, H.V. *The Life and Letters of John Galsworthy*. New York: Scribner, 1936.

Marshall, Norman. *The Producer and the Play*. MacDonald, 1962.

Martinez Sierra, Gregorio. *The Kingdom of God and Other Plays*, trans. with intro. Harley and Helen Granville-Barker. Chatto & Windus, 1929.

Masefield, John. *The Tragedy of Nan and Other Plays*. New York: Mitchell Kennerly, 1912.

Matthews, A.E. *Matty*. Hutchinson, 1952.

Maude, Cyril. *The Haymarket Theatre*. Grant Richards, 1903.

Maurois, André. *The Edwardian Era*. New York: Appleton-Century, 1933.

Mazer, Cary M. "Actors or Gramophones: The Paradoxes of Granville Barker," *Theatre Journal* 36 (1984):5–23.

    Shakespeare Refashioned: Elizabethan Plays on Edwardian Stages. Ann Arbor: UMI Research Press, 1981.

    "Treasons, Stratagems, and Spoils: Edwardian Actor-Managers and the SMNT," *Theatre Survey* 24 (1983):1–33.

Meisel, Martin. *Shaw and the Nineteenth-Century Theatre*. Princeton: Princeton Univ. Press, 1963.

Milward, Jesse. *Myself and Others*. Hutchinson, 1923.

Moore, George. *Impressions and Opinions*. David Nutt, 1891.

Morgan, Margery M. *A Drama of Political Man: A Study in the Plays of Harley Granville Barker*. Sidgwick & Jackson, 1961.

    "Edwardian Feminism and the Drama: Shaw and Granville Barker," *Cahiers Victoriens et Edouardiens* 9–10 (1979):63–85.

    Intro. to *The Madras House* (ed. Morgan). Methuen, 1977.

    The Shavian Playground. Methuen, 1972.

Murray, Gilbert (trans.). *The Collected Plays of Euripides*. Allen & Unwin, 1954. [One vol. edn, each play separately paginated.]

Nesbitt, Cathleen. *A Little Love and Good Company*. Faber, 1975.

Nicoll, Allardyce. *English Drama 1900–1930*. Cambridge: Cambridge Univ. Press, 1973.

Odell, G.C.D. *Shakespeare from Betterton to Irving*. 2 vols., 1920; rpt. New York: Dover, 1966.

Orme, Michael (pseud. for Alix A. Grein). *J.T. Grein: The Story of a Pioneer 1862–1935*. J. Murray, 1936.

Palmer, John. *The Censor and the Theatres*. T. Fisher Unwin, 1912.

Pearson, Hesketh. *Bernard Shaw*. Collins, 1942.

    The Last Actor-Managers. Methuen, 1950.

    "The Origin of 'Androcles and the Lion,' " *The Listener* 48 (1952):803–4.

Pease, Edward R. *The History of the Fabian Society*. A.C. Fifield, 1916.

Pinero, A.W. *The Collected Letters of Sir Arthur Pinero*, ed. J.P. Wearing. Minneapolis: Univ. of Minnesota Press, 1974.

    Two Plays. Heinemann, 1930.

Priestley, J.B. *The Edwardians*. Sphere Books, 1972.

Purdom, C.B. *Harley Granville Barker*. Barrie & Rockliff, 1955. Rpt. Westport, Conn: Greenwood Press, 1971.

Report from the Joint Select Committee of the House of Lords and the House of Commons on the Stage Plays (Censorship). Parliamentary Papers 1909.214. H.M. Stationery Office, 1909.

Ritchie, Harry M. "Harley Granville Barker's *The Madras House* and the Sexual Revolution," *Modern Drama* 15 (1972–3):150–8.

Robins, Elizabeth. *The Convert*. Methuen, 1907. Rpt. Women's Press, 1980, ed. Jane Marcus.

    Theatre and Friendship: Some Henry James Letters. Cape, 1932.

    Votes for Women! Mills & Boon, n.d.

Robinson, Lennox. *Curtain Up*. Michael Joseph, 1942.

Rowell, George. *Theatre in the Age of Irving*. Oxford: Blackwell, 1981.

Rutherston, Albert [Albert Rothenstein]. "Decoration in the Art of the Theatre," *The Monthly Chapbook* 1 (1919).

Sixteen Designs for the Theatre. Humphrey Milford, 1928.

St John, Christopher (ed.). *Ellen Terry and Bernard Shaw: A Correspondence*. New York: Putnam, 1931.

Salenius, Elmer W. *Harley Granville Barker*. Boston: Twayne, 1982.

Salmon, Eric. *Granville Barker: A Secret Life*. Heinemann, 1983.

Schnitzler, Arthur. *Anatol*, trans. Barker. Sidgwick & Jackson, 1911.

Scott, Dixon. "Granville Barker," *The Bookman* 44 (1914):153–62.

Sharp, Cecil. *A Midsummer Night's Dream: The Songs and Incidental Music* . . . Simkin, Marshall, Hamilton, Kent, 1914.

Shaw, G.B. *Bernard Shaw's Letters to Granville Barker*, ed. C.B. Purdom. Phoenix House, 1956. [Abbreviated in the text as *SLB*.]

Collected Letters, ed. Dan H. Laurence. 2 vols. Max Reinhardt, 1965–72. [2 further vols. projected.]

Collected Plays with Their Prefaces, ed. Dan H. Laurence. 7 vols. Max Reinhardt, The Bodley Head, 1971–4.

"Granville Barker: Some Particulars," *Drama* NS 3 (1946):7–14. Rpt. in *Shaw on Theatre*, ed. E.J. West. New York: Hill & Wang, 1958.

London Music in 1888–89 as Heard by Corno di Bassetto. Constable, 1937.

Our Theatres in the Nineties. 3 vols. Constable, 1931.

Smith, Harrison. "The Revival of Greek Tragedy in America," *The Bookman* [New York] 41 (1915):409–16.

Speaight, Robert. *William Poel and the Elizabethan Revival*. Cambridge, Mass.: Harvard Univ. Press, 1954.

Stier, Theodore. *With Pavlova Round the World*. Hurst & Blackett, n.d. [1927].

Styan, J.L. *Max Reinhardt*. Cambridge: Cambridge Univ. Press, 1982.

The Shakespeare Revolution. Cambridge: Cambridge Univ. Press, 1977.

Taylor, John Russell. *The Rise and Fall of the Well-Made Play*. Methuen, 1967.

Thomas, Noel. "Harley Granville-Barker and the Greek Drama," *Educational Theatre Journal* 7 (1955):294–300.

Trewin, J.C. *The Edwardian Theatre*. Oxford: Blackwell, 1976.

Shakespeare on the English Stage 1900–1964. Barrie & Rockliff, 1964.

Wade, Allan. "Shaw and the Stage Society," in Mander and Mitchenson, *Theatrical Companion* [which see].

Weales, Gerald. "The Edwardian Theatre and the Shadow of Shaw," *Edwardians and Late Victorians*, ed. Richard Ellmann (English Institute Essays, 1959). New York: Columbia Univ. Press, 1960.

Wearing, J.P. *The London Stage 1890–1919*. 6 vols. Metuchen, NJ: Scarecrow Press, 1976–82.

Webb, Beatrice. *Our Partnership*, ed. B. Drake and M.I. Cole. Cambridge: Cambridge Univ. Press, 1975.

Whitworth, Geoffrey. *The Making of a National Theatre*. Faber, 1951.

Williams, Harcourt. *Four Years at the Old Vic 1929–1931*. Putnam, 1935.

Old Vic Saga. Winchester Publications, 1949.

Wilson, J. Dover. "Memories of Barker and Two of His Friends," *Elizabethan and Jacobean Studies Presented to Frank Percy Wilson*, ed. Herbert Davis and Helen Gardner. Oxford: Oxford Univ. Press, 1959.

Winter, William. *Shakespeare on the Stage*. Third series, 1916. Rpt. New York: Blom, 1969.

Zucker, Irving. *Le "Court Théâtre" (1904–1914) et L'Evolution du Théâtre Anglais Contemporain*. Paris: Les Presses Modernes, 1931.

Index

Page numbers in bold type are references to illustrations (but pages that contain both text and illustrations on the same subject are given in normal type only)

VOYAGING
UNDER POWER

VOYAGING
UNDER POWER

Robert P. Beebe

SEVEN SEAS PRESS, INC.
Newport, Rhode Island

Dedication

To my wife, Linford, best of shipmates.
And to the first crew of *Passagemaker:*
Ralph Arndt, Ev Bibb and Connie Curts.

They have been there.

Published by Seven Seas Press, Inc.
524 Thames Street
Newport, Rhode Island 02840

Book Trade Distribution by
Simon and Schuster
a division of Simon & Schuster, Inc.
1230 Avenue of the Americas
New York, New York 10020

Second Printing

Library of Congress Cataloging in Publication Data

Beebe, Robert P.
Voyaging under power / Robert P. Beebe.—
1st ed.—New York: Seven Seas Press, [1975]

xvi, 256 p.: ill., 24 cm.
Bibliography: p. 240–241.
Includes index.
ISBN 0-915160-18-8: $12.50
1. Yacht-building. 2. Naval architecture. 3. Passagemaker (Yacht)
4. Ocean travel. I. Title.
VM331.B36   623.82'31   74-21847

Manufactured in the United States of America

Preface to the Second Edition

It's been ten volatile years since Capt. Robert Beebe finished writing *Voyaging Under Power*. It's been a decade of profound changes in the recreational boating industry, particularly in the power cruising segment. An energy crisis tested the will of power cruiser owners. At the same time, a recession shook everyone's financial resolve. Many came up short.

Not all the changes have been catastrophic. Thanks to the electronics revolution, cruising under power is now safer, more fun and less expensive than ever before. Engine improvements have lowered fuel consumption while the very cost of fuel has made us all wiser and more careful consumers. Finally, the development of lighter, stronger materials has increased the strength of modern hulls, while lowering building and cruising costs.

In rereading *Voyaging Under Power*, I was struck that here is tangible evidence of the truth in the old adage, "the more things change the more they stay the same." Indeed, that old saw may be the best test for what is truly "classic" in a book. *Voyaging Under Power* has withstood the test of time. It has become, in a very real way, larger than the sum of its parts. It is more than a sampling of time-honored designs; more than a set of design criteria; more than a compilation of lively narratives about successful power voyages. It has become a fundamental part of the way those who cruise under power look at their favorite pastime. This is true not because what Capt. Beebe says is chic or in vogue or because it reflects in any way the syntax of the moment. The book endures because what it contains is sensible, practical, and because it touches the precise reasons why the great majority of us put to sea—or dream of putting to sea—in whatever form of conveyance: We want the pleasure of voyaging without undue hardship. We want to be tested, but not tortured. We want to experience what is basic and elemental in voyaging and at the same time take full advantage of the wonderful technological innovations that are the birthright of 20th-century man.

So, it is with great pleasure that we at Seven Seas Press present a new edition of *Voyaging Under Power*. This is so because, in reprinting this book, we are reaffirming all *Voyaging Under Power* has come to stand for. It is a reflection of our belief that cruising in all its varied and wonderful forms is prospering on this watery planet.

Jim Gilbert, Editor
Seven Seas Press
Spring, 1984

Acknowledgements

Because yacht design and naval architecture form the basic structure of this book, I owe a considerable debt to those practitioners of the art who have helped me with advice and encouragement from my early beginnings to the present day: William Atkin, Howard I. Chapelle, L. Francis Herreshoff, Weston Farmer, William Garden, and Philip C. Bolger. This does not imply that any of them would necessarily agree with what is in this book. In fact, yacht designers being the individualists they are, I am quite sure they would not. Nevertheless, their dedication to excellence and the integrity of their work has always been an inspiration to me.

I am also especially grateful to the designers who contributed their work, which makes up the bulk of Chapter 8. Without exception, those asked responded with enough designs to make up a most interesting, instructive and diverse chapter, one that should be of continuing interest both to the informed amateur and to the student of boat design.

The experiences of many seamen, too many to acknowledge, have been incorporated into this book—experiences from many sources. But I am particularly grateful to two men, among the few with long-range motor-boat experience, who have made special contributions: Avard Fuller, with his experience in long, light vessels; and Jerrems C. Hart, whose comments on Chapter 5, Technicalities, and review of its drafts were particularly helpful.

Thanks are also due to several magazine editors who have given permission to use, in whole or part, articles originally printed in their publications: Monk Farnham of *Boating* for *"Passagemaker* Across the Atlantic," which makes up the greatest part of Chapter 12, and "Seagoing Boats for the Canals of Europe," which appears in Chapter 13; Bill Robinson of *Yachting* for "Once Over Heavily" and "Once Over Lightly," excerpts of which are used in Chapter 4 (and special thanks to Norris D. Hoyt, author of both articles); Pete Smyth of *Motor Boating & Sailing* for "Flopperstoppers for Seagoing Motorboats," portions of which are found in Chapter 6; and Joe Gribbins of *Motorboat,* who published "The Passagemaker Experience," a shortened version of material which now comprises Chapter 3.

Thanks are also due to Robert P. Sutton, whose story of *Mona Mona* was so good we persuaded him to let us use it in Chapter 10. My special appreciation goes to my wife, Linford, who not only contributed Chapter 15, "Galley Tips and Provisioning," but also acted as my long-suffering sounding board for innumerable drafts of the entire book, much of which was written on long freighter voyages.

I have been helped significantly in the production of this book, and want to express my gratitude to: Donna Doherty, who after cooking and cruising aboard *Passagemaker* on passages to New London and Montreal in 1967, contributed her considerable art talents to the design of this book; Margaret Joyce, whose copy editing contributed so much to clarity and precision, and John Stephen Doherty, editor and publisher of Seven Seas Press, who occupies a special position as the original push behind getting this book started some years ago, subsequent to his having qualified as crew in *Passagemaker.*

Contents

List of Illustrations

Introduction

By Carleton Mitchell

Voyaging Under Power is a book whose time has come. Despite the grow-ing number of yachtsmen interested in motorboats with offshore capabilities—usually called "trawlers" for lack of a better term—nothing exists as a guide, either from the viewpoint of design, or operation on long voyages. Yet Captain Robert P. Beebe, USN (Ret.) goes far beyond the nuts and bolts approach. He demonstrates that voyaging under power is not merely a time of life, but a way of life: that crossing an ocean en route to the next gunk hole can be a romantic undertaking, full of pleasure and inner satisfaction, and, once arrived, that the wanderer can enjoy the comfort of a true home afloat. In a very real sense, he tells the way to have the best of two worlds.

I first met Bob Beebe in 1964 at Newport, Rhode Island, where it was an America's Cup summer, and I was still living a good part of the year aboard my ocean racer/cruiser *Finisterre,* three-time winner of the Bermuda Race. Veteran transatlantic commuter Norris Hoyt had just completed the crossing from Plymouth via the Azores and Bermuda aboard *Passagemaker,* and was full of enthusiasm—preserved herein by an account reprinted from *Yachting* magazine. Norrie sensed I was a potential escapee from the tyranny of sail, and took me aboard my first seagoing motorboat—a vessel whose capabilities and record have never been surpassed. Bob Beebe thus not only introduced me to the possibilities of voyaging under power, thereby playing a part in my own transition, but has since counseled me in many ways.

Yet until he set down on paper his entire philosophy of design, along with precise formulas for evaluating potential performance of different types of vessels, I never fully grasped the essential qualities which must be inherent in an engine-driven vessel to be safely navigated across vast stretches of open ocean. Chapter 5, entitled "Technicalities of the Seagoing Motorboat," should be required reading by anyone interested in the type—especially Madison Avenue advertising copywriters trumpeting vessels of limited ability as "go any-where, anytime" cruisers. Beebe divides such craft into three categories: *"Pas-sagemakers"* (a term which he coined and precisely defines under a subhead of "ocean-crossers"), "trawlers" ("lighter vessels with some seagoing capability but with neither the equipment nor the range to qualify for full status as ocean-crossers"), and "seagoing motorboats" ("to cover all types when a general term is needed.").

Along with such coefficients as Displacement/Length Ratio, Speed/Length Ratio, and Above-Water/Below-Water Area Ratio, Chapter 5 adds the newly minted Beebe-ism: "Trawler/Truth Ratio," a yardstick to define how close to a true trawler is the vessel being glowingly described by salesman or advertisement. It is not that Bob Beebe has anything against such yachts if they are capable of meeting the requirements of the potential owner, but he makes possible a slide-rule-in-hand approach to make sure there will be no later disappointments. To paraphrase the title of a best-seller in another field, *Voyaging Under Power* could almost be subtitled, "Everything You Always Wanted to Know About Seagoing Motorboats but Didn't Know Whom to Ask."

A fundamental Beebe thesis is that a reliable and consistent means of reducing rolling is necessary to the enjoyment of power voyaging. Along with *Passagemaker*, Bob Beebe has done another service for prospective power voyagers by his extensive testing and development of the aptly named "flopperstoppers," anti-roll devices originally developed by Pacific coast fishermen. These are thoroughly explored, and compared with different types of stabilizers. Other chapters run the gamut from a historical background of cross-ocean passages on which the internal combustion engine first supplanted sail, through "Voyage Planning" (use of pilot charts for plotting courses through belts of light winds or calms), to "Cruising in Europe" (including maximum permissible dimensions for transiting the lesser French canals). The work of other designers is presented and analyzed, and there are two accounts of men who built their own little ships and took them to sea.

Toward the end there comes a chapter by Linford Beebe, artist both on canvas and in the galley, full of practical lore on provisioning, stowage, and the preparation of food, which might be expected from a lady with over 50,000 nautical miles astern. But equally important to someone (and his wife!) who has never cruised aboard a motorboat, is Linford's ability to convey the flavor and enjoyment of her way of life. She writes, "For the long-distance voyager, there is a special magic to a landfall: not just excitement, more like enchantment as a vision dissolves into focus and becomes reality. . . . Tomorrow you will explore the busy streets, hear the chatter, soak up the color, be startled by noise and surprised by scurry, discover the tang, aroma, fragrance, spice of the native market." Then she guides you to the goodies of some of the markets she has explored, part of the tapestry of memories that come to a voyager: Mexico, Costa Rica, Greece, Yugoslavia, France, Spain and Majorca, the Azores, Bermuda . . . and even shares a few secrets from her "Sea Fare" file, to whose excellence I can personally testify.

On only two counts do I disagree with Bob Beebe, and both are matters of personal preference. First, I would be miserable on any vessel without an outside steering station. Cruising from California to Florida aboard a Grand Banks 42-foot "trawler," with a side trip to the Galapagos, in some 16,000 miles and three years of living in the tropics, almost no time was spent buttoned-up in the pilot-house. True, slugging into Caribbean trade wind seas along the north coast of South America from the Panama Canal to Grenada I was sometimes grateful for shelter, but otherwise lived on the flying bridge, night and day, underway and anchored. Shaded by a folding canopy, it was the coolest—and most pleasant—place aboard. Second, I could never put up with an all-electric galley. On a long run, the rhythm of well-silenced engines becomes soporific, a not unpleasant background to the sigh of wind and plash of wave. Under way, the necessary 240- or 120-volts of AC current can be painlessly provided by a generator belted to the main engine. But coming to the end of the passage entails attaching an umbilical cord to the shore to brew even a cup of coffee, or listening to a generator if swinging to a hook. Propane gas stowed on deck and treated like the dangerous explosive it is can be made as safe as any other system aboard, I am convinced. Combined with carefully engineered hold-over-plate refrigeration, power requirements can be cut to a minimum. In fact, *Sans Terre* swung peacefully for weeks at a time in remote West Indian harbors with the generator running less than two hours out of 24, free from both the shore and engine noise.

Although as a present or potential powerboat operator you may never aspire to "Round-the-World Passagemaking," or even some of the lesser alternatives covered by Bob Beebe, this book is a must. Any time any vessel ventures offshore it must be ready to meet the threat of the sea, where design, equipment, and handling may become a matter of survival. Thus *Voyaging Under Power* is more than an addition to the extensive library of yachting books, even in the specialized aspect of deep-sea cruising: It is an invaluable guide into hitherto uncharted waters.

Philippine canoe the author owned as a boy.

Aircraft carrier *USS Saratoga,* author's wartime ship.

Author's Preface

It was the last day. As I came on deck for the 0400-0800 watch, a faint light in the east showed the horizon clear, with brilliant stars overhead. There would be a good fix on this, our landfall day. The bow wave chuckled softly.

Sipping a mug of coffee while waiting for sight time, I had much to think about: the years of research and theorizing, the days and weeks of drawing plans, the months of watching the vessel grow in the builder's yard—a vessel whose highly unusual make-up we hoped would prove my theories—the sea trials, the first miles of our cruise, the ports we visited, the weather—everything. Now, just ahead lay Rhodes, one of the fabled islands of Greece.

My thoughts went back even farther, to World War II when, like so many other armchair long-cruise planners, I found myself transported to the South Pacific under circumstances that had never entered my wildest dreams. There, as navigator of the aircraft carrier *Saratoga,* I observed at first hand the conditions small cruising boats would meet after the war. It was this experience that first turned me toward a vessel distinctly different from traditional long-range types. Now, as we neared Rhodes, the work begun on the bridge of the old *Saratoga* had passed from dream to reality, and the reality was carrying me and my crew across the Mediterranean on this clear, calm morning toward the castle of the Knights Hospitalers.

For the yacht *Passagemaker* was about to complete her first voyage. In six weeks to the day we had made the passage to Greece from Singapore. Almost 6000 miles of calms, brisk breezes, and gales lay astern. And through it all, our ocean-crossing motorboat had chugged steadily along, averaging exactly her designed passage speed of 7.5 knots.

I knew now that crossing oceans in owner-operated small craft in the 40- to 50-foot range, under power alone, using crews by no means made up of rough and tough seamen, worked and worked well. I had also learned what I'd only suspected before—that a very good case could be made for the power approach over sail for all long voyages.

To generations of seamen brought up on tales of long voyages in small sailing craft, such statements must sound like heresy. Some years ago I, too, would have counted myself among those seamen. But certain experiences, certain selective reading with a critical eye, and certain designing in new directions had finally convinced me that it was possible on long voyages to do better. It is the evolution of the theory, its testing with *Passagemaker,* what we learned and what can be recommended for the future that this book is all about.

The book, then, is about voyaging under power as contrasted to voyaging under sail. While a vast literature exists about deep-sea cruising under sail, there is little in print about long-range power voyaging. Of course, many of the problems encountered at sea are similar in both cases. But the power-approach does differ from sail in several important ways that need consideration. To cite just one example: The naval architecture rules that govern the speed and range of a long-range motorboat are quite rigid and must be thoroughly understood before selecting such a craft or operating it to the limits of its ability. On the other hand, the sailing cruiser, with its "free" propulsion power, is largely independent of these rules.

Of course I have nothing against cruising under sail. The long sailing cruises I have made have all been great fun. But, as will appear, there are certain conditions and certain groups of sailors for whom the power approach has definite advantages. It is for those sailors this book is written.

As for my own background in this subject, I have been a boat nut since my Army officer father gave his two small sons a dugout canoe in the Philippines over half a century ago. Class racing was my principal sport until I was almost 40. After that, the whole family did considerable cruising in 30- to 55-foot sailing craft. About 38 years ago, I began to study yacht design, first as a hobby, then as an avocation, and then, since my retirement from 30 years service in the Navy, as a full-time occupation.

It was the search for a retirement boat that led me to consider power as an alternative to sail. The more I looked into it, the more interesting it became, until the years spent pursuing the matter finally led to the building of our 50-foot *Passagemaker*. Some 60,000 miles of deep-water cruising in her, including three ocean crossings, a round trip to Hawaii, and two East Coast-West Coast passages, taught me much that can be safely passed on to those who share this interest. Of course, during those years, I exchanged experiences with the few others who had background in this narrow field, considered the features of other ocean-crossing motorboats, and studied the work of other designers.

In addition, the types of questions asked me by potential clients, as well as some features of vessels allegedly designed for ocean voyaging, all pointed to the desirability of setting down the basics of long-range power cruising as a start on a body of literature on the subject. I do not pretend to know all the answers; there is still much work to be done. And there is as much room for differences of opinion on this subject as there is on cruising under sail.

It is unfortunate that so much of the book must be made up of my experiences and my ideas. My best efforts to find men with experience in seagoing motorboats and to record their thoughts has met with only modest success: The background just is not there. So the reader should view the book in this light: A beginning is needed, and I am trying to provide it. I would be pleased to hear from anyone who can augment or rebut anything in this book.

There is one thing, though, of which I am sure: The power approach to long-range cruising makes so much sense to so many people that it is a part of the yachting scene which is certain to grow in the years ahead.

Robert P. Beebe
Carmel, California, 1974

1

Historical Background of Power Voyaging

One of the first things I undertook when I decided to embark on the design of a long-range motorboat was research in the history of the boat type. It is a scanty field, but lessons can be learned from what material is available.

There were two early small-boat voyages across the Atlantic under power; both were made to demonstrate the reliability of the internal combustion engines then coming into use in boats. The first voyage was by the *Abiel Abbot Low*, using a kerosene engine. In 1902, she crossed from New York to Falmouth, England, in 38 days. The second voyage was by the *Detroit* in 1912. She used a gasoline engine to cross from New York to Queenstown, (now Cobh), Ireland, in 28 days. What lessons can we learn from these two pioneer efforts?

My first impression after reading the logs of the *Low* and the *Detroit* was that the voyages were excellent examples of what *not* to do. With due regard for the guts of the crews, it is clear that the designers and builders had a lot to learn. This is understandable, of course, as no one had done such a thing before. Possibly more important, the men involved in these projects had had their major training in sail.

It must have been this sail background, for instance, that produced the astonishing layout of *Detroit*. She was 35 feet long with a nine-foot beam and a 4' 6" draft. She was double-ended and resembled a lifeboat in that she had high shelters bow and stern. Amidships she was low sided, and in the center of this deck space was the steering station—a stand-up wheel with no shelter whatever. The watch-stander was supposed to stand there with no handholds and steer the vessel while waves washed across the deck from either side. Fantastic! Here was a station well laid out for the watch to keep an eye on the sails—but no sails!

Understandably enough, this feature caused a good deal of discontent among the crew of four when *Detroit* entered the open Atlantic. However, the engine performed flawlessly, and *Detroit* arrived in Queenstown (Cobh) in good order.

Low was not well laid out for the crossing, either. She was 38 feet long with a 34-foot waterline, nine-foot beam, and 3' 8" draft, double-ended, with a trunk cabin forward and cockpit aft. Instead of providing some shelter by putting the wheel against the trunk cabin forward, it was placed aft as on a sailing vessel, and was wide open to the elements.

Low's principal problem was crew trouble. Her skipper, having been hired to make this engine-demonstrating voyage, chose to take his 16-year-old son as

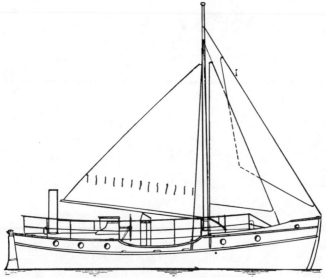

FIG. 1-1. The *Detroit.* Note the steering arrangement and the low side amidship. The *Detroit* crossed the Atlantic in 1912 in 26 days.

his only crew, then tried to do everything himself. With no relief from the tyranny of continuous steering, he soon became exhausted. This produced all sorts of crises. *Low* was also unfortunate in her weather, spending a good deal of time hove-to or riding to a sea anchor. When this was compounded by her copper fuel tanks springing numerous leaks due to the pounding of heavy seas, by kerosene getting into everything below decks, and by a constant battle to bail as much oil as possible back into the tanks, her crew was reduced almost to survival conditions. But they toughed it out, and made it. The engine ran perfectly all the way.

Nobody felt impelled to follow in the wake of these two vessels, and the way these voyages tested to the limit the endurance of hardened professional seamen, makes this reluctance understandable.

Commencing in 1912, annual motorboat "races" were held from the U.S. to Bermuda. These died after three runnings, from lack of entries. I do not think the designs of the vessels that participated show any developments of particular interest to us today.

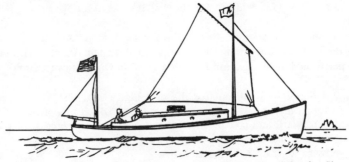

FIG. 1-2. The *Abiel Abbot Low,* first motorboat across the Atlantic. She crossed in 1902 in 38 days.

It was not until 1937 that the next crossing of the North Atlantic by a small motorboat took place. This voyage is of great interest as it was the first in a craft incorporating features found in modern ocean-crossing motorboats. The voyage was made by a Frenchman named Marin-Marie, who was the official marine painter to the French government. Marin-Marie had been a small-boat sailor all his life. In 1933, he built a double-ended cutter and sailed it singlehandedly across the Atlantic from France to New York. He enjoyed this

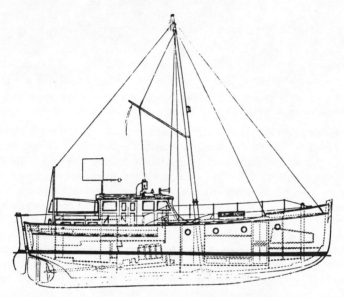

FIG. 1-3. Arielle, profile. Note the covered steering station, steadying rig, and general air of competence in this excellently planned 43-footer.

adventure so much that he wondered how the voyage would go under power. He certainly did a good job of researching the project, and made up a specification designed to correct the flaws of earlier boats, and to add features permitted by modern developments. His book, *Wind Aloft, Wind Alow,* (Scribners, 1947) is maddeningly vague about details; but it appears his *Arielle* was about 42′6″ long and drew 4′6″. She was equipped with a 75 hp four-cylinder diesel and carried 1500 gallons of fuel, a steadying and emergency propulsion rig, an enclosed steering station, a primitive form of photoelectric autopilot, and a vane-steering gear that antedated by many years the models popular today on sailing cruisers. In fact, I think the only thing missing from *Arielle*'s equipment was some method of stabilizing against rolling. She did use her steadying rig for this purpose but it was ineffective for the usual reasons (*see Chapter 6*).

In spite of dire predictions of disaster, to the point that the elders of the *Club de Yachts de France* considered having Marin-Marie restrained legally from such a foolish venture, *Arielle* left New York on July 22, 1937, and arrived in Le Havre, France, 19 days later, essentially with nothing to report—the way any well-conducted cruise should end.

PHOTO 1-4.   Arielle at sea, a photo taken from the deck of a steamer. Despite her seamanlike crossing in 1937, the feat was met by a "devastating silence."

Marin-Marie's voyage was met with devastating silence on both sides of the Atlantic. The fact that a yacht of *Arielle*'s size, under the command of a well-known yachtsman, had crossed the Atlantic to where she could now cruise the fascinating waters of Europe, and had done so in *less time and for less money than would have been required to prepare the boat and ship it across,* (and probably arrived in much better shape than if she had been shipped), didn't seem to make any impression. Marin-Marie and *Arielle* were far ahead of their time, and I want to pay tribute here to their successful pioneering effort.

In 1939, the first crossing of the Atlantic from east to west was made in a 31-foot motorboat named *Eckero*. One might say this voyage presaged things to come—*Eckero* was not designed for the voyage, nor specially fitted, nor was her crew trying to prove anything.

Eckero's owner was Uno Ekblom and he lived on the Äland Islands in the Baltic. In 1939, he decided to visit the United States, but for some reason he couldn't get a visa—and, no visa, no steamship ticket. Not one to let such a detail upset his plans, Ekblom decided to go anyway, in the motorboat *Eckero* which he had designed and built for himself 10 years previously. She was 31 feet long with a beam of 9′10″ and had a single-cylinder diesel of 10 hp—like thousands of fishing vessels in the Baltic.

Ekblom got together a crew of two friends, gave the diesel a factory overhaul, fitted a small steadying rig, and away they went on May 3, 1939.

They stopped in Copenhagen, Denmark, and Goteborg, Sweden, had their worst weather of the trip in the North Sea, and arrived in Rotterdam, Holland, on May 28. They then went to Dover, Southampton, and Falmouth, England, following Ekblom's rule of spending only one night in a port—a rule that he observed scrupulously to the end of the voyage. On June 9, they left Falmouth for Horta in the Azores, arriving at the end of a passage of 1260 miles in nine and a half days. After a day in port, they were off for Bermuda, 1800 miles away. They entered St. George on July 7, refueled and left the following day. When they arrived in New York on July 13, they had covered no less than 3725 miles in 34 days, with only two in-port days.

All of these details are from Humphrey Barton's book, *Atlantic Adventurers*. Barton called this ". . . an amazing distance to cover in 34 days," then went on to say, "I believe this to be the most outstanding voyage that has ever been carried out by a small motorboat and great credit is due to Uno Ekblom and his crew for their seamanship and endurance. Nor must the little diesel engine which served them so faithfully be forgotten. It must have run like a clock."

I certainly agree with Barton that credit is due to the ship, her crew, and her engine, but not necessarily with his comment that the performance was "amazing." Perhaps it seems so to a long-time sailor with several Atlantic crossings under sail to his credit. But the fact is, judging her voyage by the technical yardsticks to be developed later in Chapter 5, *Eckero* didn't do too well. Her time underway—if compared to standards that seem reasonable—should have been 24–26, not 34, days.

Now that the Atlantic had been crossed in both directions in small craft using the diesel engine, the stage was set for other such voyages. There have been voyages since *Eckero,* and all have been routine. Several double voyages have been reported. The British 61-foot converted lifeboat *Aries* left England for New York May 26, 1955, and made her returning landfall at Dartmouth on August 6. She had very poor luck with her weather, experiencing gales on both legs of the voyage. The motor fishing vessel (MFV) yacht *Kytra* crossed from Europe to Newport, Rhode Island, in 1963, for some North American cruising in the New England area. She spent the winter there and returned home in 1964—as described by Norris D. Hoyt in Chapter 4. She had good weather both ways.

What conclusions can we draw from these voyages? In the first place, they made such demands on the endurance of their crews that these enterprises obviously were not suitable for inexperienced seamen or their families. The greatest complaint was about rolling. *A reliable and consistent means of reducing rolling appears to be the prime factor necessary for popular participation in long-distance power voyaging.* Crew comfort is a must. Such absurdities as exclusively outside steering stations, absence of steering assistance, and hulls too small to carry the required load and still provide decent room for the crew, reduce this sort of voyage to the stunt level. Singlehanded ocean passages prove nothing, either: Not many people are interested in such feats.

PHOTO 1-5. Eckero, the first boat to cross the Atlantic from east to west. She crossed in 1939 in 34 days.

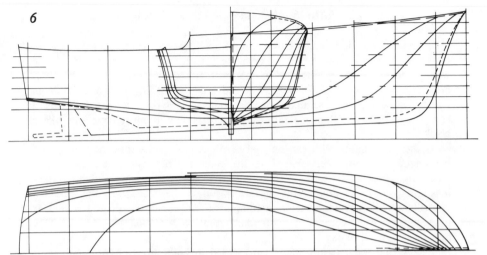

FIG. 1-6. Lines of a "Northwest Cruiser" by William Garden, showing the evolution of the early fisherman-shaped cruisers to a lighter model. Retraced by R. P. B.

On the other hand, the perfect record of the engines involved shows this part of power passage-making is a solid base on which to build. By correcting the objectionable features noted, a vessel of unique qualities can be produced with capabilities for a new sort of cruising.

Aside from the pioneering efforts that concentrated on crossing the Atlantic, a major portion of the development of true seagoing motorboats has taken place on the West Coast. This development was dictated by the characteristics of the area. From San Francisco northward the year-round weather off the coast is, on the average, worse than that of any other area except the high latitudes of the Southern Ocean. This coastal area not only has winter storms but also is bedevilled in summer by very strong winds caused by differences between pressure over the cold ocean waters and pressure over the hot interior valleys. The worst gale *Passagemaker* ever encountered, for instance, was off Cape Mendicino in the middle of August. It was not a storm, just a gradient wind.

Yet fishing vessels operate off the coast and in the Gulf of Alaska the year round, so it is possible for well-found craft to cruise these waters. It gradually became clear in the postwar years that a type of vessel was required which was not an advertised stock item.

The early examples were modified fishing boats. Designed first by Seattle designers Edwin Monk and William Garden, a type of boat began to evolve which was lighter and more economical than a true fisherman, yet offered adequate seaworthiness. "Northwest Cruisers" they were commonly called at first, though this term has about died out today.

As more and more of these boats were built, their reputation gradually became widespread and led to the sudden proliferation of vessels that today are called "trawlers." There will be a good deal to be said on *that* subject later.

This was the background, then, for the design of *Passagemaker*, and we turn now to the development of the Passagemaker concept and the design, building, and testing of the vessel herself.

2

Evolving the Passagemaker Concept

Turning to *Passagemaker* and how she grew, I mentioned earlier that the first idea of such a boat came to me during World War II when I was navigator of a large aircraft carrier in the Pacific. Years before, like so many small-craft sailors, I had built up a library of cruising tales—from Joshua Slocum on. During prewar duty in the Pacific, there had been ample opportunity to keep an eye on the activities of the comparatively few long-range sail cruisers at sea in those days. So I was reasonably well aware of their problems, and my developing designer's eye noted how few of these vessels seemed suited to their intended work.

As the war ended, and we cruised through waters hitherto forbidden to small craft, it became apparent to me that the cruising routes would differ sharply from the "standard track" so often described in cruising yarns: from Panama to the Galapagos, the Marquesas, Tahiti, and on.

For one thing, cruising among the islands the United States occupied during the war, leads one into areas having long periods of little or no wind, so considerable range under power would be useful. My own idea of a postwar cruiser, as I sketched and designed boats on the backs of old charts (as time would allow), gradually evolved into a long, slim hull of 54-foot length over all (LOA), easily driven under power, with fuel for 1500 miles, and carrying a three-masted-schooner rig. It was interesting later to see L. Francis Herreshoff's ideas of a postwar cruiser published in *Rudder*. He had come to the same conclusion as I had, producing the 55-foot *Marco Polo*, another three-masted, long, slim vessel. While comparison of our vessels ended there, I found it nice to be in such distinguished company.

But nothing came of all this at the time except the publication of my thoughts on "Postwar Pacific Cruising" in *Rudder* for August and September of 1946. Here the case for more range under power was stated as follows:

> *"The chief difference from cruises of the past is that the voyager may venture into waters where for long periods there is hardly any wind at all. He will also make passages that do not lie entirely within the Trade Wind belt. It would seem therefore that good power is essential, coupled with cruising range well above what we are accustomed to. Whether this is to be achieved by a large craft or one which achieves range from being easily driven is a matter of opinion. Personally I favor the latter, as it ties in with my ideas of a small crew and easily handled sail plan. Draft is not a problem unless one wishes to explore off the beaten track, away from islands*

7

that have been used for war purposes.

"To my mind the editor of Rudder *has done the prospective cruiser a great service by bringing forth Herreshoff's* Marco Polo. *Not only is this model a good sailing machine, adapted in every way to the use for which it is intended, but its basic design is ideally suited to the conditions to be met in a Pacific cruise. It also permits a new type of cruise, one which will fill the needs of the sailor who, however much he may dream of spending months lying under the shade of a palm, watching sarong-clad native girls dance for his amusement, must limit his cruise to a definite time and get back to the old grind where he may happily accumulate enough of the wherewithal to go cruising again."*

This statement, made in 1946, was my first step away from the conventional sailing cruiser, a step which, it will be seen, was subject to further modification. In particular, the last sentence contains the germ of an idea that was destined to grow, the idea of concentrating on passage-making.

In 1957, I jumped at the chance to be navigator of the first Herreshoff 55-footer to be completed—Joe Newcomb's *Talaria*—on a November trip from New York to the Bahamas. This rugged trip under winter conditions (described in *Rudder* for February, 1958), raised certain questions about the concept evolved during the war, and was more grist for the mill—a mill now shifting into high gear as my retirement from thirty years of Navy service drew closer.

Three years before *Passagemaker* was designed, I wrote a story about the subject, mainly as an exercise in lining up my thoughts on what I was trying to do. The editor who requested the story had not published it by the time I knew *Passagemaker* would be built, so I asked that the manuscript be returned to me, promising the editor a report on the finished boat and its performance at a later date. Now that *Passagemaker* has proved all the story's points—and more— the story has become something of a historical document, a statement of basic principles. The early developmental work that led to the concept on which *Passagemaker* was built can be illustrated by excerpts from this story.

At the suggestion of the editor, I wrote the story in the form of a conversation among three friends at a yacht club. The characters were: Tubby Watson, a dedicated ocean-racing man; Don Moore, an experienced amateur yacht designer; and Bob Reid, a "dedicated boat nut from way back who had also done some designing." Here's a condensation of the article:

> Tubby Watson walked out onto the yacht club porch in company with . . . Don Moore. Moore was a tall, spare man with the look of the sea about him. Under his arm he carried a roll of blueprints. Moore had recently moved to the West Coast and was thinking about a retirement boat that would not only be suitable for local cruising but something more. Tubby had invited him to bring his plans over to the club.
>
> Moore said, "Suppose I give you a little background first. I find it helps. When I moved to the West Coast and found I had more time for cruising, I started thinking about all the places I hadn't covered—parts of the East Coast, the Bahamas, Great Lakes, and so on. And out here,

British Columbia and Mexico. The question was how to do it?"

"Why not fly there and charter?" offered Tubby.

"That has its points, of course. But I've owned boats all my life and would feel lost without something to putter around on and fix up. My first idea was a trailerable cruiser, so you could make the long jumps by car. This is probably the cheapest way, and the boat is reasonably able. But it would be nice to have a genuine live-aboard boat when you got there. So I looked into the problems of making the trips by water."

"That's quite a project," Bob Reid said, "going from here East by boat."

"Most people think so," Moore responded. "But the more I worked on it, the more I began to see you could do a good deal to cut it down to size. The problem, of course, is making the passages. In fact, I call the final result a 'Passagemaker.' "

"It seems to me," Reid said, "there are a lot of boats that could qualify as passage-makers."

"Actually, there aren't," Don replied. "Let's really look at passage-making for a minute. Of course, many people do make long passages. But the general idea seems to be to take a well-found sailboat of some sort and start out. They get there, of course; but what most of them are really doing is *ocean cruising*. I'm not interested in that—I've been to sea. What I like to do is go to a nice area like Puget Sound and poke around from port to port. The quicker I get there the more time I'll have for cruising. Speed and dispatch is what I want. By speed I mean to keep *average speed* as high as possible. And by dispatch I mean to meet some sort of *schedule*. It is much easier to find a crew if they can be told with reasonable certainty when they will get home—"

"You mean if their wives can know—" interrupted Tubby.

"That's right! Why not face it?" relied Moore. "All these considerations *do* affect the basic idea. If you read accounts of 'voyaging' with a critical eye you will soon pick up hints that it's possible to do better . . ."

(This exchange was the first use of "Passagemaker," the word I coined to describe the type of yacht that was evolving from my thoughts on the subject.)

The group went on to discuss Moore's idea that any of the boats should be capable of singlehanded operation. Tubby didn't think much of doing that, so Moore explained that with a crew, you can single-hand by turns, so to speak; that is, run with a one-man watch. *(This remains a fundamental point.)* Tubby then suggested that Moore needed a long-range diesel motorboat.

"I considered that, of course," said Don. "The fact that so many of them are being built out here is a tribute to the good sense of some yachtsmen. The trouble is they are too expensive for me. I ran through a preliminary design of one to see how it would go in the 50-foot size. Here is the sketch I drew. She is about as 'houseboaty' as you can get and still be really seaworthy. And she has a feature I like—lots of unobstructed deck space."

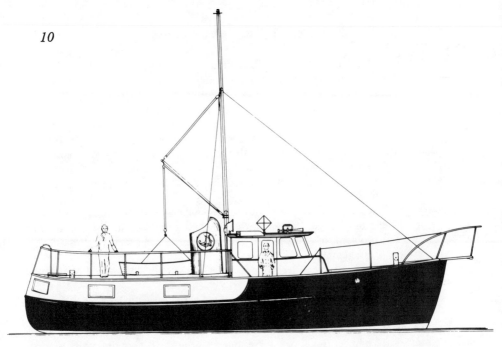

FIG. 2-1. Profile, Beebe Design 50, a sketch for a 52-ft. "oceangoing motorboat," sketched in 1959.

"Looks nice. Too bad you couldn't swing it," Reid said.

"Well, what we are doing here is facing facts, and that's one of them. But the interesting thing about these boats is the performance you can get out of them."

The group next had a thorough discussion of the significance of "hull speed," "speed/length ratio," and range. (*As all these technical matters are thoroughly explored in Chapter 5, we will hold them until later.*)

Moore said, "Now let's look at the sailing cruiser. She shows up worst of all: She is not adapted to single-handling, she can't guarantee speed *or* dispatch, and she must have a full watch-standing crew of experienced sailors before she can leave the dock."

Tubby demurred. "It's not as bad as all that!"

"Well, let's go back to the concept. In the passage to and from the East Coast, the leg from Acapulco to Panama is particularly well known for its calms and light airs. This is where the ordinary cruiser falls down on the job. You end up wishing you had a motorboat with more fuel than the auxiliary can carry so you can meet your schedule. In fact, it was considering this aspect that first turned my ideas toward what I call a 'motor-all-the-time' boat."

"What sort of a craft is that?" Reid inquired.

"The original idea came from a designer friend of mine," Moore answered. "He pointed out, in considering ocean racers, that by having something less than five horsepower available continuously for propulsion, and using only a simple rig of two or three lowers, you could lick the best of the lot carrying their load of spinnakers, jibs, genoas, mizzenstaysails and the rest—and do it a lot cheaper."

"The Race Committee wouldn't like it," Reid offered.

"The Jib Tenders Union would *never* allow anything like that," said Tubby with quiet confidence.

"Of course, it's not a practical proposition," Don answered, "and my friend hasn't done anything with it. But the principle involved looks good for what I've already called a 'Passagemaker'—where you want an assured average speed. Basically, the question was this: Would it be possible to shrink the seagoing motorboat down closer to the size, and shape, and accommodations of the sailing cruiser, with a great reduction in cost, and still get the performance desired?" He looked around the table. "Well, it turns out that you can. And then I put a rig on her suitable to the sailing you would do while singlehanded."

"So you settled on a motorsailer," said Tubby.

"No, *sir!*" said Don Moore emphatically. "I don't consider my boat a motorsailer. To me a motorsailer is something different. It has a rather large rig and is expected to use sail alone whenever the wind is at all favorable. Most of them do not carry much fuel, though more than the ordinary auxiliary, of course. And they usually compromise on propeller/hull efficiency in an attempt to provide a reasonable sailing potential. I guess you could call my boat a 'motorboat with rig.' "

"Aren't you quibbling a bit?"

"Not really. What I am referring to is the underwater body—it is wholly dedicated to efficiency under power. It is a matter of prismatic coefficient."

(This discussion reflected a tremendous amount of research and calculation. It is, of course, no great trick to take a large, burdensome hull, load it up with fuel, and achieve a very long range. What was not readily apparent in the beginning, from the available technical data, was whether this "shrinking down" process was feasible. If you don't want to be burdened with the large, heavy vessel, or your budget won't build it, shrinking down must be the answer. I recall vividly the sense of discovery and pleasure I felt when I finally found I could have Moore honestly say, "Well, it turns out that you can." There are many technical matters involved—matters such as stability when fuel is almost gone, for instance. A good deal of the research done appears again in Chapter 5 in the discussion of "displacement/length ratio.")

The three men spoke at length of the significance of the "prismatic coefficient" *(another matter covered in Chapter 5)*. Moore explained that he was trying to achieve the required range with the least fuel possible. This led to a discussion of what the range should be.

"What range are we talking about?" Reid asked.

"In the San Diego-Key West voyage, with stops at Acapulco and Panama, the longest leg is 1400 miles. But, returning from the East Coast you might want to head out to sea from Acapulco on the starboard tack and power-sail up the old sailing-ship route to California. It's rather hard to pin down, but I decided a 2400-mile 'still-water' range would be about right, and stuck to that. This would be useful coming back from Honolulu, too."

"What size boat do you need to achieve that?" Reid asked.

"I worked her up in several sizes," said Moore. "The ideal would be 48 feet overall, with a 42′6″ waterline, and a 27,000-pound displacement— with 600 gallons of diesel fuel. Here are the lines of that boat. She actually weighs about half of that 50-foot motorboat I showed you, and costs a

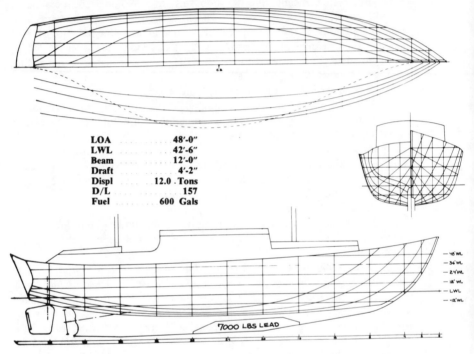

LOA	48′-0″
LWL	42′-6″
Beam	12′-0″
Draft	4′-2″
Displ	12.0 Tons
D/L	157
Fuel	600 Gals

7000 LBS LEAD

FIG. 2-2. Lines, Beebe Design 53, a 48-footer using the *Presto* midsection. This was the first of my designs called a "Passagemaker."

great deal less to build. She has the correct prismatic coefficient for a speed of eight knots, and will do the 2400 miles at that speed, using about 30 horsepower. A lot of people won't believe that, but it's true. If you back off on the speed, the range takes a tremendous jump. For instance, she could make San Diego–Panama nonstop at seven knots without stopping in Acapulco for some of that good Mexican beer."

"No nonstop for me," Tubby said fervently.

"It doesn't appeal to me, either," said Moore, "but I can think of several trips where the extra range would be useful. Unfortunately, this 48-footer proved too expensive, too, so I settled for a final design that is 40′6″ long, 36 feet on the waterline, and some 20,000 pounds displacement. She will make the 2400 miles at six knots on 300 gallons of fuel. For shorter passages, she will do 1400 miles at seven knots and 900 at eight."

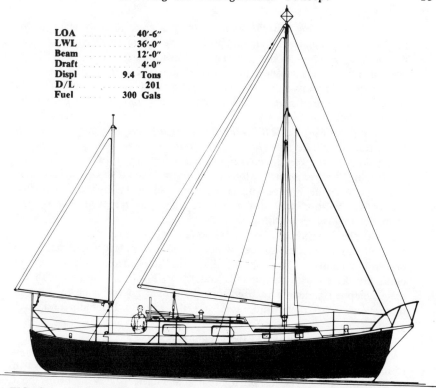

LOA	40'-6"
LWL	36'-0"
Beam	12'-0"
Draft	4'-0"
Displ	9.4 Tons
D/L	201
Fuel	300 Gals

FIG. 2-3. Profile, Beebe Design 57. A sailing Passagemaker of 40-ft. LOA. This is the design Don Moore was having built in the story in Chapter 2.

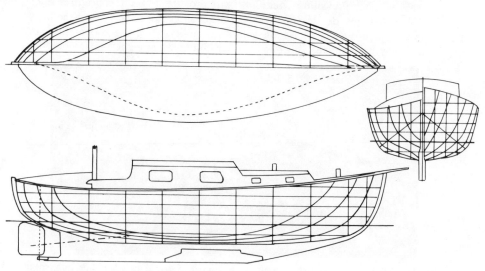

FIG. 2-4. Lines, Design 57.

(This discussion was the end result of a great deal of work which finally made it apparent that the project—designing specifically to make the desired passage—could be accomplished and made sense.) Moore pointed out that his vessel could go from San Diego to Key West in 28 days, with four days off—two each in Acapulco and Panama. Thus, a cruise to the desired area on the East Coast and return could be accomplished in less than a year.

(I still believe that 2400 miles range is a figure that makes a lot of sense. But, as will be brought out in Chapter 5, range figures must always be qualified by the speed which the operator expects to use.)

Moore then explained why it was impractical to design a boat that would do what he wanted and also be capable of Tubby's ocean racing. Moore did mention that if the big propeller was removed, sailing performance might be surprising.

"Ah, ha," exclaimed Tubby, "so you do want to race her!"

"Well, no," replied Moore, "I don't think my budget would stand two or three spinnakers, genoas, and the rest. But someone might want to outfit my design with racing sails and try it. I was all through with the design before I suddenly realized that she should do very well in some of these West Coast downwind races, like the ones to Honolulu and Acapulco."

"Why do you say that?" Reid inquired.

"Because any race off the wind, with no windward work, should go to the boat that needs the least push to exceed the speed required to win on her own rating. The instant the first boat finishes, every following boat has an average speed it *must* exceed to place first on corrected time. The less actual horsepower a boat needs to attain that speed, the more chance she has that prevailing conditions will provide it. As I concentrated on this, I saw my design should have an advantage over the round-the-buoy racers with their emphasis on windward ability. Here are two pictures of a model test I made. This one is at her hull speed of eight knots, while this

PHOTO 2-5. Model test of Design 57 showing her being towed at her hull speed of eight knots.

PHOTO 2-6. Model test of Design 57 showing her being overdriven to a speed/length ratio of about 1.6. Note minimal wave hollow amidships.

one shows her being overdriven to a speed-length ratio of about 1.6. She has a good deal less wave hollow amidships than most Cruising Club of America (CCA)-type cruiser-racers under these conditions, yet she weighs about the same."

PHOTO 2-7. A CCA-rule type ocean racer. Note how the overdriven hull has developed an extreme wave hollow amidships. (Photo by Rosenfeld.)

Moore's photos showed graphically the effect of prismatic coefficient on efficiency under power. The friends then moved on to discuss the interior of the vessel.

(In the design's accommodation, I had the chance to emphasize features that I felt, from research in long-range cruising tales, needed a new direction. As can be seen from her accommodation plan, she is laid out for singlehanded convenience, though she has bunks for four. The Root berths in the main cabin can be replaced with an ordinary transom berth-settee for local cruising.)

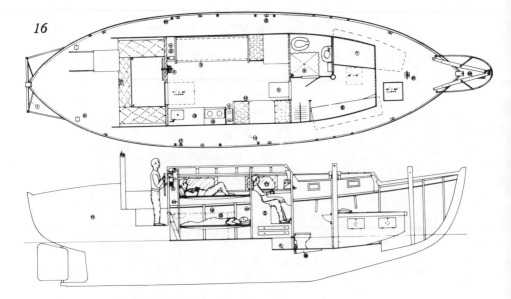

FIG. 2-8. Accommodation Plan, Design 57.

"Now, how about her cabin?"

"The main cabin is very carefully designed for the work to be done in it. It is as high as it is because all the space below the waterline is taken up by tanks. Everything in this area is dedicated to singlehanded convenience. Personally, I think it is a great advance over anything that has been used for this kind of cruising before. For instance, the skipper's bunk is up in line with the ports so he can look out while resting."

"The officers of the deck are a bunch of drunks. They stand their watches in their bunks!" chortled Tubby.

"*Mister* Watson!" Don said with mock severity. "You know very well I never touch the stuff underway. But seriously, I fail to understand why *not one* single-hander has ever done this. If you read the cruise accounts, you will be struck by how many times the skippers leap from below to see what's going on. If they could just open one eye for a look around, many vague dangers would evaporate."

"How about the cockpit?" Tubby asked. "Isn't it a bit unusual?"

"Yes, it is," Moore answered. "But I made a cruise years ago in a Francis Herreshoff yacht, the Marco Polo type, that had one like this. That spoiled me—I never want to go very far to sea again in a conventional cockpit cruiser where you sit way aft on deck without any shelter. The deep, standing-room, athwartships cockpit—with seats all around—was just wonderful. In this case, the wheel is on the forward bulkhead at stand-up height as you only use it for maneuvering."

"How do you mean?" asked Tubby.

"Why, she uses an autopilot, of course," said Don. "This is basic to the concept, and one of the great advantages of an engine-running-all-the-time vessel—you always have power for it. This is what makes a single-handed passage not only feasible but enjoyable. Your crew steers all day and never talks back, never gripes about the chow, never gets seasick.

Steering a motorboat day after day can be a terrible bore."

The three men finished their discussion with an examination of Moore's boat's proposed delivery trip. She was being built in Europe, and an interesting point developed when Don said he intended to go to the Canary Islands about September 1, then cross the Atlantic via the Cape Verde Islands.

"Why, that's right in the middle of the hurricane season," protested Tubby.

"That's right. But I can't sit around the Canary Islands until the middle of November like the sailing cruisers do before starting for the West Indies, and my 'Passagemaker' doesn't have to. We'll start out from the Cape Verdes, trying to get in a little trade-wind running with twin staysails and self-steering, but continually slanting south. Then, when we get down to latitude five or six degrees north, we'll head due west, getting what help we can from the winds, but prepared to go all the way under power. There's never been a hurricane recorded that far south.

"We'll stop at Port-of-Spain in Trinidad for fuel and some rum, then head west along the coast of South America, still south of the hurricane belt, to Panama. From there to Acapulco I'm sure we will use a lot of power. After a couple of days ashore, we'll be off on the last leg. We'll head directly for Cabo San Lucas, the southern tip of Baja California. When the wind comes ahead, I'll put her on the starboard tack with power and go out to sea. As the wind shifts around, we'll gradually come to a more northerly course and end up where the clippers used to, about 600 miles west of San Francisco. Then it's due east on a reach 'til she goes under the Golden Gate Bridge, and there we are! How about it, Tubby, want to come along? I'll make a real cruising man of you yet."

"I'd sure like to. Maybe I could make at least one leg of it—or two."

"Your ideas are very interesting, Don," Bob Reid said. "It will be fun to watch how she works out. As far as I can see you have everything you need for your 'Passagemaker.' Count me in with Tubby for part of your voyage, if you can. I'll do my best to make it."

"I'll do that, Bob," replied Moore, rolling up his prints. "You and Tubby will be hearing from me one of these days. Keep your seabags packed!"

They sat for a few minutes, thinking about Don Moore's story. Bob saw Tubby had a faraway look in his eye, a look that said he was running through the trades with Don—blue water and a fair wind, with the 'Passagemaker' chugging quietly along. Finally he sighed and looked around for a waiter.

"George," he said, "bring me the check—."

That was the end of the story. Looking back on it now, from the actual years of operating at sea that followed it, I can see that it extended the ideas first expressed in the 1946 *Rudder* article to encompass the requirement that range under power should be complete; that is, fuel for continuous motoring for any contemplated passage should be provided. Not only is this necessary for speed and dispatch but it permits the continuous use of the autopilot. The

"APE," as Carleton Mitchell calls it (for autopilot *extraordinaire*), is not simply a convenience for the crew, it is a necessity. It permits the use of a one-man watch, makes it possible to use inexperienced watch-standers, and, by taking the most onerous task off the crew's shoulders, contributes a great deal to establishing passage-making as a relaxed and pleasurable way to cross oceans.

The boats discussed in the story were full-sail vessels that could be used for sail cruising upon reaching their destinations, after exchanging their passage propellers for two-bladed sailing types. It is obvious now, though it was not then, that placing increasing emphasis on power would bring great changes to the status of the sailing rig, as will be seen.

This story was the origin of my use of the term "Passagemaker" and the "Passagemaker concept," the words I coined to differentiate my type from other classes of yachts. (The correct version of this word when applied to *voyaging* is passage-maker or passage-making.) In fact, the whole discussion was pointed toward why the vessels discussed could not be classified as of any existing type, but were really a new concept.

Before then, the terms "motor-all-the-time boat" or "motorboat with rig" were used when I had to describe this craft, one that could not properly be called a motorsailer.

In fact, what to call long-range motor cruisers still causes trouble today. In his book *Sea Sense,* Richard Henderson calls *Passagemaker* a "modified MFV Type," which she certainly is not. The term "trawler yacht" started out to mean just that—a yacht patterned after a fishing trawler. Today "trawler yacht" is used to describe boats that never in one's wildest dreams could be called true trawlers.

Let me set down here what I conceive *my* Passagemakers to be now:

1. She may carry sail or not, but in any case must carry at least enough fuel for an Atlantic crossing under power. The quantities of fuel and speeds involved are discussed in Chapter 5.

2. Her layout and equipment must be primarily for the comfort and efficiency of the crew on long passages. In-port convenience must be secondary. For some items that bear on this, see Chapter 3: Lessons Learned Nos. 2,7,8, and 14.

3. Her seaworthiness, glass areas, above water/below water areas ratio (A/B), ballast, and other factors must clearly mark her as capable of making long voyages in deep water in the proper seasons for each area. These factors are discussed in Chapter 5.

In retrospect, it is surprising but quite true that the designs I worked on were considered solely in the light of their suitability to make the San Diego–Key West passage. It was not until the work was near completion that it occurred to me to think, "If it will do that, why not extend your ambition to cross the Atlantic and cruise the Mediterranean? Or the South Seas? Or around the world?"

This was the prospect before me while I labored on the last of the series of designs. When this vessel was built and launched to test my ideas, she could hardly be called anything else but *Passagemaker*. How she was designed and built and how she worked out comes next.

3

PASSAGEMAKER: Designing, Building, & Testing— and the Lessons Learned

The design for the boat that was finally built and christened *Passagemaker* was drawn in a hectic six-week period beginning in January, 1962. Innumerable sketches and six designs taken through the lines and layout stages preceded her. Each one of these provided something for the next—it is surprising how much can be learned from a design that is never built. When *Passagemaker*'s turn came, she went together with ease, involving only the combining of concepts that had previously been tested and refined on paper.

By now the original concept had been expanded. Due to a drastic change in my personal situation it became desirable to have a vessel that not only filled the requirements of the Passagemaker concept discussed in Chapter 2, but also had room for full-time living and working aboard. Sketching with this in mind, it soon became apparent that the 50-foot size was best to fill this specification along with the basic Passagemaker concept—especially as the contemplated vessel would have no "double-decking"—a term that will become familiar later.

Fig. 3-1, 3-2, and 3-3 show what *Passagemaker* looked like. Later, we will discuss what we learned from her.

The lines show a hull of moderate deadrise, with constant deadrise aft and a perfectly straight run. The quarter beam buttock aft is literally straight. And thereby hangs a tale. Howard Chapelle, the designer and marine historian, has helped me extensively over the years by criticizing my designs and admonishing me when I needed it. One day at the Smithsonian Institution I showed the plans for *Passagemaker* to Howard.

Looking at the lines, he nodded and said, "Not bad." Then, pointing at the quarter beam buttock aft, he added, "But that should be straighter."

That gave me the opening I was looking for. "Damn it, Howard," I said, "I *knew* you would say that. That line was drawn with the straightest straight edge I could find!"

He merely answered, "Humpf."

The high stern was needed to preserve the room inside the stern cabin by providing the last seven feet with an area where the sole could be raised. The bow was the same height as the stern, which is unusual, and made her look a bit like a dhow. The entire hull shows the influence of my previous sailing experience. *PM* certainly ran nicely, with no wake to speak of, at her ocean-crossing speed of 7.5 knots. When completely built, she was somewhat over-

19

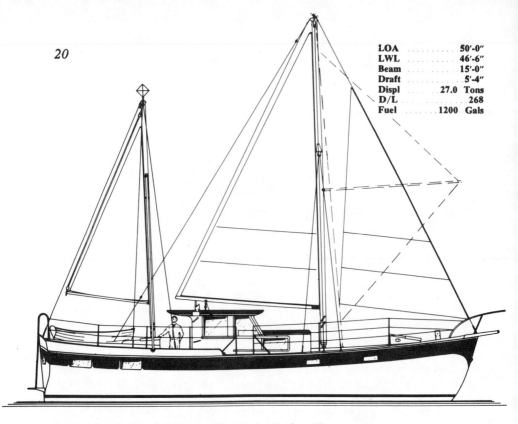

LOA	50'-0"
LWL	46'-6"
Beam	15'-0"
Draft	5'-4"
Displ	27.0 Tons
D/L	268
Fuel	1200 Gals

FIG. 3-1. Profile of *Passagemaker,* Beebe Design 67.

weight, and the significance of this will be discussed in Chapter 5 as an example of the technicalities of the business. The long keel and skeg with large rudder made her run as if on rails before a gale, and effectively handled the broaching problem so often exhibited by ordinary motorboats.

The arrangement shows the big stern cabin that was originally wide open— a combined drafting office and social center. Forward of this was the cockpit, on the same level as the pilothouse. It was designed to insure the single watch-stander a secure place to go outside and observe—something that has to be done as it is impossible to keep the pilothouse windows salt-free all the time. The pilothouse was kept small but had all required space, including a chart table and a raised settee with a good view all around. Forward of this and down three steps, was the combined galley-dinette. The dinette was raised 18 inches to put our eyes at the level of the ports while eating—a much appreciated feature. The space under it provided bins for canned goods, stores for six people for 60 days. Forward of this, was the owner's quarters with head and shower. In the stern, a convertible sofa made two berths, with a third on top of the drafting table. In this way there were four berths for the passage-making crew, the number we had on the first voyage from Singapore to Greece. Later a pipe berth was fitted up forward, increasing crew berths to five—until the aft cabin was further modified as described under Lessons Learned.

The profile shows the rig. It was quite short. Originally I had planned to have a much taller mainsail so I could attempt to sail in fair winds—motorsailer

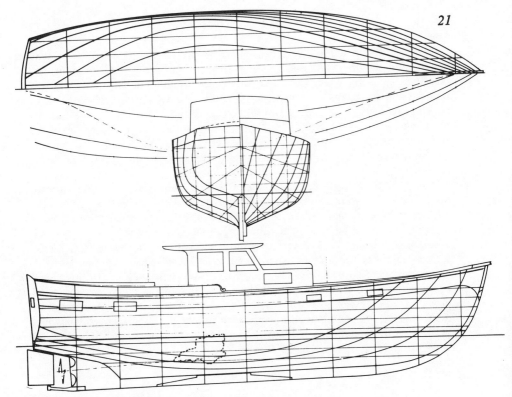

FIG. 3-2. Lines of *Passagemaker.*

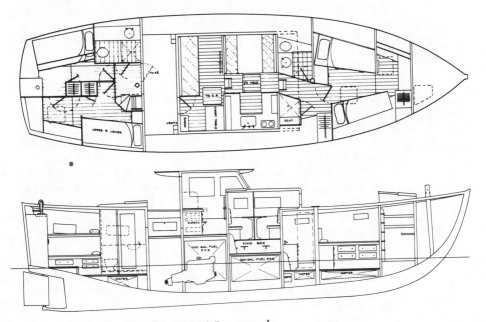

FIG. 3-3. Accommodation Plan of *Passagemaker.*

fashion—with the aid of a Hyde feathering propeller. But when the Hyde people told me they did not approve of their propeller being used in this manner, that is, on what was essentially a motor-all-the-time-boat, the rig was reduced and considered as emergency propulsion only. At that time there was no other feathering propeller I would trust. It would have been hopeless to try to sail well with her 32-inch, three-bladed prop. We did have plans to rig all the gear necessary to remove the prop at sea, but never did it. The mizzen was wholly dedicated to carrying the stabilizing rig, and its bit of sail was rarely used.

The single Ford 330, six-cylinder diesel, a Thornycroft conversion with heavy flywheel—a must with Fords—and 1200 U.S. gallons of fuel were selected to take us the required 2400 miles. Due to doubts raised in researching the problems of attaining maximum range—let alone estimating it—I made allowances everywhere I could to insure we got the range desired. These included drawing the hull to the prismatic coefficient suited to a speed of 7.5 knots; providing an oversized propeller for greatest efficiency at cruising speed —but without the ability to use all the power the engine could provide—and providing an excess of fuel over what was theoretically necessary. As a result of these precautions, she attained a range well in excess of that desired, showing, on a run from San Diego to Panama without fueling, a reserve of some 400 miles for an all-gone range of 3200 miles.

BUILDING

My research on the building problem showed the family budget could stand the cost if she was built abroad of wood with very simple equipment. The plans were sent out for bids, and a contract for the construction was ultimately awarded to John I. Thornycroft & Sons of Singapore. Work commenced in July, 1962.

I spoke of being able to swing the cost if the boat was built abroad. I planned to take advantage of all the money-saving possibilities of such a project. There are a number of steps involved that can lead to the greatest possible economy. Not everyone will be able to take advantage of all these, but here is how they worked for me:

1. The construction bid itself was lower than those from yards in the U.S.
2. I designed her myself and avoided that cost.
3. I went to Singapore and superintended the job. Not only did I live more cheaply than at home, but I feel some form of supervision is essential on a foreign contract. It is impossible to draw the details of everything, and if any solutions are left to the yard, differences in building practice are bound to make you unhappy over some of them.
4. The vessel came home under her own power. This is a saving two ways. First, you save the considerable freight bill which includes many hidden expenses. Second, you save on duty since the boat is secondhand on arrival. *Passagemaker* arrived in the U.S. 17 months after completion. The duty was reduced by 20 percent, the reduction paying the expenses of the trip. And we had a fine cruise in the bargain.

PHOTOS 3-4,5,6. Three views of *Passagemaker* during construction at the yard of John I. Thornycroft & Sons, Singapore.

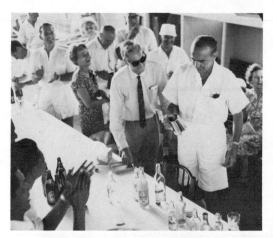

PHOTOS 3-7,8. *Left, Passagemaker's* christening party. Jack Wilde *(with tie)*, the manager of Thornycroft's has just presented the author with an inscribed pewter mug—which was promptly filled with martinis. *Right*, Mrs. Congdon Curts christens *Passagemaker* with a mighty blow. Immediately after, the huge 10-ft. string of firecrackers hanging behind the author's shoulder was fired off—a present from the yard's Chinese foremen. Firecrackers dispel devils—and bring good luck.

PHOTO 3-9. *Passagemaker* at Thornycroft's fitting-out dock, with flags flying in celebration of the christening.

PHOTO 3-10. Passagemaker during her trials in Singapore harbor. The stabilizer poles are swung out for the first time, but the stabilizers are not in the water.

Experience since 1963 shows steadily rising building costs in the Orient, reducing the differential in bid costs. But it still appears possible to save money if the boat comes home under her own power. One thing more: Supervising is not easy. I worked seven days a week all during the seven months I was there.

Thornycroft did an excellent job on the boat, using teak planking over triple-laminated *chengal* frames, plywood decking topped by Cascover sheathing. With spruce spars and English sails, and now properly christened *Passagemaker,* she lay alongside the Thornycroft pier ready to go—tanks full of fuel, provisions stowed, and crew aboard—on March 18, 1963, eight and a half months after construction began.

PASSAGEMAKER'S CRUISING

I mentioned earlier that Marin-Marie's voyage in *Arielle* resulted in his crossing the Atlantic with essentially nothing to report; this is the way it was with *Passagemaker.* Although we passed through the fringes of two hurricanes and had some gales, we always made our ETAs, suffered no damage we couldn't fix, had the engine start when the switch was turned on, and run until we stopped it.

But it will be appreciated that when we left the builder's yard in Singapore on March 18, 1963, none of the crew knew what to expect. Two of us, Captain Ralph Arndt, USN, Ret., and myself, had considerable sailing experience; Colonel Everett Bibb, USA, Ret., had extensive coastal motorboat experience; Congdon Curts, my old friend from service in Alaska, was the only man qualified as a novice. But the vessel and the ideas behind it were wholly untried.

There was at that time no other vessel that could even attempt what we were trying to do.

Any anxieties we may have felt turned out to be completely groundless. *Passagemaker* soon showed she would do all we expected and more. The log of that first voyage essentially went like this: We hurried our departure because the boat was late being completed, as is usual with yacht builders. We feared the beginning of the southwest monsoon in the Indian Ocean that would have effectively barred our way to Aden. We finished storing supplies late one night and left at dawn the next day. The three days spent running up the flat, calm Strait of Malacca were used to shake things down, get the rigging in shape, and so on, before entering the Bay of Bengal headed for Ceylon. In the Bay we found favorable winds, the remnants of the northeast monsoon, and made excellent time to Colombo, arriving before dawn on the seventh day. We had to jill around for several hours before we were able to enter port.

After a stay of four days, we were off on the 2200-mile passage to Aden. We touched the southern tip of India at Cape Comorin to get a good departure, and then headed for Minicoy island and the passage through the Maldive Island reefs. From there it was a straight shot to Cape Guardafui, the northeast tip of Somaliland, and another run of 400 miles to Aden. It took 12 days—in a flat calm most of the way. We were lucky: The southwest monsoon must have set in just a few days after we passed this critical point.

After three days in Aden, we left for Suez, experiencing the usual blow from the south at the south end of the Red Sea, and from the north at the north end. In the middle it was quite nice. Bucking the norther at the north end convinced us that we rated some time off, so we stopped for two days at Endeavour Harbor on Tawilla Island at the entrance to the Gulf of Suez. At the Canal, they were kind and efficient and we started through at the stern of a convoy the next morning, and made the usual one-night stopover at Ismailia. The next afternoon we let our pilot off with a running jump to the dock in Port Said, and headed out into the Mediterranean for Rhodes, taking care to pour a libation to Poseidon as we entered his domain. The *meltemi* from Russia to Egypt was blowing pretty hard, and we had to buck it most of the way. It took us four days, but we finally arrived in Rhodes—in a flat calm.

In a total elapsed time of six weeks we had made some 6000 miles to Greece, averaging underway exactly our designed ocean-crossing speed of 7.5 knots. We knew then that in *Passagemaker* we had something. And subsequent cruising in her has shown how right we were. There we were, 42 days from Singapore, ready for cruising in the fascinating waters of the Mediterranean. It's difficult to determine the records of sailing vessels that have made the same trip, but we had certainly arrived ahead of any of them by a matter of *months!* Even the cutter *Beyond*, mentioned in Chapter 14, would have trailed us by at least 30 days despite of her range under power of 1500 miles. Our record was achieved not only by keeping up a high average speed but also by the way the crew was rested and relaxed enough to be ready to leave port again in a matter of days. That was the start of our kind of passage-making.

For the rest of the summer, we cruised in Greece and Yugoslavia. The next spring we cruised to Malta and Italy, then moved eastward along the

Riviera to the mouth of the Rhone River. There we prepared to test another of *Passagemaker*'s features—her ability to go into the French canals (*see Chapter 13*). With her masts down and her engine turning at the maximum permitted rpm for a speed of about 9.4 knots, our vessel went up the Rhone to Lyon in two days. This was followed by an idyllic meander through France to Strasbourg on the Rhine River. Then down the Rhine and across the North Sea to England for some work at the Thornycroft plant which lies three locks up the Thames River past London.

On departure day from London, we dropped down the Thames in the middle of the night to catch the tide, put up our masts in the Medway, went to Plymouth for fuel and supplies, and crossed the Atlantic via the Azores and Bermuda to Newport, Rhode Island, in 21 steaming days.

Singlehanded, I then took her down the Inland Waterway to Miami. With a new crew, we went from Miami through the Bahamas to Panama, then up the coast to San Diego, California, in 29 days—not bad, considering we took three days off to cruise in the Bahamas. (How well I recall my earlier concern about this east-west passage in the planning and theory-stage years!) After San Diego, a crew of two took *Passagemaker* up the coast to her home port of Monterey, to end a delivery cruise of some 21 months that had been fun all the way.

After that, *Passagemaker* made a cruise to Hawaii and return via the Pacific Northwest. She also made a trip to the Pacific Northwest straight up the coast, nonstop, in seven days, our most rugged cruise.

In 1967, she went east to Expo '67 in Montreal, and was stored on the East Coast preparatory to sailing to Europe the following summer. Some months later, a gentleman who had made a long cruise with me, bought her, on the condition I would help him take her to Europe in 1969, which I did (*see Chapter 12*).

It was a wrench to let her go, but I felt I had learned all I could from her and wanted to take the next step. *PM* has been happily cruising in Europe from April to October for the past five years, covering beautiful cruising grounds from Norway to Turkey.

PHOTO 3-11. Passagemaker at anchor in Endeavour Harbour, Tawilla Island, at the entrance to the Gulf of Suez, where we took a well-earned rest.

PHOTO 3-12. *Passagemaker*'s dinghy was patterned after the Herreshoff *Columbian* model, and sized to fit the raised poop deck. Here she takes a capacity "liberty party" ashore at Delos, Greece.

WHAT WE LEARNED

The lessons learned comprise such a big file that I can only give the conclusions here. But believe me, there is much data to support every point, even if some of the conclusions sound dogmatic. So here is a list of the major items, emphasizing those that affected future design:

1. Layout. The highly specialized and personal layout of *Passagemaker* would not be anyone else's cup of tea. As a matter of fact, it did not work out and was never used for its designed purpose. We finally converted the stern cabin into two double cabins with a head. While this layout was highly satisfactory at sea, it was not a success in port.

The reason for this layout failure was that I had been so concerned about *Passagemaker*'s seaworthiness and ability to perform at sea to the required concept, that other facets of the whole-boat problem were neglected or ignored. For instance, to keep her above water/below water areas ratio as low as possible, she was not "double-decked." This concentration on performance contributed to making her a seagoing machine. I would be hard put to find some feature of her performance at sea that could be changed to advantage.

But in port, her lack of lounge space, except the galley-dinette area and the pilothouse settee, was a distinct drawback to her having any wide appeal. The fact is, such a large and expensive vessel does not make sense unless she is used the greater part of the year. This leads to the requirement that such a vessel should have good in-port living space for the owner and his wife, with all the amenities of a shore apartment if they can be fitted in. When you get right down to it, such a vessel is most suitable for a retired couple who use it as a home afloat. The problem is to combine living space with the necessary seaworthiness for ocean voyaging. I believe now that a better balance of such qualities is feasible.

I spoke above of "double-decking." This means to have one full-headroom compartment under another full-headroom compartment. *Passagemaker* was not double decked, nor is such a popular model as the Grand Banks 42. As an example of double-decking, the Grand Banks 50 takes it about as far as you can go. It is clear the amount of double-decking largely determines how much living space a vessel can have, a matter explored in depth in Chapter 7.

2. Cockpit. At sea, *Passagemaker's* cockpit—four feet deep—was one of her best features. It enabled the watch-stander to go outside to observe all around while remaining securely *in* the boat, with no possibility of falling overboard. This is a very serious problem on the seagoing motorboat. We found that the single watch-stander was alone much of the time, day as well as night. The consequences of someone falling overboard while alone, with the ship running on autopilot, are not pleasant to contemplate. On *Passagemaker* there was only one absolute rule: The watch-stander was not allowed to go on deck without someone watching him. The captain was always available for this duty. But the four-foot-long cockpit, subtracted from the overall length, certainly hurt the accommodations. In subsequent designs, I have felt it necessary to dispense with this feature. With a pilothouse placed on deck where the watch-stander can gain access to the side of the vessel, I feel it is necessary that the rails should be *not less than four feet high* and solid in any area the watch-stander is permitted to go. The presence of sailing-racer-inspired, 30-inch-high lifelines on seagoing power boats is shocking. They make sense on a sailing vessel because higher ones interfere with sails, the crew wears safety harnesses, and there is more than one watch-stander on deck. But for the single watch-stander of the oceangoing motorboat they certainly are not adequate, being a height only sufficient to trip you overboard. On *Passagemaker,* the lifeline stanchions forward were 40 inches high and on the raised after deck they were 30 inches. It was surprising how much difference the 10 inches made in the feeling of security.

PHOTO 3-13. The author, *left,* talks with Dr. James Kergen in British Columbia. This photo shows the deep cockpit, so useful at sea.

PHOTO 3-14. Aboard *Passagemaker.* The author, *left,* with Dr. John Gratiot at Mykonos Island, Greece. Note the lifelines that are 40 inches high forward, and 30 inches high aft. They are slack, preparatory to launching the dinghy.

3. Sailing Rig. This feature is hard to justify by the facts of our cruising. It is not a good emergency propulsion system for this reason: If the engine should fail, sail would get you somewhere, but the chances of its being where you wanted to go are pretty slim. Consequently, your cruise would be pretty well ruined, while an alternative power system would allow the cruise to continue. In addition an efficient sailing rig is expensive, *more* so than another diesel engine.

Sail has two things to recommend it. It gives the crew something to do, and is fun from this point of view. (But with an assured speed of 7.5 to eight knots, it is surprising how often the wind is so far ahead that the sails won't draw.) And sail gives the vessel the aspect of a motorsailer, making it more acceptable to proceed at hull speed or below without embarrassment when passed by faster coastal motorboats. I'm not being facetious here: I am convinced this is the real reason for the existence of the so-called "motorsailer." I have never seen one with its sails up in coastal waters. This is certainly a legitimate reason, but an expensive one. For vessels with sail, I now recommend they *also* have alternate engine-driven emergency drive.

4. Stabilizing Rig. *Passagemaker's* rig, the West Coast Anti-Roll Stabilizer, familiarly called "flopperstoppers," (F/S) changed the whole aspect of our cruising in ways we did not imagine before we started. For one thing, it made ocean crossing by motorboat an activity that could be thoroughly enjoyed by persons without any seagoing experience. This aspect turned out to be such a vital contribution to the success of our Passagemaker concept that there is a whole chapter devoted to it later. Now I'm sure it is a *required feature* of the ocean-crossing motorboat, so important that in the larger and more expensive vessels, an alternative means of stabilizing should be provided.

PHOTO 3-15. *Passagemaker* spreads her downwind running sails by backing down for the photographer. Note the wake at the bow. (Norris D. Hoyt Photo)

5. Freeboard. The bow was too low. We found that the measure of speed possible against the sea depended very much on the height of the bow. When encountering seas from ahead, it is mandatory that you slow down until green water does not come over the bow. If you do not, you will eventually damage the vessel. We often wished our bow was higher by a foot or so, as it could have been without esthetic damage to the profile.

6. Stern. Some people expressed concern about our broad stern in a following sea, a concern I did not share, feeling that the shape under water, not above, was the criterion. I was pleased to observe that in gales from astern we never had more than a foot or two of water over the stern platform.

7. Steering Comfort. *Passagemaker* was built with a sprocket on the wheel to provide eventually for an outside steering station. This was never installed as we felt no need for it, piloting around docks and through the canals from inside with no difficulty. While the flying bridge has its points in local cruising of the weekend variety, one must remember that the tropical sun cannot be faced day in and day out on a long voyage. In *Passagemaker* the watchstander could go outside as much as he pleased when there were others on deck.

8. Hand-Holds. Although our stabilizing gear cut rolling by two-thirds, which made ordinary rolling around five to 10 degrees at most, we found *Passagemaker*'s pipe handholds in the galley were one of her best features. At the corner of each counter and at the inboard edge of the dinette table there were brass pipes to the overhead. These were constantly in use as handgrips, particu-

PHOTO 3-16. The author's step-daughter, Gael Donovan, in *Passagemaker*'s galley. She is holding two of the galley hand-holds and the third one is visible.

larly by the cook in passing hot plates to the table, which could be reached with one hand while the other securely held a pipe.

If handholds were so useful in the intimately related galley and dinette of *Passagemaker,* it's clear that a greater separation between galley and dining table with no handholds would be quite dangerous. If a person loses his balance and starts to move across the ship, this movement must be stopped before it can accelerate to the point of injury. This is the reason why, in the days of transatlantic passenger steamers, storm-wracked ships used to reach port with extraordinary numbers of injured passengers. Yachts with wide saloons must be careful about this.

9. Propeller. *Passagemaker* was fitted with an oversize prop. That is, she could not turn up the maximum permitted rpms for continuous duty. The reason for this was to get her long-range speed of 7.5 knots at a lower rpm, 1750, which placed the engine at its most efficient fuel-consumption rate. While this provided a per cent or two of better range, I feel now it would have been better to use the conventional prop for maximum continuous hp at maximum continuous rpm. You would then not have to worry about overloading the engine, and would have a somewhat higher top speed, and be allowed a higher local cruising speed.

10. Equipment. While simplicity of equipment is an ideal given much lip service, oceangoing motorboats are often found with amazing amounts of equipment for amazing amounts of money. This is discouraging to those with small budgets.

It doesn't have to be that way; *Passagemaker* proved it. We left Singapore with hardly more equipment than one would expect to find on a 30-foot sloop making the same voyage. We did have an autopilot—but this is a necessity on an oceangoing motorboat. We had a compass, a sextant, a radio for time ticks, a small radio direction finder (RDF), a 100-foot depth-sounder, a two-burner Primus stove, hand pumps for water, and a box for ice—when we could get it. That was the lot. And we had a ball all the way, ate very well, and were able to fix any small item that went wrong.

We did not have radar, radio transmitter, watermaker, hot water, gas ovens, air conditioning, pressure water system, or any of the multitude of items so often installed today, and we never missed them. I recommend this approach, though I think it is pretty much a lost cause today. Basically you must be sure you have an answer to the question, "What will you do *when* that quits?" Not *if*, but *when*, as it will. For instance, there is the incredible story of the all-electric yacht that went to the South Seas where its *single* generator gave up the ghost. They couldn't even flush the heads. End of story—and end of cruise.

Of course, I have no objection to owners installing as much equipment as their budgets can stand. It makes sense to provide space for the later installation of equipment by building-in everything possible in the construction phase. But you don't really *need* this stuff. Get under way without it and enjoy the cruise. Once you convince yourself that warm beer is just as good as cold, refrigeration is a waste of time and money, in my opinion—but not that of my wife!

11. Night Vision. One thing I completely forgot to provide for was night vision in the pilothouse. If a light was on in the galley, the watch-stander couldn't see a thing. And the galley was the only space available for the navigator to work up his evening stars. In Ceylon we tried to fix this with a hatch cover and curtain. This helped, but a real light lock with a door is a necessity. This problem should be well up on the list in the design stage.

12. Fuel Tanks. *Passagemaker's* fuel tanks were fitted with a draw-off sump which trapped all contamination. We opened a tank after five years to see how it was doing. It was perfectly clean and free of corrosion. I feel, then, that it is permissable to build tanks without cleanout plates if a sump is used. This gets rid of a potential leak source.

13. Guard Rail. *Passagemaker* had a guard rail six inches wide outside, with full-length scarfed and glued timbers. It was considered an external sheer clamp. Inside, the frames were blocked and, with the internal clamp, there was a solid 12 inches of timber at the sheer. Knocking around ports overseas as we did, with no yacht-type moorage to speak of, we were *very* glad we had this rail. It took with aplomb some incredible knocks. It also furnished a dividend we didn't anticipate. The six-inch, flat-top surface of the rail made a convenient and safe place to run around outside the lifelines when setting fenders, lines, etc. I recommend the arrangement. Most American yachts are flimsy in this department.

14. Noise. In the planning stages, I was concerned about the possible effect of noise and vibration on the crew over long stretches. Some information on this subject indicated that noise alone can cause cumulative fatigue if the level is high enough. Consequently, as much as possible was done to suppress noise. Two inches of fiberglass insulation was used both in the engine room and in the overheads. The entire vessel from end to end inside also had acoustic tile on the overhead. The aft bulkhead of the engine room, which opened on the aft living spaces, was also heavily insulated.

No fatigue from this source was evident. In fact, the steady noise of the engine soon became a part of life and was ignored. The comment often made by sailing men, that noise would drive us crazy, turned out to be wishful thinking on their part.

I believe the acoustic tile did more to suppress noise than anything else as it stopped reflection back and forth from sole to overhead, a potent source of noise. In addition, the insulation and tile kept the interior of the boat cool on the hottest days.

15. Hot Salt Water.   Something I thought up and tried out proved to be the most popular and appreciated feature on the ship. This was to have hot salt water from the engine cooling system piped into the galley to furnish, when the engine was running, an unlimited supply of very hot water for rinsing plates and pots. The cooks and cleanup crew really missed it when the engine was shut down in port. To avoid unbalancing the engine cooling system, the water ran all the time. A two-way valve either dumped it into the sink drain or turned it into the faucet. As an added dividend, the temperature and volume of the running water gave the watch-stander a quick check on the cooling system.

16. Summary.   Finally we, and by "we" I mean all of the people who cruised aboard *Passagemaker*, discovered how much fun even long passages could be in a vessel that made no demands on one's endurance, nor required skills developed over years of experience under sail. This was something new, something worth emphasizing as we will see in Chapter 12. ". . . with speed and dispatch," the concept stated. Well, we achieved this and it does make for a different sort of cruising. On our voyage to Hawaii and return we went out in 12 days and returned in 13. By contrast, a sailing vessel that at speeds comparable to ours should have come back in 16 days, left about the same date— and took 70 days!

PHOTO 3-17. Passagemaker arriving at the dock in Monterey, California, in 1964, at the end of her passage three-quarters of the way around the world, proudly flying the flags of the 18 nations she visited.

4

The Philosophy of Power Passagemaking

So much for *Passagemaker* and what we learned from her cruising. It was a revelation to me. In my career at sea I have handled ships from El Toro dinghies to 80,000-ton aircraft carriers, and cruised in sail in all rigs from 26 feet to 55 feet. But none of this prepared me for how our long voyages in *Passagemaker* turned out to be so relaxing, such a delight to people who had never been to sea before, such an impressive demonstration that the world's cruising grounds were indeed available with "speed and dispatch." It is this side of our concept that has made me such a missionary on the subject.

Lest it be thought I am overdrawing this point, and I have certainly been accused of that, let me offer here what another sailor has said about this power passage-making business, a sailor who can by no stretch of the imagination be considered a secret power boat freak.

In August and September, 1966, *Yachting* published two articles by Norris D. Hoyt. Norrie is a writer on yachting subjects and a well-known ocean racing crew man. He has been on every Bermuda Race and transatlantic race for many years. In 1964, he broke this pattern and crossed the Atlantic in both directions in motorboats, going east in the Scottish MFV *Kytra* and returning in *Passagemaker*. He wrote about these two cruises, "I experienced revelation!" It was great fun to have him along, as well as Kitty, his wife, who has also made many crossings under sail. The reactions of the Hoyts were interesting and in some cases amusing. In his articles he set down the philosophy of the whole thing in a superb manner as these excerpts will show:

Once Over Heavily

By Norris D. Hoyt

Thirty times a year, for the last ten years, I've made speeches to Power Squadrons about crossing the Atlantic in sailboats. As I ate their dinners and drank their laughter, the slow suspicion leaked through the keelbolts of my habituation to sail that all these pleasant people must have some reason for liking motorboats. If not looks, utility; if not excitement, economy; if not complexity, stability; if not exercise, company. Awash with burgeoning curiosity, I last spring made the great decision and signed on for not one, but two crossings of the Atlantic in two different motorboats. The two boats were as unlike as boats can be: One was a massive Scottish seine-netter built from

35

fisherman molds as a yacht; the other was a sweetly subtle product of a lifetime of design development in modern powerboats. Both were superb executions of their owners' basic intentions . . .

Kytra (LOA 54 feet; beam 17 feet; draft 7.5 feet) . . . was superbly built, eloquently seaworthy, sound, round, and fully packed when we got 50 friends aboard at Newport for a final party . . . and shoved off on June 12, in the opening westerly of a large high-pressure system, for Cobh, Ireland. We hadn't a worry in the world, for the boat had come over under her own power . . . On top of that, every member of the crew had made at least one trans-atlantic trip, four were navigators, all were good cooks, and there were three conversationalists and two listeners.

. . . At 0020 we left Race Point and the United States and set course due east. It would take us 100 miles south of any known ice. With one man at a time on watch, watches were four hours, and one man was off, on rotation, to help the cook for 24 hours and sleep through an unbroken night. Hasty calculation will reveal that an average of 20 hours a day was ours to use as we would. For the next 2600 miles!

So many people cross the ocean in sailboats, and sailors are so inclined to write about it, that the world sees sailboats as passage-makers and motorboats as coastwise cruisers. Nothing could be less true. The fact is that a well-designed motor vessel makes a cinch of a passage, and offers no opportunity for heroic postures. I suspect that motor passage-makers arrive casually for lunch and move on to the next port, unnoticed—no baggywrinkle, no tattered canvas, no ragged beards, no stormcloths. There are reasons why motor passage-making is safe and easy, and there are techniques for keeping it that way.

In the first place, it *is* easy because progress is constant . . . In a sailboat, about one-fourth of your time is spent in near calms, and about a fourth of your time in headwinds—even in a traditionally downwind crossing of the Atlantic . . . A good motorboat averaging eight knots can start on the eastern edge of a high and cross the Atlantic in stable weather. Yet, if you're in a sailboat, you average eight knots only when there's fresh weather from astern; and if a storm's coming, you'll wait for it, because it will either have contrary winds or no winds in front of it . . .

Weather control, within limits, is the first great safety factor of motorboats. The second is comfort. We made a round trip of the Atlantic without getting wet or cold; in fact, Beau Wood came and went without getting out of his carpet slippers. . . . Because you're operating behind glass, and with only one man on duty at a time, you have reserve energy for emergencies.

The third factor in safety on motor passages is the variable: crew and boat preparation. If you're going offshore for long passages, the engine room and the engine must be given the same knowledgeable attention that rig and sails get from the offshore sailor. An engine tucked into a cramped space almost as an afterthought, minimal fuel tankage, and a crew that only knows how to start and stop the engine—this sailboat approach to power does not fit the ocean-crossing motorboat picture. The more sophisticated the engine room, the more sophisticated the engineer must be.

But once you truly are master of your vessel, the joys of passage-making on a motorboat are great—of them I sing.

It takes a little time, on a passage, to get used to the new tempo of sea time and sea life. When sailing, the watches change in herdlike shifts from cabin to deck, punctuated in midshift by meals, and delayed by dish washup. The boat's motion, the constant sail trimming, steering, sail-shifting, and variation of speed give a sense of involvement in the enterprise . . . At first, it's mainly busy and tiring. Then you get the rhythm, and the duty watch periods are filled with cheerful talk, instinctive activity, and the changing spectacle of the vessel heeling and running through the tireless seas.

The motorboat passage is entirely different. From the frantic business of loading, storing, fueling, checking equipment, and last minute calls, parties, and purchases, you're abruptly off into the great silence of the sea—shore, telephone and family astern, horizon ahead, nothing much to do, and less inclination to do it. Necessity has just been turned off and the silence is deafening. The autopilot clicks erratically, the diesel mumbles, the bow pushes through the yielding sea, and the duty watch-keeper sits alone, lightly clad, in a warm cabin, on an upholstered settee, half-reading a book, and half-watching the edge of the horizon rock gently through the pilothouse windows. For the first day or so you do almost nothing—make your bed, experiment with the best place to put a box

PHOTO 4-1. Kytra in a lock of the Crinian Canal, Scotland. (Norris D. Hoyt Photo)

of cameras, drink a beer every now and then, read, sleep, eat, wash up, wander around the deck looking at the gear, sunbathe, mess with watch and sextant, check WWV, read, sleep, and eat again.

The first night watch introduces you to passage-making. Out of a warm bed and into pants, slippers, and a sweater in the black pitch of midnight, you wander up to the wheelhouse, share a leisurely cup of coffee with the man you're relieving, have a little aimless conversation, and take a reluctant parting from his pleasant voice in the darkness.

Then you're alone on the pulsing, pushing boat on the dark ocean and under the open, luminous sky. You check the compass for a while, and she's hunting about four degrees across the course. You go out on deck, gaze carefully around the horizon, see nothing Creation didn't put there, and gaze in silence at the stars. Your fellow rovers are breathing trustfully in the darkness below, and you're absolutely alone in the absolute middle of peace. It's an expansive sensation.

You watch the bow wave for a while, check around the horizon every half hour, make a sandwich, check the compass again, think about important things, and go inside to repeat the process. A sensation of enormous well-being fills you. As the watch runs out, you wake your relief, and talk with him for 15 minutes or so before you wander peacefully to bed.

. . . like me, everyone somehow found amiable jobs to do and whistled away at them while *Kytra* ran along at about eight knots, string-straight across the Atlantic. For no apparent reason at all we felt euphorically happy.

It's been years and years since I've had 20 hours out of 24 to do exactly as I pleased, and *Kytra* gave them back to me for the first time since college vacations. Yet motor passage-making is a delicately balanced idleness, with enough event and opportunity for effort to flavor the day.

We ate voraciously. In fact, for the last four days, we had to. The deep freeze broke down. It was good duty—I gained 11 pounds.

On Friday, June 26, our luck broke, our idyll ended. We'd been having such a good time that we were rather shocked to see Fastnet Rock blinking, right on course, at 2308. The next morning all hands came on deck at dawn. Beau Wood in a purple silk dressing gown and slippers, to take down the steadying sails, break out the lines and fenders, and get ready to dock in Cobh—14 days from home. The passage was over; Beau had made it in his slippers. It had been a delightful milk run and, I suppose, no more than I should have expected. We were thoroughly rested, full of excitement for the land, and quite pleased with the world. Our passage had increased all our dimensions, and we were ready for Dublin the next day, the Crinian Canal the day after, and the variegated fleshpots of the Continent which stretched ahead of us.

Hoyt joined *Passagemaker* in Plymouth. We left Plymouth on July 16, went to Ponta Delgada in the Azores, picked up Kitty Hoyt, and were off to Bermuda. A few days there and a four-day passage to Newport, Rhode Island, completed the Hoyt's round trip across the Atlantic by motorboat. Norrie's article on his *Passagemaker* experience read this way in *Yachting:*

Once Over Lightly

by Norris D. Hoyt

Our pleasant voyage to Scotland aboard that solid craft *Kytra* had in no way prepared me for the trip home in a 50-foot diesel motorboat. The most exciting motorboat of my experience, *Passagemaker,* was built in Singapore and brought around to England via the Suez Canal. She was the end product of Bob Beebe's years of planning the perfect boat.

My connection with her was of long standing. After being privileged to watch *Passagemaker* develop in letters, plans, models, and photos, I was eager to settle myself on her for the return voyage . . .

As a matter of fact, I was a little apprehensive. Our trip east had been such a milk run I had premontions of averaging out with a blast of meteorological excitement. Furthermore, though *Passagemaker* was only four feet shorter than *Kytra,* she weighed less than half as much. A couple of years of messing with *Hoot Mon* had taught me that light displacement, though seaworthy, is violently active.

My apprehensions were, of course, completely groundless. She was not lightly built . . . planked with inch and three-quarters teak and all copper riveted, it was an impressive job of building. . . .

Bob is not dedicated to the proposition that he should take everyone on the block to sea with him. The boat, therefore, sleeps five in 50 feet. You could squeeze in a sixth, if he didn't mind sleeping on the duty-helmsman's seat. Still, that's not the idea, and why be subversive? Reflect, rather, on the blessings of space to spare from bow to transom. . . .

Passagemaker is an exceedingly stable boat. Her stowage patterns assert her stability everywhere, ashtrays, bowls, books, and binoculars reclining casually here and there. She'd come a third of the way around the world, and nothing had dents in it. *Passagemaker,* as the eye and mind rove over her, is superbly planned for exactly what she's intended to do . . . move comfortably and safely anywhere. Like her owner, she exudes an orderly sense of leisurely inevitability. And she does well exactly what she's supposed to. . . .

The trip down to the Azores was comfortably uneventful. After a long swell came in, we dumped the flopperstoppers in the water. Her rolling stopped entirely; the side effects were remarkable. We puzzled the local fishermen more than a little. They wander about with great wooden boats with long outriggers trolling for tuna. Boat after boat saw us steaming much too fast, looking much too new, and trailing two steel wires at the end of the booms. From three miles away they'd swing to intercept, steam suspiciously across our bows or alongside, and then line the rail and peer. The whole crew would raise their shoulders and make the Gallic gesture of bafflement with upheld palms. We puzzled the porpoises at least as much. As Bob already knew, the harmonic whine of the flopperstopper wire magnetizes schools of porpoises from afar, and they leaped after us to curvette flirtatiously alongside the singing vanes. . . .

We were not idle, however; Bob Beebe was an instinctive schoolmaster. Navigation class met each morning at 1000. Bob produced pads, notebooks,

PHOTO 4-2. *Passagemaker's* "hurricane" off Bermuda. The rain was so heavy it flattened the waves. (Norris D. Hoyt Photo)

printed worksheet forms of his own design, and diabolical exercises and ideas at any hour. Our fires banked in slumber, we were poked up for a dawn starsight; dawdling over postprandial coffee, we were snatched to sextants and the moon. Each of us had his own plotting sheet, and by the fourth day, we were checking our results against the skipper's. Without comment, he observed and lay in wait.

We were eager to try our passage sails in fresh trade winds, but we were doomed. We slid over an oiled sea. On Friday August 7, we plotted Bermuda on our charts, two days away, altered course northwest for it, and picked up a large glass fishing ball. As the day wore on it degenerated into a full gale. We carried sail and went north of the course. The gusts were hitting 55 knots. It rained torrents—visibility less than 100 yards in the midst of Niagara Falls. The barograph, reacting two hours behind the side effects, tilted over and went down at 45 degrees. In the late afternoon it dropped a vertical quarter of an inch, and abruptly the air cleared and the wind went northwest. We took the sails down, went on course, and thanked the Lord for the flopperstoppers. . . .

On August 9, Bermuda was 60 miles away. Bob had gotten an early star fix and our sun lines were north of it. We figured and refigured, little realizing he had villainously and feloniously doctored his sights to test our self-confidence. Bermuda finally showed up where it always was. . . .

We poked off for Newport the next day, had a pleasant trip home, coming in, I'm vain to say, from two days out on my fix, and sliding neatly past Block Island in the rain and haze. When we tied to the Constellation dock at the Newport Naval Base, we put on oilskins for the first time in a round trip of the Atlantic, had a last meal together at the Officer's Club, and disbanded. The simple casualness of our arrival matched the plain pleasure of our experience. Motorboats are safe, economical, comfortable (by design), companionable, and fit vehicles for Nature's noblemen as they cruise the seven seas.

5

Technicalities of the Seagoing Motorboat

In turning now from what *Passagemaker* proved to applying this experience to future vessels, the first step must be a solid grounding in the technical side of the business. The figures and how they are arrived at are not difficult—but they do require some study.

The reason why technical calculations are so important is that small, long-range motorboats must press every factor which affects performance if they are to achieve the desired results. It is one thing to design a racing sailboat and hope it will make a shambles of the opposition—all sorts of "ifs" can affect that. It is quite another thing to say, "I want a motorboat to take my wife and me, with a crew of friends, across the Atlantic. A range under power of 2400 miles at a speed/length ratio of 1.2 is about right." Here there is only one measure of success—that the vessel *does* achieve your goal.

It is the whys and wherefores of figures like those given above that concern us here. If your vessel is to be an original design, the naval architect will gladly discuss these matters with you. If you are interested in an existing boat, a knowledge of the factors involved in performance will give you a gauge of whether or not such a vessel will fill your needs, whether or not it will do what its makers say it will.

A case in my files is an example of the confusion caused by the advertisements for motorboats billed as "seagoing," or "trawlers," or "go-anywhere boats." A man and wife bought a popular brand of 42-foot "trawler" with the expectation of cruising in the South Seas, an expectation amply reinforced by the salesman who sold them the boat. It was my sad duty after much work on their project to tell them their vessel could not possibly do the job, and no feasible modification would help.

A wider understanding of the technicalities has become even more necessary because of the recent great increase in the number of designs for what are called "trawlers." What is needed is a summary of the naval architecture rules involved in the selection of *any* seagoing motorboat. The rules are not complicated when compared to designing an ocean racing yawl. But they must not be ignored! What follows is as simple an exposition as I can make, but it does take studying. My advice to a prospective owner is to approach salesmen and advertising with your slide rule in hand—ignoring Madison Avenue blurbs—and check out their figures against what is said here. If the figures are not made available, demand them. If you don't know how to use a slide rule, get one and learn. You will certainly need one later to run your long-range cruiser.

A further consequence of the expansion of interest in seagoing motorboats is that they come in such a range of sizes and performance characteristics that one term can hardly be used to cover all types. For our purposes here, let's call vessels "ocean-crossers" if their performance is roughly comparable to *Passagemaker*'s. Of course this does not mean they are useful solely for ocean-crossing. Rather, they have the range and seaworthiness to do it, the equipment and comfort at sea to make such a cruise safe and enjoyable, and are ready to cross an ocean if the owner is. You can see such characteristics are also desirable for shorter cruises. Let's apply "trawler" to lighter vessels with some seagoing capability but with neither the equipment nor the range to qualify for full status as ocean-crossers. And we will use "seagoing motorboat" to cover all types when such a general term is needed.

There is one thing more that needs to be said about "trawler." As we are going to use the term here to designate a class of motorboats that has sprung up lately—a class that has solid virtues in itself—we must first understand that the majority of today's "trawler yachts" have not even a nodding acquaintance with a real seagoing fishing trawler. Such statements as one printed in a recent article on "trawler yacht design," saying ". . . designers went to work and developed a type of hull that had none of the faults of the commercial trawler yet retained all the desirable features and the general trawler look," are pure nonsense. Don't misunderstand me. There is nothing wrong with these yachts if they meet your needs. But just because they are called "trawlers," don't imagine that the seaworthiness of the true trawler has rubbed off on them.

Now, naval architects judge hulls mostly by using "coefficients" or "ratios." There are many of these, but we will limit ourselves to four. They are:

Displacement/Length Ratio (D/L)
Speed/Length Ratio (S/L)
Above Water/Below Water Area Ratio (A/B)
Prismatic Coefficient (PC)

And we might add one I just invented. It is called the "trawler/truth ratio," (T/T). A trawler is and always has been a fishing vessel designed to tow a "trawl" (or net) that is pulled along the bottom to trap fish. To do this, she needs a husky hull with a good grip on the water and aperture space for a large, slow-turning propeller. She is expected to work the sea, winter and summer, and some of the best trawling grounds have the worst weather. Hence the seaworthiness of the North Sea and Icelandic sea trawlers made "trawler" the symbol of seaworthiness; that is, until Madison Avenue got hold of the term. Thus the need for this ratio—how near to a true trawler is the boat? There are yachts that would score quite high, as they were patterned after true trawlers. But today we see advertised as "trawlers," designs that would score, if one were charitable, one or two per cent.

Let's first consider the common way of comparing relative "heft," or weight, in boats. This is important because a relatively heavier boat must have more volume underwater to provide that weight. Hence she has more space for accommodations, fuel, stores, and the like.

What we use to measure this is called the displacement/length ratio (D/L). This is the displacement *in long tons* (2240 pounds) divided by the cube of the waterline length (LWL), divided by 100. The division by 100 is merely to keep the number small.

$$D/L = \left(\frac{D}{\frac{LWL}{100}}\right)^3$$

The ratio is useful for this reason: If you take a certain yacht and make a second model of it, twice as big but with the same lines exactly, its D/L will remain the same, although the bigger vessel will weigh eight times as much. But if you take another vessel that is not the same shape or the same length, comparing its D/L to the first model's will tell you if the new model is relatively heavier (greater D/L), or lighter (lower D/L). It is also, from experience, a good way to separate the men from the boys, so to speak. For instance, checking the D/Ls of coastal motorboats that are designed to use considerable power to attain quite respectable speeds in local cruising, you find their D/Ls range from, say, 160 to 220. Of course, these types are not expected to cross oceans.

So, taking the ocean-crossers first, what D/L should they have? This question is open to argument. But I have had certain experiences in this matter that are a good basis for my thoughts on the subject. First, let's define what we are talking about in relation to space required for crew, fuel, stores, and so forth: a space requirement that must eventually be reflected, in part, by cubic feet under water—which, of course, is displacement.

Take my client who wanted to go to the South Seas in a 42-foot "trawler." To make that cruise, in my opinion, he needed a vessel with a range of at least 2400 miles under power, permanent bunks for five or six, 60 days' supplies and, ideally, full-time live-aboard space for owner and wife. The vessel he purchased did not meet any of these requirements and could not be modified to have them—the space simply was not there. In other words, her D/L of 230 was too small.

My own *Passagemaker*'s design was supposed to be on the light side compared to the heavy diesel motorboats of the 1950s and 1960s, which were mostly fishing boat models. The idea behind her relative lightness was economy in construction and powering. The lines were drawn with a D/L of 230. But when she was built and loaded, ready to go with all the gear required for long-range cruising, we found her draft had increased so her D/L was 270. There was some overweight in construction, but most of this increase was in disposable load. Obviously, she should have been built to a D/L of 270 to begin with.

This and other data led me to the following conclusions: A satisfactory ocean-crossing vessel—a vessel to meet the requirements of the gentleman who wanted to go to the South Seas—cannot have a D/L less than 270 in the 50-foot overall size, and a bit more is desirable. A specialized vessel such as a long, slim aluminum yacht could prove me wrong. But for a conventional hull, carrying good accommodations for living on board and not stinting on equipment, supplies, and ballast, this rule is a good guide.

The shorter a vessel, the larger its D/L should be. In fact, you must increase the D/L in smaller vessels to carry the load. I see in two of my recent designs that the 50-footer has a D/L of 300, while the 42-footer has a D/L of 375. There is no particular rule here—the proportions just look right to me. Contrast the D/L of my 42-footer with that of the 42-foot "trawler" discussed above. Their respective displacements are 24 tons and 15 tons—a difference of nine tons. This essentially shows a difference in the requirements to which the boats were drawn, for I am sure the *designer* of the light 42-footer did not expect his boat to head for the South Seas.

If your demands for range, accommodations, and seaworthiness are less than those of a well-equipped ocean-crosser, you may find a "trawler type" acceptable. In the 40- to 43-foot size their D/Ls run from 156 to 230, the difference largely concentrated in the amount of fuel they carry. Naturally, these D/Ls seem low to me, but I admit to limited experience with the type. My suggestion would be to investigate these craft very thoroughly as to motion at sea and storage area, in addition to tests to be described later. Keep in mind there is a great deal of difference between a vessel fresh from the builder's yard and one fully loaded for a long cruise. I have not seen a long-range cruiser yet that did not fill every nook and cranny with stores and spares. There was absolutely no vacant space under the cabin soles of *Passagemaker,* for instance.

We have talked about low limits on D/L to emphasize the importance of enough cubic capacity to carry the loads the cruiser requires. What about high limits?

The highs, of course, would be the true fishing trawlers. Studying the three volumes of *Fishing Boats of the World,* published by the F.A.O. branch of the United Nations, which are absolute gold mines of information applicable to long-range motorboats, we find the D/Ls running from 450 for a 40-foot waterline, to 400 for 50 feet and 350 for 60 feet. Yachts that have some relation to true trawlers in their design, say a T/T ratio of 80 per cent or more, run somewhat less—about 20 per cent. This makes sense, because a yacht does not have the load problems of a fishing boat. The yacht essentially does not vary its "payload," while the trawler has to handle loads from zero to several tons. For this reason it is not at all good practice to slavishly copy a fishing boat model for a yacht.

The suggested figures for D/L must not be taken too rigidly, especially those given in relation to length overall. As the waterline length is cubed, slight variations can have a good deal of effect. In addition, the varying weights of fuel and stores are constantly changing a vessel's D/L. One must check for just what condition the displacement figures are given. Our suggested figures are for all-up weights, ready to depart on that long cruise.

So much for displacement or "heft," and for the D/L ratio. We will talk more about D/L after we take up the speed/length ratio (S/L), as the two become quite intertwined when you talk about power, range, and speed.

The speed/length ratio is the speed of the vessel in knots, divided by the square root of the waterline length in feet:

$$S/L = \sqrt{\dfrac{V \text{ knots}}{LWL}}$$

This is a very important ratio and has a powerful effect in many ways. At the same time let me define "hull speed." Strictly speaking, this is the speed at which the hull makes a wave as long as its waterline. It is an S/L of 1.34. If you find salesmen using S/L ratios of 1.4 or even 1.5 as hull speed, or telling you their pride and joy has a hull speed of *x* knots that is clearly *over* an S/L of 1.34, you have an excellent indication that they don't know what they are talking about. And if a salesman does the unspeakable and gives you speeds in *statute* miles per hour, laugh in his face and walk out! You are surely being conned.

To appreciate the importance of S/L ratio look at this typical speed/power/range curve. This curve was made for a 50-footer, and is based on one of the estimating formulas used by naval architects. In practice, it seems to be a bit on the conservative side in the area that is useful, from S/L 1.0 up. Below that, it becomes too optimistic as the formula used would produce zero power at zero speed, where, as a practical matter, around S/L 0.6 your engine would be idling and you couldn't go slower.

Although the ordinate is shaft horsepower at the engine, what we are really interested in here is gallons-per-hour, so it can be combined with speed to give range, as the curve shows. A consumption of 0.06 gallons per horsepower, per hour, is a good average figure to use here.

Note how the horsepower required starts out relatively low at the slow speed end and curves up rapidly to an S/L of about 1.2, where it becomes a straight line that continues on up. Marked on the curve are the speed/length ratios from 0.8 to 1.2 and then the hull speed of 1.34. So this curve can represent the relative changes for any craft by using S/L ratios instead of speed in knots. In fact, when discussing the performance of seagoing motorboats it is better to speak in terms of S/L ratios than in knots, so differences in size will not affect the results. We can also say this curve illustrates the "cost of speed." For instance, in this particular craft, doubling the horsepower from 100 to 200 will produce 1.7 knots more speed.

The region between S/L ratios 1.1 and 1.2 encompasses the practical speeds for long-range voyaging under power in small craft and hence are of greatest interest to us. Note how for this particular vessel the range is 2800 miles at 1.1 S/L, and 2200 miles at 1.2. Thus she can do the Bermuda-Azores run of 1850 miles easily at 8.25 knots, or S/L 1.2. But to cover the 2240 miles to Honolulu she would have to slow to eight knots, with a 200 mile reserve. And let us say you are running at an S/L ratio of 1.15. If you start to worry about fuel, dropping the speed to 1.0 will produce *50 per cent more range on what remains!* In other words—and this is important—small changes in speed make large changes in fuel consumption. In fact, the whole secret of the long-range boat is that it goes slowly, using small S/L ratios. It has to; there is just no way to lick this.

The type of curve shown, taken from mathematics, is useful in planning a boat of a certain weight. As soon as possible the new craft should be actually

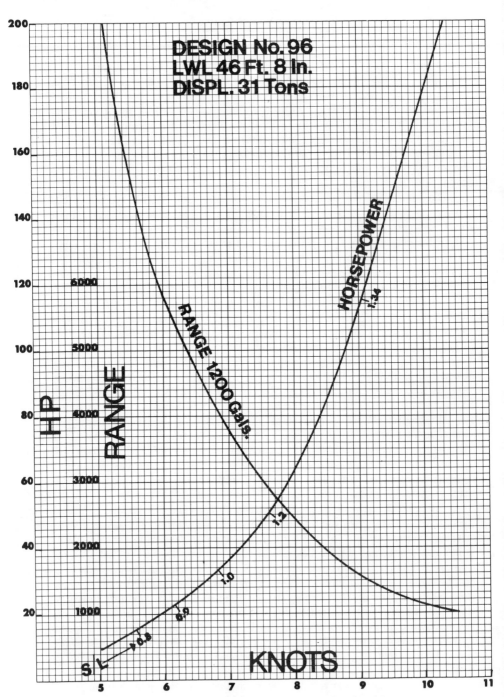

FIG. 5-1. Graph: Speed-Power-Range Curve for Beebe Design 96.

tested carrying the weights with which she will start a cruise, to develop a curve that is more useful. In fact, the careful skipper will add his experience to his curve as he goes along. Salesmen of stock boats must also be ready to furnish such a verified curve.

The simplest way to check cruising ranges is to use a calibrated standpipe that will allow accurate measuring of fuel used while the vessel is running a measured mile.

The third ratio we are going to consider is the ratio of area of the side view of the vessel *above* water to that *below* water (A/B). That is:

Area Above Water.
Area Below Water.

Obviously, the smaller this ratio the better. Thus trawlers, fishermen, may get as low as 1.0 to 1.5. It is difficult to get below 2.0 in a yacht because of the pressure for more and better accommodations. And it is this demand for more space and comfort that has gradually pushed up this ratio in contemporary yachts with an accompanying loss of seaworthiness. Several vessels that meet my ideas of being qualified as ocean-crossers range from 2.1 to 2.6. In the light "trawler" group, this ratio tends to run higher. It has to, of course, with less hull under water. In one case it ranges as high as 4.6, which scares me. Particularly as a large part of this increased area is usually glass, and thin glass at that. Steps that can be taken to hold the line after such increases are greater beam, and conversion of the largest possible proportion of the side area to watertight integrity portions of the hull.

The last item for us to consider is the prismatic coefficient (PC). This must be calculated from the lines and is not ordinarily available from salesmen. But it is well worth checking, by inquiry, the PC of any vessel you are considering.

The prismatic coefficient compares the *actual* volume of the hull below the waterline in cubic feet to what the volume *would be* if the body were a "prism" composed of the largest section from the lines carried the full length of the waterline. In effect, it is an expression of how much you sharpen the ends.

Tank-testing of hull models has shown that for each S/L ratio there is an ideal PC. That is, at each S/L a vessel designed with the correct PC will need less power to make that S/L than a vessel with an incorrect PC. It so happens that the correct PC varies most widely from one S/L to another in the very range we are interested in, S/Ls from 1.0 to 1.34, and on into the area where the light types try to drive past hull speed for local cruising, say to S/L 1.6. The table below, from D. Phillips-Birt's *Naval Architecture of Small Craft,* shows this clearly.

S/L	PC	S/L	PC	S/L	PC
1.0	0.53	1.4	0.64	1.8	0.70
1.1	0.54	1.5	0.66	1.9	0.70
1.2	0.58	1.6	0.68	2.0	0.70
1.3	0.62	1.7	0.69		

After S/L 2.0, dynamic lift becomes a major factor and the hull becomes a "planing hull." Nobody is going to go very far at sea in such a vessel. As Bill Garden said once in an article on this type of boat, "A planing hull can't carry enough fuel to get out of sight."

In heavy seagoing motorboats, the effect of the PC can be dramatic. The British Fisheries Board actually built three 62-foot waterline coastal fishing boats of exactly the same length and displacement but differing PCs. The results were as follows, from *Naval Architecture of Small Craft:*

PC	HP req. for S/L 1.14, 9 knots
0.645	123 (Many fishing boats have this PC)
0.612	105
0.537	75 (This is the correct PC)

We should not be too hard on the fishermen. The requirements of the trade may demand a larger than ideal PC. But yachts do not have this excuse for choosing the wrong PC.

If you are interested in maximum range with minimum fuel, there is no question but you should have a vessel with the PC set for the desired cruising speed. However, if you desire to cruise somewhat faster in local cruising, a compromise position might be better. You would use a little more fuel but have a hull shape designed for a slightly higher speed.

If the PC of a vessel you are interested in is more suited to the higher speeds, say from an S/L of 1.5 to 1.9, it suggests the hull is really better suited to local use than as a long-range cruiser. We might say then, the PC indicates the designer's (not the advertiser's!) intentions, and is worth checking.

So much for the four formulas that have the most effect on seagoing motorboats. We will look later at how to apply them to specific design problems. But first let's go further into the differences between the *true* trawler yacht and the lighter types we are calling "trawlers" for convenience, the name having been preëmpted by this type.

Long range passage-making essentially is aimed at reaching the desired cruising ground "with dispatch" so you have time to enjoy the local area. Once there, there is no problem of range or fuel availability (we hope!) so you can run at any speed you wish. On *Passagemaker* we habitually ran at hull speed in local cruising. This was 9.1 knots on a 46-foot waterline. Would it be possible to do better, that is cruise even faster locally and still have a vessel seaworthy enough for ocean passages?

A *true* trawler yacht is so heavy there is no question of driving her over hull speed. It simply wouldn't make sense to carry the machinery to do it. Their owners must therefore content themselves with thinking, when faster boats pass them, how their fuel bill is peanuts compared to the types that drink up hundreds of gallons per day. The hull offers enough room to be a real home afloat and the solid feel that makes for comfort at sea. This type's domain is the open sea and if they are not used there, but stick to local cruising or coastal waters, they don't make much sense. In addition, a real trawler would, at 50 feet, have a draft of around seven feet. This is excessive in many cruising grounds, particularly on the East Coast of North America. It was this draft problem, for instance, that turned me away from considering one for myself.

On the other hand, the light "trawlers" have their own advantages and drawbacks. One of their chief virtues is their ability to run somewhat over hull speed. Now, hull speed is pretty low by American standards. It takes enormous increases in waterline length to get hull speed up to the speeds ordinary coastal motorboats can achieve. In fact, to have a 12-knot hull speed takes a waterline length of some 80 feet. Yet 12 knots is an ordinary top speed for coastal motorboats. Is there a way to lick this?

What the designers of the light "trawlers" have done is to compromise between the heavy, extremely seaworthy *true* trawler on the one hand, and the coastal type on the other—so light everyone would agree it should not go to sea. In effect, they have opted for a lower "trawler/truth ratio." They say it is possible to design a hull that can exceed hull speed by a certain amount and still retain the basic seaworthiness required at sea. The steps in this process lead to lightness (relative lightness, that is) to hold down power demands, and a flat stern aft to avoid squatting at higher speeds. They contend the resulting hull form has ample seaworthiness for any reasonable cruising and cite impressive statistics to prove it. They also say that most clients who buy this type will not actually make long trips, but will be content with coastal cruising and island hopping, and be happy to have a vessel for this purpose that is clearly superior in seaworthiness to the ordinary motorboat. All of this is perfectly true, and it is not the *designers* who write those ads that imply these craft are fit to "go anywhere." Our quarrel is really with the advertisers and salesmen who produce the unhappy situation of our gentleman who wanted to take his 42-footer to the South Seas.

Obviously, the further above hull speed a light "trawler" is driven, the closer she will approach the coastal motorboat in lightness and use of large amounts of horsepower. So claims in this matter must be approached with a *really* critical eye. Taking the advertisements of seven yachts that are touted as "trawlers" or "go-anywhere boats," yet also claim they "cruise" at x knots *over* hull speed, we find they range from S/L 1.44 to 1.67, with D/Ls from 156 to 234. As "cruising-speed" has no definition in naval architecture, it really would be better to check their claimed maximum speed to see how much over hull speed they are being driven.

At the same time, these vessels claim ranges from 900 to 1500 miles. While boats with these ranges may be sufficient for many skippers' needs, it is surprising to see them advertised as go-anywhere-your-heart-desires boats when they can't even cross the smallest ocean, the Atlantic. But nothing is impossible in the advertising world, apparently. And a little slide-rule work shows they achieve these ranges not at their "cruising speed" but right down at S/L ratios around 1.1 where we would expect to find them. To improve these ranges, you would have to add fuel capacity. And, as I found out working over the 42-footer for the gentleman who wanted to go to the South Seas, there wasn't any safe place to put it; the space just wasn't there.

All of these craft have the broad, flat stern necessary to get over an S/L of 1.6. Characteristically, this type hull steers badly with seas from the quarter or aft. As the true long-range motorboat *seeks out* these conditions, keeping the wind aft as much as possible, this point is important. I recall a client who really went into this motor passage-making business, including a long trip with me, and who was talking about being able to run over hull speed locally. He took the opportunity to make a delivery trip as crew on a fine, custom-built, twin-screw flat-stern yacht from San Francisco to Puget Sound. Off Cape Mendocino, they had a gale from astern and had a wild night, handing the throttles continuously to keep her from broaching. He came home and said to me, "Forget it. From now on I'm a hull-speed boy."

Now it will be noted that this yacht made it, even if it was uncomfortable. And, in fact, the problem with this boat was not hull shape per se, but was connected with her being twin screw with small spade rudders behind each prop. These perform well at normal smooth-water speeds. But when you slow way down, they don't have enough area to "take command" properly. A single-propeller craft with deep skeg and large rudder would not have this trouble. So it's possible to avoid this steering problem.

Another problem with "trawlers" is they do not carry any ballast. Now I may be supercautious, but, to me, whether a seagoing yacht carries some ballast or not is what distinguishes the true seagoer from a vessel that is not really serious about it. My *Passagemaker* (46-foot LWL, D/L 270) carried 5000 pounds of lead on her keel, with more inside. I doubt if we needed it 98 per cent of the time and we paid good money to carry it around. But believe me, when we got into gales and the fringes of the two hurricanes we managed to find, we were delighted to have it along. A quotation from L. Francis Herreshoff's *Common Sense of Yacht Design* captures this even more graphically:

> "It is, though, interesting to note that several designers at various times have thought they had discovered the secret of designing a vee-bottom launch that went smoothly in a seaway, and this reminds me of an incident that happened to Bill Hand about 1915. Mr. Hand was one of the early big game fishermen to use high-speed gasoline launches for that purpose. Well, one fall he was fishing for tuna somewhere southeast of Block Island. It was probably pretty rough and probably Mr. Hand was quite proud of the good weather his vee-bottom launch was making of it when all of a sudden it became very much rougher (which it can do suddenly in that region). To make a short story of it, Mr. Hand finally got back to New Bedford okay, but after that he made a specialty of designing heavy auxiliary schooners much after the fashion of Gloucestermen, and this is the type he subsequently used himself for fishing southeast of Block Island, and, gentle reader, I am under the impression you will do the same thing after you have really been caught out in the same kind of weather."

CONCLUSIONS

Now that we have reviewed all this material, what have we got? All of my recommendations are arguable. Naval architects are by no means in agreement on the levels of the figures I have given. So in your quest for a vessel that meets your needs, you can expect to hear rebuttals of what is offered here. But with your slide rule in hand and a knowledge of the basics, you are much better armed to check what *they* say.

One of the first things to check is range. You simply have to decide for yourself what range you require. A realistic decision on how your boat will actually be used, not how you would like to use it, is the first step. Then the cruises you expect to take must be checked for their maximum legs. In this connection, the capabilities of the seagoing motorboat can be exploited to improve on conventional ways of doing things. For instance, instead of departing from Miami direct against wind and current to the Virgins, it would be much easier on the crew and the vessel to go north far enough to get out of the Trades, then go east until you can head south to your destination. It even appears attractive (if you plan to spend the winter cruising the Islands) to make your first hop a passage east, then south clear to Grenada to cruise up the entire island chain.

A decision on size and relative heft is next. Size is much influenced by one's budget. Any naval architect will tell you any vessel would be better if longer. But size has to stop somewhere. The number of persons to be carried is also a factor. With comfortable full-time accommodations for owner and wife, I do not believe it is possible to have more than four permanent bunks until the length reaches 46 feet, or even better, 48 feet. Long passages *can* be made with a crew of four, of course, but we found it easier with five or six.

If your vessel is to be an original design, the designer would now be in a position to come up with preliminary sketches and a speed/hp/range curve like that shown in Fig. 5–1. If you are investigating stock boats, the seller should be able to produce this curve together with certification that the vessel has been tested and will do what the curve says. If he does not have it, walk out.

Some designers make this curve at full load and half load of fuel and water. However, I prefer to make the curve for full load only. This gives you a safety factor in range from the vessel becoming lighter as she goes along. My own experience with this type of curve has shown a 10 per cent reserve is ample to take care of adverse conditions, provided you are running at S/Ls from 1.1 to 1.2. If you are thinking about stretching range to the limit for some unusual passage by running at S/L 1.0 or even 0.9, you need a larger reserve, as you haven't got the leeway to slow down—you would be too close to running the engine at idle. The curve should show the fuel rate used.

As an example, consider a vessel designed to cross the Atlantic and cruise in Europe. I would recommend for this a range of 2200 miles at S/L 1.2. It is true the longest leg is 1850 miles from Bermuda to the Azores going east. This track can be used both ways. However, returning by this route in the fall, you are squeezed between the hurricane season and the winter storms. It would be more fun and more comfortable to return over the usual track of sailing vessels. They leave Gibraltar for the Canary Islands not later than the end of September, go to Las Palmas to drink the excellent local wines until November 15, then take off like a flock of ducks for Barbados, 2800 miles down wind, and spend the winter in the Caribbean. You can see in the curve we used as an example that a vessel that can do 2200 miles at S/L 1.2 can do the 2800 miles at 1.1. And if you get nervous, say, at the two-thirds distance mark, you can drop S/L to 1.0 and gain another 300 miles of range, as the curve shows. This is the sort of figuring you do for range.

Analyzing the ads for the "trawlers," you can sort out the "cruising speed" and the "range" figures with the aid of the curve. Usually you will find "cruising speed" is well above the speed required to achieve the range claimed; that is, the boat will not actually "cruise" the "range." This is acceptable as long as you understand it.

Regarding statements of top speed, check the curve to see if top speed requires more horsepower than the maximum continuous rating of the engine. If it does, forget it. Diesels ordinarily have three ratings: Block, which means engine block only, without any accessories, not even a water pump; maximum intermittent rating, which means for one hour only—a rather useless exercise; and maximum continuous rating—the only one worth considering in a boat. It is a sad thing, really, to see manufacturers advertising diesels as 120 hp when this is the useless block rating and the engine has a continuous rating of 102 hp. It didn't used to be this way before Madison Avenue got into the act.

If the top speed is within the continuous rating of the engine, think about it a bit. Take a 46-foot waterline boat, about 50 feet overall. If it has a top speed of 12 knots it would be running at an S/L of 1.77. This is pretty high and requires a flat stern and a low D/L, not to mention lots of horsepower. Would you be willing to settle for 10 knots instead? This lowers S/L to 1.48. With this small excess over 1.34 you can have a reasonably high-deadrise, parallel-in-the-aft-sections, flat-run hull that steers like it was on rails with the seas aft, carries fuel for over 2800 miles at S/L 1.1, and has a D/L of 270. I know this is so because it describes my own boat. We didn't get *Passagemaker* up to 10 knots because her oversized prop (for range) limited her to using 85 hp. With this she reached an S/L of 1.4, or 9.4 knots—which means she could have done 10 knots on 98 horsepower.

If your range demands are more modest, say from 800–1500 miles, and you really want to cruise faster in local waters than S/L 1.48, I would certainly recommend the lighter types, particularly for their first-cost economy and lower running expenses, provided consideration is given to two items not ordinarily considered in stock boats: First, remember their motion at sea—with their smaller T/T ratios—will be worse than in the heavier boats, and certainly demand some type of stabilization to make satisfactory long voyages; and second, if it is a twin-engine type with spade rudders, adding a large central rudder will correct steering faults exhibited by these types when running off slowly before a sea.

As for the above water/below water ratio, this is pretty much of a lost cause today. I can only say again and again, *hold it down*. But perhaps it would be better to urge prospective owners to consider what they will do when each large window is broken. What is their second line of defense? I have seen some light "trawlers" that were very well equipped for this contingency and others where this danger had not been given a thought.

Certainly "areas of operation limitation" should be considered. For instance, in one of my designs destined for full-time living afloat in the Mediterranean that is double-decked full length for an A/B ratio of 3.0, I have recommended, and the owner has agreed, that the boat be limited to cruising areas south of the Bermuda-Azores-Lisbon line. She has too much glass for me to be happy if she ventures into the North Atlantic.

That's the way it goes; speed/length ratio, displacement/length ratio, and so on. Figures, figures, figures. But those pesky figures are operating all the time you are out there cruising. And it behooves the careful owner to know what they are and what influence they have.

MATHEMATICAL SUPPLEMENT TO CHAPTER 5

In this supplement we will show how to make up speed-range graphs, how to find speed/length ratios on a slide rule, and make a couple of other applications of mathematics. In recent months, now that I own a small electronic calculator, I find I use my slide rule only to work up an S/L ratio, which involves the square root of the waterline.

In estimating speed and range, we need two graphs to give us two factors, F_1 and F_2.

For F_1 enter Graph No. 1 with the vessel's displacement in long tons of 2240 pounds along the bottom line. Proceed up to the curve and read off F_1 on the edge of the graph. In the example shown the displacement is 46 tons and F_1 is 87.

For F_2 enter Graph No. 2 with speed/length ratios along the bottom line. For any given speed/length ratio there is an F_2 on the edge of the graph. The example shows that for S/L 1.25, F_2 is 1.65.

The horsepower required at any given S/L ratio is then $F_1 \times F_2$. In the cases of the examples drawn on the graphs, the horsepower required to drive the 46-ton vessel at a speed/length ratio of 1.25 would be $87 \times 1.65 = 143.5$ hp.

Regarding slide rules, get the simplest one you can, as you only use scales A,B,C, and D to do the work discussed here, and to keep track of how you are doing when at sea. To compute speed/length ratios, set the left index (1.0) of scale B next to the waterline length in feet in the right hand half of scale A. Then the index at the left end of scale C, which would be S/L 1.0, shows on D the speed, in knots, for your particular waterline length. The speeds corresponding to S/Ls over 1.0 can similarly be read off on Scale D next to the S/Ls on shown scale C. Or conversely, the speeds on scale D can be read as S/L ratios on scale C. This is what you would do in making up a table, as it is better to have speed in knots keyed to your particular waterline than in S/L ratios.

As an example, here is a table made up to produce a speed-range curve using these rules. Actually it is the one I made up to help in analyzing *Rock Bottom*'s passage from Hawaii to California as described in Chapter 11.

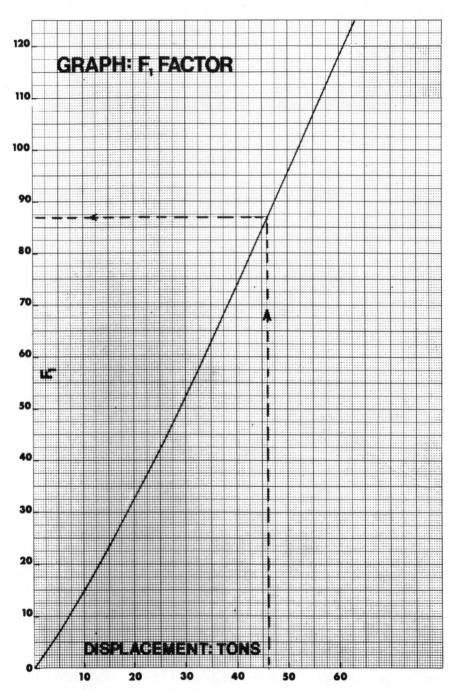

FIG. 5-2.   Graph No. 1: F_1 Factor.

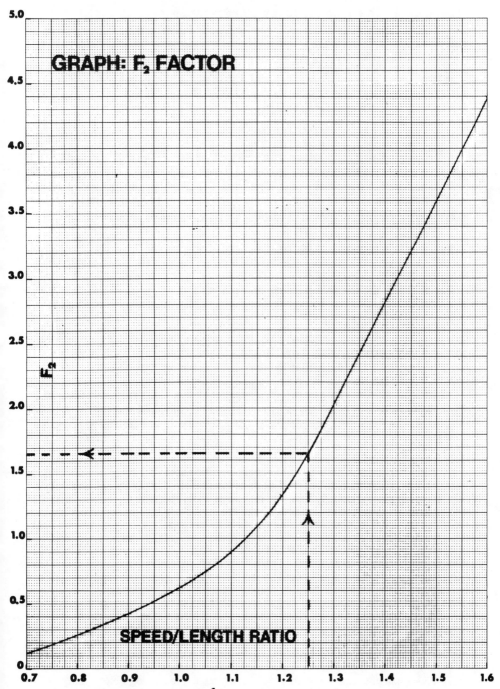

FIG. 5-3. Graph No. 2: F_2 Factor.

Displacement: 16.5 Tons; F_1: 26; LWL: 37 Ft.; Fuel: 530 Gals.

Speed Knots	S/L (slide rule)	F_2: Graph No. 2	HP $F_1 \times F_2$	Gals/hr at .06 G/hp/hr	Hours Running: 530 gals	Range
5	0.82	0.29	7.54	0.45	1178	5890
6	0.99	0.59	15.34	0.92	576	3456
7	1.15	1.09	28.34	1.70	311	2177
8	1.32	2.60	56.16	3.37	159	1256
9	1.48	3.46	89.96	5.40	98	882

Although horsepower figures in this table are given to two decimal places, it should not be assumed that the results can be depended on to be that accurate. But for plotting purposes, in making a smooth curve, it helps.

Here is the curve made from the above figures. The S/Ls of 1.0, 1.1, 1.2, and 1.34 are also indicated for reference. It will be remembered that S/L 1.0 is the limit below which the range becomes progressively more inaccurate. The ship could not possibly go 5890 miles at five knots, for example. And the range at six knots is also probably somewhat overstated.

While actually operating at sea, another useful curve is the "How-Goes-It" curve. This is a graph with total gallons at start on the left side and distance to go along the bottom. As an example, take a fuel capacity of 1200 gallons and an 1800-mile passage. Draw a line from the full-fuel mark to the zero-distance mark. Then draw a line from the full-fuel mark to the desired reserve-on-arrival figure, say 10 per cent.

It is obvious as you plot the fuel remaining each day and the distance to go, the plotted points *must* stay *above* these lines. Ideally, you want to be above the 10 per cent reserve line. But if you fall below the solid line, you *know* you are not going to reach your port unless you change what you are doing. Some fictitious plots are shown on the graph to illustrate this.

Another useful formula is the length of waves. As waves have a constant S/L of 1.34 (which is why a vessel's hull speed is S/L 1.34), then the length of the waves a boat is actually making, measured from the bow to the top of the second crest along the length of the boat, is a measure of the speed the boat is making. The formula is: $Length = \frac{V^2}{1.8}$ (1.8 is 1.34^2). The lengths, then, for the speeds we might be interested in are as follows:

V(knots)	Length	V(knots)	Length
3	5.0 ft.	8	35.5 ft.
4	8.9 "	9	45.0 "
5	13.9 "	10	55.5 "
6	20.0 "	11	67.2 "
7	27.2 "	12	80.0 "

These lengths can be marked on deck to use as a log. Note that the difference between six knots and seven knots is 7.2 feet, for instance. Surely, you

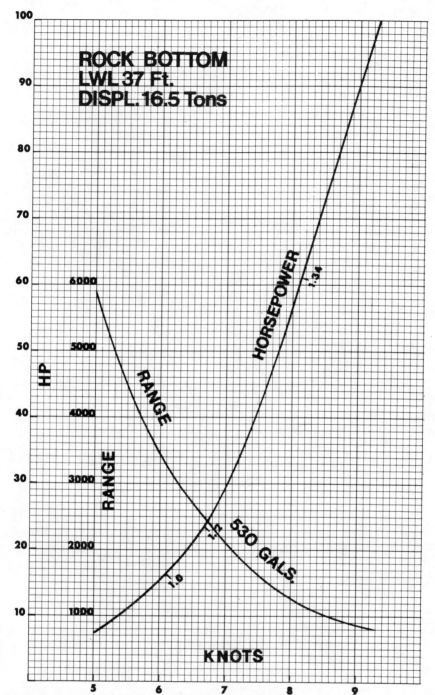

ROCK BOTTOM
LWL 37 Ft.
DISPL. 16.5 Tons

FIG. 5-4. Graph: Speed-Power-Range Curve for *Rock Bottom.*

can judge the length to the crest more accurately than that. This system was used
—to scale—finding the speeds of the model shown in Chapter 2. See if you
agree with my estimate. The scale on the model is calibrated in knots, full size.

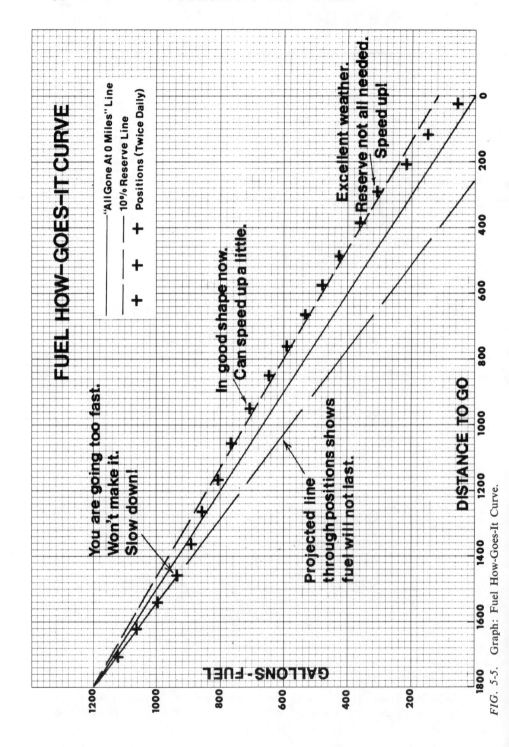

FIG. 5-5. Graph: Fuel How-Goes-It Curve.

6

Stabilizing Against Rolling

While designing *Passagemaker,* I was well aware of the infamous ability of small motorboats to roll viciously in any kind of a chop. Many hours spent holding on under these conditions and studying the problem convinced me that one basic requirement of a satisfactory power-only Passagemaker is a method of reducing rolling as much as possible in the interest of comfort and reducing fatigue.

It was apparent in the beginning, and amply proved by our later experience, that rolling is one of the principal problems of power passage-making. We must, then, devote a good deal of thought to two problems: What causes rolling, and how to reduce it.

Briefly, the technicalities of the problem are these. Small craft do not follow the rules about rolling laid down for big ships. No combination of beam, draft, displacement, hull form, or metacentric height will reduce the roll to a satisfactory degree until you reach quite large vessels, say over 150 feet. It is important to understand this, as there is still a lot of confusion on the subject, fostered by such things as a recent article on stability and rolling in a prominent boating magazine which repeated the erroneous and obsolete idea of small and large ships rolling to the same rule.

Do not misunderstand me. The factors named above *do* have an effect on the amount of roll. But the effect of variations in these factors will not in itself reduce rolling to a degree that will be satisfactory to the crew. And, returning to the militant tone of Chapter 5, don't let any salesman tell you otherwise.

The reason it cannot is embodied in the concept of "forced rolling." That is, if the period of encounter with waves is greater than the natural rolling period of the ship, the ship will tend to roll in the period of the waves, and not in its own period based on metacentric height. This condition exists for small craft almost all the time that rolling is a problem. For big ships, the reverse is true. In effect, what we call a "roll" is actually the boat trying to keep itself level with the surface of the water, as it is designed to do. But the damned sea surface keeps tilting all over!

In connection with this rolling (that is, forced rolling), some recent experience in this field has shown the existence of a seeming paradox. That is, the more stable the vessel, the more it will roll with a stabilizing gear comparable to that fitted on a vessel that is less stable.

This was demonstrated when a new vessel that was quite "stiff" due to hull dimensions, plus the temporary absence of appreciable amounts of topside weight, showed a roll period of four seconds. This compared to an older vessel of approximately the same size with less stable lines that had a period of roll of about 5.5 seconds. It so happened that the geometry of their stabilizing gear, in this case the so-called flopperstoppers, was very nearly the same. Tests at sea showed the stiffer vessel rolled more than the other vessel while their stabilizing gear was in use.

This paradox is easily explained. As noted above, the "roll" in the forced-rolling situation is actually the attempt of the vessel to keep its waterline plane parallel to the water. As the boat tilts to accomplish this, the movement is opposed by the stabilizing gear, whatever it may be. And the gears being similar, the force available is the same. But the more stable vessel has more force generated by its shape to oppose the stabilizing force and accomplish its purpose of remaining aligned with the water surface. Hence, it rolls to a greater degree.

While the two vessels were not tested simultaneously, persons who had sailed on both were quite aware of the difference. Estimates of the degree of difference varied from 25 to 40 per cent. Four seconds is clearly too short a period for comfort. The usual range is 5–7 seconds in the 40–50 foot size. Without stabilizing gear, such vessels will roll more than a stiffer vessel, but with an easier motion. When stabilizing gear is put into use, they will roll less and still retain their easier motion.

Clearly then, period of roll is an important part of an overall evaluation and should be checked on any design you investigate. Roll is measured alongside the dock. With lines slack, one man can roll a 60-foot boat by either pushing up on the guard rail in time with the period, or by stepping on the rail similarly. When the vessel is rolling appreciably, time ten over-and-back cycles, and divide by ten to give the period of roll. A vessel with a shorter period of roll is "stiffer" and has more initial stability.

Although the discussion above leads to the idea that increasing the period of roll by reducing initial stability would lead to even more comfort at sea while using stabilizing gear, this approach should be used with great caution as there are other factors involved. In particular, coupling an easily rolled vessel with extensive topside weights can well lead to catastrophic rolling due to the inertial forces involved. It was reported, for instance, that one yacht (a *true* trawler type), with extensive double- and some triple-decking, lost the use of its mechanical stabilizing gear in bad weather and rolled more than 70 degrees— with extensive internal damage. The trend in American yachts toward increasing A/B ratio, which I inveighed against in the last chapter, is an integral part of this problem.

What is needed is something external to the hull that will reduce rolling as much as possible. A good deal of work has been done on this over the years but much more could be undertaken, particularly in the field of reducing costs and enhancing simplicity. Devices in use fall into two classes: passive and active.

Passive devices essentially cause the roll to expend energy and reduce the roll by cutting down the energy left to roll the ship. They include bilge keels, keel plates, "flopperstoppers," or West Coast Anti-Roll Stabilizers, and steady-ing-rig sails.

Active devices actually produce a counterforce to the rolling force. They include "activated fins," free surface tanks, and U-tube or Frahm tanks. The tanks will not work on small craft (they must be tuned to a steady period of roll) so we are left, as a practical matter, with activated fins.

To discuss passive devices first, bilge keels are so named because they are usually fitted at the turn of the bilge in large ships and have been used on these vessels for many years with good results. They project out from the side, perpendicular to it, about one foot wide in a 60-footer. Their length is as long as possible, and theoretically they should be lined up with the streamlines of the water passing the hull. It is obvious that such an alignment is pretty hard to accomplish under all conditions and some drag other than surface friction of this keel can be expected.

It works out that bilge keels, while effective in large ships, do not suppress roll very much in small craft. Their bilge keels may be expected to reduce roll about five per cent or thereabouts. To improve on this "keel plates" have been tried. A keel plate is a horizontal plate fixed to the bottom of the keel, the plate projecting from each side about 10 inches. The idea is that the plate "turns" the water and projects it back against the motion, thereby doubling the bilge-keel effect of the ship's keel. Of course, all flat surfaces of a vessel such as the

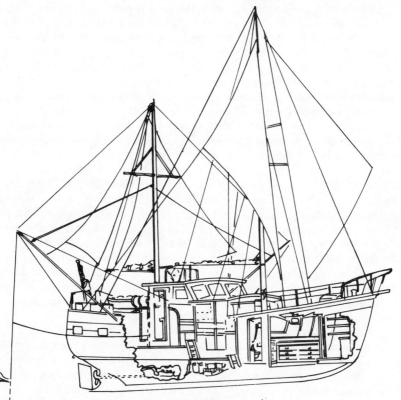

FIG. 6-1. Cross-sectional view of *Passagemaker,* showing stabilizer. (Tracing from a sketch by Kitty Hoyt.)

deadwood and the rudder have some bilge-keel effect. The evidence of keel-plate efficiency is conflicting. Some observers have reported the roll was reduced 10 per cent; others have felt the plate did little good. For both bilge keels and keel plates it should be noted their extra drag is present at all times even when roll reduction is not required. The obvious reason these two devices do not do much good is that their lever arm times the antiroll force produced is not great as they are too close to the center of the vessel.

, It is the big advantage of flopperstoppers that they greatly increase the lever arm, allowing a smaller surface to do the job. The way they work is shown in Fig. 6–1. The stabilizer, which is shaped like a delta-winged jet plane, is towed from the end of a boom projecting from the vessel's side. The stabilizer is so shaped and rigged that it will dive down with little or no resistance when the boom rolls down toward it. But when the boom attempts to pull it up, it goes flat and resists the pull very effectively. My research has convinced me that the stabilizer can generate resisting forces up to 10 pounds per square inch of surface. This is no mean item in a 300-square-inch stabilizer; until we realized what a tiger we had by the tail, and beefed up our gear to handle it, we had problems aboard *Passagemaker* with our F/S rig.

Steadying sails do a fair job when the wind is right, and can even function in a dead calm when cut flat and strapped down hard amidships. But unless the rig is quite large, its effect will not match flopperstoppers. As we had both on *Passagemaker,* we could make the comparison. The practical result was we never used sails for steadying; the F/S gear was so much better. If there was a strong beam wind, we would use the sails to steady the roll to windward and a single flopperstopper on the windward side to steady the opposite roll. This produced good results and a slight increase in speed.

Turning now to the active devices, activated fins at present comprise the only system that is tested and available. It consists of one or more fins projecting from the side of the vessel. These are controlled by a gyro unit which commands a mechanism to turn the fins to oppose the roll. In effect, the fins work like the ailerons of an airplane. When conditions favor their use, they are the champions in roll-reduction, consistently turning in records of five degrees or less under conditions where the craft might roll up to 30 degrees without them.

In summary, there are two devices that lead the field: the passive flopperstopper and the active fin. In our case, the flopperstoppers reduced rolling by two-thirds, and our cruising showed this to be highly satisfactory. Fins can do better, of course, under certain conditions. But as a specification to apply to any device, I think our experience has established that reduction of rolling by two-thirds *on all courses and at all speeds* is a satisfactory *minimum requirement.*

This two-thirds reduction brought down our rolling to less than 15° for most of the time, and days with only 5°–10° were common. We had hoped for this and we got it. What we had not realized was the significant manner this would change the whole aspect of the way we cruised. And this is what I want to talk about now.

There were two significant by-products of roll-reduction. It made going to sea in *Passagemaker* a pleasure even for persons who had never been to sea before. And it reduced the fatigue factor from motion to just about zero.

My remarks in Chapter 12 about crew and how roll-reduction made cruising with us suitable for women or inexperienced persons are based entirely on our experience in the comfortable environment produced by our roll-reduction. People cruising with us would come to the end of a long voyage and say they had never felt more fit. I finally figured out what was happening. The ship would always roll some, but the roll was not to a degree where you had to hang on, or use bunkboards, or brace yourself in a seat, or anything like that. Ordinarily one could stand without bracing if one wished, though a hand on something was more usual. At the beginning of a voyage, people would be a bit tired at the end of the day, but they soon lost this feeling. What actually happened was, there was just enough roll to give everyone a gentle isometric exercise of continuously tensing one muscle after another. This was tiring until you got used to it, then it induced a sense of fitness such as I personally have never gained in any other way. The essential thing was, there was never enough roll to cause increasing fatigue. Not for us the yearning for the arrival at the next port so we could get some rest. In fact, on one passage from Panama to San Diego, the crew caucused and voted to ask the skipper to pass up Acapulco and keep going! I've never heard of such a thing happening in any other vessel. And, en route, it was seldom the crew was not entirely satisfied to leave any port in three days. This again is in contrast with sailing voyages where days—even weeks—may be spent resting and refitting.

It is apparent there is a dividing line in average degree of roll that produces these contrasting results. It would be interesting to try and determine this limit and apply it to sailing voyages as well as power. Eric Hiscock mentioned this in his *Voyaging Under Sail* when he compared his fatigue to that of the crew of another boat that apparently rolled less than his did. It is too bad he did not examine this matter in depth. The relationship of roll reduction to long-range cruising is given in Chapter 14.

As we have seen, there are only two practical methods of roll-reduction good enough to meet our criterion of a two-thirds reduction. Let me give the advantages and disadvantages of each method. In doing this, I have nothing to sell. And I would be glad to have the ideas of anyone who could contribute to revising these judgments. This is mentioned because a couple of articles in the yachting press that praised fins and glossed over their faults while disparaging flopperstoppers, turned out to have been written by fin salesmen. This is dirty pool, to say the least.

ADVANTAGES OF FLOPPERSTOPPERS:

1. The rig is thousands of dollars more economical than fins.
2. They are not mechanical, so there can be no mechanical breakdowns.
3. They work on all courses and at all speeds. They are particularly efficient in running off before a gale at low speed, when they allow a course farther off down wind than is possible without them.
4. Using a special anchoring stabilizer, a simple device, they work when stopped or at anchor. (See Photo 6-2.)

PHOTO 6-2. Anchoring stabilizers, top and bottom views. As boat rolls one way, stabilizer moves downward in water and triangles of rubber allow water to flow upward freely. Then, as boat rolls the other way, the triangles form an unbroken surface, and resist the upward movement, damping the boat's rolling.

DISADVANTAGES OF FLOPPERSTOPPERS:

1. Their rigging has special requirements which must be part of the boat's design, and may interfere with the desired layout. The rig must be handled when put into use, a maneuver that could be difficult in heavy weather.
2. They cause drag which reduces range. *Passagemaker* lost about 0.7 knot. Other ships, larger and smaller, have reported less. This means a continuous small fuel cost.
3. The "fish" are hard to launch and retrieve without special equipment, and may damage the side of the vessel in the process.
4. In spite of continuing attempts to improve them in this respect, the fish are noisy in operation, transmitting a weird whine through the tow wire—a damned nuisance!

ADVANTAGES OF ACTIVATED FINS

1. They supply antiroll at the touch of a switch which is very convenient.
2. They stabilize better than flopperstoppers at cruising speeds in ordinary seas.
3. They require no rigging that may interfere with the rest of the vessel's layout.

DISADVANTAGES OF ACTIVATED FINS

1. The vessel must be moving at a certain velocity to make them work. The minimum speed at which they are reliable is in dispute. Fin salesmen say five–six knots. More disinterested observers have said as high as eight knots. The significance of this for running off before a gale is obvious.

2. There are reports they do not work well running directly downwind; one user felt compelled to "tack" downwind.
3. They will not work at anchor or stopped.
4. Being mechanical, they are bound to break down sometime.
5. They are expensive. While progress in reducing costs has been made lately, if *Passagemaker* had been originally equipped with them it would have increased her cost by some 20 per cent. In considering their cost, don't forget to include the spares required, and the installation charges.

CONCLUSIONS

Considering these lists, my conclusion is that, if the budget will permit, the well-equipped craft should have both roll-reducers: fins for ordinary stabilizing at the touch of a switch, flopperstoppers for the hard chance, for use at anchor, and when the fins break down. Looking back on my own cruising, the courses we followed in strong winds and gales and the speeds used, I cannot in good conscience recommend that an ocean-crossing motorboat be equipped with fins alone, equipment that would have been useless in a majority of our hard chances, due to reduced speed and the courses followed.

The plain fact is that fins, no matter how convenient, cannot fill the specification our experience dictated; that reduction of rolling by two-thirds *on all courses and at all speeds* would be a satisfactory minimum requirement. This failure is due to their dependence on speed to make them work. Hence the recommendation to have flopperstoppers for the special situations. At present there is one yacht equipped with both, and the owner has been very happy with the arrangement, particularly when his fins were out of commission for some weeks and he was awaiting spare parts.

Of course, if your budget will not cover fins, your only alternative at present is flopperstoppers. Make no mistake about it: *Stabilizing is an essential element of satisfactory passage-making.* I have had "rough and tough" sailors kid me about my concern for roll-reduction. What they forget is that the motion of an unstabilized motorboat at sea is very much worse than that of a sailing vessel. A wind-powered vessel must set its sails to have the wind impinge on them. This has a great stabilizing effect, and the sailing cruiser is usually quite steady even if she does have a large angle of heel. The exception to this is running downwind, where a sort of synchronous rolling sets in. Reports of fatigue on long runs in the Trades give this as the main factor. It would be easy to break up this rolling with a small single stabilizer in the high-speed setting, under both sail and power, as the forces rolling the ship are not large but tend to build up.

Flopperstoppers are found on most small West Coast fishing boats. Their first application to yachts was pretty haphazard, and troubles were common. As far as I know, *Passagemaker* was the first yacht designed to use them. Even then we had to make quite a few changes in the rig before we got it to its present state, where it has given no trouble for years. Our experience produced certain rules that must be followed to achieve equivalent results:

66

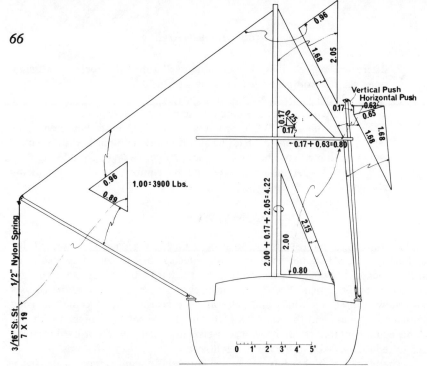

FIG. 6-3. Stress Analysis of a F/S gear, designed by the author for the 36-ft. Garden designed VEGA class trawler yacht.

1. The F/S rig should receive high priority in the design stage and not be tacked on as an afterthought. Remembering that the stabilizing force is the pull of the stabilizer times the length of the pole plus one-half beam, poles should be made as long as they conveniently can be within strength limits in this highly stressed column.

2. The proper position for the ends of the poles in the working position is 28 per cent of LWL forward of the stern. In all locations appreciably forward of this point, performance grows progressively worse. If located too far forward, when the vessel pitches up, both fish will resist, causing double drag, to no purpose.

3. Strength of rigging must be carefully worked out. A satisfactory result ensues if the breaking strength of the tow wire is used as the load, and the rig strengths are made equal or better than this by graphical statics analysis in the athwartships plane alone. This will give a safety factor of about 2.2 (*see Fig. 6-3*).

4. The tow wire should be as short as possible while still keeping the fish underwater. Our rig, on a 15-foot beam with 20-foot poles at 30 degrees up angle, put the fish 14 feet underwater at rest. As we skipped one only once in a gale in the Aegean, that was about right. For those who wonder what happens if a stabilizer is pulled out of the water, ours soared straight through the air like a porpoise, dove back in, and went back to work.

5. A nylon spring of about seven feet should be used in the tow wire to ease the strains on the rig from jerking.

6. The forward guy should be led as far forward as possible. It should be one size larger wire than the tow wire.
7. No rigging to the stabilizer other than the tow wire is required. It is absolute nonsense to have lines "to keep the stabilizer from going aft too far," or other lines suggested by some users.
8. The stabilizer sizes given in the Kolstrand Company bulletin on the subject, work out well in practice. This company is the licensee for the patented most popular type. (Address: 4739 Ballard Ave. NW, Seattle, WN 98107). We used the No. 300 size on *PM*. For trade-wind running, where the rolling force is not great but the speed may become excessive running down the long swells, we wished we had some No. 192s. All stabilizers should be ordered with the high speed arm (*see Fig. 6-4*). The hole used for towing should be as far forward as possible while still keeping the tow wire taut when diving. The set-ting is very sensitive to speed.
9. Shackles located at either end of the tow wire *must* have their pins inserted from *starboard to port*! If you don't do this, you will lose the whole assembly. Don't learn this the hard way, as we did.
10. There is a great deal of wear at the towing lug on the pole. Parts should be well oversize. *PM*s lugs are now five-eighth inch steel, two

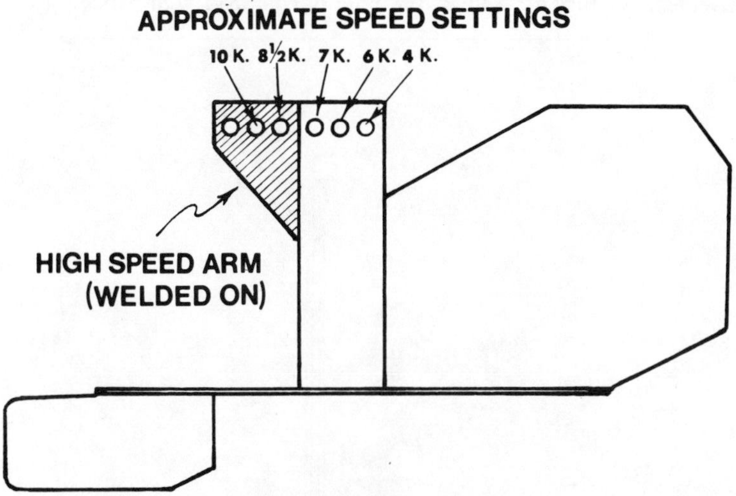

APPROXIMATE SPEED SETTINGS

10 K. 8½ K. 7 K. 6 K. 4 K.

HIGH SPEED ARM
(WELDED ON)

FIG. 6-4. The "high-speed arm" (shaded section) added to a stabilizer. The speed settings for the shackle are approximate.

inches wide, using shackles with three-quarter inch pins. When the hole wears egg-shaped at 7000 miles, it can be built up with chrome-moly weldment and will then be good indefinitely. Towing shackles last about 15,000 miles. Dab them with waterproof grease when you get the chance.
11. A hold-down strut should be fitted to prevent the poles from flipping up if they are left out when there is no fish towing.

12. Trouble with commercially produced stabilizer-towing nylon springs has occurred often, and been reported .by several users. Apparently, professional riggers do not appreciate how great and continuous the strains are on this spring. At least four vessels, to my knowledge, have had eye splices pull out. So, make your own. A satisfactory splice must have *at least five full tucks with three half tucks*! The whole should then be tightly wrapped with plastic electrician's tape (which will stretch with the nylon). A marline serving may be added, but this is mostly for appearance as the continual stretching of the splice will soon separate it—and the tape does the job.

HANDLING THE RIG

Passagemaker's rig used a pole that was held in place by forward and aft guys, the fore guy taking the strain when operating. It was a two-man job to put the poles out, as the aft guy had to have a tackle in it to adjust for the fact that the guys and the pole hinge were not in line with each other. The tackle's blocks would separate about eight feet when the pole was lowered.

That one man could not lower the pole alone was a nuisance, particularly in some of my singlehanded short trips. To fix this the "singlehanded pole" was invented. As Fig. 6-5 shows, the pole is equipped with a fixed aft guy and a

FIG. 6-5. Sketch of the Single-Handed Pole for a F/S rig.

strut to the pole that keeps it under control during the raising or lowering process. The fore guy is arranged to be taut in the down position and goes slack when the pole is raised. It can then either be cast loose and coiled up at the pole, or held down by shock cords that take up the slack. It is important that the rig be adjusted so the strut does not put a bend in the pole when in use, as any such stress could lead to rapid failure of this highly stressed compression member. Strut end connections that have considerable play would be useful in avoiding this problem.

Picking up the fish can be done in two ways: When poles are out, Kolstrand's small, smooth grapnel can be thrown out to hook the wire, which can then be drawn in until the crew can grab it and hoist the fish the rest of the way. Or, the pole can be raised, which puts the wire right in hand. The single-handed rig provides the easiest way to raise the pole and get the wire. This in-and-out drill is simple compared to the machinations we had to go through on *PM*. In the four vessels that now have the single-handed *F/S* rig, getting in the fish is accomplished routinely.

To further simplify matters, a "cable grab" (Photo 6-6, 6-7) has been invented. The fish is not particularly heavy, about 40 pounds, but pulling it up by hand while grasping the slick wire requires four hands (two people), to do it easily. The new cable grab is made so it can be attached at the cable's middle,

PHOTO 6-6. Cable Grab being fitted to a tow wire to pick up a stabilizer.

PHOTO 6-7. Cable Grab supporting stabilizer's full weight.

PHOTO 6-8. The Garden designed 67-ft. *Lady Fair,* with F/S rig by the author.

locked and slid down until it hits the stabilizer; then any upward pull will grab the wire. Attached to the grab is a piece of manila rope, the rough surface giving an excellent grip and making lifting easy for one man. To make things even easier on vessels that can use it (like *Mona Mona,* described in Chapter 10), a small crane with a snatch block can project out from the overhead to allow the fish to be pulled in with a downward pull. The cable grab was greatly appreciated on its first test cruise, the only problem being that it was horribly expensive. Modifications to make it cheaper are in hand.

At the beginning of this chapter, I suggested that much could be done to make roll-reduction more effective and cheaper. People *are* working on this, and here are brief accounts of several approaches to the problem. Perhaps others will be inspired to try their hand at it.

One of the most interesting developments is the "Lucan" stabilizing system. Essentially it is a fin system controlled as well as driven by the weight of a large pendulum. This simple system was invented by the naval architect Nils Lucander. Reports on its efficiency indicate it can reduce roll by about 75 per cent compared with gyro-controlled systems which average 85–90 per cent. It is, of course, *much* cheaper.

Mr. Samuel Burtis of Camden, Maine, has invented, tested, and obtained a patent on a hydrofoil-shaped stabilizing system. This consists of a streamlined fin which is attached to the keel and looks like a centerboard or fin keel. In his own 34-foot LWL boat, D/L 250, Mr. Burtis has two of these units on the keel. The tricky thing about this equipment is that the surface of the foil is flexible and supported in its airfoil shape by an inside structure that can move laterally. As a result, when the boat rolls, the side of the fin that presses against the water becomes flat while the other side assumes the curve appropriate to an

PHOTO 6-9. A stabilizer rig on a Garden designed 36-ft. VEGA, trawler model.

airfoil that will lift in a direction perpendicular to this curved shape. This lift is always opposed to the roll as the internal support shifts back and forth. Mr. Burtis reports roll-reduction around 60 per cent on the average, with percentage of reduction rising as the water gets rougher.

Some remarks he made in a letter to me are significant, as they bear on an important part of the stabilizing problem: "The reason for my undertaking stabilizer design was my wife's dislike of boats that 'tilt' as she phrases it . . . My best test data has been my wife's reaction to the boat with the fins operating. She is absolutely sold on them."

Another man experimented in roll reduction by taking a helicopter rotor blade and inserting it slantwise into the water from the deck. Apparently this worked pretty well and had the advantage of easy stowage when not in use.

Still another man, in the Pacific Northwest, feels it is possible to rig a streamlined fin of the symmetrical lifting type that will change its incidence to the water by careful adjustment of its axis, thus opposing roll automatically, by itself. The fin would be raised and lowered like a centerboard. I have no report of any new activity on this type to date.

In two vessels, Avard Fuller has used long daggerboards to reduce roll. These boards are fixed and do reduce roll to an extent that was considered satisfactory in a small, light vessel but which did not work as well in a larger, heavier one.

Certainly there must be other types of roll-reducers waiting to be invented. Be assured that any advances in this line will make your crew bless you; and make your wife bless you, too!

PHOTO 6-10. Carleton Mitchell's 62-ft. *Land's End,* showing her F/S rig. Note strut that prevents A-frame pole from kicking up. She also carries activated fins.

PHOTO 6-11. *Eden II,* a 50-ft. Krogen design, has an excellent F/S rig. Note that poles secure to the cabin side.

7

A New Generation of Passagemakers

Turning now from *Passagemaker* and what was learned from her, and from the general requirements of designing and stabilizing, we will discuss how this experience and these rules have been applied to a new generation of Passagemakers. This chapter shows my own ideas on design. Later chapters have examples of work by other designers.

We have already shown the plans of *Passagemaker* and some of her smaller predecessors that were essentially sailing models with extended range under power, the type of vessel envisaged in my 1946 *Rudder* article on cruising in the postwar Pacific.

In recent years, responding to the requests of clients, I have found myself concentrating on Passagemaker types that will provide a real home afloat for owner and wife. This makes sense to me—for the truth is, as already mentioned, such vessels are becoming so expensive they don't make much sense unless they are used practically full time. Ideally, they should be used as homes afloat; then their cost can be viewed as the cost of any comparable home. Granted this premise, we can see a design will not fill the need unless it provides nearly all the amenities of shoreside quarters.

We are thus faced with a demand for superior accommodations. How to supply this need? One way was mentioned in Chapter 3, the use of double-decking. This can be seen at its practical limits in Bob Sutton's *Mona Mona* in Chapter 10. She is a real home afloat for living in the Mediterranean, and with her 1200 gallons of fuel can cross the Atlantic and return.

But she does have a high A/B ratio of 3.0, with lots of glass. And she cannot use the French canals (*see Chapter 13.*) Would it be possible to develop a model that would be seaworthy enough to have no area restrictions, fit the French canals, and be a real home afloat, too? This was the problem posed by a client in Texas. What evolved is a yet-unnamed vessel, Design 96 (*see Fig. 7-1*).

This configuration comes so close to filling the specifications I don't see how she can be improved. Not only does she gain room by double-decking the pilothouse, but is greatly improved in the galley-saloon area by having the midships cabin extend out to the sides of the vessel. As a result she has almost as much galley-saloon area as *Mona Mona*, a larger owner's cabin, a larger engine room (though with less headroom), and guest cabins just slightly smaller.

Besides the extra room, she scores with the pilothouse aft—much the best position for sea work. And she is planned to fit the French canals to the limits

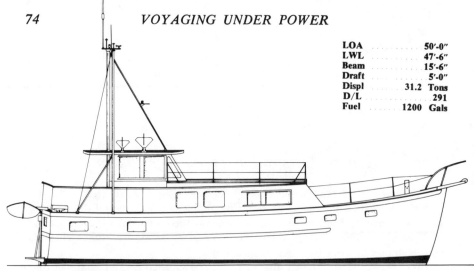

LOA	50'-0"
LWL	47'-6"
Beam	15'-6"
Draft	5'-0"
Displ	31.2 Tons
D/L	291
Fuel	1200 Gals

FIG. 7-1. Profile, Beebe Design 96.

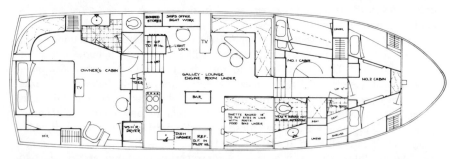

FIG. 7-2. Accommodation, Design 96.

given in Chapter 13 if the pilothouse is broken down at the lower edge of the ports. Her comparatively low A/B ratio of 2.6, together with smaller areas of glass that are amenable to shutters, allow her to operate with no area restriction other than the usual one of voyaging in each area's best season.

The penalties for all this, if you can call them that, are that one must go up and over the cabin to go forward, and her appearance is a bit unusual. As to the first, I have owned vessels built like this and found it no problem, especially in a motorboat where there should be no necessity for going forward in bad weather—there is nothing up there. As to appearance, it is interesting to note that five other designers recently have gone to the same configuration as it is the last remaining way to gain space. So I think we will see more of this design and its appearance will be accepted.

To provide reliable power, this pure motorboat uses twin engines driving to a single shaft. The persuasive reasons for this arrangement will be discussed later on.

The layout appeals to me so much I have repeated it in sizes from 42 to 50 feet. And the quest for more usable space has been carried to the logical conclusion of putting the steering gear outside on the stern where it does not

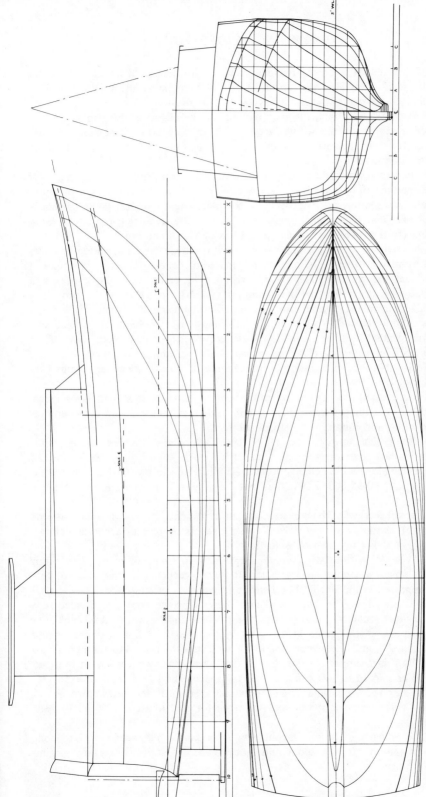

75

FIG. 7-3. Lines, Design 96. In the final version the knuckle in the bow was removed. The unique double-waterline plan was to facilitate interior accommodation planning.

intrude on the aft cabin arrangement, nor require the use of a lazarette for the rudder head. This also has the advantage of eliminating the rudder-post hole in the hull and makes the rudder accessible for repair.

As a matter of fact, the requirements of the client resulting in Design 96 forced a review of the whole layout problem before her final features were settled. Here are the various factors affecting decisions that must be made about accommodations:

The problems of the motorboat are different from the sailing cruiser. Not only does the motorboat have larger engines but their maintenance *demands* more elbow room, work benches, and the like. Then, too, fuel tanks become a major problem. If flopperstoppers are a part of the stabilizing gear, their positioning (to the rules given in Chapter 6) is of vital importance.

A sheltered steering station is essential, with an open-air station also desired by many owners. These must be capable of being completely blacked out to protect the watch-stander's night vision. The galley and dining area will generally be larger than in the sailing cruiser. The comfort of the cook is a cardinal principle. Large saloons with no convenient handholds must be viewed as dangerous at sea. With the motorboat's ability to drive hard into a head sea, an arrangement must be available for the crew berthed forward to come aft to sleep. As I learned aboard *Passagemaker,* while standing at the forward end of her fore cabin, such a vessel is quite capable of throwing you up against the overhead.

The possibilities offered by motorboat layouts for increased glass areas, compared to sailing vessels, must be approached cautiously, with consideration for location and suitability of storm shutters.

The designer must balance all of these factors, and more besides. Complicating his task immensely is one bane of his work—that human bodies do not change size along with a change in boat length. Hence a layout that might work well at, say, 50-55 feet LOA, may not be practical or desirable in a smaller version.

Looking at what has been done in this field, several distinct patterns emerge. It is thus possible to classify many yachts by type of accommodations. Figure 7-4 shows my own classifications.

"Type A" is the most common arrangement, found in many sizes, from 50 feet down, among what are called "trawler" yachts. The first boats of this type appeared in the Pacific Northwest and were sometimes called "tri-cabins," an apt description. The Type A sketch shows how the boats are divided into three distinct sections: the bow with guest cabins and head; the amidships area comprising a central cabin at, or a bit below, the sheer line with the engine room beneath, and the owner's cabin aft with its own head and shower. There is usually a lazarette aft of this, but as it is by no means necessary, it must be charged as part of the aft cabin in figuring space. The proportions of each section can be varied somewhat to suit individual owners. In the well known Grand Banks 42, for instance, the breakdown from forward to aft is 13 feet, 14 feet, 15 feet.

The advantages of this layout are: It is simple and economical to construct, it concentrates the saloon and galley amidships, it provides a large engine

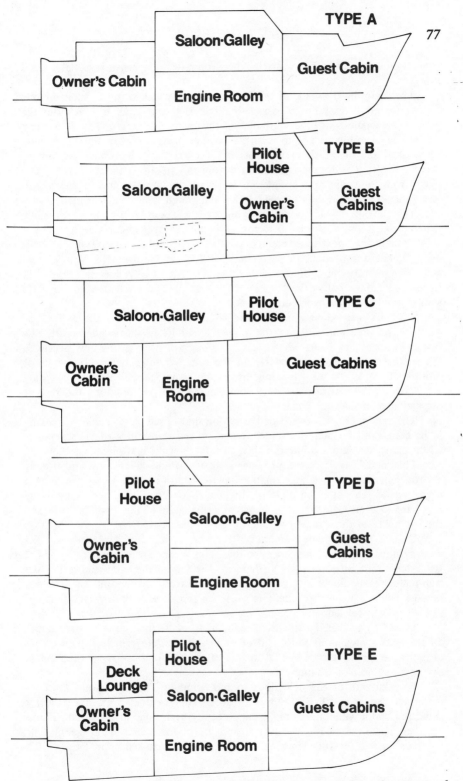

FIG. 7-4. Sketches to show the classification letters assigned to various types of motorboat layouts discussed throughout this book.

room—though with rather restricted headroom—and it has a reasonable A/B ratio.

The main disadvantage of this layout, and one that in my opinion inhibits its use for really long-range passage-making, is the inability to black out the piloting area unless all other activities in the living area cease. This is hard to manage when someone has to wash the supper dishes or work up the evening stars, or if the off-watch crew wants to play cribbage. Banishing the watchstander to the topside steering station during this period is unsatisfactory. The lights from the cabin may bother him anyway, the weather may be inclement, or a radar watch may be desirable at the set, which is normally located below.

This layout has no double-decking and is about as simple as possible. Whether it is satisfactory is up to the individual skipper and his crew.

Probably the next most popular configuration is shown as "Type B." This arrangement was brought to perfection by William Garden. His *Kaprice* and *Blue Heron* are great beauties. Unfortunately, this usually does not work out to best advantage unless the boat is 60 feet or so. Some attempts to use it in shorter models do not work out so well.

What has been done is to sink the saloon-galley down into the hull aft as much as possible and still put the engine under it. In the smaller craft, this results in the engine being what I call "sole buried." That is, the only access to the engine is through large hatches in the sole. While there are thousands of motorboats built this way, tucking the engine away inaccessibly in a seagoing vessel does not seem to me a very sensible thing to do, inhibiting the regular inspection of machinery while underway.

The pilothouse is forward of the saloon and raised to give double-decking in its area, with a stateroom under it and other cabins forward. The result is all the cabins are jammed into the bow, certainly not the best place in a blow.

This model, nevertheless, provides a superb saloon-galley area, and usually an excellent pilothouse with enough room for it also to be a social center as it is as large as the stateroom under it. In fact, for in-port living and entertaining it is hard to beat. Of course this is an important part of the whole picture and the balancing of them must be done on an individual basis.

Clearly, for the greatest amount of interior room in a given length, double-decking must be used as much as possible. This arrangement we call "Type C." Its sketch shows how much room there is. The Grand Banks 50 shows this design feature taken about as far as it can go. And it should certainly be arranged to take advantage of the superb expanse of top deck with regular stairways instead of vertical ladders.

Type C, however, is expensive, difficult to make handsome in sizes under 50 feet, has a poor A/B ratio, and other drawbacks. Nevertheless, it has a lot of appeal as a real home afloat. How one of them, *Mona Mona,* worked out at sea is the subject of Chapter 10.

To take care of the objections to the common Type A layout, the configuration shown as "Type D" was evolved. The revisions are: make the aft cabin full width without a trunk, as has recently been done in the Grand Banks 48, then place the pilothouse over it and aft of the center living cabin. The living cabin may be full width as in Design 96, or trunked as in Design 103,

(*Fig. 7-6*). The division of the three areas, (again from forward in feet), can be quite variable. In Design 96, it is 19.5, 15, 15.5. In Design 103, it is 19.5, 14.5, 20. In the 42-foot size my favorite is 14, 14, 14, with only two bunks forward. In 48 feet—considered to be the minimum length for fitting two good-sized double cabins forward with separate head and shower—a concensus of several skippers came up with 16.5, 15.5, 16. And it does appear that 16.5 feet is about the minimum for this arrangement of two doubles. But, during our cruise in *Mona Mona*, my wife and I sketched out our own ideas of a 48-footer and came up with 20, 14, 14.

As this configuration is double-decked in the pilothouse it has a clear gain in interior room of the length of the pilothouse over a similar boat not double-decked. For instance, a 42-foot boat in Type D would have the equivalent room of a 48-footer in Type A. This is an appreciable increase with no added length.

As for the size of the pilothouse, you have a deck area as long as the aft cabin to be divided between inside and outside spaces. The proportion to be alloted to each is an individual choice. One might say that a yacht expected to spend the majority of its time in warm waters could well have the outside space larger. *Passagemaker*'s pilothouse was five feet from aft bulkhead to the steering wheel bulkhead. It was about perfect for the watch-stander's convenience, but when the rest of the crew showed up for happy hour, it got a bit crowded. Six feet would have been better and seven luxurious. For outside eating on deck around a table, seven feet is about the minimum.

Would it be possible to design a configuration with as much room as a Type C, yet with a more seaworthy shape and a lower A/B ratio? Some preliminary work for a client, who eventually turned to another designer for a Type C, convinced me that the answer could be yes. The sketch shown as Type E shows this. It consists of the essentials of Type D as a base: a midships full-width saloon-galley, and the cabin on the aft deck over the owner's cabin. But instead of this cabin being the pilothouse, it is an on-deck saloon connected with the outside area. It could be a bar, library, or TV room. The pilothouse is placed forward of it, on top of the midships cabin.

It may not look it, but Type E has as much room inside as the double-decked full-length Type C. In addition, is has several other features that recommend it: The A/B ratio is smaller; the pilothouse is aft of amidships—much the best place, in my opinion—and there is enough area aft so she probably will not sail around her anchor, as Type C does mightily. If there was full headroom in the engine room, she would have a bit of triple-decking, so we must be concerned about her inertial rolling as discussed in Chapter 6. But the aft and high position of the pilothouse allows it to be made much lighter, with thinner glass than is safe when the pilothouse is far forward. Visibility for all types of maneuvering would be superb, and the seating forward of the pilothouse is a highly desirable outside lounging area in good weather.

Unfortunately, we run into trouble with our incompressible people again. It appears that the layout must be at least 55 feet long unless the draft is much increased over the usual 10 per cent of the length. But Type E has a lot of appeal and I intend to keep working at it.

There are other possible layouts, of course. Included among these would

PHOTO 7-5. William Lapworth's 50-ft. *Feng Shui.* In this vessel the engine is located in the bow and the exhaust runs up through the foremast.

be those based on unconventional engine placement. Photo 7-5 shows Bill Lapworth's *Feng Shui* that gains room by having the engine in the bow. The exhaust actually goes up the foremast. She is also interesting for the manner in which her topside cabin is kept small, with very large outside deck space. The *Mona Mona,* Chapter 10, goes the other way and places the engine in the stern with a vee drive. This was done to place the point where full 6′ 4″ headroom was required (that is, in the owner's cabin aft), farther forward where it is possible to lower the sole because the hull is deeper. There is not full headroom in the engine room, but it is quite adequate. This allows the top of the main cabin to be lower, and in fact, she has a lower silhouette than the GB-50, which has a conventional amidships engine location, although the amount of double-decking is about the same. Both *Feng Shui* and *Mona Mona* have their fuel tanks amidships with a short passageway between them. This allows the tanks to be so large in the athwartships dimension that 1200 gallons uses only 30 inches of length, a very definite contribution to living space.

All of these arrangements must be fitted into the hull itself, which is the responsibility of the naval architect. And it was to help the reader to judge the architect's work that Chapter 5 was written. In addition to the factors discussed there, several others affect the hull and can be varied within limits to make the best overall solution to your needs. These include such matters as freeboard, flare of bow, beam, draft, and deck plan.

There are no particular rules for freeboard other than to be aware of its influence on the A/B ratio. But some general remarks about the effect of variations will be useful. It is usually judged at the bow, at the stern, and at its lowest point. I have already mentioned in Chapter 3, under Lessons Learned No. 5, how we wished *Passagemaker*'s bow had been higher to increase the speed in seas from ahead without taking water over the bow. This problem actually has two parts—the height and the flare. That is, if *Passagemaker*'s bow had remained the same height but the flare of the sections had been increased, she would have been able to increase speed to some extent. But I am not at all sure I would want to do that.

Some years ago, in the 1950s as I recall, the matter of bow flare in fishing boats was a widely debated subject. The proponents of what might be called a "soft bow" claimed that such a shape would throw less spray in rough seas, and while the "flared bow" would admittedly keep solid water off the deck longer, it would also produce more spray that would be blown aboard in greater quantity. The debate was primarily concerned with the danger of icing up in freezing weather. While we do not expect yachts to encounter such conditions, the contrast between the two types of bow remains. At that time, I was inclined toward the "soft bow" school and the lines of *Passagemaker* show this.

Since then, the debate, as far as motor yachts are concerned, has been won by the advocates of flare. The advent of molded fiberglass has allowed the pro-flare forces to flare bows to their heart's content, unhindered by the shape limitations of wood planking or metal plating. It does *look* good, and, in fact, this is the main reason it is done. Naval architect Phillip Bolger, when he was working in Spain, suggested to me that I use more flare *"para la vista,"* as his clients said. Flare is recommended for "high speed launches" in *Naval Architecture of Small Craft,* but for vessels proceeding under hull speed I remain unconvinced. The problem is this: When the flared bow goes over the top of one wave and down into the trough of the next one, the flare not only reverses this "down" motion to a new "up" motion more rapidly, but also causes more deceleration in the forward motion due to the much greater relative increase in resistance as the broad part of the flare is immersed. I know from experience that flared bows can cause screams from the galley due to deceleration alone. I once went out San Francisco's Golden Gate, tide against wind, in a vessel with such extreme bow flare that it slammed very badly, throwing sheets of spray not only to the sides but forward. It seemed to me the owner was fooling himself. It's true we took no water on deck over the bow, but every time she bunted a wave we came practically to a dead stop. None of the crew appreciated it, and I don't think it was doing the vessel any good, either. So my personal preference remains that I would rather slow down slightly, so the water does not come over the bow, and have an easier motion. This conclusion is reflected in the bow of Design 105 shown in Chapter 9.

Freeboard amidships and at the stern is largely determined by desired accommodation. There seems to be no particular disadvantage to higher sterns. In fact, the high sterns of the dhow and the Chinese junk have a great deal to be said for them. Not only does the stern provide superb accommodations, but because of increased windage aft, the hull shape heaves to very well, and lies quietly at anchor, while the higher-bow types sail around their anchors to a sometimes terrifying degree—terrifying to their neighbors, that is.

Low freeboard aft is largely a legacy from fishing vessels, where it is necessary to ease the work of getting the catch aboard. This is something that does not concern the yacht. What *is* important is getting the crew aboard, not only from the dock but from the water. It is vital, for instance, that there be some way for a man overboard to be able to regain the deck unassisted. There are too many tales of crewmen, lulled by the safety of harbor, and working alone, who have fallen overboard and been unable to reach the deck of a high-sided motorboat. The minimum requirement is a series of combination handholds-steps. The ideal is the stern platform, originated on the Pacific Coast, which not only performs this function but provides a "sheltered harbor" that has to be experienced just once to be appreciated by someone climbing out of a dinghy in a blow.

Beam and draft combine to be determinants of hull volume and displacement; that is, beam at the waterline. There is no reason beam at the sheer cannot be increased separately if desired. It increases stability when a boat rolls deeply, and in this day of high dockage fees, provides space that is "free" if fees are based on overall length.

Draft is another matter that can stand variation. Shoal draft is not useful if the vessel does not go into shoal waters. But excessive draft can be troublesome in harbors. In a cruiser suitable for East Coast passage-making and crossing the Atlantic to enter French canals, my limit is five feet. Even so, in the Intracoastal Waterway and French canals you will bounce off the bottom occasionally. But these bottoms are soft—no trouble. In the Bahamas, less draft is preferable much of the time, though not strictly necessary. My observation of many boats reveals that draft usually runs about ten per cent of the length—a good general rule.

The deck plan (a view of the vessel from above) of many seagoing motorboats shows what appears to be a vestigial tendency to follow the form of sailing

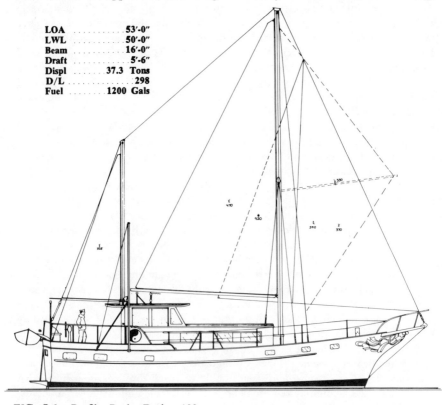

LOA	53'-0"
LWL	50'-0"
Beam	16'-0"
Draft	5'-6"
Displ	37.3 Tons
D/L	298
Fuel	1200 Gals

FIG. 7-6. Profile, Beebe Design 103.

vessels: pointed at the bow, which is necessary, and curved in at the stern, which is not. A narrow stern does give better steering in a vessel that heels under sail or rolls deeply, but stabilized motorboats don't do this so a narrow stern becomes a case of esthetics versus practicality. In a vessel with living cabins aft, the urge to broaden the stern is almost overwhelming and certainly shows in my designs. When the engine is in the stern, one can have more inward curve to the top sides aft. But in the case of *Mona Mona* with her large deckhouse, the owner wanted the cabin straight-sided for building economy, so I did not pinch in the side appreciably even though the engine room is all the way aft.

Another consideration that affects the deck plan is the placement of the stabilizing gear. When flopperstoppers are fitted using the singlehanded pole recommended in Chapter 6, especially if the pole is stowed in the up position at the spreader of a mast also used for sail, then the line between the two hinges, (pole *and* strut) must be horizontal and parallel to the center line of the hull to seat the pole in the spreader notch when hoisted. Masts used for this purpose

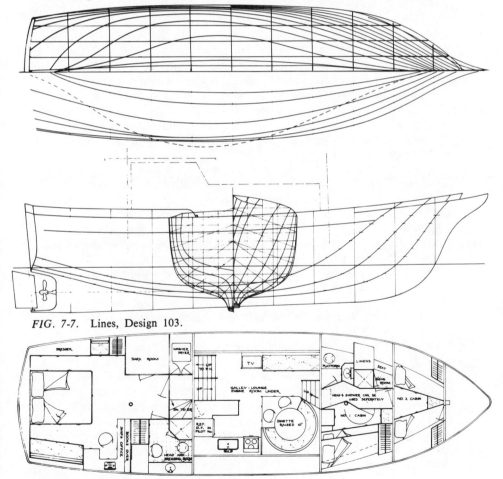

FIG. 7-7. Lines, Design 103.

FIG. 7-8. Accommodation, Design 103.

cannot have any rake. The effect of this on a vessel with this kind of mast is shown on the plan of Design 105 in Chapter 9. If the pole is secured to some other point, such as the overhang of the cabin-top, the hinges can be out of line to some extent but placed to insure that the end of the pole is exactly in line with the fastening of the topping lift to the mast in the working position. This is to insure that no fore and aft strains are put on the rig. This can be seen on the profiles of Design 96 and Design 103.

Interest in motor vessels that carry sail continues. Design 103 shows the latest such development. Although she is a bit on the large side at 54 feet, the boat in Fig. 7-6 is interesting because a basic part of her specification was to produce a new vessel that eliminated the faults we found in *Passagemaker,* as discussed in Chapter 3. In fact, there was such a close similarity between them, we started off calling her *Passagemaker II.*

The client, Dr. Donald H. Parker, of Big Sur, California, originally wanted a vessel that would perform well on all points of sailing, yet be good for long power passages also. When this was modified to *exclude* good windward ability, the project became feasible. The answer to the differing demands of power and sail is the controllable-pitch propeller. Previously, I had resisted this type propeller. Although I knew that such props had long since proved themselves abroad when working in the ahead and reverse positions, a propeller that will *also feather* (required for sailing) calls for a more delicate mechanism.

The solution was found by specifying a Hundested (Denmark) VP-5, FROA, 36-inch propeller, set to change pitch only from neutral to feathered, thereby using the sturdier operating gear. Ahead and astern is provided by a conventional hydraulic reverse gear. She carries twin engines driving one shaft in the manner of Design 96.

Dr. Parker's interest in Oriental philosophy led him to name the vessel *Yin-Yang,* with this symbol displayed on the pilothouse. He also required a clipper bow, and this will probably be decorated with the Chinese Goddess of the Winds, as shown, by my wife Linford, who is an expert in Oriental art. The 20-foot stern cabin with office and darkroom is unusual, as is the circular dinette in the saloon. The 11-foot-wide pilothouse has a seven-foot raised settee under which is located the deep freeze and chart stowage.

Because two identical engines driving a single shaft appear to make the best arrangement for a power passage-maker actually crossing oceans, let's examine this arrangement. First, there is a greatly reduced need for spares as one engine could be cannibalized to keep the other running. Second, all long voyages would be made at speeds where only one engine is needed, thus promoting efficiency by running this single engine in its best operating range. The desirability of the arrangement is shown graphically on this Engine-Propeller Curve, Fig. 7-9. It so happens that the horsepower a propeller actually uses falls off as the cube of the rpm. If, as is the custom, propeller size is selected to absorb maximum continuous horsepower at maximum permitted rpm, when the throttle is eased back it will rapidly use less horsepower—as the curve shows. This great decrease of the hp used compared to the engine's continuous horsepower rating probably accounts for the excellent service life of marine diesels. The curve shown is for Design 96, the same one for which the speed-

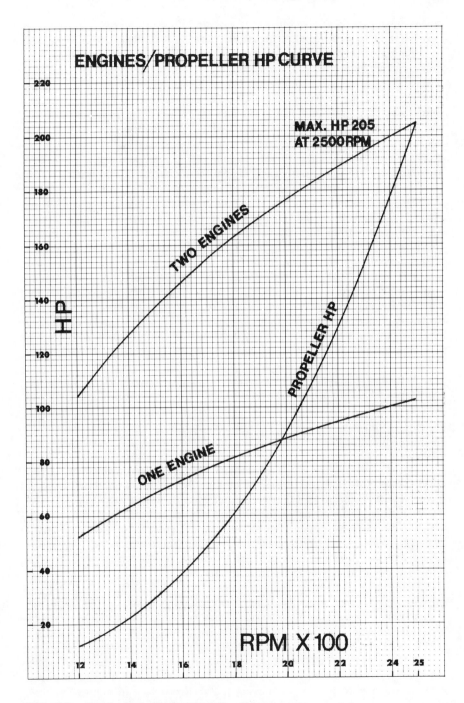

FIG. 7-9. Graph: Twin-Engine Propeller Curve.

power-range curve was given in Chapter 5. And these two curves for your own vessel should be kept together for cross reference. You will note that at 1800 rpm, the propeller uses 60 hp. On the speed curve this is eight knots. (Actually, it is 7.9 knots on the full-load curve but she should speed up enough on a long passage from burning fuel to average 8.0). This is a good speed for almost any passage except the really long ones like Canaries-Barbados. Eighteen hundred rpm is the speed generators run to produce 60-cycle AC. At this rpm the curve shows there is 22 hp available over the demands of the propeller before reaching the maximum-permitted hp curve. It is a good idea, then, to mount an AC generator on each engine. Presto—instant AC power, and with the in-port generator, it's produced three ways. Under these conditions, the watch-stander watches not engine rpm but the frequency meter, maintaining 60 cycles exactly.

The watch-stander should have a remote switch with which he can cut off the AC load instantly, so he can change vessel speed or stop the engine without hesitation. We did not have this feature on a vessel with this generating system and it was a nuisance having to worry about the load and the effects of low voltage on rotating machinery.

One should "red-line" single-engine operation at just over 1800 rpm to insure some reserve at all times for generating. When both engines are on the line, there is enough horsepower available to drive Design 96 to 10.5 knots if electric demands are cut out. In any setup where the engines can be overloaded inadvertently, such as this boat, or any vessel with a controllable-pitch propeller, it is important to have exhaust-temperature gauges prominently displayed and red-lined.

A further advantage of two engines driving a single shaft is vastly improved propeller protection. The vulnerable twins are hopeless for range as both must run all the time unless you want to go to the trouble of removing one of the props. In tests of two twin-screw vessels, shutting down one engine and dragging its prop, had this result: One boat showed increased range, the other *reduced* range!

The actual layout of the drive employs "toothed belts" in single-belt form. Earlier types of drive that depended on multiple Vee belts proved unsatisfactory. In the case mentioned, we followed the guidance of Jack Edgemond who was involved in the development of the original toothed belt. His own boat is belt-driven by two 150 hp gasoline engines, and after 12 years (6000 hours) the belts looked as good as new. Uniroyal PowerGrip High Torque Drive belts are specified, a new development in which the teeth are semicircular instead of the original trapezoids, and have a higher torque rating.

Drive is to a jackshaft that is connected to a Borg-Warner 73C 3:1 reverse-reduction gear, using the same flywheel and bell housing as the diesel engine itself. The engines must be fitted with power take-offs that are able to back-drive indefinitely (which most PTOs can't do), such as the Twin Disc SL-111-HP3. In case of trouble with the single reverse gear, this can be removed and a piece of shaft substituted. A thrust bearing is necessary. And to substitute for the 3:1 reduction, an emergency belt setup for one engine giving 2.80:1 reduction is possible by moving the sheave 0.62″, an adjustment well within the eccentricity limits of the Spicer Universal Joint coupling.

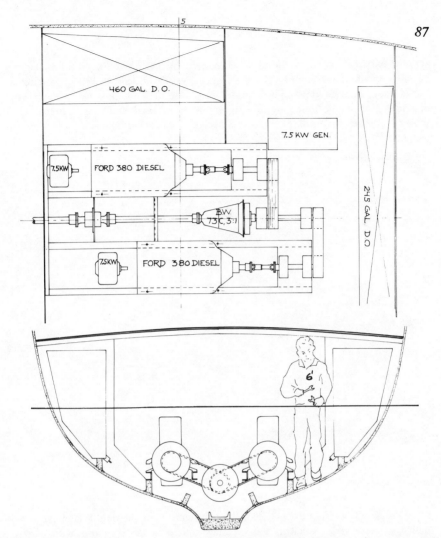

FIG. 7-10. Engine Room layout, Design 103.

In Design 103, the Palmer cruising generators are directly coupled to each engine. However, Design 96 does contemplate going west across the Atlantic under power alone by the Canaries-Barbados route, which would require cruising on one engine at 1620 rpm. So one of her generators is not coupled to an engine but to the jackshaft with belt ratios of 1:1 and 1:1.11, both easily changed.

To round out this discussion of design as a purely personal view, there are two more vessels that make different points. The first is Design 101, the 42-foot hull mentioned in Chapter 5. The genesis of this design was the search for a hull that would be suitable for a crew of four for ocean-crossing passages, one clearly more seaworthy than current 42-foot "trawlers." To provide superior room, she was given a beam of 15.5 feet, illustrating the effect of current docking fees based on length. In addition, she was made quite heavy (D/L 375) to achieve two things: Allow building in cement by the amateur, who almost invariably produces an overweight hull; and, by this added weight, producing a "solid feel" compared to lighter craft. This essentially means the "heave," or distance a vessel is tossed by encounters with waves, would be reduced. For this, of course, we must pay the penalty of greater fuel consumption due to weight.

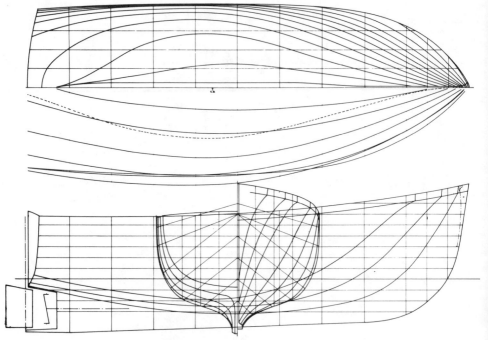

FIG. 7-11.   Lines, Beebe Design 101.

Design 101 exists now just as a lines drawing. But she could have arrangements in many styles, such as the sketches shown here—even one with berths for six. Several layouts are shown in Fig. 7-12.

The next design, No. 104, takes a different approach. She returns more to the dimensions of *Passagemaker,* having a length of 48 feet and a D/L of 275. Her accommodation was the consensus of a group of sailors who were considering the turn to power for their cruising, and it met their requirements for full-time living space for skipper and wife, plus two double cabins. It has the advantage of not exceeding the 50-foot barrier, a psychological barrier to many. The full-width cabin of Design 96 was accepted as the starting point. The preliminary sketch of this version of the 48-footer (where this design stands now) was made while Linford and I were aboard *Mona Mona* as described in Chapter 10. Working up accommodation ideas on another boat, where other layouts can be marked out and tested, is convenient.

Her three sections from forward were divided 20, 14, 14, because we returned from the *Mona Mona* cruise feeling we could reduce the size of the

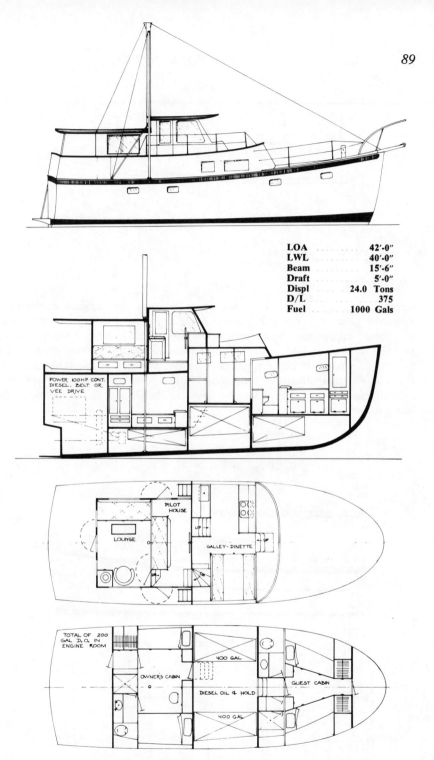

LOA	42'-0"
LWL	40'-0"
Beam	15'-6"
Draft	5'-0"
Displ	24.0 Tons
D/L	375
Fuel	1000 Gals

POWER 100HP CONT. DIESEL. BELT OR VEE DRIVE

PILOT HOUSE

LOUNGE

UP

GALLEY - DINETTE

TOTAL OF 200 GAL D.O. IN ENGINE ROOM

OWNERS CABIN

400 GAL

DIESEL OIL & HOLD

GUEST CABIN

400 GAL

FIG. 7-12 (1). A layout of Design 101, combining features of Types B and D.

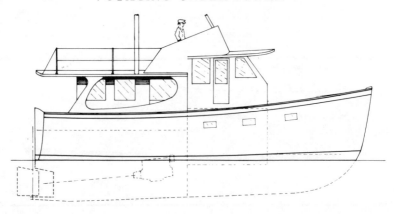

FIG. 7-12 (2). Design 101 as a Type B.

saloon/galley and aft cabin somewhat to improve the forward cabins, and move the galley aft. The galley/dinette relationship and the size of the galley were based on our experience with *Mona Mona* and a somewhat larger vessel in which we had cruised earlier. Both of these suffered in varying degree from too great a separation between galley and table, and lack of handholds between them. The circular dinette is something Linford wanted to try as she prefers a round table at home. The dinette is raised in the Passagemaker manner, with stores under.

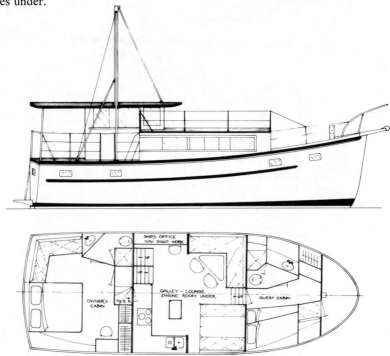

FIG. 7-12 (3). Design 101 as a Type D.

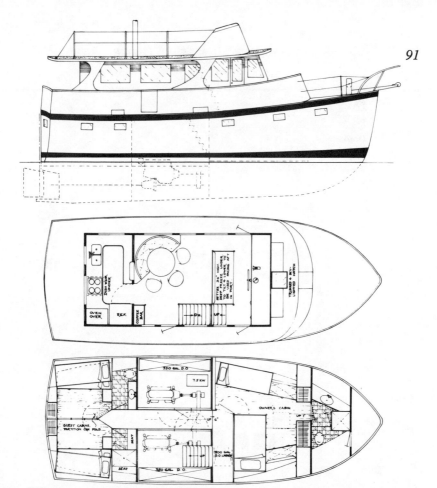

FIG. 7-12 (4). Design 101 as a Type C, with berths for six, and with galley and accommodation plan by the author's wife.

Forward, although there is plenty of room for two double cabins, we chose a different plan, with two in one cabin and one in another. We have found that a good deal of local cruising is done with only the owners aboard, or possibly another couple. So the double cabin was made really roomy. As five is the ideal crew for long passages, a small cabin does nicely for the fifth crew member. The bulkhead between these two cabins can be arranged to open in the manner discussed in Chapter 10.

The sail rig was sketched in for a man who insisted on having *some* sail, and would be fun to play with. The profile of the pilothouse came from modern freighters. While the forward slanting windshield does not look like much in a flat drawing, in actual service it's rather impressive. It really does cut down on glare and in this design, makes it possible to extend the cabin top for more area up there. The reason I wanted more space was to carry small boats better. The space would hold my 16-foot lapstrake canoe, *Japanese Doll*, which was much appreciated on *Passagemaker*'s cruise in Canada, and would also hold a 15-foot Whitehall boat for rowing by two. This would make my small-boat fleet ideal.

LOA	48'-0"
LWL	46'-8"
Beam	15'-6"
Draft	5'-0"
Displ	27.3 Tons
D/L	269
Fuel	1000 Gals

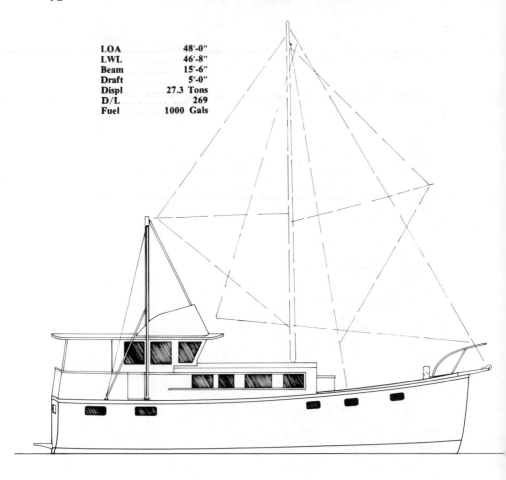

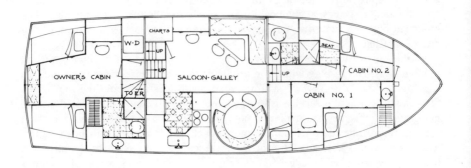

FIG. 7-13. Outboard Profile & Accommodation, Beebe Design 104.

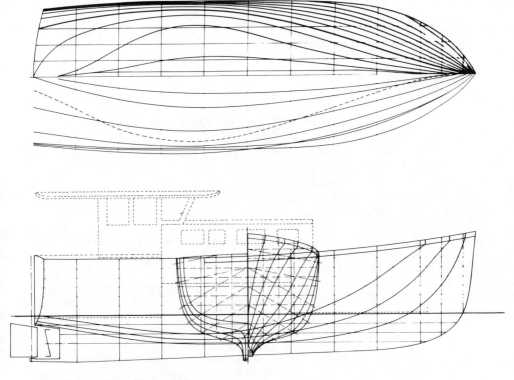

FIG. 7-14. Lines, Design 104.

The lower D/L of this vessel compared to Design 101 was chosen more for economy than anything else. She has the waterline beam of *Passagemaker* to insure that she is not too stiff (as discussed in Chapter 6) and we hope for performance of the stabilizing gear similar to her predecessor.

That's enough of my own ideas. The next chapter shows the work of several designers who kindly contributed designs and commentary to round out this book.

8

Work of Other Designers

We owe a debt of gratitude to all the designers who contributed the results of their knowledge and experience to make up this chapter. The remarkable diversity of solutions to the problem of the seagoing motorboat shows how much scope there is for different approaches to achieving what essentially is a single specification—that the product be a seaworthy motorboat with a range of X miles.

To play no favorites, the designs are arranged in alphabetical order. I do have my favorites, of course, but I hope my comments will be evenhanded enough to conceal which ones they were.

In the interest of space, vessels that are serially produced and advertised are not included, as it is felt that anyone interested in such boats gets enough information about them from the yachting press.

My request for contributions carried this specification:

> "We are interested primarily in vessels in the 40- to 50-foot class for broadest appeal. But examples of special interest in lengths both above and below these limits will also be included. While we realize the majority of seagoing motorboats will not in fact make long voyages, the designs should be capable of making passages of some days and, hopefully, be able at least to cross the Atlantic (1850 miles: Bermuda-Azores)."

We are especially grateful to the designers who have permitted us to present the lines of their creations. This permission was requested to make the book valuable to serious students of yacht design, on a continuing basis, and this objective has certainly been fulfilled.

JOHN G. ALDEN, INC.

This well-known Boston firm has provided the plans of *Ortem*. She is primarily designed as a sport fisherman, but, contrary to what we usually expect in a sport fisherman, she is not powered with twin engines for speed and maneuverability. Her basic specification called for her to fish offshore in moderate to heavy weather, have an 11-knot cruising speed (S/L 1.52), and be able to cruise at this speed for not less than 2000 miles under all weather

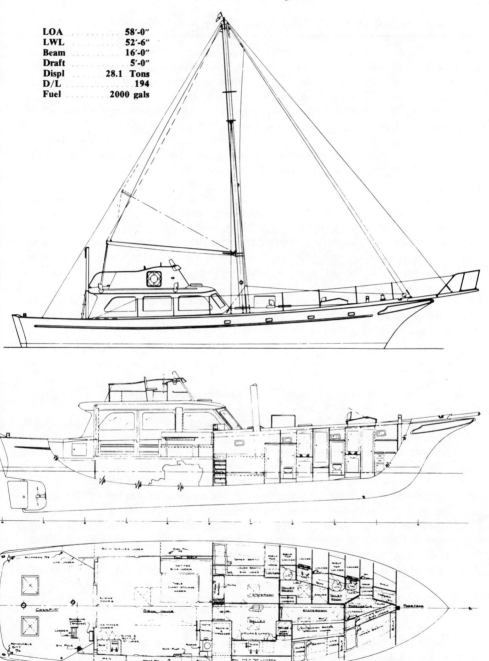

LOA		58'-0"
LWL		52'-6"
Beam		16'-0"
Draft		5'-0"
Displ		28.1 Tons
D/L		194
Fuel		2000 gals

FIG. 8-1. Profile & Accommodation, Alden 58-ft. *Ortem.*

conditions she would be likely to meet in the Gulf Stream and the Caribbean. According to her designers:

"She has filled these specifications admirably. The owner is reported to be very pleased with her capabilities to remain at sea when other boats her size are heading for shelter. She has been caught at sea off New England in a full gale, which experience only reinforced confidence in her handling and sea-keeping abilities. She has cruised from New England to the Caribbean and returned regularly for four years, making the passages offshore.

"*Ortem* is equipped with a sizable steadying and emergency propulsion rig. Although it does not show on the plans, she has been equipped with flopperstoppers, which are reported to work exceptionally well at cruising speeds."

This vessel is something of a hybrid. But aside from her fishing abilities, she shows what can be done for seaworthiness and range by holding down the A/B ratio, going to a single screw, and keeping the accommodations, particularly the cabins, somewhat on the Spartan side compared to craft more dedicated to living afloat. Her A/B ratio is about 1.98, which is excellent these days, and undoubtedly a great contributor to her reported performance in heavy weather.

The 2230 gallons of fuel needed to take *Ortem* 2000 miles at 11 knots give her a really extended range when she is slowed down: some 6,000 miles at eight knots. Pacific crossing, anyone?

JAY R. BENFORD & ASSOCIATES, INC.

I first met Jay Benford when he was doing pioneer work in ferro-cement as naval architect for Star Marine in Tacoma. Since that time he has formed his own firm and done a good deal more work in that medium. My Design 96 follows his methods of construction—with some variations, of course.

For the book, his 44-footer is an interesting variation on the "Type B" layout. He has solved the problem of the sole-buried engine by placing it boldly in the stateroom below the pilothouse, surrounded by a trunk that extends up to the pilothouse sole, thus giving direct engine-control runs. The insulated panels of this trunk can be removed for access to the engine. This is certainly a unique idea, and it would be interesting to be shipmates with it to see how it works. Perhaps the chief engineer should occupy that stateroom!

The vessel carries ballast of some 6000 pounds of inside ballast and up to 1500 gallons of fuel. With her well-proportioned profile and her shippy-looking rig, she has much appeal.

Benford's 35-foot motorsailer is an expansion of the straight motor trawler, *Strumpet,* he designed for author Ernest Gann. In the 35-footer, the full-width cabin aft adds a great deal to the space in what is essentially a small boat. Her rig looks well on her and should provide enough area for real sailing if a fully feathering, controllable-pitch propeller were provided. Her 600 gallons of fuel is enough to take her 4000 miles at six knots.

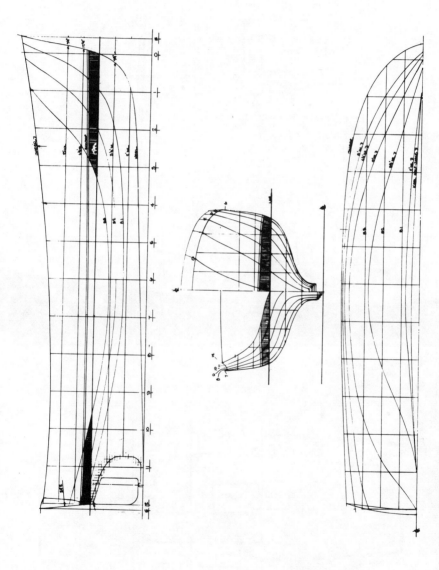

FIG. 8-2. Lines, Benford 44-ft. trawler yacht.

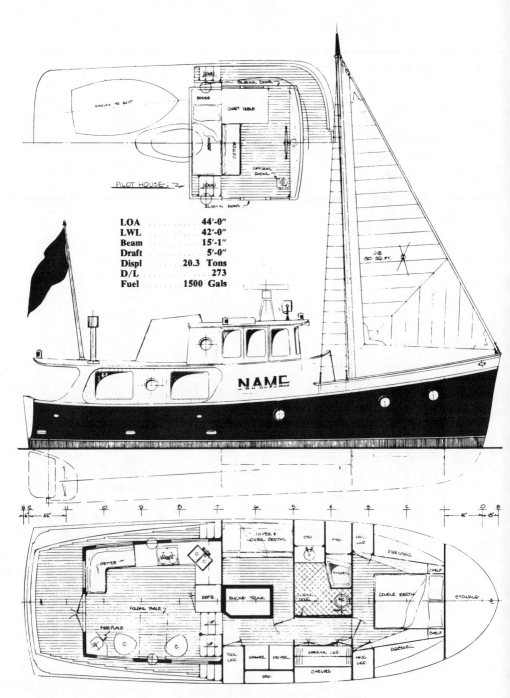

LOA	44'-0"
LWL	42'-0"
Beam	15'-1"
Draft	5'-0"
Displ	20.3 Tons
D/L	273
Fuel	1500 Gals

FIG. 8-3. Profile & Accommodation, Benford 44-ft. trawler yacht.

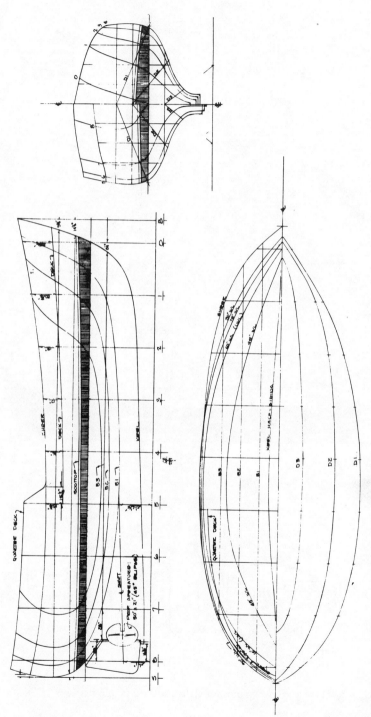

FIG. 8-4. Lines, Benford 35-ft. motorsailer.

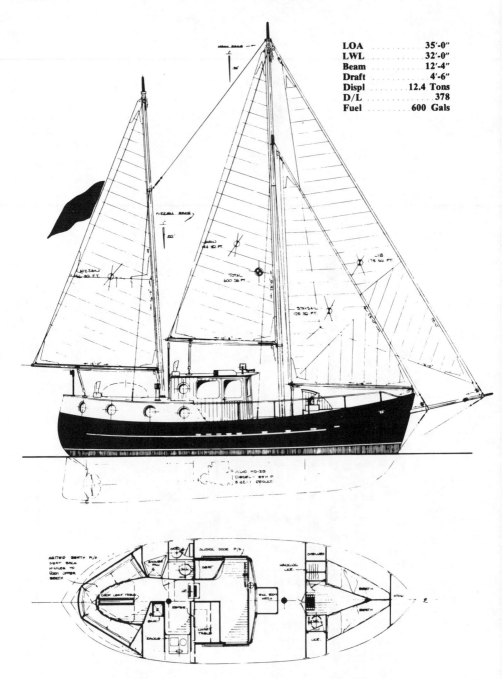

LOA	35'-0"
LWL	32'-0"
Beam	12'-4"
Draft	4'-6"
Displ	12.4 Tons
D/L	378
Fuel	600 Gals

FIG. 8-5. Profile & Accommodation, Benford 35-ft. motorsailer.

PHOTO 8-6. Benford's *Strumpet*, built for author Ernest Gann. Note the clean wake at full speed. (Roy Montgomery photo.)

PHILIP C. BOLGER

I first met Phil Bolger in 1957. At one time we discussed a loose professional association. Although this idea fell through, we still argue boats and discuss each other's designs on a no-holds-barred, no-hurt-feelings basis—if such a thing is possible!

I knew exactly which of Phil's designs I wanted for this book. The first is *Omega*. The client for this design had originally approached Phil about a larger boat, one suitable for crossing the Atlantic and entering the French canals. Phil consulted me about her because of my canal experience, and several changes had to be made in the original design. Then the client dropped the ocean-crossing requirement and decided on a "houseboaty" type for cruising in Europe, to be built over there.

The result was *Omega*, which at first glance is about as strange looking a vessel as one could imagine. But a little study shows that she makes sense. The triple-chine hull facilitates building her in steel and results in her having very fair waterlines and buttocks, with the equivalent of very good flare forward. In addition, she has a full-width cabin with reasonably small glass area. The result has been a success, and Phil speaks of her as follows:

"*Omega* is a houseboat, the year-round home for a middle-aged couple. She has cruised for a year or so in the North Sea and the Baltic, plus, I think, a trip to the Med outside, and she has met some very heavy weather. I think the owner said it was off Gotland that he had a fuel stoppage, on a lee shore with a pebble bottom that would not hold an anchor, and was almost into the breakers before he could get the engine started again. His wife reports looking into green water through the living room windows as the boat rolled in the troughs, which I take as an illustration of the advantage of the full-width house. The action of the bow shape is said to be very good and to enable her to keep up with much bigger Dutch trawlers, even in a large head sea. Her cruising speed is reported as 10 knots, which is better than I expected. Her fundamental purpose is to be a very comfortable place to live; her movements are secondary and occasional, but they are not supposed to depend on good weather or frequency of refueling points."

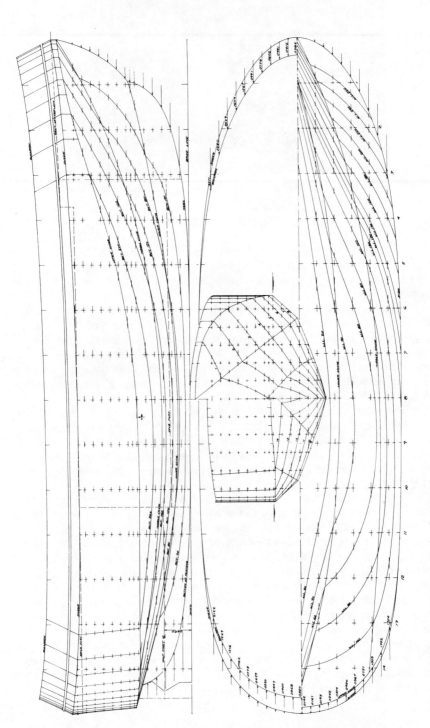

FIG. 8-7. Lines, Bolger 49-ft. Omega.

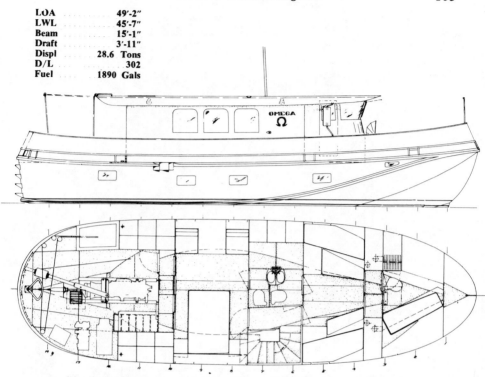

LOA		49'-2"
LWL		45'-7"
Beam		15'-1"
Draft		3'-11"
Displ		28.6 Tons
D/L		302
Fuel		1890 Gals

FIG. 8-8. Profile & Accommodation, Bolger 49-ft. *Omega.*

The other Bolger vessel, *Thorfinn,* is quite different from *Omega,* though it is possible to see some family resemblance in their lines; especially in Phil's "high chine." His remarks on *Thorfinn* are:

"*Thorfinn* was launched in Iceland and looks like she will be a success, though I hope, by tinkering, to improve on her 18.5 knot, first-trial speed. She is supposed to be a general-purpose, fast cruiser with sport-fishing ability, no different in use from the run of stock cruisers of her size, except for unusually large tankage and a range of stability almost in the lifeboat class. She's built of six mm. aluminum and displaces 32,000 lbs. I understand there were 60 people aboard her on the trial run, which apparently did not discombobulate her. She is a prototype and is somewhat different in layout from that shown on the plans."

Although at first glance neither of these vessels would seem qualified for a book on long-range motorboats, Phil went on to say this:

"Both were designed to have ocean-crossing capability if and when it is wanted, and perhaps they're both more seaworthy than vessels otherwise more suitable for long-range cruising, a distinction being drawn between seaworthiness (ability to survive in heavy weather) and seakindliness (quality of being comfortable under bad conditions). *Thorfinn* is of moderately heavy construction, with six mm. aluminum plate and all-transverse frame. Both boats have ⅜" laminated glass in exposed windows. The full-width upper works, plus

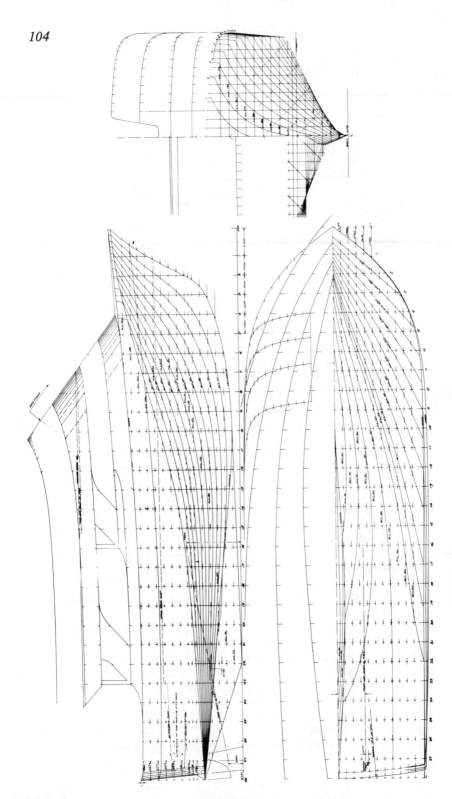

FIG. 8-9. Lines, Bolger 47-ft. *Thorfinn.*

LOA	46'-7"
LWL	42'-5"
Beam	15'-8"
Draft	3'-11"
Displ	14.3 Tons
D/L	188
Fuel	1000 Gals

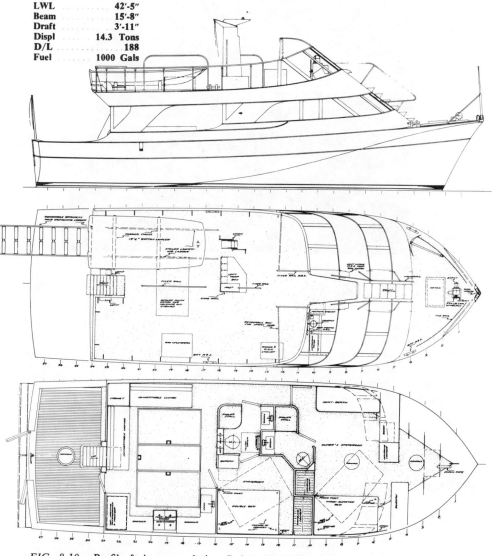

FIG. 8-10. Profile & Accommodation, Bolger 47-ft. *Thorfinn.*

some attention to location of doors, hatches, and ventilators, give ranges of stability, as with *Omega,* almost in the lifeboat class.

"As for fuel economy, it is my impression that at near-unity speeds (say 175 miles per day for the WL length of both boats), one model is almost as good as the other, though to get utmost range out of *Thorfinn,* she ought to have one of her props removed."

Thorfinn was accidentally subjected to a surprising test of her ability. This is described in Chapter 16, under "Heavy-Weather Handling."

PHOTO 8-11. Bolger 47-ft. *Thorfinn* on trials in Iceland.

EDWARD S. BREWER AND ASSOCIATES, INC.

Brewer's small cruiser, called the Grand Banks 33, is interesting for several reasons. By restricting beam and increasing draft over the averages for these dimensions, she has a hull well adapted to sea work. With a D/L of 311 she is not overly heavy. However, when this is matched with an A/B ratio of around 1.9, the whole combination works out as an extraordinarily balanced design. Brewer says of her:

"Her D/L ratio of 311 is high for a powerboat but still, of course, low by true fishing trawler standards. Nevertheless, in combination with her moderate beam, her displacement is adequate to assure comfortable motion at sea. I feel strongly that too many so-called 'trawler' yachts have insufficient displacement and excessive beam, and as a result their moment of inertia is high. This gives them a snappy and uncomfortable motion in any kind of a sea, particularly when running with waves abeam. Steadying sails or flopperstoppers can help of course, but they are of even greater benefit if fitted to a proper hull.

"Dual controls are rigged so the skipper can get outdoors in fine weather. However, the outside steering station is on the aft cabin roof rather than on a flying bridge over the pilothouse. I feel this is an important feature for at least two reasons: The weight and windage of the structure is kept as low as possible to assure safety and stability, while the helmsman, being lower, has less motion to contend with in a seaway."

Brewer's vessel is, as the accommodation plan shows, designed for a crew of two only. The large cockpit is rather unusual on such a vessel, but it does have its points, and for ardent fishermen might be advantageous. Altogether, she is a very fine little vessel. Her 250 gallons of fuel should take her 1500 miles at seven knots with a diesel of 40 to 60 hp.

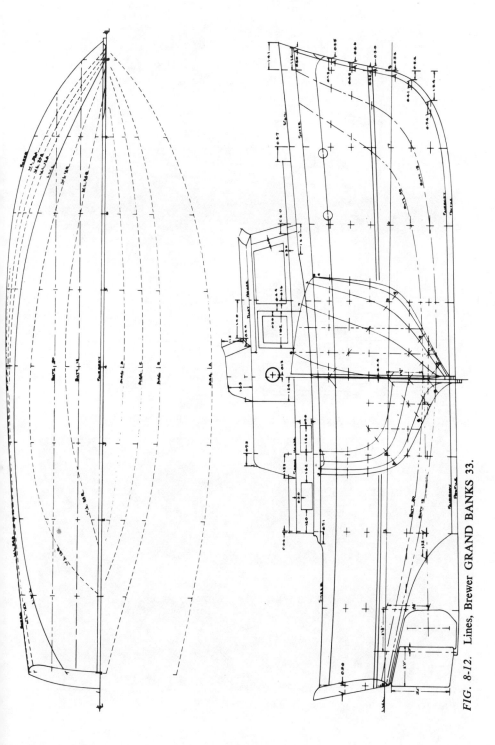

FIG. 8-12. Lines, Brewer GRAND BANKS 33.

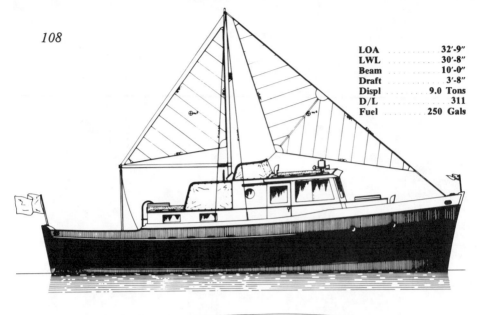

LOA	32'-9"
LWL	30'-8"
Beam	10'-0"
Draft	3'-8"
Displ	9.0 Tons
D/L	311
Fuel	250 Gals

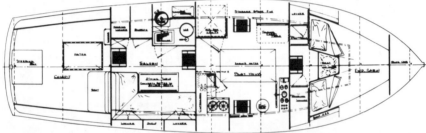

FIG. 8-13. Profile & Accommodation, Brewer GRAND BANKS 33.

PHOTO 8-14. Brewer GRAND BANKS 33.

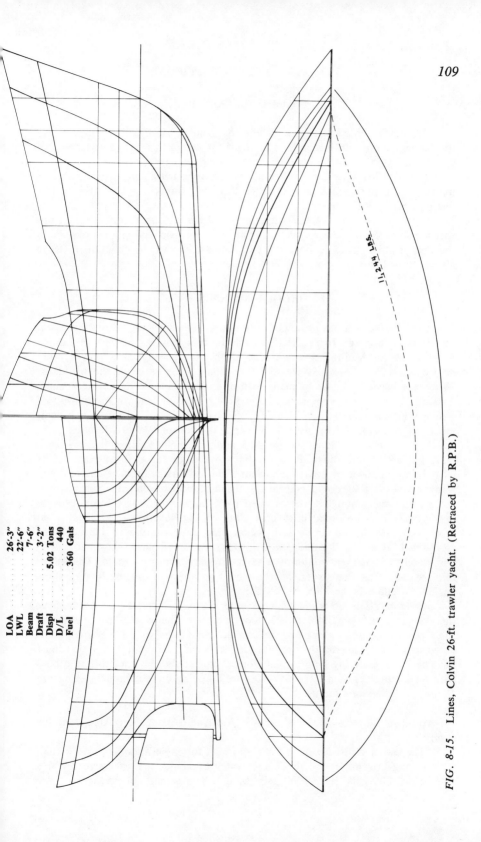

LOA	26'-3"
LWL	22'-6"
Beam	7'-6"
Draft	3'-2"
Displ	5.02 Tons
D/L	440
Fuel	360 Gals

11,244 LBS.

FIG. 8-15. Lines, Colvin 26-ft. trawler yacht. (Retraced by R.P.B.)

THOMAS E. COLVIN

We are indebted to Tom Colvin for sending us the lines of a heavy trawler model only 26 feet long. The client for whom this design was prepared was thinking of doing some singlehanded, long-distance work.

The boat has a D/L of 440, quite proper for such a small vessel. Anyone thinking of going to sea in a craft of this size, should have something like this seaworthy little bucket.

Her hull speed is 6.4 knots and it would take 16 hp to drive her at this speed. So she could power 2400 miles at hull speed on 360 gallons of fuel. If she dropped the speed to S/L 1.1 (5.2 knots), she would do 5000 miles in 40 days—*if* anyone wanted to!

ELDREDGE-McINNIS INC.

No firm has a more prestigious reputation for producing seaworthy motor vessels than this one. In the 1920s, while he was working at George Lawley & Sons, Walter McInnis, the founder of this firm, designed a power yacht named *Speejacks*. *Speejacks* was the first motor yacht to circle the world. At 98 feet she was considered by many men in those days to be dangerously small. This is nonsense, of course, as we know now. Vast numbers of 30- to 40-foot sailing craft circling the world today demonstrate that. Here are some comments on *Albacore III* by Alan J. McInnis, the son of Walter McInnis:

"This design was launched in 1955 and was modeled after the lines of a New England fishing boat. Perhaps she was one of the earliest examples of what is now known as a 'trawler yacht.' The owners cruised extensively and wanted a vessel they could take to the 'Islands,' and beyond, in comfort, and yet a boat small enough to be manned by a husband-and-wife team, because they carried a professional crew only while in the Bahamas. . . . They went from Maine to the Bahamas each winter, and one year they did head home from the Islands, via Bermuda, with just the owners aboard. They had a wild and woolly passage, encountering a severe tropical storm en route. The owner told me that after that experience he would go anywhere in the boat. I guess he felt fortunate to be alive to tell the tale."

Albacore III is a very salty, able little vessel. It surprised me to discover that her D/L is only 246, as she looks sturdier than that. The reason she fools you, of course, is her low freeboard, and cabins which are small compared to what we are used to today. Her A/B ratio is about 1.9, which must have been a mighty big help in that tropical storm! As it is hard to find a boat with A/B ratio less than 2.0 today—2.6 to 2.8 being quite common—*Albacore III* has useful lessons for us.

Another Eldredge-McInnis boat is *Narwhal*. About her, Alan McInnis says:

"The owner desired a rugged offshore boat for exploration and skin diving, with a long cruising range. Fuel and water capacities are excessive for this size boat (1800 gals. fuel; 1000 gals. water). The owner's preference was for

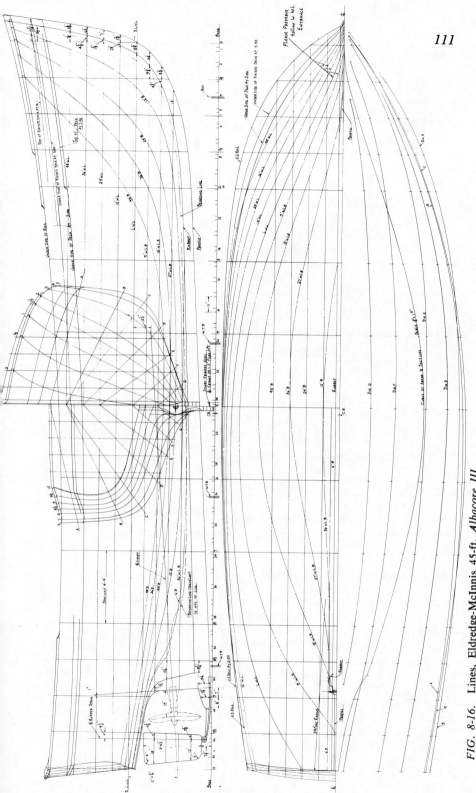

FIG. 8-16. Lines, Eldredge-McInnis 45-ft. Albacore III.

LOA .... 45'-2"
LWL .... 43'-4"
Beam .... 14'-2"
Draft .... 5'-0"
Displ ..... 20.0 Tons
D/L 246
Fuel .... 500 Gals

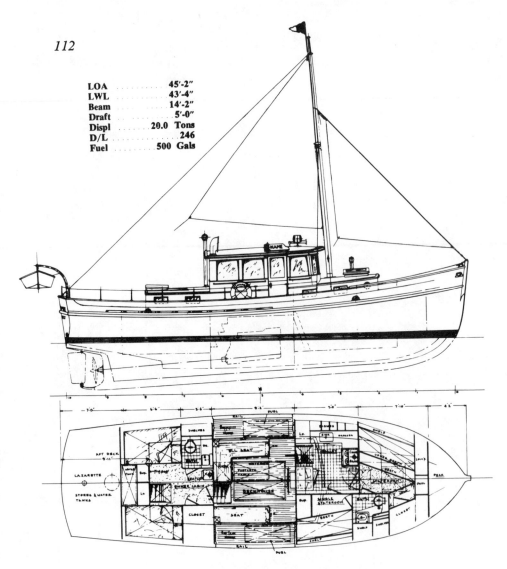

FIG. 8-17. Profile & Accommodation, Eldredge-McInnis 45-ft. *Albacore III.*

something along the lines of a Norwegian or Danish fishing boat, with the traditional double ends and extreme beam. Quarters are minimal but very comfortable for two couples, with the galley and messroom on deck, aft. The engine has a dry exhaust which also serves to heat the deck cabin. The remainder of the tank room will serve as a cargo hold."

Narwhal is a boat for dreamers—who has not thought of trading in the South Seas? She would also be an excellent candidate for the first round-the-world voyage by a motorboat under 50 feet. Her cruising to date has been confined to the Pacific Coast from Acapulco, Mexico, to Alaska. Her D/L ratio of 370 is appropriate to this type of vessel and puts her up with the true trawlers. Altogether she fills the specification nicely.

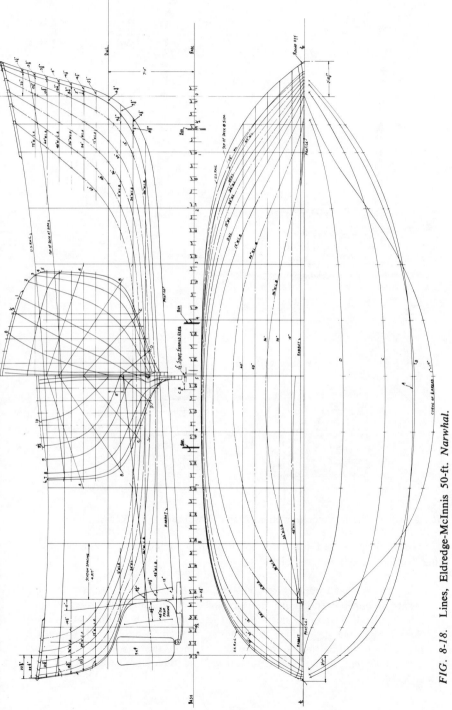

FIG. 8-18. Lines, Eldredge-McInnis 50-ft. *Narwhal.*

LOA	49'-10"
LWL	45'-2"
Beam	16'-10"
Draft	6'-1"
Displ	34.0 Tons
D/L	370
Fuel	1800 Gals

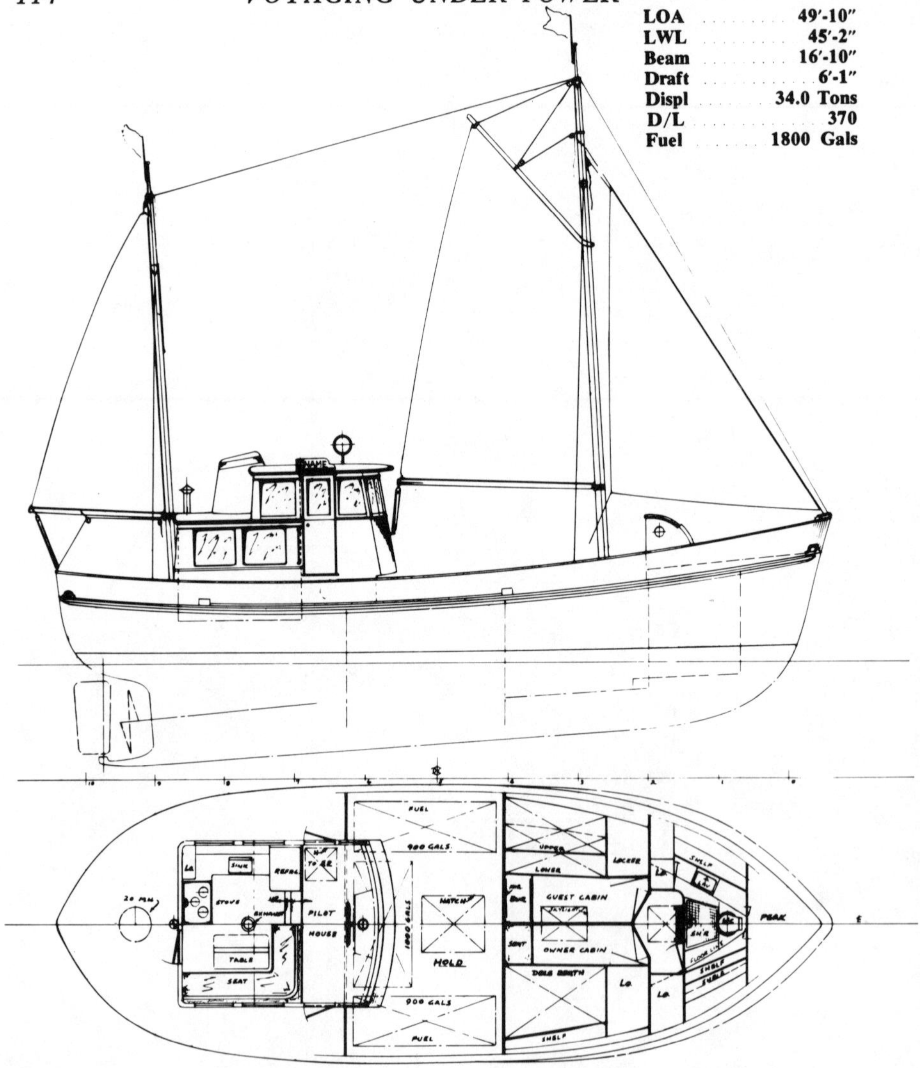

FIG. 8-19. Profile & Accommodation, Eldredge-McInnis 50-ft. *Narwhal.*

Mr. McInnis ended his letter to us with a lament that I am sure will bring "Amens" from other designers:

> "I wish that I could give you more of an insight into the accomplishments of our power yachts, but strangely enough, unless we are personally involved, owners do not see fit to keep in touch with their architects. Surprisingly, we never hear from some of them again . . . I do recall my ancient father saying that we design them to go around the world and built them strong enough to do so, and then they rarely get out of sight of land."

PHOTO 8-20. Eldredge-McInnis 50-ft. *Narwhal.*

WESTON FARMER

Westy Farmer is an old-timer at this boat-designing business, and has contributed to my design education through the years. His work in recent years has been mostly with large, expensive yachts built of aluminum. He volunteered the full working drawings of one of his creations that is within the size range we have been discussing here. Unfortunately, the large pencil tracings would not reduce legibly, so we are denied the opportunity to study how lines and construction plans are made up by a master architect working

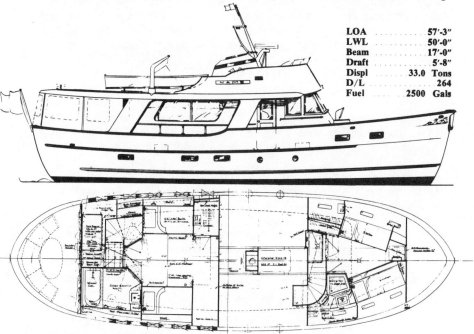

LOA	57'-3"
LWL	50'-0"
Beam	17'-0"
Draft	5'-8"
Displ	33.0 Tons
D/L	264
Fuel	2500 Gals

FIG. 8-21. Profile & Accommodation, Farmer 57-ft. *All Ten B.*

PHOTO 8-22. Farmer 57-ft. *All Ten B.*

right in the shop with the artisans who turn out these beautiful aluminum hulls.

All-Ten-B is an interesting vessel from several standpoints. She was built for Allan L. McKay, who is planning long ocean cruises when he retires in a year or two. She has been cruising the Great Lakes now for some time and has shown superior seaworthiness as well as beauty. Her layout is "Type C," though she certainly does not look double-decked for her full length. The secret here is the way her below-deck accommodations begin about nine feet forward of the stern, where the sole may be lower than if a stern cabin was used. Another vessel designed this way is shown in Chapter 10.

It does not show on the profile, but *All-Ten-B* will be equipped with a flopperstopper rig for roll-reduction at sea. And perhaps most important of all, every port and window on board is to be equipped with metal safety covers, the only vessel in this book for which this sensible precaution has been carried out completely. There are further remarks on this subject in Chapter 16.

WILLIAM GARDEN

Among designers, the name of William Garden immediately brings to mind the extraordinary versatility of his work. From dinghies to 110-foot luxury yachts, he has done everything, and done it with a style so distinctive that one is in no doubt, when one sees an example of his work, that it *is* a Garden design.

While his commercial work has been extensive and left a lasting mark on the fishing fleets of the Pacific Coast, his great love has been custom yacht work. As he stated some years ago in a brochure of his designs:

> "My work is with the experienced yachtsman, the connoisseur who wishes to develop an idea and is unable to find anything suitable in stock or in the used market—good, wholesome vessels of above average performance, and boats that reflect the character and have an identity with their owners."

We have already shown, in Chapter 1, the lines of Garden's 42-foot *WANDERER* class as an example of the type known as the "Northwest cruiser,"

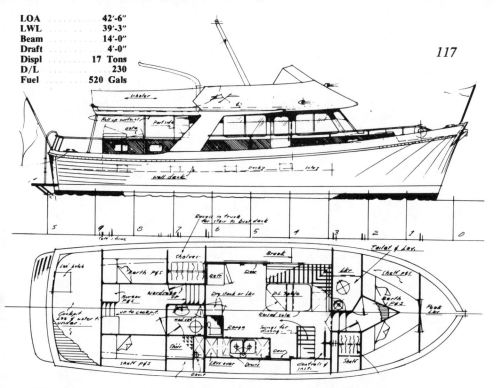

LOA	42'-6"
LWL	39'-3"
Beam	14'-0"
Draft	4'-0"
Displ	17 Tons
D/L	230
Fuel	520 Gals

FIG. 8-23. Profile & Accommodation, Garden 42-ft. WANDERER class.

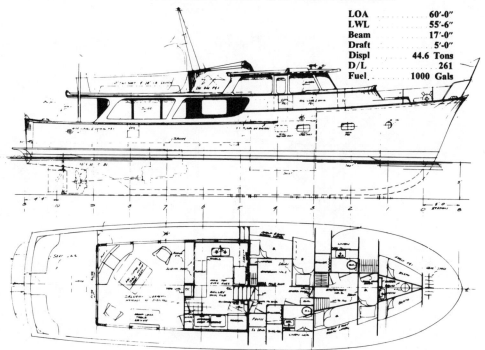

LOA	60'-0"
LWL	55'-6"
Beam	17'-0"
Draft	5'-0"
Displ	44.6 Tons
D/L	261
Fuel	1000 Gals

FIG. 8-24. Profile & Accommodation, Garden 60-ft. *Kaprice*.

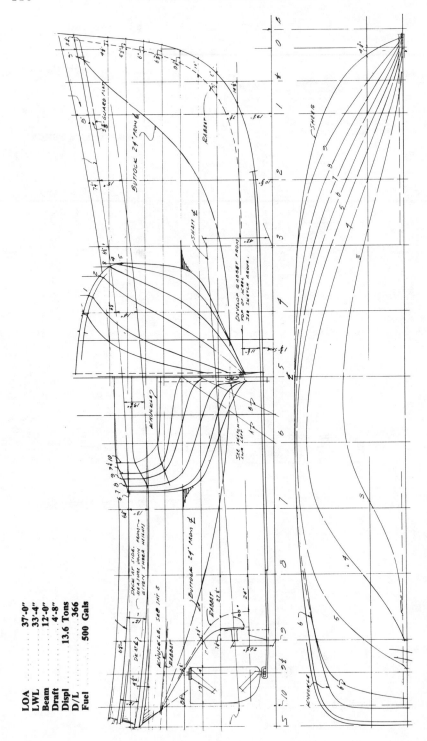

LOA ....   37'-0"
LWL ....   33'-4"
Beam ....   12'-0"
Draft ....   4'-8"
Displ .... 13.6 Tons
D/L   366
Fuel ....   500 Gals

FIG. 8-25. Lines, Garden 37-ft. troller cruiser.

the design that started the trend toward a type of yacht lighter than the fishing boat model, for use at sea. Over 100 yachts have been built to these basic lines with a variety of layouts.

Fig. 8-23 shows William Garden's *WANDERER* class cruiser, with Type A layout which exploits the space on top of the cabin to a greater degree than most of the class.

The *WANDERER* class has a D/L of 230; while this has proven ample for safety at sea, it does not allow fuel and stores room for really long passages. However, the owners of these yachts, concentrated largely on the Pacific Coast, are very happy with them as they are long-legged enough for coastal cruising from Alaska to Panama. Bill also has a 44-footer of the same family that is more burdensome, D/L 301, on which a good friend of mine has been happily cruising all over Europe for many years.

Bill has stated that his favorite among his larger yachts is *Kaprice*. Although she is pretty big for us—60 feet—she does show the "Type B" layout at its best, as discussed in Chapter 7. It is highly unusual to build so large a yacht, not really intended for long voyages, with a single engine. As Bill says, characteristically, "She has worked out very well in service. For the owner's use she seems close to ideal and has worked out to be a most useful member of his family."

Bill also contributed a set of lines for a 37-foot "troller yacht." They are presented here as an example of what will be discussed in Chapter 9, The Economical Passagemaker. They are suitable for building a combination commercial troller with cruising accommodations for a man and wife.

The troller, at 13.57 tons, has a D/L of 366, which puts her just about 20 percent below the FAO-recommended displacements for true trawlers curve, the one recommended for genuine seagoing yachts. As a matter of fact, the catch of salmon trollers is not very great in any one voyage, so these vessels do not have to be at all burdensome compared to vessels used for types of fishing that may run into schools of fish and return with catches weighing many tons. So she is well-suited for the work.

JAMES S. KROGEN AND CO., INC.

Eden II by Krogen is an excellent example of an offshore cruiser that is deliberately designed to run at S/Ls over hull speed the majority of the time. She was designed for an S/L of 1.65 (11 knots) and actually did 12.5 knots on her trials. Her D/L of 223 is not particularly light. Altogether she is a very good compromise of the factors involved.

She is also interesting in the way she tackles the main drawback of the "Type A" layout, discussed in Chapter 7. The steering station in her saloon is so arranged that it can be cut off with a curtain at night. The galley is in this area but can also be isolated by the curtain. To make it possible to use the galley at night, when necessary, it is provided with red night lighting. As it was anticipated that for most of the time owner and wife would be the only crew, this arrangement should work out well.

An organ for the wife and an office for the husband, which doubles as a

120

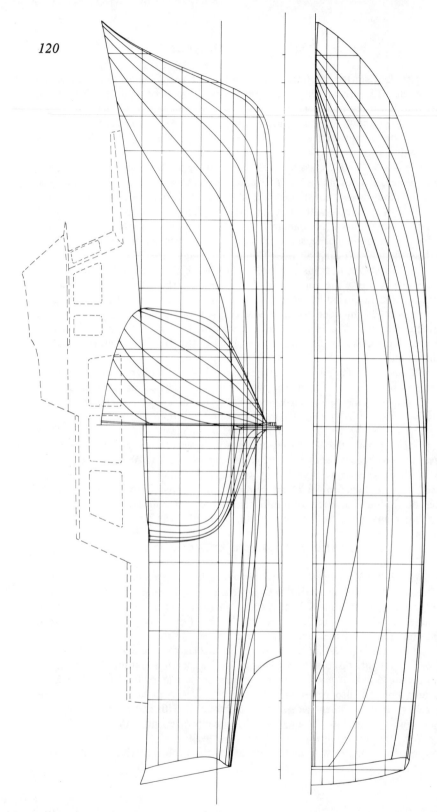

FIG. 8-26. Lines, Krogen 50-ft. *Eden II.* (Retraced by R.P.B.)

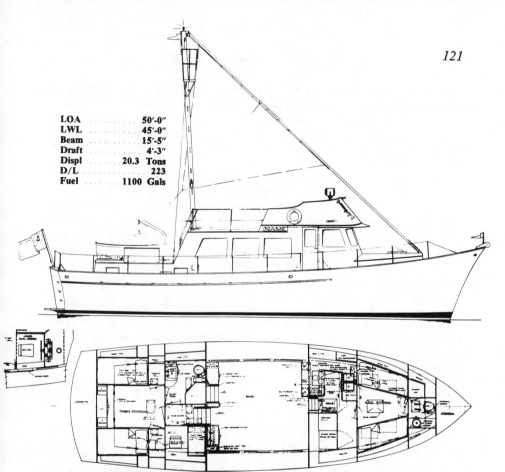

LOA	50'-0"
LWL	45'-0"
Beam	15'-5"
Draft	4'-3"
Displ	20.3 Tons
D/L	223
Fuel	1100 Gals

FIG. 8-27. Profile & Accommodation, Krogen 50-ft. *Eden II.*

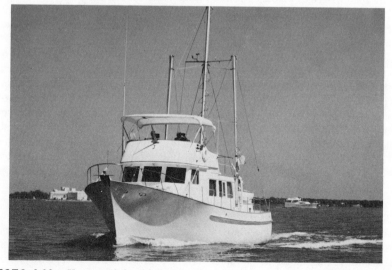

PHOTO 8-28. Krogen 50-ft. *Eden II.*

chart house, plus the big saloon and galley, do not leave much room for the guest cabin. But there are people who think such a layout is a good idea!

Eden II has quite the best flopperstopper rig of all the examples shown in Chapter 6. The fore-and-aft placement is just slightly forward of the ideal, and Mr. Krogen has not hesitated to give her a real rig with 20-foot poles that are always ready to use.

She carries 1100 gallons of fuel, an extraordinary amount for a craft with a D/L of 223 in this size. Mr. Krogen puts her range at 600 miles at 12.5 knots and 1500 miles at eight knots. By our range methods this seems greatly underestimated. Yet with two engines, either one of which can take her up close to her top speed, she could hardly expect to achieve what the graphs show. This is not a critical comment, as she is not expected to make maximum-length cruises. She has cruised widely in North America, going from Miami north into the Great Lakes and down the Mississippi. She has also made extensive cruises in the Bahamas and the Caribbean.

Altogether, *Eden II* has demonstrated a superior solution to the problems stated or implied for the higher-than-hull-speed "trawler" discussed in Chapter 5. She shows how a vessel with no double-decking can be organized for full-time living aboard—having such appliances as air conditioning, washer-dryer, all electric galley, and deep freeze.

Krogen's unnamed 62-foot motorsailer is a bit on the large side, but she does have points of interest, and we are pleased to be able to present her lines here.

James Krogen is one of the designers who has gone to the full-width cabin as the answer to demands for full-time living space. She is thus a relative of "Type D" shown in the Chapter 7 layouts, but instead of placing the pilot-house on deck aft, as shown there, she has it forward, an interesting variation that appears practical only in larger vessels.

Her lines should be of particular interest to design students. Her D/L of 318 makes her about 90 percent of the FAO recommendations for true trawlers, and thus rates her as a relatively heavier model than most of our examples. This is reflected in her midsection, which has good deadrise with the turn of the bilge well immersed. She is also relatively narrow, which also contributes to easy lines. The presence amidships of an area almost "dead flat," with both parallel sides and bottom, is unusual in yachts, but makes much sense in this case, as it is located where the extra room under the full-width cabin is most needed in the interest of keeping the A/B down. Her A/B ratio as drawn is about 2.1, which could be reduced to an excellent 1.9 by using open lifelines atop the main cabin instead of the solid lines shown.

She is also interesting for the use of bilge keels, which are provided to increase lateral resistance for sailing, and have the added advantage of holding the vessel upright if she runs aground. They will also help to some degree in roll-reduction. And, all of her large ports are provided with coverplates. Altogether this 62-footer offers a good many useful lessons.

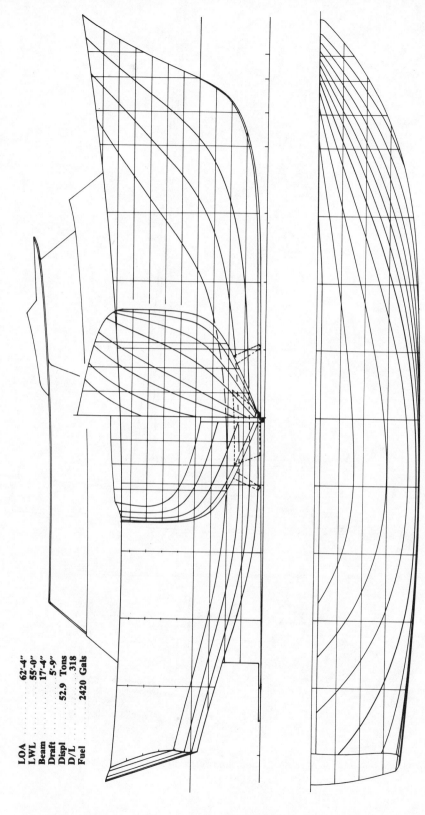

LOA	62′-4″
LWL	55′-0″
Beam	17′-4″
Draft	5′-9″
Displ	52.9 Tons
D/L	318
Fuel	2420 Gals

FIG. 8-29. Lines, Krogen 62-ft. motorboat with rig. (Retraced by R.P.B.)

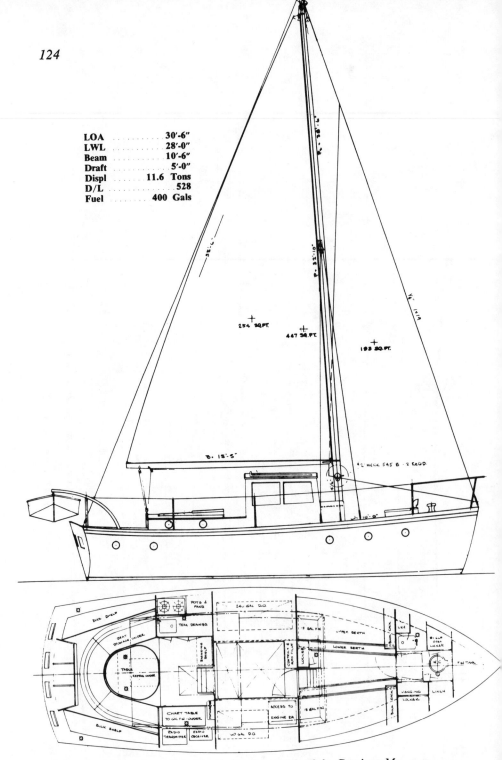

LOA	30'-6"
LWL	28'-0"
Beam	10'-6"
Draft	5'-0"
Displ	11.6 Tons
D/L	528
Fuel	400 Gals

FIG. 8-30. Profile & Accommodation, Lapworth 30-ft. *Gracious Me.*

PHOTO 8-31. Lapworth 30-ft. *Gracious Me.*

C. WILLIAM LAPWORTH

We were especially anxious to have *Gracious Me* for its historical interest, and to give recognition to a design effort that antedated *Passagemaker* by a number of years. Bill Lapworth designed this vessel for Dick Stewart in 1949. She was built in the 1950s, and hence is a pioneer among oceangoing motorboats.

Gracious Me has quite a large sailing rig, but can make 2500 miles at S/L 1.1 with her 400 gallons of fuel. She is thus a true motor-all-the-time boat, like the ones that engaged my early thoughts on the subject. Unfortunately, she never has been widely cruised in ways that would have properly demonstrated her abilities. But she did make a very workmanlike cruise from Los Angeles to the Galapagos Islands, and return, in 1958. I did not learn about this vessel until the final series of designs that led to *Passagemaker* was well along. It would be interesting to learn if there were other designers in those days whose thoughts were turning in these directions.

NILS LUCANDER

Nils Lucander is the inventor of the "Lucan" stabilizing system mentioned in Chapter 6. He has also done some work in seagoing motorboats, though his principal work is in fishing trawlers and shrimpers. Working with these types he has demonstrated the worth of the shrouded propeller combined with a controllable-pitch propeller to improve efficiency under power. These methods of improving efficiency are well worth looking into for long-range motorboats.

Some ago years Lucander designed a 50-footer called the *EMPRESS,* and several of her class have been built. One of them has been making annual passages from Maine to Trinidad for some years. The plan shown here is for the *EMPRESS 47,* which essentially is the original 50-footer with transom stern. Her chief point of interest is that the engine in the stern utilizes a Borg Warner Morse Chain "HY-VO" drive, with either single or twin engines. This

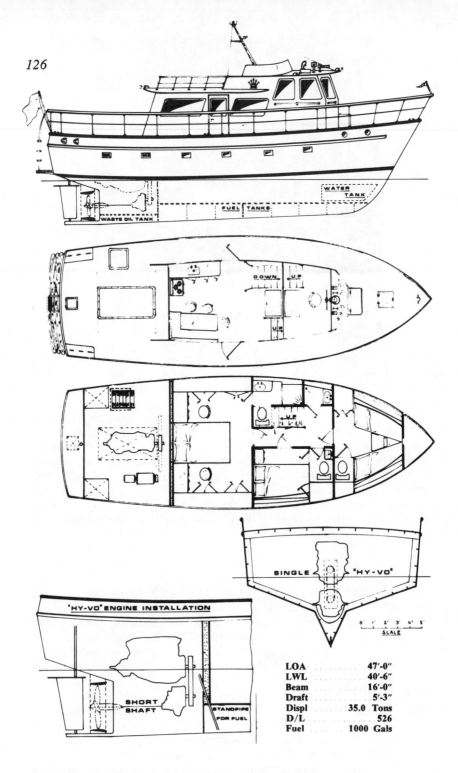

WATER TANK

FUEL TANKS

WASTE OIL TANK

DOWN UP

UP

HY-VO ENGINE INSTALLATION

SHORT SHAFT

STANDPIPE FOR FUEL

SINGLE "HY-VO"

0 1 2 3 4 5
SCALE

LOA	47'-0"
LWL	40'-6"
Beam	16'-0"
Draft	5'-3"
Displ	35.0 Tons
D/L	526
Fuel	1000 Gals

FIG. 8-32. Profile & Accommodation, Lucander EMPRESS 47 class.

PHOTO 8-33. Lucander EMPRESS 50 class.

alternative to the toothed-belt drive (discussed in Chapter 7) has its attractions. It would take less space, for instance. The casing, which is required for constant lubrication of the chain, is supplied complete with necessary bearings by Borg Warner.

The problem between Mr. Lucander and myself has been in trying to pin down the performance of these craft. He has furnished partial data which indicate, when related to the speed/power curves of Chapter 5, that his vessel uses from 26 percent to 77 percent of the power that the curves show is required to achieve stated speeds. Such a spread in test results is difficult to understand.

Even taking the higher percentage—77 percent—which is the reported fuel consumption and speed of the vessel cruising to Trinidad, we have a very interesting situation, one that bears further study. Mr. Lucander sees nothing exceptional in achieving such results. He states that his work has convinced him that conventional thinking is wrong, that weight and wetted surface have nothing to do with speed, that it is special shapes that count.

I will not comment on this. The design and the results claimed are being presented as a matter of interest. If, in the long run, he is proved correct, it could herald great changes in the design of seagoing motorboats.

A. MASON

Al Mason is generally considered to be one of the top designers and draftsmen in the country. His plans are the admiration and envy of all.

The Mason-designed trawler motor yacht *MB-48* is an excellent example of his work. In her, he shows several innovations to reduce the drawbacks of the "Type B" hull. The engine is very much "sole buried," but this is reclaimed in part by providing a small "lobby" forward of the saloon from which the engine can be observed and in which electrical installations are centered. In this way, regular inspection is facilitated, and many small problems can be taken care of without tearing up the main saloon.

In addition to providing this feature, Al is another designer who has gone to the full-width cabin for more space. In this case he has drawn a very narrow walkway with excellent handholds. This, of course, will be most useful in port. From painful experience, I can suggest that the space between house and rail

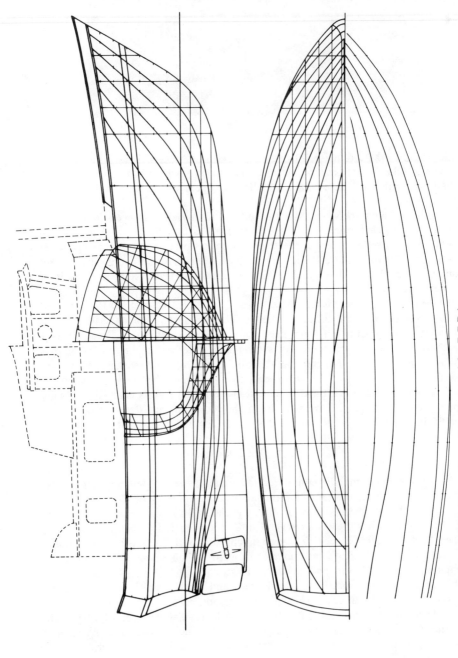

FIG. 8-34. Lines, Mason MB-48 trawler yacht. (Retraced by R.P.B.)

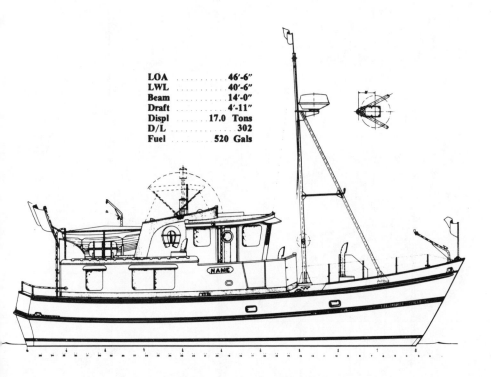

LOA	46'-6"
LWL	40'-6"
Beam	14'-0"
Draft	4'-11"
Displ	17.0 Tons
D/L	302
Fuel	520 Gals

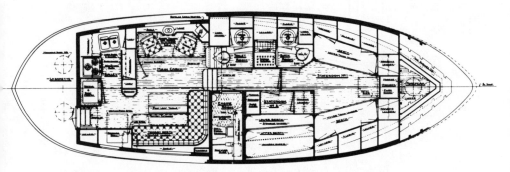

FIG. 8-35. Profile & Accommodation, Mason MB-48 trawler yacht.

should be wide enough to take the biggest shoes without jamming—even my size 12 brogans!

A third feature of this well-thought-out design is the way the watch-stander can go from the wheelhouse to the topside steering station without going outside. The best observing station is thus open to a single watch-stander, a safety factor that is ignored in too many designs.

Al Mason has kindly permitted us to show the lines of *MB-48*.

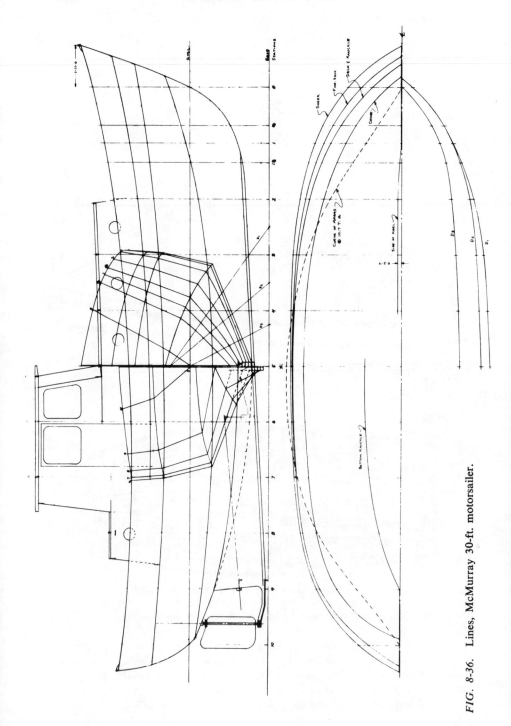

FIG. 8-36. Lines, McMurray 30-ft. motorsailer.

LOA . . . . 30'-0"
LWL . . . . 26'-8"
Beam . . . . 11'-1"
Draft . . . . 3'-10"
Displ . . . . . . 10.7 Tons
D/L 565
Fuel . . . . . . 260 Gals

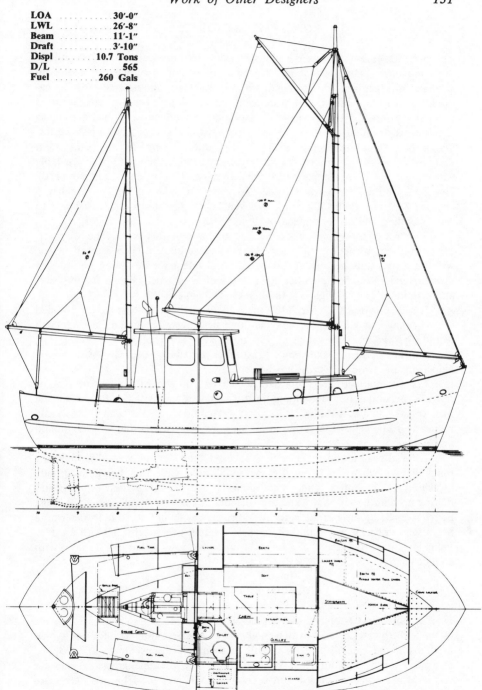

FIG. 8-37. Profile & Accommodation, McMurray 30-ft. motorsailer.

ROBERT L. McMURRAY

Mr. McMurray sent us the plans of this steel motorsailer with the following comments: "Her hard-chine, fisherman-type hull is of welded steel construction and her generous freeboard and canoe stern should make her a seakindly vessel. The hull has a watertight bulkhead between the engine room and the quarters. To avoid expensive insulation of the living quarters, her superstructure is of wood construction. The forward cabin sleeps two on V-berths, and is fitted with underberth stowage bins and shelving. In the main cabin there is a good-sized galley area, an enclosed head, a hanging locker, a table with settee, and a large single berth; the settee may be utilized as a fourth berth. Her 60 hp diesel, fed by a pair of 130 gallon fuel tanks, should give her a cruising range of about 500 miles at seven knots. The ketch rig is designed to reduce rolling and aid her speed on long passages."

This was one design we simply had to have in this book. The way Mr. McMurray has turned out a shippy looking powerboat in such a small vessel, with a rig that suits her exactly, shows his real talent for designing this sort of vessel. Her D/L of 565 puts her right in the class of true trawlers for this size, and is quite proper, though it is the highest D/L in the list.

It seems to me that Mr. McMurray is excessively modest in his claimed cruising range, as are a number of the other designers. The graphs in Chapter 5 would give this vessel a range of 750 miles at seven knots, while at S/L 1.1, for long-range cruising, she shows 1730 miles, thus being capable—with a little help from the wind—of crossing the Atlantic.

Let me interject here some data which tend to show that the formula for range is accurate. For one thing, *Passagemaker* demonstrated, by actual test over courses as long as 2800 miles, that she could do better than the formula by nearly 10 percent—the variation on the conservative side that was mentioned in Chapter 5.

Later, I was involved in testing a vessel that showed very disappointing range figures when run over the measured mile with fuel being accurately measured at the same time. After considerable checking for accuracy and finding nothing wrong, I worked the formula "backward," and stated she must be overweight by at least 12 percent. When it was finally possible to determine her displacement, it was found she was 15 percent overweight. So with a safety factor of about 10 percent, the formula does give results that can be used with confidence.

EDWIN MONK & SON

As noted in Chapter 1, the Monk firm was a pioneer in the development of the "Northwest cruiser," which might be characterized as having lines a step away from the true displacement hull, with modifications aft to allow speed to an S/L ratio of about 1.65. We are gratified to present here two examples of the Monk art. (Another design is shown in Chapter 9.) The two here were selected to illustrate development over a period of years. The designer comments:

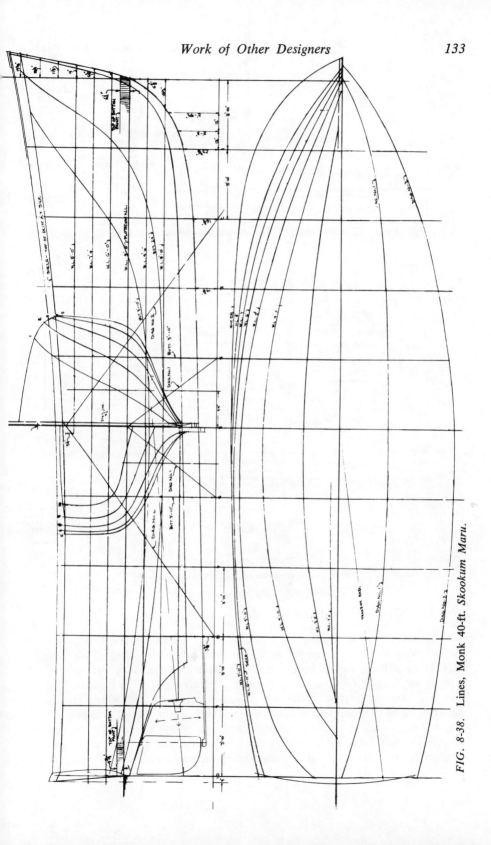

FIG. 8-38. Lines, Monk 40-ft. Skookum Maru.

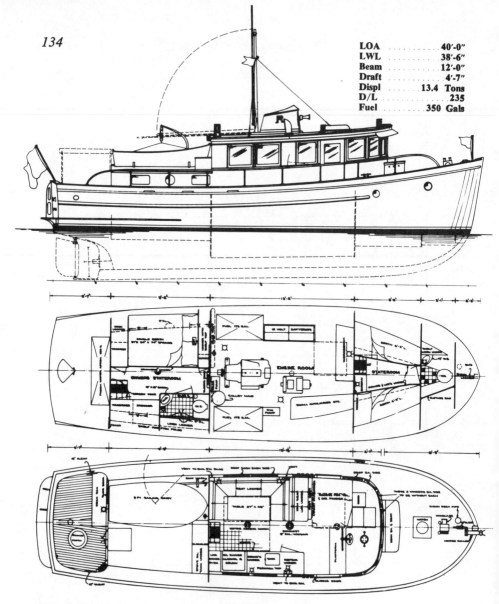

LOA	40'-0"
LWL	38'-6"
Beam	12'-0"
Draft	4'-7"
Displ	13.4 Tons
D/L	235
Fuel	350 Gals

FIG. 8-39. Profile & Accommodation, Monk 40-ft. *Skookum Maru.*

"*Skookum Maru,* designed in 1955, is one of the earlier breed of heavy-duty cruisers, and has proven her mettle in extensive coastal cruising. Mr. and Mrs. Gordon Rogers of California had her built in Japan, long before such a thing was fashionable, and shipped home. Her arrangement is interesting in that it is one of the first *COHO* or "tri-cabin" type layouts, which feature separated permanent sleeping accommodations, and a central living area combining culinary, lounging, and navigational functions in one cabin. This arrangement has proved particularly popular, both because of the sleeping privacy and comfort aft for the master stateroom, and togetherness during waking hours.

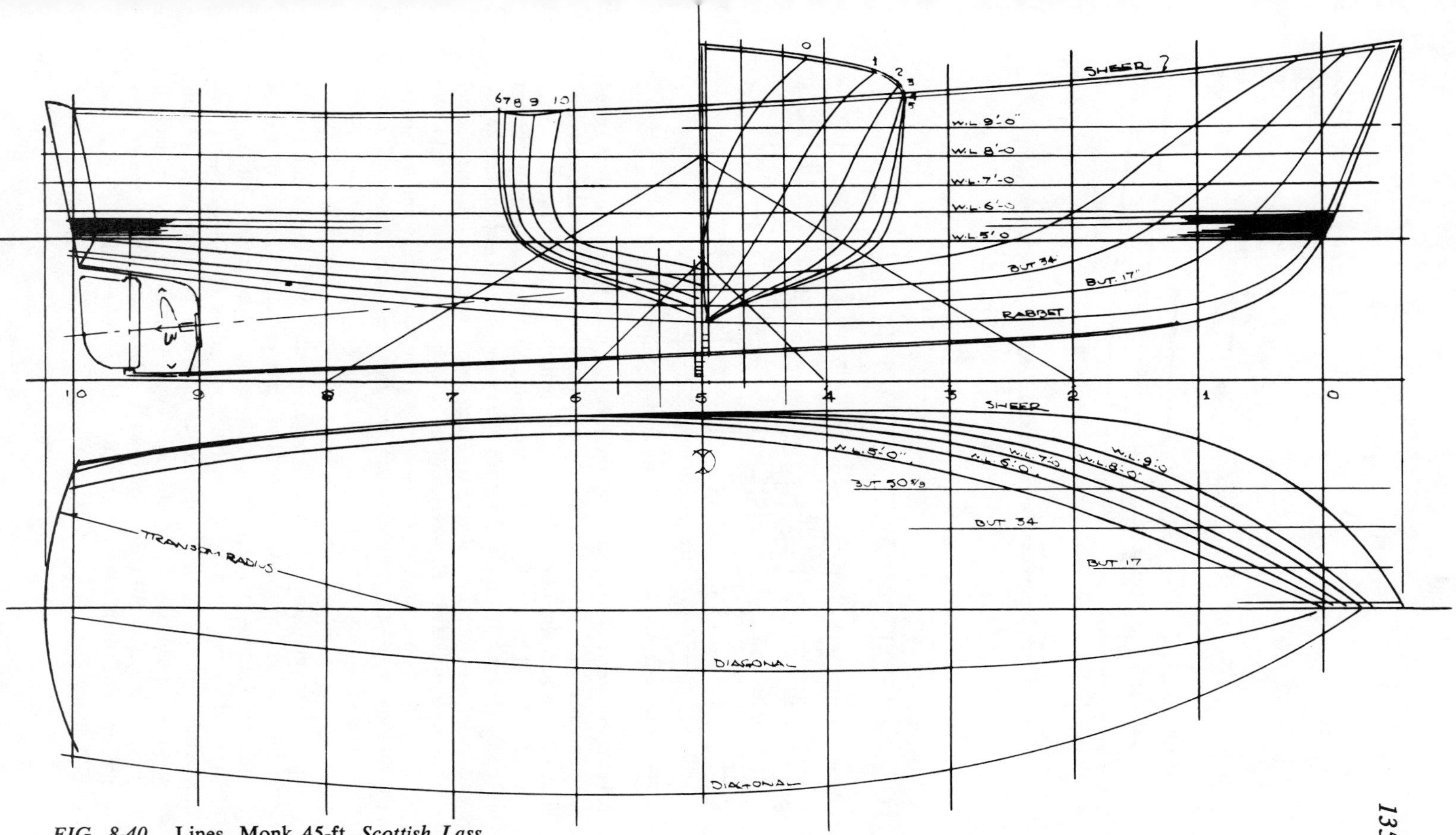

FIG. 8-40. Lines, Monk 45-ft. Scottish Lass.

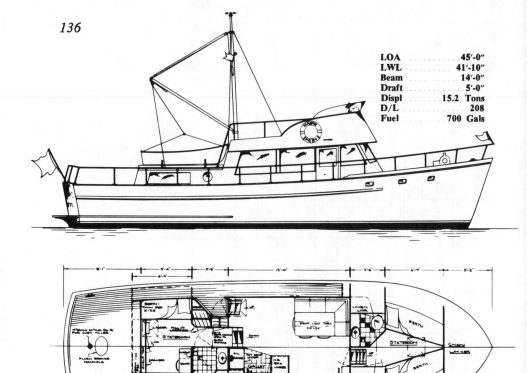

LOA	45'-0"
LWL	41'-10"
Beam	14'-0"
Draft	5'-0"
Displ	15.2 Tons
D/L	208
Fuel	700 Gals

FIG. 8-41. Profile & Accommodation, Monk 45-ft. *Scottish Lass.*

When flying bridges were accepted by the pleasure boat fraternity, they added another successful feature to this type by providing sun and excellent steering visibility, often a problem in the *COHO* arrangement. Monk writes:

"A Detroit 3-71 68 hp diesel gives a cruising speed of eight knots, though the hull could absorb a bit more power for a cruising speed closer to nine knots. Fuel and water are very small by today's standards, with 350 gallons of fuel and 120 gallons of water. However, these have proven enough to take the Rogers' where they want to go. Perhaps we waste too much space and money on tankage in today's coastal cruisers when we give them the capacity for the ocean crossing the owners rarely make."

Scottish Lass, built in 1962, was selected for this book over later vessels from the Monk board to show two features: She carries 1800 lbs. of ballast on her keel, and she uses the Gardner 6LX diesel of 121 continuous horsepower at 1500 rpm. This famous English engine is legendary for its quietness and reliability. But it was a surprise to discover that it is possible to install this engine in what is essentially a conventional "Type A" cruiser. As to the ballast, which the latest boats do not carry, Monk says: "It is more for roll smoothness and peace of mind than ultimate stability, though it would help in a bad beam-sea situation."

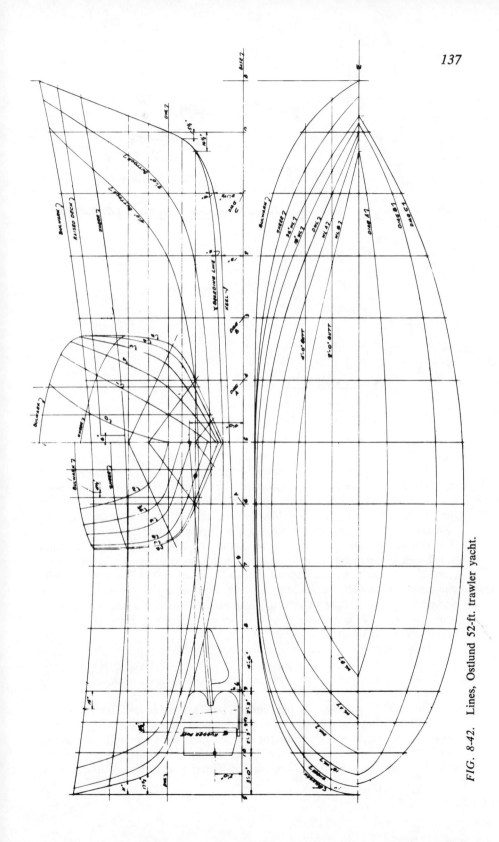

FIG. 8-42. Lines, Ostlund 52-ft. trawler yacht.

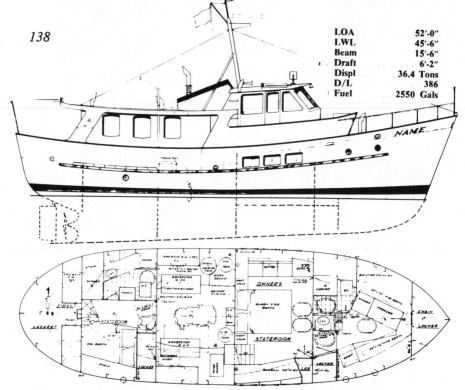

LOA	52'-0"
LWL	45'-6"
Beam	15'-6"
Draft	6'-2"
Displ	36.4 Tons
D/L	386
Fuel	2550 Gals

FIG. 8-43. Profile & Accommodation, Ostlund 52-ft. trawler yacht.

BEN OSTLUND

Ben Ostlund has provided this 52-foot vessel which makes heavier claim to being a true trawler than any other vessel in this book, except possibly *Narwhal*. She is certainly a shippy-looking vessel, and it is surprising to realize she is only 52 feet long. The way Mr. Ostlund has worked in the spaces is much facilitated by her being built of steel, and will repay careful study.

The clients, Mr. and Mrs. James Burns, of Newport Beach, California, stated their requirements as follows: "We want a vessel of about 50 feet overall, of steel, with a cruising range in the neighborhood of 4000 miles at eight knots minimum, and a 'take-home' engine in the event of main engine failure. We also desire a large master stateroom, a separate stateroom for one other couple complete with head and shower, and a utility room for the freezer, washer, and dryer; also a couple of pipe berths."

This is certainly a succinct specification, and Mr. Ostlund should be congratulated on the way he has filled it, and in a vessel of this size. Her range at eight knots, for example, works out by my calculations as 80 miles over the required 4000.

This boat *is* intended for long-range cruising, worldwide. Her equipment reflects that intention. All systems are planned to be redundant to the point where any pump, motor, or generator may be shut down for servicing without stopping any function or operation. She has anchors fore and aft, Vosper stabilizing fins, two boats, and complete electronics, including high seas SSB.

PHOTO 8-44. Ostlund 52-ft. trawler yacht, building in California, early 1974.

STEPHEN R. SEATON

Steve Seaton is a young, busy naval architect who served his apprenticeship under William Garden. He sent us three designs, all of which are worthy of note and comment. These designs by Seaton show a refreshing approach to appearance. He has not hesitated to use flat planes boldly, or to slant his windshields forward, or reverse the slant of cabin overhead supports. All this gives his vessels a distinctive look which I find esthetically pleasing.

Durbeck 45 (1970), with a D/L of 422, is the second heaviest vessel comparatively, in this book, putting her right up next to the true trawler weights in the graphs found in the FAO books. She is a variation of the "Type D" layout in that she has her pilothouse forward instead of aft. Seaton was one of the first to go to the full-width cabin, and the amount of room this provides is quite apparent.

If a critical comment on this design could be made, it would be that the galley is depressed, making it necessary to carry food up steps, something which can become a practical impossibility in heavy weather. This problem can be solved, as shown in the next design.

Mach Turtle (1972) is an interesting variation on the standard "Type B" layout in that the galley portion of the saloon is slightly depressed, and the pilothouse is placed on top of the galley. She thus approaches "Type E" and has many of its advantages, particularly the view aft.

It will be noted that the galley has a serving bar that can be used for meals in rough going. This is an excellent solution to the problem, as I can attest after cruising in a vessel thus equipped.

While *Mach Turtle* was being built, her owner asked me for advice about installing a F/S gear. My hammering away on the theme of proper location for

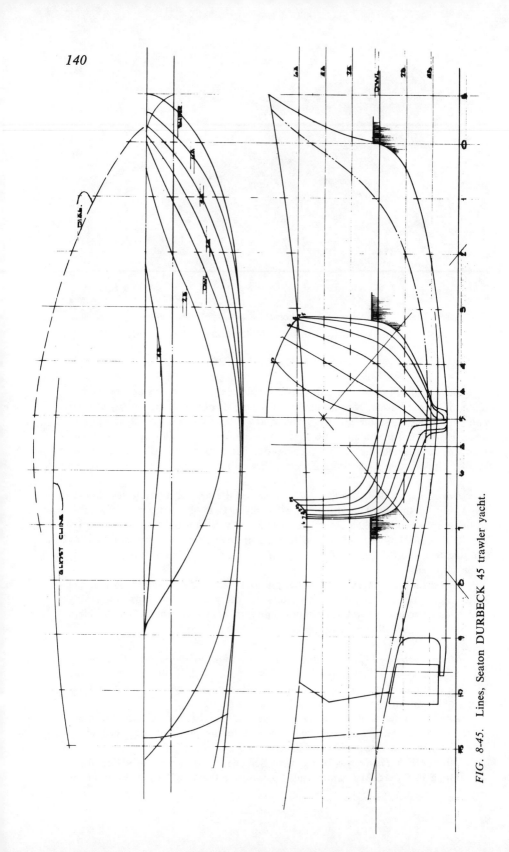

FIG. 8-45. Lines, Seaton DURBECK 45 trawler yacht.

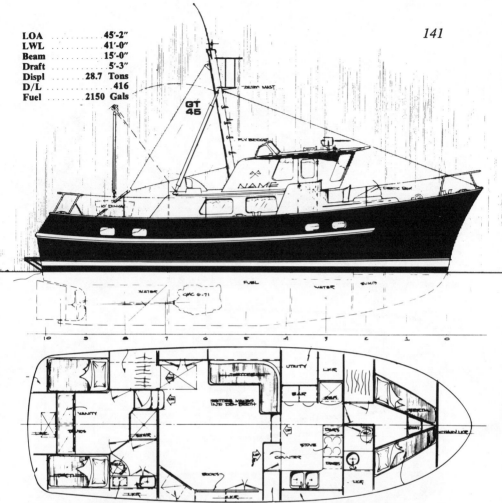

LOA	45'-2"
LWL	41'-0"
Beam	15'-0"
Draft	5'-3"
Displ	28.7 Tons
D/L	416
Fuel	2150 Gals

FIG. 8-46. Profile & Accommodation, Seaton DURBECK 45 trawler yacht.

PHOTO 8-47. Seaton DURBECK 45 trawler yacht.

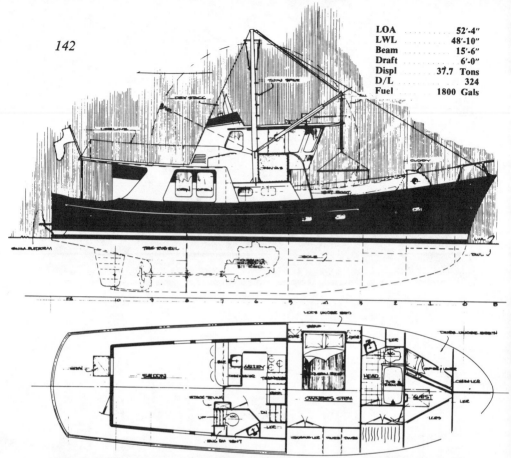

LOA	52'-4"
LWL	48'-10"
Beam	15'-6"
Draft	6'-0"
Displ	37.7 Tons
D/L	324
Fuel	1800 Gals

FIG. 8-48. Profile & Accommodation, Seaton 52-ft. trawler yacht *Mach Turtle*.

PHOTO 8-49. Seaton 52-ft. *Mach Turtle*. The F/S rig booms double as boat booms.

the mast resulted in her masts being moved aft to a position on the forward saloon bulkhead, achieving some improvement, as can be seen by comparing her picture to the plan.

Her interior is interesting. It was designed for the owner's queen-sized double bed and the bathtub, both of which were so large the vessel had to be built around them. The forward cabin is laid out for grandchildren, with other (convertible) sleeping facilities in the saloon. It is important to note the handling of the ports in the saloon. The temptation to make this area practically a "greenhouse," as is done in so many designs, has been resisted. The ports are small and concentrated in the forward part. Aft, there is the small port and a solid door. The overhead supports are wide and frame the ports—with some reduction of view, but the intent is to protect the ports as much as possible from any boarding seas. This is a much more seaworthy arrangement than the general run of designs of this type.

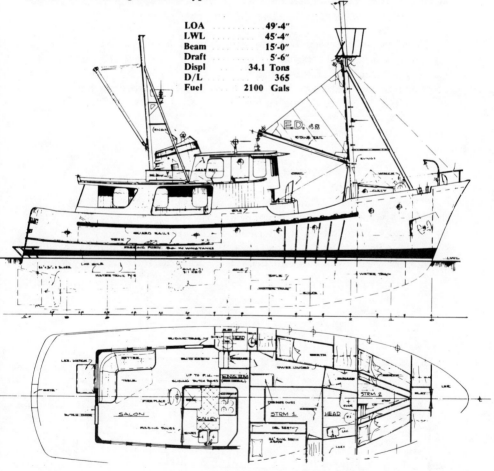

LOA	49'-4"
LWL	45'-4"
Beam	15'-0"
Draft	5'-6"
Displ	34.1 Tons
D/L	365
Fuel	2100 Gals

FIG. 8-50. Profile & Accommodation, Seaton 49-ft. trawler yacht *Nahama*.

PHOTO 8-51.   Seaton 49-ft. *Nahama.*

Seaton's 48-foot steel *Nahama* (1967) goes a long way toward giving the impression of a true trawler, and the way Steve has achieved this deserves study. The placement of masts and booms is his specialty. Not only do they contribute to the total effect, they also perform useful services as boat booms, etc. It is hard to believe this boat's overall length is only 48 feet.

SPARKMAN & STEPHENS, INC.

We are indebted to Olin Stephens for rushing to us the plans of this as-yet-unnamed 49-footer, which was still on his board as a preliminary sketch when he received our request for a contribution. He writes:

"The object of the design has been to produce a boat suited to voyaging under power which can carry auxiliary sails, primarily for steadying purposes.

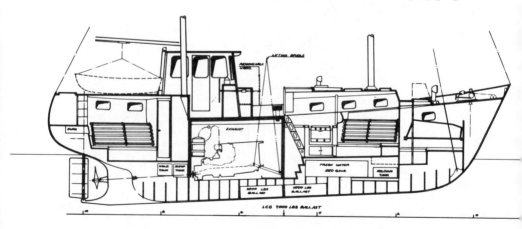

LOA	48'-5"
LWL	41'-3"
Beam	15'-4"
Draft	5'-0"
Displ	21.7 Tons
D/L	308
Fuel	1000 Gals

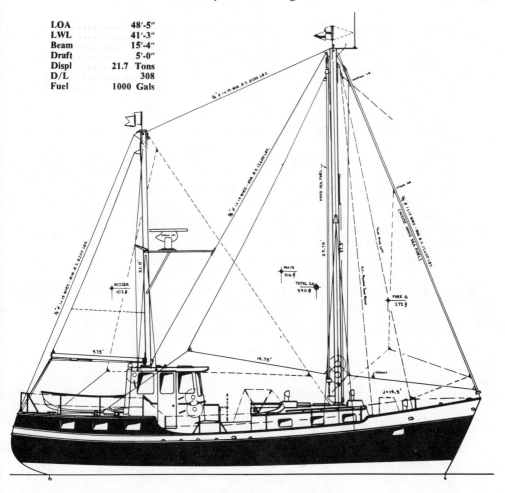

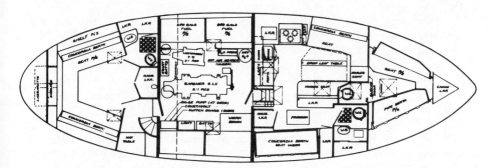

FIG. 8-52. Sparkman & Stephens 48-ft. seagoing motorboat. *Left,* Inboard Profile; *above,* Profile; *below,* Accommodation.

This aspect of the rig might be emphasized by noting that in addition to the highly dependable Gardner diesel engine, the boat is fitted with a smaller Westerbeke diesel which will combine the functions of generator and emergency propulsion system. This auxiliary engine is considerably off the centerline but is installed at a slight angle which should result in a reasonable ability to steer when the boat is moving in the open sea.

"I'd say the general design is of the trawler type, but is more closely related to the Atlantic than the Pacific trawler. While it is a heavy hull by yacht standards, the displacement is relatively light by trawler standards, as the bilge is higher than it normally would be, and there is considerable dead-rise to the midsection. Even so, about 7000 lbs. of ballast will be carried. I believe this hull will be very easily driven at moderate speeds in rough water as well as smooth, and in a seaway the boat should be dry and comfortable, although the sails will be useful in helping to minimize rolling. We estimate the cruising speed at approximately 8.5 knots at which the range would be better than 2000 miles, while at seven knots this could be stretched to 5000 miles with her 1000 gallons of fuel."

This is an interesting design from several standpoints. She carries a rig of sufficient size to be reasonably efficient in roll-reduction. In spite of my remarks about the limitations of sails as an emergency system, there is still a good deal to be said for them, especially if, as in this case, a complete engine alternate is provided as take-home power.

The provision of a small propulsion engine with its own shaft and propeller, and possibly with its own fuel tank, carries the idea of independence of the emergency system to the ultimate in reliability. Another vessel with this arrangement is shown in Chapter 10.

The arrangement plan is highly unusual and worth studying for its innovations. The advantage of a higher cabin in the stern is clearly apparent, and the placing of a cockpit *forward* of the wheelhouse is an interesting variation.

There is another Sparkman & Stephens design in Chapter 9.

CHARLES W. WITTHOLZ

We were particularly pleased to receive this design from Mr. Wittholz because he specializes in drawing husky hulls with Vee bottoms, built with wood framing and plywood planking, and covered with fiberglass. There is much to be said for this type of construction, particularly for the amateur.

This design is also interesting in its complete departure from conventional arrangement. The owner's only requirements were bunks for himself and his wife, and a darkroom/workroom. The boat is an interesting variation of the "Type B" layout in that its pilothouse is larger than the stateroom under it. This was done to place the dining and galley areas there also, and its extension allows a partial full-headroom area in the engine room, handily solving the sole-buried-engine problem. There are thus two lounge areas, and this yacht is an excellent illustration of how the "Type B" layout stars as an in-port social center.

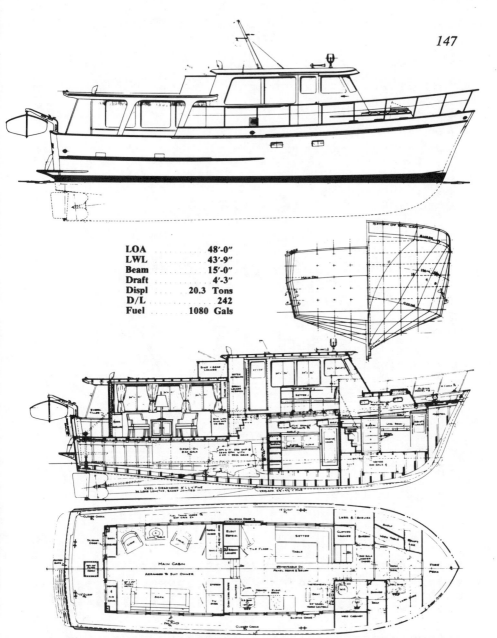

LOA	48'-0"
LWL	43'-9"
Beam	15'-0"
Draft	4'-3"
Displ	20.3 Tons
D/L	242
Fuel	1080 Gals

FIG. 8-53. Profile, Accommodation and Body Plan, Wittholz 48-ft. trawler yacht.

It should be remembered that one of the principal appeals of this craft is its economy of construction, particularly when built by a small yard. It could be turned out easily as a "Type A," a conventional "Type B," or a "Type D." It would *not* work as a "Type C" or a "Type E," because the hull is rather shoal and the D/L of 242 does not leave much room for fiddling with the A/B ratio.

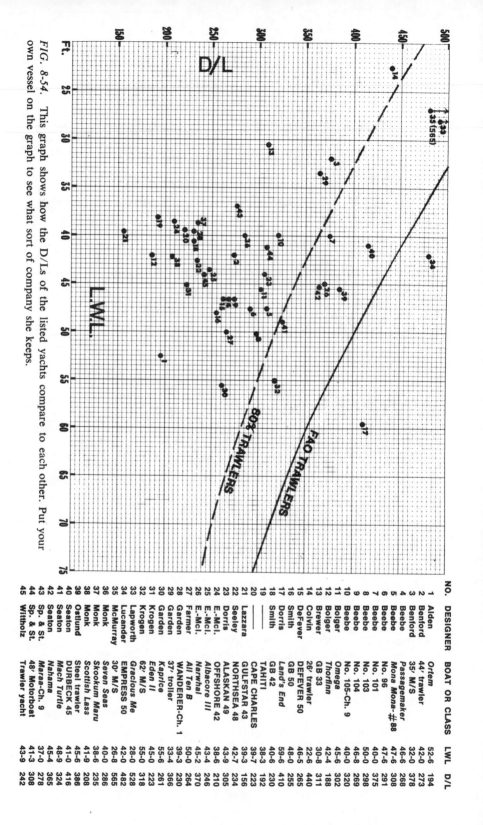

FIG. 8-54. This graph shows how the D/Ls of the listed yachts compare to each other. Put your own vessel on the graph to see what sort of company she keeps.

NO.	DESIGNER	BOAT OR CLASS	LWL	D/L
1	Alden	Ortem	52-6	194
2	Benford	44' trawler	42-0	273
3	Benford	35' M/S	32-0	378
4	Beebe	Passagemaker	46-6	268
5	Beebe	Mona Mona-#88	47-6	308
6	Beebe	No. 96	47-6	291
7	Beebe	No. 101	40-0	375
8	Beebe	No. 103	50-0	298
9	Beebe	No. 104	46-8	269
10	Beebe	No. 105-Ch. 9	40-6	320
11	Bolger	Omega	45-6	302
12	Bolger	Thorfinn	42-4	188
13	Brewer	GB 33	30-8	311
14	Colvin	26' trawler	22-6	440
15	DeFever	DEFEVER 50	46-5	265
16	Smith	GB 50	48-0	255
17	Dorris	Land's End	59-6	410
18	Smith	GB 42	40-6	230
19	—	TAHITI	38-3	192
20	—	CAPE CHARLES	39-7	223
21	Lazzara	GULFSTAR 43	39-7	156
22	Seeley	NORTHSEA 48	42-7	234
23	Dorris	ALASKAN 49	43-9	305
24	E.-Mcl.	OFFSHORE 42	38-6	210
25	E.-Mcl.	Albacore III	43-4	246
26	E.-Mcl.	Narwhal	45-2	370
27	Farmer	All Ten B	50-0	264
28	Garden	WANDERER-Ch. 1	39-3	230
29	Garden	37' troller	33-4	366
30	Garden	Kaprice	55-6	261
31	Krogen	Eden II	45-0	223
32	Krogen	62' M/S	55-0	318
33	Lapworth	Gracious Me	28-0	528
34	Lucander	EMPRESS 50	42-0	482
35	McMurray	30' M/S	26-8	565
36	Monk	Seven Seas	40-0	286
37	Monk	Skookum Maru	38-6	235
38	Monk	Scottish Lass	41-9	208
39	Ostlund	Steel trawler	45-6	386
40	Seaton	DURBECK 45	41-0	416
41	Seaton	Mach Turtle	48-9	324
42	Seaton	Nahama	45-4	365
43	Sp. & St.	Marea-Ch. 9	37-0	278
44	Sp. & St.	48' Motorboat	41-3	308
45	Wittholz	Trawler yacht	43-9	242

9

The Economy Passage-Maker

In all the discussion of passage-makers in the previous chapters, the emphasis has been on taking our fund of experience and evolving the perfect next boat, if such a thing is possible! Here, we must face the fact that a vessel with all the desirable design features plus comfort and convenience equipment to make her a true home afloat becomes quite expensive—well beyond the reach of all but a fortunate few. Can we lick this? Can we develop an economy model that will lengthen the list of owners?

Well, we can at least try, and a discussion of the factors involved may provide useful ideas. First, size. Regardless of whether a boat is commercially built or home-built, it appears that cost-per-pound tends to remain steady more or less as weight is varied. Thus we see a pressure for smaller, shorter, lighter boats as a route to economy.

But this approach immediately conflicts with several other factors: accommodation, cruising speed, and stores capacity, all of which would be better if the boat were larger. From a naval architecture point of view, for instance, waterline length is a critical factor in the speed/length ratio. That is, two boats of the same weight could attain the same S/L ratio with the same horsepower, but the longer one would make a greater speed in knots, apparently adding speed at no extra cost. But in this imperfect world, such things don't happen. Greater length means a never-ending higher cost for berthing and haul-outs. In fact, the extraordinary rise in berthing costs in certain areas is starting a trend toward vertical stems and sterns, together with increasing beam, as exemplified by my 42-footer, Design 101. Length also has a virtue at sea in that it delays the onset of pitching by "bridging" waves in higher wind speeds than the shorter vessel can. Of course, the pitching time eventually comes for every vessel, even 1000-footers. I was aboard one once when it pitched so hard in heavy weather its bow was torn up.

In ordinary coastal winds of 15- to 20-knots, wind speeds often encountered at sea, there is a marked difference of motion when steaming into the waves, between vessels of 28- to 32-foot WL and those around 46-foot WL.

The shorter WL vessels will need to slow down when the wind reaches 15-16 knots while the larger ones will forge ahead well until the sea is liberally covered with whitecaps, at say, 20 knots. As will be discussed in Voyage-Planning, Chapter 12, seagoing motorboats try to avoid these courses. But such steaming conditions are experienced by all boats, and on the West Coast they are a major fact of life. Based on the area to be cruised, a prospective owner must decide how important a longer WL would be to both motion and speed, and select these design elements accordingly. Unquestionably, this discussion tends to show the superiority of the longer waterline for those owners who will not often be subject to the tyranny of docking fees: The retired, long-range cruising folk and the like.

But if a boat is made longer, with weight remaining the same, it follows that she must have decreased beam or draft, or both. As her D/L decreases she becomes more prone to the ills of relative lightness. This leads to an increasing A/B ratio and lack of stability to carry topside weights. In fact, such a procedure soon prohibits double-decking. Can such a boat be satisfactory?

Certainly it can, if you feel you can settle for a hull without any double-decking. The amount of room required to keep the crew happy—particularly the owner's wife—is a personal thing, and can be largely the result of prior experience. We found, for example, that the people who bought *Passagemaker* thought her accommodations were huge because their former boat was a 45-foot yawl. I've met people living quite happily full time on a Grand Banks 42, yet she seemed much too small to my wife and me after five years aboard *Passagemaker*. And so it goes. I really cannot give definitive advice on this subject; each decision is too personal.

Rather than attempt that, I think it best to assemble from other parts of this book a summary of pertinent points that bear on this problem:

1. The influence of D/L on available space. It can be noted here that a 44-foot boat with 37-foot LWL, weighing 16.5 tons for a D/L of 325, has actually made voyages of 17 days underway with a crew of five, and had almost 400 miles of fuel left on arrival.

2. The length for "bridging" waves calls for as long a boat as you can afford, and militates against the ultra-small vessel for open sea work.

3. The lighter a boat is the more lively its motion and the greater the need for good stabilizing gear.

4. With more dependency on stabilizing gear, it is also more important to make careful provision for easy handling of the gear to keep it set properly for speed.

5. With the livelier motion, particularly pitching motion, it is critical to insure crew comfort. Ideally the pilothouse, galley, dinette, and sleeping accommodations should all be concentrated amidships or a bit aft. As this is impossible, be careful how you make your compromises. Consult the cook!

To further explore the question of length, we must remember that a well-designed passage-maker will do its long passages at speed/length ratios between 1.1 and 1.2, and will be able to run locally at hull speed or a bit better. So here is a table that shows these speed values:

	KNOTS			DAYS TO MAKE 1000 MILES	
LWL	**S/L 1.1**	**S/L 1.2**	**S/L 1.34**	**S/L 1.1**	**S/L 1.2**
25	5.50	6.00	6.70	7.60	6.90
30	6.03	6.58	7.35	6.90	6.33
35	6.51	7.10	7.93	6.40	5.87
40	6.95	7.59	8.48	6.00	5.49
45	7.38	8.05	9.00	5.65	5.16
50	7.78	8.48	9.48	5.36	4.91

On *Passagemaker* we did our preliminary planning on the basis of 1000 miles a week, and always did better. *Passagemaker*'s best run was 210 miles in a day with a strong beam wind and all sail set. Her worst run was 90, going up the West Coast into the teeth of the summer northwester, averaging this speed for three days until we rounded Cape Mendocino. My personal preference in balancing all the above factors would be not to go below 40 feet LWL, but I've been spoiled by longer waterlines.

THE MAN-AND-WIFE BOAT

The early long-voyage sailors who followed in the wake of Joshua Slocum were often eccentric loners, what we today frequently call "dropouts." While there are still such types sailing the Seven Seas, the tremendous proliferation of "world voyagers" in the last few decades has been primarily in man-and-wife teams. Without doubt, the foremost ocean voyagers are Eric Hiscock and his wife Susan, who in their *Wanderers* have circumnavigated the world so many times that most of us have lost count. Hiscock's *Voyaging Under Sail* is the bible of the long-range voyager.

This group is also exemplified by the Seven Seas Cruising Association. Chapter 12 urges prospective voyagers under power to read both Hiscock and the bulletins of the SSCA. Here, we will only give their comments on the matter of size for the man-and-wife boat.

Hiscock bluntly says, "The bigger the better, provided the crew can handle her," and cites couples who have handled sailing vessels up to 46 feet in voyages around the world. The SSCA did a poll of its members and arrived at an "average recommended size" of 38 to 42 feet for a man-and-wife sailing vessel.

These experts are primarily concerned with shorthanded sail-handling, which is not a motorboat problem. It is notable that this advice does set a low limit of 38 feet as suitable for full-time living and cruising for a crew of two. I agree with this because I reached the same conclusion some years ago by a different line of reasoning. There are man-and-wife teams cruising the world in smaller·boats, but I wonder if they are entirely satisfied with their space.

Throwing all this into the pot and sticking to my preference for a minimum LWL of 40 feet, a first try at an economical Passagemaker might look like this sketch, which is loosely based on the layout of *Rock Bottom* in Chapter 11.

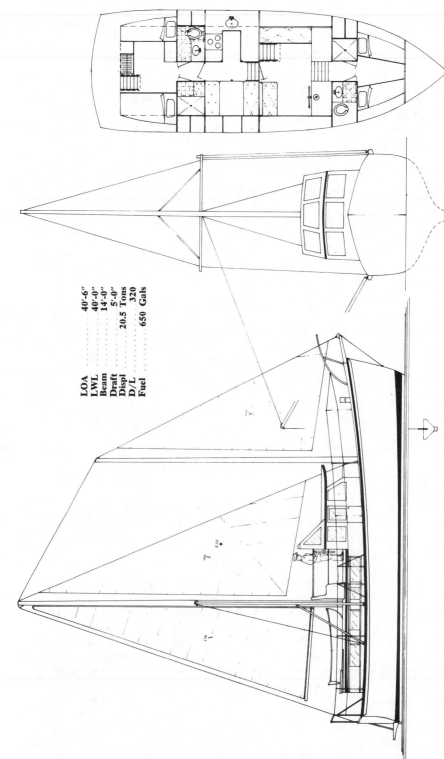

LOA		40'-6"
LWL		40'-0"
Beam		14'-0"
Draft		5'-0"
Displ		20.5 Tons
D/L		320
Fuel		650 Gals

FIG. 9-1. Profile & Accommodation, Beebe 42-ft. Design 105.

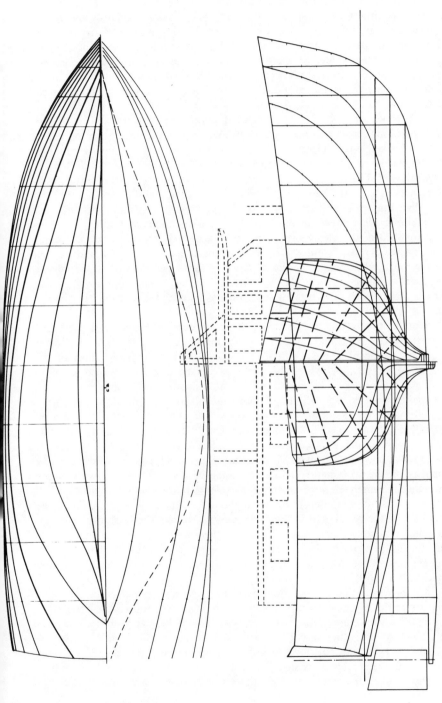

FIG. 9-2. Lines, Design 105.

Design 105 shows certain basics that I would like in any boat. No overhang aft and very little forward seems indicated by conditions previously mentioned —economy, slip rentals, etc. The vertical stern offers two advantages: It is best for a stern platform, an item I would not do without, and it makes possible an outboard-mounted rudder so there is no hole in the hull, and easy access for repairs. An anchor-handling bowsprit is also required. The heavy guard rail is needed not only for rough overseas docking, but to protect the stabilizing-gear hinge.

She is 42-feet overall. The enclosed pilothouse is from amidships forward. It is long enough to permit a high bunk in line with the ports as recommended for single-handing in Chapter 2. When not used for this, it could be lowered and used as a settee, though there is also a permanent seat for the watch-stander. The engine will be under the pilothouse with nearly full headroom. Aft, right on the center of gravity, is the galley and dinette for four, and abaft that, the owner's quarters with head and shower. The mast, primarily for the stabilizing gear, rests on the bulkhead between cabin and galley. It is located forward of the ideal position but not excessively so. The mast can carry some sails to play with, but if sails are the emergency power, it would be well to have more area, along the lines of *Rock Bottom*. We must remember that a motorboat's sailing rig is a touchy question. If large, ballast must approach sailboat amounts to prevent the vessel taking a knockdown from rig windage alone.

I prefer this layout to one having the pilothouse farther aft and the galley forward, as we have found it easier to put up with motion away from the center of gravity in the pilothouse, where everyone is or can be seated most of the time, than in the galley, where the cook has a stand-up job. It is also easier to provide a truly dark pilothouse for the watch-stander with this arrangement. The engine room is under the pilothouse with headroom of 5′ 6″.

With a displacement of 20.5 tons, she would have a D/L of 320 and need 650 gallons of fuel to go 2400 miles at S/L of 1.1. She could easily be made "French-canal Capable" (see *Chapter 13*). She is well suited to the type of cruising discussed in Chapter 14, "Round The World Passage-Making," and broadens the field of man-and-wife long-range cruising for those without the experience, strength, or inclination to consider a purely sailing voyage.

An excellent example of the same sort of design approach, in about the same size, is the Sparkman & Stephens' design *Maraa*. She is shown here because her dimensions and layout come so close to those for a man-and-wife boat. She is particularly interesting for her large open cockpit. This has advantages for ardent fishermen and would be pleasant much of the time in the tropics if furnished with an awning.

Maraa was designed to be delivered under her own power from New England to Tahiti, an assignment she executed handily. She must have acted as a pure sailboat for some of the time on this voyage as her range under power is not enough to cover the vast distance from Panama to Tahiti, as discussed in Chapter 14. Her twins for downwind running would do the trick.

Another approach to cruising with economy is the cruising boat that is basically a fisherman. The ability to earn some money in season as well as the

LOA	**40'-0"**
LWL	**37'-0"**
Beam	**12'-6"**
Draft	**4'-0"**
Displ	**14.1 Tons**
D/L	**278**
Fuel	**520 Gals**

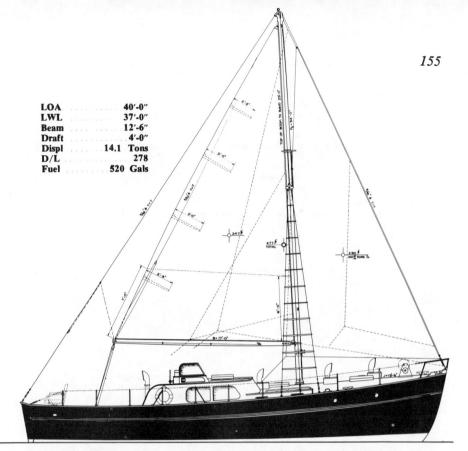

FIG. 9-3. Profile, Sparkman & Stephens 40-ft. seagoing power boat *Maraa.*

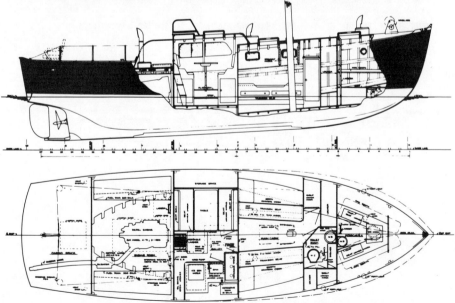

FIG. 9-4. Interior Profile & Accommodation, Sparkman & Stephens *Maraa.*

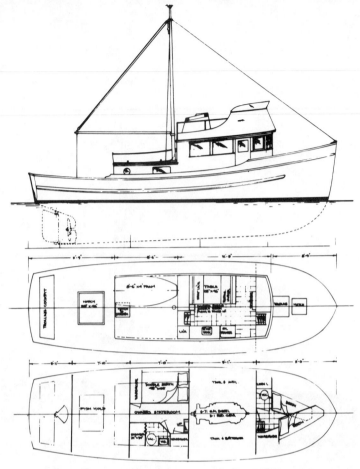

FIG. 9-5. Profile & Accommodation, Monk 42-ft. troller *Seven Seas.*

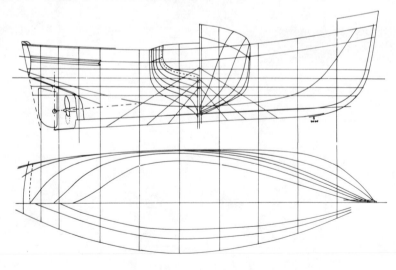

FIG. 9-6. Lines, Monk 42-ft. troller *Seven Seas.* (Retraced from original Lines.)

tax breaks available to the commercial fisherman are well worth looking into. The most suitable area for this sort of thing undoubtedly is our Pacific Northwest, where salmon trolling commercially is followed by many man-and-wife teams. So popular is this approach that designers have turned out special models for it. We have already shown the lines of a Garden troller that was designed for this purpose, and Garden has done others. Edwin Monk, in addition to his vessels shown in Chapter 8, has given us the plans of his *Seven Seas,* one of his standard troller hulls modified to be suitable for use as a cruiser when not on the trolling grounds. Mr. Monk says this about her:

"Due to the nature of their work, trollers must go to sea, often for a week or more at a time. They must provide a seakindly and seaworthy home and work platform. Trollers seldom catch great amounts of fish and therefore don't need a fat shape to carry the load, thereby allowing a more efficient and seakindly shape than many other fish boats. These characteristics as well as their salty style lend themselves well to the offshore cruiser.

"The owner of *Seven Seas* not only wanted a cruiser with the characteristics of a troller, but also wanted to supplement his income by trolling during the season. Aft of the trunk cabin is a relatively small hold capable of holding about eight tons of fish and ice. Across the stern is a trolling cockpit and just forward of that is room for gurdies and the other equipment necessary for trolling. The mast is sturdy and large, capable of carrying a steadying sail and, of course, trolling poles. The rest of *Seven Seas,* however, is all living accommodations, comfortable enough for a couple.

"The construction is pure troller: stout. There is about three tons of concrete ballast, mostly poured to form a smooth bottom in the fish hold and engine room. Power should be a diesel of about 165 continuous horsepower. She carries 775 gallons of fuel. Performance is just what could be expected of a 42-foot displacement hull, about eight to nine knots."

Applying the formulas of Chapter 5 to this hull, she should have a range of 3300 miles at S/L 1.1 (seven knots), and a range of 2400 miles at S/L 1.2 (7.6 knots).

Let's leave design for a bit and talk about costs. Whatever they are, they are sure to go up—that's about the only certain thing you can say. It has become almost a cliché among designers that the cost of the hull is only 20 per cent of the total. Thus, they argue, the cost of hull material does not matter that much. I don't think any such general statement is too useful. It was first made to me by Bill Garden in the 1960s when he was at the height of his career designing some very plush yachts for repeat clients before he retired to his island off Victoria, B.C. As I was then in the process of designing *Passagemaker,* his comment jarred me more than somewhat. Fortunately, it didn't turn out that way for me. After the hull shell, the engines, stern gear, tanks, and soles may be an equal amount. But it is equipment and furniture and its installation cost that *really* mount up. This matter has already been referred to in Chapter 3, under Lessons Learned, No. 10, which describes how *Passagemaker* left Singapore with only the most basic equipment. This was dictated by the budget mostly, but we definitely wanted to discover how well things went with such simplicity. As stated, things worked out fine. It might be well to expand on this.

The basic contract cost for *Passagemaker,* a 50-foot vessel weighing 27 tons, in 1962, was $40,000. We could have left the yard for this. But about $3000 worth of extra work was done in improvements, such as the after head and furniture generally. A three kw diesel generator was purchased at a very favorable price in the United Kingdom, and was installed by ourselves two years later. Our plan was to upgrade her interior over the years as the budget permitted. During this period she continued her cruising as has been related. (When she was sold, the new owner accelerated this program, installing a deep freeze, refrigeration, larger generator, diesel heat, radio transmitter, and other assorted goodies, none of which impressed me on the cruise I made with him. As a result, some 10 years later, the original price has about been doubled.)

I think our approach to improvements makes sense. We started cruising sooner than if I had waited till my funds could purchase a fully found vessel. We were just as comfortable in our bunks at the beginning as at the end, but the cook was happier when *PM* eventually acquired the bigger stove, refrigerator, and deep-freeze. Our meals may have had more variety then, but I don't think they were any better. Still, a happy cook is—or should be—a principal objective of any designer. We certainly did less maintenance work in the early days. Our navigation put us where we wanted to go, with only a couple of days on RDF and no need for a radar or Loran. These days, my wife and I are working up a new boat, and when she starts cruising she will be even more austere than *Passagemaker.*

In the course of planning this new vessel, I have rechecked all methods of construction in their latest form: steel, ferro-cement, one-off fiberglass, Feralite, cold-molded plywood, and others. At the end, I just felt confused. There is something good to be said about all of them, and something bad, too. The next two chapters tell the story of two owner-built boats: a large, one-off fiberglass, and a fine example of ferro-cement. I have also seen an owner-built Airex foam-core fiberglass vessel, 62 feet long, on which a gang of five laid down her lines, set up the mold, and applied the outer skin in ten working days. The ingenuity and tenacity of the better amateur builders is something to behold. I heard of a charter boat operator out of the West Indies who needed a new boat, went to the Puget Sound area, hired a Hertz truck, filled it with red cedar planks, and drove it to Florida. He found a building spot, set it up, built a triple-planked hull, and was ready to charter again in six months! (And then someone came along and made him an offer he couldn't refuse! So now he is a boat builder again.)

So we can be sure, no matter what the problems and the escalation in costs, there will always be individuals ready to tackle the difficulties and overcome them to get their dream vessels. They are a dedicated bunch and have minds of their own. If the ideas in this chapter can help them a bit, it will have served its purpose. Good luck!

10

The Building of Mona-Mona

AUTHOR'S NOTE: I can't imagine a more unlikely candidate for a "do-it-yourself" big-boat-building project than Bob Sutton. When he asked me to design a 50-foot Passagemaker for him to build personally, I'll admit I had some nagging fears that it might turn out to be one more backyard monument to a dreamer who let himself be overmatched.

At the time, Bob was in his early 60s. Thirty years of sitting behind a Columbia Broadcasting System desk had equipped him with a 30-pound spare tire, which was going to get heavier every time he climbed a scaffold. To the best of my knowledge, he had never built so much as a dinghy; he had carpenters put the bookshelves in his home, and he had never used a power tool more complicated than the electric rotisserie on his barbecue.

Later, I'll point out the things that make his backyard-built Mona Mona such a remarkably successful vessel.

What prompts a man with such a limited background to take on such a chore? I think Bob can tell it better in his own words.

Mona Mona and How She Grew

By Robert Patrick Sutton

I got hipped on Bob's Passagemaker concept in the spring of 1967. My wife, Ramona, and I were invited to crew with Bob and Linford Beebe and another couple from Newport Beach, California, to Miami aboard the original *Passagemaker*. On our arrival in Miami, I called the executive VP at CBS to whom I reported, and said, "Start plans for an early retirement—I know what I want to spend the rest of my life doing."

I had dreamed the long-distance-cruising dream for many years. But I had also crewed on some ocean-racers, including the *Queen Mab*, a lovely old Herreshoff schooner, 78 feet overall and representing my idea of just about the kind of live-aboard space I wanted on a retirement boat. I had a pretty good idea of *Mab's* upkeep costs— and I personally knew the amount of backbreaking labor 14 of us expended driving her to Honolulu in the 1955 Transpac.

World cruising means sailboat. Comfortable living aboard means *big* sailboat. Big sailboat means lots of money and lots of crew. So forget it. That's how the logic went until the Newport Beach-Miami trip aboard *Passagemaker*.

PHOTO 10-1. Mona Mona a few days after her launching.

By September of 1967 I was on the beach, blessed with a few retirement dollars and an understanding wife, ready to go passage-making. But how?

I checked boat yard costs in the U.S. I exchanged some correspondence with Hongkong and Taiwan. I looked for used boats. The fishing industry in San Diego was having real problems, so I shopped for distress sales in used work boats that I might convert. I did a tour of the Pacific Northwest to check out the ferro-cement circuit.

Meanwhile, Roger Bury of Westport, Connecticut, had acquired *Passage-maker* and was looking for a crew for an Atlantic crossing. I jumped at the chance to do some more passage-making and also to search the south of England for converted motor fishing vessels. I even flew to Malta to look at some prewar gold-platers that were reasonably priced.

There were some pretty serious objections to all of them. They just couldn't be fitted into the Passagemaker concept.

About this time, Bob Beebe sent me a clipping from *Boating* about a 65-foot schooner Lloyd Clark was building at his Glas-Dock company in Long Beach, California.

He had come up with a one-off fiberglass method which started with a big, wooden-batten basket which was then lined with fiberglass sheets. These fiberglass sheets, made right in the yard over a flat formica form, were secured to the inside of the batten basket from the outside with self-tapping metal screws. Then, using the fiberglass sheets as the exterior skin of the vessel, Clark built an outer hull of four laminations each of mat and woven roving, with extra strength at critical areas.

Then longitudinal fiberglass stiffeners were bonded into the outer hull. They were formed on 2" x 4" strips of polyurethane foam placed on 17" centers. At this point, his hull was already stronger than the Lloyds 100A1 rules for fiberglass construction.

Clark then went one step farther: He filled in between the longitudinal stringers with two-inch polyurethane foam, faired it with a Sur-form, and laid up an inner hull of the same fiberglass layup used in the outer hull.

The end result was an enormously stiff, reasonably light hull—and at a price substantially below anything comparable being offered by the kit makers.

I climbed all over Clark's hull, looked at the process and thought, "With some professional guidance and a little bit of luck, I can do that."

I prayed earnestly for the luck and made a deal with Lloyd Clark for the professional guidance. The deal included space in his yard to build *Mona Mona,* the right to hire some of his people intermittently, and materials-purchasing service through his firm.

With solid professional support assured, I commissioned Bob Beebe to start drawing.

The design problem we presented to Bob was straightforward: to design a second-generation version of *Passagemaker* for someone with no particular interest in the French canals, who never wants to lay hand on a piece of sail again and who promises to stay out of the North Atlantic and never go 'round the Horn.

Mona Mona was the result.

We got the drawings from Bob for Christmas, 1969.

Bob came south and helped me loft her lines in January, 1970.

In February, 1970, Lloyd Clark went out of business.

And there I was with plans for a 50-footer, the lines lofted full-size, and all the framing cut to build *Mona Mona* by the Lloyd Clark method—but no Lloyd Clark.

In November, 1972, at Lido Shipyard in Newport Beach, California, we launched *Mona Mona.*

And in between those two dates were three of the funniest, hardest-working, most frustrating, muscle-straining, expensive and glorious years that I reckon among the considerable number I have spent on this globe.

I worked with geniuses, hippie freaks, competent professionals, flakes, one man who was as dedicated as I to making *Mona Mona* a great boat, and a jerk who showed up on the job with an American flag sewed to the seat of his pants. I had to keep an eye out for rising costs, material shortages, and a kid with a scraggly beard who took marijuana breaks and tried to float off the end of the scaffolding because a ladder seemed too Establishment-oriented.

But it all paid off when we took our shakedown cruise to Turtle Bay in Baja California, in March, 1973. The trip of about 500 miles there and our stay, were, as our British friends put it, "without incident." Coming back, we left the shelter of Cedros Island and headed into a northwester that our navigator labeled as a "conservative Force 8." It took us 22 hours to make the 90 miles from Cedros to the shelter behind Punta Baja.

Mona Mona behaved like a lady through it all. With both flopperstoppers

PHOTO 10-2. The author laying down the lines of *Mona Mona.*

out, we seldom rolled beyond 20 degrees. Hour after hour of punching right into the weather produced no creaking and groaning; the hull just simply wasn't working at all. And everything mechanical kept right on doing its appointed thing.

We were convinced we'd gotten our own personal, hand-tooled version of *Passagemaker.*

Later tests confirmed that she was performing to specifications. Stability tests showed her metacentric height well within the limits set by the designer; she cruised at 8.5 knots using about 70 horsepower; at our economical cruising speed of 7.5 knots she burned three gph, giving us an honest 3000 mile cruising range on her 1200 gallons of fuel.

We felt we were ready to go passage-making.

We set our departure date for the big adventure: May 1, 1973.

Actually, about 1500 on April 30 we realized there was nothing more to do: Ship's stores were stowed, the ship was fueled, the crew was aboard and the goodbyes had been made.

We looked at each other and said, "Why not? We might just as well spend the night at sea as here in Newport Harbor." So at 1620 of April 30, we cranked up the main engine and departed Newport Beach on a passage which we hoped would wind up in the Mediterranean.

Starting eight hours early seemed a good omen. You *never* start a small-boat voyage on time. Always there are delays caused by tardy crew arrivals, supplies that arrive late, or last-minute repairs.

But there we were at sea early. The next morning at 1000 saw us dropping the hook in Ensenada Harbor, and weighing anchor at 1330 that afternoon with the entrance-to-Mexico formalities taken care of, and the freezer loaded with a couple of dozen of the fresh *bolillos* that are an Ensenada speciality.

We had a six-day stretch ahead of us now, with the next stop scheduled in Manzanillo. *Mona Mona* was finally doing what she was designed for: taking six people over a long stretch of ocean with reasonable comfort and privacy.

Reasonable comfort, hell! It was luxury.

The three gals put on a cooking competition that would slow the Galloping

Gourmet down to a walk. Each day, two of the ladies were on galley duty while the third one took care of one long daylight watch.

As skipper, I didn't set up a detailed watch list for the ladies; just told them that I expected the three of them to cover cooking, dishes, and the daylight watch from 0900 to 1400. How they did it, or who did what, was up to them.

I realize more authoritarian skippers would be driven up the bulkhead by this attitude, but to me it represented a victory of realism over a new gold-encrusted blue cap. I've spent much of my professional life dealing with creative people. Many of my unprofessional—and happier—moments have been spent around women. And I've never learned how to boss either group.

So I just take them up to the mountain top, show them the beautiful scene on the distant horizon, and turn them loose. This is known as the Lazy Executive's Shuffle. It's amazing how often it works.

Bob Beebe was our navigator. He took the watch from 0400 to 0800, and was on duty any other time he figured navigating chores needed doing. He was also the man to call in the middle of the night in case of an outside emergency. For an inside emergency, I still wanted to get at it personally at the earliest possible moment.

Bob Wendling, with his fine background of teaching auto shop in the San Diego high schools and his years of skippering his own boat, made a wonderful first mate. He and I shared the remaining watches. And if you think having all the males aboard ship named "Bob" doesn't make for some interesting moments, I'll put in with you.

Linford Beebe, Joan Wendling, and my own Ramona—of *Mona Mona*—cooked and cooked. And with a freezer full of food, fresh supplies, and over a ton of canned goods, the major danger on board was instant obesity.

We had all done some cruising before, and with the boat behaving so well, everything soon shook down to the succession of days and nights and watches and meals and miles made good over the bottom that passage-making is all about.

Manzanillo came up on schedule on the afternoon of May 7.

A competent ship's agent there found us cheap diesel fuel, bottled water (500 gallons worth delivered in the original bottles for $17.00), and clearance papers for Costa Rica.

Seven more days got us to Puntarenas, Costa Rica.

En route, the Gulf of Tehuantepec behaved just fine—and its waters can get sloppy. Less pleasant was the sea off the coast of Nicaragua: The land just wasn't high enough to keep the northeast Trades from coming at us, and butting into 25-30 knot headwinds is tiresome after two days.

On departing Puntarenas, a short visit to Jesusita Island gave us a proper tropical-cruising feeling, and we were off to Panama.

Now the Panama Canal transit, to a small boat, can be a real rump-buster. You get into one of the upbound locks, and the ship ahead of you starts up his propeller and if you lose a bow line, or if you have been foolish enough to tie up to the side of the lock instead of asking for "center lockage," you go through the trauma of seeing your pretty little boat get beat to hell.

Our *Mona Mona* luck held.

As we reached the first lock, there was a Panama Canal Company tug on the port hand. On instructions from our pilot, we rafted up to the tug and let his crew do all the work of line-handling. As we reached the top of the first lock, the skipper said, "Leave her lashed. I'll tow you to the next one." So we got a free and gentle ride up that one, too. Next lock? Another tug and another free ride for *Mona Mona*. It's got to be the easiest transit a small boat has ever made. We dropped our pilot in Cristobal at 1445. Fifteen minutes later we were rigged for sea and pulling out of Cristobal for Florida, all for $90 of which $25 was for a one-time measuring fee. And remember, you must be ready to pay in *cash!*

The Florida leg had a couple of memorable moments. The radar packed up just as we were approaching the west end of Cuba. The Castroites have been known to get goosey when small unidentified boats approach their island at night. The alternative was to take a big swing around the island, wasting time and fuel, so knowing exactly where you are becomes important. In spite of continuously overcast skies, Bob did some precision navigation, and we stayed just about the right distance off Cuba.

But joining that big stream of tankers that depart the ports of the Gulf of Mexico and make a U-turn around the Florida keys into the Straits of Florida bound north, makes for some tense moments. One night we had six or seven

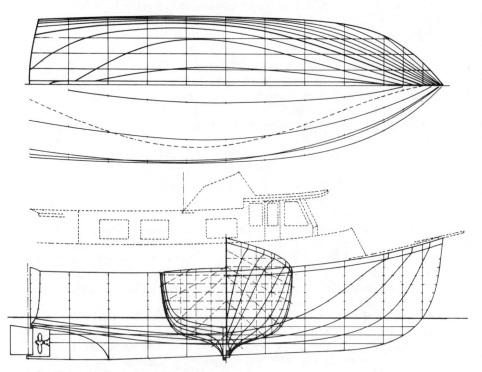

FIG. 10-3.   Lines, Beebe 50-ft. Design 88, *Mona Mona*.

LOA	50′-0″
LWL	47′-6″
Beam	16′-0″
Draft	5′-0″
Displ	33.0 Tons
D/L	308
Fuel	1200 Gals

FIG. 10-4. Profile, Design 88, *Mona Mona.*

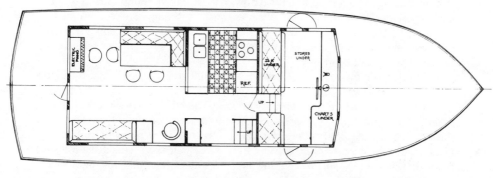

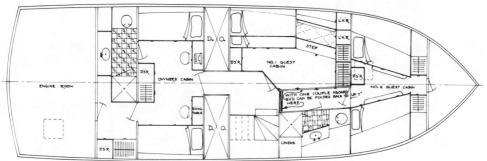

FIG. 10-5. Accommodation, Design 88, *Mona Mona.*

tankers in sight at a time. We were doing 7.5 knots and they were doing 15 to 20 knots. No radar, so you keep up all your relative bearings the old-fashioned way.

But they all did what they were supposed to do, and we did what we were supposed to do, and nobody hit nobody, and Key West showed up right where it belonged.

There was a lot of conversation in Florida and elsewhere about fuel shortages, but not once did we get turned away. An order of 800 to 1000 gallons of Number 2 diesel didn't seem to upset anyone, and the prices didn't get out of line.

However, neither in Key West, Miami, nor Fort Lauderdale were we able to find anyone to fix the radar, so we took off for Bermuda without it.

The Atlantic decided to get a little less cooperative on the Bermuda leg. We were slowed down a couple of times by some pretty good-sized swells from the east.

What with the slowing down for weather, and a few hours off for a cooling-system repair, we were just over six days going from Fort Lauderdale to Bermuda, arriving June 11. And, quite frankly, having done 5000 nautical miles in six weeks, we were a little travel-weary.

The Wendlings had to leave us in Bermuda; it was all they had signed on for. Our replacement crew member, due in from the West Coast, got involved in a business deal he just couldn't walk away from. So we found ourselves shorthanded for the Atlantic crossing. We were a week lining up new crew in Bermuda. We were lucky in the ones we found. Ray Wilson and Ron Firth both had seagoing engineering experience in big ships and were glad to take advantage of a free ride to Europe.

So we were off to the Azores—Horta 1800 miles away—six of us in a 50-foot backyard special.

The June departure was carefully chosen. The pilot charts show that in that month at those latitudes, you're right in the doldrums; you should slice precisely through the middle of the Bermuda High and find 1800 miles of millpond— ideal weather and seas for a power-driven passage-maker. That's the way we found it when we made the crossing in 1969—the ocean and the pilot charts were in perfect accord.

Not in 1973.

Something pushed the northeast Trades way north of their usual limits, and we started slugging into the so-called "reinforced trades" coming from dead ahead at 25-30 knots, and making for that miserable, tiring, fuel-consuming, hobby-horse pitching.

We were so sure that the easterlies would disappear shortly that we started off at our "fast" cruise speed—8.5 knots. This power setting had checked out to give us about 1.8 nautical miles per gallon. The slide rule showed that we should arrive in Horta with 15 per cent of our fuel remaining. We had proven she'd do 1.8 nautical miles per gallon in still water. Only problem, the water wouldn't stay still. Two days out of Bermuda we realized that with the headwinds and seas slowing us down, we were burning too much fuel. So we changed the generator pulleys on our main engine generator, slowed down to 7.5 knots, running just under a speed/length ratio of 1.1.

At the same time, we headed north to try to get out of the misplaced NE Trades. According to the pilot chart, about 200 miles north of the Bermuda-Azores rhumb line there should be wind from the west: That is the normal sailing route.

When we got there, the damned easterlies were *still* hitting us right on the bow, and fuel consumption was getting a little dicey. We kept a fuel How-Goes-It Curve. It kept showing that if everything went on exactly as it was, we would land in the Azores with zero gallons of fuel. If things got worse, we would wind up with zero gallons of fuel some miles short of the Azores. And there was no Coast Guard to come out and get us. If we made the decision now, we could turn back to Bermuda with a good margin of safety.

Or, we could plug on a couple of days, *then* turn back, and if conditions worsened *ahead*, then we could wind up with zero gallons of fuel *before* we made it back to Bermuda. Figuring conservatively, at about 700 miles from Bermuda, we had reached a point of no return.

The older I get, the fewer things I know for sure. But among those certain bits of knowledge is this one: The sea is unremittingly unforgiving of damn fools.

So we turned around and headed back for Bermuda.

And those same easterlies which had been making life so unpleasant blew us right back into Bermuda. And, after a couple of days of R & R in Bermuda, those *same* easterlies blew us right into Newport, Rhode Island.

Crew schedules got tight; the freak weather conditions of that summer might hold on long enough to prevent an Atlantic crossing that year—and we'd always wanted to cruise the coast of Maine, anyway.

The 610 miles from Bermuda to Newport were made in three days with the help of those easterlies, plus that great sense of lift you get when you and the weather are cooperating. We were only two couples aboard, which made for longer watches but less complicated shipboard routine.

The radar still wasn't working. And the scene of Bob Beebe navigating us right up to the Brenton Reef Texas Tower in 50-yard visibility without proper charts and using the Zenith All-Wave Receiver held in both hands and rotated in an effort to turn it into a radio direction finder, was a lesson in navigational improvisation.

But we found Newport, and after checking in with one of the friendliest Customs-Agriculture-Immigration officials the U.S. career bureaucracy has ever produced, we officially ended the passage-making and started the coastal cruising.

At several points in his articles on the art of passage-making, Bob Beebe has stressed that crossing ocean in a small boat is simply something to be done so that one may enjoy the local cruising. The essence of passage-making is that the great cruising grounds of the world are opened up to you if you can reach them on your own bottom: the maximum of cruising pleasure with a minimum of expense, time, and trauma.

The rest of the summer on *Mona Mona* proved that point beautifully.

The cruise went "down east to Maine" as far as Roque Island and Machias Bay; south through New England, paying particular attention to the Cape Cod area; then a little time in Long Island Sound. Then outside to the mouth of the Delaware and a month spent exploring Delaware and Chesapeake Bays.

Nights on the hook back of deserted piney islands in Maine, a week in Boston tied up in a downtown marina, down New York's East River and past the Statue of Liberty and up the Potomac to Washington—the whole great cruising ground of the east coast of the United States was there for the express purpose of giving three months of enjoyment to a crew of West Coasters.

And that cruise made the building of *Mona Mona*—the three years at hard labor, and the spending of too much of the family money—all worthwhile.

So read Bob Beebe and his book on Passagemakers and passage-making with great caution—it may be injurious to your peace of mind.

You see what happened to one couple who listened to Bob's insidious siren song of how the waters of the world can be yours even though you're heavy in the middle, light in the pocketbook, and the reverse of a horny-handed salt.

World cruising for those of middle age and pot bellies?

It'll never work.

ABOUT MONA MONA

Well, that's a good yarn by Bob Sutton. And not too far from the facts, though I thought *he* helped *me* lay down the lines. Seriously, the whole thing was a major effort that was remarkably successful. I think the secret of its success was that Bob treated it as a regular nine-to-five job, five days a week, without fail.

One thing that is not in his story is how superbly he and his wife Mona decorated the vessel, light and airy and quite superior to several larger and more expensive yachts I have inspected recently.

At the start, I was not too happy about drawing a 50-foot double-decker, but with Bob's promise to stay out of the North Atlantic and to use her as a live-aboard home in the Mediterranean, I decided it could be done, and we could still call her a Passagemaker.

The building method influenced her in two ways: The wooden form made it necessary to design her as if she were to be built of wood; and it made desirable a main deck that ran full length without a break. In addition, the main saloon area aft required an almost flat profile and we wanted a higher bow than *Passagemaker*'s for the reasons previously discussed. All this combined to produce a sheer line that didn't look like much on tracing paper, but a scale model showed it would be okay in the round, so we went ahead.

We agreed on the necessity of raising the pilothouse to give vision aft, hence the step-up here. This caused a feeling of insecurity coming out the pilothouse door. If you fell, you could quite possibly go over the side. Hence the pipe rail there which more than complies with my rule of four-foot-high rails in any area where the watch-stander can approach the side. It was a blessing while taking sights, too.

Like all *Passagemaker*-trained crewmen, Bob didn't think much of having an outside steering station. But one was drawn in topside if he wanted it. One may judge the effect of its absence from the photos. As explained in Chapter 7, the sheer line was lowered by putting the engine aft. The flopperstopper gear is 39 percent of LWL forward of the stern, instead of the ideal 28 per cent, because it had to be placed on the aft galley bulkhead, which is a major

PHOTO 10-6. Building *Mona Mona:* The batten basket in which the hull was laid up.

PHOTO 10-7. Building *Mona Mona:* Fabricating the curved fiberglass transom.

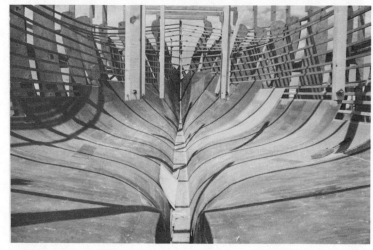

PHOTO 10-8. Building *Mona Mona:* Bottom fiberglass panels laid in the batten basket.

structural member, needed to hold it. A slight "double drag" effect was noted.

The lines were made a bit broader in beam at the waterline to make her stiffer—so as to carry the topside weights. One of these was supposed to be a small auto Bob made up. (He has been building and racing sport cars for years.) As none of this topside weight has been installed to date, she turned out to be too stiff, with the results described in Chapter 7.

Her accommodations worked out very well and show how much room is added by double-decking. In Maine, it was interesting to be visited by the crew of one of the better "trawlers," a model 50 feet long with no double-decking whatever, which had actually followed the same track from California that we had. Their expressions of astonishment and downright envy over the difference in crew's quarters, particularly forward, were revealing.

The idea of folding away the partition that separates the two forward cabins worked out very well when only two couples were aboard. Linford and I lived like that in Maine and really enjoyed the feeling of luxurious space. The way to make it perfect would be to arrange the aft top bunk to hinge down and make a settee back.

The first cruise of the *Mona Mona* was really something when you think about it. She had had a shakedown, but a short one. Yet there we were heading out for a destination some 9000 miles away, expecting to meet some people on the dock at a prearranged time. We would have pulled it off if the weather had cooperated. Everything worked, except the radar. The few troubles we had were minor and easily fixed, and altogether it was a great performance by the "Sutton Shipyard."

PHOTO 10-9.   Ramona Sutton at her electric piano aboard *Mona Mona*.

PHOTO 10-10. Bob Sutton, *left,* and the author on *Mona Mona*'s bow.

Inspection of the weather maps after we came home, shows what happened. The pilot chart shows the average pressures and position of the center to be expected in June in the North Atlantic, and how they relate to the Bermuda-Azores course. In 1969 we had several days of calm. In 1972 the racers from Bermuda to Spain complained about the light airs all the way. But in 1973, a complete reversal.

The day we left Bermuda there was a full-fledged storm up near New-foundland. Behind this storm, high pressure was forecast to press out over the ocean along Long Island, but was not forecast to push down to Bermuda. But it did—early on June 19 we experienced the frontal passage with rain and wind shifts. On June 20 the wind shifted to the east and remained there *for at least 22 days,* when I stopped checking it. What happened is shown on the map for June 20.

The front pushed down to about Latitude 30° N. and then formed waves along its length, at least two of them. With the high pressure north of us these waves reinforced the easterly winds around the high and kept this up until we had to concede defeat. On June 21, winds of 40 knots were reported ahead of us and we could see swells passing us that looked like the winds were higher than that.

On June 26, when we were back in Bermuda, the map *still* showed a high center north of our proposed track, producing easterly winds clear to Horta. And, as Bob said, we had southeast winds all the way to Newport, Rhode Island, where we arrived in the evening of July 3. Well, I've always wanted to cruise in Maine!

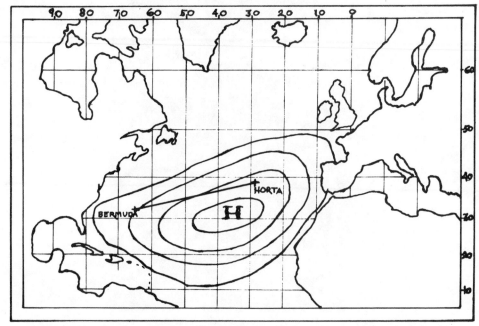

FIG. 10-11. Tracing, Weather Chart: Average Isobars for June, North Atlantic.

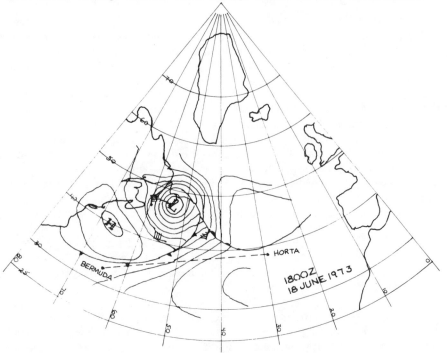

FIG. 10-12. Tracing, Weather Chart: June 18, 1973.

FIG. 10-13. Tracing, Weather Chart: June 20, 1973.

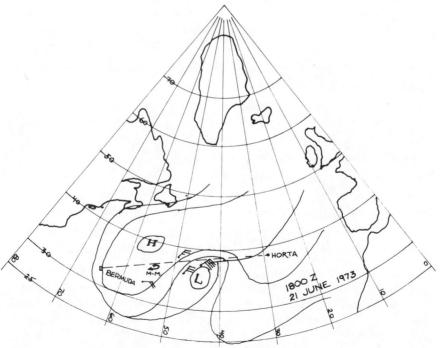

FIG. 10-14. Tracing, Weather Chart: June 21, 1973.

PHOTO 10-15. En route to Panama, *Mona Mona's* F/S gear proves the old adage: "One good tern deserves another."

AUTHOR'S NOTE: Just before this book went to press we learned from Bob Sutton that Mona Mona *had made a successful crossing of the Atlantic, from Morehead City, North Carolina, to Bermuda, Horta in the Azores, and Lisbon, Portugal, in June and July, 1974. This time they had a few rough days, but no problems with headwinds, making the crossing Bermuda-Horta on 795 gallons of fuel, in 270 hours running time.*

11

The Building of Rock Bottom

The most interesting story of building and operating an ocean-going motor-boat I have come across is that of Fred and Vera Lagier and their boat, aptly named *Rock Bottom.*

Our first contact was after Fred had read the article "On Seagoing Power-boats" written jointly by Avard Fuller and myself in *Boating,* January, 1970. In the article I had mentioned my design for a 45-footer to be built in ferro-cement. Fred wrote me a letter saying he had recently built a boat of that size after considerable experimentation with various ferro-cement layups recommended in books on the subject. He explained he did not like any of them, had developed his own, and asked would I like to see an example of his? I was very much interested and wasted no time in arranging a meeting.

The Lagier home was near Escalon, southeast of Stockton in California's San Joaquin Valley. It was a fruit and almond ranch in an area dominated by these products. And next to their pretty little ranch house stood the boat, *Rock Bottom.* The hull was plastered and work was going forward inside.

Fred's story was this: During World War II he had gone to work at the Pollock Shipyard in Stockton, which was then building Navy vessels. While there he added qualification as a shipwright (including some time in the mould loft) to his various skills in the building trades. After the war he concentrated on his ranch but continued to work in construction and lately had been a lather.

As he said, "Lathing is about the closest thing to ferro-cement in the building business, so I was interested in it. I had once built myself a 30-foot wood sailboat, but now I wanted something larger we could really cruise in."

In searching for a design that suited his ideas, he was lucky to come across William Atkin's plans for *Magpie,* a schooner-rigged motorsailer. Her dimensions are LOA 46 feet; LWL 41 feet; beam 13 feet; draft five feet. Atkin failed to include the displacement on the plan and the best I could estimate, after making some assumptions, was that her displacement was 22.4 tons, with a D/L of 326.

Fred liked the layout of this boat very much. He was thoroughly familiar with conditions on our West Coast and appreciated the importance of plenty of power and fuel. *Magpie* is more motor and less sail than most of Atkin's designs. In addition, her inside and outside steering, capability for adding fuel, an general layout really make her a good design for passage-making.

But Fred wanted something a bit smaller than *Magpie,* with a somewhat different layout. Using the skills he had learned in his wartime loft work, he

PHOTO 11-1. Fred Lagier aboard *Rock Bottom* at her dock in the Sacramento delta. (*Record* photo.)

followed *Magpie*'s general configuration and lines to produce a hull of LOA 44 feet; LWL 37 feet; beam 12'8" and draft five feet. She weighs 16.5 tons with a D/L of 325, remarkably close to *Magpie* and to my ideas on D/L for this size vessel as discussed in Chapter 5.

Now as to her construction in ferro-cement, Fred told me he had made test panels of all the recommended layups he could find and didn't think any of them would do the job. So, using his lather experience, he not only made up a test panel that suited him, but also evolved a system of construction markedly different from any other ferro-cement vessel.

This system made so much sense to me that I want to discuss it in detail. I have been studying ferro-cement for some time, both as a possible material for our next boat, and also to advise clients. It seemed to me the way things were evolving, it would make sense to have what might be called "an all steel boat with waterproof covering." That is, the steel structure, framing, longitudinals, deck beams, etc. would be strong enough to carry all loads except keeping water out. This waterproofing would be accomplished by ferro-cement or one of the new synthetic mortars. It is true, as has been noted by others, that this line of reasoning can be carried to the conclusion that the boat should be all steel in the first place. Quite so, except such a craft is limited to the chine form, where the steel frame with ferro-cement "covering" allows the use of round bilges, flared bows, and so on.

This is exactly the construction Fred decided on. In his lathing experience, particularly in the construction of heavy suspended ceilings, he noted there was a supporting longitudinal every 12 inches or so, to which the mesh was fastened. So, he reasoned, why not do the same thing in a boat? The most convenient support to use (considering the plastering problem) turned out to be ordinary

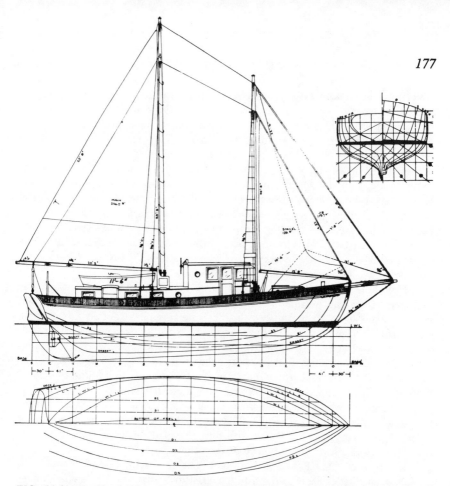

FIG. 11-2. Profile & Lines, William Atkin's 46-ft. MAGPIE, the basis for Fred Lagier's design for *Rock Bottom*. (MAGPIE'S plan from *Motor Boating & Sailing's* Ideal Series, Vol. 8.)

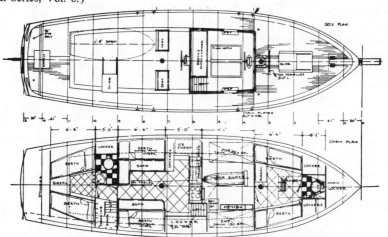

FIG. 11-3. Accommodation, William Atkin's MAGPIE, similar to the layout used by Fred Lagier in *Rock Bottom*.

water pipe (*see Photo 11–4*). The pipes were held to form either by temporary frames, or by plywood bulkheads that would remain in the boat. Her keel was cast separately, with the wire mesh crossing over it, continuous from sheer to sheer. The layup used is shown in Photo 11-5 which is a panel Fred made up for me. Note the three sections of pipe. From the inside out, the layup is: one layer of expanded metal lath, which Fred says is merely a "mudstop" for a smooth finish inside; then two layers of one-half-inch galvanized square mesh; then eight-gauge (about three-sixteenths inch) horizontal wires at three-inch intervals; finally eight-gauge vertical wires at two-inch intervals. Fred "cold worked" each piece by fastening one end and putting the other into an electric drill and giving it a big twist. The wire then became much stiffer and faired better. The outside layer was also two layers of half-inch-square mesh. Fred and Vera wire-tied the entire armature together in eight working days.

Note how fair the hull appears in mesh (*see Photo 11-6*). When she was plastered (from the outside-in) by a plasterer whom Fred considered, from his own experience, to be the best in the State, she came out so fair nothing was needed except painting. I have inspected *Rock Bottom* and another hull done by this plasterer and they are the best I have ever seen.

What with one thing and another, I didn't attend *Rock Bottom*'s christening party. The next I heard of her was Fred's letter to the editor of *Motor Boating & Sailing* for April, 1973, part of a great debate on the subject of ferro-cement, in which he gave some details on what he had done and mentioned he had been out to Hawaii and back. Thinking this would be a good story on passage-making, I got in touch with him and made arrangements to inspect *Rock Bottom* and hear how his cruises had gone.

It turned out that Fred and Vera had done considerable cruising since the launch. Their first cruise was right up the coast to Vancouver, British Columbia, and return. And, like *Passagemaker,* on their return trip they ran into the worst gale they'd ever encountered, while passing Cape Mendocino. Fred said the waves were 35 feet high. He ran off before them under bare poles, towing warps at speeds from five to ten knots—and suffered no damage.

In 1972, they made a passage to Hawaii and return. The trip out with a crew of six was routine, taking only 11 and a half days, but the trip back was really interesting. Feeling somewhat pressed for time, Fred decided the quickest return route would be a great circle course direct to San Francisco. And they made it, in 17 days, straight against the Trades!

I discussed this route with Fred. Sitting in the comfortable kitchen of his house on the ranch, with charts and plans spread out on the table, it was easy to forget what it must have been like out there, pounding into the seas day after day. We had done the same thing in *Passagemaker* for three days going north around Cape Mendocino, and for five days in *Mona Mona*. But 17!

"Actually," said Fred, "it was only fifteen. The last two days we were able to make good speed with a reaching wind."

Well, that certainly was a help!

Fred, of course, was well aware of the problem of bucking the wind. On the other hand, he and his navigator felt they did not have sufficient data on range when bucking into winds of varying velocities to estimate whether they

PHOTO 11-4. The bow section of *Rock Bottom*, showing her pipe frame in place. (Lagier photo.)

PHOTO 11-5. The panel of *Rock Bottom*'s layup made by Fred Lagier for the author.

PHOTO 11-6. *Rock Bottom*'s hull with first layers of mesh on. Note the fairness of the hull and the precast keel in place. (Lagier photo.)

could afford to go straight north from Hawaii for any appreciable distance before turning east. Another concern was that the center of the Pacific High was being reported 1300 miles due north of Honolulu, some distance more to

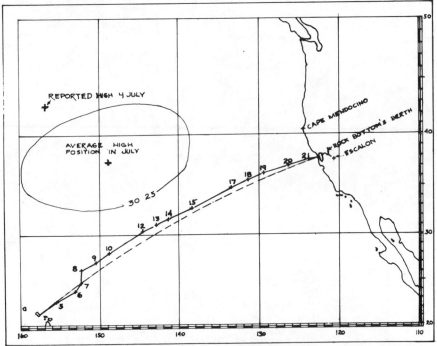

FIG. 11-7. A tracing of *Rock Bottom*'s route home from the Hawaiian Islands to California in July 1972. Note normal and unusual position of the Pacific High during the passage. The dashed line is the great circle route.

the north and west than normal, which would compound their problem. They figured going into it would take 17 days. It actually took 17 and a half, a remarkably close estimate.

So they lashed three drums of fuel on deck and on July 4 away they went. The extra fuel proved unnecessary. The normal tankage was 530 gallons for the Ford four-cylinder diesel. It is a bit difficult to calculate the fuel consumption as Fred traveled for some 260 miles in the Delta region before refueling, when the total used from Honolulu was 483 gallons.

It was a remarkable feat—the only time I have heard of a small boat that accomplished it. Others have tried it but had to turn back in defeat. This crew of five stuck it out, and the vessel performed flawlessly. However, I don't think any of them want to repeat the trip!

We spent several hours trying to figure out whether a more north-going tactic would have worked better. *Rock Bottom* was equipped only with VHF radio and consequently was unable to get any detailed weather reports for the areas they were in. But hindsight, in the form of the actual weather maps for the period, reveal an extraordinarily active High center. It *was* 1300 miles north of Hawaii on July 4 when they started, with winds of 25 knots being reported along the course. But the High center then began to move rapidly southeast until on July 11 it was at the position Latitude 33° North; Longitude 142° West, with very unsettled weather north of the center. *Rock Bottom* was then about 300 miles to the southwest and must have gotten some respite from the winds, although they would still be from ahead.

If the high had stayed put, they would have been in clover, but it didn't. The map for July 15 shows the center had retreated far to the north, a most unusual position. The way this high-pressure circulation can be accelerated by the "thermal low" of the California interior, in the manner that produces gales off Cape Mendocino in the summer, is shown on this map, with ships reporting winds of 30 to 40 knots. Hard times again for *Rock Bottom*!

Four days later on July 19 the worst of their ordeal was over. Although the High center was still far north and of extraordinary strength, with a barometric reading of 30.7 inches, they had "turned the corner" by finally reaching the area where the winds would become more and more abeam until, in the final stretch past the Farallon Islands and under the Golden Gate Bridge, they would be on the quarter. Inside, the 80-mile run up the Bay and through the Sacramento River delta to *Rock Bottom*'s mooring must have been a pure delight.

It is apparent that the weather was far from normal for that time of year. The Pacific High simply doesn't have any business being way up there in the Gulf of Alaska.

It looks, with hindsight, as if Fred's tactics paid off. If he had gone on a more northerly course to begin with, he might have had a few days of better weather around July 11. But he would have run into stronger winds from ahead on July 15 when the High was north of him.

On a time-and-distance basis, *Rock Bottom* made the trip at an average speed of five knots, which is S/L 0.82 for her. The more northerly track is about 2500 miles. If she had managed to do this at S/L 1.1 the trip would have been 15 and a half days, and presumably less wearing on ship and crew. The usual tactic is to go north, holding as much easting as possible until you can motor east in calm or near-calm weather, heading toward a point north of San Francisco until the wind comes from the north or northwest. A sailing vessels is then home free. This is the virtue of having extended range, even in a full sail vessel. The yacht mentioned in Chapter 3, which on its waterline should have made Hawaii-California in 16 days under power, but took 70, sailed too far north or had the High move down over it. It had neither the power nor the fuel to get out of it, and stayed in one spot or near it for weeks on end.

A rough range estimate for *Rock Bottom* gives her a range in smooth water of about 2500 miles at S/L 1.1. So even under "normal" conditions on a passage this long she would be close to her fuel limit. But with her sail to fall back on, she could have power-sailed north, and then powered east to about Longitude 140° West where beam winds would do the rest.

But the weather was not normal. They only got about two days of reaching winds instead of the expected five or six. The weather maps used for this analysis and also those for *Mona Mona* were those of the "Northern Hemisphere Chart," that show both the Atlantic and Pacific. It is interesting to note that if

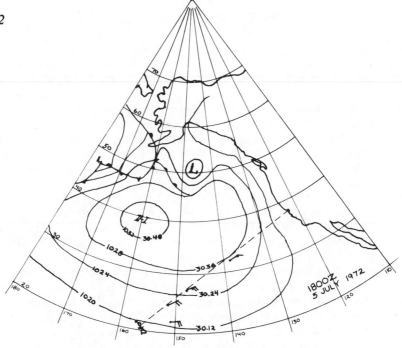

FIG. 11-8.   Tracing, Weather Chart: July 5, 1972.

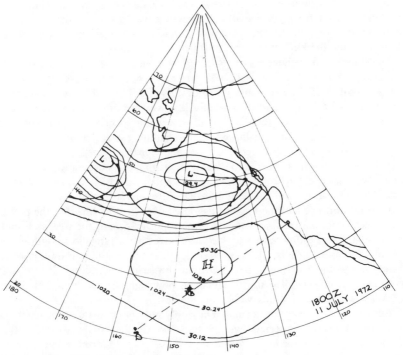

FIG. 11-9.   Tracing, Weather Chart: July 11, 1972.

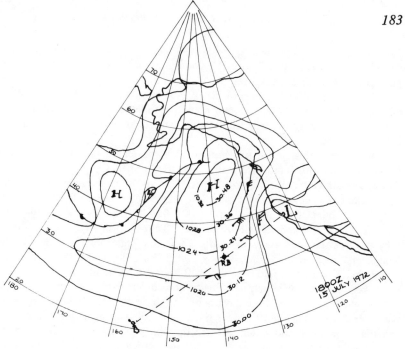

FIG. 11-10. Tracing, Weather Chart: July 15, 1972.

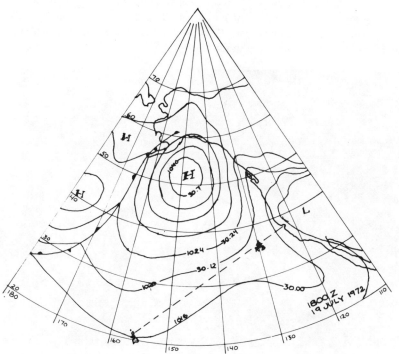

FIG. 11-11. Tracing, Weather Chart: July 19, 1972.

Fred had made his trip when *Mona Mona* made hers, or vice versa, both vessels would have experienced "normal" conditions and would have made their passages with ease. Such is life!

In 1973, Fred and Vera took *Rock Bottom* down to the Gulf of California and return. In La Paz, Mexico, their crew had to leave, so the two of them came home alone, making the trip from Cabo San Lucas to San Francisco in seven days underway.

We kicked this return trip around at some length because of its bearing on cruising by "man-and-wife teams" as discussed in Chapter 9. What makes this cruise difficult is the way all the traffic—and there is a lot of it—concentrates along the coast, making an alert watch a necessity. Fred stood watch during the hours of darkness—2100 to 0500, 1100 to 1700. Vera stood watch from 0500 to 1100 and from 1700 to 2100. That's a pretty rugged schedule, but they did not stay underway too long. Their first leg from Cabo San Lucas to Magdalena Bay took 28 hours. They rested there 20 hours, then went to Ensenada in 55 hours and laid over there 40 hours. Then eight hours to San Diego, a layover there of 16 hours, and finally nonstop to San Francisco in 74 hours.

Except for the last three days, with rough going from Point Conception to San Francisco (as it almost always is), this is not too much time underway for the effects of watch and watch to catch up with you. On the last leg, there were several suitable harbors available if it had seemed desirable to stop. So they obviously had the job well in hand since they kept going.

Their elapsed time was 10 days. This was an excellent performance of a cruise notorious in California for its potentially difficult fight against prevailing winds. Altogether the Lagiers and *Rock Bottom* are quite a team. I am sure we will hear more of their cruising in the future.

PHOTO 11-12. Fred and Vera Lagier aboard *Rock Bottom.*

12

Voyage Planning

Voyage-planning is a very large subject, one that space limitations will not allow us to cover fully in this book. It consists largely of absorbing the experience of others and applying it to your own prospective voyages. *Sailing Directions* and *Pilot Charts* are pure experience distilled over hundreds of years, for example. All books on cruising, even if under sail, will have bits and pieces of what to do and what not to do.

But the bible for this sort of thing is without doubt Eric Hiscock's *Voyaging Under Sail*. In it the Dean of Circumnavigators has set down the essentials of the business in clear and concise form. As a departure for more detailed planning, it is invaluable, and I strongly recommend it as part of any serious planner's library.

In addition to the type of file recommended later, the planner should be aware of the specialized information available from The Seven Seas Cruising Association, Box 1215, Venice, California, 90201. This unique organization's members are all live-aboard, cruising sail skippers, and to become a member one must meet those criteria. When the group was formed in 1952 the primary purpose was to exchange cruising tips and information on ports, etc., which were circulated to the members in a monthly bulletin. Over the years, the original mimeographed sheet has expanded to a monthly pamphlet of 20 pages or so. To meet the increased cost, the SSCA allows non-members to subscribe to the bulletins. This has been so successful, the subscribers now outnumber the members, and the Association is actively seeking information from subscribers as well as from its members. In effect, it is a pooling of experience that can only improve as more people become involved. Back issues of each full year are available from 1957 on. Write for current subscription price.

One of the first things I did when planning a west-to-east crossing of the Pacific was to get a complete file of these bulletins. They were a tremendous help and well worth the cost.

While much planning is common to both sail and power, the two types do differ in certain respects. And it was to these differences that I addressed myself in writing an article on voyage-planning, using a passage across the Atlantic as a guide. This article appeared in *Boating* in May, 1970, entitled "Passagemaker

Across the Atlantic." Now, some years later with more cruising under my belt, I find myself hard put to add anything of value to what I said then. Here it is:

PLANNING THE OCEAN PASSAGE

The growing interest in long voyages by seagoing motorboats of modest size is soundly based on the advantages a power-approach has over the more conventional sailing cruiser. Many of the problems in planning long voyages are common to both types, of course. Provisioning and medical, for instance, would be the same, also navigation. But the seagoing motorboat differs from the sailing cruiser in several major respects that must be considered separately. Taking our voyage across the Atlantic in the summer of 1969 as an example, let us see how the planning was done—and how it worked out.

After some 50,000 miles of deep water cruising in the 50-foot seagoing motorboat *Passagemaker,* I sold her to Roger Bury of Westport, Connecticut. Roger and his wife, Marion, had made a passage from Hawaii to Seattle with us and remained ever after interested in the whole concept of long voyages under power. I agreed at the time to help him take *Passagemaker* across the Atlantic to Scandinavia and complete his checkout of problems faced by the captain of such a vessel.

Here are some extracts from our correspondence on the approaching cruise:

(September 1968) "Dear Bob: I think it is time we started planning next summer's trip to Europe. I'd like your comments on the following: (*three pages of topics*)."

"Dear Roger: You're right, September is not too soon to start planning. When we went East to Expo in Montreal in '67, I didn't decide to go until January and when we left in May we still had annoying gaps in our planning. Here is what I think should be done: (*five pages of suggestions*). In view of the fact you have a secretary, I hope you can handle the correspondence!"

To BBC, London: "Gentlemen: We are interested in having the frequencies and times of your weather broadcasts for our forthcoming. . . ."

"Dear Al: In view of your interest in *Passagemaker,* I wonder if you and Kitty would care to join. . . ."

"Dear Roger: Your spares list is okay. But I think it needs a few additions. If the oil-cooler fails you will need a piece of copper pipe with a 90° elbow the same length as. . . ."

And so on and so on, until the lists, letters, and printed information filled two thick ring binders. Not a day passed on the voyage that these files weren't consulted for something, from the location of a spare part to the address of the next mail drop. In the end, nine months of planning proved to be none too much for our cruise!

Looking over the problems involved in voyage-planning, we find three areas in which the difference between the motor and the sailing approach to cruising is most apparent. These are: Track Selection, Mechanical Spares and Repair, and Watch-Standing/Crewing.

TRACK SELECTION

The natural habitat of the seagoing motorboat is the calm areas of the oceans. Unlike the sailing cruiser—which avoids calms as much as she can—the motorboat regards a calm day as a jewel, a day she can make her cruising speed unhindered by wind or wave. When wind cannot be avoided, she will of course seek reaching and running winds, as does the sailing cruiser. Going to windward under power in the open ocean is a frustrating exercise at best. In certain areas, such as the fully developed monsoon of the Indian Ocean, it would be impossible. In the Trades, it is possible but hardly worth the effort when your range under power enables you to get out of the Trades into areas of lighter winds.

The literature on small-boat voyaging is concerned primarily with sail. Thus what might be called the "standard tracks" for sailing vessels making worldwide cruises are well known. What is not generally appreciated is how much of the ocean has calms and light winds for the powerboat to exploit. The Azores High, the Pacific High, and the Doldrums are conspicuous examples.

What can be done is shown by past experience in *Passagemaker*. On a voyage from Honolulu to Seattle, we spent six of 12 days in glassy calm or light airs. On 10 out of 12 days, Azores to Bermuda, we had very light conditions with favorable winds. On a crossing of the Indian Ocean at the change of the monsoon, seven of 14 days were ideal for a motorboat. There are other areas waiting to be tried. For instance, it would be possible to cross the Atlantic westward with light airs and no fear of hurricanes any time of the year between Latitude 6° North and the Equator. Another route that has intrigued me since wartime service in the area, is Singapore to Hawaii via Rabaul and Canton Islands. If you were a good enough navigator to stay in the Equatorial Counter Current, you would have lots of motorboat weather plus a "free" boost of some 25 miles a day from current.

The tools for studying this matter are the wind and weather charts of the oceans, called *Pilot Charts,* plus a text on cyclonic storms, such as *Bowditch.* They will repay months of study, providing not only tracks but proper starting dates for various areas, a most important part of planning. In addition, the serious student of voyaging will maintain a file of magazine articles on cruising from the yachting press, tourist bureau literature, and the like, for the important bits of information they contain. For instance, in a British magazine bought in Bermuda, we found for the first time that yachts *do* moor to the quay wall at Horta in the Azores.

The track chosen must be within the capabilities of the vessel. The heavy displacement motorboat operates under conditions where slight changes in speed make large differences in fuel consumption. The practical speed/length ratio (speed in knots divided by the square root of the waterline length) is 1.1 to 1.2. On *Passagemaker* (46-foot waterline) this speed range is from 7.5 to 8.2 knots. We planned on the basis of 1000 miles a week, to allow for possible adverse weather, and always did better than this. An assured range of 2400 miles at S/L ratio of 1.2 means ample fuel for the longest passages. If fuel runs low, speed can be dropped to a ratio of 1.0 to give you about 50 per cent more range on what is left. If the wind comes ahead, as it is certain to do on a voyage from the East Coast to California, the only thing to do is go slow until green water stops coming over the bow, and wait it out. We found that even with a 30-knot wind we still kept forging ahead and that fuel consumption was negligible.

Applying theory to the proposed voyage worked out like this. The objective was to take *Passagemaker* to Europe with sufficient time available to cruise in Scandinavia that summer. The pilot charts show that the most settled weather in the North Atlantic is late June and July, but such a late start would seriously restrict the opportunities for further cruising overseas. We finally determined, all things considered, that leaving the East Coast on June 1 was a pretty fair compromise, particularly since we would have to spend a week in Bermuda for personal matters.

Passagemaker carries enough fuel to make a run from Newport, Rhode Island, to Ireland, direct. But this track was rejected for several reasons. Not only was the weather better farther south, but also we have found that, considering the type of crew used (a matter discussed more fully later), it is best to break up a voyage into several stages whenever possible, even if it does take longer. The final decision, then, was to leave *Passagemaker*'s yard in Virginia in late May and start down the Intracoastal Waterway toward Charleston. The purpose was twofold: Before going to sea, to get south of Hatteras to an area where the winds should be lighter and more likely to be favorable, and to give the boat a shaking down before departure in an area where anything that needed attention could be taken in hand. On June 1 we would leave for Bermuda. From Bermuda, we would steer a rhumb line for Horta in the Azores, deviating from it north or south as necessary to spend as much time as possible in the center of the Azores High. From Horta to Ireland, we would venture into a region influenced by low-pressure areas, resulting in winds predominantly from the west. By standing west of the rhumb line when the weather was good and running off to the eastward when it was bad, we hoped to finish off this leg with reasonable aplomb.

How did it work out?

Well, it worked out fine. In fact, it worked out better than we had reason to expect. We actually left one day early, on May 31 from Cape Fear, North Carolina. Three of our four days to Bermuda were flat calm. Only the last day was marred by the wind coming in from the southeast, somewhat to our surprise, with a velocity sufficient to cause us to slow to 5.5 knots for some hours.

From Bermuda to Horta, the Azores High was in great shape. We got into it shortly after leaving and basked under clear sunny skies with light winds or calm for nine of the 10 and a half days on the 1850-mile leg to Horta. At the end, the wind gradually came in from the northwest, indicating that we had reached the High's eastern limits. Only in the last six hours before arrival did it become strong enough to suggest using the whole stabilizing gear. It was the best example of the virtues of seeking out the calm areas of the oceans that *Passagemaker* has produced to date, a most enjoyable cruise.

We left Horta on June 25. Our trepidation over the last leg, to Ireland, was wasted. Although it was completely overcast the whole way, with some rain and

PHOTO 12-1. Passagemaker leaving Monterey, California, for her passage to Hawaii, with a crew of two men and four women.

fog, the winds remained light and in the main favorable. The passage ended with a bit of excitement at 0130 on July 2 when we sighted Fastnet Light through thick fog. As we coasted the green shores of the Emerald Isle to Cork, we were able to look back on a most successful track selection and timing.

MECHANICAL SPARES AND REPAIR

Unlike the sailing cruiser, where you often observe shocking neglect of the auxiliary power, the main engine of a seagoing powerboat is the heart of the ship and must be treated with the respect it deserves. Reliance on one's own resources is fundamental to offshore work. In particular, there must be alternatives for all vital systems. In the case of the main propulsion, this can be provided in various ways. It can be a sailing rig (*Passagemaker*); twin engines on twin shafts (*Jim Hawkins*); twin engines on a single shaft (Romsdal trawlers); single shaft with auxiliary drive (*Eventide*). There is only one long-range cruiser known to me that has actually returned to port under alternate power. Others have had trouble but have been able to reach port for repairs with their main engines functioning in one way or another.

After the provision of alternative drive, what other spares and repair equipment should be provided? I have often been asked this question by persons hoping to profit from my experience. My answers may not have helped very much. The truth is, of the large stock of spares on board *Passagemaker* very few were used except in the course of routine maintenance. But combining my experience with that of other owners and maintenance men shows a pattern worth thinking about:

1. Feed the engine absolutely clean fuel. *Passagemaker* had three filters ahead of the engine. A motorboat that circled the world had no less than

five. Certainly the single filter supplied with an engine is not enough.

2. The basic block of the diesel is very reliable. It is the equipment external to the engine that causes trouble. The only satisfactory way to handle trouble inside the block is, apparently, to have duplicate engines. It would be bad luck indeed if one of them could not be kept going by using parts from both.

3. An outstanding culprit is the heat-exchanger. Careful provision for alternative sources of this vital service must be made.

4. Rubber rotor pumps should be viewed with suspicion and extensive spares provided.

5. There doesn't appear to be a satisfactory wet exhaust system that will stand up under thousands of hours of running without replacement. This is particularly true of the Monel muffler. At the conclusion of her present trip, *Passagemaker* is in need of her fourth. However, this area responds well to emergency repair with epoxy compounds.

6. Belts must be constantly checked for condition, tension, and alignment. Numerous spares of correct sizes must be provided.

7. Electric tools can be vital. In particular, a small drill press has been most useful.

8. The brushes and commutators of electric equipment should be the subject of routine maintenance and not ignored until they cause trouble.

9. Be prepared as well as possible for the unexpected because it is bound to happen. Our worst trouble of the cruise happened this way. The fuel high-pressure line to No. 5 cylinder fractured at the injector one morning. Since we had a spare set of fuel lines on board, we replaced No. 5 and went on our way. Much to our horror, 24 hours later the replacement fractured in *exactly the same place,* a most astonishing occurrence. Finally, after much trial and error, we managed to bend the remnant of one of the lines so it bridged the space from pump to injector fairly well, and rein-stalled it using spare "olives" we had on board. This had to be redone several times, the last time 13 hours out of Cork. But we did enter port with all six cylinders firing merrily.

10. Take a jaundiced view of any items of equipment for which the only repair instructions are: "If it does not work, return it to our nearest service station." This is cold comfort when the nearest land is 1000 miles away. The light, compact, streamlined equipment designed for weekend boating has no place in the long-range cruiser if it is possible to find something heavier, simpler, and more fixable. This applies particularly to such items as reverse-reduction gears, horn and refrigerator compressors, steering gears, and autopilots. Although our hydraulic reverse gear has performed perfectly to date, I have always worried that there is no way to get into it and jam it ahead for "come home" ability. (There *are* gears with this facility). At any rate my policy has been not to hesitate to break into anything. If it isn't working, you can't make it worse by operating on it.

As it turned out we had an unusual amount of mechanical trouble. Much of this was in convenience features that had been added to the boat in the spring and not had a proper shaking down. In the end, we managed to fix everything so it functioned well enough for us to keep going. We replaced a broken exhaust valve in the generator, fixed the fuel lines as previously mentioned, stopped an oil leak by replacing a defective gasket, redesigned and rebuilt the mounting of the newly installed 40 amp alternator. We left port with the SeaStill not working and managed by trial and error to adapt it to *Passagemaker*'s rather peculiar cooling system.

We replaced a defective SeaStill control panel with a simple manual on-off switch, reworked the belting of its pumps, and made enough water to more than satisfy our needs. We gave the autopilot a complete overhaul when, understandably enough, it refused duty after someone spilled a glass of beer into it. We did a lot of other things, too. In fact, the "daily crisis" became something of a joke. The log shows the main engine was stopped for one reason or another during nine of the 21 days underway. But we kept going and made our ETAs. That's the important thing. And Roger Bury surely got a good checkout in coping with mechanical trouble.

WATCH–STANDING/CREWING

It is in the type of crew required and the way watches are stood that we find the greatest contrast between the seagoing motorboat and the sailing cruiser. The ideal crew for an extended sailing voyage would all be experienced in sail, young enough and rugged enough not to mind months of standing watch-and-watch, steering in an open spray-drenched cockpit, setting and taking in sail in the middle of the night. It is an activity for youth, or for those older men and selected women to whom it has become a way of life over a period of years. I know whereof I speak; I have done my time on the end of a bowsprit muzzling a jib on a black night in the middle of a squall, and enjoyed every minute of it. But even the experienced sailor arrives at a time when this sort of thing loses its appeal. And for many, the long passage under sail is effectively barred, because they have come to their love of the sea late in life or they have wives and families who do not share their enthusiasm.

This is where the seagoing motorboat comes in. Stabilized against rolling —that curse of the ordinary motorboat—she steams along in the calmest weather she can find at a rate that exceeds the average possible for a much larger sailing vessel. With the autopilot performing all the work, her single watch-stander is essentially a lookout. For this, no experience is necessary, because the only duty, until the watch-stander is qualified, is to call the captain when sighting *anything*. Standing less than one watch in three, everyone gets more rest than he can use. This type of voyaging might be called "family cruising" for lack of a better description. That is, it is suitable for women, and for interested if inexperienced persons in general, as well as for the experienced yachtsman.

Some 30 people have made long voyages in *Passagemaker*. They all liked her. But it is notable that among her most enthusiastic admirers are six women who first ventured to sea aboard her. The age of the crew has ranged from 13 to 75, the experience level from veteran ocean racers like Norrie Hoyt (and I think we almost converted *him!*), to complete tyros. They all did well.

PHOTO 12-2. Al Willis works on a new alternator mounting in *Passagemaker's* cockpit "shop" which fitted conveniently on the after deck.

Another advantage of the power voyage is that the time under way can be predicted within narrow limits, making it possible to use crew who must know when they will get back home.

A proper passage-making vessel is designed so that each member of the crew has his own permanent bunk. Convertible spaces are not allowed. For a 50-footer, this effectively limits the crew to six. In some ways, five is better. We have experimented extensively with various systems of watches in *Passagemaker* without coming to any consensus on which is best. Personally, I dislike automatically consigning women to galley duties and do prefer to give them a chance to stand watches and share the cooking. But my wife, who is a real expert in the galley, perfers to be permanent cook.

The way watches were stood on our trip with a crew of six seemed acceptable to all and can be considered typical:

Watch:	0000–0400	0400–0800	0800–1200	1200–1600	1600–2000	2000–2400
Day 1:	A	N	S	B	C	A
Day 2:	B	N	S	C	A	B
Day 3:	C	N	S	A	B	C
Day 4:	Repeats Day 1.					

"N" is the navigator, who stood the 0400–0800 watch every day because he had to be up for morning stars anyway. "S" stood for our two women. They cooked day on and day off. On the days they did not cook, they stood the

0800–1200 watch. This kept the watches dogged, and provided a lookout during the daily navigation and passage-making school for the men.

By following the fortunes of "A," you can see that the first day he stood two watches separated by 16 hours. The second and third days he stood one watch and then repeated. This is hardly working anyone to death. It is important that a watch list repeat itself; if it doesn't, things get so complicated nobody knows *when* he is on watch.

It's obvious that the problem of selecting a crew for our voyage was a bit different from manning an ocean racer for the sailing race to Ireland, which started about the same time. Of course one must be careful not to carry the use of inexperienced crew too far. Like the main engine alternative, when venturing far from shore there must be more than one person capable of taking charge and making port. In the end, we sailed with more talent—organizational, culinary, mechanical, and navigational—than had ever before put to sea in *Passagemaker.* Four of the six had previously made long cruises in her. Only one person qualified as novice.

So that's how our 1969 cruise across the Atlantic was planned and how it turned out. I often thought during those perfect days in the Azores High, lying in the sun or taking our meals on deck, what a pity it was there were not a dozen boats along with us experiencing the adventure of an Atlantic crossing under such ideal conditions. Now *Passagemaker* is in position to enjoy two years of cruising in Northern Europe and the Mediterranean. And then she will come chugging home again.

PHOTO 12-3. *Passagemaker,* well stocked for her Atlantic passage. What do you need besides soft drinks, beer, and bananas? We always carried an oversupply of canned beer. It was considered our emergency water supply. Canned beer is cheaper and keeps better than canned water. Besides, it improves the morale.

13

Cruising in Europe

AUTHOR'S NOTE: This chapter originally appeared in Boating *for May, 1971, and I am indebted to the editors for permission to reprint it here. It does give the basis of cruising in Europe, and in the canals of France. And nothing I have learned since indicates the need for any changes.*

The world being what it is, I cannot guarantee that all the article says will still be correct at whatever future date you may cruise in the fascinating areas across the Atlantic. The careful planner will make certain of the facts pertaining to canal regulations, customs, fuel, electricity, and water before leaving, by referring to the latest information available from the sources shown in the bibliography.

When Passagemaker *and her stout crew arrived in Greece direct from Singapore, we were certainly a fresh-caught bunch of innocents. And it would have been nice then to know what is in this article. But by greeting everyone with a smile, doing what we were told, and in case of doubt, exhibiting an eager but uncomprehending willingness to cooperate if somebody would only explain, we had a ball—and no trouble to speak of.*

My discussion of voyage-planning for seagoing motorboats in *Boating,* May, 1970, used for its example a crossing of the Atlantic to cruise in Europe. This was done deliberately. For I do find the greatest interest of the long-range cruising fraternity is in yachts capable of spanning the Atlantic to sample the fascinating waters that stretch from Scandinavia to Greece and Turkey. In the past, such expeditions have been largely the domain of the sailing cruiser. But a growing number of owner-operated motorboats of modest size have made this trip and blazed a trail for others to follow. The voyage of *Passagemaker* showed how such an Atlantic crossing should be done.

So, once you decide to join this group of ocean-crossing motorboaters, are there any special considerations peculiar to the European area that will affect your boat's design and equipment? The answer to this question is, "Yes." There is one major point and several minor ones.

First, let's tackle the minor problems. To start with, in the Mediterranean and to some extent in other areas, you "Mediterranean moor" routinely. To "Med moor" means an anchor is dropped ahead and the stern backed into and secured to the quay wall. This is great sport, especially with a beam wind and a single-screw vessel. The other yachtsmen, already secured, will sit smugly on deck and criticize your technique. After you are safely moored you will find yourself quite willing to join them and doing likewise to the next newcomer.

Without telling you how to handle your vessel, a few pointers may be useful. Obviously, a good view of the stern from the pilothouse should be designed-in, if possible. If this is not possible, a well-trained member of the crew, able to judge distances and communicate with the skipper, will have to do. This is how we did it on *Passagemaker* and it worked very well—after a few early disasters.

Large cleats astern with a good lead aft are essential (the hardware on most American motorboats is shockingly inadequate). And you should provide lengths of chain shackled to your mooring lines to take the chafe from the rough sea walls.

After you are moored, your next problem is to get ashore. Some people use a plank, or launch the dinghy and pull themselves back and forth. But we soon found this was inadequate for handling stores and visitors. What is required is a real gangway, complete with lifelines, a swivel fitting on the stern, and small wheels on the dock end to allow for the boat's movement. A design about 12 feet long is good.

And, finally, it wouldn't hurt to practice a few Med Moors!

While there are a growing number of marinas abroad that approach U.S. standards, in general the facilities are adapted to commercial work, especially in their extensive inland waterways. A really big, strong guard rail is a necessity and will save you much worry about your topsides. The rail provided on most American-built motorboats is little more than a bad joke.

Electricity is available to some extent. But the multiplicity of voltages and cycles, coupled with a complete lack of standardization of connections, makes it simpler for the vessel to be capable of supplying all its own needs on a continuing basis. An exception to this would be wintering over. In our winter berth, in Greece we ran in a 220V line for heat and light and managed to find a 3000 watt 220/110-transformer that enabled us to use our electric tools during overhaul.

Water is always a problem. Not only is it suspect in some areas, but it seemed to us there were not two faucets the same size on the whole continent. We got around this by using clamps on various sizes of hose feeding into 150 feet of lightweight hose, a length that proved none too long.

A relatively minor problem that caused us some trouble: Customs will sometimes want to seal up any "bonded stores" (liquor and cigarettes) that exceed their rules. The first time this happened to us, the suitable place I could find was a big locker in the stern. It wasn't until the liquor was in and sealed that I realized some tools and spares which we had badly needed were also in the locker. It took me several hours to figure out how to jimmy the locker and get the gear out without breaking the seal—but I finally managed it! *Passagemaker* now has two lockers devoted exclusively to bonded stores.

Now for the major question: Should your vessel be capable of entering the inland waterways of Europe? More specifically, because of the French canals' smaller size, should your vessel be capable of entering them? There is a good deal to be said on this point.

In contrast to the United States, Europe is literally laced with busy inland waterways which carry a large part of its commerce. They form a magnificent cruising ground in themselves. I certainly remember warmly the impressive scenery of the Caledonian Canal across Scotland, the Gota that crosses Sweden, the myriad canals of Holland, the fabled gorges of the Rhine. All of these have passed under *Passagemaker*'s keel. But it is the canals of France, which provide a link from the North Sea to the Mediterranean, that have at once the greatest charm and the greatest utility. A compelling argument for being able to traverse this network is that it enables you to cruise in Scandinavia and then retreat for the winter to the Mediterranean later than would be sensible if you had to go down the North Sea and across the Bay of Biscay to Gibraltar. Many yachts use this route every year in both directions.

Useful as such a route can be, we also found from our own experience that canal-cruising has such charm that we would like to do a whole season of it. So, in my family, the answer to this question of being able to cruise the French canals is Yes! It is interesting to note, however, that among my clients the vote is about 50-50. Designing-in a French-canal capability raises certain problems. If you don't desire to take them on, then any craft able to make the ocean crossing is well prepared for coastal cruising in Europe and for going into the larger canals. Let's discuss, then, the various pros and cons of being "French-canal-capable."

The French canals have the smallest limiting dimensions; clearance of these is critical for any vessel in which it is planned to travel through Europe. Length is not critical, it can be as great as 126 feet. But draft should be no more than five feet, beam over the guards, 16'4", and height above water, no more than 10'10". Can we meet these restrictions and still have the living room we need?

In designing a vessel capable of crossing the Atlantic under power, we find certain basics. First, these vessels are of such a size and cost that they don't make much sense unless they are used a greater part of the year. My own feeling on length is that 46 feet is about the minimum, with 50 feet a good comfortable size. With such lengths, the limits on beam and draft match well with the usual vessel proportions, and the canal capability looks attractive.

But it is the height that causes trouble. In a boat of fairly short fixed length, trying to provide excellent living space depends largely on the ability to double-deck. In the size we are talking about, it is impossible to have fixed double-decking and still go through the canals with a vessel properly shaped for ability at sea. But there is a way to lick this problem, at least in part.

The solution comprises two steps. First, we arrange the pilothouse so it can be *broken down* for the canal passage. And second, we go to a full-width cabin for the galley-lounge area. Figs. 13-1, 13-2 and 13-3 are sketches of a 46-footer with this arrangement. The 13½ x 14½ foot galley-lounge area provides 196 square feet of floor space for any arrangement you may want. The owner's cabin is 15 feet long in the full-width stern. And the pilothouse breaks down at the level of the forward cabin, the top is stowed forward on deck, and the sides in a rack on the stern. This isn't as difficult as it may sound. The cabin is put together with bolts instead of screws. A tent can be provided for the night. And, of course, the installations in the pilothouse should be treated as if they were on a flying bridge.

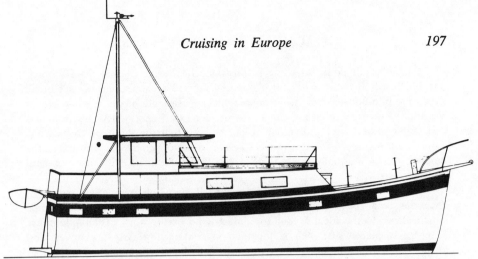

FIG. 13-1. Profile, Beebe Design 93, 46-ft. Canal Runner. Pilot house shown in normal position.

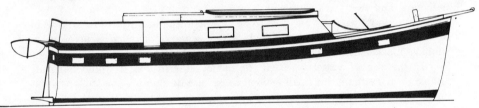

FIG. 13-2. Profile, Design 93, showing pilothouse demounted for canal work.

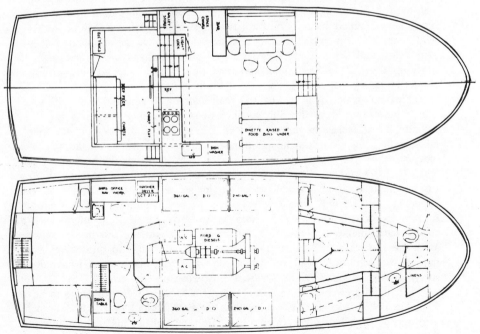

FIG. 13-3. Accommodation, Design 93.

The effect of double-decking is illustrated in the sketches of the 50-footer, for which a hull mold is now available. As Fig. 13-4 shows, she doesn't break down the pilothouse; there is no double-decking. In spite of her greater length, we find the owner's cabin must be much smaller (*see Fig. 13-5*). Whether this is acceptable is up to the individual. It can be seen that for this type to have the same room as the 46-footer she would have to be longer by the amount of the smaller model's double-decking, or a length of 53 feet, with its attendant greater costs.

But comparison by room alone doesn't tell the whole story. As a matter of fact, the canal-runners, due to the restrictions under which they labor, come much closer to the ideal layout for unrestricted ocean work. Their pilothouse is properly placed aft, their silhouette and center of gravity are lower, and their freeboard is higher. They are quite suitable for making a passage to northern Europe direct. So there is something to be said for both designs.

The choice must be a personal one, depending on the preference of the individual and the type of cruising he proposes to do. As I said, in my family there is no doubt we want our boat to be "French-capable." For those who want to explore this more fully, let me add a few remarks on what is involved in running the canals, a highly specialized nautical activity.

In the size of vessel we need for the ocean-crossing, it would be inadvisable to make the beam small enough to be sure of entering the locks without touching the sides, say about 13 feet. You might as well go to the maximum, to have a roomy hull, and just ease her through. Fenders cannot be used. The lock walls will just cut the lines. And, we found that if an air fender hits one wall hard, it can bounce you over against the opposite wall harder than the first hit. A heavy and well-shod guard rail is a must. Another advantage of the full-width boat is that once she is inside the lock she can't charge about. In fact, we found the small French locks easier to go through than wider ones, such as those on the Caledonian Canal, and used only a single spring line with the engine idling against it.

This may sound difficult but isn't really, after you get used to it. The solution to entering a lock with only an inch or two clearance each side is "inch-calling." This is used in tunnels as well. Here's the drill: An "outside man" takes station right outside the pilothouse next to you. As you head into the lock, he leans over the side until his eye is right in line with the wall of the lock. Then he glances down at the guard rail and makes an estimate of how far out he is leaning, and calls it off in inches. He can also tell if you are "opening" or "closing" with the lock wall. In the meantime, you concentrate on how the boat is moving and watch the wind on your bow pennant; even a slight breeze makes a perceptible difference when you are moving so slowly. With this inch-calling, it is surprising how often you will slip into a lock with the barest touch on the wall, or none at all. Of course, just after you have done several masterful jobs in a row—*wham!* But you can't win 'em all.

We had a crew of five on board *Passagemaker* and were fortunate to have available as "outside men" two who liked the exercise and spoke good French. The outside man has a very active life. After he finishes his inch-calling and the boat comes to a stop, he leaps up on the lock wall, drops the spring line on

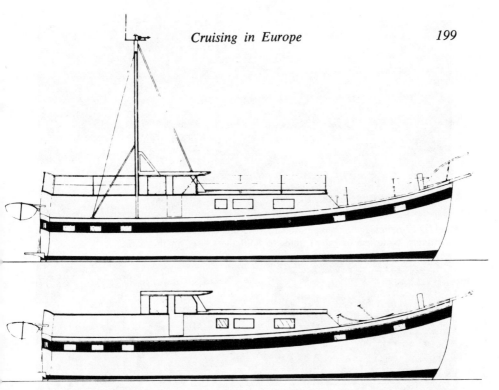

FIG. 13-4. Two Profile views, Beebe Design 92, 50-ft. Canal Runner. This design does not break down at the pilot house as there is no double-decking.

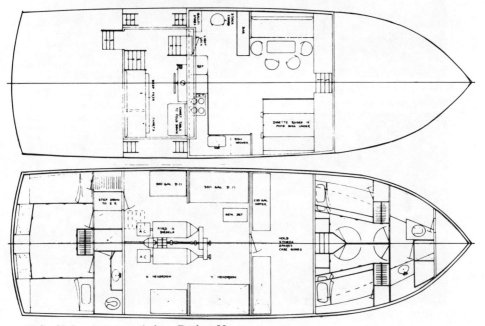

FIG. 13-5. Accommodation, Design 92.

PHOTO 13-6. *Passagemaker* moored for the night at 1200 feet elevation in the Voges Mountains. Note use of *quant* poles to hold the vessel off the bank.

PHOTO 13-7. *Passagemaker* in an "up" lock in France. Note the close fit. The "outside" man, on the port side, is Rob Poole, a Canadian medical student.

PHOTO 13-8. While passing through the French canals, *Passagemaker* often had friendly help, as from these two French boys, who "heaved with a will."

PHOTO 13-9. The author returning from a swim while at the Greek island of Hydra. Note the three types of gangways, on *Passagemaker* and on the vessels astern.

a bollard, runs to the gate opposite the lock operator and closes his half of the gate by winding on its crank. (The crew is always expected to help in locks.)

Then the outside man goes to the other end and helps open the paddle valves to let the water in or out. On board, in the meantime, your crew puts over a thin fender, *forward* on the side that has the spring line and *aft* on the other side. The pilot then goes ahead against the spring and the boat rests on these two fenders, sliding up the moss-covered lock wall easily. As the boat rises, the French-speaking outside man offers the locktender a cigarette and gossips about what's ahead and how the traffic is, sometimes gathering most valuable information. When the boat is up, he again goes to the side opposite the *éclusier* and opens his half of the gate. As the boat passes him, he swings on board, shouts, *"Bon jour,"* to the keeper, and prepares for the next lock, which may be only 100 yards away when you're going up and down hills. It's a high-speed operation, taking about four minutes when the crew is in the swing of things. Down locks are somewhat easier on everyone but the outside man.

When I called it a high-speed operation, I referred of course only to the passage through the locks; you should do this as rapidly as possible to cooperate with the waiting traffic. There's almost always someone waiting, either behind or ahead of you. The rest of the time your progress can only be called leisurely— delightfully so. The four-mile-an-hour speed limit gives you time to savor the countryside in a way that is impossible in any other means of locomotion. The ancient towns and churches, to say nothing of castles and forts, are a constant invitation to stop and explore. And, in fact, a trip planned with plenty of time to do this offers the most pleasure.

If your trip must be made quickly, as a "passage," it can still be fun, if a bit wearing. Working a full day everyday in the locks keeps all hands busy. We had to do this, passing from the Mediterranean to the North Sea via Strasbourg and the Rhine, in 22 days. With two days off in Lyons and two more in Strasbourg, we had 18 days underway, passing through 224 locks. This time could be cut several days by using the new canal from Nancy to Koblenz, but this would eliminate the Rhine gorges passage the highlight of that river.

If you have an objective to reach and want to keep going, it is a good idea to have some kind of land transportation on board. We bought a Solex motor-driven bicycle. At a likely spot the off-duty French speaker would roll this ashore as the boat sank below the level of the wall, and go shopping for delicious French bread and local wines and cheeses. He would then hunt us down four or five locks later and roll back on board.

Notice in the sketches of the boats rigged for canal-running that the life-lines have been removed. They are just a nuisance in canals. Tell your crew that if they fall overboard they can darn well swim ashore and run to the next lock in time to do their duty!

The lock-keepers quit for the day promptly at seven P.M. Whatever "pound," or water between locks you are in then, becomes your harbor for the night. About half the time, we found some place to lie alongside *something.* The rest of the time we had to tie to the bank, holding the ship off on *quants,* long poles that can be purchased along the canals. To use the *quants,* it is neces-sary to get a hand ashore. It is for this reason that, as shown in the sketches, a dinghy is carried over the stern, where it can be used with the mast down. In our case, we couldn't use the dinghy in this condition and bought a two-man rubber life raft which did the job well enough. If a barge is in the pound with you, its crew will invariably be agreeable to your tying alongside. We made some very pleasant acquaintances this way.

All in all, it was a most interesting experience and we would like to go back. The canals reveal a different France from the one seen by the ordinary tourist! They are off the beaten track and occupied by a distinct breed of people who spend their entire lives on the waterways. Without exception we found the canal people charming. When one lock tender found we had a woman on board, he went to his garden and picked flowers for her. My wife, Linford, be-came thoroughly enchanted with the French canals. And I am sure you will, too.

PHOTO 13-10. With the "outside" man standing on the starboard midship deck "inch-calling" for the helmsman, *Passagemaker* slides through a three-mile unlighted tunnel in France. Photo taken by flash arrangement devised by Ralph Arndt.

14

Round the World Passagemaking

The ultimate voyage for any vessel is around the world. But in this chapter we will also consider under this heading the problems of long voyages in general, voyages of some months that are clearly more ambitious than a trip say, from New York to the Caribbean.

At the very beginning of this book I said, ". . . a very good case could be made for the power-approach over sail for all long voyages." Here is that case. First, there are people who, for various reasons—mostly physical—cannot make long sailing voyages. Such a group is cited in my remarks on crewing in Chapter 12, Voyage Planning. This group could certainly use the power-approach to their advantage. Another group, small but likely to grow, might also find the power-approach the ideal solution to their long-distance voyaging ambitions. This group consists of people, by no means get-away-from-it-all types, who would like to make a world voyage in their own boats if the time away from home and work could be limited to a reasonable span. The period of two years is often mentioned as the goal in cruise books; this seems reasonable enough. But many who have tried it under sail didn't make it in that time; or, if they did, wore themselves out in the attempt.

In contrast, if Suez were open, a vessel with an assured speed of 7.5 knots could circle the world in six and a half months steaming time. This leaves 70 per cent of the two years for local cruising and enjoying the ports along the way. When this time-saving is combined with the crew arriving in port fresh and ready to go again, as described in Chapter 6, a power voyage should be a relaxed and enjoyable experience.

To point this up, let's turn to Hiscock's *Voyaging Under Sail* and, in its tabular record of voyages, follow a vessel that is listed almost all the way around. In fact, it was reading Hiscock and using a slide rule on his list of passages that first convinced me it was possible to do better. His book abounds in hints that more range under power would be desirable in a world-voyaging boat, though I doubt if he, himself, would ever adopt the full power approach. His leading design example, for instance, is *Beyond*, a 41-foot cutter which had a range under power of 1500 miles, autopilot, and covered steering station which did a "very workmanlike circumnavigation in two years."

Another example was *Omoo*, a 45-foot ketch with a waterline of 37 feet, which would give 6.7 knots at an S/L of 1.1. Her listed voyages actually show speeds from a high of 4.9 knots for the run from the Canaries to Barbados, to a low of 3.46 knots, in the Indian Ocean from the Keeling Cocos Islands to

Mauritius. The total time for the nine listed voyages, (about 70 per cent of the distance around), is 215 days. If she had averaged a speed/length ratio of 1.1, as *Passagemaker* proved was possible, she would have made these voyages in 126 days, leaving 89 days—almost three months!—that could have been spent in port or exploring other places. If the whole voyage was made at these averages, the extra time available would be a bit over four months. As cruising essentially is done to enjoy the ports, the people, and the scenery of the places you visit, such a gain in time is impressive. And this time advantage persists, in proportion, on less ambitious voyages, of course. The question is: How valuable is this advantage to individuals?

To a young crew in a well-found sailing vessel with no particular deadline to meet, it would seem to have *no* advantages. However, even here a couple of items need consideration. First, as John Samson noted in his book, *A New Way of Life,* which is dedicated to such people, going under power might very well turn out to be cheaper. Food cost at sea, where you consume expensive canned and prepared foods until you can get the cheaper native foods found in ports can be a big item. Second, the care and upkeep of a sailing rig is a constant expense, a heavy cost such as a blown-out sail always possible.

For the "man-and-wife teams" referred to in Chapter 9, the appeal of the power-approach would vary depending on their devotion to and experience in sail. It appears, from what little data there is on this free-wandering mass of individuals, that many of them are interested in voyaging for a definite period before moving ashore. They, too, could extend their range with power.

It is interesting to speculate on the best routes for world-girdling power passages. Going west, it appears the departure schedules and tracks of the sailing voyager would also be the best for the power cruiser, with two exceptions. One is that the long distances from Panama to the South Seas practically limit the power vessel to going Acapulco-San Diego-Hawaii before heading out to the Islands. A trip to Tahiti would take a 7.5-knot boat 16 days longer than going direct. And in the Indian Ocean, if Suez were open, its use both to shorten the voyage and to make possible a cruise of the fascinating Mediterranean, is attractive to the power vessel. Generally, sail voyagers avoid this route due to the difficulties of negotiating the Red Sea and timing conflicts with the monsoon seasons. If the power voyager elects Suez, his departure date for leaving the Pacific would be different from that of the sailing cruiser.

Occasionally some book mentions the possibility of a circumnavigation made eastward via Suez and the North Pacific to Panama. To my knowledge it has not been done to date. It looks quite practicable for the power vessel. Without investigating the route in great detail, it looks as if it would go like this, from California:

1. Leave Southern California about November 15 and go to Grenada in the West Indies, then cruise the Caribbean to June 1.
2. On June 1 leave for the Mediterranean via Bermuda and the Azores. Cruise in the Med until October 1.
3. Transit Suez about October 1 and proceed as directly as possible to Singapore during the change of the monsoon from SW to NE, arriving Singapore about November 15.

PHOTO 14-1. Linford Beebe enjoying the perfect weather in the middle of the Pacific High. There is no land in any direction for 1000 miles!

4. Leave Singapore about December 1 for Bali and Timor. Then go around Australia from the west, checking in at Darwin, then via the new western ports to Perth, Adelaide, Melbourne, Tasmania, and up the east coast (including cruising in the Great Barrier Reef), reaching Port Moresby about March 15.
5. Cruise through the Solomons to the Carolines and Guam. Then enter Japan at Nagasaki, arriving about May 1. Cruise in Japan and its Inland Sea until July 1.
6. On July 1, leave Hokkaido for Prince Rupert, B.C., Canada, fueling at Dutch Harbor, Alaska, if necessary. Cruise in British Columbia until September 15.
7. With due regard for weather, about September 15 run down the coast to San Francisco for a couple of weeks, then south to Southern California about October 15—to end a world-girdling voyage in a month less than two years.

The crux of this routing is getting through the Indian Ocean on the fall change of the monsoon. The rest is straight-forward, following the best tracks and times, and should provide good weather all the way. The only exception is the passage from Japan to Canada where a good deal of fog and some wind can be expected. Radar would be useful in this stretch, as the area abounds in fishing vessels.

Crossing the Pacific is quite a problem compared to crossing the Atlantic. The route suggested above is fine in summer but prohibited in other seasons. You can go east by an equatorial route, seeking out the countercurrent where possible, stopping at Rabaul or Honiara, Tarawa, Christmas Island, and Honolulu. But here again the passage frrom Honolulu to the mainland should be made in the summer, as one must go well north to get out of the Trades. To make a winter passage, the only possibility seems to be from Christmas Island

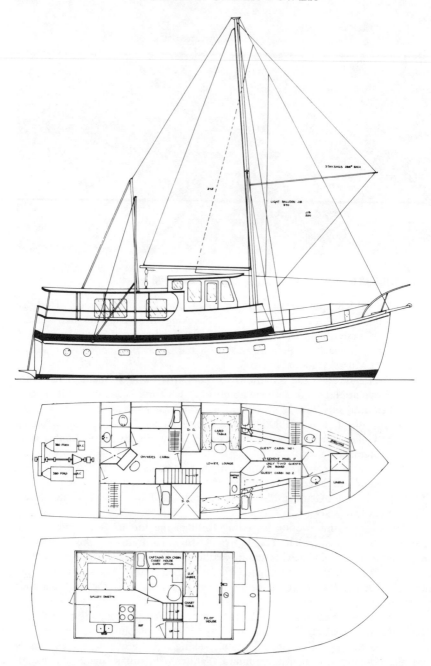

FIG. 14-2. Profile and Accommodation (both decks) of Beebe Design 90, a proposed 50-ft. motorboat for round-the-world passage-making. Note the rig for reaching and running in the Trades, captain's sea cabin, twin engines on a single shaft, and lounge spaces on the lower deck.

to Acapulco, if your vessel could make the 3715 miles of this leg. This is quite a distance, of course, and would probably bar this route to smaller craft, though use of rubber fuel tanks below and some drums on deck might make it possible. The distance would be somewhat shorter if fuel were laid on in the Marquesas. Some of the advantages this has would be lost by your having to get out of the southeast Trades immediately, and return to 6° or 8° North, where the countercurrent runs strongly to the eastward.

At these isolated islands, negotiations to lay on a supply of fuel should be undertaken 10 months to a year in advance. There is a ship from Suva to Christmas Island twice a year, for instance. If such a refueling job from drums is attempted, the vessel should be equipped with its own electric pumps, hoses several hundred feet long, and excellent filters and funnels.

What design features would characterize a round-the-world passage-maker? Fig. 14-2 shows a sketch I made as a start on this problem. Besides fuel and propulsion (two engines coupled to one shaft), she has two features specifically added for the world voyage: a sailing rig designed for reaching and running to give the crew something to do, and a layout designed to provide the maximum number of places the crew can spread out into and be by themselves when they wish, coming together only for meals. I think this is important.

Tales of crew trouble abound in sail-cruising literature and undoubtedly many more incidents go unreported. Of course, certain personalities should not go to sea in small craft at all. But most people can handle the enforced intimacy of a voyage if it is kept within reasonable limits, as it hardly can be in a small sailing cruiser. In a Passagemaker, where each person has his own bunk, with no more than two in a cabin and several spaces to "get away," the situation is much easier.

The sketch takes these ideas about as far as they can go in such a small craft, 50 feet overall. The above-deck space shows a galley-dinette where everyone gathers for meals and the cook is part of things. Forward of this, is a captain's sea cabin that doubles as a chart house for navigation work, keeping this operation out of the dinette and pilothouse. And of course the pilothouse is the domain of one person all the time. Below, there is a built-in card table, and across from it a small seat and below-decks coffee bar. There is plenty of space for friendly gatherings. But if people are not in a sociable mood they are not restricted to a single public space as in so many vessels.

So, let's visualize this craft cruising through the isles of Greece, entering Malaysia at Penang to celebrate the end of the passage across the Indian Ocean, anchoring in the little harbor at Benoa on Bali, skin diving along the Great Barrier Reef, visiting fishing villages in Japan, and mooring in that perfect spot—Princess Louisa Inlet. Then, at last, passing under the Golden Gate Bridge, and getting home again to look back on the cruise of a lifetime.

15

The Long-Range Galley

AUTHOR'S NOTE: The care that goes into provisioning, and the dedicated labor that produces fine meals day after day are as important to successful passage-making as the operation of the vessel itself.

No one is better at these duties than my wife, Linford, for years a gourmet cook of reputation. She came to boats late, and probably never in her wildest dreams did she imagine she would be preparing meals on a plunging small boat a thousand miles from land. I think it would be interesting, particularly to wives in families contemplating taking to the sea, to say a few words on how she came to join Passagemaker's crew.

We had both lost our spouses some years previously. When Linford and I met, Passagemaker *was a sheet of tracing paper on my drawing board. When we finally decided to get married, I was in Singapore finishing up* Passagemaker. *It took something of a logistic miracle to make all the pieces fall together, but they did, and we were married in the American Church in Athens, Greece, on July 6, 1963—six weeks after* Passagemaker *had arrived there.*

When Linford came aboard, her seagoing experience was limited to globe-circling steamer trips—her small-boat experience was nil. She took to it like a duck and has been Passagemaker's *most ardent fan ever since. She knows her watch-standing, handles the wheel for anchoring, does stern coaching, and handles lines for Med mooring. She can lay a boat alongside the dock if she has to, and has stood her share of night watches. As noted in Chapter 12 she doesn't care much for this last activity, preferring to be permanent cook.*

At this duty she is superb. To show how good she is, I have asked her to write this chapter on how she has organized her galleys and raised boat cookery to a fine art.

Provisioning & Galley Tips

By Linford Beebe

It was strange coming aboard *Passagemaker* at the Vouliagemeni yacht harbor in Greece, not only because I'd had no experience with such a life but also because *Passagemaker* on paper hadn't prepared me for her three-dimensional enormity. Suddenly there she was: those half-inches grown to 50 feet, a full-scale seagoing home. I loved the commodious master's quarters: I enjoyed the raised dinette where we could look out the window-sized ports at the harbor, and I was delighted with the more than adequate storage space beneath the dinette. I took pleasure in her comfort and felt secure in her dependability.

In Chapter 3 it was described how *Passagemaker* was equipped for the voyage from Singapore: A two burner Primus stove, cold water hand pump, and an icebox in the cockpit. That was my first galley. Later, during the winter in Greece, we added a sheet-metal oven that sat atop the stove for baking, and installed a pressure water system. The hand pump was retained as a standby. Surprisingly enough, I didn't find it too difficult to cope, and learned a great deal more about food preservation, recipe adapting, and food substitutions than I would have with an elaborate galley.

On other yachts, I've enjoyed sea cooking in galleys as well equipped as most kitchens ashore. And though I wouldn't trade those years on *Passagemaker,* still I find it quite easy to adjust to luxury, for duty in a galley with all the amenities is really pleasant. But I would never allow this to be the determining factor in a decision to go to sea or not.

Bob has an aversion to the use of gas in the galley, so any boat we build must have electric cooking. Other than the stove, there are three electric appliances I consider essential: a broiler-skillet, a wok, and a pressure cooker. These should be mounted on boards that can be slipped into slides that hold them immovable at sea. The frypan is used the most, especially for breakfast and lunch. Mine also has a broiler element in the lid and is a great time-saver. Stir-fried vegetables are especially fresh and tasteful when prepared in a wok. The addition of thinly sliced beef, chicken, or pork, a little soy and sherry, the whole served with rice, will make you queen of the anchorage.

The pressure cooker can be electric or the stove-top type. So much has been written about this most essential cooking pot that I'll add little here. But keep in mind that it is immune to catastrophe when the top is locked on—an important point in rough weather. Donna Doherty, who wrote *The Boatcook* for Seven Seas Press, introduced me to the cooker's food-canning capability when we cruised aboard *Mona Mona* in 1973. I have followed her directions for canning meats and am delighted with the results. The supply of good canned meats in the U.S. is pretty slim—much better abroad—and none compares in flavor and quality to those prepared from the recipes in Donna's book.

I used a microwave oven for the first time when cooking on a yacht in Hong Kong in 1972. It was well placed about eye level on a side bulkhead, out of the way of appliances and counters. I liked its performance so much we bought one after returning home to check them out further for use on a boat. It takes some relearning of cooking methods, but a week or two of experimenting will demonstrate what it can do. Short cooking time alone recommends it. Using seconds and minutes instead of hours can mean a great deal at times. In fact, I think a skipper might even change course for a few minutes if rough seas were making meal preparation an ordeal. I know Captain Bob would: He always tries to keep the cook happy. Cooking right on paper plates, warming prepare-ahead casseroles, defrosting frozen foods and preparing convenience foods quickly are just a few marks in the oven's favor. I use my microwave oven more all the time, often together with traditional cooking methods.

PHOTO 15-1. The author and his wife, Linford, on *Passagemaker*'s deck in Kotor Gulf, Jugoslavia, in 1963. They had stopped the engine to have lunch, and *Passagemaker* "sat still in the water, not seeming to move an inch."

After 10 years and some 60,000 nautical miles at sea, I've formed some definite opinions on a number of points about galley planning. Most important, the galley should be designed for the cook *at sea,* as Bob's are. The U-shape seems to work best, with stove and sink on opposite sides and just enough room between them for one person to function conveniently—about 24″ to 30″. Spacious galleys are impressive in port but may prove dangerous underway in heavy weather. The delivery of hot plates or casseroles from galley to table must be carefully thought out beforehand, and the table should have a secure spot to hold the hot casserole dish. Such procedures are rarely needed, but important when they are.

Placement, size, and shape of drawers and cabinets deserve careful consideration. I've found shallow drawers more efficient than deep ones. In fact, the only way to arrange a galley properly is to *move in* when the cabin is barely assembled, with a complete outfit of plates, glasses, and cooking utensils, and arrange proper roll-proof storage for each item, instead of leaving everything for the cabinetmaker. Drawers for flatware, placemats, napkins, and anything related to dining should be located outside the galley and near the table so helpers can assist without getting in the cook's way. This area might be combined with counter space for the electric kettle, coffeepot, and paraphernalia. Someone invariably wants coffee at the cook's busiest moment.

It seems a really great boat refrigerator has yet to be built, so I've "designed" one to avoid the faults of all the ones I've used thus far. Mine calls for two front-opening doors, one over the other, with the top section (where the cooling unit will be located) reserved for most frequently used foods. The lower section, being opened less, will help to prevent loss of cold. Both sections will be interconnected for a free downward flow of cold from the cooling unit. The interior should be specifically designed to shorten "open door" time. Since finding what you need quickly is the best way to accomplish this, the box interior should be entirely filled with roll-out wire-mesh baskets, each specifically designed for the type of food it is to hold. If a deep freeze is desired, it should be separate. The standard location for it on West Coast boats is under the pilot-house settee.

When choosing dishes, pots and pans, mixing bowls, and the like, the broader the base the greater the stability. Table fiddles are really not needed on long-distance motorboats as well-dampened placemats keep plates from sliding in rough going.

Selecting cooking utensils for their use cuts down on the number required. Heavier pans heat more slowly, cook more evenly, and are best for long, slow stewing or simmering. Cast-iron pots with glass enamel surfaces serve equally well as soup pot, bean pot, or go-to-the-table casserole, and are large enough for a party of eight to 10. Stainless steel pots with copper bottoms cook quickly and are best for range-top cooking.

Of course in flatware, stainless steel is the only thing.

STORAGE

The storage area under the raised dinette on *Passagemaker* worked out well. It held about 80 cubic feet of canned and dry foods. This was more than adequate for six persons for 60 days. On *Mona Mona,* 50 cubic feet of bin space was available under the pilothouse sole—as it was higher than the main deck. Additional cases of duplicate canned goods were stowed below decks. In both vessels storage areas were divided into bins of two to three cubic feet. These bins were easily accessible and were protected from water. Since labels were unaffected, we did not have to mark the contents of every can with indelible ink, a time-consuming job so often mentioned in the cruise accounts of sailing vessels. Bins were numbered and keyed to an inventory book.

The elaborate inventory book I found aboard *Passagemaker* when I joined her in Greece had an index to all items and their bin numbers, together with a record of daily withdrawals for future shopping lists.

What to buy and how much poses a full-scale problem for a long voyage. It's easy enough to make a provision list, with quantities, but that's not the whole story. I start with menus for seven breakfasts, 14 lunches, 14 dinners and, multiplying by the estimated number of weeks at sea, produce a Basic Provision List. Before buying, however, we make sure the bulk of anticipated purchases will fit into the available stowage spaces. We do this by estimating the cubic size of items on the list and comparing the total with the space available. If there are frozen foods, then freezer capacity comes into it. Without a freezer, you have to be an expert in how long things can be stored and how to do it properly.

There is scant information on the subject of provisioning. Most galley cookbooks seem to assume you'll be going to the market every three days. Lists of what has proved satisfactory on long voyages are hard to come by.

Passagemaker's list (*see below*) for her maiden cruise from Singapore to Greece gives the stores *actually consumed* by four men in 60 days. While some fresh vegetables were purchased in Colombo, Ceylon, and Aden, the amounts were small. All bin stores were in cans or dry packages. There was no refrigeration. If I had prepared the list and cooked on this cruise, the list would have been longer and the meals more varied, but without additional bulk of stores.

In addition, a crate each of oranges and apples were carried on deck. Fifty lbs. of potatoes, some cabbages, onions, and an unitemized number of fresh vegetables were stowed below. The Primus used 12 gallons of kerosene and 1.5 gallons of alcohol for lighting it.

PHOTO 15-2. On the Rhone River at Lyon, France. *Passagemaker*'s grocery shopping crew returns aboard. The author helps his wife, Linford, aboard, while Ralph Arndt brings up the rear, carrying a loaf of French bread.

STORES USED BY FOUR MEN IN EIGHT WEEKS:

SEAFOOD

Crab meat	4
Oysters	6
Clams	10
Sardines	8
Shrimp	6
Tuna	8

MEATS

Danish Bacon	7
Chipped Beef	4
Chopped Beef	7
Corned Beef	12
Roast Beef	7
Beef Stew	9
Pork and Beans	5
Franks and Beans	3
Whole Chicken	9
Franks	6
1 lb Hams	2
Vienna Sausage	3

VEGETABLES

Artichoke Hearts	2
Asparagus	3
Green Beans	9
Beets	4
Corn	2
Mushrooms	4
Peas	3
Sauerkraut	5
Spinach	3
Tomatoes	6
Tomato puree	3

FRUIT

Apple Sauce	3
Cherries	2
Figs	2
Fruit Salad	3
Seedless Grapes	2
Peaches	3
Pineapple	3
Plums	3
Rhubarb	4
Strawberries	1

PAPER PRODUCTS

Kleenex	12
Toilet Paper	20
Paper Towels	29

LIQUIDS

Whole Cream Avocet	7
Evaporated Milk	4
Soup Campbells	55
Olive Oil (qt.)	2
Wesson Oil (qt)	2

DRY PACKAGES

Bisquick	2
Cake Mixes	2
Coconut dessicated	1
Coffee Instant	4
Coffee Ground	4
Dutch Cookies	6
Corn Starch	1
Soda Crackers	11
Graham Crackers	3
Jello	9
Jello Pudding	3
Whole Milk (dry)	2
Noodles	4
Prunes	5
Raisins	2
Ryvita	5
Salt	1
Spaghetti	4
Powdered Sugar	1
Gran. Sugar (lbs)	40
Tea	2
White Flour	10
Rice	5
Sauces dry, Spaghetti	2
Sauces dry, Cream	3
Tang	6

JELLIES, JAMS

Marmalade	5
Chutney	1

MISC.

Tinned Butter	17
Canned Cheese	2

CLEANING

Brillo	2
Clorox	1
Lux Liquid	5
FAB flakes	15
Ajax	2

FOOD PRESERVATION

There is very little information on food preservation in cruising cookbooks. Knowledge of the subject can mean the difference between enjoying fresh fruits and vegetables for weeks at sea and depending entirely on canned stores.

Some fresh foods last best under cool, moist conditions; others need dry, dark, and cool. Some may go on the deck topside, others in shaded places or in the hold. Bins and lockers specifically designed and located for preservation of fresh stores should be prepared before they are taken aboard.

Covered deck lockers with louvered sides can be used for those foods that travel best in moderately moist conditions. Some of these are: cabbage, cauliflower, Chinese cabbage, and lettuce. They should be wrapped separately in burlap and dampened from time to time. Choose cabbage that is solid and heavy for its size. Cauliflower should be white with no yellow tinge. Lettuce must be firm, the outer leaves green, and the core end sweet smelling. Lettuce should not be stored next to fruits, for many fruits give off a gas as they ripen, causing dark spots to develop on green leafy vegetables. Oranges and grapefruit store the same way. If heat is so intense that these items start to sweat, shade the bin but allow air to circulate.

A box of moist sand kept out of the sun is a good place for many root vegetables. Choose all as fresh as possible, with crisp, green foliage. Trim foliage to within an inch of the base, as it drains moisture from the root. Small carrots with small cores are sweetest and a dark or discolored stem end is a sign of age. Bury celery in the sand so only the leafy tips are exposed.

Keep potatoes in a cool dark place; they can stand some moisture but light causes green areas to appear and turns them bitter. They should be separated from onions which steal moisture from them, and sprouting results. Keep onions dry and dark. Watch all vegetables for sprouts and remove these from time to time. Pumpkins and hard-shell squash fare well in warm weather if kept dry. When acorn squash starts to turn orange, it is showing its age.

Buy tomatoes while still green or with a slightly pinkish cast, wrap in tissue paper, and keep in a cool spot. Bring out a day or two before planning to use, but never place them in the sun. They should last six or eight weeks. Select mushrooms with tightly closed caps, the smaller the better, and store where it's dark and humid. Broccoli should have compact heads with tightly closed flowers; it will last about two weeks if wrapped in a damp cloth and kept cool. Purchase avocados while still hard, with a full stem end, and free of bruised spots. Wrap separately and bring out to ripen. You can accelerate this a bit by placing them in a paper bag for a day or two. Never refrigerate avocados before fully ripe as chilling stops the ripening process.

Apples, peaches, apricots, and plums last longer if kept dry. A box of sand stored inside the boat helps preserve them—if they are free from blemishes and completely dry before covering. Or, wrap the fruit in paper and store in a covered crock with paper between each layer. Firm, small apples keep better than large ones. Select hard, green pears; they will ripen quickly when you bring them out. Color doesn't always indicate ripeness, but a slight "give" at

PHOTO 15-3. One of the bonuses of cross-ocean voyaging with "speed and dispatch" is the extra time available for wide exploration of ports along the route. Here is the fascinating marketplace at Ponta Delgada in the Azores. (Hoyt photo.)

the stem end shows they are ready to eat. Peaches, apricots, and plums should be firm but not green. Enjoy these less durable fruits at their best as they won't last long.

Buy lemons with thin skins and slightly green. They will last indefinitely if wrapped in foil and kept in an airtight container. Limes can be kept the same way. The ones you buy in the tropics are fat, juicy, and delicious.

Many tropical fruits don't travel well and should be enjoyed as you go. Pineapple, though common in our markets, tastes sweeter and more flavorful on native soil; for export they are picked before entirely ripe and this stops the ripening process. We bought a crate of specially selected ones in Hawaii, kept them on deck under a tarp, but with good air circulation, and they lasted six weeks.

OTHER PERISHABLES AND PACKAGE GOODS

The longevity of eggs is always of special concern on long voyages for they are needed in many recipes and are an excellent source of protein. With refrigeration there is no particular problem as they are available in most ports, but for long passages some method of preservation must be used. On *Passagemaker* they were rubbed with petroleum jelly for the six-week trip from Singapore to Greece and were still edible on arrival. You test eggs by putting them in cold water: Fresh ones go to the bottom; bad ones float; and those that hover in between—well, it depends on how much you want eggs.

At home as well as at sea, I use Eggstra for many cooking needs. It is a powdered-egg product made primarily for those on low-cholesterol, low-calorie diets; I consider this just a bonus, for I use Eggstra anyway in most recipes calling for whole eggs. I also use a dry eggwhite powder, reconstituted with water. It has the quality of fresh egg white and when the two are combined they do most things an egg is supposed to do.

Butter in cans may be purchased abroad. Denmark, Great Britain, New Zealand, and Australia pack good brands. It tastes a bit like cheese when eaten as a spread, but this isn't noticeable in cooking and it lasts well even in extreme heat. In areas where water temperature is below the temperature of the air, quarter pounds of butter can be wrapped in plastic and kept in a bucket of water out of the sun. Unless the water is over 70°, the butter should stay fresh three to four weeks. This method of cooling may also be used for such perishables as peanut butter, mayonnaise, and sauces after the cans have been opened. But it is best to select small jars of these items so they will be used up quickly.

Hard Italian cheeses such as Parmesan, Provalone, and Romano are least perishable because they have the least amount of moisture. In warm weather, keep in a salt- or vinegar-saturated damp cloth in a cool place. In cool weather or when refrigerated, wrap tightly in plastic to keep the air out. Seal Cheddar, Gouda, and Swiss with paraffin, then coat again after cutting. Processed cheese keeps until opened if kept relatively cool. If mold appears on any cheese, just cut it off; it doesn't affect the taste, nor is it harmful.

Cakes, cookies, and crackers should be purchased in tins if possible, or removed from cartons, stored in airtight containers, and sealed with Scotch tape.

Bread spoils very quickly at sea, and the crew will tire of such fare as rusks and sea biscuits. The solution is to bake your own. It is very simple, whether you knead it by hand or use a bread-maker. I've made bread by hand for years but recently acquired a bread-maker that turns out five or six loaves at a time. All the ingredients go into a pot the size of a soup kettle, a lid snaps on and, after turning a hand crank for 15 minutes, the dough is put to rise. From then on the usual procedure is followed to completion. On the boat you can let the dough rise in the warmth of the engine room.

THE MAGIC OF WINE AND HERBS—IN CANNED OR PACKAGED FOODS

Adding a touch of wine or liquor, herbs or spices, can often lift an otherwise mundane dish to a gourmet level. Primitive knowledge of such culinary magic brought savor to the staple fare of peasants, and elegance to the dining of kings. A judiciously used accent can mark you as a sophisticated cook and master chef.

Most canned foods are dismally undistinguished unless some imagination is used in their preparation. I consider my bin stores only as a starting point for a meal, and constantly experiment with a pinch of this and a *soupçon* of that to achieve truly delicious dishes. Following are a few recipes and suggestions from my "Sea Fare" cooking file that have proved successful:

Welsh Rarebit.   To *1 can of Snow's Welsh Rarebit* add *1 Tbs sherry, 2 Tbs Worcestershire sauce, ½ tsp Coleman's dry mustard, ½ tsp curry*, a few grains of *cayenne pepper*. Cook according to directions. Meanwhile, gently sauté *1 can sliced tomatoes* in *garlic-seasoned butter* until heated through. Place tomatoes on *toasted English muffins* and cover with rarebit. For a more hearty dish you can put a slice of lightly browned *ham* under the tomatoes.

Chili Rarebit. Add *1 can California Green Chilies,* chopped, to *Snow's Rarebit.*

Fondue. Add ⅓ *cup dry white wine* and a little *brandy* or *bourbon* (to taste) to *1 can of Snow's Rarebit.*

Sweet-Sour Pork. (with apologies to Jenny Hung of Hong Kong). Cut *1 can Libby's Chopped Ham* into 1″ cubes. Place in plastic bag with ½ *pkg Schilling Teriyaki Sauce.* Mix. Shake bag until cubes are well coated. Allow to stand two hours. Drop in bowl and add *2 Tbs each of bourbon and soy sauce, 1 Tbs Orange Tang,* ½ *chopped onion, 2 cloves mashed garlic.* Marinate at least one more hour, turning occasionally. Mix *1 cup flour* with *2 Tbs Eggstra.* Coat meat well and brown in *hot oil.* Make *Schilling Sweet-Sour Sauce* with *1 cup pineapple juice* instead of water. Add *1 cup sliced water chestnuts* and ¼ *cup California Green Chilies* cut in squares. Cook until clear and combine with meat. Serve with *rice.*

Fish Soup. To *1 can Snow's Fish Soup* add *1 can tuna* (drained), ½ *can dry white wine,* ½ *can evaporated milk, 2 Tbs Butter,* ¼ *tsp cilantro.* Heat just to a boil. Garnish with *shrimp* and *freeze-dried chives.*

Borsch. *Blend 2 cans consommé, 2 cans sliced beets,* ½ *can dry red wine, 1 Tbs vinegar,* ½ *onion,* ¼ *tsp celery seed, 2 tsp sugar, salt and ground pepper.* Add *1 can Pet Imitation Sour Cream* and whirl until smooth. Garnish with *chives and small shrimp* or *caviar,* if you like.

Quick Cup-A-Soup. (1) To *Lipton's Instant Green Pea Soup* add ⅓ *cup skimmed milk powder, curry, chives* and *bacon bits.* (2) To *Instant Chicken Soup With Noodles,* add a little *sherry* and *soy sauce* with just *a few leaves of cilantro.* (3) Combine *Instant Cream of Chicken Soup* with *Instant Cream of Mushroom Soup,* season with *tarragon* or *curry.* This soup mixture is also a good basic cream soup for additives, such as *cream style corn,* chopped leftover *ham, bacon,* or *chicken.*

Three Sauces. (1) *Using French's White Sauce as a base: Add 1 cup clam juice* (instead of water), *butter, capers,* a little *anchovy,* a hint of *cilantro.* Serve with fish. (2) Add ½ *cup dry white wine,* ½ *cup chicken stock, butter* and ½ *cup grated cheese.* Serve on vegetables and poultry. (3) Make a mustard sauce by adding *onion juice,* ½ *cup milk,* ½ *cup white wine, 1 tsp Coleman's mustard,* a squeeze of *lemon* and a little *sugar.*

Gravy. Envelopes of gravy mixes are a good start from which some delicious gravies evolve. Instead of the water called for on the package, try using beef or chicken stock, or dry red or white wine as part of the liquid, and always add some butter. Seasonings can be tarragon, a little lemon juice, and bourbon. Or, curry, soy, and bourbon. Or, a Tbs of tomato sauce, some Pet's Sour Cream, tarragon, and bourbon. Bourbon seems to give a great lift to gravies. Gin is also good, especially with beef, but don't let any of them overwhelm other flavors.

Desserts. A great deal can be done with packaged dessert mixes. Certainly, most cake mixes are improved by adding fruit juices such as lemon, orange, apricot nectar, or sherry instead of water. Rum and instant powdered

PHOTO 15-4. Ralph Arndt returns to *Passagemaker* in a French canal after one of his forays on the Solex bike for cheese, wine and bread.

coffee are delicious in chocolate cake or brownies. Sherry, rum, and many liqueurs give pleasing flavors to pudding mixes. Add Lemon and Orange Tang to fruit pie fillings. For a real treat, try this one:

Brandied Peach Pudding.   Soak *canned peach halves* overnight in a syrup made from the canning liquid boiled down to ½ the original volume. Add ½ *cup brandy.* Flavor *vanilla pudding mix* with *sherry* and spoon into dessert dishes. When ready to serve, sprinkle peach halves with a little *Orange and Lemon Tang,* cover with *brown sugar* and put under the broiler long enough to melt the sugar. Put a peach half in each dessert dish and top with *sliced almonds.*

LANDFALL

For the long-distance voyager, there is a special magic to a landfall: not just excitement, more like enchantment as a vision dissolves into focus and becomes reality. Even men like my husband, who has worked with stars and horizons for many years, acclaims the wonder of this moment . . .

For two or three weeks you have been at sea, crew settled into jobs, ocean vast around you, high sky above, living the arts and work of the sailor. Then at some unlikely moment someone shouts, "Land ho!"

At once the crew assembles on deck, first to *find* the tiny speck on the distant horizon, then to identify it indisputably as land, finally to watch it *grow.* Abruptly you are terrestrial creatures again, eager to see your native medium, wondering about all the mysteries of the land ahead.

Awed, you see the speck swell into a mountain, stare harder as the mountain takes shape and throws out a headland, takes on a fringe of palms, acquires a coral necklace of crashing waves, and finally reveals a village: boats, people, cars, houses, shops . . .

At last, a few hours after the speck appeared, your little ship passes through a gap in the reef, curves across the harbor toward the town, slows as it nears the seawall and then—as always and remarkably—through the smiles and welcome waves, several pairs of willing hands reach for your lines and make you fast to the land . . .

Tomorrow you will explore the busy streets, hear the chatter, soak up the color, be startled by noise and surprised by scurry, discover the tang, aroma, fragrance, spice of the native market. But for the rest of today it is enough to sit and watch and marvel at being back on land again . . .

FOODS IN FOREIGN MARKET PLACES

Mexico and Central America. On the west coast of Mexico, **Ensenada, Manzanillo** and **Acapulco** were excellent stops for fresh produce. **Puntarenas, Costa Rica,** was especially charming, and the people friendly. The market was filled with tropical fruit and vegetables. There was plenty of sea food in all these ports, but the best was acquired through barter. Once it was the fisherman's idea that we trade frozen ground beef, some beans, beer, and cigarettes for four flounder and 15 lobsters. What a feast!

Greece. Just thinking about foreign ports makes me dream again. In Greece we lived like Greeks all winter. I knew the market days in the nearby towns and never failed to show up about 6:00 A.M. with string bag in hand, as all proper Greek housewives do. We enjoyed the fresh mountain spinach, an Elysian green, more delicious than our own, the *retsina*-flavored bread hot from the oven, and creamy goat milk yogurt to eat with fresh fruit. Greece is famous for its fruits, and Greek lamb is plentiful, but frozen beef is imported from Yugoslavia and frozen chickens from Denmark and the U.S. All are sold at the great market right on the waterfront at Piraeus.

Rhodes. We moored to the quay wall just in front of the arched market place, a most wonderful spot. We found everything in good supply and it was the best place for stocking canned goods. It was here in Mondraki Harbor we pulled up an *amphora* with our anchor. Bob won't take it to an expert: He says he doesn't want to know if it's *not* 2000 years old.

Yugoslavia. The market in Dubrovnik, with its cobblestone streets and surrounding ancient stone buildings, was a story-book setting with vendors in regional costume. A fine variety of produce was brought fresh from the fields each morning. There were stalls full of needlework, embroidered fur-lined jackets, fancy boots, and handmade laces. At Hvar we laid in a supply of very good local wine and excellent meats . . . The beef goulash was particularly good. We cruised the spectacular fjord to the walled town of Kotor at the foot of mountains rising 5000 feet straight up from the sea. Here we moored right in the marketplace.

France. Going up the Rhone River, as we worked our way to Strasbourg on the Rhine, we dined on local fare. When the village was far from the canal, Captain Ralph Arndt, one of our French-speaking crewmen, would take the Solex bicycle and meet us several locks later, his basket filled with local cheese, fresh-baked bread, perhaps a hen or country paté and, hanging on each handlebar, a jug of local wine. This river and canal cruise offered a feast to all senses.

Spain and Majorca deserve special comment, for nowhere in the world is there such variety, quality, and quantity of fruits and vegetables . . . We couldn't get enough of the wild asparagus that Spaniards so often tuck into an omelet. Canned goods are sensational, too. Everything is picked at its perfection for canning; artichokes, pimientos, and tuna are packed in that wonderful Spanish olive oil. Spain is definitely a place to restock canned goods.

The Azores. The market at Ponta Delgada is fabulous—large and well-stocked with fresh produce from farms specializing in quality goods for export. Horta is a small town, so, if you really need provisions, Ponta Delgada is the place. Be sure to try the *bacalhau* (codfish) dishes and the local sausages!

Bermuda has a good stock of Scandanavian and British canned goods and produce, but all are expensive as most must be flown in. I made a hit there with friends who came to dinner aboard *Mona Mona* by serving one of my deep-sea dishes: *Stuffed Baked Tomatoes.* I've found if you buy the best quality solid-pack tomatoes, seed and cut out the stems, fill with precooked stuffing, sprinkle with cheese, and pop under the broiler for a few minutes, they easily pass for fresh. Peggy Sinclair, who lives on Bermuda, commented on how good they were, but was alarmed at their probable cost at the local market. Someday I'll tell her!

The Orient. There is no lack of food both fresh and canned foods there. We spent considerable time in Hong Kong sampling the canned goods from mainland China. They were uniformly delicious and of high quality. China also offers, in cans, things you never see elsewhere. To find these items, drive far out Nathan Road until you are away from the tourist areas, and poke around in the large Chinese markets for what you want. Many U.S. canned staples are in the supermarkets. We were careful not to buy fresh produce that couldn't be peeled or cooked. Potatoes were poor, so we stuck to the dehydrated type, but local sweet potatoes are wonderful.

Japan. Here you find excellent beef and the world's best sea food. Be sure to try their many dehydrated soups—delicious.

Hong Kong and Singapore. Practically everything in the food line is available here. Being duty-free ports, goods are shipped in from all over the world. The cities are a melting pot of world culture. Most meat is imported from Australia, New Zealand, and the U.S., butter and cheese as well.

For a report on stores and food availability in the South Pacific, I will turn to a long letter I received from my niece, Betty Winter. She and her husband, Paul, cruised there in *Eolo*, a 55-foot Australian cutter, in 1970, with a crew of six to eight, and no refrigeration. Betty is also *Passagemaker*-qualified with about 5000 miles to her credit. Here are some excerpts from her letter:

"**Tahiti.** Most officials are helpful, the shops inviting, and the market colorful. We often bought a fish from a fisherman on his way to the market along the quay wall. Delicious long Chinese beans, eggplant, lettuce, tomatoes, and cilantro were available at the market, but bell peppers were hard to find. We had *pomplomous,* the grapefruit of the South Pacific, every morning for breakfast, some of them eight inches in diameter. We added some stores to our abundant supply, mainly for variety: paté, cheese, New Zealand butter in cans, *cassoulette,* and a delicious canned *ratatouille.*

"**The Leewards** of the Society Islands offered less. In Huahine, we bought vanilla beans. Tahaa had a fine agriculturist, Teka, who is experimenting with various kinds of bananas. He gave us three stalks of an unusually tart type as well as some of the delicious reds. We were in Borabora for the *fête* and enjoyed it tremendously, especially eating at all the food stands set up for the occasion.

"**Cook Islands.**   Here we found fine oranges and bananas at **Aitutaki,** but didn't stay long as the anchorage is precarious. At **Rarotonga,** the port town of Avatiu was well supplied with New Zealand frozen meats and canned goods. Vegetables were not plentiful.

"**Tonga.**   At **Nukualofa** the marketplace captivated us, especially since watermelons and salad ingredients were in good supply. The handicrafts—tapa, baskets, and mats—were especially good.

"**New Zealand.**   We entered at the Bay of Islands, and a school of porpoises piloted us in. With the grassy hills and cottages, it seemed a bit of England. This was a place of delicious tangelos and wonderful butcher shops. Later we sailed down to Auckland where meat, milk, and butter were very inexpensive, and the variety of produce remarkable. During the strawberry season we picked our own, and loaded up with every kind of apple—right at the orchard."

The beginning of this chapter tells how I came as a novice to the cruising world, and how I became happily and incurably committed. I attribute my gentle introduction to first going to sea on *Passagemaker.* Our voyages have taken us across thousands of miles of oceans and seas and into dozens of harbors. They have been a blend of many pleasures: the joy of being at sea . . . the thrill of a landfall . . . the fascination of personal discovery in each new port . . . and always, the continuing gastronomical adventure of savoring the exotic in cooking pots of the world.

But here I must stop for space limits my eager pen. All I would like to say about the good food we found, and where we found it would fill another book—and perhaps it will.

16

Operating a Seagoing Motorboat

"Operating" is a very broad term that covers just about every activity aboard a seagoing vessel once it gets underway. We cannot even begin to list *all* the captain and crew should know or should have done before they leave the dock. Instead, we will make comments on certain activities and functions which experience has shown to be important, or in which we differ from the standard texts, or where we can offer a better way of doing things.

The great majority of yachtsmen who acquire a motorboat with real seagoing ability have already had years of experience. Many have switched to power after years in sail. At any rate, they have long since graduated from "basic training."

But there are some skippers coming into the field without this basic training and without prior experience at sea. What advice can we give them?

While there is no substitute for time at sea in the making of a competent seaman, the vast store of knowledge built up over years of experience by mariners of all nations is available in books. These books should be part of the boat's "equipment" from the start. The skipper should be so familiar with their contents that he knows just where to look for any information he needs. (A recommended list of books is given in the appendix.) Courses in navigation and seamanship are available commercially, and free from such excellent organizations as the U.S. Power Squadrons and the Coast Guard Auxiliary. By volunteering for and becoming proficient as an observer in predicted log racing, a good deal of "underway time" can be acquired quickly. This activity is particularly valuable for the example experienced operators will give in operating at the highest standards of navigation, steering, and speed control.

As for sea time, there is just no substitute for getting out there. Experience as a crew member should be actively sought. If a power voyage is not available and a sail voyage is—grab it. You will learn much on either. Four of the people who have made long voyages in *Passagemaker* now skipper their own little ships.

With the commissioning of your own vessel, you should lay out a definite program for advancing your experience, doing a little more each time you go out, until a passage of several days is no longer a novelty or a cause for concern.

In observing neophyte skippers, I've noticed that they generally show wisdom by starting slowly, with respect for the sea and an understanding of their own limitations, but when finally they are qualified to take off on a passage of some days, they are somewhat reluctant to do so. This is largely a reluctance to trust their navigating ability out of sight of land. As this seems to be a common affliction, it is a good starting point for our comments on navigation.

NAVIGATION

These days, the paperwork required to work out celestial navigation fixes has been so simplified that there is quite literally "nothing to it." This is in marked contrast to the days of my initial instruction to the art, when the only connection between the earth and the stars was a horrendous term entitled "The Right Ascension of the Mean Sun Plus 12 Hours."

New, shorter methods of navigation came into use during World War II. It might be supposed that in such a huge ship as the *USS Saratoga* we would navigate in very formal fashion to the greatest accuracy. Actually, the reverse was true. The navigation department of an aircraft carrier is under tremendous pressure for accurate fixes day and night on a continuous basis to support air operations. So we concentrated on the quickest methods—which were also the easiest. The routine we developed then is the same one I use today and have taught to many students aboard *Passagemaker*. In each of her voyages, the navigating students made all the landfalls with no assistance from me. If they could do it, you can do it.

This reluctance to "take your foot off the beach" is sometimes hard to understand. It is near the shore that a vessel is in danger. The tales are legion, especially on the Pacific Coast, of vessels lost while hugging the shore for no good reason.

It is well for the reluctant navigator to remember that the only fix that *really* counts is the last one before landfall. In fact, the only difference between a 24-hour passage and one of several days is that instead of coming back in, you just keep going. The navigating done is to show you how well you are doing and what small adjustments have to be made in your courses and speeds. So even if that long voyage seems formidable, just take it a day at a time and it will not be an overwhelming problem.

The power vessel has advantages over sail cruisers when taking sights, because it is high-sided, steadier, and usually offers better shelter for sight-taking. We found we always could rely on getting good results, regardless of weather, when stars were visible. Because of the superior accuracy of star sights, it was our practice to use them almost exclusively, turning to sun lines only when necessary. I do not agree with the statements made in certain cruising and navigation books that star sights are too difficult to take from small craft: I have taken them often in a 36-foot yawl. The watch-standers, being relieved of steering duty or sail tending have plenty of time to do their own navigation. When taking sun lines has to be the main reliance (as on *Passagemaker*'s trip from the Azores to Ireland when we never saw a star), it was easy for the watch to get the five to seven sun lines needed for a good day's fix.

I have worked a good deal on organizing sight-taking so a single person can do it without having a recorder to help. This is essential with a one-man watch for morning stars; and desirable always. Recording is not easy and requires training to do properly. It is a good idea to dispense with a recorder, so you know where the responsibility lies.

The latest setup is shown in the accompanying photo. It consists of an 8″ × 3¼″ piece of plywood that is provided with two elastic straps to hold it

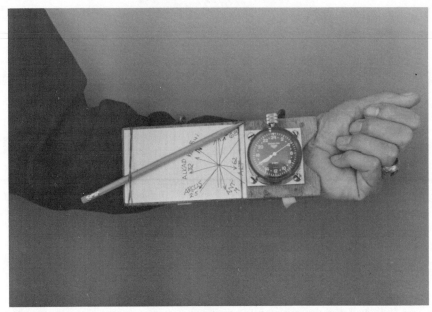

PHOTO 16-1. A view of the Beebe Sight Recorder attached to the wrist.

to your forearm. The Huer 24-hour-dial, stop-second action clock is fastened at one end, and 3″ × 5″ index cards are held by rubber bands at the other end (cards stand wetting better than paper and are less affected by wind). The other item of special equipment is a penlight worn around the neck.

The drill goes about like this: The clock is set to correct GMT just before taking sights, a step much facilitated by the stop-second action. When a sight is taken, you say "Mark!" to yourself and start mentally counting seconds until you have your eye on the clock and can read the second hand. Subtract mentally the seconds you have counted and record the reading—always seconds first, then minutes, and then the hour, the body, and the altitude. At night hold the pen-light in your mouth to point at the watch and sextant. A two-cell penlight gives just enough light to read by, yet not so much as to spoil your night vision.

For star sights, it's a good idea to make up a diagram showing the altitude and azimuth of selected stars as taken from the star-finder *HO 2102D*, or its commercial equivalent. The bearings are shown relative to the ship's bow for the course you are on as indicated by the central double-line arrow. You can then preset your sextant to the approximate altitude and look in the right direction. That gives you the maximum chance to spot the star quickly while it is still too light for general sky search in the evening. Of course, the lighter the sky the better the horizon. I always use the above method and as a result have never really learned any constellations at all. I am convinced that the emphasis placed on learning them by many navigation books is wasted effort. If you wait until you can find stars by constellation in the evening, you are bound to have horizon trouble because of darkness.

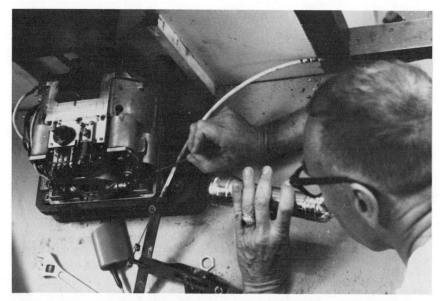

PHOTO 16-2. Repairs at sea: Aboard *Passagemaker,* a crewman is steering manually while the author chivvies a sticky relay in the autopilot motor, a job made much easier by the flopper-stopper gear, which reduced rolling this day to under 10 degrees.

Enough on navigation. As was mentioned earlier, these days the paperwork involved is so simple anyone should be able to navigate anywhere with a few weeks of drill and a little practical experience.

COMMUNICATIONS

Passagemaker did not have a radio transmitter during the time I owned her. There was little point in having one when we left Singapore because once you leave the U.S. coast, with the 2-3 MHz type of transmitter, nobody is listening. There are supposed to be stations in the Mediterranean and elsewhere, but I never heard of anyone getting a message through to one of them.

Today, the shift to VHF and Single Side Band (SSB) changes things considerably. The bridge-to-bridge capability of VHF is useful. On *Mona Mona* we discussed weather with several ships, for instance. But not all the ships we called answered at sea. VHF was useful in harbors, in Panama, and at some marinas. I would certainly have it nowadays.

As for SSB, a high-seas set with capabilities from 3-22 MHz would assure your reaching a marine operator in the U.S. from anywhere. There has been a marked rise in the number of amateur licensed operators on cruising yachts where the SSB sets have been particularly successful. Active nets exist in such areas as the west coast of Central America where they contribute to safety and convenience in such matters as ordering spares. The SSCA has details on these nets. Altogether the shift to VHF and SSB will be a boon to the long-range voyager.

We had a regular Aldis signaling lamp aboard *Passagemaker* and we used it quite a bit on our first voyage from Singapore to Suez as we were almost constantly in sight of shipping in the busy sea lanes. While most of our use was just for gossip, especially with lonesome third mates on the midwatch, it would have been handy if we had had any real need to communicate. As a standby for VHF as well as the Xenon flasher discussed later, it is my recommendation that an Aldis lamp be included in the ship's outfit, and that you practice sending and receiving flashing light.

SAFETY AT SEA

Collision Avoidance. Anyone who goes far to sea these days should be aware of two things: First, the number of ships transiting the oceans is increasing by leaps and bounds; second, the speed of ships is increasing.

What does this mean to power voyagers running at eight knots in a 40- to 50-foot boat? Obviously, it means the watch-standers must be more alert as the time available for evasive action is shortened, and there is the real possibility that the ship you've spotted will not sight you at all.

All this is compounded because many ships of all nations are running with a one-man watch, a watch that has other duties besides looking out. Even following good procedure—before taking his eyes off the sea to do something like writing up the log, the watch-stander should sweep the sea ahead very carefully with binoculars—the lights of a yacht most probably will not be visible from the distance the ship will cover while the watch-stander is not on the lookout.

You will have no trouble seeing the ship; the range lights of ships these days are much brighter than the law requires. They come up over the horizon looking like searchlights on a clear night. What is needed is some way *the ship* can see *you* as soon as possible. There is only one light available to a yacht that will do this—the Xenon flasher. I strongly recommend that you equip your vessel with one. The flasher should not be used except for its intended and legal purpose: as the "flare up light" allowed by the rules "in order to attract attention." On *Mona Mona*'s cruise, the first I made on a flasher-equipped yacht, it was not used at all.

Even with this equipment, the only safe policy, in my opinion, is to assume *nobody* can see you, and act accordingly. This means staying out of everyone's way by early and extensive changes of course if there is any possibility of another vessel coming close. In fact, any changes in course or speed should be large so they will show up quickly if you are being watched on radar.

For radar and reduced visibility it is essential you have some really good radar reflectors. It is not generally appreciated how sensitive "corner reflectors" are to the slightest deviation from a 90-degree angle. The sides must be rigidly held to this. The folding type of reflector is hardly more useful than a big tin can.

If you have a radar on your vessel, you owe it to your crew to obtain training in plotting, both on the maneuvering board and the scope so you will have a clear picture of what is happening, and can instruct the rest of the crew in this skill.

The Man-and-Wife Boat. The probable use of the seagoing motorboat for more man-and-wife cruising in the manner of the many sailing cruisers was mentioned in Chapter 9 with some further remarks on the subject in Chapter 11. Here, we are concerned about the safety of this type of operation.

Sailing yachts with crews of two, or even one, have been sailing the seas for many years. By and large, their casualty rate has not been great enough to cause concern, but they do go missing occasionally. There are good reasons to suspect some of these casualties were run down by large ships which never saw them. The problem of taking evasive action in a small sailing vessel can be compounded by sudden calms or wind shifts. So from this point of view the full-power craft is safer.

The danger of being run down varies in different parts of the oceans. For instance, from Los Angeles to Panama, the coast has an almost constant curve toward the east, causing everyone to hug the coast most of the way. On a passage I made in 1973 there was almost always traffic in sight. In the South Pacific, the traffic is still quite light. In the North Pacific, and to a lesser extent in the North Atlantic, new routing services to take advantage of weather have resulted in some scattering of shipping away from the traditional (and direct) great circle routes, so ships can be found all over the area.

With only two watch-standers, alertness is bound to deteriorate when a passage lasts more than a few days. There are some things that can be done to assist in this matter. Small radars are available that will sound an alarm if there is any contact within a certain minimum distance of the vessel. It is expected that this feature will soon become more common and cheaper. Although electronic experts keep saying it is difficult and costly, it still appears possible that without owning a full radar set, you can have a relatively cheap receiver that would alert you to the fact a radar is operating nearby. If this receiver had a reasonable bearing capability it would be a good substitute for radar on many small craft.

As another alert, a clock could be rigged to sound an alarm at any interval desired unless a reset button was pressed regularly. If this is rigged also to stop the engine, believe me, it will bring all hands up, all standing!

The idea that a fully alert watch should be stood in the dark with less alertness during the day has been advanced in several places and appears to have some merit as making the best of a bad situation. Of course, a full watch list of at least three watch-standers is even better. It is worth some inconvenience and added expense to achieve this on long passages.

MANEUVERING

Some prospective owners, while conceding the superiority of the single-screw vessel in range and propeller-protection, still want twin screws to make the vessel easier to maneuver around docks. The twins do this, of course, but not by much in a proper vessel, and by proper vessel we mean one without an excessive A/B ratio. The chief use of twin screws is to neutralize maneuvering problems caused by windage. Many popular makes of coastal motorboats have A/B ratios of 4.5 and higher, and are practically unmanageable in a good breeze of wind; *their* twin screws are a necessity.

But a seagoing vessel with an A/B ratio of about 2.6 should handle easily with a single screw under all conditions. The owners of single-screw vessels whom I know all have developed great competence in putting the ship right where they want it, and they take considerable pride in this ability. As one said to me, "Twin screws take all the sport out of it."

HEAVY-WEATHER HANDLING

The literature of sail cruising is loaded with advice and examples about handling vessels in heavy weather. For power voyaging there is not nearly as much advice available and what there is seems largely concerned with coastal motorboats and "recreational" boats—such as fishing launches. Some of this advice is applicable, particularly about running inlets and handling in thunder squalls. But for a small motor craft a thousand miles at sea, not much has been written—the experience is just not there.

Passagemaker's experience may be of some use, though her gales were not too severe. Her first hit us at the south end of the Red Sea with winds of just about gale force, around 30 knots from astern. The problem was that we had to head about 20 degrees across the wind to avoid going ashore somewhere near Mocha. And we were uncertain about how far off downwind we could safely go without tending to broach. It soon became clear that we could head as far off as we needed, except before the very biggest waves. As a matter of prudence, we took these from dead aft. It was not until this wind died out after sunset that I realized it had never occurred to me to slow down: We ran at 7.5 knots the whole time.

Our hurricane off Bermuda was a strange experience. The sky became overcast and it started to rain, the barograph went down like a rock and the wind increased. The trouble was that to us the wind appeared to be from the wrong direction for a tropical storm. It turned out later the storm had formed *over* Bermuda and headed northeast so it was already north of us. At the time, we had sail up and ran off with the wind on the port quarter, which of course is the wrong tack for a tropical storm. The rain was so heavy it flattened the waves, but as closely as we could determine, the wind reached 55 knots. It had been 85 knots at Bermuda but was dying rapidly. We eventually entered what must have been the remnants of the storm's center because the barograph started back up as rapidly as it had gone down. We were able to go to power only and head directly for Bermuda in a dying sea.

A day ahead of us, a yacht (a 77-foot motorsailer) had a very hard time of it, but she came through undamaged.

Our second hurricane was encountered on the passage from Sandy Hook, New York, to Delaware Bay; this storm was coming up the coast. The weather bureau said we could beat it if we started *right now;* but what they didn't tell us was that conditions were building up for a typical nor'easter, in addition. The result was plenty of northeast wind all night as we ran down the coast. At about 0200, when I took over, we took down the sail and continued to run with the wind and sea on the quarter, our only choice. She rode the big swells easily, and we had no real problems in a wind that got as high as about 50 knots.

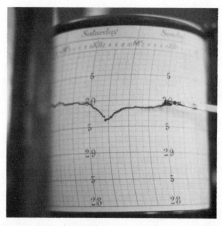

PHOTO 16-3. The barograph trace of our "hurricane" off Bermuda in 1964.

Our worst gale, which I noted earlier, was encountered off Cape Mendocino, California. After a summer in British Columbia, we were going down the Pacific Coast toward San Francisco where we had an on-board party planned for the next day. The night before, the wind started to increase from astern. By 0300 it was bad enough for me to be called. I was on the bridge for the next 27 hours. Conditions were not too bad until dawn. After that, the winds gradually increased in strength until they reached full gale. This was not a storm but a gradient wind, powered by the hot interior valleys of the West making a "thermal low," while the cold ocean air rushed in to fill the vacuum. It soon became so strong I felt it advisable to take the wheel and head off directly before the waves at low speed. Around sunset, the waves began to "roll," giving them a most frightening aspect. I was concerned about being able to stay dead before the waves after dark on a moonless night. Much to my relief, I found this was no problem: The waves could be seen well enough to achieve this.

Thus we kept on southward. The trouble was San Francisco was southeast, getting more easterly the farther we went. I had visions of the gale sweeping us right past the Golden Gate and putting us back in Monterey again. But after midnight, the wind gradually started to slacken and we could steer across it a bit more each hour, until the course was attained for San Francisco. Shortly after dawn we were steaming through a windless sea. The party was a great success. We were on schedule despite a difficult night.

Now, in all these incidents we ran off before the weather; in the last, dead before it, in the others, across the wind to varying degrees, at all times using flopperstoppers. Would it be possible to do this in winds of higher velocities, say in the 65-75 knot range? The answer is, I don't know. I rather suspect that in those conditions, the recommendations for sailing vessels under such "survival conditions," found in books on the subject, would be applicable to power vessels as well. Several books that discuss this matter are listed in the Appendix. But the essence of the argument—and there is an argument—about the best methods of meeting heavy weather is that running off raises the danger of "broaching," while lying "a-hull," that is, with engines stopped and the drifting vessel allowed to take what attitude she will to the seas, raises grave danger of heavy damage from breaking seas because, in this situation, almost every vessel will lie broadside to the seas.

Broaching means the boat turns uncontrollably beam to the wind and sea. It is caused by going too fast down the face of a wave that is coming up from astern. The bow buries deeply with enormous increase of resistance forward. The rudder is unable to provide the force necessary to stop the turning motion that results. The turn is so quickly made that large centrifugal forces are generated which, combined with a breaking wave pushing against the side, can capsize the vessel. The same forces in extreme conditions have also caused some vessels to "pitch-pole," or turn end-over-end.

It is these end results of "broaching" that have caused some experts to urge "lying a-hull." They point out that the forces acting on a hull lying broadside to the seas are very much less if the vessel is stopped than they are with the addition of centrifugal forces from the sudden broaching turn. This should make the vessel less liable to capsize. If it does, it would be better to be rolled over from the broadside position, with inertial forces helping to bring the vessel upright through a full roll, than it would be to chance the damage from "Pitch-poling.'" Actual incidents are cited to show the difference in danger and damage.

All of this sounds quite grim, and of course it is. Although many professional seamen have gone to sea all their lives without meeting such conditions, nevertheless one must realize that it can happen. What is really needed in this case is something like a submarine. Vessels going far to sea should have extensive preparation for preserving their water-tight integrity under any condition. The roster of sailing vessels that have pitch-poled or been capsized, yet righted themselves and returned safely to port, is quite lengthy. So we can see such an incident need not mean certain death—no matter how traumatic the experience. The key, of course, is keeping the sea out of the boat. It is this concern that inspired my earlier remarks on glass areas.

Some further information on the heavy weather problem I have found includes the contrasting results of two vessels being turned bottom up.

Thorfinn, shown in Chapter 8 and designed by Philip Bolger, was shipped to the United States to be exhibited at the Miami Boat Show. While being unloaded in Norfolk, Va., by crane, the sling broke. According to the report the vessel fell 40 feet and struck her side on the edge of the dock, then fell into the water almost upside down. She immediately righted herself with very little water in the hull. The engines remained on their mounts and the shafts could be turned. She is of course, a "constructive" total loss.

Thorfinn has a full-width cabin, and Phil Bolger feels that this has a lot to do with her quick return to normal trim. With her large glass area (three-eighths inch laminated glass) it remains a question whether her entering the water on the cabintop preserved the integrity of this glass to produce such a satisfactory righting result.

In contrast to this incident is the loss of the yacht *Grundl* in 1968. It appears that she was struck broadside by a breaking sea while making an approach to Grey's Harbor, Washington. *Grundl* was a 50-foot yacht of the "Northwest Cruiser" type with a moderate amount of glass area. The press accounts are not clear but she undoubtedly was rolled bottom up, throwing the skipper off the flying bridge, and then sank without fully righting herself.

Of the crew of four, three were lost.

Returning to broaching, our experiences with *Passagemaker* showed she had less tendency to broach than I had hitherto experienced. The "rooting" tendency was there—you could feel it as she put her bow down and accelerated before a wave. But her big rudder proved to have enough "command" to keep her from actually running off course. The drill was to watch the waves astern, and when a particularly vicious one appeared, to put the stern dead before it. As the bow went down, the helmsman's line of sight was shifted to dead ahead. If the bow showed the slightest tendency to turn to either side, the rudder was immediately slapped hard in the opposite direction. This always worked, yet I hesitate to imply that it always would, the sea being so full of surprises.

PAPERWORK AND OFFICIALS

"Going foreign" means inevitable contact with the maritime officials of countries much different from your own. This is nothing to worry about, provided your papers are in order and your heart is pure.

For a vessel built abroad, a consul may issue a "Certificate of American Ownership." If he does not remember what this is, tell him it is in his form book. Ordinarily, permission to issue the certificate must be obtained from Washington after the sale is completed. But for a brand-new vessel obviously being built for an American citizen, it is possible to obtain permission in advance from the State Department for the consul to issue the certificate when he is satisfied all conditions are fulfilled. We did this, and were able to leave Singapore immediately after completion of the sale. Be sure to invite the consul to your christening party.

See that the consul binds all your papers with yards of red tape and the biggest seal he has. I think this does more good than anything. You will often be asked for gross and net tonnage figures. If you don't know them, give displacement for gross and half that for net. I had *Passagemaker* measured by the British, and although the paper was clearly marked "not for British Registry" this impressive form seemed to do a lot of good. The yard's hull number was mentioned on this form and in the certificate and was successfully pointed out as the "registry number" more than once. A consul can issue a "Temporary Certificate of Registry," but this document is only good for six months and hardly any owner would want to return home in that short time.

All hands should have passports; don't fool with "seaman's papers" on a yacht. The only place we went where a visa was required in 1963 was Yugoslavia. That country, Greece, and possibly other countries have a restricted list of ports where a yacht can enter and clear. If there is any doubt, you should plan your entry into a country at a port that has facilities for regular shipping.

Every port will want crew lists with passport numbers, dates of birth, and so on. Make up plenty of them in advance on a typewriter. I have been asked for as many as six. Be sure all hands have International Immunization Certificates and that shots are up to date. Have a locker where "spirits" and cigarettes can be sealed up in case Customs thinks you have too much.

The best time to enter port is 0900 on a working day. I had reason to regret the occasions we did not follow this rule. Overtime charges are quite high in some places.

Flying a good-sized national (not merchant) flag of the country, steam right into the port. If no one tells you what to do, it is always legal for the captain to go ashore and make his presence known. But *only* the captain.

If, as is usually the case, the officials come on board for check-in, have everything ready in advance: all papers and passports laid out in an area such as the dinette where writing can be done. The area should be cleared of all crew members except the captain, with one other member prepared to come if the captain summons him to serve coffee or beer. During the time the officials are on board, no crew members other than the captain should speak to them. If questions are asked they should be referred to the captain. He alone should speak for the ship, and he should limit himself to answering questions. After all business is concluded, it is in order to offer some refreshment. It is surprising how often this will be refused. Even if no one on board smokes, it is a good idea to have cigarettes on board to offer to the officials.

This may all sound a bit formal and stuffy, but it is a good idea to exhibit a brisk, businesslike manner, be dressed in clean clothes, and have the yacht all ship-shape in order to make a good impression. Unfortunately, there are enough sailors who *don't* make a good impression to raise suspicion of yachts among customs men, and to lead to remarks like this in an SSCA bulletin: ". . . and find some freaked-out creep in a sailing pasteboard box has queered it for everybody else."

FIRE

Fire is an ancient terror of seamen. Many of the sea's great tragedies have been caused by fire, not by the sea itself. The possibility of fire must always be present in the captain's mind and every precaution taken against it. Extensive discussions of equipment and precautions are contained in books listed in the Bibliography.

What I want to emphasize here is something these books neglect: The diesel-driven vessel, while much safer than gasoline, is *not* immune to fire caused by fuel. Carelessness in handling diesel fuel or control of leakage is no more tolerable than it would be with gasoline. Under certain conditions the fumes from diesel oil *can* explode. And high-pressure fuel-injector leakage that can drain into the sump has caused "base explosions."

I personally know of two small vessels that were destroyed by diesel-fuel fires. A 50-foot twin-engine (in the stern), long-range yacht burned and sank while underway in the Mediterranean when it was about three months old. During the short period the crew was able to fight the fire with ordinary fire extinguishers before they were driven off the vessel, no investigation could be made of how or where the fire started.

In the second instance, the engine room was equipped with a CO_2 flooding system. It was also equipped with powerful engine-room blowers which were in operation. The cause was a fuel-line break right over an uncooled section of exhaust line, a situation that should have been foreseen. The CO_2 automatically functioned—and the engine-room blowers automatically blew the CO_2 out the vents! Result: an uncontrollable fire. This gives you something to think about.

Diesel-fuel fires can be fought using techniques the Navy developed during the war. The principal reliance was on the "fog nozzle" at the end of a "wand," a section of pipe about seven feet long. The fog nozzle can be approximated by the ordinary adjustable spray nozzle used on rubber hose. The main point is to get it into action as quickly as possible. On *Passagemaker,* the hose with nozzle was always hooked up with the valve open. Full pressure could be obtained instantly by flipping a switch that was outside the engine room in the galley. Some such arrangement is recommended.

I will personally not ever have propane or butane gas aboard for cooking. There are enough things to worry about at sea without the threat of explosion, which is inherent in propane. In certain areas, it is now possible to buy compressed natural gas which, being lighter than air, is much safer.

If gas is to be used, the vessel's whole design should be drawn with this in mind, rather than being a tacked-on afterthought. For instance, in one yacht, belonging to a very experienced seaman, which uses propane for cooking and heating water, the appliances are confined to one compartment of the vessel which is completely sealed off from the rest of the ship and has a blower in the bilge running constantly.

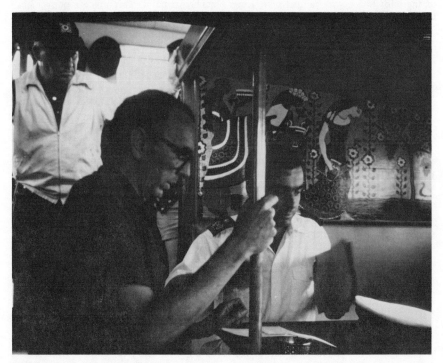

PHOTO 16-4. Customs check-in at Ponta Delgada, Azores Islands. While the captain answers questions, Col. Bibb stands by to assist if necessary.

PHOTO 16-5. *Passagemaker's* Data Board. To reduce glare the entire forward part of the pilot house was painted with green blackboard paint. This made a convenient surface on which to post data.

KEEPING TIME

Your vessel should be run on zone time, using the numbered zones as described in *Bowditch*.

The time we use to regulate our own routines is called local time, and usually corresponds nearly to the ancient idea that noon is when the sun is highest. In the U.S.A., what we call Eastern Standard Time is the time of zone +5, while Eastern Daylight Time is time of zone +4. But what happens when we leave our home boundaries to go out on the sea and disappear into the distance? What is the *local* time then?

Well, the answer is perfectly simple. *The local time aboard a ship is what the captain says it is.* This is literally true. In the old days, before accurate time pieces, when the captain observed the sun at its highest, he would say "Strike eight bells." This would be done and the hourglass turned over to start another cycle of watches.

So it ill behoves me to tell you, the captain of your vessel, what time to use. But let me respectfully suggest, as the result of my experience, that you do what we did on *Passagemaker:* Run your ship on zone time.

To handle this, the data board shows four things: the local time in the form of the presently used zone description; the local date, which means just that; the time of sunset; and the time of sunrise, which is for the next day.

Sunrise and sunset are useful for several reasons. They show when star sights will be taken when combined with the duration of twilight you experienced the previous day. (This is more accurate than the tables in the almanac.)

And they show how the local time being used works in with the ship's routine. For example, steaming steadily eastward across the Atlantic, if you do not change your zone time, you will eventually find all the navigators on deck taking star sights just when the cook announces supper at the scheduled hour of 1800. And there is nothing madder than a cook who has fixed a masterpiece and finds no one to eat it! As one of the basic principles of cruising is to keep the cook happy, you are due for a time zone change, but quick!

Another thing to keep in mind is that it is desirable to arrive at your destination using the time zone *there*. For instance, in going from Bermuda to Horta you would change three hours on the way to be on Horta time. So as a practical matter you are limited to three changes of one hour each in a passage of about 10 days. The timing of the changes is arranged with consideration of the factors mentioned.

On vessels with varnished woodwork rather than *Passagemaker's* black-board paint, the data described above was kept on cards and posted near the wheel.

WATCH-STANDING RULES

A few remarks were made on watch-standing in Chapter 12. It would be useful to expand somewhat on these. The position of watch officer (or officer of the deck as it is called in the Navy), is unique among duties in that a single person is solely responsible for the safety of the ship and its crew. It is quite true that in a vast majority of cases, when a situation arises it can be solved by calling the captain to bring his experience to bear on the problem. Nevertheless it must be kept in mind that situations will arise that demand the watch-stander take immediate and correct action on his own. Thus a certain amount of training of watch-standers is a vital ingredient of safety. Each person on the watch list should be able to perform such maneuvers as stopping the engine, changing course or speed, using autopilot "dodgers," taking bearings on approaching ships, and so on, as each vessel's makeup demands. Each watch-stander should also have specific instructions about log entries, inspections to be made, and degree of alertness required.

I know from our experience that the crew does appreciate having things spelled out, and appreciates even more the opportunity to maneuver the ship. As to what rules you should have, I can only give for the reader's consideration some we have followed.

One traditional emergency is "man overboard." I recall being taken to task by a sailing man because I did not have the ocean-racer's two horseshoe life preservers on *Passagemaker's* stern, ready to be thrown over by the helmsman. Perhaps they would be useful, but I pointed out to this gentleman that in the first place, the helmsman was about 25 feet from the stern, and in the second place, our orders were immediately to turn the rudder hard over *toward* the side the man fell from and proceed in a full circle back to the place he was, a maneuver that took only a few seconds and something the sailing vessel cannot do. I note that the new owner of *Passagemaker* has put horseshoe preservers on her stern where they do look very salty.

As regards degree of alertness, we allowed the watch-stander to read during the day when there was clear visibility and no traffic. At night, this was not possible as we emphasized protecting night vision by eschewing all light other than small penlights which give just enough light to read dials without spoiling your night vision. I have been on vessels that were quite slack about this, and I thought it a mistake.

We had the engine room inspected each hour. On *PM,* this was done from the pilothouse, looking down the hatch with a five-cell flashlight that was trained on certain spots, such as the one place you could see the bilge. For the purpose of visiting the engine room, using the head, etc., it was permissable for the watch-stander—after examining the whole horizon with binoculars—to go below for not more than 10 minutes since it takes about 18 minutes for a freighter to pass after first seeing its range lights. With the increases in speed of ships, already mentioned, perhaps this is now too long.

Each watch-stander should be trained as a helmsman to the point where he can steer the course by hand easily. One of the most common mishaps on the long-range seagoing motorboat is autopilot trouble. While it is being fixed, hand steering is required. This is particularly necessary if any of the crew are novices or if the compass reads from the rear, as in *PM,* where people trained in steering with a forward lubber line have a terrible time at first.

PORTS

In 1966, while *Passagemaker* was crossing the Trades north of Hawaii en route to Seattle, a combination of two or three small waves on the face of a larger swell interacted to produce what for want of a better term I called a "jet break," striking her side in a limited area. In this area was a Wilcox-Crittenden 8″ x 18″ "marine window." The glass in this port shattered into literally a million pieces with the major ones looking like daggers. These were propelled across the ship onto Linford's bunk and she was cut in several places, luckily not very severely, though she carries a scar on her cheek to this day.

Now I was remiss in assuming that a marine port advertised as "built to meet the severe conditions of marine use," was actually that. Instead, it was equipped with the cheapest sort of plain glass, dime-store stuff. My complaints to the company were met by the statement that competitive conditions in the industry made it impossible for them to use better and more expensive glass because they would be priced out of the market. This incredible statement is probably true—*caveat emptor* is still the rule.

Subsequently, *Passagemaker's* forward ports were refitted with quarter-inch, heat-tempered safety plate. In 1967, off Nicaragua, that same port was struck again in the same manner—the blow so severe that the man on watch stopped, thinking we had hit something. While water spurted in around the port, it did not break.

It is up to the individual, apparently, to see that his ports are safe and matched in thickness to their size. Large "picture windows" of quarter-inch glass, even if safety glass, give me the shudders. *Passagemaker's* ports, other than forward, were all half-inch, heat-tempered safety glass. In a gale in the Aegean, we were seeking shelter by going alternately 45 degrees upwind and downwind to reach a destination across the wind. By my own mismanagement during one of these turns, we were struck broadside by a breaking sea. The pilothouse ports were covered entirely with green water—no foam—yet we suffered no damage or inconvenience, just a good scare. After that, we had every confidence in our glass.

Plastic ports are now appearing and use of plastic in metal-framed ports has been suggested. Certainly it would be a lesser hazard if it did break, but it also lays claim to being stronger than glass. *Mona Mona* is equipped in her hull with the Fuller Brush Company plastic ports. They work very well, being tight and easy to open and close. They took a few good blows during the three months I observed them, but have not yet been tested by the extreme "jets" we had in *Passagemaker*.

Because *PM*'s stern cabin ports were made up of simple panes of glass held in a frame that could be tilted open 15 degrees at the top for ventilation in rain, we provided covers for storm use. The covers were bolted on from the outside. This was not easy to do in a rough sea, and such ports should be provided with covers that can be put on from the inside—an easy thing to arrange. After our first gale, we never again applied the port covers in the actual stern as they were not necessary.

CONCLUSION

Writing these notes, and in fact writing the whole book, has forced me to review all that happened over a period of years in order to insure that nothing of prime importance to successful passage-making in seagoing motorboats has been forgotten, or misstated, or is not found somewhere in the recommended reading. In the course of this review, both Linford and I had many nostalgic memories about our cruising. Like our first cruise with just the two of us in Greece, from Athens to Rhodes with the *meltemi* blowing furiously. And how Linford got seasick for the first and last time—bravely trying to brown slices of delicious Yugoslavian fillets in the galley below. And how our new stabilizer pennants began to unravel, and we took shelter briefly behind a rocky reef to put safety lines on the wires in case the pennants let go. And how we spent half a day making up new ones, with Linford learning to "pass the ball" as I served. And how the wind shifted and chased us out of our harbor before we swung onto the shore. And how we then took refuge in what was just a cleft in a sheer cliff on the south side of Nis Nikouria and got the anchor to hold after four attempts. And how Linford hoisted me up the mast so I could install the new pennants with the winds whistling down the gully, almost pushing us against the rocks, first one side then the other. And how these hectic-wonderful days are now just a note in Chapter 6, Stabilizer Pennants.

The same thread runs through the whole book, of experiences shared and lessons learned. But one lesson is most important of all—we are glad we have done it and hope to do more. And so we will leave you with one simple thought: "*Go!*"

PHOTO 16-6. Passagemaker leaving Millwall Lock, Plymouth, England, on the beginning of her trans-Atlantic passage to the United States.

Appendix

Alphabetical list of the addresses of all designers mentioned in this book:

ALDEN. John G. Alden, Inc., 89 Commercial Wharf, Boston, MA 02110.

BEEBE. Robert P. Beebe, Box 1452, Carmel, CA 93921.

BENFORD. Jay R. Benford & Associates, Inc., 1101 N. Northlake Way, Seattle, WA 98103.

BOLGER. Philip C. Bolger, 250 Washington St., Gloucester, MA 01930.

BREWER. Edward S. Brewer & Associates, Inc., Brooklin, ME 04616.

COLVIN. Thomas E. Colvin, Miles P.O., VA 23114.

ELDREDGE-McINNIS. Eldredge-McInnis, Inc., 57 Water St., Hingham, MA 02043.

FARMER. Weston Farmer, 18970 Azure Road, Wayzata, MN 55391.

GARDEN. William Garden, 2071 Kendal Ave., Victoria, B.C., Canada.

KROGEN. James S. Krogen & Co., Inc., 2500 South Dixie Highway, Miami, FL 33133.

LAGIER. Fred Lagier, 21613 South Sexton Rd., Escalon, CA 95320.

LAPWORTH. C. William Lapworth, Box 1756, Newport Beach, CA 92663.

LUCANDER. Nils Lucander, Box 3184, Brownsville, TX 78520.

MASON. A. Mason, Box 5177, Virginia Beach, VA 23455.

McMURRAY. Robert L. McMurray, 427 Marin Ave., Mill Valley, CA 94941.

MONK. Edwin Monk & Son, 616 National Building, Seattle, WA 98104.

OSTLUND. Ben Ostlund, 515 Signal Road, Newport Beach, CA 92660.

SEATON. Stephen R. Seaton, 2506 Cortez Road, Bradenton, FL 33507.

SPARKMAN & STEPHENS. Sparkman & Stephens, Inc., 79 Madison Ave., New York, NY 10016.

WITTHOLZ. Charles W. Wittholz, 315 Lexington Drive, Silver Spring, MD 20901.

Bibliography

Books and articles consulted during the writing of this book, or which are recommended for additional reading.

HISTORY

Atkin, William. "The First Motor Launch To Cross The Atlantic." *Motor Boating,* July 1962.

Barton, Humphrey. *Atlantic Adventurers.* New York: D. Van Nostrand, 1953.

Davin, Tom, ed. *The Rudder Treasury,* "The Log of the *Abiel Abott Low."* New York: Sheridan House, 1953.

Day, Thomas Fleming. *The Voyage of the Detroit.* New York: Rudder Publishing Co., 1929.

Harcourt-Smith, C. "Twice Across The Atlantic." *Yachting,* Aug. 1955.

"The Race To Bermuda." *Motor Boating.* June 1913.

Marin-Marie. *Wind Aloft, Wind Alow.* New York: Charles Scribner's Sons, 1947.

TECHNICAL DETAILS

Beebe, Robert P. "Flopperstoppers For Seagoing Motorboats." *Motor Boating,* Feb. 1967.

Beebe, Robert P. and Fuller, Avard. "On Seagoing Powerboats," *Boating,* Jan. 1970.

Monk, Edwin. "The Fisherman's Stabilizer." *Yachting,* Aug. 1960.

Phillips-Birt, Douglas. *Naval Architecture of Small Craft.* London: Hutchinson, I. Co. Ltd., 1957.

Fishing Boats of the World. Vols. I, II, III. New York: Food and Agricultural Organization, United Nations.

West, Jack. "To Roll or Not To Roll." *Motor Boating,* Aug. 1968.

PASSAGEMAKER & PASSAGE-MAKING

Beebe, Robert P. "The Passagemaker." *Yachting,* Oct. 1964.

————. "You Can Cross Oceans In A Motorboat." *Motor Boating,* May, 1966.

————. "Passagemaker Across The Atlantic." *Boating,* May 1970.

Doherty, John Stephen. "Secrets of the Long-Distance Motorboat." *Rudder,* Dec. 1967.

Hoyt, Norris D. "Once Over Heavily." *Yachting,* Aug. 1966.

————. "Once Over Lightly." *Yachting,* Sept. 1966.

CRUISING IN EUROPE

Beebe, Robert P. "Seagoing Boats For The Canals of Europe." *Boating,* May 1971.
Bury, Roger. "Passagemaker Explores the Eastern Med." *Cruising Club News,* Jan. 1974.
Imray, Laurie, Norrie & Wilson. *The Inland Waters of France.* St. Ives (Hunts), England.
————. *The Inland Waters of Holland.* St. Ives (Hunts), England.
————. *The Inland Waters of Belgium.* St. Ives (Hunts), England.
Johnson, Irving. *Yankee Sails Across Europe.* New York: W. W. Norton, 1962.
Marriner, John. *Afloat In Europe.* London: Adlard Coles Ltd.
Pilkington, Roger. *Waterways of Europe.* New York: Charles Scribner's Sons, 1973. Gives technical information on the waterways.
————. *Small Boat To* ————. New York: St Martin's Press, Inc Each book in this series gives the history and points of interest of different areas of Europe you can cruise in a small boat. Eight volumes in the series published to date.

Books on cruising in the Mediterranean and Scandinavia are so numerous they cannot be listed. A good source of supply is Captain O. M. Watts, Ltd., 45 Albermarle St., Picadilly, London, England W1X, 4BJ.

VOYAGE PLANNING

Beebe, Robert P. "Postwar Pacific Cruising." *Rudder.* Aug. & Sept. 1946.
Bowditch, Nathaniel. *The American Practical Navigator.* Washington: U. S. Navy Hydrographic Office.
Bulletins, Seven Seas Cruising Association. By subscription from Box 1215, Venice, CA 90291.
Hiscock, Eric. *Voyaging Under Sail.* London: Oxford University Press, 1970.
Pilot Charts of the Oceans. Washington, D. C.: U. S. Navy Hydrographic Office.

SEAMANSHIP & OPERATION

Bruce, Errol. *Deep Sea Sailing.* New York: D. Van Nostrand Co., 1953.
Chapman, Charles F. *Piloting, Seamanship & Small Boat Handling. Motor Boating & Sailing* (periodically revised).
Coles, K. Adlard. *Heavy Weather Sailing.* Tuckahoe, New York: John de Graff, 1968.
Henderson, Richard. *Sea Sense.* Camden, Maine: International Marine Publishing Co., 1972.
Hiscock, Eric. *Cruising Under Sail.* London: Oxford University Press, 1967.
Street, Donald M., Jr. *The Ocean Sailing Yacht.* New York: W. W. Norton & Co., Inc., 1973.

Metric Conversion Table: Lengths

1 inch = 0.025 meters   **2 inches = 0.051 meters**

Ft.-In.	Meters	Ft.-In.	Meters	Ft.-In.	Meters	Ft.-In.	Meters	Ft.-In.	Meters
1-0	0.31	14-0	4.27	27-0	8.24	40-0	12.20	53-0	16.17
1-3	0.38	14-3	4.35	27-3	8.31	40-3	12.28	53-3	16.24
1-6	0.46	14-6	4.42	27-6	8.39	40-6	12.35	53-6	16.32
1-9	0.53	14-9	4.50	27-9	8.46	40-9	12.43	53-9	16.39
2-0	0.61	15-0	4.56	28-0	8.54	41-0	12.51	54-0	16.47
2-3	0.69	15-3	4.65	28-3	8.62	41-3	12.58	54-3	16.55
2-6	0.76	15-6	4.73	28-6	8.69	41-6	12.66	54-6	16.62
2-9	0.84	15-9	4.80	28-9	8.77	41-9	12.73	54-9	16.70
3-0	0.92	16-0	4.88	29-0	8.85	42-0	12.81	55-0	16.76
3-3	0.99	16-3	4.96	29-3	8.92	42-3	12.89	55-3	16.85
3-6	1.07	16-6	5.03	29-6	9.00	42-6	12.96	55-6	16.93
3-9	1.14	16-9	5.11	29-9	9.07	42-9	13.04	55-9	17.00
4-0	1.22	17-0	5.19	30-0	9.15	43-0	13.12	56-0	17.08
4-3	1.30	17-3	5.26	30-3	9.23	43-3	13.19	56-3	17.16
4-6	1.37	17-6	5.34	30-6	9.30	43-6	13.27	56-6	17.23
4-9	1.45	17-9	5.41	30-9	9.38	43-9	13.34	56-9	17.31
5-0	1.53	18-0	5.49	31-0	9.46	44-0	13.42	57-0	17.39
5-3	1.60	18-3	5.57	31-3	9.53	44-3	13.50	57-3	17.46
5-6	1.68	18-6	5.64	31-6	9.61	44-6	13.57	57-6	17.54
5-9	1.75	18-9	5.72	31-9	9.68	44-9	13.65	57-9	17.61
6-0	1.83	19-0	5.80	32-0	9.76	45-0	13.73	58-0	17.69
6-3	1.91	19-3	5.87	32-3	9.84	45-3	13.80	58-3	17.77
6-6	1.98	19-6	5.95	32-6	9.91	45-6	13.88	58-6	17.84
6-9	2.06	19-9	6.02	32-9	9.99	45-9	13.95	58-9	17.92
7-0	2.14	20-0	6.10	33-0	10.07	46-0	14.03	59-0	18.00
7-3	2.21	20-3	6.18	33-3	10.14	46-3	14.11	59-3	18.07
7-6	2.29	20-6	6.25	33-6	10.22	46-6	14.18	59-6	18.15
7-9	2.36	20-9	6.33	33-9	10.29	46-9	14.26	59-9	18.22
8-0	2.44	21-0	6.41	34-0	10.37	47-0	14.34	60-0	18.30
8-3	2.52	21-3	6.48	34-3	10.45	47-3	14.41	60-3	18.37
8-6	2.59	21-6	6.56	34-6	10.52	47-6	14.49	60-6	18.45
8-9	2.67	21-9	6.63	34-9	10.60	47-9	14.56	60-9	18.53
9-0	2.75	22-0	6.71	35-0	10.68	48-0	14.64	61-0	18.61
9-3	2.82	22-3	6.79	35-3	10.75	48-3	14.72	61-3	18.68
9-6	2.90	22-6	6.86	35-6	10.83	48-6	14.79	61-6	18.76
9-9	2.97	22-9	6.94	35-9	10.90	48-9	14.87	61-9	18.83
10-0	3.05	23-0	7.02	36-0	10.98	49-0	14.95	62-0	18.91
10-3	3.13	23-3	7.09	36-3	11.06	49-3	15.02	62-3	18.99
10-6	3.20	23-6	7.17	36-6	11.13	49-6	15.10	62-6	19.06
10-9	3.28	23-9	7.24	36-9	11.21	49-9	15.17	62-9	19.14
11-0	3.36	24-0	7.32	37-0	11.29	50-0	15.25	63-0	19.22
11-3	3.43	24-3	7.40	37-3	11.36	50-3	15.33	63-3	19.29
11-6	3.51	24-6	7.47	37-6	11.44	50-6	15.40	63-6	19.37
11-9	3.58	24-9	7.55	37-9	11.51	50-9	15.48	63-9	19.44
12-0	3.66	25-0	7.63	38-0	11.59	51-0	15.56	64-0	19.52
12-3	3.74	25-3	7.70	38-3	11.67	51-3	15.63	64-3	19.60
12-6	3.81	25-6	7.78	38-6	11.74	51-6	15.71	64-6	19.67
12-9	3.89	25-9	7.85	38-9	11.82	51-9	15.78	64-9	19.75
13-0	3.97	26-0	7.93	39-0	11.90	52-0	15.86	65-0	19.83
13-3	4.04	26-3	8.00	39-3	11.97	52-3	15.94	65-3	19.90
13-6	4.12	26-6	8.08	39-6	12.05	52-6	16.01	65-6	19.98
13-9	4.19	26-9	8.16	39-9	12.12	52-9	16.09	65-9	20.05

Metric Conversion Table: Weights

Long Tons	=	Metric Tons	Long Tons	=	Metric Tons	Long Tons	=	Metric Tons
1.0	=	1.016	31.0	=	31.497	61.0	=	61.979
2.0	=	2.032	32.0	=	32.514	62.0	=	62.995
3.0	=	3.048	33.0	=	33.530	63.0	=	64.011
4.0	=	4.064	34.0	=	34.546	64.0	=	65.027
5.0	=	5.080	35.0	=	35.562	65.0	=	66.043
6.0	=	6.096	36.0	=	36.578	66.0	=	67.059
7.0	=	7.112	37.0	=	37.594	67.0	=	68.075
8.0	=	8.128	38.0	=	38.610	68.0	=	69.091
9.0	=	9.144	39.0	=	39.626	69.0	=	70.107
10.0	=	10.160	40.0	=	40.642	70.0	=	71.123
11.0	=	11.177	41.0	=	41.658	71.0	=	72.139
12.0	=	12.193	42.0	=	42.674	72.0	=	73.155
13.0	=	13.209	43.0	=	43.690	73.0	=	74.171
14.0	=	14.225	44.0	=	44.706	74.0	=	75.187
15.0	=	15.241	45.0	=	45.722	75.0	=	76.204
16.0	=	16.257	46.0	=	46.738	76.0	=	77.220
17.0	=	17.273	47.0	=	47.754	77.0	=	78.236
18.0	=	18.289	48.0	=	48.770	78.0	=	79.252
19.0	=	19.305	49.0	=	49.786	79.0	=	80.268
20.0	=	20.321	50.0	=	50.802	80.0	=	81.280
21.0	=	21.337	51.0	=	51.818	81.0	=	82.300
22.0	=	22.353	52.0	=	52.834	82.0	=	83.316
23.0	=	23.370	53.0	=	53.850	83.0	=	84.332
24.0	=	24.385	54.0	=	54.867	84.0	=	85.348
25.0	=	25.401	55.0	=	55.883	85.0	=	86.364
26.0	=	26.417	56.0	=	56.899	86.0	=	87.380
27.0	=	27.433	57.0	=	57.915	87.0	=	88.396
28.0	=	28.449	58.0	=	58.931	88.0	=	89.412
29.0	=	29.465	59.0	=	59.947	89.0	=	90.428
30.0	=	30.481	60.0	=	60.963	90.0	=	91.444

NOTE: To convert tenths of long tons into kilograms, add the following:

Tenths of Long Tons	0.1	0.2	0.3	0.4	0.5	0.6	0.7	0.8	0.9
Add Kilograms	101	203	305	406	508	610	711	713	914

METRIC CONVERSION TABLE: Inches to Centimeters

Inches:	1	2	3	4	5	6	7	8	9	10	11
Centimeters:	2.5	5.1	7.6	10.2	12.7	15.2	17.8	20.3	22.9	25.4	27.9

METRIC CONVERSION TABLE: Volume of Liquids

To convert U.S. Gals. to Liters, multiply U.S. Gals. × 3.785.

To convert U.S. Gals. to English (Imperial) Gals., multiply U.S. Gals. × 0.833.

Index